ethics in perspective / a reader

ethics in perspective

KARSTEN J. STRUHL

Long Island University

PAULA ROTHENBERG STRUHL

William Paterson College

Random House/New York

a reader

First Edition
98765432
Copyright © 1975 by Random House, Inc.

Library of Congress Cataloging in Publication Data

Struhl, Karsten J   comp.
  Ethics in perspective: a reader.

  1. Ethics—Addresses, essays, lectures. I. Struhl, Paula Rothenberg, joint
comp. II. Title.
BJ21.S8   170   74–19274
ISBN 0–394–31852–8

Manufactured in the United States of America

acknowledgments

"Self-Interest and Morality," from *The Moral Point of View,* Abridged Edition, by Kurt Baier. Copyright © 1958 by Cornell University. Copyright © 1965 by Random House, Inc. Reprinted by permission of Cornell University Press and Random House, Inc.

"Self-Interest and Social Welfare," from *The Morality of Self-Interest* by Robert Olson. Reprinted by permission of the author.

"Selfishness, Self-Love and Self-Interest," from *Man For Himself* by Erich Fromm. Copyright 1947 by Erich Fromm. Reprinted by permission of Holt, Rinehart and Winston, Inc.

"Inhumanity As A Way Of Life," by Maitland Edey, from LIFE Magazine (November 10, 1972), © 1972 Time, Inc. Reprinted with permission of the publisher.

"On Cultural Relativism," by Ija Lazari-Pawlowska, from *The Journal of Philosophy* 67 (September 3, 1970). Reprinted by permission of the publisher and the author.

"Ethical Absolutism and Ethical Relativism," reprinted with permission of Macmillan Publishing Co., Inc. from *The Concept of Morals* by Walter Stace. Copyright 1937 by Macmillan Publishing Co., Inc., renewed 1965 by Macmillan Publishing Co., Inc.

"The Vanity of Humanism," by Ronald Sampson, from *The Nation* (December 29, 1969). Reprinted by permission of the publisher.

"God and the Good: Does Morality Need Religion?," by Kai Nielsen, from *Theology Today* 21 (April 1964). Reprinted by permission of the publisher and the author.

"A Good Will," from Immanuel Kant: *Fundamental Principles of the Metaphysics of Morals,* translated by Thomas K. Abbott, copyright, 1949, by The Liberal Arts Press, Inc., reprinted by permission of The Bobbs-Merrill Company, Inc.

"Utilitarianism," from John Stuart Mill: *Utilitarianism,* edited by Oskar Piest, copyright © 1957, by The Liberal Arts Press, Inc., reprinted by permission of The Bobbs-Merrill Company, Inc.

"The Right and the Good," from *The Right and the Good* by W. D. Ross, 1930, pp. 16–22, 28–34, 39–41. Reprinted by permission of The Clarendon Press, Oxford.

"Rule-Utilitarianism," abridged from *Human Conduct,* 2nd Edition, by John Hospers, © 1961, by Harcourt Brace Jovanovich, Inc., and reprinted with their permission.

"Against Moral Conservativism," by Kai Nielsen, from *Ethics* 82 (April 1972). Reprinted by permission of the publisher, the University of Chicago Press, and the author.

"The Subject-Matter of Ethics," from *Principia Ethica* by G. E. Moore. Reprinted by permission of the publisher, Cambridge University Press.

"Emotivism," from *Language, Truth, and Logic* by A. J. Ayer. Reprinted by permission of Victor Gollancz Ltd.

"You Ought to Derive 'Ought' from 'Is'," by Robert V. Hannaford, from *Ethics* 82 (January 1972), pp. 155–162. Reprinted by permission of the publisher, the University of Chicago Press, and the author.

"Master and Slave Morality," from *Beyond Good and Evil,* by Friedrich Nietzsche, translated with commentary by Walter Kaufmann, Copyright © 1966 by Random House, Inc. Reprinted by permission of the publisher.

"Morality as Class Interest," from *Anti-Dühring* by Frederick Engels. Reprinted by permission of International Publishers.

"Morality and Ideology" by Henry David Aiken from the book *Ethics and Society,* edited by Richard T. DeGeorge. Copyright © 1966 by The Kansas University Endowment Association. Reprinted by permission of Doubleday & Company, Inc.

"Powerlessness" and "Violence," excerpted from *The New Socialist Revolution* by Michael P. Lerner. Copyright © 1973 by Michael P. Lerner. Reprinted with permission of Delacorte Press and *The Wall Street Journal,* © Dow Jones & Company, Inc. 1971.

"Visceral Racism," by Irving Thalberg, reprinted from *The Monist,* Vol. 56, No. 1 (1972), LaSalle, Illinois, with the permission of the author and publisher.

"The Nature of Freedom," by Angela Y. Davis, first published in *American Dialogue,* Vol. 6 (Autumn 1971). This paper is an unrevised, unedited lecture by Angela Y. Davis. Reprinted by permission of the National Alliance.

"Homogenizing the American Woman: The Power of an Unconscious Ideology," by Sandra L. Bem and Daryl J. Bem. Copyright © Sandra and Daryl Bem, 1973. Reprinted by permission of the authors.

"The Oppression of Children," reprinted by permission of William Morrow & Company, Inc. from *The Dialectic of Sex* by Shulamith Firestone. Copyright © 1970 by Shulamith Firestone.

"Animal Liberation," by Peter Singer from *The New York Review of Books* (April 5, 1973). Reprinted with permission from the author and *The New York Review of Books.* Copyright © 1973 Nyrev, Inc.

"Abortion: Parameters for Decision," by R. J. Gerber from *Ethics* (January 1972). Reprinted by permission of the publisher, the University of Chicago Press.

"Abortion and Infanticide," by Michael Tooley, from *Philosophy and Public Affairs,* Vol. 2, No. 1 (1972). Reprinted by permission of Princeton University Press.

"The Force of Nonviolence," by Howard Zinn, from *The Nation* (March 17, 1962). Reprinted by permission of the publisher.

"Alienated Labor," from *Karl Marx: Early Writings* translated and edited by T. B. Bottomore. Copyright © 1963 by T. B. Bottomore. Used with permission of McGraw-Hill Book Company.

" 'Work' and 'Play'," by Richard Burke, from *Ethics* 82 (October 1971). Reprinted by permission of the publisher, the University of Chicago Press, and the author.

"Rationality in Sexual Morality," by Albert Ellis. This article first appeared in *The Humanist,* September/October 1969 issue, and is reprinted by permission.

"Monogamy: A Critique," by John McMurtry. Reprinted from *The Monist,* Vol. 56, No. 4 (1972), LaSalle, Illinois, with the permission of the author and publisher.

"Communes as Experiments in Human and Sexual Relationships," excepted from *Becoming Partners* by Carl R. Rogers. Copyright © 1972 by Carl R. Rogers. Reprinted by permission of Delacorte Press.

"Philosophical Reflections on Experiments on Human Subjects," by Hans Jonas. Reprinted by permission of *Daedalus,* Journal of the American Academy of Arts and Sciences, Boston, Massachusetts, Spring 1969.

"On the Birth of a Severely Handicapped Infant," by Warren T. Reich and Harmon Smith. Reprinted with permission from the series, Case Studies in Bioethics, *Hastings Center Report,* Vol. 3, No. 4, September 1973.

"Psychosurgery," excerpted from "Brain Surgery in Aggressive Epileptics," by Vernon H. Mark, *Hastings Center Report,* Vol. 3, No. 1. © 1973 by the Institute of Society, Ethics and the Life Sciences.

"Prison Psychiatry: The Clockwork Cure," by Bernard Weiner, from *The Nation* (April 3, 1972). Reprinted by permission of the publisher.

"The Myth of Mental Illness," by Thomas S. Szasz, from *The New York Times Magazine* (June 12, 1966). © 1966 by The New York Times Company. Reprinted by permission.

"Advertising as a Philosophical System," from *Culture Against Man,* by Jules Henry. Copyright © 1963 by Random House, Inc. Reprinted by permission of the publisher.

"Competition and Planning," from *The Road to Serfdom* by Friedrich A. Hayek. Reprinted by permission of the publisher, the University of Chicago Press, and the author.

"Profit versus Social Utility," from *Strategy for Labor* by André Gorz. French text © 1964 by Éditions du Seuil, English translation Copyright © 1967 by Beacon Press. Reprinted by permission of Beacon Press.

"Deterring Corporate Crime," by Gilbert Geis, from *Corporate Power in America* edited by Ralph Nader and Mark J. Green. Copyright © 1973 by Ralph Nader. Reprinted by permission of Grossman Publishers.

"Justice as Fairness," reprinted by permission of the publishers from John Rawls, *A Theory of Justice,* Cambridge, Mass.: The Belknap Press of Harvard University Press, Copyright, 1971, by the President and Fellows of Harvard College.

"Economic Justice," by Joel Feinberg from *Social Philosophy* © 1973. Reprinted by permission of Prentice-Hall, Inc., Englewood Cliffs, New Jersey.

"The Ethics of Distribution," from *Capitalism and Freedom* by Milton Friedman. Reprinted by permission of the publisher, the University of Chicago Press, and the author.

"To Each According to His Needs," from Karl Marx, "Critique of the Gotha Program," in *Marx and Engels: Selected Works.* Reprinted by permission of International Publishers.

"On Justice under Socialism," by Edward and Onora Nell from *Dissent* (Summer 1972). Reprinted by permission of the authors.

preface

For some time we have found courses in ethics difficult or at least frustrating to teach. This is because students often have little idea of what is expected of them when they do philosophy and almost no idea of what it might mean to do ethics. The present text is our attempt to remedy the problem. We feel it is not enough to provide an interesting collection of essays about contemporary moral problems; unless those essays are presented within the context of a comprehensive theoretical framework that focuses on what doing ethics is all about, class discussions can never really get off the ground. Students often begin the semester convinced that there is no room for serious discussion of "right" and "wrong" ("It's all a matter of opinion," "It's up to the individual"), or that ethics must depend upon religion, or that moral judgments can only be viewed relative to a particular society. A successful course in ethics must begin, therefore, by bringing these issues out into the open and coming to terms with them if a stimulating and productive discussion of contemporary moral issues is to follow.

Even more basic to the success of a course in ethics is some preliminary discussion of what kinds of problems are moral problems and how to go about resolving them. This is the reason for our Introduction, "A Few Moral Dilemmas," with its capsule ethical problems and its suggestions on how to approach them. Through a discussion of these dilemmas at the start of a course in ethics, the need for some kind of conceptual framework in which to place moral problems will become apparent; and the material in Part 1, "The Status of Ethics," will thus be made relevant for the student who wishes to systematize the moral judgments provoked by the dilemmas. He or she can then proceed to Part 2, "Contemporary Moral Problems," with a developed sense of what it means to discuss contemporary social and personal issues within the philosophical tradition of ethics. Furthermore, because some of the problems that are presented in skeletal form in the Introduction appear again in essays in Parts 1 and 2, later discussion will profit from this earlier, anticipatory introduction of them.

The contemporary moral problems presented in this book flow from our conception of ethics as a discipline that analyzes the nature of the good life in its broadest terms. Sections like "Work and Play and the Protestant Ethic," "Medical and Psychiatric Ethics," "Business Ethics and Social Responsibility," and "Just Distribution and the Social Good," reflect our belief that ethics has something important to say about the conduct of everyday life in our advanced technological society. These sections also suggest that we need not accept the existing social framework and its prevailing norms as defining the only conditions under which people can live. They suggest that we consider alternative forms of social relationships, arrangements, and institutions.

The essays in this volume have been chosen because they are highly readable, because they should provoke student interest, and because they should permit a genuinely philosophical discussion of contemporary value conflicts. Regrettably, but understandably, some of these essays reflect the unconscious prejudices of the societies in which they were written. You will find some sexist language (most contributors have used the male pronoun exclusively) and sexist assumptions about human capacities, and you will find some insensitivity to other kinds of exploitative relationships. Were articles excluded because of such flaws, it would be difficult, perhaps impossible, to compile a complete anthology. It is our hope that these are problems which future editors will not have to confront.

Many thanks to the students, friends, and people at Random House who helped make this volume possible. Special thanks to Eli Hirsch, Barbara Chasin, Dick Franke, Richard Garretson, Jim Wall, Peter Deane, Susan Phillips, Joe Morse, Nancy Barton, and Pat Klossner.

And last but not least, to Timothy Dingman who bears responsibility for some of the more outlandish moral dilemmas in the Introduction.

And last and certainly least, to Byron who did the typing.

contents

introduction

a few moral dilemmas

All of us spend a considerable portion of each day making choices. Some of these choices are trivial, so trivial and so habitual that we scarcely notice them: Shall I take a jacket or not? Do I want a second cup of coffee? Other choices are not trivial; they are fewer in number, but vastly more important in terms of our own future and the future of others. These nontrivial choices are often fairly difficult to make—if I choose wrongly about taking my jacket I will simply be uncomfortable for a short period, but if I choose wrongly about whether to marry or have children or work for a particular social cause, I shall have to live with the consequences of that choice for a good many years.

For the purpose of our discussion let us agree that virtually all nontrivial choices can be understood as *moral* choices. Generally, such choices will (1) have fairly long-term consequences, (2) affect others in a significant way, (3) contribute to defining the kind of person we are, (4) contribute to defining the kinds of relations we want people to have and the kind of world we think ought to exist, and (5) contribute to creating the kinds of values we think ought to operate in the world. At first glance, this definition of what counts as a moral choice or moral dilemma may seem too broad. For example, someone might suggest that, while the choice of which car to buy may be important to us, it hardly seems to qualify as a moral choice. But is this really so? For instance, should you purchase a large car or small car: should gasoline consumption be a serious consideration; should you feel an obligation to purchase optional devices that would significantly decrease the pollution emitted by the car? In fact, we might ask whether there should be any cars at all in our large urban centers and whether the present emphasis on private modes of transportation should be placed more appropriately on the creation of efficient mass transportation systems. All these considerations have far-reaching consequences for yourself and the well-being of others and are significant because they entail a commitment to the creation of a particular kind of society.

Let us look at another example. How about the decision of where to live? Certainly it is not trivial, and it will have long-term consequences, but can it qualify as a moral dilemma? Under certain conditions it clearly can; for example, would you be willing to move into an apartment building where Jewish tenants were excluded? Would you live in a house in a neighborhood where blacks and

Spanish-speaking people were not welcome? Is it important to deliberately choose an integrated neighborhood in which to live? When considered in light of these kinds of questions, the choice of where to live can clearly be seen as having implications that qualify it as a moral choice.

And one last example—choosing what to eat. At first glance, choosing between a salad or a soup, a pork roast or an eggplant parmigiana, may not seem to involve any moral issues, but what if the salad is made with nonunion lettuce and a national boycott has been called because of the oppressive conditions under which farm workers must labor. This choice clearly involves more than just suiting our tastes of the moment. And how about our choice of an entree? Pork is not just a food, it was once a living animal, one that was capable of suffering and feeling pain and which is about as intelligent as your pet dog. This animal was raised under unpleasant and confining conditions and was killed purposely so that it could appear on your table. Further, it takes an average of fifteen to twenty pounds of vegetable protein to produce one pound of animal protein. Considering the limited food resources of the earth and the actual fact of starvation in the world, should you knowingly commit yourself to this allocation of resources by choosing meat? Viewed in this way it becomes clear that something more than a matter of taste is involved in our choice of entrees.

So what to buy, where to live, and what to eat can all involve moral decisions, and we can add innumerable other choices to this list: whether to keep a promise, to go to war, to join a revolutionary movement, to support various social policies, to let people suffer when it is in our power to do something about it, to have many lovers (or one or none), to cheat the boss, and so forth.

If we understand moral decisions in this way, we are returning to a conception of ethics held by Aristotle. For Aristotle, ethics was a branch of politics because it concerned how people ought to live within a community. Using such a definition to guide us, we can see that many choices are, in fact, moral decisions, even though they are not ordinarily thought to be so. The moral dilemmas that are presented in this chapter grow out of such a conception of ethics.

What, then, is a moral dilemma? Sometimes the word "dilemma" is used very loosely to mean any difficult problem but, in a more specific sense, it presents a conflict between several alternatives, all of which seem to have undesirable consequences. As a category of logic, a dilemma is an argument that presents the unhappy consequences of *two* seemingly exhaustive alternatives. For our purposes, a dilemma may involve any number of alternatives, so long as each of them seems to present difficulties. A moral dilemma, then, is a situation in which all the alternatives have consequences that seem unsatisfying. In other words, moral dilemmas arise because we find ourselves faced, not with clear-cut choices between good and bad (no problem there—choose the good!), but between competing goods and competing bads, between competing standards of value, between competing obligations, between competing loyalties. What if someone must be hurt? What if helping one person requires that I not help someone else? What if saving the lives of many persons requires the commission of an act usually understood to be profoundly immoral? What if loyalty to a friend (to a country, religion, ethnic group, or family) conflicts with some principle of justice? What if the rights of the individual conflict with the overall welfare of the society? What if doing good to others requires that I sacrifice my well-being? What if lying (stealing, committing adultry, and breaking other commandments) will make me very happy and will cause no one to suffer?

A moral dilemma is experienced as a conflict within ourselves. In daily life, each of us acts on the basis of a variety of moral intuitions and principles. For the most part, we like to pretend that these intuitions and principles are compatible. A moral dilemma makes us aware that this is not always the case, that when applied to concrete situations, our most deeply felt intuitions appear to demand two opposing courses of actions. What seems right from one perspective, seems wrong from the other. And our intuitions push us to adopt both perspectives simultaneously. Thus, a moral dilemma has a crucial existential dimension. Although we can and do simultaneously hold contradictory intuitions in our mind, we cannot act on them both simultaneously. The choice to act on one principle may leave us feeling guilty about our inability to fulfill the demands of the other. Our very sense of self is at stake. For who we are is not simply a matter of what we profess to believe, but how those beliefs manifest themselves in our choices and our actions.

Of course, reflecting on the moral dilemmas presented in this book is not the same as living through them. Here, the main task is moral clarification; we need to make our intuitions explicit, to analyze the practical implications of certain moral principles, to determine the conditions under which they apply, to recognize when they conflict with other principles, to determine which ought to take precedence, and so forth. In so doing, we would hope to be able to resolve at least some of the moral dilemmas presented here.

Although there is no definitive way to resolve a moral dilemma, we shall offer some suggestions in the hope that they will serve as useful guideposts. Later your own reading of the essays in Parts 1 and 2 should help you formulate some additional guideposts.

First, when considering a moral dilemma, you should attempt to imagine yourself in the place of those affected by the moral decision, as well as in the place of the one making the decision. These two categories necessarily overlap, because persons making moral decisions affect not only others but themselves in the very process of decision making.

Second, although the starting point of moral deliberation is often intuition, it cannot end with intuition alone. For one thing, as we have already discussed, our intuitions are often in conflict; for another, our moral intuitions are sometimes nothing more than internalized cultural prejudices. Moral reflection requires not merely that we draw out the principles implicit in our intuition, but that we be willing to place those principles in doubt. This does not mean that we can doubt all our moral beliefs simultaneously, for to be able to doubt some of our beliefs requires that we hold others constant. In other words, we need to retain some of our moral intuitions in order to question and evaluate others. Moral reflection is a complex process by which we reflect on the theoretical and practical implications of acting in accord with certain intuitions in the light of still other intuitions which, in turn, can be the subject of critical scrutiny. While there is no ultimate stopping point to this process, we can reach a tentative conclusion when we arrive at a moral position that seems satisfactory on balance in terms of all presently conceivable consequences.

This brings us to a third consideration—how to calculate consequences. While this is partially a causal question, it is not entirely so. We may understand the results (both long-range and short-range) of various alternative courses of action and still be unable to decide which results are, on balance, more desirable. In its simplest form, this occurs when the alternative consequences are both good or both bad and we must decide which is the greater good or the lesser evil. In a more complex form, each course of action may have both good and bad consequences and the balance of these may seem different depending on how much weight we give to short-range or long-range concerns. (A good example is the dilemma entitled "Violence/Nonviolence" presented below.) This problem may be further complicated by the fact that the social position we occupy— for example, whether we are relatively privileged and comfortable or extremely impoverished—greatly determines our attitudes toward these consequences. This is why, as we have suggested, it is especially important to attempt to imagine oneself in the place of all those affected. Thus, not only do we need to focus on the multiplicity of consequences that may arise, but we should also attempt to arrive at a moral position that would be satisfactory, if not to the person least privileged, at least to an impartial observer. Ideally, we need a general theoretical framework within which the varying kinds of consequences can be translated into a common moral quality. This quality would, then, serve as the basis by which they can be compared and provides a temporal calculus for balancing short- and long-range goals.

A similar difficulty confronts us when we attempt to mediate between competing obligations. Even when we are clear about the origin and nature of these obligations (this in itself may require an extensive analysis of institutional arrangements and a variety of personal relationships), it is not always clear which obligation is to take precedence. The obligations themselves do not wear the mark of their own moral priority. In fact, what is particularly troublesome about obligations is that there is no preestablished hierarchy between them; that one obligation overrides another is determined by a multiplicity of variables within a given situation. Hence, we need an independent moral criterion by which these variables can be evaluated in relation to the competing obligations.

Finally, we need to consider if the dilemma is genuine. In some cases, what appears to be a conflict may rest on a misunderstanding. An obligation that holds in one kind of situation may be forfeit in another (we are not obliged to keep a promise made under duress; it might be claimed that we are not obligated to respect the rights of those who do not respect our rights). Although certain moral principles may be appropriate to the evaluation of certain kinds of problems, they may be inappropriate in another context. Ideals such as justice, liberty, and the public good do not have unlimited range of application; therefore, what appears as a moral conflict may rest on an inadequate understanding of the concept and an inability to accurately delineate moral boundary lines.

Nonetheless, many moral dilemmas are genuine and, of these, some will perhaps be incapable of any fully satisfactory resolution. For these last, we may reserve the term "tragedy."

The suggestions given above should give the reader a sense of the complexity of attempting to take a moral stand and to defend that stand. The dilemmas presented here should afford the reader the opportunity to begin such moral reflection in a concrete manner. But even more important, what should emerge from a consideration of the moral dilemmas that follow is a clear sense of the need to develop a theoretical perspective from which we can turn our moral intuitions into rationally defensible moral positions. The readings in Parts 1 and 2 of this volume are designed to do just that. It should be interesting to return to some of the dilemmas presented in this introduction after you have finished the course and to see whether you are then better equipped to formulate an articulate defense of the kinds of moral choices they elicit.

A FEW MORAL DILEMMAS

Shall We Torture?

For weeks a diabolical murderer has been planting bombs at random in a large Midwestern city, and to date seventeen people have been killed in the explosions. At this moment the city is in an uproar because this fiend has called the city's daily newspaper and announced that he has planted five bombs set to go off at three in the afternoon. He predicts that hundreds of people will lose their lives in the blast. By extraordinary good luck, the bomber is apprehended at twelve-thirty in the afternoon. By one-thirty all attempts to make him divulge the locations of the bombs have failed. Only an hour and a half remain before the bombs are set to explode. Someone proposes that we use torture in a last desperate attempt to get him to tell us where the bombs are and thus avert a tragedy of mind-boggling proportions.

QUESTIONS: Would it be morally right to use torture?
Would your answer be different if the bomber were setting off the bombs for a political cause of which you approve?

Privileged Information

You are a lawyer defending your client, Rock Toothsome, who is charged with the premeditated murder of his pregnant wife. On the day of his trial you are in top form; your summation brings tears to the eyes of several jurors and even the judge seems moved by your emotional account of your client's innocence. While the jury is deliberating, Rock leans over and whispers in your ear that he appreciates the brilliant way you have handled his defense. He says you almost convinced him that he was innocent, even though he had of course committed the murder. Having believed him to be not guilty, you are shocked by this revelation. At this very moment the jury begins filing in to announce their verdict. What, if anything, should you do?

House for Sale

In July, Jones places an advertisement in the newspaper announcing that his home is for sale. Smith, a lifetime apartment dweller, answers the ad and finds the house to his liking. Jones is scrupulously honest in answering all of Smith's queries about the condition of the house; however, in part because it is summer, and in part because of his inexperience, Smith never asks about the condition of the boiler. As it happens, the boiler is in very poor condition and Jones knows this.

He has been told that it will not last another winter, and he has received an estimate of $1,200 as the cost of installing a new one. But Smith never asks and
Jones never tells.

QUESTION: Has Jones behaved in a morally acceptable manner?

Responsibility

Dr. Ficktnicht was considered by his contemporaries to be the consummate scientist. His work, microbiology, was his life. He was so dedicated to his research
that he never found time to marry. His colleagues frequently found it necessary to
remind him to take nourishment. In 1950, Dr. Ficktnicht stumbled on an amaz-
ingly deadly bacterium during the course of his search for new antibiotics. The
good doctor found that the culture produced painful but inevitable death in 100
percent of all laboratory animals tested. He documented his findings, turned them
over to his government's Bacteriological Warfare Division, and proceeded with his
work. Two years later, Dr. Ficktnicht's government launched an aggressive war
against several of its neighbors. Within ninety days the aggressors were defeated,
but not before they had wiped out hundreds of thousands of the victor's civilian
population. The victor's first act upon occupation was to arrest Dr. Ficktnicht in
his laboratory.

QUESTION.   Should Dr. Ficktnicht be tried with the aggressor's military personnel for
genocide?

Flesh

You are living on an island with seven people. The island has lush vegetation;
fruits and vegetables grow in abundance, and a balanced diet of them will provide you with complete nutrition.

QUESTIONS: Would it be right to kill a human being and eat its flesh?
Would it be right to kill an animal and eat its flesh?

Profits and Pollution

José Diaz works for the XYZ corporation, which makes Frizelheimers. One day,
Diaz's boss calls him in and announces that it will be necessary to alter the production conditions and thus produce more Frizelheimers per hour. Diaz points out
that if they increase production, the XYZ corporation will be causing 30 percent

more air and water pollution than it currently does. His boss agrees but points out that the corporation has an obligation to its stockholders to make as high a rate of profit as possible.

QUESTIONS: Should the corporation make the changes?
Should Diaz carry out the changes knowing that severe pollution will result?

A Tribal Ceremony

You find yourself the guest of a tribe living on a remote island. Custom has it that once each year a ten-year-old child is killed as part of the tribe's most sacred ceremony. The child and its family regard being chosen for sacrifice as the highest honor they can receive and as a guarantee that they will have an afterlife with the gods. As guest of the tribe, you are asked to participate in the ceremony and are given the equally high honor of wielding the spear that strikes the death blow.

QUESTION: Would it be wrong to participate?

Omission and Commission

Marcia Stevens, a championship sw   is out for a leisurely stroll. During the course of her walk she passes by the   n which, a moment earlier, a small child has fallen. The child is waving its   calling for help. No other people are present. Marcia continues on her walk   he child drowns.

QUESTIONS: Was it morally wrong for Stevens to walk by? Did she have an obligation to save the child?
Would your answer be different if Stevens could not swim at all? If she were a poor swimmer?
Compare her action or failure to act with the act of someone who deliberately pushes the child into the river and then leaves. Is Stevens' action (1) equivalent to, (2) not as bad as, (3) worse than the action of the person who pushes the child in and leaves it to drown?

The Greater Good

Two hundred Sioux Indians, the remainder of a once populous and powerful nation, have claimed sole ownership of several thousand acres of land, including a four-mile stretch of the Grand Canyon. They declare that they are going to alter the landscape and the water course to raise crops and livestock for the tribe, and that they will use force to assert and maintain their claim if necessary. The government, distressed by the possibility of losing this landmark (which they assert is public domain), hands the problem to a game-theory computer in the Pentagon subbasement. The computer predicts that the government will have to kill 41.3 Indians before the group will relent.

QUESTIONS: Is the Grand Canyon worth the lives of 41.3 Sioux Indians?
Is the Grand Canyon worth the lives of 12.3 Sioux Indians?

A Pregnancy

Hester Prim, an unmarried college senior, finds herself pregnant. Does she have a moral obligation to inform the baby's father and allow him to participate in the decision about whether to have the child?

QUESTIONS: Would your answer be different if:
1. the man were someone with whom Prim was having a long-term relationship?
2. Prim were married and her husband was the baby's father?
3. the man were someone Prim hardly knew and did not like?

Privacy

While on assignment in East McKeesport, Pennsylvania, ace reporter Inky Pressfingers recognizes Dr. Eldritch Rites. When Dr. Rites disappeared in 1971, he was on the verge of discovering a method of male contraception so perfect that it promised to solve the population problem for even the most underdeveloped nations of the world. Dr. Rites tells Pressfingers he has suffered a great personal tragedy which convinced him that the human race is not deserving of his knowledge. He wants to be left alone and in peace.

QUESTIONS: Does Pressfingers have either the right or the duty to reveal the whereabouts of Dr. Rites?
Does Dr. Rites have the right to withhold his knowledge?

Making a Profit

Garley Gogetter's job, making deliveries, pays him $1.75 an hour. One day he is offered a better job that pays $2.25 an hour. He hires Billy Downenout to make the deliveries and pays him $1.25 an hour, thus assuring himself an immediate profit of $.50 an hour in addition to the wages from his new job.

QUESTIONS: Is there anything immoral about this?

Would your answer be different if he offered Billy $1.50 an hour?

What if he offered Billy $1.65 an hour?

Violence/Nonviolence

Group X is living under conditions of brutal exploitation, oppression, and suffering. It can be liberated in thirty years if nonviolent means are employed; however, it can be liberated in ten years if violent means are used.

QUESTION: Would it be more moral to employ violent or nonviolent means to bring about the group's liberation?

Euthanasia

Angel O'brien, a former profootball star, is dying of cancer. The cancer has spread throughout his body and he has already lost fifty pounds. As his doctor, you are convinced that he cannot live more than a few weeks. During one of your visits, O'brien pleads with you to put him to death. He is in constant pain and is using up the limited savings of his family. He wishes his wife and children to remember him as he once was, not as an emaciated man, semiconscious be-cause of prescribed painkillers.

QUESTIONS: Should you put O'brien to death?

Would your answer be different if you were his best friend instead of his doctor?

Hijacking

You are Prime Minister of a major world power, the Continuous State of Ambi-ance. Word has just reached you that a group of political opponents has hijacked an Ambiance Airlines plane and is threatening to destroy it along with the passen-gers and crew on board unless you release five political prisoners.

QUESTIONS: What would be the right course of action?

Would your answer be different if the hijackers requested a half million dollars in medical supplies for the poor instead of the prisoners' release?

Would your answer be different if one of your children were on board the plane?

Dividing the Pie

What is the most just way of dividing an apple pie among four people?

> Would your answer be different if:
> 1. two of the people had just finished eating large meals and two of the people had not eaten for some time and were very hungry?
> 2. the pie were the property of one of the four?

Quantity versus Quality

You are a manager of The Amalgamated Sweatshop Company. One day the fore-man comes to you and announces that morale is very low because the workers find their jobs tedious and boring. Some workers have even resorted to using barbiturates to make their time on the job endurable. Under a new plan for reorganization of the plant, workers will find their participation in the productive process 100 percent more challenging and interesting; however, this change will result in the factory producing fewer goods.

QUESTION: Should the change be instituted?

A Lesser Evil

You are the mayor of a town occupied by enemy forces during a war. The leader of the occupying troops calls all the townspeople together and announces that all men between the ages of fifteen and sixty-five are to be exterminated. In response to the entreaties of the citizenry, he modifies his order and announces that he will permit most of the men to live on the condition that you, the mayor, choose three men from the town's population and kill them yourself publicly.

QUESTION: What does morality require?

Cheating

Stuart Slyguiler is a college senior slated to graduate next month. He postponed taking biology until his last semester because he believed that he would have trouble with it. Stuart's reservations proved correct. He is on the borderline between a C and a D, and he must receive the C in order to graduate. On the day of the final exam he finds himself sitting next to Wendy Winsomewinner, the best student in the class. Stuart can see Wendy's paper clearly, and if he copies from her no one will ever know.

QUESTIONS: Would it be right for him to cheat on the exam?
Would your answer be different if Stuart were a sophomore and this were just another exam?

Accident

You are an attorney-at-law in the state of New Jersey. On your way to court in Newark one morning, you witness a rear-end automobile collision. At least one of the two people in the struck vehicle appears to be injured. Traffic is heavy. There must be twenty witnesses, but no one seems to be stopping. You yourself are in a hurry to reach the courthouse. As an attorney, you know how unpleasant and time-consuming it can be to become involved in this sort of thing, especially if the case goes to court.

QUESTIONS: Should you drive on, feeling certain that someone else will surely stop?
Should you drive to the nearest telephone and report the accident anonymously?
Should you stop, even though you have no first-aid training and realize that you could come under professional criticism for appearing to be an "ambulance chaser"?

Obligation to Parents

Frankie and Johnny are college students who have been going together for two years. They have just figured out that by continuing to work at the part-time jobs they now hold and by moving in together they can manage to move out of their parents' homes and into a place of their own. Although they are very emotionally involved with each other, they have no intention of getting married. In fact, they consider marriage an unequal and oppressive relationship. Upon hearing the couple's intentions, their parents become distraught and plead with them not to live together unless they get married.

QUESTION: Do Frankie and Johnny have an obligation to consider their parents' concern in deciding whether to live together?

Blood

A multiple car accident has occured near your campus involving several cars driven by college students. As a result, the local hospital puts out an emergency call for blood donors. You are in excellent health.

QUESTIONS: Do you have a moral obligation to donate blood?

Would it be all right to accept payment for the blood?

Kidney Machine

Seven patients are suffering acute kidney failure and require the use of a kidney machine if they are to survive. The hospital has only one kidney machine available, and there is only enough time on it for two patients to be treated. Five of the seven will die. The patients are

1. a ten-year-old child
2. a twenty-seven-year-old mother of three
3. a twenty-seven-year-old father of three
4. a sixty-year-old neurosurgeon
5. a thirty-five-year-old Nobel prizewinning author
6. a nineteen-year-old college sophomore
7. a seventy-two-year-old retired carpenter

QUESTION: How should the two patients be chosen?

Fur

Adrienne Fox is a copywriter for Harkwell, Horwell and Dithers, a large advertising agency. The agency acquires the account of a major furrier who is interested in promoting his line of sealskin coats. Adrienne believes that it is immoral to kill animals and use their skins for decoration. In addition, she knows that baby seals are brutally slaughtered to make coats by having their heads bashed in.

QUESTION: Even though Adrienne is not assigned to work on the fur account, should she resign her job with the agency?

Cancer Cure

Theodore Brand, an eminent scientist, announces that he is on the verge of discovering a cure for cancer. His final experiment will require five hundred subjects. We know in advance that some of the subjects will die in the course of the research. Brand proposes using prisoners with life sentences in his experiments. They will be given the opportunity to volunteer and will know all the facts. In addition, those who survive the experiment will have their sentences commuted.

QUESTION: Would it be morally right to invite life-term prisoners to volunteer for the experiment?

God's Will

Abraham Brown kills his infant son while the child sleeps. Later he explains, with tears streaming down his cheeks, that he had to do so because God came and ordered him to kill the child and he could not disobey God's will. You are completely convinced of Brown's sincerity.

QUESTION: What would be the right course of action to adopt in relation to Brown?
1. try him for murder
2. commit him for psychiatric observation
3. honor him as a mortal chosen by God for special communication

Benevolence

Horace Moneymuncher is out for a walk. He comes upon a frail-looking woman carrying a small, emaciated child. The woman sways on her feet and Horace comes to her assistance. He asks if she is ill and she replies that neither she nor her child has eaten for some time because they are penniless. Horace sympathizes with her and bids her goodbye. On the way home he happens to pass a Jaguar dealer and, on a whim, purchases a canary-yellow car that catches his fancy. He already owns five cars, but none of them is yellow, and he is partial to yellow.

QUESTION: Was it morally wrong to buy the car but not to buy the woman and her child some food?

Population Control

In the year 2000, scientists tell us that if population growth is not radically curtailed within ten years, the food, water, and energy supply will not be capable of fulfilling the population's needs.

QUESTION: Given such a crisis, would it be right to prohibit some people from having children? If so, what criterion would be the most just for choosing who would be permitted to have offspring and who would not?
Some possible criteria:
1. random lottery
2. IQ tests
3. wealth
4. age
5. educational background
6. health

Promise Keeping

Your closest friend extracts a promise from you that you will not repeat what she is about to tell you. You promise. She then confesses that she has become hooked on heroin and is resorting to petty crime to support her habit, and she tells you that she has just stolen money from a neighbor's wallet. The next day you find out that the local delivery boy has been arrested on charges of stealing money from this neighbor while making a delivery.

QUESTION: Should you keep your promise to your friend?

Justice and the Limits of the System

A magistrate at Queens Bench in England has a strange case before him. Mr. Schmedrick is found dead on the sidewalk in front of Gottbaum's Grainery. There is a 250-pound bag of grain on top of Mr. Schmedrick's body, and a second-story loading door directly above the body is open. The magistrate believes it is obvious that Mr. Schmedrick was killed by a falling bag of negligently handled grain. He wants to make some award to Mrs. Schmedrick, widow of the deceased, but to this date all such awards have been based on the testimony of witnesses, and no one saw the death of Mr. Schmedrick. The magistrate is afraid that if he sets a precedent, thousands of similar cases will flood the court system.

QUESTION: Should the judge "open the flood gates" by making what he considers a just award to Widow Schmedrick?

Ending the Human Race

Incredibly, fifty people somehow manage to survive a nuclear war. Looking back over human civilization, they decide that the centuries have provided a record of brutality, exploitation, oppression, and incalculable suffering. Looking back over their own lives, each believes that he or she has lived through more pain and unhappiness than pleasure. As a result they agree not to produce any offspring so that when the last of them dies the human race will cease to exist.

QUESTION: Is it morally legitimate for these people to decide to end the human race?

part
1

the status of ethics

Those who claim to be doing ethics do an extraordinary variety of things under that title. Some talk of God, some scrutinize language, some go off in search of anthropological data, and so forth. The diversity of these activities leads us to begin our study of ethics, not by directly considering moral problems, but by focusing on ethics itself as a particular kind of discipline; by asking how it functions in its own right, what its relation is to other disciplines, and what ethical thinkers have themselves claimed to be doing. But even before we can begin so basic an inquiry, a preliminary question awaits us. Ethics, however else we define it, is concerned with right and wrong, good and bad. The first question that arises is, why should I be concerned with what is right or good, or, to put it another way, why be moral?

Since ethical demands are generally presented as motives for action, they suggest that there is a conflict between desire and what is right; for the need to mention that something is right already assumes that there may be a tendency not to do it. Thus, the question "Why be moral?" suggests a conflict between morality and my desires, or, to put it another way, between morality and self-interest. In fact, some like Kurt Baier have insisted that moral rules are precisely designed to overrule considerations of self-interest. This distinction, however, may be drawn too sharply: The self is not an isolated unit but a social self—an entity created originally by social interactions (would we have a sense of self without society?) and constantly involved in these interactions. Thus, if there is a conflict between morality and self-interest, it may be the responsibility not so much of the individual, but, as Robert Olson argues, of a society which is so imperfectly and unjustly structured that the individual good tends to be in opposition to the social good. The conflict, then, requires not a motive for individual action so much as a demand for social change. Conversely, the way we define self-interest depends on how we understand the concept of self. A self intimately connected with the social world need not be selfish in the narrow sense. And, as Erich Fromm points out, whereas a narrow sense of self may conflict with morality, a more developed sense of self will find morality to its self-interest.

Once we decide that there is a reason to be moral, we must ask what can provide the foundation for morality. Is such a foundation to be discovered by philosophical reflection alone? In other words, is ethics, as the philosophical study of morality, an autonomous discipline? Or, rather, does ethics depend in turn on some other discipline?

It is not uncommon for persons new to the study of ethics to argue that morality is simply a reflection of whatever one's society happens to approve or disapprove and, therefore, words like "right" and "wrong" can mean nothing more than what a particular culture happens to believe is right and wrong. In this mode of thinking, what is generally believed to be right *is* right (for that society), and no more can be said about the matter. Morality, then, becomes relative to whatever meaning a culture gives to it; there can be no universal moral standard; and ethics, thus, becomes a branch of sociology and anthropology. This is the thesis of ethical relativism, and it is often thought to be derived from a corresponding anthropological thesis—the thesis of cultural relativism. This latter thesis holds that different cultures do in fact have very different moral standards and practices; they believe very different things about what is right and what is wrong. Anthropologists will observe that while a given culture A approves of *x* and disapproves of *y*, another culture B approves of *y* and disapproves of *x*. In other words, while *x* is considered "right" in culture A, it is considered "wrong" in culture B, and, reversely, while *y* is considered "right" in culture B, it is considered "wrong" in culture A. This, claim the cultural relativists, is not the exception but the general rule.

Two questions need to be asked here. First, to what extent is the thesis of cultural relativism correct? This involves not only a consideration of whether there are some value differences between various cultures—and the overwhelming evidence indicates that there are—but whether there are any differences in the fundamental underlying values of different cultures. This requires not merely that we collect certain anthropological data, but that we understand how to interpret that data, and, for this, we need a criterion to determine what constitutes a fundamental ethical disagreement across cultural boundaries. Second, even if different cultures do have fundamentally different values, the thesis of *ethical* relativism is not thereby established. For, as Walter Stace argues, the ethical absolutist can still claim that what a given culture *believes* to be right is not *actually* right. Morality, then, is not relative to whatever a given culture happens to believe, but can, in fact, be used to challenge the values of that culture as a whole. Ethics cannot merely report the values of a given society; it must devise a criterion by which to evaluate those values and that society.

It is at this point that the theologian enters. If moral values are transcendent to the beliefs of any given culture, we must, it is claimed, turn to religion for guidance; for where else can we find the basis for universal values? Without belief in God as the source of all morality, even humanistic ethics must flounder without roots, and the world will continue on its course of moral decay. Thus, the important question that confronts us in Section Three is whether ethics is dependent on religion in some ultimate sense or whether, as Kai Nielsen argues, even religious morality requires an independent ethical criterion.

It is interesting to note that Nielsen's position in Section Three parallels Stace's position in Section Two about the independence of ethics from anthropology. If both positions are correct, then ethics can be regarded as an autonomous discipline in search of its own criterion for moral action.

Historically, there have been two basic approaches to the development of an independent ethical criterion. Deontologists, like Kant and Ross, insist that ethics must focus on the nature of certain kinds of moral acts which are right in themselves and which it is our duty or obligation to perform. Some of these duties grow out of specific kinds of relationships and institutional arrangements, such as the duty of a parent to a child, duties entailed by friendship, the duties of a husband or a wife, the duties of a teacher to his or her students, the duties of citizenship, and the like: Other duties are of a more general nature—to be honest, to keep promises, to help others in distress, to respect other persons, and so forth. The good human being is the person who understands these duties and obligations and acts accordingly. The task of ethics, according to the deontological view, is to inquire into the nature and source of these moral duties. In contrast, utilitarians argue that our assessment of the moral worth of an act can only proceed by examining the consequences that flow from it and, therefore, no act can be right in itself. What makes an act right is not that it fulfills certain primary moral obligations, but that it leads to good consequences, generally understood as the greatest amount of happiness, of pleasure, and the least amount of pain for all concerned. From this point of view, rules of moral obligation are mere rules of thumb; they become a shorthand summary of the kinds of acts that *usually* produce the greatest amount of happiness for the greatest number. However, when in a particular situation it is clear that the greatest happiness will not be achieved by following the standard moral rules, the utilitarian argues that there is no need to do so. Thus, deontology and utilitarianism imply conflicting evaluations of many concrete situations. Some deontologists may well admit that we have a duty to promote the general good, but they would insist that we have other duties which may conflict with this goal and which are, in some cases, overriding. The utilitarian emphatically denies this, arguing instead that in all situations the only thing we ought to do is whatever will result in the greatest amount of good (happiness). Because many actions produce both good and bad consequences, because to do good may require doing some bad and to bring about happiness for some may entail bringing about unhappiness for others, the utilitarian needs to effect a balance, and this balance may require violating what we ordinarily understand to be our moral obligation. It may require deceit, broken promises, stealing, and even killing innocents. Thus, the utilitarian is, again, often in the position of advocating actions that the deontologist would regard with moral reproach.

Turning to contemporary ethical thought, we find that a number of philosophers tend to focus their attention less on the question of what is good or bad, right or wrong, than on the question of how such "value words" function in our language. Unlike those engaged in normative ethics, who argue for particular moral positions, these thinkers attempt to analyze what people are doing when they argue for moral positions or make moral pronouncements. This is not to say that they spend their time simply looking up words in the dictionary and reporting certain linguistic facts. Their fundamental concern is with the relation between the world and ethical language. This attempt to analyze the meaning of ethical statements is called metaethics, and it proceeds on the assumption that ethical terms function differently than factual terms; that is, terms like "good" and "bad" cannot be defined by reference to any empirically observable objects. This has led some thinkers to conclude with G. E. Moore that the fundamental ethical term, "good," refers to a simple nonnatural (nonempirical) property and, therefore, it is inherently indefinable. Among the implications of this position is a challenge to the utilitarian attempt to define good in terms of happiness, or pleasure. Other philosophers have concluded with A. J. Ayer that, inasmuch as ethical statements do not report facts, they do not refer to anything whatsoever (what, after all, is a nonempirical property?) and therefore are to be considered neither true nor false but meaningless. Statements such as "Lieutenant Calley was wrong to kill unarmed men, women, and children at My Lai" are, by this analysis, merely expressions of emotional preference. So that, whereas for Moore, what is good and bad can be known (by means of nonempirical intuition), for Ayer, ethical statements do not give us any knowledge whatsoever. Contemporary ethics, then, would seem to arrive at the conclusion that no foundation for morality can be found. More recently, however, there have been attempts to rediscover the foundations of morality within the metaethical tradition. These attempts, while recognizing that ethical terms cannot be *defined* by reference to any given facts, suggest that ethical claims can be *derived* from certain basic facts about human needs and interests within a social framework, thus narrowing the gap between facts and values, between the "is" and the "ought." Robert Hannaford's article in Section Five is representative of this position.

Finally, if morality is to be derived from human needs and interests, we need to ask whose needs and interests are to count. The answer that everyone's needs and interests are to count equally tends to mask the real social conflicts that we confront, for the social world has not been and is not now a cooperative enterprise among equal partners, all of whom can participate in deciding what is to their mutual benefit. The social world tends to be divided into those who dominate and those who are dominated, into the oppressors and the oppressed. It is to the interest of the former to maintain and reinforce the kind of social organization upon which their power and privilege rest. It is to the interest of the oppressed to alter, even to overthrow, the system of social domination. Hence, what poses as a universal ethic may, on closer examination, turn out to be the ideology of a social group. Seen in this way, ethics performs a fundamentally political role—that of stabilizing the society in the interests of those who hold power or of undermining its dominant ideological fabric. The conflicts in ethical theory may, ultimately, represent conflicts in ideology. That is why, in the last section of Part 1, we explore the relation of morality to ideology.

section one

morality and self-interest

SELF-INTEREST AND MORALITY

Kurt Baier

. . .

The Supremacy of Moral Reasons

Are moral reasons really superior to reasons of self-interest as we all believe? Do we really have reason on our side when we follow moral reasons against self-interest? What reasons could there be for being moral? Can we really give an answer to 'Why should we be moral?' It is obvious that all these questions come to the same thing. When we ask, 'Should we be moral?' or 'Why should we be moral?' or 'Are moral reasons superior to all others?' we ask to be given a reason for regarding moral reasons as superior to all others. What is this reason?

Let us begin with a state of affairs in which reasons of self-interest are supreme. In such a state everyone keeps his impulses and inclinations in check when and only when they would lead him into behavior detrimental to his own interest. Everyone who follows reason will discipline himself to rise early, to do his exercises, to refrain from excessive drinking and smoking, to keep good company, to marry the right sort of girl, to work and study hard in order to get on, and so on. However, it will often happen that people's interests conflict. In such a case, they will have to resort to ruses or force to get their own way. As this becomes known, men will become suspicious, for they will regard one another as scheming competitors for the good things in life. The universal supremacy of the rules of self-interest must lead to what Hobbes called the state of nature. At the same time, it will be clear to everyone that universal obedience to certain rules overriding self-interest would produce a state of affairs which serves everyone's interest much better than his unaided pursuit of it in a state where everyone does the same. Moral rules are universal rules designed to override those of self-interest when following the latter is harmful to others. 'Thou shalt not kill,' 'Thou shalt not lie,' 'Thou shalt not steal' are rules which forbid the inflicting of harm on someone else even when this might be in one's interest.

The very *raison d'être* of a morality is to yield reasons which overrule the reasons of self-interest in those cases when everyone's following self-interest would be harmful to everyone. Hence moral reasons are superior to all others.

"But what does this mean?" it might be objected. "If it merely means that we do so regard them, then you are of course right, but your contention is useless, a mere point of usage. And how could it mean any more? If it means that we not only do so regard them, but *ought* so to regard them, then there must be *reasons* for saying this. But there could not be any reasons for it. If you offer reasons of self-interest, you are arguing in a circle. Moreover, it cannot be true that it is always in my interest to treat moral reasons as superior to reasons of self-interest. If it were, self-interest and morality could never conflict, but they notoriously do. It is equally circular to argue that there are moral reasons for saying that one ought to treat moral reasons as superior to reasons of self-interest. And what other reasons are there?"

The answer is that we are now looking at the world from the point of view of *anyone*. We are not examining particular alternative courses of action before this or that person; we are examining two alternative worlds, one in which moral reasons are always treated by everyone as superior to reasons of self-interest and one in which the reverse is the practice. And we can see that the first world is the better world, because we can see that the second world would be the sort which Hobbes describes as the state of nature.

This shows that I ought to be moral, for when I ask the question 'What ought I to do?' I am asking, 'Which is the course of action supported by the best reasons?' But since it has just been shown that moral reasons are superior to reasons of self-interest, I have been given a reason for being moral, for following moral reasons rather than any other, namely, they are better reasons than any other.

But is this always so? Do we have a reason for being moral whatever the conditions we find ourselves in? Could there not be situations in which it is not true that we have reasons for being moral, that, on the contrary, we have reasons for ignoring the demands of morality? Is not Hobbes right in saying that in a state of nature the laws of nature, that is, the rules of morality, bind only *in foro interno?*

Hobbes argues as follows.

(i) To live in a state of nature is to live outside society. It is to live in conditions in which there are no common ways of life and, therefore, no reliable expectations about other people's behavior other than that they will follow their inclination or their interest.

(ii) In such a state reason will be the enemy of co-operation and mutual trust. For it is too risky to hope that other people will refrain from protecting their own interests by the preventive elimination of probable or even possible dangers to them. Hence reason will counsel everyone to avoid these risks by preventive action. But this leads to war.

(iii) It is obvious that everyone's following self-interest leads to a state of affairs which is desirable from no one's point of view. It is, on the contrary, desirable that everybody should follow rules overriding self-interest whenever that is to the detriment of others. In other words, it is desirable to bring about a state of affairs in which all obey the rules of morality.

(iv) However, Hobbes claims that in the state of nature it helps nobody if a single person or a small group of persons begins to follow the rules of morality, for this could only lead to the extinction of such individuals or groups. In such a state, it is therefore contrary to reason to be moral.

(v) The situation can change, reason can support morality, only when the presumption about other people's behavior is reversed. Hobbes thought that this could be achieved only by the creation of an absolute ruler with absolute power to enforce his laws. We have already seen that this is not true and that it can also be achieved if people live in a society, that is, if they have common ways of life, which are taught to all members and somehow enforced by the group. Its members have reason to expect their fellows generally to obey its rules, that is, its religion, morality, customs, and law, even when doing so is not, on certain occasions, in their interest. Hence they too have reason to follow these rules.

Is this argument sound? One might, of course, object to step (i) on the grounds that this is an empirical proposition for which there is little or no evidence. For how can we know whether it is true that people in a state of nature would follow only their inclinations or, at best, reasons of self-interest, when nobody now lives in that state or has ever lived in it?

However, there is some empirical evidence to support this claim. For in the family of nations, individual states are placed very much like individual persons in a state of nature. The doctrine of the sovereignty of nations and the absence of an effective international law and police force are a guarantee that nations live in a state of nature, without commonly accepted rules that are somehow enforced. Hence it must be granted that living in a state of nature leads to living in a state in which individuals act either on impulse or as they think their interest dictates. For states pay only lip service to morality. They attack their hated neighbors when the opportunity arises. They start preventive wars in order to destroy the enemy before he can deliver his knockout blow. Where interests conflict, the stronger party usually has his way, whether his claims are justified or not. And where the relative strength of the parties is not obvious, they usually resort to arms in order to determine "whose side God is on." Treaties are frequently concluded but, morally speaking, they are not worth the paper they are written on. Nor do the partners regard them as contracts binding in the ordinary way, but rather as public expressions of the belief of the governments concerned that for the time being their alliance is in the interest of the allies. It is well understood that such treaties may be canceled before they reach their predetermined end or simply broken when it suits one partner. In international affairs, there are very few examples of *Nibelungentreue,* although statesmen whose countries have kept their treaties in the hope of profiting from them usually make such high moral claims.

It is, moreover, difficult to justify morality in international affairs. For suppose a highly moral statesman were to demand that his country adhere to a treaty obligation even though this meant its ruin or possibly its extinction. Suppose he were to say that treaty obligations are sacred and must be kept whatever the consequences. How could he defend such a policy? Perhaps one might argue that someone has to make a start in order to create mutual confidence in international affairs. Or one might say that setting a good example is the best way of inducing others to follow suit. But such a defense would hardly be sound. The less skeptical one is about the genuineness of the cases in which nations have adhered to their treaties from a sense of moral obligation, the more skeptical one must be about the effectiveness of such examples of virture in effecting a change of international practice. Power politics still govern in international affairs.

We must, therefore, grant Hobbes the first step in his argument and admit that in a state of nature people, as a matter of psychological fact, would not follow the dictates of morality. But we might object to the next step that knowing this psychological fact about other people's behavior constitutes a reason for behaving in the same way. Would it not still be immoral for anyone to ignore the demands of morality even though he knows that others are likely or certain to do so, too? Can we offer as a justification for morality the fact that no one is entitled to do wrong just because someone else is doing wrong? This argument begs the question whether it *is* wrong for anyone in this state to disregard the demands of morality. It cannot be wrong to break a treaty or make preventive war if we have no reason to obey the moral rules. For to say that it is wrong to do so is to say that we ought not to do so. But if we have no reason for obeying the moral rule, then we have no reason overruling self-interest, hence no reason for keeping the treaty when keeping it is not in our interest, hence it is not true that we have a reason for keeping it, hence not true that we ought to keep it, hence not true that it is wrong not to keep it.

I conclude that Hobbes's argument is sound. Moralities are systems of principles whose acceptance by everyone as overruling the dictates of self-interest is in the interest of everyone alike, though following the rules of a morality is not of course identical with following self-interest. If it were, there could be no conflict between a morality and self-interest and no point in having moral rules overriding self-interest. Hobbes is also right in saying that the application of this system of rules is in accordance with reason only under social conditions, that is, when there are well-established ways of behavior.

The answer to our question 'Why should we be moral?' is therefore as follows. We should be moral because being moral is following rules designed to overrule reasons of self-interest whenever it is in the interest of everyone alike that such rules should be generally followed. This will be the case when the needs and wants and aspirations of individual agents conflict with one another and when, in the absence of such overriding rules, the pursuit of their ends by all concerned would lead to the attempt to eliminate those who are in the way. Since such rules will always require one of the rivals to abandon his pursuit in favor of the other, they will tend to be broken. Since, *ex hypothesi* it is in everyone's interest that they should be followed, it will be in everyone's interest that they should not only be taught as "superior to" other reasons but also adequately enforced, in order to reduce the temptation to break them. A person instructed in these rules can acknowledge that such reasons are superior to reasons of self-interest without having to admit that he is always or indeed ever attracted or moved by them.

But is it not self-contradictory to say that it is in a person's interest to do what is contrary to his interest? It certainly would be if the two expressions were used in exactly the same way. But they are not. We have already seen that an enlightened egoist can acknowledge that a certain course of action is in his enlightened long-term, but contrary to his narrow short-term interest. He can infer that it is "in his interest" and according to reason to follow enlightened long-term interest, and "against his interest" and contrary to reason to follow short-term interest. Clearly, "in his interest" and "against his interest" here are used in new ways. For suppose it is discovered that the probable long-range consequences and psychological effects on others do not work out as predicted. Even so we need not admit that, in this new and extended sense, the line of action followed merely seemed but really was not in his interest. For we are now considering not merely a single action but a policy.

All the same, we must not make too much of this analogy. There is an all-important difference between the two cases. The calculations of the enlightened egoist properly allow for "exceptions in the agent's favor." After all, his calculus is designed to promote his interest. If he has information to show that in his particular circumstances it would pay to depart from a well-established general canon of enlightened self-interest, then it is proper for him to depart from it. It would not be a sign of the enlightened self-interest of a building contractor, let us say, if he made sacrifices for certain subcontractors even though he knew that they would or could not reciprocate, as subcontractors normally do. By contrast, such information is simply irrelevant in cases where moral reasons apply. Moral rules are not designed to serve the agent's interest directly. Hence it would be quite inappropriate for him to break them whenever he discovers that they do not serve his interest. They are designed to adjudicate primarily in cases where there is a conflict of interests so that from their very nature they are bound to be contrary to the interest of one of the persons affected. However, they are also bound to serve the interest of the other person, hence his interest in the other's observing them. It is on the assumption of the likelihood of a reversal of roles that the universal observation of the rule will serve everyone's interest. The principle of justice and other principles which we employ in improving the moral rules of a given society help to bring existing moralities closer to the ideal which is in the interest of everyone alike. Thus, just as following the canons of enlightened self-interest is in one's interest only if the assumptions underlying it are correct, so following the rules of morality is in everyone's interest only if the assumptions underlying it are correct, that is, if the moral rules come close to being true and are generally observed. Even then, to say that following them is in the interest of everyone alike means only that it is better for everyone that there should be a morality generally observed than that the principle of self-interest should be acknowledged as supreme. It does not of course mean that a person will not do better for himself by following self-interest than by doing what is morally right, when others are doing what is right. But of course such a person cannot *claim* that he is following a superior reason.

It must be added to this, however, that such a system of rules has the support of reason only where people live in societies, that is, in conditions in which there are established common ways of behavior. Outside society, people have no reason for following such rules, that is, for being moral. In other words, outside society, the very distinction between right and wrong vanishes.

. . .

SELF-INTEREST AND SOCIAL WELFARE

Robert G. Olson

. . .

Formally, the position I wish to argue for . . . may be stated in the following terms: A man is legitimately subject to moral censure for performing an act only if he has good reason to regard that act as detrimental to his own best long-range interests, whereas a man is entitled to moral commendation for performing an act only if he has good reason to regard that act as conducive to his own best long-range interests. The defense of this position, very briefly stated, is that the general adoption of this policy for the distribution of praise and blame serves not only the interests of the individual but also the interests of the community. Three arguments will be presented in defense of this view. In order to follow these arguments more easily, it will be helpful to keep the two following hypothetical cases in mind.

A person of low intelligence and repulsive physical features from a slum district in one of our larger cities grows up in a poverty-stricken, broken home, neglected by his parents and despised by those around him. He resorts to theft, believing for good reasons that he will probably not be caught or that even life in jail is preferable to the life to which he has otherwise been condemned. Now, according to the traditional view, the interests of society would best be served in this case by a generous use of moral censure. According to my view, the interests of society cannot be served in this way. It is even likely that society would benefit by praising the man.

Again, we have a man of low intelligence and repulsive physical features from a slum district. Again, he grows up in a poverty-stricken, broken home, neglected by his parents and despised by those around him. This time, however, we shall endow him with an intuition that one ought to sacrifice one's own welfare to that of others, with a hope that he will be rewarded in an afterlife for so doing, or, finally, with a belief that "virtue is its own reward." He thus drudges away a weary existence, eking out an "honest living" for himself and three abandoned nephews whom he loathes, refusing to indulge his appetites for women, drink, and decent food—almost the only pleasures that, given his background, he is capable of enjoying. According to the traditional view, this man ought to be praised. In my view, society cannot expect to benefit by praising this man. In all likelihood social interests require that he be censured.

The first argument in support of the position adopted here turns on the belief that most socially dangerous acts have their source in impulsive and ill-considered action, for which the corrective is deliberate and rational pursuit of true self-interest. As many traditional philosophers have pointed out, morality requires more, not less, regard for our own all-round personal well-being. Since, however, the only grounds they have ever given for putting social welfare above one's own long-range interests are the beliefs that there are rewards and punishments after death, that no reasons are required beyond intuition of some allegedly impersonal moral law, and that virtue is its own reward, they have tacitly sanctioned faith, intuition, and confidence in a thoroughly implausible psychological generalization as legitimate motives for behavior. The result has been that those who pride themselves on their rationality often tend to develop contempt for conventional moral rules, while those who pride themselves on their moral earnestness often tend to develop contempt for reason. The danger to social well-being in the first case is obvious; and although the danger in the second case is less obvious, it is no less serious. One cannot lose respect for reason without weakening one's precious but usually feeble habits of rational self-control. A man who is taught to accept faith or intuition as legitimate bases of belief cannot be expected to develop a healthy respect for rationality, and neither can a man who is taught not to question psychological generalizations simply because they appear initially to favor "virtue." Our cognitive life is not easily compartmentalized, and who or what will adjudicate the disputes that arise when faith or intuition inclines us to one belief and reason to a different belief? On the other hand, by praising a man for acting consistently in his own best interests one encourages him to cultivate habits of rationality and rational self-control with all of the social advantages which this entails.

Second, it frequently happens that in the long and complex chain of causes culminating in antisocial behavior the most significant are individual attitudes or dispositions which society can effectively control by the use of moral sanctions. This is especially the case when the behavior is inspired by disregard of individual self-interest. It also and by no means infrequently happens that the significant causal factors are not personal attitudes or dispositions but rather social institutions or circumstances which can be effectively counteracted only by concerted social action. This, I maintain, is almost invariably the case when an individual has been led to perform a socially undesirable act because the prevailing system of rewards and penalties renders that act in his own best all-around interests. Since, however, by blaming a man for his behavior we usually imply that the principal source of the difficulty lies within him and can best be corrected by him, we cannot urge the individual to put the social welfare above his own best long-range interests without tending to divert attention from the social causes of his embarrassment and fixing upon him individually a responsibility that belongs to all of us collectively as members of society.

A related distinction is between blaming an individual for performing an act with socially undesirable effects and blaming society for a complacent tolerance of the conditions that led him to perform the act. Although in some cases this is wholly or very nearly an either-or proposition, it would be a mistake to suppose that the occurrence of a socially injurious act ought never to serve as an occasion for blaming both the individual who performed it *and* society. In many cases both reproaches would be justified. To the extent that the socially undesirable act is not in the best interests of the agent, the agent ought to be blamed for performing it. To the extent that the act is produced by conditions that others would find it in their own best interests to eliminate, they ought to be blamed. The point is simply that the criterion by which we decide which reproach is legitimate or how much weight should be accorded to each ought to be the best long-range interests of the individuals concerned. The disinterested altruist who preaches the sacrifice of the individual in the name of society allows little, if any, place for efforts at social reform and undermines the individual's sense of his own dignity and personal worth. At the opposite extreme old-style social reformers and humanitarians have all too readily adopted some scheme of social or economic determinism that gives us little, if any, hold upon the individual and jeopardizes the concept of individual moral responsibility altogether.

Despite the influence of this latter group, however, we still tend overmuch to focus blame upon the individual agent rather than society whenever the agent performs an act with socially undesirable consequences. There are three principal reasons for this. First, the agent has in almost all cases of the kind under consideration here performed an act that most persons would not have found it in their own best interests to perform, and we do not always appreciate the unusual circumstances that obtain in a particular case. Second, although social institutions or circumstances are as important to a causal understanding of socially undesirable behavior as individual attitudes or personality traits, the latter, being more immediate and often more dramatically interesting causes, tend to crowd the former out of mind. This is especially true in a highly moralistic, apolitical, and psychologically oriented society such as our own. Third, moral indignation is usually accompanied by a pleasing sentiment of superiority and can often serve as a mask for our own shortsightedness and complacency with respect to social injustice. But this tendency to blame the agent rather than society is often in conflict with our desire for a more equitable and harmonious social order and must be controlled in our own best long-range interests.

The simple fact is that moral censure is not often an effective means of promoting the general welfare when an individual performs an act dictated by rational consideration of his own best long-range interests. If we succeed in persuading the individual that he is at fault in so acting, it will probably be at the cost of jeopardizing his and our own rational habits. If we do not succeed, we will probably embitter the offender of the conventional code and reinforce his antisocial attitudes. The best thing to do at this point if we wish to promote the general welfare is to remind ourselves of the social imperfections that have given rise to the conflict and to censure ourselves and others for having tolerated the conditions producing these tragic cases.

When, on the other hand, we praise an individual for acting consistently in his own best long-range interests even though this sometimes involves the performance of socially disapproved behavior, we not only encourage the individual violently to protest against the injustices of which he is a victim, but we also protest against these injustices ourselves in a highly dramatic way. Some persons will, no doubt, regard this remedy as unduly drastic. In the example above, it would involve condoning the agent if he abandoned his nephews and took to theft, since by hypothesis theft is in his own best long-range interests. If we remember, however, (a) that the alternative to deliberate pursuit of long-range self-interest is abject acquiescence to social injustice and impoverishment of the human personality and (b) that we ordinarily postulate as the goal of the moral life the greatest possible coincidence of private and social welfare not merely in the present but in the future as well, then my position is very difficult to refute.

Third, and finally, there is the following argument. In distributing praise and blame according to how a man acts or fails to act in his own best long-range interests, we oblige ourselves to take the interests of other individuals into fuller consideration than we would if we distributed praise and blame in some other fashion, thereby eliminating a very considerable source of friction and bitterness in human relationships. As we saw earlier, the probable effect of urging a man to act contrary to what he rationally regards as his own best interests is either to embitter him or to inspire contempt for reason. The probable effect of urging a man consistently to act in his own best rational interests, however, is to establish a relationship of mutual respect with him, thus creating conditions that favor a reasonable and co-operative endeavor to reconcile differing interests and disposing the agent to regard with greater sympathy moral rules designed to promote the general welfare. A man whom fortune has not favored is far more likely to co-operate with others and far less likely to adopt a solution to his problems that runs counter to their interests if he knows that they are acutely aware of his misfortune and are acting to ameliorate his lot.

      . . .

It was earlier stated that although my position does imply a greater coincidence between private and public good than is usually supposed to exist, it does not necessarily imply a perfect, or invariable, coincidence between private and public good. But, it might be asked, if the coincidence between private and public good is not perfect, how can you recommend praise for those who follow self-interest at the expense of society or blame for those who follow the opposite course? To this question the answer is that no such policy is recommended. My position is that self-interest is a *necessary* condition of morally correct behavior, not a *sufficient* condition. Moreover, as I said above, social well-being is an equally necessary condition. If a case should arise in which an individual must choose between serving the public interest at the expense of his personal well-being or promoting his private interest at the expense of society, his choice, whatever it might be, would, on my view, merit neither praise nor blame. The person who faces such a choice and the second parties who would like to advise him are confronted by an insoluble moral dilemma. We cannot praise a man for an act unless it is right, but an act is not right unless it promotes both the interests of the agent and the interests of the community. We cannot blame a man for an act unless it is wrong, but an act is not wrong unless it fails to promote either his own personal interests or the interests of the community. The humanly appropriate reaction when we discover a case of ultimate conflict between private and social interest, if we ever do, is to dedicate ourselves to preventing the recurrence of similar situations rather than to attempt the impossible task of moral appraisal of the individual involved.

Fortunately, as the arguments presented [previously] were designed to make clear, such socially valuable consequences usually follow from a consistently rational pursuit of self-interest that in any reasonably well-ordered society cases of ultimate conflict between the individual and society are either nonexistent or exceedingly rare. It is only in a very imperfectly ordered society where rewards for socially valuable behavior or penalties for its opposite are virtually nonexistent and where the social conscience is so poorly developed that the society's members are unwilling to make any serious effort to correct the situation that ultimate conflicts between the individual and society are likely to occur.

      . . .

SELFISHNESS, SELF-LOVE, AND SELF-INTEREST

Erich Fromm

. . .

The doctrine that selfishness is the arch-evil and that to love oneself excludes loving others is by no means restricted to theology and philosophy, but it became one of the stock ideas promulgated in home, school, motion pictures, books, indeed in all instruments of social suggestion as well. "Don't be selfish" is a sentence which has been impressed upon millions of children, generation after generation. Its meaning is somewhat vague. Most people would say that it means not to be egotistical, inconsiderate, without any concern for others. Actually, it generally means more than that. Not to be selfish implies not to do what one wishes, to give up one's own wishes for the sake of those in authority. "Don't be selfish," in the last analysis, has the same ambiguity that it has in Calvinism. Aside from its obvious implication, it means, "don't love yourself," "don't be yourself," but submit yourself to something more important than yourself, to an outside power or its internalization, "duty." "Don't be selfish" becomes one of the most powerful ideological tools in suppressing spontaneity and the free development of personality. Under the pressure of this slogan one is asked for every sacrifice and for complete submission: only those acts are "unselfish" which do not serve the individual but somebody or something outside himself.

This picture, we must repeat, is in a certain sense one-sided. For besides the doctrine that one should not be selfish, the opposite is also propagandized in modern society: keep your own advantage in mind, act according to what is best for you; by so doing you will also be acting for the greatest advantage of all others. As a matter of fact, the idea that egotism is the basis of the general welfare is the principle on which competitive society has been built. It is puzzling that two such seemingly contradictory principles could be taught side by side in one culture; of the fact, however, there is no doubt. One result of this contradiction is confusion in the individual. Torn between the two doctrines, he is seriously blocked in the process of integrating his personality. This confusion is one of the most significant sources of the bewilderment and helplessness of modern man.

The doctrine that love for oneself is identical with "selfishness" and an alternative to love for others has pervaded theology, philosophy, and popular thought; the same doctrine has been rationalized in scientific language in Freud's theory of narcissism. Freud's concept presupposes a fixed amount of libido. In the infant, all of the libido has the child's own person as its objective, the stage of "primary narcissism," as Freud calls it. During the individual's development, the libido is shifted from one's own person toward other objects. If a person is blocked in his "object-relationships," the libido is withdrawn from the objects and returned to his own person; this is called "secondary narcissism." According to Freud, the more love I turn toward the outside world the less love is left for myself, and vice versa. He thus describes the phenomenon of love as an impoverishment of one's self-love because all libido is turned to an object outside oneself.

These questions arise: Does psychological observation support the thesis that there is a basic contradiction and a state of alternation between love for oneself and love for others? Is love for oneself the same phenomenon as selfishness, or are they opposites? Furthermore, is the selfishness of modern man really a *concern for himself* as an individual, with all his intellectual, emotional, and sensual potentialities? Has "he" not become an appendage of his socioeconomic role? *Is his selfishness identical with self-love or is it not caused by the very lack of it?*

Before we start the discussion of the psychological aspect of selfishness and self-love, the logical fallacy in the notion that love for others and love for oneself are mutually exclusive should be stressed. If it is a virtue to love my neighbor as a human being, it must be a virtue—and not a vice—to love myself since I am a human being too. There is no concept of man in which I myself am not included. A doctrine which proclaims such an exclusion proves itself to be intrinsically contradictory. The idea expressed in the Biblical "Love thy neighbor as thyself!" implies that respect for one's own integrity and uniqueness, love for and understanding of one's own self, can not be separated from respect for and love and understanding of another individual. The love for my own self is inseparably connected with the love for any other self.

We have come now to the basic psychological premises on which the conclusions of our argument are built. Generally, these premises are as follows: not only others, but we ourselves are the "object" of our feelings and attitudes; the attitudes toward others and toward ourselves, far from being contradictory, are basically *conjunctive*. With regard to the problem under discussion this means: Love of others and love of ourselves are not alternatives. On the contrary, an attitude of love toward themselves will be found in all those who are capable of loving others. *Love, in principle, is indivisible as far as the connection between "objects" and one's own self is concerned.* Genuine love is an expression of productiveness and implies care, respect, responsibility, and knowledge. It is not an "affect" in the sense of being affected by somebody, but an active striving for the growth and happiness of the loved person, rooted in one's own capacity to love.

To love is an expression of one's power to love, and to love somebody is the actualization and concentration of this power with regard to one person. It is not true, as the idea of romantic love would have it, that there is only *the* one person in the world whom one could love and that it is the great chance of one's life to find that one person. Nor is it true, if that person be found that love for him (or her) results in a withdrawal of love from others. Love which can only be experienced with regard to one person demonstrates by this very fact that it is not love, but a symbiotic attachment. The basic affirmation contained in love is directed toward the beloved person as an incarnation of **essentially** human qualities. Love of one person implies love of man as such. The kind of "division of labor" as William James calls it, by which one loves one's family but is without feeling for the "stranger," is a sign of a basic inability to love. Love of man is not, as is frequently supposed, an abstraction coming after the love for a specific person, but it is its premise, although, genetically, it is acquired in loving specific individuals.

From this it follows that my own self, in principle, must be as much an object of my love as another person. *The affirmation of one's own life, happiness, growth, freedom, is rooted in one's capacity to love,* i.e., in care, respect, responsibility, and knowledge. If an individual is able to love productively, he loves himself too; if he can love *only* others, he can not love at all.

Granted that love for oneself and for others in principle is conjunctive, how do we explain selfishness, which obviously excludes any genuine concern for others? The *selfish* person is interested only in himself, wants everything for himself, feels no pleasure in giving, but only in taking. The world outside is looked at only from the standpoint of what he can get out of it; he lacks interest in the needs of others, and respect for their dignity and integrity. He can see nothing but himself; he judges everyone and everything from its usefulness to him; he is basically unable to love. Does not this prove that concern for others and concern for oneself are unavoidable alternatives? This would be so if selfishness and self-love were identical. But that assumption is the very fallacy which has led to so many mistaken conclusions concerning our problem. *Selfishness and self-love, far from being identical, are actually opposites.* The selfish person does not love himself too much but too little; in fact he hates himself. This lack of fondness and care for himself, which is only one expression of his lack of productiveness, leaves him empty and frustrated. He is necessarily unhappy and anxiously concerned to snatch from life the satisfactions which he blocks himself from attaining. He seems to care too much for himself but actually he only makes an unsuccessful attempt to cover up and compensate for his failure to care for his real self. Freud holds that the selfish person is narcissistic, as if he had withdrawn his love from others and turned it toward his own person. *It is true that selfish persons are incapable of loving others, but they are not capable of loving themselves either.*

It is easier to understand selfishness by comparing it with greedy concern for others, as we find it, for instance, in an oversolicitous, dominating mother. While she consciously believes that she is particularly fond of her child, she has actually a deeply repressed hostility toward the object of her concern. She is overconcerned not because she loves the child too much, but because she has to compensate for her lack of capacity to love him at all.

This theory of the nature of selfishness is borne out by psychoanalytic experience with neurotic "unselfishness," a symptom of neurosis observed in not a few people who usually are troubled not by this symptom but by others connected with it, like depression, tiredness, inability to work, failure in love relationships, and so on. Not only is unselfishness not felt as a "symptom"; it is often the one redeeming character trait on which such people pride themselves. The "unselfish" person "does not want anything for himself"; he "lives only for others," is proud that he does not consider himself important. He is puzzled to find that in spite of his unselfishness he is unhappy, and that his relationships to those closest to him are unsatisfactory. He wants to have what he considers are his symptoms removed—but not his unselfishness. Analytic work shows that his unselfishness is not something apart from his other symptoms but one of them; in fact often the most important one; that he is paralyzed in his capacity to love or to enjoy anything; that he is pervaded by hostility against life and that behind the façade of unselfishness a subtle but not less intense self-centeredness is hidden. This person can be cured only if his unselfishness too is interpreted as a symptom along with the others so that his lack of productiveness, which is at the root of both his unselfishness *and* his other troubles, can be corrected.

The nature of unselfishness becomes particularly apparent in its effect on others and most frequently, in our culture, in the effect the "unselfish" mother has on her children. She believes that by her unselfishness her children will experience what it means to be loved and to learn, in turn, what it means to love. The effect of her unselfishness, however, does not at all correspond to her expectations. The children do not show the happiness of persons who are convinced that they are loved; they are anxious, tense, afraid of the mother's disapproval and anxious to live up to her expectations. Usually, they are affected by their mother's hidden hostility against life, which they sense rather than recognize, and eventually become imbued with it themselves. Altogether, the effect of the "unselfish" mother is not too different from that of the selfish one; indeed, it is often worse because the mother's unselfishness prevents the children from criticizing her. They are put under the obligation not to disappoint her; they are taught, under the mask of virtue, dislike for life. If one has a chance to study the effect of a mother with genuine self-love, one can see that there is nothing more conducive to giving a child the experience of what love, joy, and happiness are than being loved by a mother who loves herself.

Having analyzed selfishness and self-love we can now proceed to discuss the concept of *self-interest,* which has become one of the key symbols in modern society. It is even more ambiguous than selfishness or self-love, and this ambiguity can be fully understood only by taking into account the historical development of the concept of self-interest. The problem is what is considered to constitute self-interest and how it can be determined.

There are two fundamentally different approaches to this problem. One is the objectivistic approach most clearly formulated by Spinoza. To him self-interest or the interest "to seek one's profit" is identical with virtue. "The more," he says, "each person strives and is able *to seek his profit,* that is to say, to preserve his being, the more virtue does he possess; on the other hand, in so far as each person neglects his own profit he is impotent." [1] According to this view, the interest of man is to preserve his existence, which is the same as realizing his inherent potentialities. This concept of self-interest is objectivistic inasmuch as "interest" is not conceived in terms of the subjective feeling of what one's interest is but in terms of what the nature of man is, objectively. Man has only one real interest and that is the full development of his potentialities, of himself as a human being. Just as one has to know another person and his real needs in order to love him, one has to know one's own self in order to understand what the interests of this self are and how they can be served. It follows that man can deceive himself about his real self-interest if he is ignorant of his self and its real needs and that the science of man is the basis for determining what constitutes man's self-interest.

In the last three hundred years the concept of self-interest has increasingly been narrowed until it has assumed almost the opposite meaning which it has in Spinoza's thinking. It has become identical with selfishness, with interest in material gains, power, and success; and instead of its being synonymous with virtue, its conquest has become an ethical commandment.

This deterioration was made possible by the change from the objectivistic into the erroneously subjectivistic approach to self-interest. Self-interest was no longer to be determined by the nature of man and his needs; correspondingly, the notion that one could be mistaken about it was relinquished and replaced by the idea that what a person *felt* represented the interest of his self was necessarily his true self-interest.

The modern concept of self-interest is a strange blend of two contradictory concepts: that of Calvin and Luther on the one hand, and on the other, that of the progressive thinkers since Spinoza. Calvin and Luther had taught that man must suppress his self-interest and consider himself only an instrument for God's purposes. Progressive thinkers, on the contrary, have taught that man ought to be only an end for himself and not a means for any purpose transcending him. What happened was that man has accepted the contents of the Calvinistic doctrine while rejecting its religious formulation. He has made himself an instrument, not of God's will but of the economic machine or the state. He has accepted the role of a tool, not for God but for industrial progress; he has worked and amassed money but essentially not for the pleasure of spending it and of enjoying life but in order to save, to invest, to be successful. Monastic asceticism has been, as Max Weber has pointed out, replaced by an *inner-worldly asceticism* where personal happiness and enjoyment are no longer the real aims of life. But this attitude was increasingly divorced from the one expressed in Calvin's concept and blended with that expressed in the progressive concept of self-interest, which taught that man had the right—and the obligation—to make the pursuit of his self-interest the supreme norm of life. The result is that modern man *lives* according to the principles of self-

[1] Spinoza, *Ethics,* IV, Prop. 20.

denial and *thinks* in terms of self-interest. He believes that he is acting in behalf of *his* interest when actually his paramount concern is money and success; he deceives himself about the fact that his most important human potentialities remain unfulfilled and that he loses himself in the process of seeking what is supposed to be best for him.

The deterioration of the meaning of the concept of self-interest is closely related to the change in the concept of self. In the Middle Ages man felt himself to be an intrinsic part of the social and religious community in reference to which he conceived his own self when he as an individual had not yet fully emerged from his group. Since the beginning of the modern era, when man as an individual was faced with the task of experiencing himself as an independent entity, his own identity became a problem. In the eighteenth and nineteenth centuries the concept of self was narrowed down increasingly; the self was felt to be constituted by the property one had. The formula for this concept of self was no longer "I am what I think" but "I am what I have," "what I possess."

In the last few generations, under the growing influence of the market, the concept of self has shifted from meaning "I am what I possess" to meaning "I am as you desire me." Man, living in a market economy, feels himself to be a commodity. He is divorced from himself, as the seller of a commodity is divorced from what he wants to sell. To be sure, he is interested in himself, immensely interested in his success on the market, but "he" is the manager, the employer, the seller—and the commodity. His self-interest turns out to be the interest of "him" as the subject who employs "himself," as the commodity which should obtain the optimal price on the personality market.

The "fallacy of self-interest" in modern man has never been described better than by Ibsen in *Peer Gynt*. Peer Gynt believes that his whole life is devoted to the attainment of the interests of his *self*. He describes this self as:

> "The Gyntian Self!
> —An army, that, of wishes, appetites, desires!
> The Gyntian Self!
> It is a sea of fancies, claims and aspirations;
> In fact, it's all that swells within my breast
> And makes it come about that I am I and live as such."

At the end of his life he recognizes that he had deceived himself; that while following the principle of "self-interest" he had failed to recognize what the interests of his real self were, and had lost the very self he sought to preserve. He is told that he never had been himself and that therefore he is to be thrown back into the melting pot to be dealt with as raw material. He discovers that he has lived according to the Troll principle: "To thyself be enough"—which is the opposite of the human principle: "To thyself be true." He is seized by the horror of nothingness to which he, who has no self, can not help succumbing when the props of pseudo self, success, and possessions are taken away or seriously questioned. He is forced to recognize that in trying to gain all the wealth of the world, in relentlessly pursuing what seemed to be his interest, he had lost his soul—or, as I would rather say, his self.

The deteriorated meaning of the concept of self-interest which pervades modern society has given rise to attacks on democracy from the various types of totalitarian ideologies. These claim that capitalism is *morally* wrong because it is governed by the principle of selfishness, and commend the moral superiority of their own systems by pointing to their principle of the unselfish subordination of the individual to the "higher" purposes of the state, the "race," or the "socialist fatherland." They impress not a few with this criticism because many people feel that there is no happiness in the pursuit of selfish interest, and are imbued with a striving, vague though it may be, for a greater solidarity and mutual responsibility among men.

We need not waste much time arguing against the totalitarian claims. In the first place, they are insincere since they only disguise the extreme selfishness of an "elite" that wishes to conquer and retain power over the majority of the population. Their ideology of unselfishness has the purpose of deceiving those subject to the control of the elite and of facilitating their exploitation and manipulation. Furthermore, the totalitarian ideologies confuse the issue by making it appear that they represent the principle of unselfishness when they apply to the state as a whole the principle of ruthless pursuit of selfishness. Each citizen ought to be devoted to the common welfare, but the state is permitted to pursue its own interest without regard to the welfare of other nations. But quite aside from the fact that the doctrines of totalitarianism are disguises for the most extreme selfishness, they are a revival—in secular language—of the religious idea of intrinsic human powerlessness and impotence and the resulting need for submission, to overcome which was the essence of modern spiritual and political progress. Not only do the authoritarian ideologies threaten the most precious achievement of Western culture, the respect for the uniqueness and dignity of the individual; they also tend to block the way to constructive criticism of modern society, and thereby to constructive criticism of modern society, and thereby to necessary changes. The failure of modern culture lies not in its principle of individualism, not in the idea that moral virtue is the same as the pursuit of self-interest, but in the deterioration of the meaning of self-interest; not in the fact that people are *too much concerned with their self-interest,* but that they are *not concerned enough with the interest of their real self; not in the fact that they are too selfish, but that they do not love themselves.*

If the causes for persevering in the pursuit of a fictitious idea of self-interest are as deeply rooted in the contemporary social structure as indicated above, the chances for a change in the meaning of self-interest would seem to be remote indeed, unless one can point to specific factors operating in the direction of change.

Perhaps the most important factor is the inner dissatisfaction of modern man with the results of his pursuit of "self-interest." The religion of success is crumbling and becoming a façade itself. The social "open spaces" grow narrower; the failure of the hopes for a better world after the First World War, the depression at the end of the twenties, the threat of a new and immensely destructive war so shortly after the Second World War, and the boundless insecurity resulting from this threat, shake the faith in the pursuit of this form of self-interest. Aside from these factors, the worship of success itself has failed to satisfy man's ineradicable striving to be himself. Like so many fantasies and daydreams, this one too fulfilled its function only for a time, as long as it was new, as long as the excitement connected with it was strong enough to keep man from considering it soberly. There is an increasing number of people to whom everything they are doing seems futile. They are still under the spell of the slogans which preach faith in the secular paradise of success and glamour. But doubt, the fertile condition of all progress, has begun to beset them and has made them ready to ask what their real self-interest as human beings is.

This inner disillusionment and the readiness for a revaluation of self-interest could hardly become effective unless the economic conditions of our culture permitted it. I have pointed out that while the canalizing of all human energy into work and the striving for success was one of the indispensable conditions of the enormous achievement of modern capitalism, a stage has been reached where the problem of *production* has been virtually solved and where the problem of the *organization* of social life has become the paramount task of mankind. Man has created such sources of mechanical energy that he has freed himself from the task of putting all his human energy into work in order to produce the material conditions for living. He could spend a considerable part of his energy on the task of living itself.

Only if these two conditions, the subjective dissatisfaction with a culturally patterned aim and the socioeconomic basis for a change, are present, can an indispensable third factor, rational insight, become effective. This holds true as a principle of social and psychological change in general and of the change in the meaning of self-interest in particular. The time has come when the anesthetized striving for the pursuit of man's real interest is coming to life again. Once man knows what his self-interest is, the first, and the most difficult, step to its realization has been taken.

Suggested Readings

Falk, W. D. "Morality, Self and Others," in Hector-Neri Castañeda and George Nakhnikian (eds.), *Morality and the Language of Conduct.* Detroit: Wayne State University Press, 1963.

Lemos, Ramon. "Egoism and Non-Egoism in Ethics," *Southern Journal of Philosophy* 9 (Winter 1971).

Nielsen, Kai. "A Short Way with Psychological Egoism," *Journal of Social Philosophy* 4 (April 1973).

Rand, Ayn. *The Virtue of Selfishness.* New York: Norton, 1965.

section two

ethical and cultural relativism

INHUMANITY AS A WAY OF LIFE *

Maitland Edey

Is it conceivable that, under extreme conditions, human beings can exist without any consideration of others at all? This is the chilling question raised by anthropologist Colin Turnbull. He has found a group of human beings who actually live in this "inhuman" way.

His people are the Ik, an obscure tribe of East African hunter-gatherers who formerly followed a roving way of life in Northern Uganda. For countless generations they made a slow seasonal circle across semidesert, mountains and open grassland in pursuit of game, wild vegetables and water.

Suddenly, and for them catastrophically, they had to stop. Forty or 50 years ago, part of their ancient territory was turned into a government game preserve. The Ik were forbidden to hunt and told instead to support themselves as farmers on some steep stony hillsides. This they could not do. They slowly began to starve. Under the goad of hunger their society broke down. Parents could no longer take care of children if they expected to survive themselves. Old and worn out at 30, they, in turn, could expect no help from their own children or relatives. By the time Turnbull arrived to study them, they had become a terrifying loveless group of totally selfish individuals.

Today, Ik children are turned out of the hut at 3 or 4. They join small bands of juvenile foragers, and subsist on bark, berries, the remains of fruit nibbled and discarded by baboons. When desperately hungry, they eat mud and small pebbles. They

* This article originally appeared as a book review of *The Mountain People* by Colin M. Turnbull.—Eds.

44

quickly discover that friendship is a luxury and learn to betray one another, to exist alone in utter selfishness.

When Turnbull tried to sustain life in one frail old man (who might have been 40) by giving him food and water every few days, the man's son regularly took it away from him and he died. One little girl was crazy by Ik standards, because she could not get it through her head that others were not to be loved and trusted, that her parents would not take care of her. Starved, she kept creeping back to their hut. Finally they said they would get her some food, told her to wait, and walled her in. When they came back two weeks later, what was left of her had almost completely rotted away.

Turnbull spent two years with the Ik, at last learning "not to hate them." He realized that under any alternative to their awful way of life—poaching, stealing, fomenting quarrels and rustling the cattle of neighboring tribes—all would die. Now, having given up everything else for survival, some do survive.

This poses an agonizing question for Turnbull: are love and generosity just icing, expendable when one gets down to the bare bone? "Yes," he says, "the Ik prove it." Furthermore, Turnbull sees disturbing parallels in modern society, where community life has also broken down under the weight of urban gigantism, where work is not rewarding, where families are fractured, where custom is frayed, where belief is gone. The uncaring acceptance of atrocities in Vietnam, the callous turning of one's back to the screams of a woman being murdered in an alley, the general loss of concern, the substitution of mechanization for rewarding work, care of the individual by soulless agencies instead of by personal cooperation, sacrifice and forethought—all these things increasingly reveal the Ik that is in us.

Is Turnbull right? The Ik could prove him so by continuing to survive, and by demonstrating that their inhuman way of life is indeed viable. More likely it is not. They may be getting by right now, but in the long run, in another few generations, all may be extinct—not archetypes of true humanity after all, but small losers in the bigger evolutionary struggle.

Whether he is right or wrong in his larger concern, Turnbull has produced a magnificent book, beautifully written, compassionate, absorbingly interesting. Best of all, it has the priceless quality of making the reader pause and think about his own society and its values, and what kind of human being he himself really is.

ON CULTURAL RELATIVISM

Ija Lazari-Pawlowska

The literature concerning the problems of cultural relativism is voluminous. It deals with many different problems. The present article will concentrate entirely upon the problem known as the *cultural diversity of morals.*

The opinions of cultural anthropologists vary with respect to the problem of whether we can discover some uniformity in human nature which could be reflected in universally accepted moral standards.

It is easy to understand the fascination of some authors with the striking differences between cultures, which have been so vividly presented, for example, by Frazer in "The Golden Bough"; yet it is also easy to understand the inevitable impression forcing itself upon other authors: that there exists some basic identity manifesting itself in human societies, independent of time and place.

Some authors maintain that the actual range of the differences anthropology has discovered is enormous: they point out that the same kind of act is praised in one culture and blamed in another. "Sometimes, when we look at all that ethnography and history have recorded about customs and institutions, it seems as though there had developed varieties of moral judgment so different from one another as to force the conclusion that there is no common human nature but only a multitude of human natures." [1]

People are in fact the same everywhere—this is another opinion represented in the works of anthropologists. And indeed, it is enough to see a mother despairing over her dead child in any spot of our globe, to be impressed by the identity of human experience.

It must be mentioned that, in the course of controversy, in supporting or denying the universal existence of certain moral phenomena, the disagreeing authors are often discussing what are not exactly the same phenomena.

In *Anthropology and Ethics* by May and Abraham Edel we find the following statement: "Birth and death, love and sorrow and fear are the lot of all men; all are capable of desires and dreams, and use symbolic thinking, identification, reaction-formation." [2] And Robert Redfield writes: "All people feel shame or guilt or, probably, some combination of these; all take satisfaction in or feel dissatisfaction with regard to their enterprises and productions; all dislike, under some conditions, public humiliation and enjoy recognized success; and so on" (*op. cit.,* 450). Many similar statements could be quoted here. They seem to aim at claiming that there exists some range of psychic dispositions common to all people (common statistically rather than absolutely) which could be recognized as a component of human nature. This range of dispositions is treated by these authors as being of special interest for the ethical philosopher, since they relate these dispositions to the sphere of morality. Unfortunately, the authors do not explain how they move from pointing out certain common dispositions—which are, moreover, cited only by way of example (the examples being very divergent)—to the statement of an identity in the sphere of morals, although this problem obviously requires some comment.

[1] Robert Redfield, *Human Nature and the Study of Society* (Chicago: University Press, 1962), p. 440.

[2] *Anthropology and Ethics* (Springfield, Ill.: Charles C Thomas, 1959), p. 30.

Besides the common dispositions, Edel and Edel also mention, in the sentence quoted above, some basic facts from the sphere of human existence: birth and death. In another place they say: "Common needs, common social tasks, common psychological processes, are bound to provide some common framework for the wide variety of human behaviors that different cultures have developed" (31). It seems to me, however, that a statement of this kind of fact can serve only as a hypothesis accounting for all human communities' having worked out *some* rules of conduct, having *some* morality, and that it cannot properly be treated as an argument supporting the notion of a genuine identity of people of different cultures with respect to their morals. The same attitude is represented, for example, by Morris Ginsberg,[3] who says that morality is universal in the formal sense that everywhere we find rules of conduct prescribing what is to be done or not to be done. Behind this similarity of form there is considerable diversity of content.

Besides, the anthropologists do not insist upon the identity of moral rules—they agree in recognizing their great diversity. Nevertheless, some of them proclaim the thesis of the basic similarity of people of different cultures with respect to morals. According to them, the diversity of rules is a nonessential fact, there being many reasons for this nonessentiality. I will discuss these reasons later in the paper.

There are also some authors who try to establish at least a small list of norms valid in all cultures. "In our times we again go back, with great persistency, to the problem of generally accepted moral norms"—declares M. Ossowska, and she associates the new interest in these problems with, among others, the cruel experiences of the twentieth century and with the desire to find a basis for humanitarian ideas in some "universal and deeply human needs."[4]

A formulation of this problem in more precise form (for example: What is meant by the universal character of norms or by their acceptance? What is the criterion for incompatibility of norms? etc.) and some improvement in methods of investigation will probably enable us to obtain reliable empirical data concerning the existence or nonexistence of a certain number of elements common to all cultures, at least to those cultures which are accessible at present to direct observation. I think, however, that a possible register of such common elements will not settle the question whether there are universal moral norms. For there will remain a major controversial question, namely: On the basis of which features should we distinguish from among those common elements the range of *moral* elements, that is, the range of elements to which we would apply terms like 'moral norm', 'moral behavior', 'moral motive', etc.? The term 'moral' is nowadays used by anthropologists in reference to various ranges.

Let us assume that among the generally accepted universals we would find the following:

---

[3] *On the Diversity of Morals: Approaches to Ethics* (London: Heinemann, 1962), p. 485.

[4] *Socjologia moralności (Sociology of Morals)* (Warszawa 1969), p. 243.

1. Everywhere a new-born human child is unable to exist by itself, and everywhere mothers take care of those of their children whom they want to survive.
2. Everywhere people condemn homicide committed upon a mature healthy member of one's own group, who has not committed any crime and whose death is not treated as a means of gaining some benefit for the group (for example, restoring the mercy of gods).

I think that opinion about whether these two phenomena should be included within the category of *moral* phenomena would differ.

I have given here examples of two possible cultural universals (the first is biological-cultural in character), aiming at the greatest possible specificity. Most authors, however, confine themselves to general impressions. For example, S. E. Asch says: "We do not know of societies in which bravery is despised and cowardice held up to honor, in which generosity is considered a vice and ingratitude a virtue." [5] The author does not take into consideration the obvious fact that the idea of bravery, although it may be known everywhere, refers to different acts in different cultures. An act that is not approved of is called not brave but rash, inconsiderate, etc. What some people condemn and call cowardice, others approve of and call prudent, careful behavior, behavior that takes into account the real conditions of life, etc. Thus, the statement that everywhere men value bravery is too vague to be included in the list of the universals in question. We should rather try to find out whether a certain kind of act strictly defined will be everywhere approved of as "brave." On the other hand, Clyde Kluckhohn's opinion that every culture has a concept of murder, distinguishing this from "justifiable homicide," [6] quite obviously contains elements of tautology.

According to some anthropologists there are no *essential* differences among people of different cultures from the point of view of morality. But I think that the way in which actual differences are classified as essential or nonessential depends not only upon knowledge of the facts, but also upon the author's own moral feelings. If one author appreciates in people a certain formal disposition—for example, the ability to serve an idea disinterestedly—while another appreciates that ability only when he approves of the idea in question, then, having at their disposal the same information, one will be inclined to consider nonessential the differences between people serving disinterestedly ideas that are antagonistic, whereas the other will consider those differences essential indeed. The idea of being essential is not explicit in the anthropologists' discussions; its actual use is determined by the moral intuition of the investigators, and it varies according to the situation.

I would like to accentuate three kinds of differences from among those regarded by

---

[5] "A Critique of the Psychology of Cultural Relativism," in Richard Brandt, ed., *Value and Obligation* (New York: Harcourt, Brace & World, 1961), p. 483.

[6] "Ethical Relativity: *Sic et Non*," [*The Journal of Philosophy*], LII, 23 (Nov. 10, 1955): 663–677, p. 672.

some anthropologists as nonessential. They are: (1) differences of behavior resulting from dispositions that are treated as identical; (2) differences of means that are treated as chosen with respect to the same end; and (3) differences in the hierarchy of accepted values.

1. Redfield writes: "About whatever primitive or ancient people you may read, you will find something already familiar to you—mothers who cherished their children, or men proud of their achievements. The children cherished may later be killed as offerings to supernaturals, and the proud man may be proud of the number of heads he has taken; but it is still mothers' love about which you have read, and it is still a pride in one's achievement that is characteristic of all humanity" (*op. cit.*, 440). According to Redfield, even the strangest customs are only "various costumes" expressing the same dispositions, which are common to all people. A given culture decides about which elements from a wide scale of possible human behaviors (a scale common to all people) are actually realized by individuals.

Let us assume that everywhere people are capable of love and hatred, joy and sorrow, pride and shame. That is: everywhere people love *somebody* and hate *somebody;* they are happy about *something,* and unhappy about *something;* they are proud of one thing, and ashamed of another. This is why some authors speak of a basic moral similarity among people, whereas others point to basic differences, considering it important *whom* people love, *what* they are happy about, *what* they are proud of—the number of heads taken or the number of patients successfully operated on.

2. Some anthropologists maintain that moral differences depend mainly on differences of opinion concerning matters of fact and that those differences are nonessential. Divergence of opinion regarding facts is undoubtedly a very important factor within the sphere of morality, and the unification of empirical knowledge favors the process of making the postulates uniform. Wherever people do not have sound empirical knowledge they try to use various magical practices in matters important for an individual or a group, basing their behavior upon imaginary relations. When, for instance, the achievements of agronomy become popularized, people will probably cease to observe norms imposing various religious ceremonies which are practiced in order to increase the crop or to bring rain—ceremonies described in the works of anthropologists.

The authors under consideration treat the differences we are discussing now as consisting in using different means in order to achieve the same ends, and they consider nonessential any differences among norms that serve (or at least are meant to serve) the realization of the same ends. Thus they mention together norms recommending ritual dances in order to increase the crop and norms introducing bloody rituals, human sacrifice, because in each of these cases the ends are the same, the difference concerning "only the means." Such an attitude, however, evokes objections resulting probably from the moral factor. I think Gunnar Myrdal is right when he says: "It is simply not true that only ends are the object of valuations and that means are valued only as instrumental to ends. In any human valuation means have, in addition to their instrumental value, independent values as well." [7] Killing a man in order to increase the crop is recommended in one culture; in another (for instance, among the Jains of India), a man would die of hunger rather than kill another man or even an animal to save his own life. Richard Brandt suggests: "Perhaps those who condemn cannibalism would not do so if they thought that eating the flesh of an enemy is necessary for the survival of the group. If we are to estimate whether there is ultimate disagreement of ethical principle, we must have information about this, about the beliefs, more or less conscious, of various peoples about what they do." [8] Yet there are authors who consider extremely significant the question of the *admissibility* of means serving (whether seemingly or actually) to realize the desired ends.

Treating the differences caused by diversity of belief as nonessential, A. C. Ewing says: "Why did the medieval inquisitors think it their duty to burn people alive for their theological beliefs, while I should think it very wicked? Chiefly because they differed from me in holding that in the case of certain beliefs theirs was the only way to save more people from being burnt eternally. Why have savages practised human sacrifice? Chiefly because they thought it to be the only way of stopping pestilences, which we do not." [9] According to this author, the inquisitors had in mind the good of the people whom they tortured to death; so their guiding principle was the same end that, in different circumstances, is achieved by other means. Yet the idea of good appears here as a rather vague general notion, and if we tried to specify it and analyze it in a complete axiological context, taking into consideration, for instance, opinions concerning the problem of whether we ought to make somebody happy against his will, it would appear that the values and ends of the inquisitor were quite different from those of a man tolerant toward other people's beliefs.

3. The controversy concerning the importance of the differences is also related to the hierarchy that holds among particular norms in particular cultures. Some authors focus their attention upon the fact of the general acceptance of these norms without considering the differences in their ordering. Yet this difference may be considered very important; surely it is the decisive element in conflict situations involving choice. "Such differences not only make for misunderstanding but also for mutual recriminations on moral grounds and for feelings of contempt and hostility." [10] Two persons may both accept, for example, the two norms of being faithful to one's own convictions and being approved of by the society; yet their behavior may be different, for their choices will depend upon the value that each person considers primary in the case of conflict. We may agree with a statement that, both in the culture of India and in that of the western

---

[7] *Value in Social Theory* (London: Routledge & Paul, 1958), p. 49.

[8] *Ethical Theory* (Englewood Cliffs, N.J.: Prentice-Hall, 1959), p. 102.

[9] "The Nature of Ethical Judgment," in Milton K. Munitz, ed., *A Modern Introduction to Ethics* (Glencoe, Ill.: Free Press, 1958), p. 560.

[10] R. Linton, "The Problem of Universal Values," in Brandt, *Value and Obligation,* p. 472.

world, men approve of soothing the suffering of both people and animals. Yet the hierarchy of moral duties toward animals in India is quite different from the western one. King Asoka (third century B.C.) ordered an inscription to be cut in stone, saying that, according to his disposition, public roads are to be lined with trees of thick foliage to provide shade "for animals and people." He ordered stations to be built providing drinking water "for animals and people." The order in which the king mentions the creatures he cares for—the order which has a long tradition in India and which has been accepted there—results in significant consequences in the sphere of people's behavior; consequences which prevail today, as in the time of Asoka.

I have pointed out some differences in regard to which opinions vary as to whether they are essential or not.

We must, however, admit that, in spite of the great variety of moral attitudes of people belonging to different cultures and also of people within one culture, it is a right and vital thing to emphasize the existence of dispositions common to all people. For these common dispositions may be looked upon as a fact supporting the idea of people's *potential* unanimity of a kind stronger than the unanimity that prevails at present. The common dispositions are often a source of hope for moralists and reformers who, having noticed in people the capacity for being sympathetic toward *somebody,* toward *some* people, believe that, by means of proper influence, this disposition could be developed to such an extent as to embrace a much greater number of people than it does today.

There seems to be general agreement that, at the present time within the primary group, there is everywhere a "natural solidarity," i.e., a measure of mutual forbearance, helpfulness, and trust,[11] resulting in certain accepted moral rules. But these rules often do not apply outside the primary group; in any case there are variations in the range of persons to whom these rules are held to be applicable. It is the great dream of many moralists to widen the moral community, at least in the sense of treating all people, however different or alien, as human individuals who count.

ETHICAL ABSOLUTISM AND ETHICAL RELATIVISM

Walter Stace

There is an opinion widely current nowadays in philosophical circles which passes under the name of "ethical relativity." Exactly what this phrase means or implies is certainly far from clear. But unquestionably it stands as a label for the opinions of a group of ethical philosophers whose position is roughly on the extreme left wing among

[11] Cf. Ginsberg, *op. cit.,* p. 486.

the moral theorizers of the day. And perhaps one may best understand it by placing it in contrast with the opposite kind of extreme view against which, undoubtedly, it has arisen as a protest. For among moral philosophers one may clearly distinguish a left and a right wing. Those of the left wing are the ethical relativists. They are the revolutionaries, the clever young men, the up to date. Those of the right wing we may call the ethical absolutists. They are the conservatives and the old-fashioned.

According to the absolutists there is but one eternally true and valid moral code. This moral code applies with rigid impartiality to all men. What is a duty for me must likewise be a duty for you. And this will be true whether you are an Englishman, a Chinaman, or a Hottentot. If cannibalism is an abomination in England or America, it is an abomination in central Africa, notwithstanding that the African may think otherwise. The fact that he sees nothing wrong in his cannibal practices does not make them for him morally right. They are as much contrary to morality for him as they are for us. The only difference is that he is an ignorant savage who does not know this. There is not one law for one man or race of men, another for another. There is not one moral standard for Europeans, another for Indians, another for Chinese. There is but one law, one standard, one morality, for all men. And this standard, this law, is absolute and unvarying.

Moreover, as the one moral law extends its dominion over all the corners of the earth, so too it is not limited in its application by any considerations of time or period. That which is right now was right in the centuries of Greece and Rome, nay, in the very ages of the cave man. That which is evil now was evil then. If slavery is morally wicked today, it was morally wicked among the ancient Athenians, notwithstanding that their greatest men accepted it as a necessary condition of human society. Their opinion did not make slavery a moral good for them. It only showed that they were, in spite of their otherwise noble conceptions, ignorant of what is truly right and good in this matter.

The ethical absolutist recognizes as a fact that moral customs and moral ideas differ from country to country and from age to age. This indeed seems manifest and not to be disputed. We think slavery morally wrong, the Greeks thought it morally unobjectionable. The inhabitants of New Guinea certainly have very different moral ideas from ours. But the fact that the Greeks or the inhabitants of New Guinea think something right does not make it right, even for them. Nor does the fact that we think the same things wrong make them wrong. They are *in themselves* either right or wrong. What we have to do is to discover which they are. What anyone thinks makes no difference. It is here just as it is in matters of physical science. We believe the earth to be a globe. Our ancestors may have thought it flat. This does not show that it *was* flat, and is *now* a globe. What it shows is that men having in other ages been ignorant about the shape of the earth have now learned the truth. So if the Greeks thought slavery morally legitimate, this does not indicate that it was for them and in that age morally legitimate, but rather that they were ignorant of the truth of the matter.

The ethical absolutist is not indeed committed to the opinion that his own, or our own, moral code is the true one. Theoretically at least he might hold that slavery is ethically justifiable, that the Greeks knew better than we do about this, that ignorance of the true morality lies with us and not with them. All that he is actually committed to is the opinion that, whatever the true moral code may be, it is always the same for all men in all ages. His view is not at all inconsistent with the belief that humanity has still much to learn in moral matters. If anyone were to assert that in five hundred years the moral conceptions of the present day will appear as barbarous to the people of that age as the moral conceptions of the middle ages appear to us now, he need not deny it. If anyone were to assert that the ethics of Christianity are by no means final, and will be superseded in future ages by vastly nobler moral ideals, he need not deny this either. For it is of the essence of his creed to believe that morality is in some sense objective, not man-made, not produced by human opinion; that its principles are real truths about which men have to learn—just as they have to learn about the shape of the world—about which they may have been ignorant in the past, and about which therefore they may well be ignorant now.

Thus although absolutism is conservative in the sense that it is regarded by the more daring spirits as an out of date opinion, it is not necessarily conservative in the sense of being committed to the blind support of existing moral ideas and institutions. If ethical absolutists are sometimes conservative in this sense too, that is their personal affair. Such conservativism is accidental, not essential to the absolutist's creed. There is no logical reason, in the nature of the case, why an absolutist should not be a communist, an anarchist, a surrealist, or an upholder of free love. The fact that he is usually none of these things may be accounted for in various ways. But it has nothing to do with the sheer logic of his ethical position. The sole opinion to which he is committed is that whatever is morally right (or wrong)—be it free love or monogamy or slavery or cannibalism or vegetarianism—is morally right (or wrong) for all men at all times.

Usually the absolutist goes further than this. He often maintains, not merely that the moral law is the same for all the men on this planet—which is, after all, a tiny speck in space—but that in some way or in some sense it has application everywhere in the universe. He may express himself by saying that it applies to all "rational beings"—which would apparently include angels and the men on Mars (if they are rational). He is apt to think that the moral law is a part of the fundamental structure of the universe. But with this aspect of absolutism we need not, at the moment, concern ourselves. At present we may think of it as being simply the opinion that there is a single moral standard for all human beings.

This brief and rough sketch of ethical absolutism is intended merely to form a background against which we may the more clearly indicate, by way of contrast, the theory of ethical relativity. Up to the present, therefore, I have not given any of the reasons which the absolutist can urge in favour of his case. It is sufficient for my purpose at the moment to state *what* he believes, without going into the question of *why* he believes it. But before proceeding to our next step—the explanation of ethical relativity—I think it will be helpful to indicate some of the historical causes (as distinguished from logical reasons) which have helped in the past to render absolutism a plausible interpretation of morality as understood by European peoples.

Our civilization is a Christian civilization. It has grown up, during nearly two thousand years, upon the soil of Christian monotheism. In this soil our whole outlook upon life, and consequently all our moral ideas, have their roots. They have been moulded by this influence. The wave of religious scepticism which, during the last half century, has swept over us, has altered this fact scarcely at all. The moral ideas even of those who most violently reject the dogmas of Christianity with their intellects are still Christian ideas. This will probably remain true for many centuries even if Christian theology, as a set of intellectual beliefs, comes to be wholly rejected by every educated person. It will probably remain true so long as our civilization lasts. A child cannot, by changing in later life his intellectual creed, strip himself of the early formative moral influences of his childhood, though he can no doubt modify their results in various minor ways. With the outlook on life which was instilled into him in his early days he, in large measure, lives and dies. So it is with a civilization. And our civilization, whatever religious or irreligious views it may come to hold or reject, can hardly escape within its lifetime the moulding influences of its Christian origin. Now ethical absolutism was, in its central ideas, the product of Christian theology.

The connection is not difficult to detect. For morality has been conceived, during the Christian dispensation, as issuing from the will of God. That indeed was its single and all-sufficient source. There would be no point, for the naïve believer in the faith, in the philosopher's questions regarding the foundations of morality and the basis of moral obligation. Even to ask such questions is a mark of incipient religious scepticism. For the true believer the author of the moral law is God. What pleases God, what God commands—that is the definition of right. What displeases God, what he forbids—that is the definition of wrong. Now there is, for the Christian monotheist, only one God ruling over the entire universe. And this God is rational, self-consistent. He does not act upon whims. Consequently his will and his commands must be the same everywhere. They will be unvarying for all peoples and in all ages. If the heathen have other moral ideas than ours—inferior ideas—that can only be because they live in ignorance of the true God. If they knew God and his commands, their ethical precepts would be the same as ours.

Polytheistic creeds may well tolerate a number of diverse moral codes. For the God of the western hemisphere might have different views from those entertained by the God of the eastern hemisphere. And the God of the north might issue to his worshippers commands at variance with the commands issued to other peoples by the God of the south. But a monotheistic religion implies a single universal and absolute morality.

This explains why ethical absolutism, until very recently, was not only believed by philosophers but *taken for granted without any argument*. The ideas of philosophers, like the ideas of everyone else, are largely moulded by the civilizations in which they live. Their philosophies are largely attempts to state in abstract terms and in self-consistent language the stock of ideas which they have breathed in from the atmosphere of their social environment. This accounts for the large number of so-called "unrecognized presuppositions" with which systems of philosophy always abound. These pre-suppositions are simply the ideas which the authors of the systems have breathed in with the intellectual atomospheres by which they happen to be surrounded—which they have taken over therefore as a matter of course, without argument, without criticism, without even a suspicion that they might be false.

It is not therefore at all surprising to find that Immanuel Kant, writing in the latter half of the eighteenth century, not only took the tenets of ethical absolutism for granted, but evidently considered that no instructed person would dispute them. It is a notice-able feature of his ethical philosophy that he gives no reasons whatever to support his belief in the existence of a universally valid moral law. He assumes as a matter of course that his readers will accept this view. And he proceeds at once to enquire what is the metaphysical foundation of the universal moral law. That alone is what interests him. *Assuming* that there does exist such a law, how, he asks, can this be the case, and what, in the way of transcendental truth, does it imply? It never occurs to him to reflect that any philosopher who should choose to question his fundamental assumption could outflank his whole ethical position; and that if this assumption should prove false his entire moral philosophy would fall to the ground like a pack of cards.

We can now turn to the consideration of ethical relativity which is the proper subject [here]. The revolt of the relativists against absolutism is, I believe, part and parcel of the general revolutionary tendency of our times. In particular it is a result of the decay of belief in the dogmas of orthodox religion. Belief in absolutism was supported, as we have seen, by belief in Christian monotheism. And now that, in an age of widespread religious scepticism, that support is withdrawn, absolutism tends to collapse. Revolu-tionary movements are as a rule, at any rate in their first onset, purely negative. They attack and destroy. And ethical relativity is, in its essence, a purely negative creed. It is simply a denial of ethical absolutism. That is why the best way of explaining it is to begin by explaining ethical absolutism. If we understand that what the latter asserts the former denies, then we understand ethical relativity.

Any ethical position which denies that there is a single moral standard which is equally applicable to all men at all times may fairly be called a species of ethical relativity. There is not, the relativist asserts, merely one moral law, one code, one standard. There are many moral laws, codes, standards. What morality ordains in one place or age may be quite different from what morality ordains in another place or age. The moral code of Chinamen is quite different from that of Europeans, that of African savages quite different from both. Any morality, therefore, is relative to the age, the place, and the circumstances in which it is found. It is in no sense absolute.

This does not mean merely—as one might at first sight be inclined to suppose—that the very same kind of action which is *thought* right in one country and period may be *thought* wrong in another. This would be a mere platitude, the truth of which everyone would have to admit. Even the absolutist would admit this—would even wish to emphasize it—since he is well aware that different peoples have different sets of moral ideas, and his whole point is that some of these sets of ideas are false. What the relativist means to assert is, not this platitude, but that the very same kind of action which *is* right in one country and period may *be* wrong in another. And this, far from being a platitude, is a very startling assertion.

It is very important to grasp thoroughly the difference between the two ideas. For there is reason to think that many minds tend to find ethical relativity attractive because they fail to keep them clearly apart. It is so very obvious that moral ideas differ from country to country and from age to age. And it is so very easy, if you are mentally lazy, to suppose that to say this means the same as to say that no universal moral standard exists—or in other words that it implies ethical relativity. We fail to see that the word "standard" is used in two different senses. It is perfectly true that, in one sense, there are many variable moral standards. We speak of judging a man by the standard of his time. And this implies that different times have different standards. And this, of course, is quite true. But when the word "standard" is used in this sense it means simply the set of moral ideas current during the period in question. It means what people *think* right, whether as a matter of fact it *is* right or not. On the other hand when the absolutist asserts that there exists a single universal moral "standard," he is not using the word in this sense at all. He means by "standard" what *is* right as distinct from what people merely think right. His point is that although what people think right varies in different countries and periods, yet what actually is right is everywhere and always the same. And it follows that when the ethical relativist disputes the position of the absolutist and denies that any universal moral standard exists he too means by "standard" what actually is right. But it is exceedingly easy, if we are not careful, to slip loosely from using the word in the first sense to using it in the second sense; and to suppose that the variability of moral beliefs is the same thing as the variability of what really is moral. And unless we keep the two senses of the word "standard" distinct, we are likely to think the creed of ethical relativity much more plausible than it actually is.

The genuine relativist, then, does not merely mean that Chinamen may think right what Frenchmen think wrong. He means that what *is* wrong for the Frenchman may *be* right for the Chinaman. And if one enquires how, in those circumstances, one is to know what actually is right in China or in France, the answer comes quite glibly. What is right in China is the same as what people think right in China; and what is right in France is the same as what people think right in France. So that, if you want to know what is moral in any particular country or age all you have to do is to ascertain what are the moral ideas current in that age or country. Those ideas are, *for that age or country,* right. Thus what is morally right is identified with what is thought to be morally right, and the distinction which we made above between these two is simply denied. To put the same thing in another way, it is denied that there can be or ought to be any distinction between the two senses of the word "standard." There is only one kind of standard of right and wrong, namely, the moral ideas current in any particular age or country.

Moral right *means* what people think morally right. It has no other meaning. What Frenchmen think right is, therefore, right *for Frenchmen.* And evidently one must conclude—though I am not aware that relativists are anxious to draw one's attention to such unsavoury but yet absolutely necessary conclusions from their creed—that cannibalism is right for people who believe in it, that human sacrifice is right for those races which practice it, and that burning widows alive was right for Hindus until the British stepped in and compelled the Hindus to behave immorally by allowing their widows to remain alive.

When it is said that, according to the ethical relativist, what is thought right in any social group is right for that group, one must be careful not to misinterpret this. The relativist does not, of course, mean that there actually is an objective moral standard in France and a different objective standard in England, and that French and British opinions respectively give us correct information about these different standards. His point is rather that there are no objectively true moral standards at all. There is no single universal objective standard. Nor are there a variety of local objective standards. All standards are subjective. People's subjective feelings about morality are the only standards which exist.

To sum up. The ethical relativist consistently denies, it would seem, whatever the ethical absolutist asserts. For the absolutist there is a single universal moral standard. For the relativist there is no such standard. There are only local, ephemeral, and variable standards. For the absolutist there are two senses of the word "standard." Standards in the sense of sets of current moral ideas are relative and changeable. But the standard in the sense of what is actually morally right is absolute and unchanging. For the relativist no such distinction can be made. There is only one meaning of the word "standard," namely, that which refers to local and variable sets of moral ideas. Or if it is insisted that the word must be allowed two meanings, then the relativist will say that there is at any rate no actual example of a standard in the absolute sense, and that the word as thus used is an empty name to which nothing in reality corresponds; so that the distinction between the two meanings becomes empty and useless. Finally— though this is merely saying the same thing in another way—the absolutist makes a distinction between what actually is right and what is thought right. The relativist rejects this distinction and identifies what is moral with what is thought moral by certain human beings or groups of human beings.

It is true that the relativist may object to my statement of his case on the ground that it does not specify precisely *who* the human beings are whose thinking makes what is right right and what is wrong wrong; and that he himself would not think of defining right as "that which people think right"—using the vague word "people" as if morality were determined by what any chance persons, anyone or everyone, happen to think moral. . . . there is a real and incurable ambiguity in the relativist's position here (and not merely in my statement of it), and that he himself has difficulty in saying who are the "people" whose ideas are to constitute moral standards. But he cannot deny, at any rate, that his creed does identify morality with the subjective thinking of human beings. And that is the only point which I am at present trying to make clear. . . .

In the preceding pages I have attempted to place absolutism and relativism over against one another in sharp contrast. In order not to blur the contrast I shall refrain . . . from mentioning or discussing other possible and intermediate views on the matters in dispute. In the end neither absolutism nor relativism will be upheld . . . as being the truth. They are both, in my opinion, unreasonable extremes of opinion. Between black and white there are many shades of grey. For the present, however, I shall continue, for the sake of simplicity, to talk as if there were only the two views, absolutism and relativism, in existence. I trust the reader will not be misled by this procedure into supposing that, if I reject ethical relativity, this must be because I wish to embrace absolutism and to argue in favour of it. This would be a complete misapprehension of my position.

. . .

[One of the main arguments in favour of ethical relativity] relies upon the actual varieties of moral "standards" found in the world. It was easy enough to believe in a single absolute morality in older times when there was no anthropology, when all humanity was divided clearly into two groups, Christian peoples and the "heathen." Christian peoples knew and possessed the one true morality. The rest were savages whose moral ideas could be ignored. But all this is changed. Greater knowledge has brought greater tolerance. We can no longer exalt our own morality as alone true, while dismissing all other moralities as false or inferior. The investigations of anthropologists have shown that there exist side by side in the world a bewildering variety of moral codes. On this topic endless volumes have been written, masses of evidence piled up. Anthropologists have ransacked the Melanesian Islands, the jungles of New Guinea, the steppes of Siberia, the deserts of Australia, the forests of central Africa, and have brought back with them countless examples of weird, extravagant, and fantastic "moral" customs with which to confound us. We learn that all kinds of horrible practices are, in this, that, or the other place, regarded as essential to virtue. We find that there is nothing, or next to nothing, which has always and everywhere been regarded as morally good by all men. Where then is our universal morality? Can we, in face of all this evidence, deny that it is nothing but an empty dream?

This argument, taken by itself, is a very weak one. It relies upon a single set of facts—the variable moral customs of the world. But this variability of moral ideas is admitted by both parties to the dispute, and is capable of ready explanation upon the hypothesis of either party. The relativist says that the facts are to be explained by the non-existence of any absolute moral standard. The absolutist says that they are to be explained by human ignorance of what the absolute moral standard is. And he can truly point out that men have differed widely in their opinions about all manner of topics including the subject-matters of the physical sicences—just as much as they differ about morals. And if the various different opinions which men have held about the shape of the earth do not prove that it has no one real shape, neither do the various opinions which they have held about morality prove that there is no one true morality.

Thus the facts can be explained equally plausibly on either hypothesis. There is nothing in the facts themselves which compels us to prefer the relativistic hypothesis to that of the absolutist. And therefore the argument fails to prove the relativist conclusion. If that conclusion is to be established, it must be by means of other considerations.

This is the essential point. But I will add some supplementary remarks. The work of the anthropologists, upon which ethical relativists seem to rely so heavily, has as a matter of fact added absolutely nothing *in principle* to what has always been known about the variability of moral ideas. Educated people have known all along that the Greeks tolerated sodomy, which in modern times has been regarded in some countries as an abominable crime; that the Hindus thought it a sacred duty to burn their widows; that trickery, now thought despicable, was once believed to be a virtue; that terrible torture was thought by our own ancestors only a few centuries ago to be a justifiable weapon of justice; that it was only yesterday that western peoples came to believe that slavery is immoral. Even the ancients knew very well that moral customs and ideas vary—witness the writings of Herodotus. Thus the principle of the variability of moral ideas was well understood long before modern anthropology was ever heard of. Anthropology has added nothing to the knowledge of this principle except a mass of new and extreme examples of it drawn from very remote sources. But to multiply examples of a principle already well known and universally admitted adds nothing to the argument which is built upon that principle. The discoveries of the anthropologists have no doubt been of the highest importance in their own sphere. But in my considered opinion they have thrown no new light upon the special problems of the moral philosopher.

Although the multiplication of examples has no logical bearing on the argument, it does have an immense *psychological* effect upon people's minds. These masses of anthropological learning are impressive. They are propounded in the sacred name of "science." If they are quoted in support of ethical relativity—as they often are—people *think* that they must prove something important. They bewilder and over-awe the simple-minded, batter down their resistance, make them ready to receive humbly the doctrine of ethical relativity from those who have acquired a reputation by their immense learning and their claims to be "scientific." Perhaps this is why so much ado is made by ethical relativists regarding the anthropological evidence. But we must refuse to be impressed. We must discount all this mass of evidence about the extraordinary moral customs of remote peoples. Once we have admitted—as everyone who is instructed must have admitted these last two thousand years without any anthropology at all—the principle that moral ideas vary, all this new evidence adds nothing to the argument. And the argument itself proves nothing for the reasons already given.

. . .

Suggested Readings

Benedict, Ruth. *Patterns of Culture.* Boston: Houghton Mifflin, 1934.

Emmet, Dorothy. *Rules, Roles and Relations.* New York: St. Martin's Press, 1966.

Ginsberg, Morris. *Essays in Sociology and Social Philosophy.* Middlesex, England: Penguin, 1968.

Herskovits, Melville J. *Cultural Relativism.* New York: Random House, 1973.

Westermarck, Edward A. *Ethical Relativity.* New York: Harcourt, 1932.

section three

ethics and religion

THE VANITY OF HUMANISM

Ronald Sampson

Susan Stebbing wrote in 1941: "But it is also no illusion but uncontested fact that here and now we know that hatred, cruelty, intolerance and indifference to human misery are evil; that love, kindliness, tolerance, forgiveness and truth are good, so unquestionably good that we do not need God or heaven to assure us of their worth." When I first read this, it struck a responsive chord; I remember quoting it with approval a decade ago. Virtue, I felt, was self-evident, beyond the possibility of sincere disputation; moreover, this was all that was truly important: that we should get on with the business of doing what we so clearly knew. For if our lives were loving and honorable, if we were kind, tolerant, forgiving and truthful, there would be no problems of an urgent or serious kind.

Moreover, so it then seemed to me—it was not merely that morality was self-sufficient and that discussion of the nature or existence of God was unnecessary. Theological discussion was positively harmful. It was precisely when men began to dispute about the nature of God that they showed their worst qualities, and for good reason. Men become most bitter and intolerant at the point where the touchstone of evidence, to which appeal can be made, breaks down. In the absence of evidence the will to self-assertion, the desire to subjugate one's opponent, find free rein. "God" is such a nebulous, unverifiable concept, meaning all things to all men, I thought, that it is bound to be a bone of inexhaustible contention. In morals, the appeal to universal experience offers itself as an inescapable arbiter; in theology, on the other hand, there is no such arbiter, and so it is not surprising that religion brings out the worst in man.

Consider the record of man's search for God. All history indicates not only that there are apparently no limits to what men will worship under this label but also that men have committed and still commit some of their more atrocious crimes in pursuit of their worship and in their intolerance of other men's differing concepts of what is appropriate or required of them in matters of a religious nature. And among wars it is notorious that none is more calculated to bring out new depths of cruelty than the religious war.

Nor is it simply that religious belief has been intimately associated with fear, superstition and irrationality, spawning innumerable mystical cults and rituals to act as magnets for fanaticism and ignorance. Religion is also intimately associated with the apparatus of political domination and economic exploitation. When reason and persuasion fail of their purpose, the temptation is immediate to seek to buttress one's unacknowledged or weak authority by appealing to divine command. Countless rulers have sought to validate their authority by asserting a divine right, and have tried to make the claim credible through ritual and pomp associated with such hallowed symbols as scepter, miter and orb. After World War I, men began to recognize the full price of this folklore, and their bitterness found expression in sardonically humorous verse:

> God save the king. Gott strafe England,
> God this, God that and God the other thing.
> Good God! said God, I've got my work cut out.

Even in the age of Cromwell, some among the radical Puritans were aware of the sociological function of religion as the "opium of the people." The bare bones of Marx's argument two centuries later are found in Gerrard Winstanley's *The Law of Freedom in a Platform or True Magistracy Restored* (1652):

The elder brother replies, What, will you be an Atheist, and a factious man, will you not believe God?

Yes, saith the younger brother, if I knew God said so I should believe, for I desire to serve him.

Why, saith the elder brother, this is his word, and if you will not believe it, you must be damned; but if you will believe it, you must go to Heaven.

Well, the younger brother being weak in spirit, and having not a grounded knowledge of the Creation, nor of himself, is terrified, and lets go his hold in the Earth, and submits himself to be a slave to his brother . . . and so his eyes are put out, and his Reason is blinded.

In our time the major emphasis has probably been focused on the psychology of religion. Stimulated by psychoanalytic theories, men have been increasingly inclined to construe God as a projection of fears, need for consolation, inability to look the unknown unflinchingly in the face, failure to achieve emotional autonomy from parental control and consequent need for an eternal Father. Common to Marxist theories of alienation and Freudian psychoanalysis is the reduction of God to the status of a morbid symbol of man's immaturity as an exploited worker or as a possessed and dominated son. In philosophy, molded largely by the 20th-century reverence for science, concern has been with precision and clarity of linguistic usage. Tests of meaning of the most rigorous nature, acceptable to the scientist, were devised. If a statement were neither a definition nor verifiable by appeal to any possible sense experience, it was held to be meaningless. Under attack, minor concessions were made to avoid manifest absurdity, but only to safeguard the purity of the central positivist principle. If God is to pass such a test before being admitted to the status of meaningful concepts, the onus is on the believer to supply evidence of God's transcendent reality. What evidence of a falsifiable nature can be adduced to prove that man is not alone in the universe, that God would still exist if the human species were to perish? In this way the whole 19th-century debate between immanentists and transcendentalists has been neatly headed off.

The theologians themselves have long been in full retreat before the positivist onslaught, bringing their teachings up to date, rethinking, rationalizing, salvaging what crumbs they could, or even—on the notorious principle that if you cannot beat your opponent, join him—producing ultra-sophistications of their own about what they are pleased to call the death of God. In short, the twin streams of the European Enlightenment, the liberal empiricist stream and the dialectical materialist stream, have united in an immensely powerful river to wash away the last remnants of man's traditional beliefs about the existence and nature of God. Since, however, most of us recognize that man cannot live without some guiding metaphysic, a new "religion," Humanism, is rapidly being evolved in the West and appears to be growing increasingly fashionable. The essential argument is admittedly persuasive and is implicit in the preceding analysis. Since the evidence is overwhelming that nothing is more difficult to secure than agreement among men concerning the nature of *reality,* and since it is a matter of urgency to secure some measure of agreement about the nature of *morality,* where common yardsticks of appeal are potentially within reach, let us put the religious debate into cold storage, if it is not possible to get rid of it altogether, so that we can get on with the practical and urgent business of hammering out an agreed morality. To hope that Christians and Marxists, for example, might one day agree upon the nature of reality or the nature of God, is obviously futile and in any case unnecessary. But since they do share common problems, it is urgent and far from utopian that we should begin to try to establish mutual understanding about problems of conduct in the interests of harmony and peace. Let us agree to avoid the *odium theologicum* and settle for concord about important matters like peace, security and productivity. Ronald Fletcher, professor of sociology at the University of York writes:

If morality is to wait upon agreement about religious or metaphysical matters then men are in a serious plight indeed, for every religion and ideology in the world differs on these matters, and very radically. Men are everywhere faced, however, with common economic, social, political problems, and are involved—from the personal, right up to the international, level—in issues of reciprocal obligation.

Ethics is an autonomous discipline, he states, and therefore asks rhetorically: "Who is right about 'reality' is a question which can surely wait?" What could sound more reasonable?

It is the purpose of this essay to deny this thesis, to argue that Humanism, be it agnostic or atheistic, is a false religion, that men *are* "in a serious plight indeed," that this plight has arisen ultimately from false religious belief, that the liberation from false metaphysics only to fall into new forms of error will not alleviate our existing grave situation, but will on the contrary produce even more deadly consequences; that morality is not an autonomous discipline, that the argument about the nature of reality is fundamental, that error about the nature and purpose of God must necessarily lead to avoidable suffering and death, and that the metaphysical debate, so far from being a luxury to be postponed indefinitely, is the most urgent task, now more than ever, confronting men.

That men have worshipped false gods is abundantly evident; the targets against which Marx and Freud launched their arrows were shrewdly chosen. But the fact that men in their blindness have conceived an infinitude of false gods, does not entitle us to infer that therefore God does not exist. That is as though we were to infer from the innumerable instances of men's false reasoning that man is incapable of distinguishing truth from falsehood. Let us return to the original quotation from Susan Stebbing and ask why, notwithstanding the fact that the distinction between good and evil is self-evident, men after millennia of struggle show as yet but faint signs of overcoming evil. We know here and now indisputably that "hatred, cruelty, intolerance and indifference to human misery are evil. . . ." Had Dr. Stebbing stopped there, none could gainsay her. But we must ask why, given this knowledge, we *appear* to be incapable of acting upon it. Is it that this knowledge has come to us only recently, that we have not had sufficient time to gird our loins? Clearly not. "War of any kind is evil," wrote Herodotus a very long time ago. But we wage it today with apparently undiminished zest. Sexual immorality and depravity also lead to geat evil, but when theologians discuss morality solely in the context of sexual relations and to the exclusion of war, we rightly feel that there is something odd—that they are being less than honest to us, let alone to God.

Of the very many ills which afflict humanity one evil dwarfs all the others. Throughout human history men have lived in organized groups under governments which have feared and competed with one another by means of arms, and the resultant arms races have erupted at more or less regular intervals into wars. The present arms race is consuming $183 billion a year, and it is beyond the power of any human imagination to foresee the extent of the holocaust which will ensue if it continues until it erupts into war. In the childhood of our species it was no doubt possible to delude men that evil occurred because the gods were angry or because exceptionally wicked men held sway; but it is no longer possible to deceive in this way. Today, men know that when very great evil threatens to overtake them, it is and can only be because very large numbers of men are contributing their share to that evil, that is to say, are living their lives on a false and evil basis. And this, notwithstanding that we all know, indeed cannot *not* know, that "love, kindliness, tolerance, forgiveness and truth are good . . . unquestionably good." So where is all the evil coming from?

At this point I find it difficult not to resort to the first person singular, not because the evidence is in any way private or less than general but because it is more likely to touch the imagination when translated into the idiom in which we as individuals experience it. In my childhood it was the practice in my part of the world for children to go to day school on weekdays and to Sunday school on Sunday. It was in the latter school that I was first exposed to the four Gospels of the New Testament, and they immediately reached into my profoundest emotions—not the absurd and manifestly false tales about people rising physically from the dead, walking on the water and conjuring water into wine, but stories such as that of the woman taken in adultery, the good Samaritan, the prodigal son, and the lucid, yet poetic simplicity of the Beatitudes. But although these readings, repeated many times, were to make an ineffaceable impression, another and different lesson was also taught me, one that was the more powerful because it was never openly expressed. I noticed that while I was required to attend Sunday school and while interest was expressed if I received a prize for attendance or diligence in memorizing required lessons, the interest was nevertheless essentially polite. But the interest shown by everyone in my circle to success achieved in lessons and examinations at the day school was of the genuine variety which quickened the pulse.

In short, I learned that "religion" played in life some part that was never made plain beyond the fact that it was peripheral and wrapped around with much that was evidently irrational—dogma, miracle and ritual which inspired not respect but contempt. On the other hand, I learned that to make a successful career, that is to say, to "get on" in the world, was a matter of central and enduring importance, commanding the immediate and genuine respect of everyone I knew. That there might ever be a conflict between these two planes of experience never seriously occurred to me. That there had been such conflicts in history, I was of course aware, but that was on the public stage and in the past, and clearly had nothing to do with my own private, personal existence. The real purpose of life was to be successful, as the world and I measured success. As for virtue, that was something which largely took care of itself; one did as one's neighbor did and as professional standards required, and no one could pretend that such requirements were especially onerous. I knew, of course, that injustice and inequality existed in the world, and that this was wrong; but my obligations in that respect were wholly covered by my tacit membership in and support of the reformist party, which was working, admittedly slowly but nevertheless steadily— Rome was not built in a day—to set matters right. So I had been sedulously taught, and so I believed.

It is not necessary here to describe the gradual and painful process whereby I awoke from this dream. Everyone of my generation knows how the organized parties of reform not only betrayed their "principles" but themselves became active agents in the committing of atrocity and crime. And as the wars and the famines, the arms race and irresponsible technology, the hangings and assassinations continued, it became more and more evident that the dissidents, the protesters, "the stage army of the good," who were called upon to protest again and again, with enduring stamina, were not drawn at random from all levels of society. They were drawn always from the ranks of the "powerless," the people who had no positions of authority to jeopardize or lose. Those who consistently sought allies against recurring wrong and injustice quickly learned that the reservoir of potential support shrank visibly as one ascended the hierarchy of prestige and power. It would be useful to get X's signature; it would carry a lot of weight, we fondly imagined. But we soon discovered that X's signature was not to be had. Privately he might well be with us, but we must appreciate that for a person in his position, well . . . we did understand, didn't we? So we had to make do with poor old Z's signature, which allegedly carried little or no weight, but which was always to be relied upon.

One other facet of my experience also sharply impressed me. Although great and growing evil occurred in the world, yet, wherever I moved in society, be it among teachers, soldiers, churchmen, criminals, housewives, policemen, workmen, politicians, foreigners, doctors, I never met anyone who struck me as essentially an evil man. Men who were weak and pompous, who dissembled and were evasive, who were self-important, vain and ambitious, who were self-contradictory, self-deceiving, unreliable, acquisitive, these I met in plenty at every level of society; but nowhere was it my misfortune to find an unmistakably evil man. So evil occurred in the world, very great and unbelievable evil, and yet there were no evil men, it appeared. Whenever we sought support to protest against an evil, it was very rare indeed to find anyone who wished to identify himself, least of all publicly, with the evil in question. To be sure, halfhearted attempts at casuistry would sometimes be made, but these would soon fade under the pressure of honest logic. Nevertheless, it was not easy to enlist support against the evil from people of "influence" in the community. For people of influence and position, of power or wealth, had their positions and their power to lose, whereas those unencumbered by such positions were more free to listen to the voice of conscience within. Or, to put the matter the other way round, if a man were consistently to heed and act upon the voice of conscience, he would inevitably be required to pay a price in the shape of growing ineligibility for promotion to positions of authority, increased emolument and "influence."

In short, a clash, a conflict, a dilemma was inherent in the logic of things, and it was inescapable that every man had to choose. He could choose to aspire toward fortune or preferment, a successful career, high status, position; or he could listen consistently to and try to act upon the voice of conscience which urged him to protest against the injustice of the world. But what he could not have—as I had so fondly hoped to be the case—was both. A man could not have both power over others and genuine love for others. And while it was obvious which one should choose, it was unfortunately by no means easy to make the right choice, as was attested both by my own backsliding and by the large number of those who were unwilling because of their positions, actual or hoped for, to oppose publicly the evils which they would repudiate privately.

In brief I had learned the ancient lesson that, while all human beings are more than adequately equipped to distinguish good from evil, nevertheless a price is to be paid for choosing the good rather than the evil. There is a reward, too, of course, in the shape of a tranquil conscience and the serenity of spirit that is alone born of a tranquil consicence; but most human beings appear to be more immediately impressed by the nature of the sacrifice than by the reality of the reward, for the former is tangible and the latter is not. And any discussion of the autonomy of ethics which fails to take this dilemma for mortal man adequately into account must be condemned as facile and not very helpful. It is not enough to know that kindliness is good and cruelty is bad. It is also necessary to be able to answer correctly the question: why am I alive and what is the purpose of this life that has been temporarily entrusted to me?

Every man must be bound by some conviction, conscious or unconscious, about the significance he attaches to his life in order to live it, to direct it, to make plans or merely to drift. Whatever a man may say, his behavior over a prolonged period will under close study inevitably reveal the real values sustaining it. And this metaphysic is the most important thing that we must know of a man if we need to assess his basic character or to predict how he will act in a given situation. Since every man is endowed with very powerful appetites, it is perfectly possible to find the meaning of one's life in a ceaseless pursuit of gratification. In practice, most of us are in varying degree aware both that appetites ceaselessly pampered are apt to cloy and that unrestrained egoism on the part of large numbers of individuals is calculated to bring about conditions of misery and discomfort to all concerned. Therefore a policy of unrelieved individualism is generally tempered to some degree by a further extension of this principle. That is to say, the individual finds the meaning of his life not solely in self-indulgence but also in satisfying the wants of a group or groups with which he identifies emotionally. The most universal form of ego identification with a group is of course with the family, but the principle extends in a lesser degree to schools, villages, social classes, religious and ethnic groups and political nationalities.

The difficulty with all these "goods" sought for oneself or one's group is that they are particularistic or exclusive; they displace a like good for somebody else or some other group. They are not compatible with the principle of universalism and therefore violate the principle of justice. They stimulate competition; they are keenly sought just because they confer privilege or special status; they differentiate favorably the success-ful from those who fail. They are therefore of the very stuff of strife, of envy, of the struggle for power, of the resentments of inferiority, of the war of all against all.

Unfortunately, the energies which are harnessed to these secular goals are very powerful, and sustain the central efforts of a man's striving and struggle over a lifetime. If they are rejected as having morally indefensible consequences to mankind as a whole, inevitably an immense problem makes itself felt. To what is a man to devote his energies? What shall be the central goal of his life? If he ceases to find it in the quest for power, privilege, status, "authority," wealth, what substitute is there that *is* morally acceptable and which can realistically evoke a comparable single-mindedness and consistently sustained application of energy? In whatever way we seek to answer this question, one thing is certain: the first step consists in renouncing what have hitherto been powerfully felt desires, animating the individual's main aspirations and life goals. And such a task is calculated to daunt even strong people. Resistance cannot but be profound, as St. Augustine testified with a disarming candor and wry humor:

And when Thou didst on all sides shew me, that what Thou saidst was true, I, convicted by the truth, had nothing at all to answer but only those dull and drowsy words, "Anon, anon," "presently"; "leave me but a little." But "presently, presently" had no present, and my "little while" went on for a long while. . . .

It is important to analyze why it is so difficult. Consider the case: A man has been living his life according to goals arising out of emotions of egoism, sexual gratification, acquisitiveness or group loyalty, emotions laid deep within the psychic life of every human being, emotions which therefore reinforce themselves by the very frequency with which we find them exemplified in the behavior of others. A man has not only to overcome the resistances within himself; he must overcome his initial fear of the resistance of those among whom he lives, often by no means least the resistance of those nearest and dearest. When Christian decided as a result of his dream to hasten forth from the city of destruction, the discovery that he could not persuade his wife and family to accompany him must have been bitter indeed, although Christian's own previous life could scarcely have been such as to prepare them for so strange a develop-ment. When Tolstoy at the age of 50, in all the agony of soul he has imperishably described in his *Confession,* discovered the real nature of the city of destruction and hastened accordingly to flee it, he too found himself in almost complete isolation from his wife and family, although, as he himself realized, the sins of his youth were in no small part to blame.

To follow the voice of truth, as it struggles to make itself heard within the quietude of the individual soul, is difficult because of our instinctive awareness that to do so will not simply fail to add to our popularity, but will evoke strong resistance from those around us, leading at best to a degree of isolation. "There is a saying among children," testified Joan of Arc at her trial, "that men are sometimes hanged for having spoken the truth." There is also an old saw to the effect that if God were to live on earth, people would break His windows. Is not the experience of Socrates, Jesus, Arnold of Brescia, the Maid herself, More, Huss, Giordano Bruno, Servetus, enough to stand in perpetual warning of this terrible truth? But martyrdom requires not only innocence and courage on the part of the victim and cruelty on the part of his persecutors; it requires in addition the acquiescence of the multitude. And a few cannot intimidate multitudes solely by fear. "Ye are many, they are few," as Shelley reminded us. The multitudes must themselves first be morally confused. That this is commonly the case derives from the deceitfulness of the human heart. Men commonly will the good, but are easily gulled. To come to a conclusion that will convict us ourselves of immorality is exceedingly hard, because of the great strength of our vanity and self-love. Paul Tillich has expressed the nature of this inner resistance of the soul with exceptional clarity in his *The Shaking of the Foundations:*

Our entire inner life, our thoughts and desires, our feelings, and imaginations, are known to God. The final way of escape, the most intimate of all places, is held by God. That fact is the hardest of all to accept. The human resistance against such relentless observation can scarcely be broken. Every psychiatrist and confessor is familiar with the tremendous force of resistance in each personality against even trifling self-revelations. Nobody wants to be known, even when he realizes that his health and salvation depend upon such a knowledge. We do not even wish to be known by ourselves. We try to hide the depth of our souls from our own eyes. We refuse to be our own witness. How then can we stand the mirror in which nothing can be hidden?

But if it is difficult to acknowlege the truth and follow it, it is not impossible. To do what I will may not always lie within my power, but what surely does always lie within my power is the ability to will the good. And it is the peculiar and unique power of the truth that, if acknowledged freely and honestly, ultimately it will of its own accord rectify our existing false situation. Truth is impregnable against all forms of attack, all mockery, all satire; it is immune to self-contradiction; it is impervious to the emotions of cunning, deceit, self-doubt. It commands universal attention, and ultimately the obedience of all honest men. "Truth," wrote James Russell Lowell in the *Biglow Papers,* "is quite beyond the reach of satire. There is so brave a simplicity in her, that she can no more be made ridiculous than an oak or a pine."

Nevertheless, truth is a hard taskmaster, for it demands as the first step in its service a willingness to transcend the claims of the self in the service of other selves. Its first and last law is that of renunciation, which though possible for man, does not come naturally to him. And the paradox is that insofar as a man succeeds in his aspiration to obey truth, he inevitably puts himself at the mercy of all who suffer from no such inhibitions and who accordingly take advantage of him. One man's truth has to confront another man's falsehood; one man's forbearance is met with another's will to dominion; the one's agony of conscience contends with him who is without scruple; the one man's love and nonviolence has to brave the threats of hatred and violence; the total vulnerability of the one stands against the bludgeon of a Cain or Raskolnikov.

In logic, the only possible remedy to the arms race based on fear is unilateral disarmament based on trust. The truth of renunciation which is the key to all goodness is pre-eminently demonstrated here, yet nowhere are there apparently so few willing takers. At no point does human skepticism and despair appear more intractable. The reason is to be found in the conviction, so deep in this world, that evil must inevitably triumph over good. From the author of the seventy-third Psalm to Gerard Manley Hopkins men have lamented the evident fact that the ungodly prosper in the world while the godly are chastened for their pains.

> Why do sinners' ways prosper? and why must
> Disappointment all I endeavour end?
> Wert thou my enemy, O thou my friend,
> How wouldst thou worse, I wonder, than thou dost
> Defeat, thwart me? . . .

Many have found in this fact alone the most eloquent of all testimony to the necessity of the immortality of the soul. Something other must exist to redress the balance of this vale of tears. "Had I no other proof of the immaterial nature of the soul," affirmed Rousseau's Savoyard vicar, "the triumph of the wicked and the oppression of the righteous in this world would be enough to convince me."

But on reflection we must surely see that there was no other way in which man could be taught the truth. If to avoid defeat we resist evil violently, we provide yet another alibi for wrongdoing, we do something dubious, we teach a wrong lesson. Men see only that a battle of wills is taking place, and they understand that well enough from long familiarity. It is essential that we show that we struggle not that our will should prevail but that the truth of justice or equality should prevail. *Not my will but Thy will!* Will it is that we must obey—and it is clearly not the will of organized men, nor is it the natural will of the individual. Then whose will? What is the will we follow in the quest for self-perfection? If it were our own will, would not the skeptics be right who accuse those who strive after perfectibility of vanity or self-righteousness?

We can abdicate all "power" means of implementing our will, only if we have confidence that by following the way indicated by conscience and reason as the true way, thus paradoxically putting ourselves at the mercy of the evil will, good will ultimately be advanced and the truth prevail. *Not my will but Thy will!* But what confidence can we have in the presence of so much violence, a vast surrounding ocean of evil? Faith? Yes, perhaps, but not blind faith—it must be reasonable faith based on evidence and reasoning conducted as always by rigorous adherence to the logic of the argument to the end. After all, if we are to have faith, it may well cost us our lives. The evil one, soldier or criminal, whom men fear as the potential agent of violent death, may well take advantage of our self-chosen vulnerability to dispatch us forthwith. And these are no academic possibilities but actual contingencies being experienced in the flesh by many here and now. Are we to sacrifice our all on the basis of blind faith, where reason would surely call at best for agnosticism?

It is inescapable that so long as one man survives who is willing to take advantage of his physically weaker brother to slay him, this world must remain the kingdom of power. But might it not be that an unknown X factor could, if found, trusted and relied upon, ultimately prevail over the forces of power, of evil, even in this world, the only world we know? But what if this X factor becomes efficacious only if we trust it even unto possible acceptance of a violent, premature and otherwise escapable death? And if such an X factor is found by all testable experience to exist, a factor before which power itself is rendered impotent by entirely nonpower means, what name must we give it? Truth? Yes, but it is the very core of truth that we are seeking to define. *Magna est veritas et praevalebit.* Yes, indeed, if we always scrupulously follow it, but what is its essence and what is the evidence? What is the one thing that overcomes all our resistance, our pride, our self-love, our self-seeking, our power? Everyone knows the answer to this—it is love.

> Was neverë werre in this worldë
> Ne wikkednessë so kenë
> That ne love, an him liste,
> To laughyngë ne broughtë

But what is love? Again its inmost essence, its great strength, turns out to be powerlessness. When the barrier of our self-pride is broken down, when we become as little children, with the natural, naive humility of the child, it is then and only then, when power has fled us completely, that ultimately we move even the most hardened.

When Joan of Arc rode at the head of her troops, when she was hailed by all France as the maid sent to liberate Orléans, to secure the crowning of the Dauphin, when she mounted her white charger to hurl herself upon the English, she constitutes the very stuff of romance, of legend, of glory, but the truth is not in her. On the contrary, it was during this period that Joan's inimitable qualities of simplicity, common sense, truthfulness, courage first began to show signs of being undermined and corroded by her elevation to a position of leadership among the "great" ones of the earth. As Michelet carefully noted, the banner she originally carried had by the time she was taken at Compiègne been put aside for the sword, "excellent both to thrust and cut." The Christian Maid had become coarsened by military conquest to the point where she could surrender a captured Burgundian freebooter to the royal bailiff for execution. It is only after her capture, after she has been brought low and subjected to base brutality, that she puts on the lineaments of truth—so much so that across half a thousand years she still speaks to our most lucid reason and plumbs the profoundest emotions. Abandoned by the world, entirely alone, exposed to the coarsest insult, sick, wracked by fear and doubt, in mortal physical peril, humbled, she achieves her apotheosis. Treacherously asked if she believed herself to be in a state of grace, she replied: "If I am not, may it please God to to bring me into it; if I am, may He preserve me in it." And asked why she had recanted, she defeated guile with the irrefutable courage and simplicity of the truth: "Because I was afraid of the fire."

If we turn back to the story of Jesus himself, we feel compelled to ask if it is mere coincidence that the account of the cursing of the fig tree because it failed to bear fruit out of season, and the hounding of the moneychangers out of the temple—both of them acts out of character and less than edifying—come immediately after Jesus' triumphant ride into Jerusalem, acclaimed by the multitude. Be that as it may, it is certainly not the success which has captured the imagination of the world for two millennia. What moves mankind is the vision of a child cradled in a cattle manger, because there was no room at the inn, which the well-to-do had already occupied. That was the significant beginning; the end was the crucifixion between two thieves. The man taught with unmistakable clarity: *Resist not evil,* and the forgiveness of sin. "Neither do I condemn thee. Go thy way and sin no more." And when Pilate marveled that a man being tried for his life, should make no attempt to defend himself, thrice called on him to answer, he met only with silence. "God forgive them, for they know not what they do." And indeed it is the case: we do not know, we do not really know what it is we do, or we could not inflict such astounding and unbelievable cruelties on one another. Men behold one another incomprehendingly. The Bishop of Linz confronted by the heroic Jägerstätter could see only a young man with a lust for martyrdom; and Jägerstätter could in charity only conceive of the bishop as one who had not received the grace to see things as they really were. But through it all runs the consistent thread of the truth, simple, void of ambiguity, unmistakable to all with eyes to see. On the one hand the sword of Caesar, the governor's crown, the armed might of the centurion, the cry for blood that arises when power feels itself threatened; and confronting it, what? An emaciated, disarmed, defenseless carpenter's son, whose only crime has been the continuous, quiet yet impassioned eloquence of his plea that we should love one another.

To all of which no doubt the reply from those who pride themselves on being what is called "tough-minded" will be that emotion is emotion and reason is reason, and reason indicates that, whatever the truth of the foregoing, we have done nothing to demonstrate that ethics is not an autonomous discipline. We have been discussing morals, not theology. Let it be conceded for the sake of argument: humility and forgiveness, especially of enemies, are high virtues, high guarantors of moral excellence. Where does that leave us? Agnostics have never denied that morality exists, nor would they necessarily quarrel with this definition of the content of morality. The question at issue is whether or not morals are self-sufficient.

Let us recapitulate the central argument. It comes naturally to man to attend to what appear to be in his own interests or conducive to the pleasures of himself or the group with which he emotionally identifies. But all experience testifies that such conduct on the part of individuals and groups leads directly and inevitably to competition, strife, fear, hatred, rivalry, self-deception, greed, xenophobia. In short, they are destructive of man's real interests. Therefore the true form of conduct, which will promote man's genuine interests, is the opposite of self-interest. It consists in finding the meaning of one's life, not in the quest for wealth, power and prestige but in engaging in activities prompted by consideration of the needs of one's fellows. And this policy, although productive of great and enduring satisfaction, does not appear to come naturally and easily to man, although it is certainly possible for him to achieve it. The former metaphysic is the law of power and/or violence and leads to evil; the latter is the law of love and equality and leads to good. And the meaning of every individual's life consists in the choice which he is of necessity required to make between these alternatives. The balance of forces is never more than precariously poised between the two; and in the nature of things if the forces of power are sufficiently ruthless, the *immediate* victory must always go to them. And this means that the individual who chooses the good must not only overcome the disposition of his own natural egocentric passions but must also overcome his own natural fears of the powerful, who are in a position to do him great harm, and are very likely to attempt to do so because they are effectively threatened only by the individual who seeks the good and evokes a like response in the conscience of others.

But the question remains: why should the individual choose the good, when it is a path full of difficulties and pitfalls, and may well lead him into a position of discomfort, hardship, persecution or even peril to his life? Because it is the good? But why should I prefer the good to my own immediate comfort, appetites and security? Even if I am capable of willing the good, why should I? Why should I not will what is natural to me? The good is clearly not the fruit of my own spontaneous will, nor is it the will of nature, whose law is one that is indeed "red in tooth and claw"; still less is it the will of human law, which is at all times and everywhere based on fear and violence. Then why should I obey this will? Whose will is it? I should obey it, because it is the will of God. There is no other possible answer. If God did not exist, I would have no reason for obeying this law; it would be no more than the idle dream, which is what vain, presumptuous and wicked men have always cynically claimed it to be.

Nor would this be all. If God did not exist, it would be possible to secure everlasting peace by mutual deterrence through the balance of terror—that is to say, to bring about good by doing evil, as the casuists and sophists would always have us believe. But it is not so possible. As men sow, so shall they always reap. Nothing and no one can disturb this law. And this is the answer to Man Friday's celebrated question to Robinson Crusoe: "Why God not kill the devil?" Man's only protection lies in his obedience to the moral law; were it possible to disobey it with impunity without bringing about evil consequences in its wake, the last barrier between the soul of man and his total depravity would go down. It may be asked why, if God exists, man be not given tangible proof of the fact, authentic evidence verifiable through the senses, scientifically warranted; a Day of Judgment, perhaps? Could we not each of us have been permitted to draw up one day at "A siding at a railway station" with James Anthony Froude, and see with our own eyes the first-class passengers receiving their sentences, and the philosopher who believed that we lived in the best of all possible worlds being condemned to renew his life once more, only this time as one "born blind and paralytic"? Of course the answer is "no," since virtue ceases to be virtue immediately it is followed for reasons of prudence, of calculation or utility.

If God did not exist, then the individual's struggle to perfect himself would indeed be no more than a form of moral vanity or egocentric spiritual pride, which is how the enemies of perfectibility are so eager to construe it. When we fail in our moral striving, we are humbled, and that is good for us. When we succeed—and if success were impossible, aspiration itself would be fatally undermined—we are threatened by pride. When Bunyan was once complimented on the quality of the sermon he had just delivered, he replied: "You need not remind me of that. The Devil told me of it before I was out of the pulpit." If God did not exist, we would indeed be caught in a "double bind" from which no moral escape would be possible. But this is not so, as Job discovered when by his self-righteousness he brought upon himself the voice out of the whirlwind, whose awe-inspiring admonition left him no alternative but to acknowledge that he was "of small account," that he abhorred himself and repented "in dust and ashes."

Finally, if God did not exist, then ultimately we should unavoidably feel impelled to look not simply to our own truthfulness, integrity and humility but to our own *power* to implement the good and ward off the evil. And this quest for power, commonly disguised by what appear to be good or disinterested motives, is the primal source of the evil which we feel ourselves called upon to overcome. We can overcome it completely only if we can say with genuine conviction: *Not my will but Thy will!*

In the context of a discussion concerning the probable outcome of the existing "defense" policies of the world's governments, I was once asked by a clergyman:

"Supposing mankind proves unable to turn back the clock of the suicidal arms race of the governments, and the consequences prove as dire as we fear; suppose in fact that all life on our planet were to perish, would it matter?" My immediate response was one of incredulous shock at a question seemingly resting on brutal, callous, cosmic indifference. But the man was kindly, humane, responsible, concerned, and he posed his question with deliberation and a grave serenity. I began to grasp his point. All life is mortal, all living things are destined to perish utterly, leaving no trace. This we know incontrovertibly. So in what sense can it be said to matter if life itself were ultimately destined to perish? I have often attempted to formulate an answer, and have found myself groping inarticulately, for it is as difficult as it is necessary that such a question be faced and honestly answered. I was therefore grateful when I came across the following passage in the *Journal of Amiel*, which seems to me to put the heart of the matter with great clarity and force, and speaks for my own deepest feeling:

It is by no means necessary that the universe should exist, but it is necessary that justice should be done, and atheism is bound to explain the fixed obstinacy of conscience on this point. Nature is not just; we are the products of nature: why are we always claiming and prophesying justice? Why does the effect rise up against its cause? It is a singular phenomenon. Does the protest come from any puerile blindness of human vanity? No, it is the deepest cry of our being, and it is for the honour of God that the cry is uttered. Heaven and earth may pass away, but good *ought* to be, and injustice ought *not* to be. Such is the creed of the human race. Nature will be conquered by spirit: the eternal will triumph over time.

GOD AND THE GOOD: DOES MORALITY NEED RELIGION?

Kai Nielsen

It is the claim of many influential Christian and Jewish theologians (Brunner, Buber, Barth, Niebuhr and Bultmann—to take outstanding examples) that the *only* genuine basis for morality is in religion. And any old religion is not good enough. The only truly adequate foundation for moral belief is a religion that acknowledges the absolute sovereignty of the Lord found in the prophetic religions.

These theologians will readily grant what is plainly true, namely, that as a matter of fact many non-religious people behave morally, but they contend that without a belief in God and his Law there is no *ground* or *reason* for being moral. The sense of moral relativism, skepticism, and nihilism rampant in our age is due in large measure to the general weakening of religious belief in an age of science. Without God there can be no objective foundation for our moral beliefs. As Brunner puts it, "The believer *alone* clearly perceives that the Good, as it is recognized in faith, is the sole Good, and all that is otherwise called good cannot lay claim to this title, at least in the ultimate sense of the word." "The Good consists in always doing what God wills at any particular moment." This "Good" can only "take place in unconditional obedience" to God, the ground of our being. Without God life would have no point and morality would have no basis. Without religious belief, without the Living God, there could be no adequate answer to the persistently gnawing questions: What ought we to do? How ought I to live?

Is this frequently repeated claim justified? Are our moral beliefs and conceptions based on or grounded in a belief in the God of Judaism, Christianity, and Islam? More specifically still, we need to ask ourselves three very fundamental questions: (1) Is being willed by God the or even a *fundamental* criterion for that which is so willed being morally good or for its being something that ought to be done? (2) Is being willed by God the *only* criterion for that which is so willed being morally good or for its being something that ought to be done? (3) Is being willed by God the only *adequate* criterion for that which is so willed being morally good or being something that ought to be done? I shall argue that the fact that God wills something—if indeed that is a fact—cannot be a fundamental criterion for its being morally good or obligatory and thus it cannot be the only criterion or the only adequate criterion for moral goodness or obligation.

I

By way of preliminaries we first need to get clear what is meant by a "fundamental criterion." When we speak of the criterion for the goodness of an action or attitude we speak of some *measure* or *test* by virtue of which we may decide which actions or attitudes are good or desirable, or, at least, are the least undesirable of the alternative actions or attitudes open to us. A moral criterion is the measure we use for determining the value or worth of an action or attitude. We have such a measure or test when we have some generally relevant considerations by which we may decide whether something is whatever it is said to be. A fundamental moral criterion is (a) a test or measure used to judge the legitimacy of moral rules and/or acts or attitudes, and (b) a measure that one would give up last if one were reasoning morally. (In reality, there probably is no *single* fundamental criterion, although there are fundamental criteria.)

There is a further preliminary matter we need to consider. In asking about the basis or authority for our moral beliefs we are not asking about how we came to have them. If you ask someone where he got his moral beliefs, he should answer that he got them from his parents, parent surrogates, teachers, etc.[1] They are beliefs which he has simply been conditioned to accept. But the validity or soundness of a belief is independent of its origin. When one person naively asks another where he got his moral beliefs,

[1] P. H. Nowell-Smith, "Morality: Religious and Secular," *The Rationalist Annual* (1961), pp. 5–22.

he is most likely not asking how he came by them; he is, in effect, asking: (a) on what authority does he hold these beliefs?, or (b) what good reasons or justification does he have for these moral beliefs? He should answer that he does not and cannot hold these beliefs on *any authority.* It is indeed true that many of us turn to people for moral advice and guidance in moral matters, but if we *simply* do what we do because it has been authorized, we cannot be reasoning and acting as moral agents; for to respond as a moral agent, to treat a principle as one's moral principle, it must be something which is subscribed to by one's own deliberate commitment, and it must be something for which one is prepared to give reasons.

With these preliminaries out of the way we can return to my claim that the fact (if indeed, it is a fact) that God has commanded, willed, or ordained something cannot, in the very nature of the case, be a fundamental criterion for claiming that whatever is commanded, willed, or ordained *ought* to be done.

II

Some perceptive remarks made by A. C. Ewing can carry us part of the way.[2] Theologians like Barth and Brunner claim that ethical principles gain their justification simply because they are God's decrees. But as Ewing points out, if "being obligatory" *means* just "willed by God," it becomes unintelligible to ask why God wills one thing rather than another. In fact, there can be no *reason* for his willing one thing rather than another, for his willing it *eo ipso* makes whatever it is he wills good, right, or obligatory. "God wills it because it ought to be done" becomes "God wills it because God wills it"; but the first sentence, even as used by the most ardent believer, is not a tautology. "If it were said in reply that God's commands determined what we ought to do but that these commands were only issued because it was good that they should be or because obedience to them did good, this would still make judgments about the good, at least, independent of the will of God, and we should not have given a definition of all fundamental ethical concepts in terms of God or made ethics dependent on God." [3] Furthermore, it becomes senseless to say what the believer very much wants to say, namely, "he ought always to do what God wills" if "what he ought to do" and "what God wills" have the same meaning. And to say I ought to do what God wills because I love God makes the independent assumption that I ought to love God and *that I ought* to do what God wills if I love him.

Suppose we say instead that we ought to do what God wills because God will punish us if we do not obey him. This may very well be a cogent self-interested or prudential reason for doing what God commands, but we hardly have a morally good reason for doing what he commands since such considerations of self-interest cannot be an ade-

---

[2] A. C. Ewing, "The Autonomy of Ethics," in *Prospect for Metaphysics* (ed. Ian Ramsey; London: 1961).
[3] *Ibid.,* p. 39.

quate basis for morality. A powerful being—an Omnipotent and Omniscient being—speaking out of the whirlwind cannot by his *mere commands* create an *obligation.* Ewing goes on to assert: "Without a prior conception of God as good or his commands as right God would have no more claim on our obedience than Hitler or Stalin except that he would have more power than even they had to make things uncomfortable for those who disobey him." [4] Unless we assume that God is morally perfect, unless we assume the perfect goodness of God, there can be no necessary "relation between being commanded or willed by God and being obligatory or good." [5]

To this it is perfectly correct to reply that as believers we must believe that God is wholly and completely good, the most perfect of all conceivable beings.[6] It is not open for a Jew or Christian to question the goodness of God. He must start with that assumption. Any man who seriously questions God's goodness or asks why he should obey God's commands shows by this very response that he is not a Jew or a Christian. Believers must indeed claim that God is wholly and utterly good and that what he wills or commands is of necessity good, though this does not entail that the believer is claiming that the necessity here is a *logical* necessity. For a believer, God is all good; he is the Perfect Good. This being so, it would seem that the believer is justified in saying that he and we—if his claim concerning God is correct—ought to do what God wills and that our morality is after all grounded in a belief in God. But this claim of his is clearly dependent on his assumption that God is good (a "given" for Jewish and Christian belief). Yet I shall argue that even if God is good, even if God is the perfect good, it does not follow that morality can be based on religion and that we can know what we ought to do simply by knowing what God wishes us to do.

III

To see the rationale for these last "dark sayings" we must consider the logical status of "God is good." Is it a non-analytic and in some way substantive claim, or is it analytic? (Can we say that it is neither?) No matter what we say, we get into difficulties.

Let us first try to claim that it is a non-analytic, that is to say, that it is in some way a substantive statement. So understood, God cannot then be by *definition* good. If the statement is synthetic and substantive, its denial cannot be self-contradictory, that is, it cannot be self-contradictory to assert that x is God but x is not good. It would always *in fact* be wrong to assert this, for God is the Perfect Good, but the denial of this claim is not self-contradictory, it is just false or in some way mistaken. The "is" in "God is the Perfect Good" is not the "is" of identity, perfect goodness is being predicated of God in some *logically* contingent way. It is the religious experience of

[4] *Ibid.,* p. 40.
[5] *Ibid.,* p. 41.
[6] See D. A. Rees, "Metaphysical Schemes and Moral Principles," *Prospect for Metaphysics,* p. 23.

the believer and the events recorded in the Bible that lead the believer to the steadfast conviction that God has a purpose or vocation for him which he can fulfill only by completely submitting to God's will. God shall lead him and guide him in every thought, word, and deed. Otherwise he will be like a man shipwrecked, lost in a vast and indifferent universe. Through careful attention to the Bible, he comes to understand that God is a wholly good being who has dealt faithfully with his chosen people. God is not *by definition* perfectly good or even good, but in reality, though not of logical necessity, he never falls short of perfection.

Assuming "God is good" is not a truth of language, how, then, do we know that God is good? Do we know or have good grounds for believing that the remarks made at the end of the above paragraph are so? The believer can indeed make a claim like the one we have made above, but how do we or how does he know that this is so? What grounds have we for believing that God is good? Naive people, recalling how God spoke to Job out of the whirlwind, may say that God is good because he is omnipotent and omniscient. But this clearly won't do, for, as Hepburn points out, there is nothing logically improper about saying "X is omnipotent and omniscient and morally wicked." [7] Surely in the world as we know it there is no logical connection between being powerful and knowledgeable, on the one hand, and, on the other, being good. As far as I can see, all that God proved to Job when he spoke to him out of the whirlwind was that God was an immeasurably powerful being; but, he did not prove his moral superiority to Job, and he did nothing at all even to exhibit his moral goodness. (One might even argue that he exhibited moral wickedness.) We need not assume that omnipotence and omniscience bring with it goodness or even wisdom.

What other reason could we have for claiming that God is good? We might say that he is good because he tells us to do good in thought, word, and deed and to love one another. In short, in his life and in his precepts God exhibits for us his goodness and love. Now one might argue that children's hospitals and concentration camps clearly show that such a claim is false. But let us *assume* that in some way God does exhibit his goodness to man. Let us assume that if we examine God's works we cannot but affirm that God is good. [8] We come to understand that he isn't cruel, callous, or indifferent. But in order to make such judgments or to gain such an understanding, we must use our own logically independent moral criteria. On our present assumption in asserting "God is good" we have of necessity made a moral judgment, a moral appraisal, using a criterion that cannot be based on a knowledge that God exists or that he issues commands. We *call* God "good" because we have experienced the goodness of his acts, but in order to do this, in order to know that he is good or to have any grounds for believing that he is good, we must have an independent moral criterion which we use in making this predication of God. So if "God is good" is taken

---

[7] Ronald Hepburn, *Christianity and Paradox* (London: 1958), p. 132.

[8] This is surely to assume a lot.

to be synthetic and substantive then morality cannot simply be based on a belief in God. We must of logical necessity have some criterion of goodness that is not derived from any statement asserting that there is a Deity.

IV

Let us alternatively, and more plausibly, treat "God is good" as a truth of language. Now some truths of language (some analytic statements) are statements of identity as in "puppies are young dogs" or "a father is a male parent." Such statements are definitions and the "is" is the "is of identity." But "God is good" is clearly not such a statement of identity, for that "God" does not equal "good" or "God" does not have the same meaning as "good" can easily be seen from the following case: Jane says to Betsy, after Betsy helps an old lady across the street, "That was good of you." "That was good of you" most certainly does not mean "that was God of you." And when we say "conscientiousness is good" we do not mean to say "conscientiousness is God." To say, as a believer does, that God is good is not to say that God is God. This clearly indicates that the word "God" does not have the same meaning as the word "good." When we are talking about God we are not simply talking about morality.

"God is the Perfect Good" is somewhat closer to "a father is a male parent," but even here "God" and "the Perfect Good" are not identical in meaning. "God is the Perfect God" is like "a triangle is a trilateral" in some important respects. Though something is a triangle if and only if it is a trilateral, it does not follow that "triangle" and "trilateral" have the same meaning. Similarly, something is God if and only if that something is the Perfect Good, but it does not follow that "God" and "the Perfect Good" have the same meaning. When we speak of God we wish to say other things about him as well, though indeed what is true of God will also be true of the Perfect Good. Yet what is true of the evening star will also be true of the morning star for they both refer to the same object, namely Venus, but, as Frege has shown, it does not follow that the two terms have the same meaning if they have the same referent.

And even if it could be made out that "God is the Perfect Good" is in some way a statement of identity, (1) it would not make "God is good" a statement of identity, and (2) we could know that x is the Perfect Good only if we already knew how to decide that x is good.[9] Even on the assumption that "God is the Perfect Good" is a statement of identity, we need some independent way of deciding whether something is good, that is to say, we must have an independent criterion for goodness.

Surely it is more plausible to interpret "God is good" to be analytic in the way "puppies are young," "a bachelor is unmarried," or "unjustified killing is wrong" are

---

[9] Finally we must be quite clear that x's being good is but a necessary condition for x's being the perfect good, but what would be a sufficient condition? Do we really know? I don't think we do. We do not know how to identify the referent of "the Perfect Good." Thus in one clear sense we do not understand what such a phrase means.

analytic. These statements are not statements of identity; they are not definitions, though they all follow from definitions and to deny any of them is self-contradictory.

In short it seems to me correct to argue "God is good," "puppies are young," and "triangles are three-sided" are all truths of language; the predicates *partially* define their subjects. That is to say—to adopt for a moment a Platonic *sounding* idiom—goodness is partially definitive of Godhood, as youngness is partially definitive of puppyhood, and as three-sidedness is partially definitive of triangularity.

To admit this is not at all to admit that we can have no understanding of "good" without an understanding of "God," and the truth of the above claim about "God is good" will not show that God is the or even a fundamental criterion for goodness.

Let us first see how it does *not* show that we could not have an understanding of "good" without having an understanding of "God." We couldn't understand the full religious sense of what is meant by "God" without knowing that whatever is denoted by this term is said to be good, but, as "young" or "three-sided" are understood without reference to "puppies" or "triangles," though the converse cannot be the case, so "good" is also understood quite independently of any reference to "God," but again the converse cannot be the case. We can intelligibly say, "I have a three-sided figure here that is most certainly not a triangle" and "colts are young but they are not puppies." Similarly, we can well say "conscientiousness, under most circumstances at least, is good even in a world without God." Such an utterance is clearly intelligible, to believer and non-believer alike. It is a well-formed English sentence with a use in the language. But here we can use "good" without implying anything about the reality of God. Such linguistic evidence clearly shows that good is a concept which can be understood quite independently of any reference to the Deity and that morality without religion, without theism, is quite possible. In fact quite the reverse is the case. Christianity, Judaism, and theistic religions of that sort could not exist if people did not have a moral understanding that was, logically speaking, quite independent of such religions. We could have no understanding of the truth of "God is good" or of the concept God unless we had an independent understanding of goodness.

That this is so can be seen from the following considerations. If we had no grasp of the use of the word "young," and if we did not know the criteria for deciding whether a dog was young, we could not know how correctly to apply the word "puppy." Without such a prior understanding of what it is to be young we could not understand the sentence "puppies are young." Similarly, if we had no grasp of the use of the word "good," and if we did not know the criteria for deciding whether a being (or if you will, a power or a force) was good, we could not know how correctly to apply the word "God." Without such a prior understanding of goodness we could not understand the sentence "God is good." This clearly shows that our understanding of morality and knowledge of goodness is independent of any knowledge that we may or may not have of the Divine. In fact the very converse is the case. Without a prior and logically independent understanding of "good" and without some non-religious criterion for judging something to be good, the religious person could have no knowledge of God, for he could not know whether that powerful being who spoke out of the whirlwind and laid the foundations of the earth was in fact worthy of worship and perfectly good.

From the argument we have made so far we can conclude that we cannot decide whether something is good or whether it ought to be done simply from finding out (assuming that we can find out) that God commanded it, willed it, enjoined it, and the like. Furthermore, whether "God is good" is synthetic (substantive) or analytic (a truth of language), the concept of good must be understood as something distinct from the concept of God; that is to say, a man could know how to use "good" properly and still not know how to use "God." In fact, quite the reverse is the case. A man could not know how to use "God" correctly unless he already understood how to use "good." An understanding of goodness is logically prior to and is, as such, independent of any understanding or acknowledgment of God.

V

In attempting to counter my argument for the necessary independence of morality—including a central facet of religious morality—from any beliefs about the existence or powers of the Deity, the religious moralist might begin by conceding that (1) there are secular moralities that are logically independent of religion, and (2) that we must understand the *meanings* of moral terms independently of understanding what it means to speak of God. He might even go so far as to grant that only a man who understood what good and bad were could come to believe in God. "Good," he might concede, does not mean "willed by God" or anything like that; and "there is no God, but human happiness is nonetheless good" is indeed perfectly intelligible as a moral utterance. But granting that, it is still the case that Jews and Christians do and must—on pain of ceasing to be Jews or Christians—take God's will as their final court of appeal in the making of moral appraisals or judgments. Any rule, act, or attitude that conflicts with what the believer sincerely believes to be the will of God must be rejected by him. It is indeed true that in making moral judgments the Jew or Christian does not always use God's will as a criterion for *what* is good or *what* ought to be done. When he says "fluoridation is a good thing" or "the resumption of nuclear testing is a crime" he *need* not be using God's will as a criterion for his moral judgment but *where any moral judgment whatsoever or where any other moral criterion conflicts with God's ordinances, or with what the person making the judgment honestly takes to be God's ordinances, he must accept them or he is no longer a Jew or a Christian.* Accepting this is a crucial test of his faith. In this way God's will is his fundamental moral criterion.

That orthodox Jews and Christians would reason in this way is perfectly true, but though they *say* that God's will is their most fundamental criterion (and in the way already referred to it is) it is still plain, from the very way the Christian must argue, that he has a yet more fundamental criterion which he *must use* in order to use God's will as a moral criterion. Such a religious moralist must believe and thus be prepared to make (be committed to) the *moral* claim that there exists a being whom he deems to be *perfectly good* or *worthy* of worship and whose will should always be obeyed. But to do this he must have a moral criterion (a standard for *what* is morally good) that is independent of God's will or what people believe to be God's will. In fact the believer's moral criterion—"because it is willed by God"—is in logical dependence on some *distinct* criterion in virtue of which the believer *judges that* something is *perfectly good,* is *worthy* of worship. And in making this very crucial judgment he cannot appeal to God's will as a criterion, for, that there is a being *worthy* of the appellation "God," depends in part on the above prior moral claim. Only if it is correct, can we justifiably say that there is a God.

It is important to keep in mind that "a wholly *good* being exists who is *worthy* of worship" is *not* analytic, is not a truth of language, though "God is wholly good" is. It is rather a substantive moral statement (expressing a moral judgment) and a very fundamental one indeed, for the believer's whole faith rests on it. Drop this and the whole works go.

It is tempting to reply to my above argument in this vein: "But it is *blasphemy* to *judge* God; no account of the logical structure of the believer's argument can be correct if it says that the believer must *judge* that God is good." Here we must beware of verbal magic and attend very carefully to exactly what it is we are saying. I did not—and could not on pain of contradiction—say, "God must be judged worthy of worship, perfectly good," for God by definition is worthy of worship, perfectly good. I said something quite different, namely that the believer and non-believer alike must decide for [themselves] whether there exists or could *conceivably* exist a force, a being ("ground of being"?) that is worthy of worship or perfectly good; and I further said that in deciding this one makes a moral judgment that can in no way be logically dependent on God's will. In fact it is exactly the reverse that is the case. The moral standard, "because it is willed by God," is dependent for its validity on the acceptance of the claim that there is a being worthy of worship. And, as our little word "worthy" indicates, this is unequivocally a moral judgment for believer and non-believer alike.

Suggested Readings

Altizer, Thomas J. J., and William Hamilton (eds.). *Radical Theology and the Death of God.* Indianapolis: Bobbs-Merrill, 1966.

Feigl, Herbert. "Scientific Humanism," *The Humanist* 28 (September–October 1968).

Huxley, Aldous. *The Perennial Philosophy.* New York: Meridian, 1962, chap. 11.

Mayberry, Thomas C. "God and Moral Authority," *The Monist* 54 (January 1970).

Ramsey, Ian (ed.). *Christian Ethics and Contemporary Philosophy.* New York: Macmillan, 1966. Includes essays by R. B. Braithwaite, P. H. Nowell-Smith, and A. Boyce Gibson.

section four

utility and deontology

A GOOD WILL

Immanuel Kant

Nothing can possibly be conceived in the world, or even out of it, which can be called good without qualification, except a *good will*. Intelligence, wit, judgment, and the other *talents* of the mind, however they may be named, or courage, resolution, perseverance, as qualities of temperament, are undoubtedly good and desirable in many respects; but these gifts of nature may also become extremely bad and mischievous if the will which is to make use of them, and which, therefore, constitutes what is called *character,* is not good. It is the same with the *gifts of fortune.* Power, riches, honor, even health, and the general well-being and contentment with one's condition which is called *happiness,* inspire pride, and often presumption, if there is not a good will to correct the influence of these on the mind, and with this also to rectify the whole principle of acting, and adapt it to its end. The sight of a being who is not adorned with a single feature of a pure and good will, enjoying unbroken prosperity, can never give pleasure to an impartial rational spectator. Thus a good will appears to constitute the indispensable condition even of being worthy of happiness.

There are even some qualities which are of service to this good will itself, and many facilitate its action, yet which have no intrinsic unconditional value, but always presuppose a good will, and this qualifies the esteem that we justly have for them, and does not permit us to regard them as absolutely good. Moderation in the affections and passions, self-control, and calm deliberation are not only good in many respects, but even seem to constitute part of the intrinsic worth of the person; but they are far from deserving to be called good without qualification, although they have been so unconditionally praised by the ancients. For without the principles of a good will, they may become extremely bad; and the coolness of a villain not only makes him far more dangerous, but also directly makes him more abominable in our eyes than he would have been without it.

A good will is good not because of what it performs or effects, not by its aptness for the attainment of some proposed end, but simply by virtue of the volition—that is, it is good in itself, and considered by itself is to be esteemed much higher than all that can be brought about by it in favor of any inclination, nay, even of the sum-total of all inclinations. Even if it should happen that, owing to special disfavor of fortune, or the niggardly provision of a step-motherly nature, this will should wholly lack power to accomplish its purpose, if with its greatest efforts it should yet achieve nothing, and there should remain only the good will (not, to be sure, a mere wish, but the summoning of all means in our power), then, like a jewel, it would still shine by its own light, as a thing which has its whole value in itself. Its usefulness or fruitlessness can neither add to nor take away anything from this value. It would be, as it were, only the setting to enable us to handle it the more conveniently in common commerce, or to attract to it the attention of those who are not yet connoisseurs, but not to recommend it to true connoisseurs, or to determine its value.

There is, however, something so strange in this idea of the absolute value of the mere will, in which no account is taken of its utility, that notwithstanding the thorough assent of even common reason to the idea, yet a suspicion must arise that it may perhaps really be the product of mere high-flown fancy, and that we may have misunderstood the purpose of nature in assigning reason as the governor of our will. Therefore we will examine this idea from this point of view.

In the physical constitution of an organized being, that is, a being adapted suitably to the purposes of life, we assume it as a fundamental principle that no organ for any purpose will be found but what is also the fittest and best adapted for that purpose. Now in a being which has reason and a will, if the proper object of nature were its *conservation,* its *welfare,* in a word, its *happiness,* then nature would have hit upon a very bad arrangement in selecting the reason of the creature to carry out this purpose. For all the actions which the creature has to perform with a view to this purpose, and the whole rule of its conduct, would be far more surely prescribed to it by instinct, and that end would have been attained thereby much more certainly than it ever can be by reason. Should reason have been communicated to this favored creature over and above, it must only have served it to contemplate the happy constitution of its nature, to admire it, to congratulate itself thereon, and to feel thankful for it to the beneficent cause, but not that it should subject its desires to that weak and delusive guidance, and meddle bunglingly with the purpose of nature. In a word, nature would have taken care that reason should not break forth into *practical exercise,* nor have the presumption, with its weak insight, to think out for itself the plan of happiness and of the means of attaining it. Nature would not only have taken on herself the choice of the ends but also of the means, and with wise foresight would have entrusted both to instinct.

And, in fact, we find that the more a cultivated reason applies itself with deliberate purpose to the enjoyment of life and happiness, so much the more does the man fail of true satisfaction. And from this circumstance there arises in many, if they are candid enough to confess it, a certain degree of *misology,* that is, hatred of reason, especially in the case of those who are most experienced in the use of it, because after calculating all the advantages they derive—I do not say from the invention of all the arts of common luxury, but even from the sciences (which seem to them to be after all only a luxury of the understanding)—they find that they have, in fact, only brought more trouble on their shoulders rather than gained in happiness; and they end by envying rather than despising the more common stamp of men who keep closer to the guidance of mere instinct, and do not allow their reason much influence on their conduct. And this we must admit, that the judgment of those who would very much lower the lofty eulogies of the advantages which reason gives us in regard to the happiness and satisfaction of life, or who would even reduce them below zero, is by no means morose or ungrateful to the goodness with which the world is governed, but that there lies at the root of these judgments the idea that our existence has a different and far nobler end, for which, and not for happiness, reason is properly intended, and which must, therefore, be regarded as the supreme condition to which the private ends of man must, for the most part, be postponed.

For as reason is not competent to guide the will with certainty in regard to its objects and the satisfaction of all our wants (which it to some extent even multiplies), this being an end to which an implanted instinct would have led with much greater certainty; and since, nevertheless, reason is imparted to us as a practical faculty, that is, as one which is to have influence on the *will,* therefore, admitting that nature generally in the distribution of her capacities has adapted the means to the end, its true destination must be to produce a *will,* not merely good as a *means* to something else, but *good in itself,* for which reason was absolutely necessary. This will then, though not indeed the sole and complete good, must be the supreme good and the condition of every other, even of the desire of happiness. Under these circumstances, there is nothing inconsistent with the wisdom of nature in the fact that the cultivation of the reason, which is requisite for the first and unconditional purpose, does in many ways interfere, at least in this life, with the attainment of the second, which is always conditional—namely, happiness. Nay, it may even reduce it to nothing, without nature thereby failing of her purpose. For reason recognizes the establishment of a good will as its highest practical destination, and in attaining this purpose is capable only of a satisfaction of its own proper kind, namely, that from the attainment of an end, which end again is determined by reason only, notwithstanding that this may involve many a disappointment to the ends of inclination.

We have then to develop the notion of a will which deserves to be highly esteemed for itself, and is good without a view to anything further, a notion which exists already in the sound natural understanding, requiring rather to be cleared up than to be taught, and which in estimating the value of our actions always takes the first place and constitutes the condition of all the rest. In order to do this, we will take the notion of duty, which includes that of a good will, although implying certain subjective restrictions and hindrances. These, however, far from concealing it or rendering it unrecognizable, rather bring it out by contrast and make it shine forth so much the brighter.

I omit here all actions which are already recognized as inconsistent with duty, although they may be useful for this or that purpose, for with these the question whether they are done *from duty* cannot arise at all, since they even conflict with it. I also set aside those actions which really conform to duty, but to which men have *no* direct *inclination,* performing them because they are impelled thereto by some other inclination. For in this case we can readily distinguish whether the action which agrees with duty is done *from duty* or from a selfish view. It is much harder to make this distinction when the action accords with duty, and the subject has besides a *direct* inclination to it. For example, it is always a matter of duty that a dealer should not overcharge an inexperienced purchaser; and wherever there is much commerce the prudent tradesman does not overcharge, but keeps a fixed price for everyone, so that a child buys of him as well as any other. Men are thus *honestly* served; but this is not enough to make us believe that the tradesman has so acted from duty and from principles of honesty; his own advantage required it; it is out of the question in this case to suppose that he might besides have a direct inclination in favor of the buyers, so that, as it were, from love he should give no advantage to one over another. Accordingly the action was done neither from duty nor from direct inclination, but merely with a selfish view.

On the other hand, it is a duty to maintain one's life; and, in addition, everyone has also a direct inclination to do so. But on this account the often anxious care which most men take for it has no intrinsic worth, and their maxim has no moral import. They preserve their life *as duty requires,* no doubt, but not *because duty requires.* On the other hand, if adversity and hopeless sorrow have completely taken away the relish for life, if the unfortunate one, strong in mind, indignant at his fate rather than desponding or dejected, wishes for death, and yet preserves his life without loving it—not from inclination or fear, but from duty—then his maxim has a moral worth.

To be beneficent when we can is a duty; and besides this, there are many minds so sympathetically constituted that, without any other motive of vanity or self-interest, they find a pleasure in spreading joy around them, and can take delight in the satisfaction of others so far as it is their own work. But I maintain that in such a case an action of this kind, however proper, however amiable it may be, has nevertheless no true moral worth, but is on a level with other inclinations, for example, the inclination to honor, which, if it is happily directed to that which is in fact of public utility and accordant with duty, and consequently honorable, deserves praise and encouragement, but not esteem. For the maxim lacks the moral import, namely, that such actions be done *from duty,* not from inclination. Put the case that the mind of that philanthropist was clouded by sorrow of his own, extinguishing all sympathy with the lot of others, and that while he still has the power to benefit others in distress, he is not touched by their trouble because he is absorbed with his own; and now suppose that he tears himself out of this dead insensibility and performs the action without any inclination to it, but simply from duty, then first has his action its genuine moral worth. Further still, if nature has put little sympathy in the heart of this or that man, if he, supposed to be an upright man, is by temperament cold and indifferent to the sufferings of others, perhaps because in respect of his own he is provided with the special gift of patience and fortitude, and supposes, or even requires, that others should have the same—and such a man would certainly not be the meanest product of nature—but if nature had not specially framed him for a philanthropist, would he not still find in himself a source from whence to give himself a far higher worth than that of a good-natured temperament could be? Unquestionably. It is just in this that the moral worth of the character is brought out which is incomparably the highest of all, namely, that he is beneficent, not from inclination, but from duty.

To secure one's own happiness is a duty, at least indirectly; for discontent with one's condition, under a pressure of many anxieties and amidst unsatisfied wants, might easily become a great *temptation to transgression of duty.* But here again, without looking to duty, all men have already the strongest and most intimate inclination to happiness, because it is just in this idea that all inclinations are combined in one total. But the precept of happiness is often of such a sort that it greatly interferes with some inclinations, and yet a man cannot form any definite and certain conception of the sum of satisfaction of all of them which is called happiness. It is not then to be wondered at that a single inclination, definite both as to what it promises and as to the time within which it can be gratified, is often able to overcome such a fluctuating idea, and that a gouty patient, for instance, can choose to enjoy what he likes, and to suffer what he may, since, according to his calculation, on this occasion at least, he has [only] not sacrificed the enjoyment of the present moment to a possibly mistaken expectation of a happiness which is supposed to be found in health. But even in this case, if the general desire for happiness did not influence his will, and supposing that in his particular case health was not a necessary element in this calculation, there yet remains in this, as in all other cases, this law—namely, that he should promote his happiness not from inclination but from duty, and by this would his conduct first acquire true moral worth.

It is in this manner, undoubtedly, that we are to understand those passages of Scripture also in which we are commanded to love our neighbor, even our enemy. For love, as an affection, cannot be commanded, but beneficence for duty's sake may, even though we are not impelled to it by any inclination—nay, are even repelled by a natural and unconquerable aversion. This is *practical* love, and not *pathological*—a love which is seated in the will, and not in the propensions of sense—in principles of action and not of tender sympathy; and it is this love alone which can be commanded.

The second [1] proposition is: That an action done from duty derives its moral worth, *not from the purpose* which is to be attained by it, but from the maxim by which it is determined, and therefore does not depend on the realization of the object of the action, but merely on the *principle of volition* by which the action has taken place, without regard to any object of desire. It is clear from what precedes that the purposes which we may have in view in our actions, or their effects regarded as ends and springs of the will, cannot give to actions any unconditional or moral worth. In what, then, can their worth lie if it is not to consist in the will and in reference to its expected effect? It cannot lie anywhere but in the *principle of the will* without regard to the ends which can be attained by the action. For the will stands between its *a priori* principle, which is formal, and its *a posteriori* spring, which is material, as between two roads, and as it must be determined by something, it follows that it must be determined by the formal principle of volition when an action is done from duty, in which case every material principle has been withdrawn from it.

The third proposition, which is a consequence of the two preceding, I would express thus: *Duty is the necessity of acting from respect for the law.* I may have *inclination* for an object as the effect of my proposed action, but I cannot have *respect* for it just for this reason that it is an effect and not an energy of will. Similarly, I cannot have respect for inclination, whether my own or another's; I can at most, if my own, approve it; if another's, sometimes even love it, that is, look on it as favorable to my own interest. It is only what is connected with my will as a principle, by no means as an effect—what does not subserve my inclination, but overpowers it, or at least in case of choice excludes if from its calculation—in other words, simply the law of itself, which can be an object of respect, and hence a command. Now an action done from duty must wholly exclude the influence of inclination, and with it every object of the will, so that nothing remains which can determine the will except objectively the *law,* and subjectively *pure respect* for this practical law, and consequently the maxim [2] that I should follow this law even to the thwarting of all my inclinations.

Thus the moral worth of an action does not lie in the effect expected from it, nor in any principle of action which requires to borrow its motive from this expected effect. For all these effects—agreeableness of one's condition, and even the promotion of the happiness of others—could have been also brought about by other causes, so that for

---

[1] [The first proposition was that to have moral worth an action must be done from duty.]

[2] A *maxim* is the subjective principle of volition. The objective principle (*i.e.*, that which would also serve subjectively as a practical principle to all rational beings if reason had full power over the faculty of desire) is the practical *law.*

this there would have been no need of the will of a rational being; whereas it is in this alone that the supreme and unconditional good can be found. The pre-eminent good which we call moral can therefore consist in nothing else than *the conception of law* in itself, *which certainly is only possible in a rational being,* in so far as this conception, and not the expected effect, determines the will. This is a good which is already present in the person who acts accordingly, and we have not to wait for it to appear first in the result.[3]

But what sort of law can that be the conception of which must determine the will, even without paying any regard to the effect expected from it, in order that this will may be called good absolutely and without qualification? As I have deprived the will of every impulse which could arise to it from obedience to any law, there remains nothing but the universal conformity of its actions to law in general, which alone is to serve the will as a principle, that is, I am never to act otherwise than so *that I could also will that my maxim should become a universal law.* Here, now, it is the simple conformity to law in general, without assuming any particular law applicable to certain actions, that serves the will as its principle, and must so serve it if duty is not to be a vain delusion and a chimerical notion. The common reason of men in its practical judgments perfectly coincides with this, and always has in view the principle here suggested. Let the question be, for example: May I when in distress make a promise with the intention not to keep it? I readily distinguish here between the two significations which the question may have: whether it is prudent or whether it is right to make a false promise? The former may undoubtedly often be the case. I see clearly indeed that it is not enough to extricate myself from a present difficulty by means of this subterfuge, but it must be well considered whether there may not hereafter spring from this lie much greater inconvenience than that from which I now free myself, and as, with all my supposed *cunning,* the consequences cannot be so easily foreseen but that credit once lost may be much more injurious to me than any mischief which I seek to avoid at present, it should be considered whether it would not be more *prudent* to

---

[3] It might be here objected to me that I take refuge behind the word *respect* in an obscure feeling, instead of giving a distinct solution of the question by a concept of the reason. But although respect is a feeling, it is not a feeling *received* through influence, but is *self-wrought* by a rational concept, and, therefore, is specifically distinct from all feelings of the former kind, which may be referred either to inclination or fear. What I recognize immediately as a law for me, I recognize with respect. This merely signifies the consciousness that my will is *subordinate* to a law, without the intervention of other influences on my sense. The immediate determination of the will by the law, and the consciousness of this, is called *respect,* so that this is regarded as an *effect* of the law on the subject, and not as the *cause* of it. Respect is properly the conception of a worth which thwarts my self-love. Accordingly it is something which is considered neither as an object of inclination nor of fear, although it has something analogous to both. The *object* of respect is the *law* only, that is, the law which we impose on *ourselves,* and yet recognize as necessary in itself. As a law, we are subjected to it without consulting self-love; as imposed by us on ourselves, it is a result of our will. In the former aspect it has an analogy to fear, in the latter to inclination. Respect for a person is properly only respect for the law (of honesty, etc.) of which he gives us an example. Since we also look on the improvement of our talents as a duty, we consider that we see in a person of talents, as it were, the *example of a law* (viz. to become like him in this by exercise), and this constitutes our respect. All so-called moral *interest* consists simply in *respect* for the law.

act herein according to a universal maxim, and to make it a habit to promise nothing except with the intention of keeping it. But it is soon clear to me that such a maxim will still only be based on the fear of consequences. Now it is a wholly different thing to be truthful from duty, and to be so from apprehension of injurious consequences. In the first case, the very notion of the action already implies a law for me; in the second case, I must first look about elsewhere to see what results may be combined with it which would affect myself. For to deviate from the principle of duty is beyond all doubt wicked; but to be unfaithful to my maxim of prudence may often be very advantageous to me, although to abide by it is certainly safer. The shortest way, however, and an unerring one, to discover the answer to this question whether a lying promise is consistent with duty, is to ask myself, Should I be content that my maxim (to extricate myself from difficulty by a false promise) should hold good as a universal law, for myself as well as for others; and should I be able to say to myself, "Every one may make a deceitful promise when he finds himself in a difficulty from which he cannot otherwise extricate himself"? Then I presently become aware that, while I can will the lie, I can by no means will that lying should be a universal law. For with such a law there would be no promises at all, since it would be in vain to allege my intention in regard to my future actions to those who would not believe this allegation, or if they over-hastily did so, would pay me back in my own coin. Hence my maxim, as soon as it should be made a universal law, would necessarily destroy itself.

I do not, therefore, need any far-reaching penetration to discern what I have to do in order that my will may be morally good. Inexperienced in the course of the world, incapable of being prepared for all its contingencies, I only ask myself: Canst thou also will that thy maxim should be a universal law? If not, then it must be rejected, and that not because of a disadvantage accruing from it to myself or even to others, but because it cannot enter as a principle into a possible universal legislation, and reason extorts from me immediate respect for such legislation. I do not indeed as yet *discern* on what this respect is based (this the philosopher may inquire), but at least I understand this—that it is an estimation of the worth which far outweighs all worth of what is recommended by inclination, and that the necessity of acting from *pure* respect for the practical law is what constitutes duty, to which every other motive must give place because it is the condition of a will being good *in itself,* and the worth of such a will is above everything.

. . .

UTILITARIANISM

John Stuart Mill

There are few circumstances among those which make up the present condition of human knowledge more unlike what might have been expected, or more significant of the backward state in which speculation on the most important subjects still lingers, than the little progress which has been made in the decision of the controversy respecting the criterion of right and wrong. From the dawn of philosophy, the question concerning the *summum bonum,* or, what is the same thing, concerning the foundation of morality, has been accounted the main problem in speculative thought, has occupied the most gifted intellects and divided them into sects and schools carrying on a vigorous warfare against one another. And after more than two thousand years the same discussions continue, philosophers are still ranged under the same contending banners, and neither thinkers nor mankind at large seem nearer to being unanimous on the subject than when the youth Socrates listened to the old Protagoras and asserted (if Plato's dialogue be grounded on a real conversation) the theory of utilitarianism against the popular morality of the so-called sophist.

. . .

To inquire how far the bad effects of this deficiency have been mitigated in practice, or to what extent the moral beliefs of mankind have been vitiated or made uncertain by the absence of any distinct recognition of an ultimate standard, would imply a complete survey and criticism of past and present ethical doctrine. It would, however, be easy to show that whatever steadiness or consistency these moral beliefs have attained has been mainly due to the tacit influence of a standard not recognized. Although the nonexistence of an acknowledged first principle has made ethics not so much a guide as a consecration of men's actual sentiments, still, as men's sentiments, both of favor and of aversion, are greatly influenced by what they suppose to be the effects of things upon their happiness, the principle of utility, or, as Bentham latterly called it, the greatest happiness principle, has had a large share in forming the moral doctrines even of those who most scornfully reject its authority. Nor is there any school of thought which refuses to admit that the influence of actions on happiness is a most material and even predominant consideration in many of the details of morals, however unwilling to acknowledge it as the fundamental principle of morality and the source of moral obligation. I might go much further and say that to all those *a priori* moralists who deem it necessary to argue at all, utilitarian arguments are indispensable. It is not my present purpose to criticize these thinkers; but I cannot help referring, for illustration, to a systematic treatise by one of the most illustrious of them, the *Metaphysics of Ethics* by Kant. This remarkable man, whose system of thought will long remain one of the landmarks in the history of philosophical speculation, does, in the treatise in question, lay down a universal first principle as the origin and ground of moral obligation; it is this: "So act that the rule on which thou actest would admit of being adopted as a law by all rational beings." But when he begins to deduce from this precept any of the actual duties of morality, he fails, almost grotesquely, to show that there would be any contradiction, any logical (not to say physical) impossibility, in the adoption by all rational beings of the most outrageously immoral rules of conduct. All he shows is that the *consequences* of their universal adoption would be such as no one would choose to incur.

On the present occasion, I shall, without further discussion of the other theories, attempt to contribute something toward the understanding and appreciation of the "utilitarian" or "happiness" theory, and toward such proof as it is susceptible of. It is evident that this cannot be proof in the ordinary and popular meaning of the term. Questions of ultimate ends are not amenable to direct proof. Whatever can be proved to be good must be so by being shown to be a means to something admitted to be good without proof. The medical art is proved to be good by its conducing to health; but how is it possible to prove that health is good? The art of music is good, for the reason, among others, that it produces pleasure; but what proof is it possible to give that pleasure is good? If, then, it is asserted that there is a comprehensive formula, including all things which are in themselves good, and that whatever else is good is not so as an end but as a means, the formula may be accepted or rejected, but is not a subject of what is commonly understood by proof. We are not, however, to infer that its acceptance or rejection must depend on blind impulse or arbitrary choice. There is a larger meaning of the word "proof," in which this question is as amenable to it as any other of the disputed questions of philosophy. The subject is within the cognizance of the rational faculty; and neither does that faculty deal with it solely in the way of intuition. Considerations may be presented capable of determining the intellect either to give or withhold its assent to the doctrine; and this is equivalent to proof.

We shall examine presently of what nature are these considerations; in what manner they apply to the case, and what rational grounds, therefore, can be given for accepting or rejecting the utilitarian formula. But it is a preliminary condition of rational acceptance or rejection that the formula should be correctly understood. I believe that the very imperfect notion ordinarily formed of its meaning is the chief obstacle which impedes its reception, and that, could it be cleared even from only the grosser misconceptions, the question would be greatly simplified and a large proportion of its difficulties removed. Before, therefore, I attempt to enter into the philosophical grounds which can be given for assenting to the utilitarian standard, I shall offer some illustrations of the doctrine itself, with the view of showing more clearly what it is, distinguishing it from what it is not, and disposing of such of the practical objections to it as either originate in, or are closely connected with, mistaken interpretations of its meaning. Having thus prepared the ground, I shall afterwards endeavor to throw such light as I can call upon the question considered as one of philosophical theory.

. . .

A passing remark is all that needs be given to the ignorant blunder of supposing that those who stand up for utility as the test of right and wrong use the term in that restricted and merely colloquial sense in which utility is opposed to pleasure. An apology is due to the philosophical opponents of utilitarianism for even the momentary appearance of confounding them with anyone capable of so absurd a misconception; which is the more extraordinary, inasmuch as the contrary accusation, of referring everything to pleasure, and that, too, in its grossest form, is another of the common charges against utilitarianism: and, as has been pointedly remarked by an able writer, the same sort of persons, and often the very same persons, denounce the theory "as impracticably dry when the word 'utility' precedes the word 'pleasure,' and as too practically voluptuous when the word 'pleasure' precedes the word 'utility.' " Those who know anything about the matter are aware that every writer, from Epicurus to Bentham, who maintained the theory of utility meant by it, not something to be contradistinguished from pleasure, but pleasure itself; together with exemption from pain; and instead of opposing the useful to the agreeable or the ornamental, have always declared that the useful means these, among other things. Yet the common herd, including the herd of writers, not only in newspapers and periodicals, but in books of weight and pretension, are perpetually falling into this shallow mistake. Having caught up the word "utilitarian," while knowing nothing whatever about it but its sound, they habitually express by it the rejection or the neglect of pleasure in some of its forms: of beauty, of ornament, or of amusement. Nor is the term thus ignorantly misapplied solely in disparagement, but occasionally in compliment, as though it implied superiority to frivolity and the mere pleasures of the moment. And this perverted use is the only one in which the word is popularly known, and the one from which the new generation are acquiring their sole notion of its meaning. Those who introduced the word, but who had for many years discontinued it as a distinctive appellation, may well feel themselves called upon to resume it if by doing so they can hope to contribute anything toward rescuing it from this utter degradation.

The creed which accepts as the foundation of morals "utility" or the "greatest happiness principle" holds that actions are right in proportion as they tend to promote happiness; wrong as they tend to produce the reverse of happiness. By happiness is intended pleasure and the absence of pain; by unhappiness, pain and the privation of pleasure. To give a clear view of the moral standard set up by the theory, much more requires to be said; in particular, what things it includes in the ideas of pain and pleasure, and to what extent this is left an open question. But these supplementary explanations do not affect the theory of life on which this theory of morality is grounded—namely, that pleasure and freedom from pain are the only things desirable as ends; and that all desirable things (which are as numerous in the utilitarian as in any other scheme) are desirable either for pleasure inherent in themselves or as means to the promotion of pleasure and the prevention of pain.

Now such a theory of life excites in many minds, and among them in some of the most estimable in feeling and purpose, inveterate dislike. To suppose that life has (as they express it) no higher end than pleasure—no better and nobler object of desire and pursuit—they designate as utterly mean and groveling, as a doctrine worthy only of swine, to whom the followers of Epicurus were, at a very early period, contemptuously likened; and modern holders of the doctrine are occasionally made the subject of equally polite comparisons by its German, French, and English assailants.

When thus attacked, the Epicureans have always answered that it is not they, but their accusers, who represent human nature in a degrading light, since the accusation supposes human beings to be capable of no pleasures except those of which swine are capable. If this supposition were true, the charge could not be gainsaid, but would then be no longer an imputation; for if the sources of pleasure were precisely the same to human beings and to swine, the rule of life which is good enough for the one would be good enough for the other. The comparison of the Epicurean life to that of beasts is felt as degrading, precisely because a beast's pleasures do not satisfy a human being's conceptions of happiness. Human beings have faculties more elevated than the animal appetites and, when once made conscious of them, do not regard anything as happiness which does not include their gratification. I do not, indeed, consider the Epicureans to have been by any means faultless in drawing out their scheme of consequences from the utilitarian principle. To do this in any sufficient manner, many Stoic, as well as Christian, elements require to be included. But there is no known Epicurean theory of life which does not assign to the pleasures of the intellect, of the feelings and imagination, and of the moral sentiments a much higher value as pleasures than to those of mere sensation. It must be admitted, however, that utilitarian writers in general have placed the superiority of mental over bodily pleasures chiefly in the greater permanency, safety, uncostliness, etc., of the former—that is, in their circumstantial advantages rather than in their intrinsic nature. And on all these points utilitarians have fully proved their case; but they might have taken the other and, as it may be called, higher ground with entire consistency. It is quite compatible with the principle of utility to recognize the fact that some kinds of pleasure are more desirable and more valuable than others. It would be absurd that, while in estimating all other things quality is considered as well as quantity, the estimation of pleasure should be supposed to depend on quantity alone.

If I am asked what I mean by difference of quality in pleasures, or what makes one pleasure more valuable than another, merely as a pleasure, except its being greater in amount, there is but one possible answer. Of two pleasures, if there be one to which all or almost all who have experience of both give a decided preference, irrespective of any feeling of moral obligation to prefer it, that is the more desirable pleasure. If one of the two is, by those who are competently acquainted with both, placed so far above the other that they prefer it, even though knowing it to be attended with a greater amount of discontent, and would not resign it for any quantity of the other pleasure which their nature is capable of, we are justified in ascribing to the preferred enjoyment a superiority in quality so far outweighing quantity as to render it, in comparison, of small account.

Now it is an unquestionable fact that those who are equally acquainted with and equally capable of appreciating and enjoying both do give a most marked preference to the manner of existence which employs their higher faculties. Few human creatures would consent to be changed into any of the lower animals for a promise of the fullest allowance of a beast's pleasures; no intelligent human being would consent to be a fool, no instructed person would be an ignoramus, no person of feeling and conscience would be selfish and base, even though they should be persuaded that the fool, the dunce, or the rascal is better satisfied with his lot than they are with theirs. They would not resign what they possess more than he for the most complete satisfaction of all the desires which they have in common with him. If they ever fancy they would, it is only in cases of unhappiness so extreme that to escape from it they would exchange their lot for almost any other, however undesirable in their own eyes. A being of higher faculties requires more to make him happy, is capable probably of more acute suffering, and certainly accessible to it at more points, than one of an inferior type; but in spite of these liabilities, he can never really wish to sink into what he feels to be a lower grade of existence. We may give what explanation we please of this unwillingness; we may attribute it to pride, a name which is given indiscriminately to some of the most and to some of the least estimable feelings of which mankind are capable; we may refer it to the love of liberty and personal independence, an appeal to which was with the Stoics one of the most effective means for the inculcation of it; to the love of power or to the love of excitement, both of which do really enter into and contribute to it; but its most appropriate appellation is a sense of dignity, which all human beings possess in one form or other, and in some, though by no means in exact, proportion to their higher faculties, and which is so essential a part of the happiness of those in whom it is strong that nothing which conflicts with it could be otherwise than momentarily an object of desire to them. Whoever supposes that this preference takes place at a sacrifice of happiness—that the superior being, in anything like equal circumstances, is not happier than the inferior—confounds the two very different ideas of happiness and content. It is indisputable that the being whose capacities of enjoyment are low has the greatest chance of having them fully satisfied; and a highly endowed being will always feel that any happiness which he can look for, as the world is constituted, is imperfect. But he can learn to bear its imperfections, if they are at all bearable; and they will not make him envy the being who is indeed unconscious of the imperfections, but only because he feels not at all the good which those imperfections qualify. It is better to be a human being dissatisfied than a pig satisfied; better to be Socrates dissatisfied than a fool satisfied. And if the fool, or the pig, are of a different opinion, it is because they only know their own side of the question. The other party to the comparison knows both sides.

It may be objected that many who are capable of the higher pleasures occasionally, under the influence of temptation, postpone them to the lower. But this is quite compatible with a full appreciation of the intrinsic superiority of the higher. Men often, from infirmity of character, make their election for the nearer good, though they know it to be the less valuable; and this no less when the choice is between two bodily pleasures than when it is between bodily and mental. They pursue sensual indulgences to the injury of health, though perfectly aware that health is the greater good. It may be further objected that many who begin with youthful enthusiasm for everything noble, as they advance in years, sink into indolence and selfishness. But I do not believe that those who undergo this very common change voluntarily choose the lower description of pleasures in preference to the higher. I believe that, before they devote themselves exclusively to the one, they have already become incapable of the other. Capacity for the nobler feelings is in most natures a very tender plant, easily killed, not only by hostile influences, but by mere want of sustenance; and in the majority of young persons it speedily dies away if the occupations to which their position in life has devoted them, and the society into which it has thrown them, are not favorable to keeping that higher capacity in exercise. Men lose their high aspirations as they lose their intellectual tastes, because they have not time or opportunity for indulging them; and they addict themselves to inferior pleasures, not because they deliberately prefer them, but because they are either the only ones to which they have access or the only ones which they are any longer capable of enjoying. It may be questioned whether anyone who has remained equally susceptible to both classes of pleasures ever knowingly and calmly preferred the lower, though many, in all ages, have broken down in an ineffectual attempt to combine both.

From this verdict of the only competent judges, I apprehend there can be no appeal. On a question which is the best worth having of two pleasures, or which of two modes of existence is the most grateful to the feelings, apart from its moral attributes and from its consequences, the judgment of those who are qualified by knowledge of both, or, if they differ, that of the majority among them, must be admitted as final. And there needs be the less hesitation to accept this judgment respecting the quality of pleasures, since there is no other tribunal to be referred to even on the question of quantity. What means are there of determining which is the acutest of two pains, or the intensest of two pleasurable sensations, except the general suffrage of those who are familiar with both? Neither pains nor pleasures are homogeneous, and pain is always heterogeneous with pleasure. What is there to decide whether a particular pleasure is worth purchasing at the cost of a particular pain, except the feelings and judgment of the experienced? When, therefore, those feelings and judgment declare the pleasures derived from the higher faculties to be preferable *in kind,* apart from the question of intensity, to those of which the animal nature, disjoined from the higher faculties, is susceptible, they are entitled on this subject to the same regard.

I have dwelt on this point as being a necessary part of a perfectly just conception of utility or happiness considered as the directive rule of human conduct. But it is by no means an indispensable condition to the acceptance of the utilitarian standard; for that standard is not the agent's own greatest happiness, but the greatest amount of happiness altogether; and if it may possibly be doubted whether a noble character is always the happier for its nobleness, there can be no doubt that it makes other people happier, and that the world in general is immensely a gainer by it. Utilitarianism, therefore, could only attain its end by the general cultivation of nobleness of character, even if each individual were only benefited by the nobleness of others, and his own, so far as happiness is concerned, were a sheer deduction from the benefit. But the bare enunciation of such an absurdity as this last renders refutation superfluous.

According to the greatest happiness principle, as above explained, the ultimate end, with reference to and for the sake of which all other things are desirable—whether we are considering our own good or that of other people—is an existence exempt as far as possible from pain, and as rich as possible in enjoyments, both in point of quantity and quality; the test of quality and the rule for measuring it against quantity being the preference felt by those who, in their opportunities of experience, to which must be added their habits of self-consciousness and self-observation, are best furnished with the means of comparison. This, being according to the utilitarian opinion the end of human action, is necessarily also the standard of morality, which may accordingly be defined "the rules and precepts for human conduct," by the observance of which an existence such as has been described might be, to the greatest extent possible, secured to all mankind; and not to them only, but, so far as the nature of things admits, to the whole sentient creation.

. . .

It has already been remarked that questions of ultimate ends do not admit of proof, in the ordinary acceptation of the term. To be incapable of proof by reasoning is common to all first principles, to the first premises of our knowledge, as well as to those of our conduct. But the former, being matters of fact, may be the subject of a direct appeal to the faculties which judge of fact—namely, our senses and our internal consciousness. Can an appeal be made to the same faculties on questions of practical ends? Or by what other faculty is cognizance taken of them?

Questions about ends are, in other words, questions what things are desirable. The utilitarian doctrine is that happiness is desirable, and the only thing desirable, as an end; all other things beings only desirable as means to that end. What ought to be required of this doctrine, what conditions is it requisite that the doctrine should fulfill—to make good its claim to be believed?

The only proof capable of being given that an object is visible is that people actually see it. The only proof that a sound is audible is that people hear it; and so of the other sources of our experience. In like manner, I apprehend, the sole evidence it is possible to produce that anything is desirable is that people do actually desire it. If the end which the utilitarian doctrine proposes to itself were not, in theory and in practice, acknowledged to be an end, nothing could ever convince any person that it was so. No reason can be given why the general happiness is desirable, except that each person, so far as he believes it to be attainable, desires his own happiness. This, however, being a fact, we have not only all the proof which the case admits of, but all which it is possible to require, that happiness is a good, that each person's happiness is a good to that person, and the general happiness, therefore, a good to the aggregate of all persons. Happiness has made out its title as *one* of the ends of conduct and, consequently, one of the criteria of morality.

. . .

THE RIGHT AND THE GOOD

W. D. Ross

The real point at issue between hedonism and utilitarianism on the one hand and their opponents on the other is not whether 'right' means 'productive of so and so'; for it cannot with any plausibility be maintained that it does. The point at issue is that to which we now pass, viz. whether there is any general character which makes right acts right, and if so, what it is. Among the main historical attempts to state a single characteristic of all right actions which is the foundation of their rightness are those made by egoism and utilitarianism. But I do not propose to discuss these, not because the subject is unimportant, but because it has been dealt with so often and so well already, and because there has come to be so much agreement among moral philosophers that neither of these theories is satisfactory. A much more attractive theory has been put forward by Professor Moore: that what makes actions right is that they are productive of more *good* than could have been produced by any other action open to the agent.

This theory is in fact the culmination of all the attempts to base rightness on productivity of some sort of result. The first form this attempt takes is the attempt to base rightness on conduciveness to the advantage or pleasure of the agent. This theory comes to grief over the fact, which stares us in the face, that a great part of duty consists in an observance of the rights and a furtherance of the interests of others, whatever the cost to ourselves may be. Plato and others may be right in holding that a regard for the rights of others never in the long run involves a loss of happiness for the agent, that 'the just life profits a man'. But this, even if true, is irrelevant to the rightness of the act. As soon as a man does an action *because* he thinks he will promote his own interests thereby, he is acting not from a sense of its rightness but from self-interest.

To the egoistic theory hedonistic utilitarianism supplies a much-needed amendment. It points out correctly that the fact that a certain pleasure will be enjoyed by the agent is no reason why he *ought* to bring it into being rather than an equal or greater pleasure to be enjoyed by another, though, human nature being what it is, it makes it not unlikely that he *will* try to bring it into being. But hedonistic utilitarianism in its turn needs a correction. On reflection it seems clear that pleasure is not the only thing in life that we think good in itself, that for instance we think the possession of a good character, or an intelligent understanding of the world, as good or better. A great advance is made by the substitution of 'productive of the greatest good' for 'productive of the greatest pleasure'.

Not only is this theory more attractive than hedonistic utilitarianism, but its logical relation to that theory is such that the latter could not be true unless *it* were true, while it might be true though hedonistic utilitarianism were not. It is in fact one of the logical bases of hedonistic utilitarianism. For the view that what produces the maximum pleasure is right has for its bases the views (1) that what produces the maximum good is right, and (2) that pleasure is the only thing good in itself. If they were not assuming that what produces the maximum *good* is right, the utilitarians' attempt to show that pleasure is the only thing good in itself, which is in fact the point they take most pains to establish, would have been quite irrelevant to their attempt to prove that only what produces the maximum *pleasure* is right. If, therefore, it can be shown that productivity of the maximum good is not what makes all right actions right, we shall *a fortiori* have refuted hedonistic utilitarianism.

When a plain man fulfils a promise because he thinks he ought to do so, it seems clear that he does so with no thought of its total consequences, still less with any opinion that these are likely to be the best possible. He thinks in fact much more of the past than of the future. What makes him think it right to act in a certain way is the fact that he has promised to do so—that and, usually, nothing more. That his act will produce the best possible consequences is not his reason for calling it right. What lends colour to the theory we are examining, then, is not the actions (which form probably a great majority of our actions) in which some such reflection as 'I have promised' is the only reason we give ourselves for thinking a certain action right, but the exceptional cases in which the consequences of fulfilling a promise (for instance) would be so disastrous to others that we judge it right not to do so. It must of course be admitted that such cases exist. If I have promised to meet a friend at a particular time for some trivial purpose, I should certainly think myself justified in breaking my engagement if by doing so I could prevent a serious accident or bring relief to the victims of one. And the supporters of the view we are examining hold that my thinking so is due to my thinking that I shall bring more good into existence by the one action than by the other. A different account may, however, be given of the matter, an account which will, I believe, show itself to be the true one. It may be said that besides the duty of fulfilling promises I have and recognize a duty of relieving distress,[1] and that when I think it right to do the latter at the cost of not doing the former, it is not because I think I shall produce more good thereby but because I think it the duty which is in the circumstances more of a duty. This account surely corresponds much more closely with what we really think in such a situation. If, so far as I can see, I could bring equal amounts of good into being by fulfilling my promise and by helping some one to whom I had made no promise, I should not hesitate to regard the former as

---

[1] These are not strictly speaking duties, but things that tend to be our duty, or *prima facie* duties.

my duty. Yet on the view that what is right is right because it is productive of the most good I should not so regard it.

There are two theories, each in its way simple, that offer a solution of such cases of conscience. One is the view of Kant, that there are certain duties of perfect obligation, such as those of fulfilling promises, of paying debts, of telling the truth, which admit of no exception whatever in favour of duties of imperfect obligation, such as that of relieving distress. The other is the view of, for instance, Professor Moore and Dr. Rashdall, that there is only the duty of producing good, and that all 'conflicts of duties' should be resolved by asking 'by which action will most good be produced?' But it is more important that our theory fit the facts than that it be simple, and the account we have given above corresponds (it seems to me) better than either of the simpler theories with what we really think, viz. that normally promise-keeping, for example, should come before benevolence, but that when and only when the good to be produced by the benevolent act is very great and the promise comparatively trivial, the act of benevolence becomes our duty.

In fact the theory of 'ideal utilitarianism', if I may for brevity refer so to the theory of Professor Moore, seems to simplify unduly our relations to our fellows. It says, in effect, that the only morally significant relation in which my neighbours stand to me is that of being possible beneficiaries by my action.[2] They do stand in this relation to me, and this relation is morally significant. But they may also stand to me in the relation of promisee to promiser, of creditor to debtor, of wife to husband, of child to parent, of friend to friend, of fellow countryman to fellow countryman, and the like; and each of these relations is the foundation of a *prima facie* duty, which is more or less incumbent on me according to the circumstances of the case. When I am in a situation, as perhaps I always am, in which more than one of these *prima facie* duties is incumbent on me, what I have to do is to study the situation as fully as I can until I form the considered opinion (it is never more) that in the circumstances one of them is more incumbent than any other; then I am bound to think that to do this *prima facie* duty is my duty *sans phrase* in the situation.

. . .

There is nothing arbitrary about these *prima facie* duties. Each rests on a definite circumstance which cannot seriously be held to be without moral significance. Of *prima facie* duties I suggest, without claiming completeness or finality for it, the following division.[3]

---

[2] Some will think it, apart from other considerations, a sufficient refutation of this view to point out that I also stand in that relation to myself, so that for this view the distinction of oneself from others is morally insignificant.

[3] I should make it plain at this stage that I am *assuming* the correctness of some of our main convictions as to *prima facie* duties, or, more strictly, am claiming that we *know* them to be true. To me it seems as self-evident as anything could be, that to make a promise, for instance, is to create a moral claim on us in someone else. Many readers will perhaps say that they do *not* know this to be true. If so, I certainly cannot prove it to them; I can only ask them to reflect again, in the hope that they will ultimately agree that they

(1) Some duties rest on previous acts of my own. These duties seem to include two kinds, (*a*) those resting on a promise or what may fairly be called an implicit promise, such as the implicit undertaking not to tell lies which seems to be implied in the act of entering into conversation (at any rate by civilized men), or of writing books that purport to be history and not fiction. These may be called the duties of fidelity. (*b*) Those resting on a previous wrongful act. These may be called the duties of reparation. (2) Some rest on previous acts of other men, i.e. services done by them to me. These may be loosely described as the duties of gratitude. (3) Some rest on the fact or possibility of a distribution of pleasure or happiness (or of the means thereto) which is not in accordance with the merit of the persons concerned; in such cases there arises a duty to upset or prevent such a distribution. These are the duties of justice. (4) Some rest on the mere fact that there are other beings in the world whose condition we can make better in respect of virtue, or of intelligence, or of pleasure. These are the duties of beneficence. (5) Some rest on the fact that we can improve our own condition in respect of virtue or of intelligence. These are the duties of self-improvement. (6) I think that we should distinguish from (4) the duties that may be summed up under the title of 'not injuring others'. No doubt to injure others is incidentally to fail to do them good; but it seems to me clear that non-maleficence is apprehended as a duty distinct from that of beneficence, and as a duty of a more stringent character. It will be noticed that this alone among the types of duty has been stated in a negative way. An attempt might no doubt be made to state this duty, like the others, in a positive way. It might be said that it is really the duty to prevent ourselves from acting either from an inclination to harm others or from an inclination to seek our own pleasure, in doing which we should incidentally harm them. But on reflection it seems clear that the primary duty here is the duty not to harm others, this being a duty whether or not we have an inclination that if followed would lead to our harming them; and that when we have such an inclination the primary duty not to harm others gives rise to a consequential duty to resist the inclination. The recognition of this duty of non-maleficence is the first step on the way to the recognition of the duty of beneficence; and that accounts for the prominence of the commands 'thou shalt not kill', 'thou shalt not commit adultery', 'thou shalt not steal', 'thou shalt not bear false witness', in so early a code as the Decalogue. But even when we have come to recognize the duty of beneficence, it appears to me that the duty of non-maleficence is recognized as a distinct one, and as *prima facie* more binding. We should not in general consider it justifiable to kill one person in order to keep another alive, or to steal from one in order to give alms to another.

---

also know it to be true. The main moral convictions of the plain man seem to me to be, not opinions which it is for philosophy to prove or disprove, but knowledge from the start; and in my own case I seem to find little difficulty in distinguishing these essential convictions from other moral convictions which I also have, which are merely fallible opinions based on an imperfect study of the working for good or evil of certain institutions or types of action.

The essential defect of the 'ideal utilitarian' theory is that it ignores, or at least does not do full justice to, the highly personal character of duty. If the only duty is to produce the maximum of good, the question who is to have the good—whether it is myself, or my benefactor, or a person to whom I have made a promise to confer that good on him, or a mere fellow man to whom I stand in no such special relation—should make no difference to my having a duty to produce that good. But we are all in fact sure that it makes a vast difference.

. . .

It is necessary to say something by way of clearing up the relation between *prima facie* duties and the actual or absolute duty to do one particular act in particular circumstances. If, as almost all moralists except Kant are agreed, and as most plain men think, it is sometimes right to tell a lie or to break a promise, it must be maintained that there is a difference between *prima facie* duty and actual or absolute duty. When we think ourselves justified in breaking, and indeed morally obliged to break, a promise in order to relieve some one's distress, we do not for a moment cease to recognize a *prima facie* duty to keep our promise, and this leads us to feel, not indeed shame or repentance, but certainly compunction, for behaving as we do; we recognize, further, that it is our duty to make up somehow to the promisee for the breaking of the promise. We have to distinguish from the characteristic of being our duty that of tending to be our duty. Any act that we do contains various elements in virtue of which it falls under various categories. In virtue of being the breaking of a promise, for instance, it tends to be wrong; in virtue of being an instance of relieving distress it tends to be right. Tendency to be one's duty may be called a parti-resultant attribute, i.e. one which belongs to an act in virtue of some one component in its nature. *Being* one's duty is a toti-resultant attribute, one which belongs to an act in virtue of its whole nature and of nothing less than this. . . .

. . .

Something should be said of the relation between our apprehension of the *prima facie* rightness of certain types of act and our mental attitude towards particular acts. It is proper to use the word 'apprehension' in the former case and not in the latter. That an act, *qua* fulfilling a promise, or *qua* effecting a just distribution of good, or *qua* returning services rendered, or *qua* promoting the good of others, or *qua* promoting the virtue or insight of the agent, is *prima facie* right, is self-evident; not in the sense that it is evident from the beginning of our lives, or as soon as we attend to the proposition for the first time, but in the sense that when we have reached sufficient mental maturity and have given sufficient attention to the proposition it is evident without any need of proof, or of evidence beyond itself. It is self-evident just as a mathematical axiom, or the validity of a form of inference, is evident. The moral order expressed in these propositions is just as much part of the fundamental nature of the universe (and, we may add, of any possible universe in which there were moral agents at all) as is the spatial or numerical structure expressed in the axioms of geometry or arithmetic. In our confidence that these propositions are true there is involved the same trust in our reason that is involved in our confidence in mathematics; and we should have no justification for trusting it in the latter sphere and distrusting it in the former. In both cases we are dealing with propositions that cannot be proved, but that just as certainly need no proof.

Some of these general principles of *prima facie* duty may appear to be open to criticism. It may be thought, for example, that the principle of returning good for good is a falling off from the Christian principle, generally and rightly recognized as expressing the highest morality, of returning good for evil. To this it may be replied that I do not suggest that there is a principle commanding us to return good for good and forbidding us to return good for evil, and that I do suggest that there is a positive duty to seek the good of all men. What I maintain is that an act in which good is returned for good is recognized as *specially* binding on us just because it is of that character, and that *ceteris paribus* any one would think it his duty to help his benefactors rather than his enemies, if he could not do both; just as it is generally recognized that *ceteris paribus* we should pay our debts rather than give our money in charity, when we cannot do both. A benefactor is not only a man, calling for our effort on his behalf on that ground, but also our benefactor, calling for our *special* effort on *that* ground.

Our judgements about out actual duty in concrete situations have none of the certainty that attaches to our recognition of the general principles of duty. A statement is certain, i.e. is an expression of knowledge, only in one or other of two cases: when it is either self-evident, or a valid conclusion from self-evident premises. And our judgements about our particular duties have neither of these characters. (1) They are not self-evident. Where a possible act is seen to have two characteristics, in virtue of one of which it is *prima facie* right, and in virtue of the other *prima facie* wrong, we are (I think) well aware that we are not certain whether we ought or ought not to do it; that whether we do it or not, we are taking a moral risk. We come in the long run, after consideration, to think one duty more pressing than the other, but we do not feel certain that it is so. And though we do not always recognize that a possible act has two such characteristics, and though there *may* be cases in which it has not, we are never certain that any particular possible act has not, and therefore never certain that it is right, nor certain that it is wrong. For, to go no further in the analysis, it is enough to point out that any particular act will in all probability in the course of time contribute to the bringing about of good or of evil for many human beings, and thus have a *prima facie* rightness or wrongness of which we know nothing. (2) Again, our judgements about our particular duties are not logical conclusions from self-evident premises. The only possible premises would be the general principles stating their *prima facie* rightness or wrongness *qua* having the different characteristics they do have; and even if we could (as we cannot) apprehend the extent to which an act will tend on the one hand, for example, to bring about advantages for our benefactors, and on the other hand to bring about disadvantages for fellow men who are not our benefactors, there is no principle by which we can draw the conclusion that it is on the whole right or on the whole wrong. In this respect the judgement as to the rightness of a particular act is just like the judgement as to the beauty of a particular natural object or work of art. A poem is, for instance, in respect of certain qualities beautiful and in respect of certain others not beautiful; and our judgement as to the degree of beauty it possesses on the whole is never reached by logical reasoning from the apprehension of its particular beauties or particular defects. Both in this and in the moral case we have more or less probable opinions which are not logically justified conclusions from the general principles that are recognized as self-evident.

There is therefore much truth in the description of the right act as a fortunate act. If we cannot be certain that it is right, it is our good fortune if the act we do is the right act. This consideration does not, however, make the doing of our duty a mere matter of chance. There is a parallel here between the doing of duty and the doing of what will be to our personal advantage. We never *know* what act will in the long run be to our advantage. Yet it is certain that we are more likely in general to secure our advantage if we estimate to the best of our ability the probable tendencies of our actions in this respect, than if we act on caprice. And similarly we are more likely to do our duty if we reflect to the best of our ability on the *prima facie* rightness or wrongness of various possible acts in virtue of the characteristics we perceive them to have, than if we act without reflection. With this greater likelihood we must be content.

. . .

The general principles of duty are obviously not self-evident from the beginning of our lives. How do they come to be so? The answer is, that they come to be self-evident to us just as mathematical axioms do. We find by experience that this couple of matches and that couple make four matches, that this couple of balls on a wire and that couple make four balls; and by reflection on these and similar discoveries we come to see that it is of the nature of two and two to make four. In a precisely similar way, we see the *prima facie* rightness of an act which would be the fulfilment of a particular promise, and of another which would be the fulfilment of another promise, and when we have reached sufficient maturity to think in general terms, we apprehend *prima facie* rightness to belong to the nature of any fulfilment of promise. What comes first in time is the apprehension of the self-evident *prima facie* rightness of an individual act of a particular type. From this we come by reflection to apprehend the self-evident general principle of *prima facie* duty. From this, too, perhaps along with the apprehension of the self-evident *prima facie* rightness of the same act in virtue of its having another characteristic as well, and perhaps in spite of the apprehension of its *prima facie* wrongness in virtue of its having some third characteristic, we come to believe something not self-evident at all, but an object of probable opinion, viz. that this particular act is (not *prima facie* but) actually right.

In this respect there is an important difference between rightness and mathematical properties. A triangle which is isosceles necessarily has two of its angles equal, whatever other characteristics the triangle may have—whatever, for instance, be its area, or the size of its third angle. The equality of the two angles is a parti-resultant attribute. And the same is true of all mathematical attributes. It is true, I may add, of *prima facie* rightness. But no act is ever, in virtue of falling under some general description, necessarily actually right; its rightness depends on its whole nature [4] and not on any element in it. The reason is that no mathematical object (no figure, for instance, or angle) ever has two characteristics that tend to give it opposite resultant characteristics, while moral acts often (as every one knows) and indeed always (as on reflection we must admit) have different characteristics that tend to make them at the same time *prima facie* right and *prima facie* wrong; there is probably no act, for instance, which does good to any one without doing harm to some one else, and *vice versa*.

. . .

In what has preceded, a good deal of use has been made of 'what we really think' about moral questions; a certain theory has been rejected because it does not agree with what we really think. It might be said that this is in principle wrong; that we should not be content to expound what our present moral consciousness tells us but should aim at a criticism of our existing moral consciousness in the light of theory. Now I do not doubt that the moral consciousness of men has in detail undergone a good deal of modification as regards the things we think right, at the hands of moral theory. But if we are told, for instance, that we should give up our view that there is a special obligatoriness attaching to the keeping of promises because it is self-evident that the only duty is to produce as much good as possible, we have to ask ourselves whether we really, when we reflect, *are* convinced that this is self-evident, and whether we really *can* get rid of our view that promise-keeping has a bindingness independent of productiveness of maximum good. In my own experience I find that I cannot, in spite of a very genuine attempt to do so; and I venture to think that most people will find the same, and that just because they cannot lose the sense of special obligation, they cannot accept as self-evident, or even as true, the theory which would require them to do so. In fact it seems, on reflection, self-evident that a promise, simply as such, is something that *prima facie* ought to be kept, and it does *not*, on reflection, seem self-evident that production of maximum good is the only thing that makes an act obligatory. And to ask us to give up at the bidding of a theory our actual apprehension of what is right and what is wrong seems like asking people to repudiate their actual experience of beauty, at the bidding of a theory which says 'only that which satisfies such and such

[4] To avoid complicating unduly the statement of the general view I am putting forward, I have here rather overstated it. Any act is the origination of a great variety of things many of which make no difference to its rightness or wrongness. But there are always many elements in its nature (i.e. in what it is the origination of) that make a difference to its rightness or wrongness, and no element in its nature can be dismissed without consideration as indifferent.

conditions can be beautiful'. If what I have called our actual apprehension is (as I would maintain that it is) truly an apprehension, i.e. an instance of knowledge, the request is nothing less than absurd.

I would maintain, in fact, that what we are apt to describe as 'what we think' about moral questions contains a considerable amount that we do not think but know, and that this forms the standard by reference to which the truth of any moral theory has to be tested, instead of having itself to be tested by reference to any theory. I hope that I have in what precedes indicated what in my view these elements of knowledge are that are involved in our ordinary moral consciousness.

It would be a mistake to found a natural science on 'what we really think', i.e. on what reasonably thoughtful and well-educated people think about the subjects of the science before they have studied them scientifically. For such opinions are interpretations, and often misinterpretations, of sense-experience; and the man of science must appeal from these to sense-experience itself, which furnishes his real data. In ethics no such appeal is possible. We have no more direct way of access to the facts about rightness and goodness and about what things are right or good, than by thinking about them; the moral convictions of thoughtful and well-educated people are the data of ethics just as sense-perceptions are the data of a natural science. Just as some of the latter have to be rejected as illusory, so have some of the former; but as the latter are rejected only when they are in conflict with other more accurate sense-perceptions, the former are rejected only when they are in conflict with other convictions which stand better the test of reflection. The existing body of moral convictions of the best people is the cumulative product of the moral reflection of many generations, which has developed an extremely delicate power of appreciation of moral distinctions; and this the theorist cannot afford to treat with anything other than the greatest respect. The verdicts of the moral consciousness of the best people are the foundation on which he must build; though he must first compare them with one another and eliminate any contradictions they may contain.

. . .

RULE-UTILITARIANISM

John Hospers

. . .

A district attorney who has prosecuted a man for robbery chances upon information which shows conclusively that the man he has prosecuted is innocent of the crime for which he has just been sentenced. The man is a wastrel who, if permitted to go free, would almost certainly commit other crimes. Moreover, the district attorney has fairly conclusive evidence of the man's guilt in prior crimes, for which, however, the jury has failed to convict him. Should he, therefore, "sit on the evidence" and let the conviction go through in this case, in which he knows the man to be innocent? We may not be able to articulate exactly *why,* but we feel strongly that the district attorney should not sit on the evidence but that he should reveal every scrap of evidence he knows, even though the revelation means releasing the prisoner (now known to be innocent) to do more crimes and be convicted for them later.

x: It seems to me that some acts are right or wrong, not *regardless* of the consequences they produce, but *over and above* the consequences they produce. We would all agree, I suppose, that you should break a promise to save a life but not that you should break it whenever you considered it probable (even with good reason) that more good effects will come about through breaking it. Suppose you had promised someone you would do something and you didn't do it. When asked why, you replied, "Because I thought breaking it would have better results." Wouldn't the promisee condemn you for your action, and rightly? This example is quite analogous, I think, to the example of the district attorney; the district attorney might argue that more total good would be produced by keeping the prisoner's innocence secret. Besides, if he is released, people may read about it in the newspaper and say, "You see, you can get by with anything these days" and may be encouraged to violate the law themselves as a result. Still, even though it would do more total good if the man were to remain convicted, wouldn't it be wrong to do so in view of the fact that he is definitely innocent of *this* crime? The law punishes a man, not necessarily because the most good will be achieved that way, but because he has committed a crime; if we don't approve of the law, we can do our best to have it changed, but meanwhile aren't we bound to follow it? Those who execute the law are sworn to obey it; they are *not* sworn to produce certain consequences.

Y: Yes, but remember that the facts *might* always come out after their concealment and that we can never be sure they won't. If they do, keeping the man in prison will be far worse than letting the man go; it will result in a great public distrust for the law itself; nothing is more demoralizing than corruption of the law by its own supposed enforcers. Better let a hundred human derelicts go free than risk that! You see, *one* of the consequences you always have to consider is the effect of *this* action on the *general practice* of lawbreaking itself; and when you bring in *this* consequence, it will surely weigh the balance in favor of divulging the information that will release the innocent man. So utilitarianism will still account quite satisfactorily for this case. I agree that the man should be released, but I do so on utilitarian grounds; I needn't abandon my utilitarianism at all to take care of this case.

x: But your view is open to one fatal objection. You say that one never can be sure that the news *won't* leak out. Perhaps so. But suppose that in a given case one *could* be sure; would that really make any difference? Suppose you are the only person that knows and you destroy the only existing evidence. Since *you* are not going to talk, there is simply no chance that the news will leak out, with consequent damage to public morale. Then is it all right to withhold the information? You see, I hold that if it's wrong not to reveal the truth when others might find out, then it's equally wrong not to reveal it when *nobody* will find out. You utilitarians are involved in the fatal error of making the rightness or wrongness of an act depend on whether performing it will ever be publicized. And I hold that it is immoral even to consider this condition; the district attorney should reveal the truth regardless of whether his concealing it would ever be known.

Y: But surely you aren't saying that one should *never* conceal the truth? not even if your country is at war against a totalitarian enemy and revealing truths to the people would also mean revealing them to the enemy?

X: Of course I'm not saying that—don't change the subject. I am saying that *if* in situation S it is wrong to convict an innocent man, then it is equally wrong whether or not the public knows that it is wrong; the public's knowledge will certainly have bad consequences, but the conviction would be wrong anyway even *without* these bad consequences; so you can't appeal to the consequences of the conviction's becoming public as grounds for saying that the conviction is wrong. I think that you utilitarians are really stuck here. For you, the consideration "but nobody is ever going to know about it anyway" *is* a relevant consideration. It has to be; for the rightness of an act (according to you) is estimated in terms of its total consequences, and its total consequences, of course, include its effects (or lack of effects) on other acts of the same kind, and there won't be any such effects if the act is kept absolutely secret. You have to consider *all* the consequences relevant; the matter of keeping the thing quiet is one consequence; so you have to consider this one relevant too. Yet I submit to you that it isn't relevant; the suggestion "but nobody is going to know about it anyway" is not one that will help make the act permissible if it wasn't before. If anything, it's the other way round: something bad that's done publicly and openly is not as bad as if it's done secretly so as to escape detection; secret sins are the worst. It is just as bad, if not worse, for the explorer to break his promise to the dying man in secret, as for him to break it publicly, even if publicly announcing it may tend to lead to more breaches of faith in the future.

Y: I deny what you say. It seems to me worse to betray a trust in public, where it may set an example to others, than to do so in secret, where it can have no bad effects on others.

X: And I submit that you would never say that if you weren't already committed to the utilitarian position. Here is a situation where you and practically everyone else would not hesitate to say that an act done in secret is no less wrong than when done in public, were it not that it flies in the face of a doctrine to which you have already committed yourself on the basis of quite different examples.

Here is a still different kind of example. We consider it our duty in a democracy to vote and to do so as wisely and intelligently as possible, for only if we vote wisely can a democracy work successfully. But in a national election my vote is only one out of millions, and it is more and more improbable that *my* vote will have any effect upon the outcome. Nor is my failure to vote going to affect other people much, if at all. Couldn't a utilitarian argue this way: "My vote will have no effect at all—at least far, far less than other things I could be doing instead. Therefore, I shall not vote." Each and every would-be voter could argue in exactly the same way. The result would be that nobody would vote, and the entire democratic process would be destroyed.

What conclusion emerges from these examples? If the examples point at all in the right direction, they indicate that there are some acts which it is right to perform, even though by themselves they will not have good consequences (such as my voting), and that there are some acts which it is wrong to perform, even though by themselves they would have good consequences (such as sitting on the evidence). But this conclusion is opposed to utilitarianism as we have considered it thus far.

· · ·

A. Rule-Utilitarianism and Objections to It

The batter swings, the ball flies past, the umpire yells "Strike three!" The disappointed batter pleads with the umpire, "Can't I have four strikes just this once?" We all recognize the absurdity of this example. Even if the batter could prove to the umpire's satisfaction that he would be happier for having four strikes this time, that the spectators would be happier for it (since most of the spectators are on his side), that there would be little dissatisfaction on the side of the opposition (who might have the game clinched anyway), and that there would be no effect on future baseball games, we would still consider his plea absurd. We might think, "Perhaps baseball would be a better game—i.e., contribute to the greatest total enjoyment of all concerned—if four strikes were permitted. If so, we should change the rules of the game. But until that time, we must play baseball according to the rules which are now the accepted rules of the game."

This example, though only an analogy, gives us a clue to the kind of view we are about to consider—let us call it *rule-utilitarianism*. Briefly stated (we shall amplify it gradually), rule-utilitarianism comes to this: Each act, in the moral life, falls under a *rule;* and we are to judge the rightness or wrongness of the act, not by *its* consequences, but by the consequences of its universalization—that is, by the consequences of the adoption of the *rule* under which this act falls. . . .

Thus: The district attorney may do more good in a particular case by sitting on the evidence, but even if this case has no consequences for future cases because nobody ever finds out, still, the general policy or *practice* of doing this kind of thing is a very bad one; it uproots one of the basic premises of our legal system, namely that an innocent person should not be condemned. Our persistent conviction that it would be wrong for him to conceal the evidence in this case comes *not* from the conviction that concealing the evidence will produce less good—we may be satisfied that it will produce more good in this case—but from the conviction that the *practice* of doing this kind of thing will have very bad consequences. In other words, "Conceal the evidence when you think that it will produce more happiness" would be a bad rule to follow, and it is because this *rule* (if adopted) would have bad consequences, not because *this act* itself has bad consequences, that we condemn the act.

The same applies in other situations: Promises solemnly made, for which a man has paid his life, should be kept; if a policy of not doing so when nobody knew about it were to be introduced, the results would be bad, for nobody would any longer have reason to believe that a promise would be kept if the person who made the promise could break it in secret and thought he could do the most good by breaking it. . . . The same considerations apply also to the voting example: if Mr. Smith can reason that his vote won't make any difference to the outcome, so can Mr. Jones and Mr. Robinson and every other would-be voter; but if everyone reasoned in this way, no one would vote, and this *would* have bad effects. It is considered one's duty to vote, not because the consequences of one's not doing so are bad, but because the consequences of the general practice of not doing so are bad. To put it in Kantian language, the maxim of the action, if universalized, would have bad consequences. But the individual act of *your* not voting on a specific occasion—or of any *one* person's not voting, as long as *others* continued to vote—would probably have no bad consequences.

There are many other examples of the same kind of thing. If during a water shortage there is a regulation that water should not be used to take baths every day or to water gardens, there will be virtually no bad consequences if only *I* violate the rule. Since there will be no discernible difference to the city water supply and since my plants will remain green and fresh and pleasant to look at, why shouldn't I water my plants? But if everyone watered his plants, there would not be enough water left to drink. My act is judged wrong, not because of *its* consequences, but because the consequences of everyone doing so would be bad. If I walk on the grass where the sign says, "Do not walk on the grass," there will be no ill effects; but if everyone did so it would destroy the grass. There are some kinds of act which have little or no effect if any one person (or two, or three) does them but which have very considerable effects if everyone (or even just a large number) does them. Rule-utilitarianism is designed to take care of just such situations.

Rule-utilitarianism also takes care of situations which are puzzling in traditional utilitarianism, situations which we have already commented on, namely, the secrecy with which an act is performed. "But no one will ever know, so my act won't have any consequences for future acts of the same kind," the utilitarian argued; and we felt that he was being somehow irrelevant, even immoral: that if something is wrong when people know about it, it is just as wrong when done in secret. Yet this condition *is* relevant according to traditional utilitarianism, for if some act with bad consequences is never known to anyone, this ignorance does mitigate the bad consequences, for it undeniably keeps the act from setting an example (except, of course, that it may start a habit in the agent himself). Rule-utilitarianism solves this difficulty. . . .

Rule-utilitarianism is a distinctively twentieth-century amendment of the utilitarianism of Bentham and Mill, often called *act-utilitarianism.* . . . Since this pair of labels is brief and indicates clearly the contents of the theories referred to, we prefer these terms to a second pair of labels, which are sometimes used for the same theories: *restricted utilitarianism* as opposed to *unrestricted* (or *extreme,* or *traditional*) *utilitarianism.* (Whether or not Mill's theory is strictly act-utilitarianism is a matter of dispute. Mill never made the distinction between act-utilitarianism and rule-utilitarianism, and his doctrine has always been interpreted as being act-utilitarianism. This is the interpretation taken by G. E. Moore in his very precise account of act-utilitarianism in Chapters 1 and 2 of his *Ethics.* Some of Mill's examples, however, have to do not with individual acts but with general principles and rules of conduct. Mill and Bentham were both legislators, interested in amending the laws of England into greater conformity to the utilitarian principle; and to the extent that Mill was interested in providing a criterion of judging rules of conduct rather than individual acts, he may be said to have been a rule-utilitarian.)

. . .

AGAINST MORAL CONSERVATIVISM

Kai Nielsen

I

It is sometimes claimed that any consequentialist view of ethics has monstrous implications which make such a conception of morality untenable. What we must do—so the claim goes—is reject all forms of consequentialism and accept what has been labeled 'conservativism' or 'moral absolutism.' By 'conservativism' is meant, here, a normative ethical theory which maintains that there is a privileged moral principle or cluster of moral principles, prescribing determinate actions, with which it would always be wrong not to act in accordance no matter what the consequences. A key example of such a principle is the claim that it is always wrong to kill an innocent human, whatever the consequences of not doing so.

I will argue that such moral conservativism is itself unjustified and, indeed, has morally unacceptable consequences, while consequentialism does not have implications which are morally monstrous and does not contain evident moral mistakes.

A consequentialist maintains that actions, rules, policies, practices, and moral principles are ultimately to be judged by certain consequences: to wit (for a very influential kind of consequentialism), by whether doing them more than, or at least as much as doing anything else, or acting in accordance with them more than or at least as much as acting in accordance with alternative policies, practices, rules or principles, tends, on the whole, and for *everyone* involved, to maximize satisfaction and minimize dissatisfaction. The states of affairs to be sought are those which maximize these things to the greatest extent possible for all mankind. But while this all sounds very humane and humanitarian, when its implications are thought through, it has been forcefully argued, it will be seen actually to have inhumane and morally intolerable implications. Circumstances could arise in which one holding such a view would have to assert that one was justified in punishing, killing, torturing, or deliberately harming the innocent, and such a consequence is, morally speaking, unacceptable.[1] As Anscombe has put it,

[1] Alan Donagan, "Is There a Credible Form of Utilitarianism?" and H. J. McCloskey, "A Non-Utilitarian Approach to Punishment," both in *Contemporary Utilitarianism*, ed. Michael D. Bayles (Garden City, N.Y.: Doubleday & Co., 1968).

anyone who "really thinks, *in advance,* that it is open to question whether such an action as procuring the judicial execution of the innocent should be quite excluded from consideration—I do not want to argue with him; he shows a corrupt mind." [2]

At the risk of being thought to exhibit a corrupt mind and a shallow consequentialist morality, I should like to argue that things are not as simple and straightforward as Anscombe seems to believe.

Surely, every moral man must be appalled at the judicial execution of the innocent or at the punishment, torture, and killing of the innocent. Indeed, being appalled by such behavior partially defines what it is to be a moral agent. And a consequentialist has very good utilitarian grounds for being so appalled, namely, that it is always wrong to inflict pain for its own sake. But this does not get to the core considerations which divide a conservative position such as Anscombe's from a consequentialist view. There are a series of tough cases that need to be taken to heart and their implications thought through by any reflective person, be he a conservative or a consequentialist. By doing this, we can get to the heart of the issue between conservativism and consequentialism. Consider this clash between conservativism and consequentialism arising over the problem of a 'just war.'

If we deliberately bomb civilian targets, we do not pretend that civilians are combatants in any simple fashion, but argue that this bombing will terminate hostilities more quickly, and will minimize all around suffering. It is hard to see how any brand of utilitarian will escape Miss Anscombe's objections. We are certainly killing the innocent . . . we are not killing them for the sake of killing them, but to save the lives of other innocent persons. Utilitarians, I think, grit their teeth and put up with this as part of the logic of total war; Miss Anscombe and anyone who thinks like her surely has to either redescribe the situation to ascribe guilt to the civilians or else she has to refuse to accept this sort of military tactics as simply wrong. [3]

It is indeed true that we cannot but feel the force of Anscombe's objections here. But is it the case that anyone shows a corrupt mind if he defends such bombing when, horrible as it is, it will quite definitely lessen appreciably the total amount of suffering and death in the long run, and if he is sufficiently nonevasive not to rationalize such a bombing of civilians into a situation in which all the putatively innocent people—children and all—are somehow in some measure judged guilty? Must such a man exhibit a corrupt moral sense if he refuses to hold that such military tactics are never morally justified? Must this be the monstrous view of a fanatical man devoid of any proper moral awareness? It is difficult for me to believe that this must be so.

Consider the quite parallel actions of guerrilla fighters and terrorists in wars of national liberation. In certain almost unavoidable circumstances, they must deliberately kill the innocent. We need to see some cases in detail here to get the necessary

---

[2] Elizabeth Anscombe, "Modern Moral Philosophy," *Philosophy* 23 (January 1957): 16–17.

[3] Alan Ryan, "Review of Jan Narveson's *Morality and Utility,*" *Philosophical Books* 9, no. 3 (October 1958): 14.

contextual background, and for this reason the motion picture *The Battle of Algiers* can be taken as a convenient point of reference. There we saw Algerian women—gentle, kindly women with children of their own and plainly people of moral sensitivity—with evident heaviness of heart, plant bombs which they had every good reason to believe would kill innocent people, including children; and we also saw a French general, also a human being of moral fiber and integrity, order the torture of Arab terrorists and threaten the bombing of houses in which terrorists were concealed but which also contained innocent people, including children. There are indeed many people involved in such activities who are cruel, sadistic beasts, or simply morally indifferent or, in important ways, morally uncomprehending. But the characters I have referred to from *The Battle of Algiers* were not of that stamp. They were plainly moral agents of a high degree of sensitivity, and yet they deliberately killed or were prepared to kill the innocent. And, with inessential variations, this is a recurrent phenomenon of human living in extreme situations. Such cases are by no means desert-island or eso-teric cases.

It is indeed arguable whether such actions are always morally wrong—whether anyone should ever act as the Arab women or French general acted. But what could not be reasonably maintained, *pace* Anscombe, by any stretch of the imagination, is that the characters I described from *The Battle of Algiers* exhibited corrupt minds. Possibly morally mistaken, yes; guilty of moral corruption, no.

Dropping the charge of moral corruption but sticking with the moral issue about what actions are right, is it not the case that my consequentialist position logically forces me to conclude that under some circumstances—where the good to be achieved is great enough—I must not only countenance but actually advocate such violence toward the innocent? But is it not always, no matter what the circumstances or consequences, wrong to countenance, advocate, or engage in such violence? To answer such a question affirmatively is to commit oneself to the kind of moral absolutism or conservativism which Anscombe advocates. But, given the alternatives, should not one be such a conservative or at least hold that certain deontological principles must never be overridden?

I will take, so to speak, the papal bull by the horns and answer that there are circumstances when such violence must be reluctantly assented to or even taken to be something that one, morally speaking, must do. But, *pace* Anscombe, this very much needs arguing, and I shall argue it; but first I would like to set out some further but simpler cases which have a similar bearing. They are, by contrast, artificial cases. I use them because, in their greater simplicity, by contrast with my above examples, there are fewer variables to control and I can more conveniently make the essential con-ceptual and moral points. But, if my argument is correct for these simpler cases, the line of reasoning employed is intended to be applicable to those more complex cases as well.

II

Consider the following cases embedded in their exemplary tales:

1. The Case of the Innocent Fat Man

Consider the story (well known to philosophers) of the fat man stuck in the mouth of a cave on a coast. He was leading a group of people out of the cave when he got stuck in the mouth of the cave and in a very short time high tide will be upon them, and unless he is promptly unstuck, they all will be drowned except the fat man, whose head is out of the cave. But, fortunately or unfortunately, someone has with him a stick of dynamite. The short of the matter is, either they use the dynamite and blast the poor innocent fat man out of the mouth of the cave or everyone else drowns. Either one life or many lives. Our conservative presumably would take the attitude that it is all in God's hands and say that he ought never to blast the fat man out, for it is always wrong to kill the innocent. Must or should a moral man come to that conclusion? I shall argue that he should not.

My first exemplary tale was designed to show that our normal, immediate, rather absolutistic, moral reactions need to be questioned along with such principles as 'The direct intention of the death of an innocent person is never justifiable.' I have hinted (and later shall argue) that we should *beware* of our moral outrage here—our naturally conservative and unreflective moral reactions—for here the consequentialist has a strong case for what I shall call 'moral radicalism.' But, before turning to a defense of that, I want to tell another story taken from Phillipa Foot but used for my own purposes.[4] This tale, I shall argue, has a different import than our previous tale. Here our unrehearsed, commonsense moral reactions will stand up under moral scrutiny. But, I shall also argue when I consider them in Section III, that our commonsense moral reactions here, initial expectations to the contrary notwithstanding, can be shown to be justified on consequentialist grounds. The thrust of my argument for this case is that we are not justified in opting for a theistic and/or deontological absolutism or in rejecting consequentialism.

2. The Magistrate and the Threatening Mob

A magistrate or judge is faced with a very real threat from a large and uncontrollable mob of rioters demanding a culprit for a crime. Unless the criminal is produced, promptly tried, and executed, they will take their own bloody revenge on a much smaller and quite vulnerable section of the community (a kind of frenzied pogrom). The judge knows that the real culprit is unknown and that the authorities do not even have a good clew as to who he may be. But he also knows that there is within easy reach a disreputable, thoroughly disliked, and useless man, who, though innocent, could easily be framed so that the mob would be quite convinced that he was guilty and would be pacified if he were promptly executed. Recognizing that he can prevent

---

[4] Phillipa Foot, "The Problem of Abortion and the Doctrine of the Double Effect," *Oxford Review*, no. 5 (Trinity 1967), pp. 5–15.

the occurrence of extensive carnage only by framing some innocent person, the magistrate has him framed, goes through the mockery of a trial, and has him executed. Most of us regard such a framing and execution of such a man in such circumstances as totally unacceptable.[5] There are some who would say that it is categorically wrong—morally inexcusable—*whatever the circumstances.* Indeed, such a case remains a problem for the consequentialist, but here again, I shall argue, one can consistently remain a consequentialist and continue to accept commonsense moral convictions about such matters.

My storytelling is at an end. The job is to see what the stories imply. We must try to determine whether thinking through their implications should lead a clearheaded and morally sensitive man to abandon consequentialism and to adopt some form of theistic absolutism and/or deontological absolutism. I shall argue that it does not.

III

I shall consider the last case first because there are good reasons why the consequentialist should stick with commonsense moral convictions for such cases. I shall start by giving my rationale for that claim. If the magistrate were a tough-minded but morally conscientious consequentialist, he could still, on straightforward consequentialist grounds, refuse to frame and execute the innocent man, even knowing that this would unleash the mob and cause much suffering and many deaths. The rationale for his particular moral stand would be that, by so framing and then executing such an innocent man, he would, in the long run, cause still more suffering through the resultant corrupting effect on the institution of justice. That is, in a case involving such extensive general interest in the issue—without that, there would be no problem about preventing the carnage or call for such extreme measures—knowledge that the man was framed, that the law had prostituted itself, would, surely, eventually leak out. This would encourage mob action in other circumstances, would lead to an increased skepticism about the incorruptibility or even the reliability of the judicial process, and would set a dangerous precedent for less clearheaded or less scrupulously humane magistrates. Given such a potential for the corruption of justice, a utilitarian or consequentialist judge or magistrate could, on good utilitarian or consequentialist grounds, argue that it was morally wrong to frame an innocent man. If the mob must rampage if such a sacrificial lamb is not provided, then the mob must rampage.

Must a utilitarian or consequentialist come to such a conclusion? The answer is no. It is the conclusion which is, as things stand, the most reasonable conclusion, but that he *must* come to it is far too strong a claim. A consequentialist could *consistently*—I did not say successfully—argue that, in taking the above tough-minded utilitarian

---

[5] Later, I shall show that there are desert-island circumstances—i.e., highly improbable situations—in which such judicial railroading might be a moral necessity. But I also shall show what little force desert-island cases have in the articulation and defense of a normative ethical theory.

position, we have overestimated the corrupting effects of such judicial railroading. His circumstance was an extreme one: a situation not often to be repeated even if, instead of acting as he did, he had set a precedent by such an act of judicial murder. A utilitarian rather more skeptical than most utilitarians about the claims of common-sense morality might reason that the lesser evil here is the judicial murder of an innocent man, vile as it is. He would persist in his moral iconoclasm by standing on the consequentialist rock that the lesser evil is always to be preferred to the greater evil.

The short of it is that utilitarians could disagree, as other consequentialists could disagree, about what is morally required of us in that case. The disagreement here between utilitarians or consequentialists of the same type is not one concerning fundamental moral principles but a disagreement about the empirical facts, about what course of action would in the long run produce the least suffering and the most happiness for *everyone* involved.[6]

However, considering the effect advocating the deliberate judicial killing of an innocent man would have on the reliance people put on commonsense moral beliefs of such a ubiquitous sort as the belief that the innocent must not be harmed, a utilitarian who defended the centrality of commonsense moral beliefs would indeed have a strong utilitarian case here. But the most crucial thing to recognize is that, to regard such judicial bowing to such a threatening mob as unqualifiedly wrong, as morally intolerable, one need not reject utilitarianism and accept some form of theistic or deontological absolutism.

It has been argued, however, that, in taking such a stance, I still have not squarely faced the moral conservative's central objection to the judicial railroading of the innocent. I allow, as a consequentialist, that there could be circumstances, at least as far as logical possibilities are concerned, in which such a railroading would be justified but that, as things actually go, it is not and probably never in fact will be justified. But the conservative's point is that in *no circumstances, either actual or conceivable, would it be justified.* No matter what the consequences, it is unqualifiedly unjustified. To say, as I do, that the situations in which it might be justified are desert-island, esoteric cases which do not occur in life, is not to the point, for, as Alan Donagan argues, "Moral theory is *a priori,* as clear-headed utilitarians like Henry Sidgwick recognized. It is, as Leibniz would say, 'true of all possible worlds.' "[7] Thus, to argue as I have and as others have that the counterexamples directed against the consequentialist's appeal to conditions which are never in fact fulfilled or are unlikely to be fulfilled is beside the point.[8] Whether "a moral theory is true or false depends on

---

[6] 'Everyone' here is used distributively; i.e., I am talking about the interests of each and every one. In that sense, everyone's interests need to be considered.

[7] Alan Donagan (n. 1 above), p. 189.

[8] T. L. S. Sprigge argues in such a manner in his "A Utilitarian Reply to Dr. McCloskey," in *Contemporary Utilitarianism,* ed. Michael D. Bayles (Garden City, N.Y.: Doubleday & Co., 1968).

whether its implications for all possible worlds are true. Hence, whether utilitarianism (or consequentialism) is true or false cannot depend on how the actual world is." [9] It is possible to specify logically conceivable situations in which consequentialism would have implications which are monstrous—for example, certain beneficial judicial murders of the innocent (whether they are even remotely likely to obtain is irrelevant)—hence consequentialism must be false.

We should not take such a short way with consequentialists, for what is true in Donagan's claim about moral theory's being a priori will not refute or even render implausible consequentialism, and what would undermine it in such a claim about the a priori nature of moral theory and presumably moral claims is not true.

To say that moral theory is a priori is probably correct if that means that categorical moral claims—fundamental moral statements—cannot be deduced from empirical statements or nonmoral theological statements, such that it is a contradiction to assert the empirical and/or nonmoral theological statements and deny the categorical moral claims or vice versa. [10] In that fundamental sense, it is reasonable and, I believe, justifiable to maintain that moral theory is autonomous and a priori. It is also a priori in the sense that moral statements are not themselves a kind of empirical statement. That is, if I assert 'One ought never to torture any sentient creature' or 'One ought never to kill an innocent man,' I am not trying to predict or describe what people do or are likely to do but am asserting what they are *to do.* It is also true that, if a moral statement is true, it holds for all possible worlds *in which situations of exactly the sort characterized in the statement obtain.* If it is true for one, it is true for all. You cannot consistently say that *A* ought to do *B* in situation *Y* and deny that someone exactly like *A* in a situation exactly like *Y* ought to do *B.*

In these ways, moral claims and indeed moral theory are a priori. But it is also evident that none of these ways will touch the consequentialist or utilitarian arguments. After all, the consequentialist need not be, and typically has not been, an ethical naturalist—he need not think moral claims are derivable from factual claims or that moral claims are a subspecies of empirical statement and he could accept—indeed, he must accept—what is an important truism anyway, that you cannot consistently say that *A* ought to do *B* in situation *Y* and deny that someone exactly like *A* in a situation exactly like *Y* ought to do *B.* But he could and should deny that moral claims are a priori in the sense that rational men must or even will make them without regard for the context, the situation, in which they are made. We say people ought not to drive way over the speed limit, or speed on icy roads, or throw knives at each other. But, if human beings had a kind of metallic exoskeleton and would not be hurt, disfigured, or seriously inconvenienced by knives sticking in them or by automobile crashes, we

---

[9] Alan Donagan, p. 194.

[10] There is considerable recent literature about whether it is possible to derive moral claims from nonmoral claims. See W. D. Hudson, ed., *The Is-Ought Question: A Collection of Papers on the Central Problem in Moral Philosophy* (New York: St. Martin's Press, 1969).

would not—so evidently at least—have good grounds for saying such speeding or knife throwing is wrong. It would not be so obvious that it was unreasonable and immoral to do these things if these conditions obtained.

In the very way we choose to describe the situation when we make ethical remarks, it is important in making this choice that we know what the world is like and what human beings are like. Our understanding of the situation, our understanding of human nature and motivation cannot but effect our structuring of the moral case. The consequentialist is saying that, as the world goes, there are good grounds for holding that judicial killings are morally intolerable, though he would have to admit that if the world (including human beings) were very different, such killings could be something that ought to be done. But, in holding this, he is not committed to denying the universalizability of moral judgments, for, where he would reverse or qualify the moral judgment, the situation must be different. He is only committed to claiming that, where the situation is the same or relevantly similar and the persons are relevantly similar, they must, if they are to act morally, do the same thing. However, he is claiming both (1) that, as things stand, judicial killing of the innocent is always wrong and (2) that it is an irrational moral judgment to assert of reasonably determinate actions (e.g., killing an innocent man) that they are unjustifiable and morally unacceptable in all *possible* worlds, whatever the situation and whatever the consequences.

Donagan's claims about the a priori nature of moral theories do not show such a consequentialist claim to be mistaken or even give us the slightest reason for thinking that it is mistaken. What is brutal and vile, for example, throwing a knife at a human being just for the fun of it, would not be so, if human beings were invulnerable to harm from such a direction because they had a metallic exoskeleton. Similarly, what is, as things are, morally intolerable, for example, the judicial killing of the innocent, need not be morally intolerable in all conceivable circumstances.

Such considerations support the utilitarian or consequentialist skeptical of simply taking the claims of our commonsense morality as a rock-bottom ground of appeal for moral theorizing. Yet it may also well be the case—given our extensive cruelty anyway—that, if we ever start sanctioning such behavior, an even greater callousness toward life than the very extensive callousness extant now will, as a matter of fact, develop. Given a normative ethical theory which sanctions, *under certain circumstances,* such judicial murders, there may occur an undermining of our moral disapproval of killing and our absolutely essential moral principle that all human beings, great and small, are deserving of respect. This is surely enough, together with the not unimportant weight of even our unrehearsed moral feelings, to give strong utilitarian weight *here* to the dictates of our commonsense morality. Yet, I think I have also said enough to show that someone who questions their 'unquestionableness' in such a context does not thereby exhibit a 'corrupt mind' and that it is an open question whether he must be conceptually confused or morally mistaken over this matter.

IV

So far, I have tried to show with reference to the case of the magistrate and the threatening mob how consequentialists can reasonably square their normative ethical theories with an important range of commonsense moral convictions. Now, I wish by reference to the case of the innocent fat man to establish that there is at least a serious question concerning whether such fundamental commonsense moral convictions should always function as 'moral facts' or a kind of moral ground to test the adequacy of normative ethical theories or positions. I want to establish that careful attention to such cases shows that we are not justified in taking the principles embodied in our commonsense moral reasoning about such cases as normative for all moral decisions. That a normative ethical theory is incompatible with some of our 'moral intuitions' (moral feelings or convictions) does not refute the normative ethical theory. What I will try to do here is to establish that this case, no more than the case examined in Section III, gives us adequate grounds for abandoning consequentialism and for adopting moral conservativism.

Forget the levity of the example and consider the case of the innocent fat man. If there really is no other way of unsticking our fat man and if plainly, without blasting him out, everyone in the cave will drown, then, innocent or not, he should be blasted out. This indeed overrides the principle that the innocent should never be deliberately killed, but it does not reveal a callousness toward life, for the people involved are caught in a desperate situation in which, if such extreme action is not taken, many lives will be lost and far greater misery will obtain. Moreover, the people who do such a horrible thing or acquiesce in the doing of it are not likely to be rendered more callous about human life and human suffering as a result. Its occurrence will haunt them for the rest of their lives and is as likely as not to make them more rather than less morally sensitive. It is not even correct to say that such a desperate act shows a lack of respect for persons. We are not treating the fat man merely as a means. The fat man's person—his interests and rights—are not ignored. Killing him is something which is undertaken with the greatest reluctance. It is only when it is quite certain that there is no other way to save the lives of the others that such a violent course of action is justifiably undertaken.

Alan Donagan, arguing rather as Anscombe argues, maintains that "to use any innocent man ill for the sake of some public good is directly to degrade him to being a mere means" and to do this is of course to violate a principle essential to morality, that is, that human beings should never merely be treated as means but should be treated as ends in themselves (as persons worthy of respect).[11] But, as my above remarks show, it need not be the case, and in the above situation it is not the case, that in killing such an innocent man we are treating him *merely* as a means. The action is universalizable, all alternative actions which would save his life are duly considered, the blasting

---

[11] Alan Donagan (n. 1 above), pp. 199–200.

out is done only as a last and desperate resort with the minimum of harshness and indifference to his suffering and the like. It indeed sounds ironical to talk this way, given what is done to him. But if such a terrible situation were to arise, there would always be more or less humane ways of going about one's grim task. And in acting in the more humane ways toward the fat man, as we do what we must do and would have done to ourselves were the roles reversed, we show a respect for his person.[12]

In so treating the fat man—not just to further the public good but to prevent the certain death of a whole group of people (that is to prevent an even greater evil than his being killed in this way)—the claims of justice are not overidden either, for each individual involved, if he is reasoning correctly, should realize that if he were so stuck rather than the fat man, he should in such situations be blasted out. Thus, there is no question of being unfair. Surely we must choose between evils here, but is there anything more reasonable, more morally appropriate, than choosing the lesser evil when doing or allowing some evil cannot be avoided? That is, where there is no avoiding both and where our actions can determine whether a greater or lesser evil obtains, should we not plainly always opt for the lesser evil? And is it not obviously a greater evil that all those other innocent people should suffer and die than that the fat man should suffer and die? Blowing up the fat man is indeed monstrous. But letting him remain stuck while the whole group drowns is still more monstrous.

The consequentialist is on strong moral ground here, and, if his reflective moral convictions do not square either with certain unrehearsed or with certain reflective particular moral convictions of human beings, so much the worse for such common-sense moral convictions. One could even usefully and relevantly adapt here—though for a quite different purpose—an argument of Donagan's. Consequentialism of the kind I have been arguing for provides so persuasive "a theoretical basis for common morality that when it contradicts some moral intuition, it is natural to suspect that intuition, not theory, is corrupt." [13] Given the comprehensiveness, plausibility, and overall rationality of consequentialism, it is not unreasonable to override even a deeply felt moral conviction if it does not square with such a theory, though, if it made no sense or overrode the bulk of or even a great many of our considered moral convictions, that would be another matter indeed.

Anticonsequentialists often point to the inhumanity of people who will sanction such killing of the innocent, but cannot the compliment be returned by speaking of the even greater inhumanity, conjoined with evasiveness, of those who will allow even more death and far greater misery and then excuse themselves on the ground that they did not intend the death and misery but merely forbore to prevent it? In such a context, such reasoning and such forbearing to prevent seems to me to constitute a moral

---

[12] Again, I am not asserting that we would have enough fortitude to assent to it were the roles actually reversed. I am making a conceptual remark about what as moral beings we must try to do and not a psychological observation about what we can do.

[13] Alan Donagan (n. 1 above), p. 198.

evasion. I say it is evasive because rather than steeling himself to do what in normal circumstances would be a horrible and vile act but in this circumstance is a harsh moral necessity, he allows, when he has the power to prevent it, a situation which is still many times worse. He tries to keep his 'moral purity' and avoid 'dirty hands' at the price of utter moral failure and what Kierkegaard called 'doublemindedness.' It is understandable that people should act in this morally evasive way but this does not make it right.

My consequentialist reasoning about such cases as the case of the innocent fat man is very often resisted on the grounds that it starts a very dangerous precedent. People rationalize wildly and irrationally in their own favor in such situations. To avoid such rationalization, we must stubbornly stick to our deontological principles and recognize as well that very frequently, if people will put their wits to work or just endure, such admittedly monstrous actions done to prevent still greater evils will turn out to be unnecessary.

The general moral principles surrounding bans on killing the innocent are strong and play such a crucial role in the ever-floundering effort to humanize the savage mind—savage as a primitive and savage again as a contemporary in industrial society— that it is of the utmost social utility, it can be argued, that such bans against killing the innocent not be called into question in any practical manner by consequentialist reasoning.

However, in arguing in this way, the moral conservative has plainly shifted his ground, and he is himself arguing on consequentialist grounds that we must treat certain nonconsequentialist moral principles as absolute (as principles which can never *in fact,* from a reasonable moral point of view, be overridden, for it would be just too disastrous to do so).[14] But now he is on my home court, and my reply is that there is no good evidence at all that in the circumstances I characterized, overriding these deontological principles would have this disastrous effect. I am aware that a bad precedent could be set. Such judgments must not be made for more doubtful cases. But my telling my two stories in some detail, and my contrasting them, was done in order to make evident the type of situation, with its attendant rationale, in which the overriding of those deontological principles can be seen clearly to be justified and the situations in which this does obtain and why. My point was to specify the situations in which we ought to override our commonsense moral convictions about those matters, and the contexts in which we are not so justified or at least in which it is not clear which course of action is justified.[15]

---

[14] Jonathan Bennett, "Whatever the Consequences," *Analysis,* vol. 26 (1966), has shown that this is a very common equivocation for the conservative and makes, when unnoticed, his position seem more plausible than it actually is.

[15] I have spoken, conceding this to the Christian absolutist for the sake of the discussion, as if (1) it is fairly evident what our commonsense moral convictions are here and (2) that they are deontological principles taken to hold no matter what the consequences. But that either (1) or (2) is clearly so seems to me very much open to question.

If people are able to be sufficiently clearheaded about these matters, they can see that there are relevant differences between the two sorts of cases. But I was also carefully guarding against extending such 'moral radicalism'—if such it should be called—to other and more doubtful cases. Unless solid empirical evidence can be given that such a 'moral radicalism' would—if it were to gain a toehold in the community—overflow destructively and inhumanely into the other doubtful and positively unjustifiable situations, nothing has been said to undermine the correctness of my consequentialist defense of 'moral radicalism' in the contexts in which I defended it.[16]

---

[16] I do not mean to suggest that I am giving a blanket defense to our commonsense morality; that is one of the last things I would want to do. Much of what we or any other tribe take to be commonsense morality is little better than a set of magical charms to deal with our social environment. But I was defending the importance of such cross-culturally ubiquitous moral principles as that one ought not to harm the innocent or that promises ought to be kept. However, against Christian absolutists of the type I have been discussing, I take them to be prima facie obligations. This means that they always hold *ceteris paribus;* but the *ceteris paribus* qualification implies that they can be overridden on occasion. On my account, appeal to consequences and considerations about justice and respect for persons determines when they should on a given occasion be overridden.

Suggested Readings

Bayles, Michael D. (ed.). *Contemporary Utilitarianism.* New York: Doubleday, 1968.

Broad, C. D. *Ethics and the History of Philosophy.* London: Routledge & Kegan Paul, 1952.

Isenberg, Arnold. "Deontology and the Ethics of Lying," *Philosophy and Phenomenological Research* 24 (1964).

Schneewind, J. B. (ed.). *Mill: A Collection of Critical Essays.* New York: Doubleday, 1968.

Smart, J. J. C., and Bernard Williams. *Utilitarianism: For and Against.* New York: Cambridge University Press, 1973.

Smith, James M., and Ernest Sosa (eds.). *Mill's Utilitarianism: Text and Criticism.* Belmont, Calif.: Wadsworth, 1969.

Toulmin, Stephen. *An Examination of the Place of Reason in Ethics.* New York: Cambridge University Press, 1950.

Wolf, Robert Paul (ed.). *Kant: Foundations of the Metaphysics of Morals, Text and Critical Essays.* Indianapolis: Bobbs-Merrill, 1969.

section five

the language of ethics

THE SUBJECT-MATTER OF ETHICS

G. E. Moore

. . .

Ethics is undoubtedly concerned with the question what good conduct is; but, being concerned with this, it obviously does not start at the beginning, unless it is prepared to tell us what is good as well as what is conduct. For 'good conduct' is a complex notion: all conduct is not good; for some is certainly bad and some may be indifferent. And on the other hand, other things, beside conduct, may be good; and if they are so, then, 'good' denotes some property, that is common to them and conduct; and if we examine good conduct alone of all good things, then we shall be in danger of mistaking for this property, some property which is not shared by those other things: and thus we shall have made a mistake about Ethics even in this limited sense; for we shall not know what good conduct really is. This is a mistake which many writers have actually made, from limiting their enquiry to conduct. And hence I shall try to avoid it by considering first what is good in general; hoping, that if we can arrive at any certainty about this, it will be much easier to settle the question of good conduct: for we all know pretty well what 'conduct' is. This, then, is our first question: What is good? and What is bad? and to the discussion of this question (or these questions) I give the name of Ethics, since that science must, at all events, include it.

. . .

What, then, is good? How is good to be defined? Now, it may be thought that this is a verbal question. A definition does indeed often mean the expressing of one word's meaning in other words. But this is not the sort of definition I am asking for. Such a definition can never be of ultimate importance in any study except lexicography. If I wanted that kind of definition I should have to consider in the first place how people generally used the word 'good'; but my business is not with its proper usage, as established by custom. I should, indeed, be foolish, if I tried to use it for something which it did not usually denote: if, for instance, I were to announce that, whenever I used the word 'good,' I must be understood to be thinking of that object which is usually denoted by the word 'table.' I shall, therefore, use the word in the sense in which I think it is ordinarily used; but at the same time I am not anxious to discuss whether I am right in thinking that it is so used. My business is solely with that object or idea, which I hold, rightly or wrongly, that the word is generally used to stand for. What I want to discover is the nature of that object or idea, and about this I am extremely anxious to arrive at an agreement.

But, if we understand the question in this sense, my answer to it may seem a very disappointing one. If I am asked 'What is good?' my answer is that good is good, and that is the end of the matter. Or if I am asked 'How is good to be defined?' my answer is that it cannot be defined, and that is all I have to say about it. But disappointing as these answers may appear, they are of the very last importance. To readers who are familiar with philosophic terminology, I can express their importance by saying that they amount to this: That propositions about the good are all of them synthetic and never analytic; and that is plainly no trivial matter. And the same thing may be expressed more popularly, by saying that, if I am right, then nobody can foist upon us such an axiom as that 'Pleasure is the only good' or that 'The good is the desired' on the pretence that this is 'the very meaning of the word.'

Let us, then, consider this position. My point is that 'good' is a simple notion, just as 'yellow' is a simple notion; that, just as you cannot, by any manner of means, explain to any one who does not already know it, what yellow is, so you cannot explain what good is. Definitions of the kind that I was asking for, definitions which describe the real nature of the object or notion denoted by a word, and which do not merely tell us what the word is used to mean, are only possible when the object or notion in question is something complex. You can give a definition of a horse, because a horse has many different properties and qualities, all of which you can enumerate. But when you have enumerated them all, when you have reduced a horse to his simplest terms, then you can no longer define those terms. They are simply something which you think of or perceive, and to any one who cannot think of or perceive them, you can never, by any definition, make their nature known. It may perhaps be objected to this that we are able to describe to others, objects which they have never seen or thought of. We can, for instance, make a man understand what a chimaera is, although he has never heard of one or seen one. You can tell him that it is an animal with a lioness's head and body, with a goat's head growing from the middle of its back, and with a snake in place of a tail. But here the object which you are describing is a complex object; it is entirely composed of parts, with which we are all perfectly familiar—a snake, a goat, a lioness; and we know, too, the manner in which those parts are to be put together, because we know what is meant by the middle of a lioness's back, and where her tail is wont to grow. And so it is with all objects, not previously known, which we are able to define: they are all complex; all composed of parts, which may themselves, in the first instance, be capable of similar definition, but which must in the end be reducible to simplest parts, which can no longer be defined. But yellow and good, we say, are not complex: they are notions of that simple kind, out of which definitions are composed and with which the power of further defining ceases.

When we say, as Webster says, 'The definition of horse is "A hoofed quadruped of the genus Equus," ' we may, in fact, mean three different things. (1) We may mean merely: 'When I say "horse," you are to understand that I am talking about a hoofed quadruped of the genus Equus.' This might be called the arbitrary verbal definition: and I do not mean that good is indefinable in that sense. (2) We may mean, as Webster ought to mean: 'When most English people say "horse," they mean a hoofed quadruped of the genus Equus.' This may be called the verbal definition proper, and I do not say that good is indefinable in this sense either; for it is certainly possible to discover how people use a word: otherwise, we could never have known that 'good' may be translated by 'gut' in German and by 'bon' in French. But (3) we may, when we define horse, mean something much more important. We may mean that a certain object, which we all of us know, is composed in a certain manner: that it has four legs, a head, a heart, a liver, etc., etc., all of them arranged in definite relations to one another. It is in this sense that I deny good to be definable. I say that it is not composed of any parts, which we can substitute for it in our minds when we are thinking of it. We might think just as clearly and correctly about a horse, if we thought of all its parts and their arrangement instead of thinking of the whole: we could, I say, think how a horse differed from a donkey just as well, just as truly, in this way, as now we do, only not so easily; but there is nothing whatsoever which we could so substitute for good; and that is what I mean, when I say that good is indefinable.

. . .

'Good,' then, if we mean by it that quality which we assert to belong to a thing, when we say that the thing is good, is incapable of any definition, in the most important sense of that word. The most important sense of 'definition' is that in which a definition states what are the parts which invariably compose a certain whole; and in this sense 'good' has no definition because it is simple and has no parts. It is one of those innumerable objects of thought which are themselves incapable of definition, because they are the ultimate terms by reference to which whatever *is* capable of definition must be defined. That there must be an indefinite number of such terms is obvious, on reflection; since we cannot define anything except by an analysis, which, when carried as far as it will go, refers us to something, which is simply different from anything else, and which by that ultimate difference explains the peculiarity of the whole which we are defining: for every whole contains some parts which are common to other wholes also. There is, therefore, no intrinsic difficulty in the contention that 'good' denotes a simple and indefinable quality. There are many other instances of such qualities.

Consider yellow, for example. We may try to define it, by describing its physical equivalent; we may state what kind of light-vibrations must stimulate the normal eye, in order that we may perceive it. But a moment's reflection is sufficient to shew that those light-vibrations are not themselves what we mean by yellow. *They* are not what we perceive. Indeed we should never have been able to discover their existence, unless we had first been struck by the patent difference of quality between the different colours. The most we can be entitled to say of those vibrations is that they are what corresponds in space to the yellow which we actually perceive.

Yet a mistake of this simple kind has commonly been made about 'good.' It may be true that all things which are good are *also* something else, just as it is true that all things which are yellow produce a certain kind of vibration in the light. And it is a fact, that Ethics aims at discovering what are those other properties belonging to all things which are good. But far too many philosophers have thought that when they named those other properties they were actually defining good; that these properties, in fact, were simply not 'other,' but absolutely and entirely the same with goodness. This view I propose to call the 'naturalistic fallacy' and of it I shall now endeavour to dispose.

. . .

Suppose a man says 'I am pleased'; and suppose that is not a lie or a mistake but the truth. Well, if it is true, what does that mean? It means that his mind, a certain definite mind, distinguished by certain definite marks from all others, has at this moment a certain definite feeling called pleasure. 'Pleased' *means* nothing but having pleasure, and though we may be more pleased or less pleased, and even, we may admit for the present, have one or another kind of pleasure; yet in so far as it is pleasure we have, whether there be more or less of it, and whether it be of one kind or another, what we have is one definite thing, absolutely indefinable, some one thing that is the same in all the various degrees and in all the various kinds of it that there may be. We may be able to say how it is related to other things: that, for example, it is in the mind, that it causes desire, that we are conscious of it, etc., etc. We can, I say, describe its relations to other things, but define it we can *not.* And if anybody tried to define pleasure for us as being any other natural object; if anybody were to say, for instance, that pleasure *means* the sensation of red, and were to proceed to deduce from that that pleasure is a colour, we should be entitled to laugh at him and to distrust his future statements about pleasure. Well, that would be the same fallacy which I have called the naturalistic fallacy. That 'pleased' does not mean 'having the sensation of red,' or anything else whatever, does not prevent us from understanding what it does mean.

It is enough for us to know that 'pleased' does mean 'having the sensation of pleasure,' and though pleasure is absolutely indefinable, though pleasure is pleasure and nothing else whatever, yet we feel no difficulty in saying that we are pleased. The reason is, of course, that when I say 'I am pleased,' I do *not* mean that 'I' am the same thing as 'having pleasure.' And similarly no difficulty need be found in my saying that 'pleasure is good' and yet not meaning that 'pleasure' is the same thing as 'good,' that pleasure *means* good, and that good *means* pleasure. If I were to imagine that when I said 'I am pleased,' I meant that I was exactly the same thing as 'pleased,' I should not indeed call that a naturalistic fallacy, although it would be the same fallacy as I have called naturalistic with reference to Ethics. The reason of this is obvious enough. When a man confuses two natural objects with one another, defining the one by the other, if for instance, he confuses himself, who is one natural object, with 'pleased' or with 'pleasure' which are others, then there is no reason to call the fallacy naturalistic. But if he confuses 'good,' which is not in the same sense a natural object, with any natural object whatever, then there is a reason for calling that a naturalistic fallacy; its being made with regard to 'good' marks it as something quite specific, and this specific mistake deserves a name because it is so common. As for the reasons why good is not to be considered a natural object, they may be reserved for discussion in another place. But, for the present, it is sufficient to notice this: Even if it were a natural object, that would not alter the nature of the fallacy nor diminish its importance one whit. All that I have said about it would remain quite equally true: only the name which I have called it would not be so appropriate as I think it is. And I do not care about the name: what I do care about is the fallacy. It does not matter what we call it, provided we recognise it when we meet with it. It is to be met with in almost every book on Ethics; and yet it is not recognised: and that is why it is necessary to multiply illustrations of it, and convenient to give it a name. It is a very simple fallacy indeed. When we say that an orange is yellow, we do not think our statement binds us to hold that 'orange' means nothing else than 'yellow,' or that nothing can be yellow but an orange. Supposing the orange is also sweet! Does that bind us to say that 'sweet' is exactly the same thing as 'yellow,' that 'sweet' must be defined as 'yellow'? And supposing it be recognised that 'yellow' just means 'yellow' and nothing else whatever, does that make it any more difficult to hold that oranges are yellow? Most certainly it does not: on the contrary, it would be absolutely meaningless to say that oranges were yellow, unless yellow did in the end mean just 'yellow' and nothing else whatever —unless it was absolutely indefinable. We should not get any very clear notion about things, which are yellow—we should not get very far with our science, if we were bound to hold that everything which was yellow, *meant* exactly the same thing as yellow. We should find we had to hold that an orange was exactly the same thing as a stool, a piece of paper, a lemon, anything you like. We could prove any number of absurdities; but should we be the nearer to the truth? Why, then, should it be different with 'good'? Why, if good is good and indefinable, should I be held to deny that pleasure is good?

Is there any difficulty in holding both to be true at once? On the contrary, there is no meaning in saying that pleasure is good, unless good is something different from pleasure. . . .

. . .

I propose, then, to begin by an examination of Mill's *Utilitarianism*. That is a book which contains an admirably clear and fair discussion of many ethical principles and methods. Mill exposes not a few simple mistakes which are very likely to be made by those who approach ethical problems without much previous reflection. But what I am concerned with is the mistakes which Mill himself appears to have made, and these only so far as they concern the Hedonistic principle. Let me repeat what that principle is. It is, I said, that pleasure is the only thing at which we ought to aim, the only thing that is good as an end and for its own sake. And now let us turn to Mill and see whether he accepts this description of the question at issue. 'Pleasure,' he says at the outset, 'and freedom from pain, are the only things desirable as ends' (p. 10 [1]); and again, at the end of his argument, 'To think of an object as desirable (unless for the sake of its consequences) and to think of it as pleasant are one and the other thing' (p. 58). These statements, taken together, and apart from certain confusions which are obvious in them, seem to imply the principle I have stated; and if I succeed in shewing that Mill's reasons for them do not prove them, it must at least be admitted that I have not been fighting with shadows or demolishing a man of straw.

It will be observed that Mill adds 'absence of pain' to 'pleasure' in his first statement, though not in his second. There is, in this, a confusion, with which, however, we need not deal. I shall talk of 'pleasure' alone, for the sake of conciseness; but all my arguments will apply *a fortiori* to 'absence of pain': it is easy to make the necessary substitutions.

Mill holds, then, that 'happiness is desirable, and *the only thing desirable*,[2] as an end; all other things being only desirable as means to that end' (p. 52). Happiness he has already defined as 'pleasure, and the absence of pain' (p. 10); he does not pretend that this is more than an arbitrary verbal definition; and, as *such*, I have not a word to say against it. His principle, then, is 'pleasure is the only thing desirable,' if I may be allowed, when I say 'pleasure,' to include in that word (so far as necessary) absence of pain. And now what are his reasons for holding that principle to be true? He has already told us (p. 6) that 'Questions of ultimate ends are not amenable to direct proof. Whatever can be proved to be good, must be so by being shewn to be a means to something *admitted to be good without proof.*' With this, I perfectly agree . . . Anything which is good as an end must be admitted to be good without proof. We are agreed so far. Mill even uses the same examples . . . 'How,' he says, 'is it possible to prove that health is good?' 'What proof is it possible to give that pleasure is good?' Well,

---

[1] My references are to the 13th edition, 1897.

[2] My italics.

in Chapter IV, in which he deals with the proof of his Utilitarian principle, Mill repeats the above statement in these words: 'It has already,' he says, 'been remarked, that questions of ultimate ends do not admit of proof, in the ordinary acceptation of the term' (p. 52). 'Questions about ends,' he goes on in this same passage, 'are, in other words, questions what things are desirable.' I am quoting these repetitions, because they make it plain what otherwise might have been doubted, that Mill is using the words 'desirable' or 'desirable as an end' as absolutely and precisely equivalent to the words 'good as an end.' We are, then, now to hear, what reasons he advances for this doctrine that pleasure alone is good as an end.

'Questions about ends,' he says (pp. 52–3), 'are, in other words, questions what things are desirable. The utilitarian doctrine is, that happiness is desirable, and the only thing desirable, as an end; all other things being only desirable as means to that end. What ought to be required of this doctrine—what conditions is it requisite that the doctrine should fulfil—to make good its claim to be believed?

'The only proof capable of being given that a thing is visible, is that people actually see it. The only proof that a sound is audible, is that people hear it; and so of the other sources of our experience. In like manner, I apprehend, the sole evidence it is possible to produce that anything is desirable, is that people do actually desire it. If the end which the utilitarian doctrine proposes to itself were not, in theory and in practice, acknowledged to be an end, nothing could ever convince any person that it was so. No reason can be given why the general happiness is desirable, except that each person, so far as he believes it to be attainable, desires his own happiness. This, however, being the fact, we have not only all the proof which the case admits of, but all which it is possible to require, that happiness is a good: that each person's happiness is a good to that person, and the general happiness, therefore, a good to the aggregate of all persons. Happiness has made out its title as *one* of the ends of conduct, and consequently one of the criteria of morality.'

There, that is enough. That is my first point. Mill has made as naïve and artless a use of the naturalistic fallacy as anybody could desire. 'Good,' he tells us, means 'desirable,' and you can only find out what is desirable by seeking to find out what is actually desired. This is, of course, only one step towards the proof of Hedonism; for it may be, as Mill goes on to say, that other things beside pleasure are desired. Whether or not pleasure is the only thing desired is, as Mill himself admits (p. 58), a psychological question . . . The important step for Ethics is this one just taken, the step which pretends to prove that 'good' means 'desired.'

Well, the fallacy in this step is so obvious, that it is quite wonderful how Mill failed to see it. The fact is that 'desirable' does not mean 'able to be desired' as 'visible' means 'able to be seen.' The desirable means simply what *ought* to be desired or *deserves* to be desired; just as the detestable means not what can be but what ought to be detested and the damnable what deserves to be damned. Mill has, then, smuggled in, under cover of the word 'desirable,' the very notion about which he ought to be quite clear.

'Desirable' does indeed mean 'what it is good to desire'; but when this is understood, it is no longer plausible to say that our only test of *that,* is what is actually desired. Is it merely a tautology when the Prayer Book talks of *good* desires? Are not *bad* desires also possible? Nay, we find Mill himself talking of a 'better and nobler object of desire' (p. 10), as if, after all, what is desired were not *ipso facto* good, and good in proportion to the amount it is desired. Moreover, if the desired is *ipso facto* the good; then the good is *ipso facto* the motive of our actions, and there can be no question of finding motives for doing it, as Mill is at such pains to do. If Mill's explanation of 'desirable' be *true,* then his statement (p. 26) that the rule of action may be *confounded* with the motive of it is untrue: for the motive of action will then be according to him *ipso facto* its rule; there can be no distinction between the two, and therefore no confusion, and thus he has contradicted himself flatly. These are specimens of the contradictions, which, as I have tried to shew, must always follow from the use of the naturalistic fallacy; and I hope I need now say no more about the matter.

. . .

EMOTIVISM

A. J. Ayer

. . .

We begin by admitting that the fundamental ethical concepts are unanalysable, inasmuch as there is no criterion by which one can test the validity of the judgements in which they occur. So far we are in agreement with the absolutists. But, unlike the absolutists, we are able to give an explanation of this fact about ethical concepts. We say that the reason why they are unanalysable is that they are mere pseudo-concepts. The presence of an ethical symbol in a proposition adds nothing to its factual content. Thus if I say to someone, "You acted wrongly in stealing that money," I am not stating anything more than if I had simply said, "You stole that money." In adding that this action is wrong I am not making any further statement about it. I am simply evincing my moral disapproval of it. It is as if I had said, "You stole that money," in a peculiar tone of horror, or written it with the addition of some special exclamation marks. The tone, or the exclamation marks, adds nothing to the literal meaning of the sentence. It merely serves to show that the expression of it is attended by certain feelings in the speaker.

If now I generalise my previous statement and say, "Stealing money is wrong," I produce a sentence which has no factual meaning—that is, expresses no proposition which can be either true or false. It is as if I had written "Stealing money!!"—where the shape and thickness of the exclamation marks show, by a suitable convention, that a special sort of moral disapproval is the feeling which is being expressed. It is clear that there is nothing said here which can be true or false. Another man may disagree with me about the wrongness of stealing, in the sense that he may not have the same feelings about stealing as I have, and he may quarrel with me on account of my moral sentiments. But he cannot, strictly speaking, contradict me. For in saying that a certain type of action is right or wrong, I am not making any factual statement, not even a statement about my own state of mind. I am merely expressing certain moral sentiments. And the man who is ostensibly contradicting me is merely expressing his moral sentiments. So that there is plainly no sense in asking which of us is in the right. For neither of us is asserting a genuine proposition.

What we have just been saying about the symbol "wrong" applies to all normative ethical symbols. Sometimes they occur in sentences which record ordinary empirical facts besides expressing ethical feeling about those facts: sometimes they occur in sentences which simply express ethical feeling about a certain type of action, or situation, without making any statement of fact. But in every case in which one would commonly be said to be making an ethical judgement, the function of the relevant ethical word is purely "emotive." It is used to express feeling about certain objects, but not to make any assertion about them.

It is worth mentioning that ethical terms do not serve only to express feeling. They are calculated also to arouse feeling, and so to stimulate action. Indeed some of them are used in such a way as to give the sentences in which they occur the effect of commands. Thus the sentence "It is your duty to tell the truth" may be regarded both as the expression of a certain sort of ethical feeling about truthfulness and as the expression of the command "Tell the truth." The sentence "You ought to tell the truth" also involves the command "Tell the truth," but here the tone of the command is less emphatic. In the sentence "It is good to tell the truth" the command has become little more than a suggestion. And thus the "meaning" of the word "good," in its ethical usage, is differentiated from that of the word "duty" or the word "ought." In fact we may define the meaning of the various ethical words in terms both of the different feelings they are ordinarily taken to express, and also the different responses which they are calculated to provoke.

We can now see why it is impossible to find a criterion for determining the validity of ethical judgements. It is not because they have an "absolute" validity which is mysteriously independent of ordinary sense-experience, but because they have no objective validity whatsoever. If a sentence makes no statement at all, there is obviously no sense in asking whether what it says is true or false. And we have seen that sentences which simply express moral judgements do not say anything. They are pure expressions of feeling and as such do not come under the category of truth and falsehood. They are unverifiable for the same reason as a cry of pain or a word of command is unverifiable—because they do not express genuine propositions.

Thus, although our theory of ethics might fairly be said to be radically subjectivist, it differs in a very important respect from the orthodox subjectivist theory. For the orthodox subjectivist does not deny, as we do, that the sentences of a moralizer express genuine propositions. All he denies is that they express propositions of a unique non-empirical character. His own view is that they express propositions about the speaker's feelings. If this were so, ethical judgements clearly would be capable of being true or false. They would be true if the speaker had the relevant feelings, and false if he had not. And this is a matter which is, in principle, empirically verifiable. Furthermore they could be significantly contradicted. For if I say, "Tolerance is a virtue," and someone answers, "You don't approve of it," he would, on the ordinary subjectivist theory, be contradicting me. On our theory, he would not be contradicting me, because, in saying that tolerance was a virtue, I should not be making any statement about my own feelings or about anything else. I should simply be evincing my feelings, which is not at all the same thing as saying that I have them.

The distinction between the expression of feeling and the assertion of feeling is complicated by the fact that the assertion that one has a certain feeling often accompanies the expression of that feeling, and is then, indeed, a factor in the expression of that feeling. Thus I may simultaneously express boredom and say that I am bored, and in that case my utterance of the words, "I am bored," is one of the circumstances which make it true to say that I am expressing or evincing boredom. But I can express boredom without actually saying that I am bored. I can express it by my tone and gestures, while making a statement about something wholly unconnected with it, or by an ejaculation, or without uttering any words at all. So that even if the assertion that one has a certain feeling always involves the expression of that feeling, the expression of a feeling assuredly does not always involve the assertion that one has it. And this is the important point to grasp in considering the distinction between our theory and the ordinary subjectivist theory. For whereas the subjectivist holds that ethical statements actually assert the existence of certain feelings, we hold that ethical statements are expressions and excitants of feeling which do not necessarily involve any assertions.

We have already remarked that the main objection to the ordinary subjectivist theory is that the validity of ethical judgements is not determined by the nature of their author's feelings. And this is an objection which our theory escapes. For it does not imply that the existence of any feelings is a necessary and sufficient condition of the validity of an ethical judgement. It implies, on the contrary, that ethical judgements have no validity.

There is, however, a celebrated argument against subjectivist theories which our theory does not escape. It has been pointed out by Moore that if ethical statements were simply statements about the speaker's feelings, it would be impossible to argue about questions of value. To take a typical example: if a man said that thrift was a virtue, and another replied that it was a vice, they would not, on this theory, be disputing with one another. One would be saying that he approved of thrift, and the other that *he* didn't; and there is no reason why both these statements should not be true. Now Moore held it to be obvious that we do dispute about questions of value, and accordingly concluded that the particular form of subjectivism which he was discussing was false.

It is plain that the conclusion that it is impossible to dispute about questions of value follows from our theory also. For as we hold that such sentences as "Thrift is a virtue" and "Thrift is a vice" do not express propositions at all, we clearly cannot hold that they express incompatible propositions. We must therefore admit that if Moore's argument really refutes the ordinary subjectivist theory, it also refutes ours. But, in fact, we deny that it does refute even the ordinary subjectivist theory. For we hold that one really never does dispute about questions of value.

This may seem, at first sight, to be a very paradoxical assertion. For we certainly do engage in disputes which are ordinarily regarded as disputes about questions of value. But, in all such cases, we find, if we consider the matter closely, that the dispute is not really about a question of value, but about a question of fact. When someone disagrees with us about the moral value of a certain action or type of action, we do admittedly resort to argument in order to win him over to our way of thinking. But we do not attempt to show by our arguments that he has the "wrong" ethical feeling towards a situation whose nature he has correctly apprehended. What we attempt to show is that he is mistaken about the facts of the case. We argue that he has misconceived the agent's motive; or that he has misjudged the effects of the action, or its probable effects in view of the agent's knowledge; or that he has failed to take into account the special circumstances in which the agent was placed. Or else we employ more general arguments about the effects which actions of a certain type tend to produce, or the qualities which are usually manifested in their performance. We do this in the hope that we have only to get our opponent to agree with us about the nature of the empirical facts for him to adopt the same moral attitude towards them as we do. And as the people with whom we argue have generally received the same moral education as ourselves, and live in the same social order, our expectation is usually justified. But if our opponent happens to have undergone a different process of moral "conditioning" from ourselves, so that, even when he acknowledges all the facts, he still disagrees with us about the moral value of the actions under discussion, then we abandon the attempt to convince him by argument. We say that it is impossible to argue with him because he has a distorted or undeveloped moral sense; which signifies merely that he employs a different set of values from our own. We feel that our own system of values is superior, and therefore speak in such derogatory terms of his. But we cannot bring forward any arguments to show that our system is superior. For our judgement that it is so is itself a judgement of value, and accordingly outside the scope of argument. It is because argument fails us when we come to deal with pure questions of value, as distinct from questions of fact, that we finally resort to mere abuse.

In short, we find that **argument** is possible on moral questions only if some system of values is presupposed. If our opponent concurs with us in expressing moral disapproval of all actions of a given type *t*, then we may get him to condemn a particular action A, by bringing forward arguments to show that A is of type *t*. For the question whether A does or does not belong to that type is a plain question of fact. Given that a man has certain moral principles, we argue that he must, in order to be consistent, react morally to certain things in a certain way. What we do not and cannot argue about is the validity of these moral principles. We merely praise or condemn them in the light of our own feelings.

If anyone doubts the accuracy of this account of moral disputes, let him try to construct even an imaginary argument on a question of value which does not reduce itself to an argument about a question of logic or about an empirical matter of fact. I am confident that he will not succeed in producing a single example. And if that is the case, he must allow that its involving the impossibility of purely ethical arguments is not, as Moore thought, a ground of objection to our theory, but rather a point in favour of it.

Having upheld our theory against the only criticism which appeared to threaten it, we may now use it to define the nature of all ethical enquiries. We find that ethical philosophy consists simply in saying that ethical concepts are pseudo-concepts and therefore unanalysable. The further task of describing the different feelings that the different ethical terms are used to express, and the different reactions that they customarily provoke, is a task for the psychologist. There cannot be such a thing as ethical science, if by ethical science one means the elaboration of a "true" system of morals. For we have seen that, as ethical judgements are mere expressions of feeling, there can be no way of determining the validity of any ethical system, and, indeed, no sense in asking whether any such system is true. All that one may legitimately enquire in this connection is, What are the moral habits of a given person or group of people, and what causes them to have precisely those habits and feelings? And this enquiry falls wholly within the scope of the existing social sciences.

. . .

YOU OUGHT TO DERIVE "OUGHT" FROM "IS"

Robert V. Hannaford

Contemporary philosophers—weaned on G. E. Moore—have been ignoring the connection between factual assertions and norms of action, no doubt because they have been anxious to maintain the distinction between facts and norms.[1] I want to maintain

---

[1] Many have argued against attempts to show a connection between one's principles and any kind of factual assertion, arguing first that one is not strictly *deducible* from the other and then concluding that one's choice of moral principles cannot be based on factual consideration. See, e.g., R. M. Hare (p. 303) in "Universalizabil-

the distinction while focusing on the connection. If "ought" typically implies "can," "can be" and "must be" often lead normally and naturally to "ought." Arguments which proceed from empirical accounts of human behavior and needs may be the most cogent and persuasive arguments which can be used for reaching moral and political agreement. I want to maintain that arguments based on empirically confirmed assertions about the conditions of human action can provide a common and objective basis for a commitment to uphold moral and political rights.

I want to argue (Part I) that such assertions about men can be employed to lead toward agreement on—can be employed to derive—general norms of action, norms which define conditions and freedoms that ought to be preserved in community practices. Subsequently (Part II), I would like to argue that, since we often have the need of reliable guidance in deciding what moral norms to adopt, we ought to avail ourselves of this derivation where possible.

I

It is clear that empirical accounts of behavior can be used in deciding questions of value when one is employing hypothetical value judgments. Such value judgments take the form: if you want to do any specific thing, then (if you are to be consistent [2] and if you are to achieve your goal) you must employ whatever conditions are indispensable to achieving that goal and you must defend or protect those means or conditions. It is obvious how these judgments apply to particular acts: if one wants to do anything, one must take the means required to do it.

However, arguments of roughly the same form may be employed in support of general norms of action. For such arguments it is crucial that we establish what conditions (rather than what means) are necessary to subsequent action. If we can

---

ity," *Proceedings of the Aristotelian Society* 55, n.s. (1954–55): 295–312. He argues against the view that we can show a connection between moral principles and "statements describing what sort of person I am. This would be to offend against Hume's Law . . . (I cannot) set about choosing between moral principles by first asking what sort of person I am and then deducing the correct principles from premisses giving this information."

[2] One could remove the phrase "if we are to be consistent" from the argument without destroying its logical force. For, as Carl Wellman observed in commenting on the paper, the logical connection is not contingent on the determination or ability of the reader to be consistent. I retain the phrase ("if we are to be consistent") in order to mark the fact that we must be able to be—and concerned to be—consistent in order for us to accept the resulting moral judgments. One does not derive or accept judgments about what one ought to do unless one is able and willing to accept the logical connection. Ever since Aristotle, philosophers have been observing that men are less likely to reason clearly about matters that affect their own obligation. Thus, without the ability to accept a logical connection as binding, we will not be prepared to move from a knowledge of our wants and a knowledge of the conditions necessary to their fulfillment to an acceptance of the derived moral judgment. Wellman and others might want to counter that we need not be willing to acknowledge that a moral judgment is valid in order for it to *be* valid—and with that statement I agree. But I would add that we could not reach moral agreement about such judgments without the ability and concern to be consistent and that we are especially prone to fail of consistency in matters affecting our own obligations.

establish that some conditions are necessary to any subsequent action, we can give good (hypothetically stated) reasons for wanting to preserve those conditions. In defining conditions which must be preserved for any subsequent action, we will thereby have formulated norms or principles to direct all subsequent action: and thus we, by this reasoning, would have reason to commit ourselves to upholding that norm on future occasions. From the knowledge of what is necessary to human action in general we can derive judgments of what we ought to do if we are to continue to engage in that action.

What are some of these necessary conditions?—A politically significant and pervasive feature of human action is that it involves other people: every stage of a person's life involves him with other people—for nurture, for education, for goods and services to be used, for self-expression and communication.

To be human is to use language, and language exists only through the mutual response of persons in a community. We typically rely on language to develop a conception of a course of action, and we rely on it for a conception of ourselves. If we think of being human as involving thought and expression about action, there is no human life apart from a community to persons who are language users.

If we want to engage in any activity that involves other people—and almost all our activities do—then, if we are to be consistent, we must defend and preserve the persons with whom we must act. Other persons are to be revered, not simply as instruments to our goals, but rather as integral to our own. A human life, in the standard and usual sense of the term "human," is a texture of associations and relationships with other people. One cannot wash other people out of the life and still have a human life. Thus one cannot coherently value one's own life without valuing his relationships with other people that are constitutive of it.

One may object that this reasoning provides no basis for valuing the lives and freedoms of *all* persons in one's community but only of those with whom we are to act. However, the difficulty with this objection is that we cannot know all those with whom we shall be acting. We may need to act with and feel the effects of the action of any person in the community: our common daily activities are possible only through a far-flung network of activities and responses.

If one values his relationships with others in a community, he should protect or defend the conditions which are necessary for community life. Among those necessary conditions are those that permit people to act in accord with some community practices. If none were to adhere to recognized practices or roles, we could not share or cooperate, we could not have a relationship *with* people. Unless men placed restrictions on their impulses to act, life would be as Hobbes described it.

What conditions and freedoms are required in order for men to be able to govern their behavior in accord with community practices? Certainly a great many are, and the argument could be extended to show these.

If one wants to engage in any of the usual human activities, he must employ the conditions or relationships which are integral to the responses of persons in a community. Thus, he ought to preserve those conditions. Usually one cannot by one's own actions guarantee that all these conditions will be preserved. However, one will have good reason for not destroying them. One ought not do anything that would be destructive of those relationships, and one ought to do what he can to prevent others from such destruction.

If one is to preserve (or avoid the destruction of) those conditions, he must understand what the essential conditions are and he must—ought to—preserve the conditions which contribute to that understanding. Thus, one ought not to undermine freedom of expression, access to information and ideas of others, and access to other resources for education and investigation.

What conditions and freedoms are required for education and investigation? Certainly a great many are, and we could extend the argument to show what some of them are.

The pattern for extending such arguments is: If you want *a* (any human activity) then you ought to preserve *b* (the conditions or relationships shown to be essential to *a*). If you want to preserve *b*, then you ought to preserve *c* (the conditions essential to *b*), and so on. The argument would continue, identifying all the conditions and freedoms which are essential to any of the standard human activities.

The derivation or supporting argument is applicable generally because it appeals to human action taken generally. In showing the conditions which are essential to *any* of the standard or usual kinds of human activities, it shows that those who want to engage in those activities have reason for defending those conditions. In showing the general conditions or freedoms which are necessary for the ordinary and generically human interpersonal responses, it gives a reason for upholding those conditions or freedoms in subsequent action. In doing so, in short, it gives a generally applicable support for general norms of action.

The argument (being a support for general norms) does not, of itself, indicate what specific actions are to be undertaken in any given circumstances. Its conclusion will be relevant to such determinations in that the conclusion will justify those specific actions which uphold the general norms under the given circumstances and the conclusion will condemn those actions which fail to do so. As more of the essential conditions or freedoms are identified and made explicit, it will be easier for us to identify the conditions or freedoms to be preserved in our actions, and thus it will be easier for us to say what ought to be done in any specific situation. But, of course, the situation and conditions in which we must act are continually changing so that we could never extend the argument for moral norms to the point where we could derive specific moral rules or instructions for action for each situation.

If we were to extend the argument we would find reason to preserve various freedoms, freedoms that cannot always be granted and freedoms whose desirability gives rise to conflicting claims. This fact raises questions which I cannot explore in any detail here; one such question is: How does one choose between conflicting claims? While I do not propose this method of derivation as a method of resolving all ethical questions, I do think it reasonable to hope that such investigation will help us solve this one. For by such investigation and derivation, we may be able to identify some of the circumstances under which the exercise of a freedom is most crucial. To the extent that we can do so, we will be able to define the order of importance of the various freedoms and to define the circumstances in which it is most necessary that they be defended. To that extent such investigation and derivation will enable us to choose between conflicting claims.

II

If the above investigation and derivation were extended, it would indicate what ought to be protected in community life. Each part of the argument may be described as one in which we derive an "ought" judgment from "is" judgments, or as one in which we derive norms or principles of value from factual assertions.

One may object that it is not, strictly speaking, a logical derivation, for, from the truth of the factual assertions, we cannot guarantee that everyone who understands the factual assertions will adopt the moral commitment. The objection has some force in that we have no guarantee that everyone will feel the force of the imperative, since some will not fulfill the conditions of the antecedent clauses. That is to say, some will not *want* to engage in any continuing human activity, and some may not have the will or capacity to be consistent in what they want.

Although it is possible to make this kind of objection to speaking of the derivation of an "ought" judgment, the objection is attenuated. For this is a normal and natural kind of derivation, although it is not a strictly logical one. The fact is that one could not engage in any discussion which sought to direct action unless those he addressed wanted to engage in some kind of action in the human community and were capable of consistent thought. Indeed, unless a person fulfilled these requirements he could not be regarded as a sane or responsible person. Thus, when we are discussing what is to be done, it is appropriate to assume that those with whom we speak want to do something and that they can entertain consistent thought. Otherwise, moral discourse could have no point.

It is standard and usual for us to take account of the intentions and desires of those with whom we speak, even though we do not make explicit reference to those intentions and desires. Thus, we may calm a child who is waiting for a parade by saying only, "Now you can hear the drums." We are able to read desires and intentions of people generally, often taking other cues from the context. An example is to be found on the road up Pike's Peak; near the summit is a sign which reads simply, "Oh yes you can." It is not necessary to add "make it to the top," and frequently we do not find it necessary to add "if you want to."

In normal moral discourse we assume that our listeners have the desire to live and the capacity for consistent thought. Thus we employ factual statements as warnings: to warn we say simply, "Those are high voltage wires," or "That gun is loaded." And the factual statement carries the force of a warning or an imperative. If a fellow passenger said to you, "If you turn here, we'll all go over the cliff," you would think it odd if he *bothered* to add the moral judgment, "So you ought not to turn here." When I say, "The water has poison in it," I do not normally find it necessary to add "so you ought not to drink it." Neither is it usually necessary to add "if you want to continue living." Wanting to continue living is the common condition of moral discourse.

Thus, we commonly derive the "ought" judgment from the "is" judgment and would think the failure to do so extraordinary. If we inform another person that what he is about to do will hurt another person, then, barring unusual circumstances, we would think it odd if he failed to conclude that he ought not to do it. If a person were judged to be of sound mind and if he understood that by throwing a certain switch he would electrocute all the residents of his street, we would judge him guilty if he threw it.

Moral discussion is standardly conducted within a context where action is to be directed. Clearly no direction as to how to act would be possible where no activity was wanted. And no statements giving direction could be intelligible if one could not see any consequences of a statement. Thus we do not normally hesitate in deriving an "ought" judgment from a description of perilous conditions, and we would find the failure to do so peculiar.

. . .

Stated briefly, the argument shows that, if we can identify conditions or features that are necessary for subsequent action, we will have identified conditions which everyone (who wants to engage in subsequent activity) [3] will have *good reasons* for defending and protecting. In a community where one must choose between conflicting norms and where all other allegedly justifying moral authorities are set aside, these reasons seem to provide the only coherent motive for adopting a norm.

Thus we should not be hesitant about making the move to "ought": if we can identify conditions that are necessary for subsequent human action, we will have identified conditions which everyone (who wants to engage in subsequent activity) *ought* to defend. In a community where allegedly justifying authorities are in conflict, such support makes an ethical "ought" intelligible. Under these circumstances, we ought to investigate and then defend those conditions which are, in fact, necessary to continued human life.

---

[3] It may be that one would regard the discussion with a person who contemplated suicide as a moral discussion. If so, it might be regarded as an exception. (The effective response to a would-be suicide is to try to *create* in him a desire to live by showing one's concern, reminding him of his possibilities, etc.)

Suggested Readings

Edwards, Paul. *The Logic of Moral Discourse*. New York: Free Press, 1955.

Hare, R. M. *The Lanaguage of Morals*. New York: Oxford University Press, 1964.

Nowell-Smith, P. H. *Ethics*. Middlesex, England: Penguin, 1954.

Searle, John R. "How to Derive 'Ought' from 'Is,' " *Philosophical Review* 73 (January 1964).

Stevenson, Charles L. *Facts and Values*. New Haven: Yale University Press, 1963.

section six

ethics and ideology

MASTER AND SLAVE MORALITY

Friedrich Nietzsche

Refraining mutually from injury, violence, and exploitation and placing one's will on a par with that of someone else—this may become, in a certain rough sense, good manners among individuals if the appropriate conditions are present (namely, if these men are actually similar in strength and value standards and belong together in *one* body). But as soon as this principle is extended, and possibly even accepted as the *fundamental principle of society,* it immediately proves to be what it really is—a will to the *denial* of life, a principle of disintegration and decay.

Here we must beware of superficiality and get to the bottom of the matter, resisting all sentimental weakness: life itself is *essentially* appropriation, injury, overpowering of what is alien and weaker; suppression, hardness, imposition of one's own forms, incorporation and at least, at its mildest, exploitation—but why should one always use those words in which a slanderous intent has been imprinted for ages?

Even the body within which individuals treat each other as equals, as suggested before—and this happens in every healthy aristocracy—if it is a living and not a dying body, has to do to other bodies what the individuals within it refrain from doing to each other: it will have to be an incarnate will to power, it will strive to grow, spread, seize, become predominant—not from any morality or immorality but because it is *living* and because life simply *is* will to power. But there is no point on which the

143

ordinary consciousness of Europeans resists instruction as on this: everywhere people are now raving, even under scientific disguises, about coming conditions of society in which "the exploitative aspect" will be removed—which sounds to me as if they promised to invent a way of life that would dispense with all organic funtions. "Exploitation" does not belong to a corrupt or imperfect and primitive society: it belongs to the *essence* of what lives, as a basic organic function; it is a consequence of the will to power, which is after all the will of life.

If this should be an innovation as a theory—as a reality it is the *primordial fact* of all history: people ought to be honest with themselves at least that far.

Wandering through the many subtler and coarser moralities which have so far been prevalent on earth, or still are prevalent, I found that certain features recurred regularly together and were closely associated—until I finally discovered two basic types and one basic difference.

There are *master morality* and *slave morality*—I add immediately that in all the higher and more mixed cultures there also appear attempts at mediation between these two moralities, and yet more often the interpenetration and mutual misunderstanding of both, and at times they occur directly alongside each other—even in the same human being, within a *single* soul. The moral discrimination of values has originated either among a ruling group whose consciousness of its difference from the ruled group was accompanied by delight—or among the ruled, the slaves and dependents of every degree.

In the first case, when the ruling group determines what is "good," the exalted, proud states of the soul are experienced as conferring distinction and determining the order of rank. The noble human being separates from himself those in whom the opposite of such exalted, proud states finds expression: he despises them. It should be noted immediately that in this first type of morality the opposition of "good" and *"bad"* means approximately the same as "noble" and "contemptible." (The opposition of "good" and *"evil"* has a different origin.) One feels contempt for the cowardly, the anxious, the petty, those intent on narrow utility; also for the suspicious with their unfree glances, those who humble themselves, the doglike people who allow themselves to be maltreated, the begging flatterers, above all the liars: it is part of the fundamental faith of all aristocrats that the common people lie. "We truthful ones"—thus the nobility of ancient Greece referred to itself.

It is obvious that moral designations were everywhere first applied to *human beings* and only later, derivatively, to actions. Therefore it is a gross mistake when historians of morality start from such questions as: why was the compassionate act praised? The noble type of man experiences *itself* as determining values; it does not need approval; it judges, "what is harmful to me is harmful in itself"; it knows itself to be that which first accords honor to things; it is *value-creating*. Everything it knows as part of itself it honors: such a morality is self-glorification. In the foreground there is the feeling of fullness, of power that seeks to overflow, the happiness of high tension, the consciousness of wealth that would give and bestow: the noble human being, too, helps the unfortunate, but not, or almost not, from pity, but prompted more by an urge begotten by excess of power. The noble human being honors himself as one who is powerful, also as one who has power over himself, who knows how to speak and be silent, who delights in being severe and hard with himself and respects all severity and hardness. "A hard heart Wotan put into my breast," says an old Scandinavian saga: a fitting poetic expression, seeing that it comes from the soul of a proud Viking. Such a type of man is actually proud of the fact that he is *not* made for pity, and the hero of the saga therefore adds as a warning: "If the heart is not hard in youth it will never harden." Noble and courageous human beings who think that way are furthest removed from that morality which finds the distinction of morality precisely in pity, or in acting for others, or in *désintéressement;* faith in oneself, pride in oneself, a fundamental hostility and irony against "selflessness" belong just as definitely to noble morality as does a slight disdain and caution regarding compassionate feelings and a "warm heart."

It is the powerful who *understand* how to honor; this is their art, their realm of invention. The profound reverence for age and tradition—all law rests on this double reverence—the faith and prejudice in favor of ancestors and disfavor of those yet to come are typical of the morality of the powerful; and when the men of "modern ideas," conversely, believe almost instinctively in "progress" and "the future" and more and more lack respect for age, this in itself would sufficiently betray the ignoble origin of these "ideas."

A morality of the ruling group, however, is most alien and embarrassing to the present taste in the severity of its principle that one has duties only to one's peers; that against beings of a lower rank, against everything alien, one may behave as one pleases or "as the heart desires," and in any case "beyond good and evil"—here pity and like feelings may find their place. The capacity for, and the duty of, long gratitude and long revenge—both only among one's peers—refinement in repaying, the sophisticated concept of friendship, a certain necessity for having enemies (as it were, as drainage ditches for the affects of envy, quarrelsomeness, exuberance—at bottom, in order to be capable of being good *friends*): all these are typical characteristics of noble morality which, as suggested, is not the morality of "modern ideas" and therefore is hard to empathize with today, also hard to dig up and uncover.

It is different with the second type of morality, *slave morality.* Suppose the violated, oppressed, suffering, unfree, who are uncertain of themselves and weary, moralize: what will their moral valuations have in common? Probably, a pessimistic suspicion about the whole condition of man will find expression, perhaps a condemnation of man along with his condition. The slave's eye is not favorable to the virtues of the powerful: he is skeptical and suspicious, *subtly* suspicious, of all the "good" that is honored there—he would like to persuade himself that even their happiness is not genuine. Conversely, those qualities are brought out and flooded with light which serve to ease existence for those who suffer: here pity, the complaisant and obliging hand, the warm heart, patience, industry, humility, and friendliness are honored—for here these are the most useful qualities and almost the only means for enduring the pressure of existence. Slave morality is essentially a morality of utility.

Here is the place for the origin of that famous opposition of "good" and "evil": into evil one's feelings project power and dangerousness, a certain terribleness, subtlety, and strength that does not permit contempt to develop. According to slave morality, those who are "evil" thus inspire fear; according to master morality it is precisely those who are "good" that inspire, and wish to inspire, fear, while the "bad" are felt to be contemptible.

The opposition reaches its climax when, as a logical consequence of slave morality, a touch of disdain is associated also with the "good" of this morality—this may be slight and benevolent—because the good human being has to be *undangerous* in the slaves' way of thinking: he is good-natured, easy to deceive, a little stupid perhaps, *un bonhomme.* Wherever slave morality becomes preponderant, language tends to bring the words "good" and "stupid" closer together.

One last fundamental difference: the longing for *freedom,* the instinct for happiness and the subtleties of the feeling of freedom belong just as necessarily to slave morality and morals as artful and enthusiastic reverence and devotion are the regular symptom of an aristocratic way of thinking and evaluating.

. . .

MORALITY AS CLASS INTEREST

Frederick Engels

. . .

. . . The conceptions of good and bad have varied so much from nation to nation and from age to age that they have often been in direct contradiction to each other. But all the same, someone may object, good is not bad and bad is not good; if good is confused with bad there is an end to all morality, and everyone can do and leave undone whatever he cares. This is also, stripped of all oracular phrases, Herr Dühring's opinion.* But the matter cannot be so simply disposed of. If it was such an easy business there would certainly be no dispute at all over good and bad; everyone would know

---

* Eugen Dühring was a Professor at the University of Berlin and a socialist thinker who had a small following within the Social Democratic Party of Germany. He claimed to derive socialist theory from a more abstract philosophical system in which there were, among other things, ultimate and eternal moral truths. *The Anti-Dühring,* from which this essay is taken, is a collection of polemical articles attacking Dühring written by Engels between the years 1877 and 1878.—Eds.

what was good and what was bad. But how do things stand today? What morality is preached to us today? There is first Christian-feudal morality, inherited from past periods of faith; and this again has two main subdivisions, Catholic and Protestant moralities, each of which in turn has no lack of further subdivisions from the Jesuit-Catholic and Orthodox-Protestant to loose "advanced" moralities. Alongside of these we find the modern bourgeois morality and with it too the proletarian morality of the future, so that in the most advanced European countries alone the past, present and future provide three great groups of moral theories which are in force simultaneously and alongside of one another. Which is then the true one? Not one of them, in the sense of having absolute validity; but certainly that morality which contains the maximum of durable elements is the one which, in the present, represents the overthrow of the present, represents the future: that is, the proletarian.

But when we see that the three classes of modern society, the feudal aristocracy, the bourgeoisie and the proletariat, each have their special morality, we can only draw the conclusion, that men, consciously or unconsciously, derive their moral ideas in the last resort from the practical relations on which their class position is based—from the economic relations in which they carry on production and exchange.

But nevertheless there is much that is common to the three moral theories mentioned above—is this not at least a portion of a morality which is externally fixed? These moral theories represent three different stages of the same historical development, and have therefore a common historical background, and for that reason alone they necessarily have much in common. Even more. In similar or approximately similar stages of economic development moral theories must of necessity be more or less in agreement. From the moment when private property in movable objects developed, in all societies in which this private property existed there must be this moral law in common: Thou shalt not steal. Does this law thereby become an eternal moral law? By no means. In a society in which the motive for stealing has been done away with, in which therefore at the very most only lunatics would ever steal, how the teacher of morals would be laughed at who tried solemnly to proclaim the eternal truth: Thou shalt not steal!

We therefore reject every attempt to impose on us any moral dogma whatsoever as an eternal, ultimate and forever immutable moral law on the pretext that the moral world too has its permanent principles which transcend history and the differences between nations. We maintain on the contrary that all former moral theories are the product, in the last analysis, of the economic stage which society had reached at that particular epoch. And as society has hitherto moved in class antagonisms, morality was always a class morality; it has either justified the domination and the interests of the ruling class, or, as soon as the oppressed class has become powerful enough, it has represented the revolt against this domination and the future interests of the oppressed. That in this process there has on the whole been progress in morality, as in all other branches of human knowledge, cannot be doubted. But we have not yet passed beyond class morality. A really human morality which transcends class antagonisms and their legacies in thought becomes possible only at a stage of society which has not only overcome class contradictions but has even forgotten them in practical life. And now it is possible to appreciate the presumption shown by Herr Dühring in advancing his claim, from the midst of the old class society and on the eve of a social revolution, to impose on the future classless society an eternal morality which is independent of time and changes in reality. Even assuming—what we do not know up to now—that he understands the structure of the society of the future at least in its main outlines.

Finally, one more revelation which is "absolutely original" but for that reason no less "going to the roots of things." With regard to the origin of evil, we have "the fact that the *type of the cat* with the guile associated with it is found in animal form, and the similar fact that a similar type of character is found also in human beings. . . . There is therefore nothing mysterious about evil, unless someone wants to scent out something mysterious in the existence of that *cat* or of any animal of prey." Evil is—the cat. The devil therefore has no horns or cloven hoof, but claws and green eyes. And Goethe committed an unpardonable error in presenting Mephistopheles as a black dog instead of the said cat. Evil is the cat! That is morality, not only for all worlds, but also—of no use to anyone!

. . .

The idea that all men, as men, have something in common, and that they are therefore equal so far as these common characteristics go, is of course primeval. But the modern demand for equality is something entirely different from that; this consists rather in deducing from those common characteristics of humanity, from that equality of men as men, a claim to equal political or social status for all human beings, or at least for all citizens of a state or all members of a society. Before the original conception of relative equality could lead to the conclusion that men should have equal rights in the state and in society, before this conclusion could appear to be something even natural and self-evident, however, thousands of years had to pass and did pass. In the oldest primitive communities equality of rights existed at most for members of the community; women, slaves and strangers were excluded from this equality as a matter of course. Among the Greeks and Romans the inequalities of men were of greater importance than any form of equality. It would necessarily have seemed idiotic to the ancients that Greeks and barbarians, freemen and slaves, citizens and dependents, Roman citizens and Roman subjects (to use a comprehensive term) should have a claim to equal political status. Under the Roman Empire all these distinctions gradually disappeared, except the distinction between freemen and slaves, and in this way there arose, for the freemen at least, that equality as between private individuals on the basis of which Roman law developed—the complete elaboration of law based on private property which we know. But so long as the distinction between freemen and slaves existed, there could be no talk of drawing legal conclusions from the fact of general equality *as men;* and we saw this again quite recently, in the slave-owning states of the North American Union.

Christianity knew only *one* point in which all men were equal: that all were equally born in original sin—which corresponded perfectly with its character as the religion of the slaves and the oppressed. Apart from this is recognised, at most, the equality of the elect, which however was only stressed at the very beginning. The traces of common ownership which are also found in the early stages of the new religion can be ascribed to the solidarity of a proscribed sect rather than to real equalitarian ideas. Within a very short time the establishment of the distinction between priests and laymen put an end even to this tendency to Christian equality. The overrunning of Western Europe by the Germans abolished for centuries all ideas of equality, through the gradual building up of a complicated social and political hierarchy such as had never before existed. But at the same time the invasion drew Western and Central Europe into the course of historical development, created for the first time a compact cultural area, and within this area also for the first time a system of predominantly national states exerting mutual influence on each other and mutually holding each other in check. Thereby it prepared the ground on which alone the question of the equal status of men, of the rights of man, could at a later period be raised.

The feudal Middle Ages also developed in its womb the class which was destined in the future course of its evolution to be the standard-bearer of the modern demand for equality: the bourgeoisie. Itself in its origin one of the "estates" of the feudal order, the bourgeoisie developed the predominantly handicraft industry and the exchange of products within feudal society to a relatively high level, when at the end of the fifteenth century the great maritime discoveries opened to it a new and more comprehensive career. Trade beyond the confines of Europe, which had previously been carried on only between Italy and the Levant, was now extended to America and India, and soon surpassed in importance both the mutual exchange between the various European countries and the internal trade within each separate country. American gold and silver flooded Europe and forced its way like a disintegrating element into every fissure, hole and pore of feudal society. Handicraft industry could no longer satisfy the rising demand; in the leading industries of the most advanced countries it was replaced by manufacture.

But this mighty revolution in the economic conditions of life in society was not followed immediately by any corresponding change in its political structure. The state order remained feudal, while society became more and more bourgeois. Trade on a large scale, that is to say, international and, even more, world trade, requires free owners of commodities who are unrestricted in their movements and have equal rights as traders to exchange their commodities on the basis of laws that are equal for them all, at least in each separate place. The transition from handicraft to manufacture presupposes the existence of a number of free workers—free on the one hand from the fetters of the guild and on the other from the means whereby they could themselves utilise their labour power: workers who can contract with their employers for the hire of their labour power, and as parties to the contract have rights equal with his. And finally the equality and equal status of all human labour, because and in so far as it is *human* labour, found its unconscious but clearest expression in the law of value of modern bourgeois economics, according to which the value of a commodity is measured by the socially necessary labour embodied in it. But where economic relations required freedom and equality of rights, the political system opposed them at every step with guild restrictions and special privileges. Local privileges, differential duties, exceptional laws of all kinds affected in trading not only foreigners or people living in the colonies, but often enough also whole categories of the nationals of each country; the privileges of the guilds everywhere and ever anew formed barriers to the path of development of manufacture. Nowhere was the path open and the chances equal for the bourgeois competitors—and yet this was the first and ever more pressing need.

The demand for liberation from feudal fetters and the establishment of equality of rights by the abolition of feudal inequalities was bound soon to assume wider dimensions from the moment when the economic advance of society first placed it on the order of the day. If it was raised in the interests of industry and trade, it was also necessary to demand the same equality of rights for the great mass of the peasantry who, in every degree of bondage from total serfdom upwards, were compelled to give the greater part of their labour time to their feudal lord without payment and in addition to render innumerable other dues to him and to the state. On the other hand, it was impossible to avoid the demand for the abolition also of feudal privileges, the freedom from taxation of the nobility, the political privileges of the various feudal estates. And as people were no longer living in a world empire such as the Roman Empire had been, but in a system of independent states dealing with each other on an equal footing and at approximately the same degree of bourgeois development, it was a matter of course that the demand for equality should assume a general character reaching out beyond the individual state, that freedom and equality should be proclaimed as *human rights*. And it is significant of the specifically bourgeois character of these human rights that the American Constitution, the first to recognize the rights of man, in the same breath confirmed the slavery of the coloured races in America: class privileges were proscribed, race privileges sanctified.

As is well known, however, from the moment when, like a butterfly from the chrysalis, the bourgeoisie arose out of the burghers of the feudal period, when this "estate" of the Middle Ages developed into a class of modern society, it was always and inevitably accompanied by its shadow, the proletariat. And in the same way the bourgeois demand for equality was accompanied by the proletarian demand for equality. From the moment when the bourgeois demand for the abolition of class *privileges* was put forward, alongside of it appeared the proletarian demand for the abolition of the *classes themselves*—at first in religious form, basing itself on primitive Christianity, and later drawing support from the bourgeois equalitarian theories themselves. The proletarians took the bourgeoisie at their word: equality must not be merely apparent, must not apply merely to the sphere of the state, but must also be real, must be extended to the social and economic sphere. And especially since the time when the French bourgeoisie, from the Great Revolution on, brought bourgeois equality to the forefront, the French proletariat has answered it blow for blow with the demand for social and economic equality, and equality has become the battle-cry particularly of the French proletariat.

The demand for equality in the mouth of the proletariat has therefore a double meaning. It is either—as was especially the case at the very start, for example in the peasants' war—the spontaneous reaction against the crying social inequalities, against the contrast of rich and poor, the feudal lords and their serfs, surfeit and starvation; as such it is the simple expression of the revolutionary instinct, and finds its justification in that, and indeed only in that. Or, on the other hand, the proletarian demand for equality has arisen as the reaction against the bourgeois demand for equality, drawing more or less correct and more far-reaching demands from this bourgeois demand, and serving as an agitational means in order to rouse the workers against the capitalists on the basis of the capitalists' own assertions; and in this case it stands and falls with bourgeois equality itself. In both cases the real content of the proletarian demand for equality is the demand for the *abolition of classes*. Any demand for equality which goes beyond that, of necessity passes into absurdity. . . .

The idea of equality, therefore, both in its bourgeois and in its proletarian form, is itself a historical product, the creation of which required definite historical conditions which in turn themselves presuppose a long previous historical development. It is therefore anything but an eternal truth. And if today it is taken for granted by the general public—in one sense or another—if, as Marx says, it "already possesses the fixity of a popular prejudice," this is not the consequence of its axiomatic truth, but the result of the general diffusion and the continued appropriateness of the ideas of the eighteenth century. . . .

MORALITY AND IDEOLOGY

Henry David Aiken

. . .

I wish now to examine, all too briefly and schematically, certain interesting dialectical relationships between morality and ideology. To this end, let me introduce two parallel distinctions, first between the moral agent, or man of conscience as I shall sometimes call him, and the moralist, and then between the ideologue, or agent of some ideology, and the ideologist.

By a moral agent, or man of conscience, I mean of course simply any individual in his daily activity of trying, according to his lights, to determine what he ought to do in his dealings with other persons, what principles he should try to live by, and how he ought to comport himself toward the otherwise non-moral or extra-moral enterprises that impinge upon his moral concerns, and hence create for him genuine problems of moral choice. On the other hand, the moralist, as I conceive him here, is one whose concern is to understand morality and, so to say, to represent it at that court of reason where philosophical critiques are supposedly conducted. When he performs his role systematically and with a view to all the limiting questions which the moral agent may raise, the moralist of course becomes by stages the moral philosopher. My concern here, however, is not directly with the moral philosopher who, just because he is a philosopher, must have already moved beyond the perspectives afforded by morality alone, but simply the moralist whose whole loyalty is to the moral agent. In passing it is worth emphasizing that the moral agent, not the moralist, is the fundamental moral reality; moralists and moral philosphers, however valuable their services, always ride piggyback on his shoulders. They can make sense in the end only to the extent that he already has made a sense for them to examine and to represent. Accordingly they should keep their place and not try, as some moralists have done, to usurp his role and hence to give to morality a bad name which should be reserved for bad moralists and moral philosophers.

By analogy, an ideologue is one who, like the original ideologues of France or like the Marxists, the Fascists, or the liberal democrats, advocates and represents some particular ideology. Any ideologue always faces other ideologues as a partisan. His role, therefore, is not to explain or defend ideology, but only to employ the forms and resources of ideological discourse or action in making his ideological commitments prevail. By an ideologist, on the other hand, is to be understood, by analogy with the moralist, one whose role is to explain and to represent ideology at the philosophical court of reason.[1]

What I wish first to consider now are the relations between the moralist and the ideologist in their own somewhat abstract confrontations. Now it seems to me plain enough that the moralist cannot oppose ideology as such on the grounds that it is prone

---

[1] By a series of obvious inversions we may envisage the pure anti-ideologist who opposes, or professes to oppose, ideology as a form of thought and of life, as well as the anti-moralist as one who opposes the whole notion of personal moral activity, including moral judgment, justification, and agency and who, if he could, would root out the whole complex of moral sentiments, including, for example, indignation, guilt, gratitude, and respect. The immoralist, however, is a more difficult and elusive notion. For present purposes it may suffice to define the immoralist as a moral agent who, on principle, systematically acts against the moral principles of persons with whom he stands ordinarily in close and permanent moral relations. Thus, for example, the concept of the anti-moralist emerges fairly clearly in some of the writings of Nietzsche and, on some interpretations, in those of Freud, whereas that of the immoralist is perhaps best exemplified in the work of such writers as André Gide. I know of no established term for the ideologue who, by analogy to the immoralist, seeks systematically to undermine an ideology accepted by a group of persons with whom he is deeply and permanently involved and whose affairs are of constant concern to him. For the sake of discussion I shall call him simply a counter-ideologue. Now it seems to me, that in some veins Gabriel Marcel and Martin Buber and perhaps Albert Camus may be viewed as genuine anti-ideologists, whereas most representatives of the end-of-ideology school in America and England are not anti-ideologists but counter-ideologues who do not fully understand the nature of their own position.

to irrationalism, that it involves the use of myths or appeals to supernatural authorities, or that it is extremist or utopian. For some forms of ideology do not exemplify these characteristics; moreover, some forms of moral thought do exemplify them. There are ideological extremists such as the Populists who are prepared to sacrifice every other social or political end to the will of the many. But there are also ideological moderates such as James Madison who seek a social system that balances the will of the many against the need for a rule of law and the passion for liberty against the need for security and social justice. Likewise, there are moral extremists, who, like Antigone, would sacrifice every other right or good upon the altar of a particular principle. But there are moral compromisers who, like Aristotle, defend on principle the principles of adjustment and reconciliation. Thus the tension between the moralist and the ideologist must be located elsewhere.

Now there is a great passage in the first chapter of G. E. Moore's *Principia Ethica* which, as it seems to me, provides a clue to what we are looking for. In summarizing his objections to the tendency of ethical naturalists (as he calls them) to define moral goodness in terms of some objective property that is, or is alleged to be, common to morally good things, Moore goes beyond the point which he has hitherto been making, namely, that the naturalist is guilty of the logical error of confusing distinct ideas, to the new and extremely important contention that the tendency to identify moral goodness as such with some prevailing standard or criterion of moral goodness, some factor or property of things which is, or may be thought to make them good, can also be a source of grave moral error. Thus, says Moore, "If we start with the conviction that a definition of good can be found, we start with the conviction that good *can mean* nothing else than some one property of things; and our only business will then be to discover what that property is. But if we recognize that, so far as the meaning of good goes, anything whatever may be good, we start with a much more open mind." I myself am not suggesting, as Moore seems to be doing here, that the individual moral agent himself must be an advocate of the open mind. The advocate of extreme open-mindedness in morals represents a particular moral point of view which could easily lead to moral skepticism and paralysis of the will. However, Moore's statement supplies the text for a very different thesis, namely that the kind of extreme open-mindedness which Moore himself apparently advocates here is at least morally possible. If this thesis is correct, as I believe it to be, then the moralist, as an advocate of the moral life, is bound to defend a form of life that *makes* such open-mindedness possible. In short, the moralist is defending, among other things, not the obligation of the moral agent to keep his infernal open question "but is it good?" going in the face of all difficulties including possible alienation from all of his peers, but his prerogative to do so. And in defending this prerogative, this moral possibility, he is bound on principle to be suspicious of the tendency inherent in any ideology, liberal as well as illiberal, to require of its devotees unquestioning submission to its own creed. A liberal ideology may be as individualistic as you please; but, as an ideology, it is to that extent hostile to any moral agent who questions whether he ought to adhere to its premises. And, in short, the moralist, concerned as he is to defend the prerogatives of first-personal moral judgment and decision, and hence the fundamentality of purely first-personal relations and first-personal responsibilities among men, is bound to be hostile to the tendency of every ideologue to adopt the impersonal tone of the functionary and the official spokesman, even when the latter speaks as an exponent of something called "the free society," "democratic liberalism," or "the rule of law." Again, every ideologue, just because he represents an orthodoxy to which he is committed as the member of a class or group, is bound to resent precisely those limiting questions which even the most sympathetic moral agent, in no name but his own, is capable of raising. Hence, the moralist who, for his part, is bound to defend such questions, as well as the prerogatives, the self-constituting and self-construed authority of him who raises them, will inevitably be suspicious of any ideologue, however liberal or open-ended the point of view he represents, who as an ideologue, is bound impersonally to censure any member of his party who, peremptorily and without a by-your-leave, raises the ancient first-person scruple, "But after all is said and done, ought I really to be all that liberal and open-minded in my thought and action?" It is, in short, the orthodoxy of the ideologue, not the principles which he orthodoxly adheres to, which the moralist must resent. And it is precisely this resentment which even the orthodox liberal finds it so hard to understand or to forgive. "In God's name," we can hear him cry, "what does the moralist want that we liberals are not prepared to grant his blasted moral agent?" And to this the moralist can only reply. "Nothing really, except acknowledgment of the possibility that the moral agent, the man of conscience may seriously ask whether after all liberalism may be wrong, and thus to treat himself in relation to liberalism as, in principle, an independent moral agent and critic."

The moralist, it should be understood, is not necessarily defending subjectivism as against objectivism. The ordinary moral agent, as I have tried to show elsewhere, is by no means a principled subjectivist; on the contrary, he has his own conscientious way of being, or trying to be objective, through reconsideration and sober second thought. But objectiv*ism,* which precludes the very possibility of untrammeled first-personal reconsideration and appraisal, is inherent in every form of ideological thought, no matter how liberal may be its principles. The ideologue, even at his most visionary and utopian, never speaks merely for his own visions but always in behalf of a group; he never gives us simply his own sober second thoughts, never tells us simply what he, as a person, considers to be right or good or true or beautiful. And in a word, it is not the objectivity of the ideologue which the moralist may seem to oppose, but his objectivism. And what makes him uneasy in the presence of all ideological discourse is the incessant, impersonal drone of the establishmentarian, the representative man, the wholly public personage.

On the other side, the ideologist is as naturally and properly suspicious of the very conscientiousness of the moral agent who, in reserving his judgment or his question, makes it clear that he cannot be absolutely trusted as the member of any party, however splendid its cause, or the absolute adherent to any orthodoxy, however ancient its lineage. What galls the ideologist in the case of Socrates is not that he has gone whoring after false or foreign gods but that he has his own daemon, not his opinions, but his opinionatedness, his presumption of a right or an obligation to stand alone even against the liberal, democratic orthodoxy of the *polis*. Again, what worried the spokesmen of the ancient regime in the case of Voltaire was not so much his social and political opinions as his presumption of a duty to offer them on his own. The French ideologues regarded him as a cultural hero; yet they would have found him, just as the Athenians found Socrates, a thorn in their flesh. The moralist must find something reassuring and refreshing, something incomparably choice, in a Thoreau. But the ideologist is bound to regard Thoreau as, at best, a kind of fool, absurdly going his own way even when he has, really, nowhere to go, and at worst as a kind of symbol of the unsafe, the untrustworthy, unrepresentative man who refuses to pay his taxes just to prove a point. What gravels the ideologist in a word is not the objective behavior, the substantive public acts of the Thoreaus of the world, most of whom, of course, are harmless enough, but simply the fact that they have consciences of their own.

At this point I can imagine that some one will exclaim, as did the reader of an earlier version of this paper, "But don't you see? You yourself have destroyed ideology. The ideologist is a golem, a pure example of the organization man who believes in organization for its own sake and at all costs. The moralist, whatever his faults, is defending the little fellow, the individual person. In an age of ideologies, he represents the spirit of the resistance which you yourself have often extolled. He is the original, final enemy of totalitarianism, of the soul-destroying collective in which all independence and all personal freedom is lost." There is power in this criticism. Can anything be said in reply?

Let us recall our distinctions between the ideologist and the ideologue and the moralist and the moral agent, the man with a conscience. The man with a conscience is not called upon to defend something called morality at all costs; nor is he bound *a priori* to be a moralist. Suppose now we take another look at the moralist, against his own protests, from an ideological point of view. Who, among the varieties of idoelogue, is his counterpart? I think the answer is plain. He is the absolute anarchist, the utopian counter-ideologue who, abstractly and on principle, despises and condemns the bureaucrat, the functionary, the organization man and the forms of life generally associated with the social system. In a word, he is the ideologue to end all ideologues. Americans are traditionally and sentimentally attracted to such a figure. He is the Henry David Thoreau of *Civil Disobedience* and *Walden;* he is also Huckleberry Finn, the Outcast of Poker Flat, the Lone Ranger, and a thousand and one other free spirits that live out of time, out of history, in the literary imagination.

Let us recall also that the actual moral agent finds himself, as is and in context, bound by certain particular moral judgments and decisions. Regardless of his inclination, like you or me, he finds, willy-nilly, that he has assumed certain responsibilities and, accordingly, that he *ought* to fulfill them. Or else he perceives that he has failed to do what he should have done and so is in conscience bound to make amends. His commitment is to what, according to his conscience, he finds to be right, not to an abstract idea entitled "morality." It is not difficult to conceive a moral agent, a man of conscience, who finds himself, as matters stand, profoundly committed to certain historical institutional practices or activities, such as a rule of law or a bill of rights, and to the covering ideological traditions that have been their doctrinal shields. Nor is it hard to imagine that such a person might find it simply frivolous, in a situation where such traditions and practices are under systematic and continual attack, merely to represent the moralist, that is to say, the ahistorical anarchist who is so obsessed by the idea of the *tête à tête*, the dialogical, or I-Thou, relationship that he ignores the only historical institutions that, in reality, have enabled such relationships to exist. The historical Socrates, be it recalled, elected to stay in Athens and to submit to the verdict of the ideologues, the functionaries, the public men who had condemned him to death.

My conclusion is this. Few men of good will, when they examine their consciences, can condemn the ideologue out of hand. The ideologue may not be loveable; undoubtedly he is a tedious dinner companion. But if the ideology which he professes is, on the whole, beneficent and will, in practice, serve the cause of peace and the amelioration of the lot of the great masses of suffering humanity, I will take him any time in preference to the moralist whose only concern is the good conscience itself. There are ideologies and ideologies, some bad, some indifferent, a few useful. Ideologies, like other forms of life, are as they do. And by their fruits so should we judge them. Meanwhile, we have our consciences to live with as we can in an age of perpetual crisis in which each of us is faced with moral problems of unprecedented difficulty, and the whole world is confronted with tasks of ideological reconstruction and creation which will not be finished for many generations.

Suggested Readings

Corbett, Patrick. *Ideologies.* New York: Harcourt, Brace, 1965.

Mannheim, Karl. *Ideology and Utopia.* New York: Harcourt, Brace, 1936.

Marx, Karl, and Frederick Engels. *The German Ideology.* New York: International Publishers, 1960.

Nietzsche, Friedrich. *The Genealogy of Morals.* Translated by Francis Golffing. New York: Doubleday Anchor, 1956.

part
2

contemporary moral problems

Our society receives its unique historical character from the extraordinary technological development that has marked the last fifty years. This development has given rise to new moral concerns in a number of ways. First, the technological development itself presents possibilities for human achievement that were, at the most, merely dreams in the past: an abundance of goods that creates the potential for a society where no one need want for the basic necessities and where the historical emphasis on increased productivity may no longer be meaningful or relevant; advances in medicine and psychiatry that raise questions about the use to which this knowledge should or should not be put; contraceptive techniques that have transformed our sexual mores; the development of television and print media of such vast proportions that they can manipulate the consciousness of a nation. Second, the same technology has created problems that threaten the very existence of the human race—terrifying instruments of war and an industrial waste that is on the verge of making the earth uninhabitable by most forms of life. Finally, modern technology has provided the base for new social forces and has given impetus to social and political tendencies that are now just beginning to come into their own.

What all this means is that ethical considerations now occur in a setting where large numbers of people are demanding fundamental changes in our attitudes and institutions. The first section of Part 2, "Oppression and Liberation," is concerned with understanding what it means to be oppressed and what it might mean to be free. Through these readings we focus on two aspects of oppression: the first consists of objectively real power relations that rob us of power over our lives and turn our physical selves into instruments to be used by others for their own ends; the second is concerned with mental attitudes toward ourselves and others that render all of us less free. Racism, sexism, and other forms of oppression must be dealt with in terms of these two components if we are ever to move toward the kind of personal and social liberation that the writers of these essays seem to envision.

One of the consequences of the various movements for social change in conjunction with the technological advances we have been considering is that we must rethink our concept of murder (see Section Two, "Killing and Murder").

By "murder" we do not refer to *any* act of killing, but specifically to *unjustified* or *wrongful* killing. So we must ask, when and under what conditions is killing unjustified (wrong)? Most people would agree that it is perfectly legitimate to kill trees in order to get paper and firewood, to kill insects that are destroying crops, and to use antibiotics to kill bacteria that cause disease. But beyond these sorts of examples we find extensive disagreement, intensified by the social movement of the last decade. Is abortion a form of murder? Most women's liberation groups argue that it is not and that a woman's right to the control of her own body overrides the so-called right of the fetus. Is it wrong to kill in time of war? The traditional answer is that it is not only proper to kill for one's country but it is one's duty. In contrast, the pacifist answers that no authority can legitimize the taking of human life. In recent years, every newspaper we read, every news broadcast we hear forces us to face the question of violence. When those who are disenfranchised and desperate employ increasingly violent means to secure their liberation, we are forced to ask when and if violence against the state can be justified. How are we to understand the desperate acts of terrorist groups in America and abroad who cry out for justice and dignity, but who are also convinced that these ends can only be achieved through the use of violence? The American civil rights movement of the early sixties followed Gandhi's example of nonviolent civil disobedience. So, at first, did the antiwar movement. But by the end of the sixties we had witnessed ghetto rebellions, bombings, and forms of confrontation and political disobedience that no longer had the same scrupulous respect for the principle of nonviolence. Are things getting out of hand? Have the original ideals of these movements for social justice been depreciated? Can a just cause ever justify these violent means? Are we, as Howard Zinn suggests, too quick to jump to a violent solution when a nonviolent alternative may be as effective?

Let us take a closer look at the violence/nonviolence dichotomy. What kinds of acts should count as acts of violence? In the past, attacks on property by persons opposed to the system have been called "violent," while even direct physical assaults committed by the system's representatives have been masked by other words (for example, "protective reaction"). Now, some like Michael Lerner ask us to redefine the concept of violence so that it includes the effects of the system itself when it deprives some of its citizens of lives of dignity and health. When this is the case, the choice is not between violence and nonviolence, but between violence in the interest of oppression and violence in the interest of liberation.

The third and fourth sections of Part 2 ("Work and Play and the Protestant Ethic" and "Sexual Morality") confront the changing ideology of our era. With the coming of automation and with scientists predicting that in the not very distant future a very small percentage of the world's population may be able to produce all that is necessary for the world's needs, the work ethic seems strangely out of place. Increasingly, labor unions are placing their emphasis, not on demands for higher pay, but on achieving better working conditions—ones that will help overcome the increasing alienation, boredom, and frustration of the worker. The four-day workweek is being discussed as a real possibility for the seventies. And many of today's youth are seeking to experiment with new forms of living arrangements in which both work and leisure become more integrated into their lives. Similarly, with the greater emphasis on leisure time and the kinds of contraceptive devices available, a significant offensive has been launched against traditional sexual attitudes. Not only have such concepts as "virginity before marriage," "infidelity," and "sexual perversion" come under attack, but also marriage itself, and even the value of a monogamous relationship (with or without marriage), is called into question. Again, as the increase in communal sexual experiments suggests, the challenge to traditional sexual morality is taking place not only in theory but in practice.

Sections Five and Six ("Medical and Psychiatric Ethics" and "Business Ethics and Social Responsibility") examine the moral implications of two fundamental institutions that have been profoundly affected by the development of scientific knowledge and industry. Given the phenomenal advances that have been made in modern medicine in the past few years, and the potential for still more amazing discoveries, under what conditions is it legitimate to experiment with human subjects? Are there times when we should refrain from using all the means within our power to preserve human life? When, if at all, should we employ the medical techniques devised to control human behavior (drug therapy, electric shock, psychosurgery)? Do we have the right to forcibly confine someone for psychiatric reasons? Is "mental illness" primarily a medical or a moral category?

Similarly, when gargantuan monopolies condition so many aspects of our lives, we must begin to evaluate business practices under moral categories. What, for instance, constitutes a legitimate use of advertising techniques, and how far should advertisers be permitted to go in developing their own particular kind of "truth" (for example, "Use brand X cologne and women will drop at your feet."). At what point should shady business practices, which are technically legal, become subject to moral criticism and censure, and at what point should such moral censure be reflected in the law? More significantly, the rise of corporate conglomerates presses us to ask what the corporation's responsibility is to the public at large. Does the corporate executive have a primary obligation to his or her stockholders or does he or she have a more basic obligation to promote the public good? What is the relation between the pursuit of the public good and an economy that operates in the interest of maximizing private profits? What is the relation between government controls and economic competition? Two of the selections in Section Six confront these last two problems directly. While Friedrich Hayek looks with alarm at the movement toward a planned economy and argues that state intervention is legitimate only as a means to develop more optimum conditions for economic competition, André Gorz contends that the public good can be achieved only through a system which produces in the interest of human need and not in the interest of profit. Ultimately, this becomes a debate between the respective merits of capitalism and socialism.

Finally, the last section, "Just Distribution and the Social Good," raises what may be the most basic moral problem that confronts us today. It is a problem at least as old as Plato, who, in *The Republic,* set out to find the nature of Justice; but it is one that receives a new impetus from the achievements of contemporary industrial society in the output of goods and services and a new sense of urgency from the increasingly militant movements for social change. Specifically, insofar as we are confronted with a tremendous productive capacity and, at least in American society, with a huge wealth of goods, we must ask: How should these goods be distributed? Should we give more to those who work hardest, or to those who have special skills, or to those who have inherited great wealth? Shall we simply let people compete and allow luck together with some combination of the above to win out? Shall we divide the wealth equally, giving each person an identical share? Or shall we give "to each according to his needs," no matter what his or her talents and abilities may be? These questions are at once practical and moral: practical, in that we must consider how a society based on any of these principles would function (or, indeed, if it could function); moral, in that to opt for any one of these principles is to choose the kind of society we would most want to live in and, if this choice is not to be based simply on personal, self-serving interests, to choose the kind of society we think most reasonable and just.

section one

oppression and liberation

POWERLESSNESS

Michael Lerner

On July 22, 1971, the *Wall Street Journal* carried a report that captures the flavor of the situation of American workers today. Consider some excerpts from that story:

It was 1940 when Elmer Novak walked out of his sophomore year in high school and into the coal mines, just as his brothers had before him and father before them. Thirty-one years later, Elmer Novak has a mortgage, 10 kids and black lung. Looking back, he says he would never have gone down to the mines if he hadn't felt he had to. But there was not then—and there is not now—much else to do around Edensburg, Pa., a tiny town on the western slopes of the Allegheny mountains. As a 100 pound, 17-year-old, Elmer Novak started as a track layer's helper at $6.75 a day and graduated in a few months to pick-and-shovel miner at 65¢ a ton. . . . Today Elmer Novak is a member of the rock crew at Number 32 mine of Bethlehem Mines Corp., where he timbers walls. He takes home $120 a week, often works in water up to his ankles, never has a coffee break, takes half an hour to eat lunch from a tin bucket and works a rotating shift. After three decades, he is still not used to the danger or the coal dust or the chill in a mine shaft 1000 feet under ground. At home, he never talks about his job, and his wife never asks. He has never had a new car or a savings account, and he says there is "no way I could raise $100 in an emergency." Elmer Novak has 14 years to go before he can retire on a union pension that currently is $150 a month—unless his illness worsens before that time and he can apply for black lung benefits. . . . Why does Elmer Novak continue to work at a job that has cost him his health and paid him a wage that he had to struggle on all his grown life? "There aren't many jobs around here for a high school dropout," he says. "I'd leave in a minute, but where would I go?" That is the dilemma of millions of relatively unskilled manual laborers across the country. They mine coal, shovel steel slag, gut animal carcasses, sort mail, clean hotel rooms, bend over sewing machines and perform a thousand other grueling or mind-deadening tasks. . . . And when they are asked, as several dozen of them recently were by *Wall Street Journal* reporters, why they keep at it, most of them echo Elmer Novak: Where else would I go? . . . Most of them know they are not on the very bottom of the economic heap: they are *not* among the 17 million workers in the country—over 30% of the work force—who earn less than $5000 a year. But for the privilege of escaping poverty they have paid the price of accepting labor that ranges from grinding to merely monotonous, under conditions that range from uncomfortable to miserable. Few of them hope anymore for anything better. All of them say they learned long ago to simply stop thinking about the way things might have been. . . . Many of them hate every minute on the job. But a surprising number of them take a measure of pride in performing well jobs that can only be described as either back-breaking or deadly dull. . . .

Marvin Conyers works the 3:30 to midnight shift on "the line"—the assembly line at Chrysler Corporation's Jefferson Avenue plant in Detroit. Mr. Conyers, 34 years old and the father of five, has been on the line for seven years now, and he says bluntly and with considerable despair, that it is brutal. Mr. Conyers' job involves physical effort and strain, but unlike Elmer Novak . . . he doesn't lift heavy loads all day long. What he does is perform a job so monotonous and bleak that it drives him into a mental trance daily. . . . For eight years, he worked selling insurance or as a helper at his aunt's restaurant. He says he enjoyed that, but with a growing family he decided in 1964 to return to the line. Mr. Conyers is better off now than he was then. At first, "I had to climb over into the trunk, weld in the back window, climb down, and get ready for the next car. I did that eight or nine hours a day, about one car every fifty seconds. . . . I think about everything, just everything, to keep my mind occupied. The day goes by real slow. It seems like 16 hours." . . . Alcohol and drugs are rampant, and Mr. Conyers admits he once or twice has been drunk on the job himself. Nearly 6% of the workers at the Jefferson plant don't show up on any given day, and nearly 30% of the work force turns over every year. But for most, the alternatives are worse. Money brought them to the line, and it keeps them there.

Mrs. Malindia Boykin, age 53, is a worker in a Los Angeles laundry and has been for 21 years. Until recently she was a press operator—a job that involves working in heat over 100 degrees and keeping a swift pace, turning out 250 pieces an hour on a cuff and collar press, 225 shirts an hour on a "body press" or 150 pairs of pants an hour on the pants press. Like all laundry workers, Mrs. Boykin is among the lowest paid of manual workers, earning a meager $2.19 an hour. That's $87.60 a week—gross. . . . Mrs. Boykin claims no sense of pride. She has found a better way to endure the job. She simply accepts it; like the sun rising in the morning and setting at night, the job, to her, is just "there," a fact of life that is unpleasant but uncontrovertible. When she is questioned about the job, Mrs. Boykin is sunny, cooperative, and says, yes, the pay is terrible and the work is dangerous and the routine monotonous—in much the manner one might comment on the weather. . . . Malindia Boykin has no complaints. And no hopes. . . . The kind of resignation Malindia Boykin has learned may be the best defense against the drudgery of a mindless job. It is a defense many have learned.[1]

This report highlights a central claim of the radical analysis of American society: the most important feature of the internal life of America is the total powerlessness of the overwhelming majority of people to control the circumstances of their lives. And this powerlessness stems not from "the human condition" or from the inevitable

[1] "News Roundup," *Wall Street Journal,* 22 July 1971, p. 1.

circumstances of a complex society, but from the specific form of economic-social-political organization that develops in an advanced industrial capitalist society.

To prove my point this [article] documents three facts: (1) a small number of Americans have vast economic power while the overwhelming majority have almost no power in the economic realm; (2) economic power gives the small group that wields it a huge amount of political power while, for most Americans, political power is very limited and exists within a very narrow framework; and (3) powerlessness in the economic and political spheres affects people's daily lives in a large number of ways, permitting the development of a society in which the human needs of most people are largely ignored so that the wealthy and powerful can benefit. Additionally, I argue that most of the problems Americans think of as individual are in fact shared by most other people and are rooted in the nature of the system itself.

Capitalism and Classes

What exactly is capitalism? We can define it as an economic system in which small numbers of people, through their ownership and control of the means of production (e.g., factories, farms, mines), are able to buy the labor power of most other people and to direct that labor power into the production of goods to be sold for the profit of the owners. Typically, capitalism involves competition among the capitalists for a share of the market, though in the present advanced stages of capitalism several areas of production are governed by large monopolies that try to limit competition so that they can rationalize their production over long periods of time and control prices and profits. As was the case with previous forms of social organization, capitalist society is divided into classes: the very small ruling class owns and controls the means of production and the very large working class sells its labor power. Ownership of the means of production and the vast wealth that it brings provides the class of owners with a vastly disproportionate amount of political power which they use to sustain their own privileged postition and to govern the lives of everyone else.

You may want to stop right here. I know I did when I first heard these ideas presented. I had recently graduated from Columbia college at the time and was proud to be an intellectual and a liberal. I had heard all these "tired old Marxist ideas" before, and had taken several classes in which they had been "disproved." Moreover, to accept them would lead me to conclusions that would upset the pleasant plans I had for myself as a detached scholar. Nevertheless, my own experience over the next several years, and the intellectual work that accompanied it, forced me to rethink these ideas in light of the empirical evidence. And so I ask the reader: Read on. See if you, too, will find that these ideas make sense of your own experience in a way that high school civics courses or *Time* magazine or liberal college professors never did.

America is a class society. The two fundamental classes are the owners of the means of production—variously referred to as the bourgeoisie or the ruling class—and the wage laborers—usually called the working class or the proletariat—who use the productive apparatus to create material or service goods. Within each class is a high degree of differentiation between sections or strata

The ruling class can be differentiated from the working class in two important ways. First, there is a crucial structural fact: a small group of people have control over the banks and corporations, and that control gives them a huge amount of power over the lives of nearly everyone else. Second, these people do not have to sell their labor power to someone else, as does almost everyone else. The working class *has* to work—otherwise its members would literally starve (unemployment and welfare benefits do run out, and people are slowly starving in the United States even as you are reading this book). The "free" marketplace has always had this ambiguity: It is free in the sense that no one is required by law to take any particular job, as, for instance, the feudal serf was required by law to work the land on which he was born. But there are only a limited number of jobs available (in the United States in 1972, nearly 6 percent of the work force could not get jobs); and if you do not get a job you will shortly get hungry and live pretty miserably. If you are confused about which of the two fundamental classes you belong to, try the following test: Lie in bed and just listen to music for the next two months. If you start getting hungry during that time you're a worker. On the other hand, if two months of recumbent music listening does not interfere with your ability to live comfortably and feed yourself and your family adequately, you're probably not a member of the working class.

In addition to the two fundamental classes, a few other groups have interests that sometimes put them on the side of the working class and sometimes on the side of the ruling class. For example, there is a group called the lumpen proletariat, composed of those who do not seek employment—petty crooks, gamblers, "bums," etc. And there is the petite bourgeoisie—small-time entrepreneurs such as independent artisans, small farmers, small shopkeepers, and self-employed providers of services, selling some skill or service or product directly to the public.

One reason people hesitate to talk about class structure is that they see so many obvious differences among workers with regard to pay, status, and the like. Another is that many recently developed jobs require skilled, college-educated personnel, and it seems difficult to assimilate such workers as engineers and scientists into a category reserved for the hardcore industrial workers on the assembly lines and in the mines. Many American workers like to describe themselves as middle class, and in some ways their life styles are similar to those of the "middle-class" elements—such as lawyers and doctors, for example. After all, at least some American workers live in expensive suburbs, own big, expensive cars and other trappings of luxury. But this similarity is often exaggerated. In 1969 the average union scale in the building trades, generally considered the "aristocracy of labor," was $5.67 an hour, which would yield an income of $11,794 a year for a full year's employment—and a full year's employment is a rare occurrence for most workers in the building trades. Nevertheless, it points to an important fact: large differences exist among the standards of living of members of the working class. The person who sells his labor power at $15,000 a year can have quite a different kind of life from the person who sells it at half that much. Over 80 percent of U.S. families earned less than $15,000 a year in 1971, and in most of the families that did earn $15,000 two people were working. The differences in income that exist mean a lot to the people involved. In the main, it is these differences that give rise to the popular notion that some workers are "middle class": some are able to sell their labor power at a higher price than others.

It is understandable why so much attention is paid to the differences in price at which people sell their labor power. After all, ordinary workers or professionals do not have much basis on which to compare their lives to the lives of the Rockefellers or Duponts. But they *can* compare their lives with one another's. And as long as people focus their attention on these gradations of wealth between the lower paid workers and higher paid workers or small enterpreneurs, they miss the really crucial differences between themselves and the rulers, whose vast wealth and power remain outside public scrutiny.

Another cause for confusion is the existence of a small percentage of the population that has to work and has no control over the means of production but nevertheless makes a great deal of money. A wealthy doctor or lawyer is not usually a member of the ruling class in the strict sense. But by and large, doctors and lawyers identify with the ruling class and its interests. And this could also be true of a medium-size store owner who nets $20,000 a year, or a worker who wins a large sum in the sweepstakes and retires from work, or a hard-working adviser to the president, etc. It is a mistake to assume that because the boundary lines for a concept are hard to draw, the concept is meaningless. This kind of reasoning misses the "open-texture" nature of our language: often a concept is perfectly workable even when borderline cases exist. Consider the concept of baldness. It is often difficult to decide whether or not to call a given man "bald"; there are, after all, no agreed-upon criteria—as, for example, counting his hairs individually. But we would not on those grounds toss out the concept, because it points to a fundamental reality. Similarly, in talking about the differences between David Rockefeller or Ted Kennedy on the one hand and a bus driver or a store clerk on the other, the notion of working class makes a lot of sense. We may be puzzled about what to call the owner of a small or medium-size farm or business, and we may want to make it clear that teachers and mine workers perceive themselves differently. But the notion of classes *does* help to unravel many of the apparent mysteries of American political and economic life.

Just as there is much stratification within the working class, so the ruling class has a series of differentiated strata and interests. Some people have much more wealth and, consequently, much more power than others. Nor is the ruling class organized democratically: those with more wealth have much more power than those with less. Moreover, wealth and power are greatly concentrated in one small section of the ruling class. In 1969, the latest year for which figures are presently available, a very large number of small corporations in the United States (906,458, or 59 percent of the total number of corporations) held only a tiny portion of corporate assets ($31 billion, or 1.5 percent of the total), while at the top a few giant corporations (958, or 0.06 percent of the total) held a majority of all corporate assets ($1.07 trillion, or 53.2 percent of the total).[2]

Is there really a class in the United States that has disproportionate amounts of wealth and power? Yes. Let us consider, for example, income distributions. As G. William Domhoff points out, "The top 0.1% were 45,000 families who received an average of $110,000 per year, or 15 times as much as their numbers would warrant if income were equally distributed under conditions of equality."[3] The government no longer makes available information about personal wealth, but for 1953, the last year when such figures were published, the top 1.04 percent of the population owned 28.5 percent of all the wealth, while the bottom 20 percent of the population owned less than 2.5 percent (actually a slight reduction from its percentage fifty years before).

According to the 1970 census data, the poorest fifth of families in the United States received 5.5 percent of the total money income. The second poorest fifth received 12 percent of the total money income, so together the poorest 40 percent of American families in 1970 received 17.5 percent of money income. On the other hand, the richest fifth of American families received 41.6 percent of all money income. In money terms, the average income of the 10.4 million families in the top fifth was $23,100. (Had money income been divided equally among families, the average income for each family would have been over $11,000.) And this picture has remained relatively constant since World War II, despite much-heralded fair deals, great societies, and poverty programs. In 1947, for example, the poorest fifth received 5 percent and the richest fifth received 43 percent of the total money income, very slight fluctuations from the picture twenty-three years later.[4]

[2] Figures cited in Howard Sherman, *Radical Political Economy* (New York: Basic Books, 1972).

[3] G. William Domhoff, *Who Rules America?* (Englewood Cliffs, N.J.: Prentice-Hall, 1967), p. 41.

[4] Data compiled here from the U.S. Bureau of the Census. *Current Population Reports,* 4 October 1971, is latest available. Information has been compiled on these matters by Letitia Upton and Nancy Lyons of the Cambridge Institute and issued as a pamphlet entitled "Basic Facts: Distribution of Personal Income and Wealth in the United States," available by writing to the Cambridge Institute, 1878 Massachusetts Avenue, Cambridge, Massachusetts.

    A key point about all these figures: they show a general trend and overall configuration. Obviously, they will change somewhat from year to year. Incomes will rise, but often not as fast as inflation. A liberal Democrat may be elected president and submit plans for slightly revising the total distribution picture. What is interesting about the proposals made by even the most liberal Democrats is that they make only slight alterations in the total picture and would not change the basic class structure, but only smooth off some of its more piercing edges. McGovern, for example, has repudiated the National Welfare Rights Organization's plan for a minimum income of $6,500 for a family of four and is embarrassed that his income assistance plan is seen as too radical. But even the minimal programs that liberal politicians promise will be much scaled down by the time they emerge from congressional committees. The likely prognosis is for much fanfare about income redistribution and tax reform, with conservatives yelling that the vastly inadequate programs of the liberals constitute outright socialism, but the basic picture will not be altered to the degree that it would make sense to drop the categories of "class" that have been central to an understanding of capitalist societies for the past few hundred years.

John Kenneth Galbraith's famous celebration of American capitalism, *The Affluent Society,* together with a barrage of magazine and newspaper propaganda, has created the popular notion that in America we live in an "affluent society" where almost everybody has become "middle class." But, for most working people, the reality is quite different. According to the 1962 Conference on Economic Progress in the United States, 38 million Americans were living in poverty, as defined by the U.S. Labor Department's standards. Another 37 million were living in conditions of "deprivation" (defined as living above the stark poverty level but below the Labor Department's description of a "modest but adequate" family budget). In 1969 the median income of all families in the United States, based on the income of all wage earners in the family, was $8,632. While in that same year the U.S. Bureau of Labor Statistics estimated that a family of four needed $10,077 a year to live in an urban area at a "moderate living standard." Tens of millions of Americans that year could not even claim a moderate living standard. Furthermore, more than one person in the family usually has to work to achieve even a below-moderate living standard. In 1967, for example, more than 60 percent of white families needed two or more earners to reach an income of $5,000 or more a year. The so-called middle-class worker may read accolades to his new status in *Time* magazine or his children's sociology textbooks, but the words do not correspond to the reality. In 1967 the median income of craftsmen—skilled workers—was only $7,227; in 1968 the average auto worker made $7,280; and in 1969 the U.S. Department of Agriculture estimated that over 12 million Americans were severely undernourished and hungry. In 1965 there were 12 million workers (in farm, domestic, retail trade, restaurant, laundry, factory, and hospital jobs) whose hourly wages were less than $1.50: if these men and women managed to work 50 weeks of the year they would still have earned only $3,000.

And things have not been getting more equal. Despite all the claims about the effects of the New Deal and the Progressive Era before it, the basic contours of wealth distribution in America have remained largely constant throughout the past fifty years. The relative inequalities still exist. True, over the past thirty years things have been getting better in material terms for many people. Part of the reason is that, although each class's share of the pie has remained about the same, the pie as a whole has grown considerably . . . But there has been no "democratization of wealth," as the apologists for American capitalism like to pretend.

But what about taxes? Don't they change all that by redistributing income from the wealthy to the poor? No. Despite all the rhetoric, the percentages of wealth distribution after income tax are virtually the same as before. And most taxes hit hardest at those least able to pay. A 1960 income study showed that those who made under $2,000 per year paid 38 percent of their income in all types of taxes; those who made from $2,000 to $5,000 paid from 38 percent to more than 41 percent; and those who made above $10,000 paid only 31.6 percent. And, typically, those who made over $750,000 a year paid a percentage of their income to income taxes not much greater than the percentage paid by the average wage earner. Moreover, large corporations are permitted to spend millions of dollars each year that are not reported as income but are written off as business expenses. In fact, the tax system actually works to redistribute wealth from the poor to the rich, because the wealthy control the state legislatures, the Congress, and the governmental bodies. The rich are often able to use tax money to subsidize their own business ventures or to defend their investments abroad.[5]

Every few years there is some talk about reforming the tax system, and occasionally an obvious abuse is modified. But in the process, other benefits are arranged for the rich. There can be no clearer testimony to the powerlessness of most working people in America than the fact that it is *their* taxes, rather than corporate and wealth taxes, that are raised to fund vitally needed social services. And when taxes are lowered, it is the corporation that benefits most. Consider the 1971 tax relief passed by the Democratic Congress. According to political scientist James Ridgeway, the measure gives an estimated $7.5 *billion* to corporations. The bill grants a $500 million tax subsidy to the big international corporations that do most of U.S. trading abroad, by setting up dummy corporations called Domestic International Sales Corporations, through which sales can be channeled. The bill was driven through Congress not by conservative Republicans but by the Democratic leadership, specifically by Wilbur Mills in the House and Russell Long in the Senate, both of whom describe themselves as "populists." It is not impossible that in the future, reformers will be elected who will reverse this latest subsidy to the corporations, but that is not the point. What is important is that tax law is written by and for the rich, and hence is not likely to have any effect on changing the concentration of wealth in the hands of a very few.

. . .

Earned Wealth

Someone may now concede, "Sure, there are social and economic classes, and the upper class has a vastly disproportionate amount of wealth and power, but don't the members of that class deserve their great wealth and power because they worked harder, and isn't there a great deal of social mobility today among classes?" No, on both counts, Most people with large fortunes in America today did not achieve their fortunes because they worked hard—although this is more likely to be true of the upper-middle-class professionals and small entrepreneurs than of the upper 0.5 percent of the population that controls the banks, corporations, and industries. But even if they were hard

---

[5] See Joseph A. Pechman, "The Rich, the Poor, and the Taxes They Pay," *Public Interest,* no. 17 (Fall 1969). Pechman points out that "the effective rate of tax paid in 1967 by the top 1% was only 26% of their total reported income, including all of their realized capital gains." Now, obviously, 26 percent of $125,000 a year leaves quite a healthy share for the rich person, whereas the same or even a lesser percentage of taxes paid on an income of $11,000 or less is really going to hurt the struggling-to-make-ends-meet working person.

workers, they were not the only ones. What distinguishes them from the large numbers of people with equally high (or higher) intelligence who worked equally hard (or harder) is some combination of the following factors: (1) access to large sums of capital which they could use to invest, either through familial wealth or through special access to credit institutions; (2) access to educational opportunity often unavailable to people from working-class families; (3) influence with businessmen and politicians needed to initiate their own business ventures; (4) ruthlessness in competition; (5) exploitation of their workers in order to maximize their own profits. Most wealthy people today either inherited their wealth or depended on family or bank connections for large sums of initial capital. This money was available to their families and to banks because previous generations had managed to accumulate surplus wealth through a variety of tactics, important among which were enslaving black men and women; importing Irish, Italian, Chinese, and other immigrant groups as sources of cheap labor; and profiting from the labor of those they employed. If anybody "deserves" to have wealth either because of previous family accomplishments or because of work done earlier in life, it is clearly the working people of this country whose back-breaking, tedious, and insipid labor in this and previous generations has built and sustained modern America.

Social Mobility and Competition

At this point you may object, "At least our children can make it out of the working class if they try hard enough." But the facts do not support your thesis. "Studies on the basis of data up to 1960 have found that the number of sons of manual workers who were able to make . . . 'the big leap' into higher business and independent professional occupations . . . was nearly 8% for the United States. It may not be essential, in order to achieve material or professional success, to be born of wealth, or even of well-to-do parents; but it is certainly an enormous advantage, rather like joining a select club, membership of which offers unrivaled opportunities for the consolidation and enhancement of the advantages which it in any case confers." [6] True, a higher level of education is now available to working-class children than in the past, but this is largely because advanced capitalism requires more highly trained personnel. We now have junior or community colleges to train working-class people, state universities and college systems to train business and professional men, and a small group of elite universities that still provide "recruits for the command posts of society." The university system as presently constructed reinforces the pattern of class structure.

None of this denies that a small percentage of working people *do* make it, *do* switch classes in a real sense. But these switches, far from undermining the class system,

[6] Ralph Miliband, *The State in Capitalist Society* (New York: Basic Books, 1969), pp. 39–40.

actually strengthen it by assuring that the most highly competitive and ambitious people will not be operating against the interests of the ruling class, but in concert with them. These individual advances are made against a background of general class stability in which the system of maldistribution of wealth and power remains intact. This is true at virtually every level of the class system. When an economic system has a level of involuntary unemployment approaching 6 percent, three out of every fifty people simply cannot get a job. In fact, the government officially considers an unemployment rate of 4 percent to be "full employment." The individual's ability to be employed depends at least in part on the fact that someone else is unemployed. In short, whenever any particular person makes it, other people necessarily lose out. Hence, from childhood on, Americans are carefully indoctrinated by the family, school, and media to compete with other people and to see others as impediments to their own success. Nor is this view of others the product of some irrational "urge to evil" in human nature. In the context of capitalist society it is quite rational. For you really *do* have to compete in order to survive, and you really *do* have to beat out others in the process. In such a context, being sly, scheming, deceptive, self-protective, guarded, self-centered, and distrustful all become quite rational. What is irrational is the context.

The best clue to human relationships in capitalist society is to understand how the basic economic institutions function and then see how these institutions affect the rest of human life. Consider the way the individual is treated by the large corporations: as a means to make profit for the few. Capitalists use everybody for their own personal gain. When they can no longer use a person as a worker, they simply throw him out of work. When he is too old to be used, he is dismissed as irrelevant. (Hence the "tragedy of old age." Death is a problem for any society, but old age is a "tragedy" only because a capitalist society measures human worth in terms of the individual's usefulness to the ruling class for its own ends.) Human needs are important only to the extent that they help create a workforce capable of producing more wealth for the capitalists.

Needless to say, if people are formed, and form themselves, in order to succeed and survive in this context, they become unsuited for human relationships which require precisely the opposite kinds of qualities. If you have been pushed to compete in school, in seeking employment, and in advancing yourself at your job, you are ill prepared to see others as ends in themselves, as individuals to be respected because they are human beings. It often becomes extremely difficult to establish friendships. You may find a few friends and perhaps a sexual partner with whom you can become a single economic unit (and hence enhance each other's buying power), but most of the outside world is likely to appear indifferent or even hostile to you. This is not paranoia—the rest of the world really is indifferent or even hostile to you. Why? Because you stand in its way. You have to stop caring about others, because if you get too involved with them you yourself won't survive. As theologian A. J. Heschel points out, "Suspect your neighbor as yourself" has become the motto of the present age. What could be a greater indictment of a social system than this: it makes humane and loving relationships between people less likely and more difficult?

Political Democracy?

"Granted that there are economic classes in society and that some have vastly more power than others. But this can't really be as bad for the people as you say, because otherwise they would simply vote and change things. So people obviously like things the way they are!" The critical assumption in this statement is that we live in a society in which the people have the political power to make basic decisions. But this is not true. In fact, most citizens are never asked to make decisions of any importance to them except which of two candidates who agree on almost everything shall represent them. When the people look at the men in power from one administration to the next, they see basically the same men and the same policies. No wonder many people end up by not voting at all or by treating the elections as a spectator sport. In 1968 about 38 percent of eligible citizens failed to vote in the presidential election and about 44 percent failed to vote in the congressional election. The folk wisdom embodied in the notion that things will not change no matter who wins any particular election is an insightful reflection on the actual limits of power that most people have.

One way in which the wealthy minority exercises disproportionate political power is by dominating the key decision-making posts in the state. This is demonstrated by G. William Domhoff: "Of the 13 men who have been Secretary of War since 1932, eight have been listed in the Social Register. The others are bankers and corporation executives, and clearly members of the power elite." [7] Gabriel Kolko studied the key American foreign policy decision makers from 1944 through 1960—234 individuals who held 678 posts in a 16-year period, nearly all of them high-level and policy-making posts. Kolko writes:

The net result of this study, however imperfect, revealed that foreign policy decision-makers are in reality a highly mobile sector of the American corporate structure, a group of men who frequently assume and define high level policy tasks in government, rather than routinely administer it, and then return to business. Their firms and connections are large enough to afford them the time to straighten out or formulate government policy while maintaining their vital ties with giant corporate law, banking or industry. . . . Of the 234 officials examined, 35.8% . . . held 63.4% of the posts. Thirty men from law, banking and investment firms accounted for 22% of all the posts which we studied, and another 57 from this background held an additional 14.1% or a total 36.1% of the key posts. Certain key firms predominated among this group: members of Sullivan & Cromwell or Carter, Ledyard & Milburn, and Coudert Brothers [all large corporate law firms serving the giant corporations], in that order among law firms, held twenty-nine posts, with other giant corporate-oriented law firms accounting for most of the remainder. Dillon, Read & Co. [one of the largest investment firms] with four men, and the Detroit Bank, with only Joseph

[7] Domhoff, *Who Rules America?*, p. 99.

M. Dodge, accounted for eighteen and ten posts, respectively, and two men from Brown Brothers, Harriman [another huge investment firm] held twelve posts—or forty posts for three firms. . . .[8]

In all, men who came from big business, investment firms, and the law firms that serve these interests held 59.6 percent of all posts.

But what about elective offices? Certainly the wealthy do not play such an important role here. The evidence, however, is to the contrary. The wealthy do not always serve in the chief elective positions, but the people who get elected are almost always those who are acceptable to the wealth and power elites and who have been able, thereby, to accumulate sufficient capital to run an election campaign. Needless to say, if all wealthy owners of newspapers have decided to ignore you, and the media in general consider your candidacy irrelevant because you are "irresponsible," you have only a very slight chance of getting the large sums of money an election campaign requires. And the key to being "responsible" is to accept the basic contours of the distribution of wealth and power in this society and the basic requirements of American imperialism abroad.

. . .

Happiness and Ideology

"But if Americans are so powerless in both the economic and political sphere, why don't they seem more unhappy about the system as a whole?" The answer to this problem is complicated. . . . For one thing, it is not quite true to suggest that people are happy with the current arrangements in America. In the late 1950s, there did not seem to be any basic discontent. But the 1960s changed all that. Moreover, people who feel discontent find it difficult to express their feelings in ways that make any difference. Sometimes, in desperation, they turn to a George Wallace or to other political figures who seem to be speaking to some of their anxieties. But many people take no social action at all. Americans have been heavily indoctrinated to believe that the problems they feel are not social, but personal, and reflect their own inner difficulties. When they sense something wrong with their lives, they are instructed to look inward, whether through the old forms of religion or psychoanalysis, or the more hip version of encounter groups. Besides, people are able to acquire at least some of the material things they need, and are constantly reminded of how much more they have than those below them and those in other countries. Finally, the system validates itself by setting forth a persuasive ideological line about the virtues of American society. Not only does American society institutionalize democracy, we are told, but also liberty: men are free to do as they will. So why complain since you are free to do whatever you want?

It is only later that we learn through experience that the alternatives are chosen by

[8] Gabriel Kolko, *The Roots of American Foreign Policy* (Boston: Beacon Press, 1970), pp. 17–19.

someone else, and that, in fact, we are free to sell our labor power or starve. We are told that all men are equal, though it is conceded this equality does not exist in any real, material sense but only in the formal sense that we all have equal rights before the law. Even if we did have formal equality (though any black person can show how false that claim is) it would mean something quite different than what we originally thought was embodied in the notion of a society based on equality. Equality before the law now can be seen to mean that the beggar and Rockefeller are both prohibited from sleeping under the bridge when they are homeless, from trespassing on another's property to pick berries if they are hungry, from shoplifting from a department store when they need clothes, from forcibly keeping scabs from taking their jobs when they are on strike for higher wages. But Rockefeller does not have to do any of these things since he has inherited enough money to sustain him for his entire life. So, in practice, the law works against the poor, protecting those who have made it against those who have not. Any society needs some safeguards. The point is that in this society the people who are really protected are the rich. Crime runs rampant against working people and the poor. And most of that crime is motivated by economic need generated by the capitalist maldistribution of wealth. Law and order maintain stability, but in America that stability is a *class*-oriented stability, a stability that favors the wealthy and oppresses the downtrodden.

One of the greatest ideological myths in the United States is the myth of free speech. Free speech is granted only as long as it has no significant effect. Thus, in the late 50s and early 60s nearly everyone could criticize freely, without fear of being called a "kook" or "bum" by the president. When speech was used simply to express dissent, freedom of speech was acceptable—it was, in fact, a key tool in the ideological struggle against the Left. The U.S. Information Service took movies of protest demonstrations, sent them around the world, and proclaimed "This is what we are fighting for in Vietnam—the right to have differing points of view and to be able to express them freely." While the Left was obeying the polite rules of the game, the government was ordering greater escalations of the war or more efficient bombings or intensified pacification programs. *Our* speech was being used to pacify us while *their* speech was used to mask a policy of murder. But when free speech was used to organize, as it was in the late 60s, the Left faced outright oppression: the use of naked violence against demonstrators and the use of conspiracy and criminal anarchy charges to imprison organizers. Formal freedoms quickly disappear when anyone threatens to use them effectively against the interests of the ruling class. The irony is that civil liberties have been withdrawn just at those times when they are most necessary: when there is serious political conflict about the direction of American society. True, in some cases an appeals court may later reverse a conviction. But the years spent in jail or in litigation have a markedly restraining effect. The government often succeeds in intimidating people from participating in activity that is theoretically protected by the Constitution. A vindication years later in the courts really doesn't change the reality of repression.

. . .

Consequences of Powerlessness

Every important social problem and most important individual problems become intelligible against the background of powerlessness that pervades the economic and political life of capitalist society. There was an obvious reason for Marx to stress the relations that exist between people in production as the key to understanding all the rest of the things that happen during any historical epoch: the relations that obtain between people during the greatest number of their hours of peak consciousness—the hours when they are engaged in making a living—must inevitably have an effect on the quality of their lives and their consciousness during the few hours when they are neither working, commuting to work, sleeping, nor relaxing in exhaustion from the work activity.

The combined effects of a competitive marketplace and the daily powerlessness of people to affect their world is shown most dramatically in the relations between men and women. The man, frustrated and made to feel insignificant by the outside world, finds his opportunity to seem important and powerful by dominating and controlling a woman. The hierarchy of the outside world is re-created in the family, with the mother often finding her sole power in being able to make her children dependent on her in some way. Human relations are treated as if they were relations between marketable things: the chief criteria being How much can I get out of him (her)? and What's in it for me? How else are people to react to other people when their whole lives and the entire structure of society combines to make them view one another as threats to survival, and as objects to be manipulated?

The neuroses afflicting so many people (and which keep psychiatrists rich) are a direct consequence of a society in which people are forced to compete with each other, and in which they perceive the utter impossibility of controlling their own lives and the utter waste of so much of their time in useless or even destructive production. To be "normal" in a society that exploits people all around the world, that suppresses people at home, that renders human beings into mere objects for manipulation and control—requires a human being so insensitive that his very humanity may be in question. Whoever is not abnormal in such a society has either no feelings or no mind. Insanity is one possible response to these conditions. Another is to ape the characteristics of the system in your own life by finding some group—be it Vietnamese, blacks, women, children—over whom you can play out the inhumanities that have been inflicted upon you.

The vast majority of crimes committed in this society stem from the economic structure. Crime is almost nonexistent in the pseudo-socialist societies of Eastern Europe or in Cuba, North Vietnam and the Israeli kibbutz, which are somewhat closer to socialism. In addition to the crimes that shouldn't be crimes even by capitalist standards (e.g., smoking marijuana), there are those that stem from people's needs for more money (hence the petty ripoffs, bank robberies, grocery store holdups, etc.) or from their feelings of frustration in society (from which so many crimes of passion derive). The biggest criminals are the ones who have managed to rob whole classes and whole countries—the people who sit on the boards of corporations, banks, and universities and who administer the federal government. Perhaps cognizant of the fact that any attack on the big criminals might lead to embarrassing questions, the FBI and other law enforcement agencies bend over backward not to attack the Mafia and other centers of organized crime: the "most wanted" become the small-time bankrobbers, the muggers and the political organizers. Honor among thieves.

Nor are the crimes of the rich without danger to the rest of the population. In their frenzy for profits, the rich are willing to go to any lengths of destructiveness, from bombing the Vietnamese to building unsafe industrial plants. In 1968 a total of 14,300 Americans died in industrial accidents; between 1961 and 1969, 126,000 Americans were killed this way. In 1968, 90,000 workers suffered permanent impairments and a total of 2,100,000 suffered total but temporary disability. Minimal precautions could have prevented most of these accidents and deaths. But such precautions would have required capital outlays and hence cut into corporate profit, so they were often deemed not worth it. Congress made a great fanfare of passing an industrial health and safety bill in 1970, but it has been virtually unenforced. In any sane society the men who run factories and mines and who knowingly refuse to provide adequate safety controls would be treated as the worst of criminals. But in capitalist America, they become the secretaries of defense and state, or advisers to governmental agencies. And, ironically, they are the ones who cry most loudly for "law and order."

Even those who do not turn to crime or racism or insanity or neuroses are plagued with an overriding sense of the meaninglessness of their lives. Existentialism describes this as a general problem, built into the structure of human existence. But in fact it is societal in origin and is true for a certain historical period. Within a society in which men cannot control their own lives, there is no way for them to introduce any meaning into their daily affairs. In a society in which the criterion of production is profitability, when people's talents can never be developed but only "exploited" by the large corporations, when people's human potentialities are stunted and underdeveloped unless someone can "use" them, it is inevitable that people will feel dissatisfied and unfulfilled. The task of religion or patriotism or chauvinism or psychoanalysis is to channel this feeling in a direction that does not challenge its fundamental source: the capitalist economic structure.

In the face of these conditions, the worker protests in the only way he can: by demanding more money for the time he is wasting in production. The worker must sell his skin, so why not sell it at the highest price possible? This direction of protest is taken because it is only with regard to wages that management seems willing to bargain at all. But the price the worker gets will never be high enough to compensate for a lost life, and his willingness to accept this channel plays directly into the hands of management, which (while imperialism is still functioning well) can often afford to raise pay and then raise prices.

Powerlessness is not merely an insignificant fact about the economy or the political realm. It pervades every area of people's lives, ensuring that their human potential for creativity, freedom, rationality, love, and human sympathy will not be realized.

. . .

VISCERAL RACISM

Irving Thalberg

At a meeting shortly before his death, Malcolm X was asked by a young white listener: "What contribution can youth, especially students who are disgusted with racism, make to the black struggle for freedom?" Malcolm X's reply has become a familiar one: "Whites who are sincere should organize among themselves and figure out some strategy to break down prejudice that exists in white communities. . . . This has never been done." [1]

I will not offer strategies, but I will do what I can with fairly standard philosophical techniques to delineate one target for action. I hope that the social phenomenon I analyze is what polemical writers had in view when they coined the term 'visceral racism'. At any rate the phenomenon is worth bringing into sharper focus; and therefore I will keep the emotively charged term 'racism' out of my discussion as much as possible. Nevertheless when I do for convenience use the expression 'visceral racism', I want it to be clear that I am not belaboring old-fashioned white supremacy doctrines and practices. Adherents of white supremacy are still both numerous and influential; but I doubt that further analysis is needed to understand or to attack their position. What I examine here is more protectively camouflaged and philosophically challenging.

1. *Not a 'latent' form of white supremacy.* The main components of the earlier tradition I take to be: (a) factual claims that, in various respects, black people are 'inferior'; (b) normative conclusions, drawn from such factual claims, about how others ought to treat black Americans; (c) regional and national customs of discriminatory treatment that are vindicated by these normative conclusions. All three elements appear in Chief Justice Taney's account of the status of slaves and free Negroes under the U.S. Constitution. Writing immediately before the Civil War in the *Dred Scott* decision, Taney says:

[1] In G. Breitman, ed., *Malcolm X Speaks* (New York: Grove Press, 1966), p. 221.

They had for more than a century . . . been regarded as beings of an inferior order, and altogether unfit to associate with the white race . . . ; and so far inferior, that they had no rights which the white man was bound to respect (19 How. [60 U.S.] 392 [1857]).

An equally frank statement is Senator Tillman's apology for the discriminatory post-Reconstruction customs of his state:

In 1876, . . . the people of South Carolina had been living under negro rule for eight years. There was a condition bordering upon anarchy. . . . There was no incentive to labor. . . .

They were taxing us to death and confiscating our property. We felt the very foundations of our civilization crumbling beneath our feet, [sic] that we were sure to be engulfed by the black flood of barbarians . . . In desperation we determined to take the government away from the negroes.

We organized the Democratic party with one plank, . . . namely that "this is a white man's country and white men must govern it" (*Congressional Record,* 59th Congress, 1907, pp. 1440–1).

In more recent times, 'respectable' white supremacists have been less forthright about their intention to subjugate blacks. On the other hand, a few biologists and social scientists have plugged *lacunae* in the vague theory of racial inferiority. Their most interesting hypotheses are that Negroid *homo sapiens* evolved much later, and from different sub-*sapiens* ancestors, than Caucasoids; and that the resulting differences in Negroid and Caucasoid brain morphology still determine such things as school achievement and crime rates. Along with data from archeology and brain physiology, comparative psychometric studies of children in the Georgia public schools from 1954 to 1962 have been introduced as evidence for such 'inferiority' hypotheses. This evidence, the leading theories, and especially the normative conclusions that have been drawn from scientific theories of racial inferiority, all have received thorough criticism in scientific and popular journals. So I will turn to contrasts between white supremacist and visceral racist attitudes. This calls for a preliminary characterization of the visceral syndrome, to which I will add all-important details later.

By visceral racism I will mean a set of unacknowledged attitudes that afflict me and most other 'unprejudiced' whites, especially middle-class liberals. These attitudes are mainly dispositions to perceive and to describe social events in which black people figure. Our most noticeable proclivities are, first, to structure and report such events in a manner that 'screens out' social inequalities which are glaringly evident to black observers; and secondly to represent black people as helplessly dependent upon the white majority. The overall tendency is for 'visceral' whites to regard themselves as doing just about as well as can be expected with 'the race problem'. Of course they never regard themselves as the problem! Examples will exphasize how the visceral racist does not want to think of himself as hostile toward blacks or indifferent to their individual and collective aspirations.

This sketch explains why the visceral inclinations that I shall analyze here are not dissimulated white supremacy attitudes. To recognize your viscerally racist dispositions is *not* to avow that deep down you think black people are all over-sexed savages, or that you really like the caste system we have. It is to notice the protective cocoon of ignorance and distortion that we have spun about ourselves.

Before I review the inequities that we thereby manage to ignore, I want to answer a natural objection from liberal white readers. Many will indignantly complain, "I've never had any hostile feelings toward black people, so how can you call me a visceral or any other kind of racist?"

2. *Not 'feelings'.* The visceral dispositions I'm analyzing do not consist in sensations or emotions. In this regard, white supremacist and viscerally racist inclinations are similar. Neither type of attitude—or any other attitude I can think of—is made up of twinges, glows, tingles, tugs, fantasy images, and similar 'inner sensations'. Perhaps feelings of tension come over a Southern sheriff when he sees a 'mixed' couple. But these feelings are never all, or even part, of what we mean when we say that the sheriff has a white supremacist outlook, and that he displays his attitude in his responses and conduct toward the couple. One proof is that it is not self-contradictory to assert that he displayed white supremacist reactions but was perfectly calm—felt serene or 'felt nothing'—inside. Another proof is that the couple are in no danger from his 'inner feelings'. The threat to their rights and dignity comes from his tendency to respond with insults and worse. As for the visceral racist, we have an even stronger reason for denying that his attitude consists in feelings. However confused our notion of inner sensations may be, one thing is sure: they cannot occur while the person who has them is totally unaware of them. Now the peculiarity of viscerally racist attitudes, according to the hypothesis I will develop, is that a person with these attitudes systematically ignores features of the social situation of black people in this country. If his attitudes were 'inner sensations', he would be aware of them, and presumably his tendency to misperceive would to that extent diminish. But, as I will illustrate, there are people who systematically distort things and yet seem totally unaware that they do. Therefore their disposition to distort things cannot consist in 'inner sensations'. The other two arguments also prove that viscerally racist attitudes cannot be 'inner sensation' feelings.

How about emotions? Aren't these kinds of 'feelings' part of what we mean when we talk of white supremacist and viscerally racist attitudes? Again, no. The sheriff may be agitated by surges of hatred and malevolence. Visceral racists might experience a rush of embarrassment when they meet the 'mixed' couple. More generally, they may be troubled by emotions ranging from 'guilt' to uneasiness whenever they deal with black people who do not occupy a subordinate role. But such emotions are only concomitants; they are not essential to, much less identical with, white supremacist and visceral attitudes.

The 'no contradiction' argument again suffices to prove this. If you have a female sibling, then you must have a sister. It is inconsistent for anyone to assert that you have a female sibling and deny that you have a sister. By contrast, it is never inconsistent to report that a white supremacist, or a visceral racist, was free of emotion when he displayed his attitude. Indeed, one sinister aspect of both types of attitude is that people who have them go about their business in such an unemotional, matter-of-fact way.

Although this explains why you can be a visceral racist and have no 'feelings' of hostility toward black people, some philosophers may complain that I have made the case too easy by assimilating all emotion to episodes of turbulence and agitation. Aren't some emotions, such as resentment and hatred, long-term dispositions? No doubt we can classify a white supremacist's hatred as a settled disposition, which only comes to be displayed on certain occasions. For example, we could say that he began despising black people when he was a child, that he only ceased briefly during military service, because he was in a combat team with black soldiers, and that his hatred developed again when he returned to his old neighborhood. Perhaps you want to stretch the concept of an emotion to comprise such cases. But then what would it mean to insist that the attitudes of a white supremacist and a visceral racist are emotions? Surely not that, during all times when they have these dispositions they are constantly—or intermittently—stirred by hostility or uneasiness? That is precisely the implication you avoided by broadening the concept of emotion. So you are left with an altogether vacuous account. Moreover, it sounds odd to characterize a man as having a particular *emotion* since childhood. To speak of attitudes in this way is standard.

These negative remarks, to the effect that viscerally racist attitudes are neither 'inner sensations' nor emotions, give us minimal insight. As soon as I explain briefly what we are disposed to ignore and to distort when we are afflicted by viscerally racist attitudes, I will offer a more positive analysis.

3. *What the visceral racist overlooks.* Militant readers will have lost patience by now. To them my investigation will appear worthlessly academic, because admittedly there is so little practical difference between the familiar old white supremacist and the 'well-meaning' people whose attitudes I'm analyzing. The visceral racist will not throw a brick through the window of a new black neighbor. He won't assault black children who are bussed to the neighborhood school. But what does he do to protect them? Doesn't he let the redneck do his dirty-work for him? In general, doesn't he support institutions that oppress black people in nearly every area of social life? Right; and that is why I want to diagnose his visceral inclinations to misperceive our society as progressing with all deliberate speed toward equality.

For the benefit of nonmilitants, I will explain briefly the claim that there is almost no practical difference for the majority of blacks under liberals and their 'reformed' institutions, in comparison with the old days. No doubt there are more lucky blacks who 'make it' nowadays. Certainly more vote. Fewer lynchings occur. Blacks are no longer obliged to display humility and gratitude. Otherwise the statistics on the vast *majority* of black people in America show little alteration. Except for temporary economic gains during World War II and the Korean War, most blacks have continued to enjoy a very small share of the nation's fabled prosperity. Typically, the 500 largest industrial corporations earn around 40% of the gross national product. About 7,000 companies with 100 or more employees do 90% of manufacturing and 80% of the sales. About 1.6% of the population owns more than 80% of the stock of these top corporations and others. As you would expect, members of this group control corporate and government policy. Blacks have not gotten into this 1.6% group that owns and runs the country. The few whites who belong to it are usually inheritors of wealth. Most stock ends up in the hands of white women, because of their longevity.

Turning to black wage-earners, experts attribute to them between 55% and 70% of the salary that whites receive for equivalent work.[2] Incidentally, the percentage *declines* when we consider blacks with 'higher' positions and more formal education, thus refuting the myth that serious study and 'drive' will be differentially rewarded. Working-class blacks are twice as likely to be unemployed or laid off. In nearly every profession—including our own, academic philosophy—blacks are grossly under-represented. The same is true with skilled trades. Labor unions have driven blacks out of some fields. This happened with locomotive engineers and firemen in the South. Construction workers' unions have kept blacks out. And in automotive industry, unions have confined blacks to low-paying, no-seniority positions.

Black consumers face similar hindrances. They pay more to buy or rent deteriorated housing. Mortgages are nearly unavailable to a black home-buyer. If he obtains one, he will pay higher interest than whites do. Neighborhood segregation is rising, and black children attend increasingly segregated schools, where considerably less is spent per pupil than in white areas. Barely 2% of elective offices at all levels of government are held by blacks—and this marks a relatively big step forward during the last few years. In their relations with government, notably police, most blacks have made no progress at all. Black citizens and property-owners are virtually without police protection, while harrassment from police has grown. Ten to seventeen times as many black people are arrested for major violent crimes.[3] Large numbers, including 'bystanders', fall victims of unprovoked attacks by police. Their property rights, and Fourth Amendment immunity to arbitrary search and seizure, are violated constantly by police. Blacks still constitute the majority of the more than 200,000 inmates of federal and

---

[2] The lower figure is given by Thomas F. Mayer, on the basis of U.S. Bureau of Census figures for 1939 and 1947–62, in his useful résumé, "The Position and Progress of Black America," reprinted by Radical Education Project (Ann Arbor, 1967). *The Report of the National Advisory Commission on Civil Disorders* (Washington, D.C.: Government Printing Office, 1968) gives the higher figure for 23 cities it surveyed. Since Mayer draws upon a wide variety of official and scholarly sources, I generally paraphrase his summary of the situation in jobs, housing, and education.

[3] This last figure comes from a report by the National Commission on the Causes and Prevention of Violence, summarized in the *Chicago Sun-Times,* November 24, 1969, pp. 5, 18.

state prisons and reformatories, and are the least likely to have received an impartial trial.

All in all, this lack of progress since the passing of white supremacy appears to confirm Dr. King's foreboding. He wrote in 1963:

I have almost reached the regrettable conclusion that the Negro's great stumbling block in the stride toward freedom is not the White Citizen's Council-er or the Ku Klux Klanner, but the white moderate who is more devoted to "order" than to justice. . . . Shallow understanding from people of goodwill is more frustrating than absolute misunderstanding from people of ill will.[4]

It's hard to believe that the visceral racist manages to ignore all this. But as I shall illustrate, he sometimes even turns the situation upside down, and imagines that with all the current 'favoritism' toward blacks, there is discrimination against whites! In any case, my method is straightforward. Rather than suspect most 'well-meaning' whites of hypocrisy, I will look for patterns of selective and distorted perception of this background when they describe social occurrences involving black people. Since these epistemic and linguistic patterns have been stamped into me, and since I have lived for years among the whites whose attitudes I'm analyzing, I will not burden this part of my essay with much documentation. But presumably sociologists can verify whether the patterns are as widespread as this native thinks they are. Sociologists will also have to decide whether the attitudes I delineate are important causes of white complacency toward the grim situation I've reviewed.

4. *Visceral racism and language.* Whatever their causal role may be, the attitudes which concern me are manifest in reports that 'unprejudiced' whites spontaneously give of what blacks do and undergo. Reports of a black observer are likely to be at variance. The psychiatrist C. A. Pinderhughes expresses this neatly:

What most whites preceive as an orderly American social system most blacks experience as unresponsive, unremitting, dehumanized, well-rationalized, quiet, courteous, institutionalized violence not unlike colonialism.[5]

A visceral racist's description will also clash with his own account of similar events which feature whites. You will notice these disparities with respect to what is emphasized and neglected; what causes and effects of the occurrence are recorded; and what motives are ascribed to participants.

5. *A hackneyed illustration* of these discrepancies is easiest to start with. Consider the type of event that engulfed the Watts district of Los Angeles in August 1965; Detroit and Newark in July 1967; and Prague, Czechoslovakia, in August 1968. Why

---

[4] "Letter from a Birmingham City Jail," reprinted in *Civil Disobedience,* ed. by H. A. Bedau (New York: Pegasus, 1969), p. 81.

[5] "Understanding Black Power: Processes and Proposals," *American Journal of Psychiatry,* 125, No. 11 (1969), 1555.

throw Prague into the same basket? Weren't the Czechs rising up against Soviet tyranny? Indeed they were. And the black commentators I've read are nearly unanimous in saying that the residents of Watts rebelled too. By the following summer, for example, Stokely Carmichael was interpreting such events as "rebellion" (*New York Times,* July 29, 1966, p. 13:1). Of course the inhabitants of Watts, and hundreds of other black communities since 1964, had little chance of overcoming police and National Guard firepower. But weren't the Czechs, the Hungarians in 1956, before them the East Berliners in 1953, and the Warsaw Jews in 1944, just as disorganized, just as unlikely to free themselves? So far, then, I find no reason for the visceral racist to withhold the laudatory term 'uprising' when he describes the behavior of Watts residents. Ironically enough, insurance companies tried to avoid compensating local property-owners by appealing to "insurrection" clauses in their policies! (*New York Times,* August 16, 1965, p. 16:5, 6, 8.) The closest that white spokesmen came to this was when Los Angeles Police Chief Parker reported "guerrilla warfare" (*New York Times,* August 14, 1965, p. 1:8), and California Governor Brown admitted "guerrilla fighting with gangsters" in Watts (*New York Times,* August 17, 1965, p. 1:8).

Nowhere in the white media do you find echoes of the indignation that was expressed when Soviet troops and tanks "invaded" Prague. On that occasion, Senator Tower declared that the USSR had shown it could not maintain its "hegemony without military force" (*New York Times,* August 23, 1968, p. 8:3). Watts, Detroit and Newark surely illustrate the same point. In admiration of the Czechs, the *New York Times* said that the "populace openly voices its defiance and hostility" to the Russian occupiers (August 22, 1968, p. 1:3–7). It lamented that a mood of "sadness, fear and helplessness" was descending on Prague (August 30, 1968, p. 2:7). How about the mood of an occupied black community? The visceral racist seems to block out these aspects of such incidents. He focuses instead on ghetto dwellers removing the proverbial color television set from their local credit store.

6. *Disguising politically significant acts as 'ordinary crimes'.* Here you might ask: "Weren't the so-called 'rebels' of Watts, Detroit and Newark only interested in looting, and in destroying rather than liberating their ghettos? Weren't they simply criminals?" I won't attempt to devise general criteria for distinguishing between criminal and political acts. I assume that a single item of behavior might qualify as both. What I am trying to get at is the distortion that occurs when behavior is written off as *merely* a violation of the property rights of merchants and landlords by looters and arsonists. Perhaps the simplest antidote would be to notice how these same acts appear in the context of ghetto life. Psychiatrists W. H. Grier and P. M. Cobbs take such a view:

The goods of America, piled high in the neighborhood stores, had been offered to [black people] with a price tag that made work slavery and made balancing a budget a farce . . . The available jobs paid so poorly and the prices (plus interest) of goods were so high that if one made a purchase he was entering upon years of indebtedness. . . .

. . . At bottom, America remains a slave country which happens to have removed the slave laws from the books. The question we must ask is: What held the slave rebellion in check for so long? [6]

Besides ignoring the exploitation of black community residents by merchants and landlords, the visceral racist 'filters out' crimes by police that have contributed to nearly all the hundreds of ghetto outbreaks since the 1964 Harlem 'riots'. This ingredient has been recognized by the National Advisory Commission on Civil Disorders, although the Commission did not talk of police 'crimes'. Well-known books on Watts, Detroit and Newark document the background of official lawlessness in those black communities.[7] I won't go over that material; but I will take a 'miniature' illustration from local newspaper reporting of a more limited clash between blacks and authorities.

7. *Police crimes 'screened out'*. The general background of this story is conflict between black youth 'gangs' and police in the South Chicago suburb of Robbins. The situation became newsworthy when the Mayor of Robbins was shot in the leg as he answered the doorbell Halloween evening, 1970. Naturally a search was on for the miscreants. An article in *Chicago Tribune* for November 7 begins: "Four street gang members were charged yesterday with last Saturday's shooting of Marion Smith, Robbins mayor." Further along, and altogether secondary to the wounding of Mayor Smith, we read that Smith had called in special sheriff's investigators

to patrol the suburb after two persons were shot to death Monday [Nov. 2, 1970], in a shoot-out with [Robbins] police outside the Richard Flowers Housing Project. . . .

According to sheriff's police one of the two, Ronald Lee, 29, . . . was shot by a Robbins policeman, Sgt. Melvin Jessup, as he stood outside the doorway from which Robbins police said shots were fired at them. Lee was found to be unarmed.

However, sheriff's police still are investigating who fired the shot which killed Miss Barbara Franks, 18, as she was riding past in a car toward her home. . . .

Police Chief Porter McKamey of Robbins said no disciplinary action was planned against Jessup (p. 5).

In an interview reported by *Chicago Today,* there is another priceless statement by chief McKamey: "If a shot from a policeman killed the girl, it's one of those unfortunate incidents" (November 6, p. 5). The surprise ending is that Mayor Smith discharged Chief McKamey, Sergeant Jessup and two other patrolmen who were involved in the housing project gunplay.

This story recapitulates, in miniature, our perception of Watts-type incidents. We see black violence, and overlook the history of official lawlessness toward blacks. Next we subordinate the major consequences of official lawlessness, such as the death

---

[6] *Black Rage* (New York: Bantam Books, 1969), pp. 58–59.

[7] Robert Conot, *Rivers of Blood, Years of Darkness* (New York: Bantam Books, 1967); John Hersey, *The Algiers Motel Incident* (New York: Alfred A. Knopf, 1968); Tom Hayden, *Rebellion in Newark* (New York: Random House, 1967).

of black people, to comparatively minor results of black violence. Finally, when we cannot ignore a case of police violence, we agree with Chief McKamey to the extent that we *isolate* the case. Calling this an "unfortunate incident" is not enough for outraged liberals. They would rank it as 'tragic'. McKamey's choice of adjectives suggests that he may be either a disguised or an honest white supremacist. However that may be, notice that McKamey and outraged liberals fail to mention the fact that this "incident" is typical rather than isolated. Liberals agree with McKamey in not recognizing that this sort of thing happens regularly to blacks of Robbins and other communities.

A similar distortion crops up when the liberal sees this 'tragic incident' as rectified when a few 'bad cops' like McKamey and Jessup are weeded out. More precisely, he distorts things when he believes that further incidents of this kind will not occur if enlightened 'professionals' replace hostile and trigger-happy policemen.

More generally, when the outraged liberal reads that these and other 'bad cops' have been discharged or 'transferred to less sensitive work', and concludes that 'real progress is being made in police-community relations', he misperceives things again. Mayor Smith's action against McKamey and Jessup is far from typical. Crimes by authorities against black people almost never result in legal or disciplinary sanctions for official lawbreakers. Here is the more typical case. Three black students were killed, and 27 wounded, at the State College in Orangeburg, South Carolina, in February 1968. Nine State Highway patrolmen who were charged with shooting them have been promoted. But Cleveland Sellars, a young Student Non-Violent Coordinating Committee organizer, was sentenced to a year in jail for participating in a riot two nights before the killings.

If the visceral response is, "But that happened in the South," then more Northern 'incidents' are easy to find.[8] What I'm concerned to prove, however, is not the obvious point that violence against blacks is widespread and largely unpunished, but that most whites systematically overlook it, or subordinate it to black violence. These violent outbursts in turn are perceived as ordinary crimes, not rebellions. The epistemic pattern at least has the virtue of consistency. If you ignore conditions that provoke and justify it, you can more easily ignore an uprising.

Perhaps I have called too much attention to crimes by police against blacks. As I suggested earlier, policemen are not the only sources of oppression. Blacks must contend with other hostile and uncomprehending officials: welfare investigators, hospital admissions personnel, school administrators and teachers. Then there are various nongovernmental agents of white society: the neighborhood credit store owner; the loan shark; bill collectors; landlords. Even if some of these agents have dark skins, most

---

[8] See Eliot Asinof, *People v. Butcher* (New York: Viking Press, 1970); and Gene Marine, *The Black Panthers* (New York: Ramparts Books, 1969).

are oppressing their brothers for the benefit of whites. The 'take' of black intermediaries is negligible. Anyway, the important point is that such official and nonofficial agents, both black and white, frequently behave lawlessly toward residents of the black community. Besides violating constitutional rights to due process, and immunities to arbitrary search and seizure, these agents of white society commit numerous 'ordinary' crimes against blacks. For instance, tenement owners commonly violate fire and safety regulations. Thus you realize why it is a distortion to perceive blacks as engaged in violent and criminal activities, such as looting. A more accurate description would be to say they are responding lawlessly toward the lawless agents of white society.

Maybe it sounds odd, in the cumulative setting of the 350 years that I evoked, to distinguish between legality and illegality. Is there enough contrast in the behavior of white Americans toward blacks to draw the distinction? If you don't think so, then you may find the terminology of insurrection more appropriate. In that case, you would *not* say that black community residents occasionally violate, *en masse,* a system of laws; for how can a system of laws be said to exist in the black community when officials deal as American officials do with blacks? Taking this perspective, you would report that black community residents are trying to overthrow, not a system of laws but a system of oppression. What is the goal of their uprising? Perhaps, among other things, some approximation to the system of law that was promised in the Constitution and its Amendments but not delivered. I won't pursue that inquiry, however, because we should be analyzing visceral racist attitudes *toward* black aspirations, not the goals themselves.

And here we must contend with white liberals and moderates who say: "I agree with their goals, and I admit that they are oppressed; but I just can't agree with their methods. Why are they so impatient?" We have already noticed distortions in the view that black people have used unlawful and violent methods. But the ascription of motives like impatience is revealing.

8. *The norm of submissiveness for blacks.* The visceral racist seems to be implying that black people should be more patient. Apparently he thinks that it would be both normal and right for black people to go on waiting and protesting 'through legal channels'. But why? Does he think that *people in general* do and ought to go on waiting, when for 350 years they have been systematically deprived of many basic constitutional rights, not to mention dignity and a sense of control over their collective destiny? Would he admit that the poor in America are oppressed, and then expect them to be patient? Would he say this of American women? He might describe the Catholics of Northern Ireland as 'angry' and 'violent', but never as 'impatient'. I do not want to pursue any of these overworked analogies. I'm attempting to track down our perceptual distortions of black people in America. And my suggestion now is that the visceral racist unconsciously imposes a norm of submissiveness upon black people alone. He both expects and requires them to be unusually passive, or else to have superhuman

control over their frustrations. For when blacks deviate from this twofold standard of docility, the visceral racist perceives them as behaving abnormally—for blacks. The norm is his, not theirs.

9. *Confusion about threats to defend oneself.* The visceral racist will raise a further objection here which is equally revealing. He will deny that he is imposing a norm of submissiveness upon blacks. What bothers him now is that their reactions to frustration nowadays are becoming so aggressive. He is particularly apprehensive of black leaders, and organized groups like the Blank Panther Party, who endorse violence. After all, don't they tell black people to arm themselves and to shoot down policemen? Next thing you know they will be invading the suburbs and attacking every white they see!

Aside from the strange reversal of National Guardsmen besieging Watts, Detroit and Newark, what is philosophically interesting about this visceral fantasy is the way it distorts black self-defense. Advocates of this policy have always been unequivocal. Malcolm X contended:

It is criminal to teach a man not to defend himself when he is the constant victim of brutal attacks. It is legal and lawful to own a shotgun or a rifle. . . .

In areas where our people are the constant victims of brutality, and the government seems unable or unwilling to protect them, we should form rifle clubs that can be used to defend our lives and our property, in times of emergency, such as happened [in 1963] in Birmingham.[9]

He illustrated more poignantly at a meeting where Mrs. Fannie Lou Hamer spoke of the treatment she received as a result of her work for the Mississippi Freedom Democratic Party. Malcolm X said:

When I listen to Mrs. Hamer, a black woman—could be my mother, my sister, my daughter—describe what they had done to her in Mississippi, I ask myself: How in the world can we ever expect to be respected as *men* when we will allow something like that to be done to our women?[10]

The 'furthest' he went toward advocating attacks was in case authorities would not prosecute known murderers of black people. This was selective retaliation.[11] So far as I can tell, the Black Panther Party follows Malcolm X on these as well as many other points. As of mid-November 1970, their retaliatory attacks appear to have been limited to undercover policemen and informants in their midst; and at most one man may have died in this way. Scores of Party members have died in police attacks. How many have defended themselves? That is unclear. When police raiders killed Illinois Chairman Fred Hampton and Mark Clark in a 'shootout' December 4, 1969, one shot was fired

[9] In Breitman, ed., *Malcolm X Speaks*, p. 22.

[10] *Ibid.,* p. 107.

[11] *Ibid.,* pp. 7 8, 33, 43–44, 133–136, 160–165.

from inside, while police riddled their apartment. A 'moderate' local newspaper quotes "Justice Department figures" to the effect that eleven Party members and nine policemen were killed between November 1968 and November 1970.

Exact figures are of less importance for my analysis than perceptual distortions. The profoundest one is that you are never legally entitled to use 'violence' to defend yourself against a policeman. Malcolm X remarked: "Nowadays, our people don't care who the oppressor is; whether he has on a sheet or whether he has on a uniform"; in other words, "a uniform does not give him the right to come and shoot up your neighborhood." [12] If the uniformed man is acting illegally, while you are not, and there is a serious risk that he will kill you if you do not resist, you have a right to defend yourself. You may have difficulty proving your factual and legal claims; but the principle is obviously rooted in the Common Law regarding self-defense.

Other distortions are less profound but more evident in the visceral racist's account of self-defense: he confuses advocacy of self-defense with practicing it; then he confuses defensive violence with indiscriminately going on the warpath against policemen or whites generally. If this sounds too incredible, then I would say that at a minimum, the visceral racist either neglects the official violence which blacks say they will resist, or else he describes the situation so that it would appear to be the duty of black people, rather than their uniformed attackers, to restrain themselves. This last interpretation brings out the norm of submissiveness once again.

10. *Misperception of black 'demands'.* Before now the unacknowledged visceral racist will have asked, "What do they want anyhow? Will anything satisfy them?" One distortion here is the assumption that black people have to *ask* their oppressors for anything, as if it were a favor or privilege for them to have the same rights and opportunities that other groups do! A related distortion is to imagine that black people are 'demanding'—violently or nonviolently—deep alterations of American statutory and Common Law traditions. The changes they seem to be after are more changes in the behavior of officials and others who are covered by the laws we have. It is time civil rights laws and policies were obeyed! But what if we aren't legal experts? Then a minimal change would be that black people get at least the economic and other opportunities that 'poor whites' and working-class whites have.

In a minute I will analyze the troubling attitude of some of these whites to that suggestion. But first I want to correct one remaining visceral distortion that may have been encouraged by my analysis so far.

11. *Residual imagery of black victimization.* Suppose that we recognize and overcome the attitudes I have noted so far. We reject the norm of docility; we admit that policemen and other officials sometimes act lawlessly toward blacks; we recognize that blacks are already entitled by law to what they 'demand'. Unfortunately my own line of argumentation has nourished an attitude that meshes neatly with many of the

---

[12] *Ibid.,* pp. 67 and 164.

attitudes I've been challenging, particularly the norm of submissiveness. For example, I began by calling attention to the ways they are oppressed and exploited in our society. In discussing the 'riot'-'insurrections' I highlighted police crimes against them. On the whole it may appear that, despite these outbursts of anger, black Americans are unwilling but helpless victims of white brutality and cunning; helpless, that is, unless their fellow citizens decide to let up.

Why are these descriptions viscerally racist? What specifically do they distort? Surely black Americans are victimized. Otherwise why bother to analyze our visceral inclinations to ignore their situation? I agree that they suffer unbearable injustices. But it is a distortion to cast them as merely victims. They have resisted too—and long before Watts. Instead of screening it out, one should underscore their determination to survive. Is that word-magic? No, I believe that this is an objective, empirical dispute. There are historical reasons to stress resistance instead of victimization. Many kidnapped Africans killed themselves and their children, rather than accept slavery. Slaves revolted on numerous occasions from 1529 onwards. Sabotage was practiced endlessly by slaves and later by oppressed black servants and laborers. From the earliest times, black freemen agitated for their rights and against slavery. Segregated schools were challenged by blacks as early as 1844 (*Sarah C. Roberts v. The City of Boston*, 59 Mass. 198 [1849]). Between 'Emancipation' and the full development of Jim Crow law in the South, blacks seized a fair amount of political power—although defenders of Jim Crow, like Senator Tillman, whom I quoted in Section 1, tend to exaggerate this. During the Jim Crow era, blacks courageously formed civil rights organizations. Most recently they have assumed fuller control of their own movements. And as we noticed, some groups have armed to repel official and unofficial attacks on their people. So while they can use aid from whites, they are not supine without it.

Along the same lines, it is a distortion to assume that every aspect of life among the majority of blacks is second-rate, so that their only hope rests in becoming 'integrated'. By way of illustration, notice how we often refer to black neighborhoods as 'ghettos'. Black children are said to be 'culturally deprived'; we describe their relatively matriarchal living groups as 'broken homes', not 'complete' families. But why assume that all blacks would prefer and be better off with the dominant society's culture and life styles? Taking that for granted is the visceral equivalent of a white supremacist's belief that his civilization is superior. Of course it is *not* visceral racism to insist that black Americans must have the same opportunities as others to choose between life styles, and to participate in all cultural activities.

No doubt there are other deposits of viscerally racist attitudes in myself and fellow liberals that I have failed to spot. But I think I have given a sufficiently detailed diagnosis so that the reader can 'go on by himself', and social scientists can investigate these attitudes and their linguistic manifestations. As a concluding exercise, however, I want to test out my account. I have been considering mainly the relatively verbalized and 'ideological' dispositions of white liberals. Now I want to see how we can use my analysis to characterize various well-known and deeply troubling attitudes of Northern white industrial laborers and craftsmen toward blacks who threaten them.

12. *'Why should white workers sacrifice the advantages they struggled for?'* The exclusion of blacks from these sectors was documented earlier. The test for my analysis is therefore simple. I will ask, of readily available though relatively crude data, whether or not they qualify as evidence for a viscerally racist outlook. Take this pungent interview:

Ray Walczak, 44, works as a gig grinder . . . in Milwaukee. As he walked off his shift not long ago, he saw across the street the Rev. James Groppi and a group of black militants picketing for more jobs.

"Look at that," Ray Walczak said. "Bastards don't want jobs. If you offered them jobs now, 90 per cent of them would run like hell. I tell you, people on relief get better jobs, got better homes, than I've got. You're better off now not working. The colored people are eating steak, and this Polack bastard is eating chicken.

"Damn right I'm bitter. The Polish race years ago didn't go out and riot and ruin people's property. I've been in the shops since I was 16 . . . if I live to be a hundred I'll probably be doing the same job.

"The only raise I ever got was a union raise . . . never a merit raise . . . We're peons, just numbers." [13]

That particular worker does not think himself privileged; but if you compare his situation with that of his potential black competitors, he is. There is an interesting distortion in his claim that blacks do not really want the meagre opportunities he has. There is even a slight contradiction between his statement that they "don't want jobs" and his complaint that "people on relief get better jobs"; but perhaps this indicates that he is candidly expressing attitudes that conflict. Naturally he assumes that black protesters are on relief!

More explicit animosity toward blacks appears in another interview:

Ernest (Pee Wee) Hayes is 58, and for 37 years he has worked at the Armco steel plant in Middletown, Ohio. . . .

"We do all the work and the niggers have got it made. They keep closing and closing in, working their way into everything. Last 3 or 4 months you can't even turn on that damn TV without seeing a nigger. They're even playing cowboys. We briarhoppers ain't gonna stand for it. And 90% of Middletown is briarhoppers.

"My man got beat, Wallace. We need someone to wake 'em up. Shake 'em up. Kill 'em." [14]

[13] From Richard Lemon, *The Troubled American* (New York: Simon & Schuster, 1970), as serialized in the Chicago *Daily News,* October 29, 1970, p. 6.

[14] Lemon, *The Troubled American,* as serialized in the Chicago *Daily News,* October 30, 1970, p. 6.

This second worker is clearly a white supremacist, because in addition to being hostile toward blacks, he rocognizes that they do not presently have the same opportunities he has, and he intends to keep things that way.

How about the first worker? I think that my analysis helps us notice distortions as well as white supremacist elements in his diatribe. One particular theme in that interview is worth examining further, because it is so common in discussions I've heard. The theme is that workers like this man have suffered to win the few advantages they have. They started working before they could complete high school, and they accepted miserable wages for long hours, under hazardous conditions. They joined the union movement, got fired and took beatings. How can you expect them to give up the few advantages they won, and step aside to benefit blacks? On this view, schemes for preferential recruitment of blacks, admission to apprenticeship programs, and promotion, all seem like 'favoritism' and 'discrimination in reverse'.

Why are these misdescriptions of economic reality? First, while it is true that white workers suffered, fought and took their knocks, it is a distortion to forget that black workers did also. Moreover, as we noticed in Section 3, labor unions regularly betrayed black workers, forcing companies to put them out of jobs they already had, and refusing to admit and represent them. Thus fatal ambiguities begin to appear in the claim that white workers gained the advantages they have by struggling. If you ask, "Struggling against whom, and advantages over whom?," the answer in each case is: "Employers *and* black workers." Now the struggle does not sound so much like 'the good fight' any more. And the privileges no longer appear to be *privileges for laborers in general.* We notice that they are to a considerable extent 'white-skin privileges', unfair advantages over potential black competitors. The case for white workers looks very twisted.

How about the 'sacrifice' and 'favoritism' themes? These are again gross distortions. In the first place, there is a confusion between actuality and possibility. So far, very few blacks have gotten into industrial and craft unions, apprenticeship programs and supervisory positions. Thus in actual fact, whites have made no sacrifices, and no favoritism has been shown to black workers. At most the complaint might be that *if* blacks eventually get what they demand, this *would be* the result. But the second point to raise here is: "Would it be favoritism, and would there be sacrifices?" If you agree that white workers' advantages are unfair advantages, then how can you describe it as a 'sacrifice' when they must renounce them? Black workers have not called for the firing of whites. No renunciation of their legitimate privileges *as workers* is at issue: only their undeserved privileges as *white* workers. To end these privileges is no more a sacrifice than it is a sacrifice when you must return someone's property, whether you took it deliberately or by mistake, or whether you got it from your parents.

In connection with the 'favoritism' theme, what distorts things is the omission of all-important historical background. Consider preferential hiring programs in the setting of 350 years of gross favoritism toward white laborers and craftsmen. Then it hardly sounds unfair when blacks announce: "Until we get our share, you will have to *wait longer* than usual for the new jobs, for promotions and for admission to apprenticeship programs." It is not favoritism toward blacks when whites lose their illegal monopoly.

White workers and their union representatives who describe economic circumstances in the manner I've been analyzing certainly display visceral racism. But the hitch is that when you expose these and similar distortions, many workers will become explicitly antagonistic toward blacks. How many? That is for trained interviewers to find out. At this stage of exploring a person's attitudes, does it make any difference whether you have a visceral racist or a white supremacist on your hands? Besides the ideological and theoretical differences I've noted, there might be a practical difference when someone is intellectually 'up against the wall'. The acknowledged white supremacist will want to preserve current inequalities. Visceral racists like ourselves, once we have stopped misperceiving things, have strong professed reasons to work for immediate and drastic change.

THE NATURE OF FREEDOM *

Angela Davis

The idea of freedom has justifiably been a dominating theme in the history of Western ideas. Man has been repeatedly defined in terms of his inalienable freedom. One of the most acute paradoxes present in the history of Western society is that while on a philosophical plane freedom has been delineated in the most lofty and sublime fashion, concrete reality has always been permeated with the most brutal forms of unfreedom, of enslavement. In ancient Greece where, so we are taught, democracy had its source, it cannot be overlooked that in spite of all the philosophical assertions of man's freedom, in spite of the demand that man realize himself through exercising his freedom as a citizen of the polis, the majority of the people in Athens were not free. Women were not citizens and slavery was an accepted institution. Moreover, there was definitely a form of racism present in Greek society, for only Greeks were suited for the benefits of freedom: all non-Greeks were called barbarians and by their very nature could not be deserving or even capable of freedom.

In this context, one cannot fail to conjure up the image of Thomas Jefferson and the other so-called Fathers formulating the noble concepts of the Constitution of the United States while their slaves were living in misery. In order not to mar the beauty

* This article was part of Angela Davis's initial lecture for her course, "Recurring Philosophical Themes in Black Literature," delivered at UCLA.—Eds.

of the Constitution and at the same time to protect the institution of slavery, they wrote about "persons held to service or labor," a euphemism for the word slavery, as being exceptional types of human beings, persons who do not merit the guarantees and rights of the Constitution.

Is man free or is he not? Ought he be free or ought not he be free? The history of Black Literature provides, in my opinion, a much more illuminating account of the nature of freedom, its extent and limits, than all the philosophical discourses on this theme in the history of Western society. Why? For a number of reasons. First of all, because Black Literature in this country and throughout the world projects the consciousness of a people who have been denied entrance into the real world of freedom. Black people have exposed, by their very existence, the inadequacies not only of the practice of freedom, but of its very theoretical formulation. Because, if the theory of freedom remains isolated from the practice of freedom or rather is contradicted in reality, then this means that something must be wrong with the concept—that is, if we are thinking in a dialectical manner.

The pivotal theme of this course will thus be the idea of freedom as it is unfolded in the literary undertaking of Black people. Starting with *The Life and Times of Frederick Douglass* we will explore the slave's experience of his bondage and thus the negative experience of freedom. Most important here will be the crucial transformation of the concept of freedom as a static, given principle into the concept of liberation, the dynamic, active struggle for freedom. We will move on to W. E. B. Du Bois, to Jean Toomer, Richard Wright and John A. Williams. Interspersed will be poetry from the various periods of Black History in this country, and theoretical analyses such as Fanon and Du Bois' *A.B.C. of Color.* Finally I would like to discuss a few pieces by African writers and poems by Nicolas Guillen, a Black Cuban poet, and compare them to the work of American Blacks.

Throughout the course, I have said, the notion of freedom will be the axis around which we will attempt to develop other philosophical concepts. We will encounter such metaphysical notions as identity, the problem of self-knowledge. The kind of philosophy of history which emerges out of the works we are studying will be crucial. The morality peculiar to an oppressed people is something we will have to come to grips with. As we progress along the path of the unfolding of freedom in Black Literature, we should retrieve a whole host of related themes.

Before I get into the material, I would like to say a few words about the kinds of questions we ought to ask ourselves when we delve into the nature of human freedom. First of all, is freedom totally subjective, totally objective, or is it a synthesis of both poles? Let me try to explain what I mean. Is freedom to be conceived merely as an inherent, given characteristic of man, is it a freedom which is confined within the human mind, is freedom an internal experience? Or, on the other hand, is freedom only the liberty to move, to act in a way one chooses? Let us pose the original question as to the subjectivity or objectivity of freedom in the following manner: Is freedom the freedom of thought or the freedom of action? Or more important, is it possible to conceive of the one without the other?

This leads us directly to the problem of whether freedom is at all possible within the bounds of material bondage. Can the slave be said to be free in any way? This brings to mind one of the more notorious statements which the French existentialist, Jean-Paul Sartre, has made. Even the man in chains, he says, remains free—and for this reason: he is always at liberty to eliminate his condition of slavery even if this means his death. That is, his freedom is narrowly defined as the freedom to choose between his state of captivity and his death. Now, this is extreme. But we have to decide whether or not this is the way in which we are going to define that concept. Certainly, this would not be compatible with the notion of liberation, for when the slave opts for death, he does much more than obliterate his condition of enslavement, for at the same time he is abolishing the very condition of freedom, life. Yet there is more to be said, when we take the decision to die out of an abstract context and examine the dynamics of a real situation in which a slave meets his death in the fight for concrete freedom. That is to say, the choice, slavery or death, could either mean slavery or suicide, or on the other hand slavery or liberation at all costs. The difference between the two situations is crucial.

The authentic consciousness of an oppressed people entails an understanding of the necessity to abolish oppression. The slave finds at the end of his journey towards understanding a real grasp of what freedom means. He knows that it means the destruction of the master-slave relationship. And in this sense, his knowledge of freedom is more profound than that of the master. For the master feels himself free and he feels himself free because he is able to control the lives of others. He is free at the expense of the freedom of another. The slave experiences the freedom of the master in its true light. He understands that the master's freedom is abstract freedom to suppress other human beings. The slave understands that this is a pseudo concept of freedom and at this point is more enlightened than his master for he realizes that the master is a slave of his own misconceptions, his own misdeeds, his own brutality, his own effort to oppress.

Now I would like to go into the material. The first part of *The Life and Times of Frederick Douglass,* called "Life of a Slave," constitutes a physical voyage from slavery to freedom which is both the conclusion and reflection of a philosophical voyage from slavery to freedom. We will see that neither voyage would have been possible alone; they are mutually determinant.

The point of departure for his voyage is the following question Frederick Douglass asks himself as a child: "Why am I a slave? Why are some people slaves and others masters?" (page 50). His critical attitude when he fails to accept the usual answer—that God had made Black people to be slaves and white people to be masters—is the basic condition which must be presented before freedom can become a possibility in the mind of the slave. We must not forget that throughout the history of Western society there is an abundance of justifications for the existence of slavery. Both Plato and Aristotle felt that some men were born to be slaves, some men are not born into a state of freedom. Religious justifications for slavery are to be found at every turn.

Let's attempt to arrive at a philosophical definition of the slave: we have already stated the essence: he is a human being who, by some reason or another is denied freedom. But is not the essence of the human being his freedom? Either the slave is not a man or his very existence is a contradiction. We can rule out the first alternative, although we should not forget that the prevailing ideology defined the Black man as sub-human. The failure to deal with the contradictory nature of slavery, the imposed ignorance of reality is exemplified in the notion that the slave is not a man, for if he were a man, he should certainly be free.

We all know of the calculated attempts to rob the Black man of his humanity. We know that in order to maintain the institution of slavery, Black people were forced to live in conditions not fit for animals. The white slave-owners were determined to mold Black people into the image of the sub-human being which they had contrived in order to justify their actions. A vicious circle emerges in which the slave-owner loses all consciousness of himself.

The vicious circle continues to turn, but for the slave there is a way out: Resistance. Frederick Douglass seems to have had his first experience of this possibility of a slave becoming free upon observing a slave resist a flogging:"That slave who had the courage to stand up for himself against the overseer, although he might have many hard stripes at first, became while legally a slave virtually a free man. 'You can shoot me,' said a slave to Rigby Hopkins, 'but you can't whip me,' and the result was he was neither whipped nor shot."

Already we can begin to concretize the notion of freedom as it appeared to the slave. The first condition of freedom is the open act of resistance—physical resistance, violent resistance. In that act of resistance, the rudiments of freedom are already present. And the violent retaliation signifies much more than the physical act: it is refusal not only to submit to the flogging, but refusal to accept the definitions of the slave-master; it is implicitly a rejection of the institution of slavery, its standards, its morality, a microcosmic effort towards liberation.

The slave is actually conscious of the fact that freedom is not a fact, it is not given, but rather something to be fought for, it can exist only through a process of struggle. The slave-master, on the other hand, experiences his freedom as inalienable and thus as a fact: he is not aware that he too has been enslaved by his own system.

To begin to answer a question we posed earlier—is it possible for a man to be in chains and at the same time be free—we can now say that the path towards freedom can only be envisioned by the slave when he actively rejects his chains. The first phase of liberation is the decision to reject the image of himself which the slave-owner has painted, to reject the conditions which the slave-owner has created, to reject his own existence, to reject himself as slave.

. . .

HOMOGENIZING THE AMERICAN WOMAN: THE POWER OF AN UNCONSCIOUS IDEOLOGY

Sandra L. Bem and Daryl J. Bem

"In the beginning God created the heaven and the earth. . . . And God said, Let us make man in our image, after our likeness; and let him have dominion over the fish of the sea, and over the fowl of the air, and over the cattle, and over all the earth. . . . And the rib, which the Lord God had taken from man, made he a woman and brought her unto the man. . . . And the Lord God said unto the woman, What is this that thou hast done? And the woman said, The serpent beguiled me, and I did eat. . . . Unto the woman God said, I will greatly multiply thy sorrow and thy conception; in sorrow thou shalt bring forth children; and thy desire shall be to thy husband, and he shall rule over thee." (Gen. 1, 2, 3)

There is a moral to that story. St. Paul spells it out even more clearly.

"For a man . . . is the image and glory of God; but the woman is the glory of the man. For the man is not of the woman, but the woman of the man. Neither was the man created for the woman, but the woman for the man." (1 Cor. 11)

"Let the woman learn in silence with all subjection. But suffer not a woman to teach, nor to usurp authority over the man, but to be in silence. For Adam was first formed and then Eve. And Adam was not deceived, but the woman, being deceived, was in the transgression. Nothwithstanding, she shall be saved in childbearing, if they continue in faith and charity and holiness with sobriety." (1 Tim. 2)

Now one should not assume that only Christians have this kind of rich heritage of ideology about women. So consider now, the morning prayer of the Orthodox Jew:

"Blessed art Thou, oh Lord our God, King of the Universe, that I was not born a gentile."

"Blessed art Thou, oh Lord our God, King of the Universe, that I was not born a slave."

"Blessed art Thou, oh Lord our God, King of the Universe, that I was not born a woman."

Or, consider the Koran, the sacred text of Islam:

"Men are superior to women on account of the qualities in which God has given them pre-eminence."

Because they think they sense a decline in feminine "faith, charity, and holiness with sobriety," many people today jump to the conclusion that the ideology expressed in these passages is a relic of the past. Not so, of course. It has simply been obscured by an equalitarian veneer, and the same ideology has now become unconscious. That is, we remain unaware of it because alternative beliefs and attitudes about women, until very recently, have gone unimagined. We are very much like the fish who is unaware of the fact that his environment is wet. After all, what else could it be? Such is the nature of all unconscious ideologies in a society. Such, in particular, is the nature of America's ideology about women.

What we should like to do in this paper is to discuss today's version of this same ideology.

When a baby boy is born, it is difficult to predict what he will be doing 25 years later. We can't say whether he will be an artist, a doctor, a lawyer, a college professor, or a bricklayer, because he will be permitted to develop and fulfill his own unique potential—particularly, of course, if he happens to be white and middle class. But if that same newborn child happens to be a girl, we can predict with almost complete confidence how she is likely to be spending her time some 25 years later. Why can we do that? Because her individuality doesn't have to be considered. Her individuality is irrelevant. Time studies have shown that she will spend the equivalent of a full working day, 7.1 hours, in preparing meals, cleaning house, laundering, mending, shopping and doing other household tasks. In other words, 43 percent of her waking time will be spent in activity that would command an hourly wage on the open market well below the federally set minimum for menial industrial work.

Of course, the point really is not how little she would earn if she did these things in someone else's home. She will be doing them in her own home for free. The point is that this use of time is virtually the same for homemakers with college degrees and for homemakers with less than a grade-school education, for women married to professional men, and for women married to blue-collar workers. Actually, that's understating it slightly. What the time study really showed was that college-educated women spend slightly *more* time cleaning their houses than their less-educated counterparts!

Of course, it is not simply the full-time homemaker whose unique identity has been rendered largely irrelevant. Of the 31 million women who work outside the home in our society, 78 percent end up in dead-end jobs as clerical workers, service workers, factory workers, or sales clerks, compared to a comparable figure of 40 percent for men. Only 15 percent of all women workers in our society are classified by the Labor Department as professional and technical workers, and even this figure is misleading— for the single, poorly-paid occupation of non-college teacher absorbs half of these women, and the occupation of nurse absorbs an additional quarter. In other words, the two jobs of teacher and nurse absorb three-quarters of all women classified in our society as technical or professional. That means, then, that fewer than 5 percent of all professional women—fewer than 1 percent of all women workers—fill those positions which to most Americans connote "professional": Physician, lawyer, engineer, scientist, college professor, journalist, writer, and so forth.

Even an I.Q. in the genius range does not guarantee that a woman's unique potential will find expression. There was a famous study of over 1,300 boys and girls whose I.Q.'s averaged 151.[1] When the study began in the early 1900s, these highly gifted youngsters were only ten years old, and their careers have been followed ever since. What are they today? 86 percent of the men have now achieved prominence in professional and managerial occupations. In contrast, only a minority of the women were even employed. Of those who were, 37 percent were nurses, librarians, social workers, and non-college teachers. An additional 26 percent were secretaries, stenographers, bookkeepers, and office workers! Only 11 percent entered the higher professions of law, medicine, college teaching, engineering, science, economics, and the like. And even at age 44, well after all their children had gone to school, 61 percent of these highly gifted women remained full-time homemakers. Talent, education, ability, interests, motivations: all irrelevant. In our society, being female uniquely qualifies an individual for domestic work—either by itself or in conjunction with typing, teaching, nursing, or (most often) unskilled labor. It is this homogenization of America's women which is the major consequence of our society's sex-role ideology.

It is true, of course, that most women have several hours of leisure time every day. And it is here, we are often told, that each woman can express her unique identity. Thus, politically interested women can join the League of Women Voters. Women with humane interests can become part-time Gray Ladies. Women who love music can raise money for the symphony. Protestant women play canasta; Jewish women play mahjongg; brighter women of all denominations and faculty wives play bridge.

But politically interested *men* serve in legislatures. *Men* with humane interests become physicians or clinical psychologists. *Men* who love music play in the symphony. In other words, why should a woman's unique identity determine only the periphery of her life rather than its central core?

Why? Why nurse rather than physician, secretary rather than executive, stewardess rather than pilot? Why faculty wife rather than faculty? Why doctor's mother rather than doctor? There are three basic answers to this question: (1) discrimination; (2) sex-role conditioning; and (3) the presumed incompatibility of family and career.

Discrimination

In 1968, the median income of full-time women workers was approximately $4,500. The comparable figure for men was $3,000 higher. Moreover, the gap is widening. Ten years ago, women earned 64 percent of what men did; that percentage has now shrunk

[1] L. M. Terman and M. H. Oden, *The Gifted Group at Mid-Life: Thirty-Five Years' Follow-up of the Superior Child,* Genetic Studies of Genius, V (Stanford, Calif.: Stanford University Press, 1959).

to 58 percent. Today, a female college graduate working full-time can expect to earn less per year than a male high-school dropout.

There are two reasons for this pay differential. First, in every category of occupation, women are employed in the lesser-skilled, lower-paid positions. Even in the clerical field, where 73 percent of the workers are women, females are relegated to the lowest status positions and hence earn only 65 percent of what male clerical workers earn. The second reason for this pay differential is discrimination in its purest form: unequal pay for equal work. According to a survey of 206 companies in 1970, female college graduates were offered jobs which paid $43 per month less than those offered to their male counterparts in the same college major.

New laws should begin to correct both of these situations. The Equal Pay Act of 1963 prohibits employers from discriminating on the basis of sex in the payment of wages for equal work. In a landmark ruling on May 18, 1970, the U.S. Supreme Court ordered that $250,000 in back pay be paid to women employed by a single New Jersey glass company. This decision followed a two-year court battle by the Labor Department after it found that the company was paying men selector-packers 21.5 cents more per hour than women doing the same work. In a similar case, the Eighth Circuit Court of Appeals ordered a major can company to pay more than $100,000 in back wages to women doing equal work. According to the Labor Department, an estimated $17 million is owed to women in back pay. Since that estimate was made, a 1972 amendment extended the Act to cover executive, administrative, and professional employees as well.

But to enjoy equal pay, women must also have access to equal jobs. Title VII of the 1964 Civil Rights Act prohibits discrimination in employment on the basis of race, color, religion, national origin—and sex. Although the sex provision was treated as a joke at the time (and was originally introduced by a Southern Congressman in an attempt to defeat the bill), the Equal Employment Opportunities Commission discovered in its first year of operation that 40 percent or more of the complaints warranting investigation charged discrimination on the basis of sex.[2]

Title VII has served as one of the most effective instruments in helping to achieve sex equality in the world of work. According to a report by the E.E.O.C., nearly 6,000 charges of sex discrimination were filed with that agency in 1971 alone, a 62 percent increase over the previous year.

But the most significant legislative breakthrough in the area of sex equality was the passage of the Equal Rights Amendment by both houses of Congress in 1972. The ERA simply states that "Equality of rights under the law shall not be denied or abridged by the United States or by any state on account of sex." This amendment has been introduced into every session of Congress since 1923, and its passage now is clearly an indication of the changing role of the American woman. All of the various ramifica-

[2] C. Bird, *Born Female: The High Cost of Keeping Women Down* (New York, Pocket Books, 1969).

tions are hard to predict, but it is clear that it will have profound consequences in private as well as public life.

Many Americans assume that the recent drive for equality between the sexes is primarily for the benefit of the middle-class woman who wants to seek self-fulfillment in a professional career. But in many ways, it is the woman in more modest circumstances, the woman who *must* work for economic reasons, who stands to benefit most from the removal of discriminatory barriers. It is *she* who is hardest hit by unequal pay; it is *she* who so desperately needs adequate day-care facilities; it is *her* job which is often dead-ended while her male colleagues in the factory get trained and promoted into the skilled craft jobs. And if both she and her husband work at unfulfilling jobs eight hours a day just to make an adequate income, it is still *she* who carries the additional burden of domestic chores when they return home.

We think it is important to emphasize these points at the outset, for we have chosen to focus our remarks in this particular paper on those fortunate men and women who can afford the luxury of pursuing self-fulfillment through the world of work and career. But every societal reform advocated by the new feminist movement, whether it be the Equal Rights Amendment, the establishment of child-care centers, or basic changes in America's sex-role ideology, will affect the lives of men and women in every economic circumstance. Nevertheless, it is still economic discrimination which hits hardest at the largest group of women, and it is here that the drive for equality can be most successfully launched with legislative and judicial tools.

Sex-Role Conditioning

But even if all discrimination were to end tomorrow, nothing very drastic would change. For job discrimination is only part of the problem. It does impede women who choose to become lawyers or managers or physicians. But it does not, by itself, help us to understand why so many women "choose" to be secretaries or nurses rather than executives or physicians; why only 3 percent of ninth-grade girls as compared to 25 percent of the boys "choose" careers in science or engineering; or why 63 percent of America's married women "choose" not to work at all. It certainly doesn't explain those young women whose vision of the future includes only marriage, children, and living happily ever after; who may, at some point, "choose" to take a job, but who almost never "choose" to pursue a career. Discrimination frustrates choices already made. Something more pernicious perverts the motivation to choose.

That "something" is an unconscious ideology about the nature of the female sex, an ideology which constricts the emerging self-image of the female child and the nature of her aspirations from the very beginning; an ideology which leads even those Americans who agree that a black skin should not uniquely qualify *its* owner for a janitorial or domestic service to act as if the possession of a uterus uniquely qualifies *its* owner for precisely such service.

Consider, for example, the 1968 student rebellion at Columbia University. Students from the radical Left took over some administration buildings in the name of equalitarian ideals which they accused the university of flouting. Here were the most militant spokesmen one could hope to find in the cause of equalitarian ideals. But no sooner had they occupied the buildings than the male militants blandly turned to their sisters-in-arms and assigned them the task of preparing the food, while they—the menfolk—would presumably plan future strategy. The reply these males received was the reply that they deserved—we will leave that to your imagination—and the fact that domestic tasks behind the barricades were desegregated across the sex line that day is an everlasting tribute to the class consciousness of these ladies of the Left. And it was really on that day that the campus women's liberation movement got its start— when radical women finally realized that they were never going to get to make revolution, only coffee.

But these conscious co-eds are not typical, for the unconscious assumptions about a woman's "natural" talents (or lack of them) are at least as prevalent among women as they are among men. A psychologist named Phillip Goldberg demonstrated this by asking female college students to rate a number of professional articles from each of six fields.[3] The articles were collated into two equal sets of booklets, and the names of the authors were changed so that the identical article was attributed to a male author (e.g., John T. McKay) in one booklet and to a female author (e.g., Joan T. McKay) in the other booklet. Each student was asked to read the articles in her booklet and to rate them for value, competence, persuasiveness, writing style, and so forth.

As he had anticipated, Goldberg found that the identical article received significantly lower ratings when it was attributed to a female author than when it was attributed to a male author. He had predicted this result for articles from professional fields generally considered the province of men, like law or city planning, but to his surprise, these women also downgraded articles from the fields of dietetics and elementary-school education when they were attributed to female authors. In other words, these students rated the male authors as better at everything, agreeing with Aristotle that "we should regard the female nature as afflicted with a natural defectiveness." Such is the nature of America's unconscious ideology about women.

When does this ideology begin to affect the life of a young girl? Research now tells us that from the day a newborn child is dressed in pink, she is given "special" treatment. Perhaps because they are thought to be more fragile, six-month-old infant girls are actually touched, spoken to, and hovered over more by their mothers while they are playing than are infant boys.[4] One study even showed that when mothers and babies are still in the hospital, mothers smile at, talk to, and touch their female infants more

[3] Phillip Goldberg, "Are Women Prejudiced Against Women?" *Transaction* 5 (April 1968), 28–30.

[4] S. Goldberg and M. Lewis, "Play Behavior in the Year-old Infant: Early Sex Differences," *Child Development* 40 (1969), 21–31.

than their male infants at two days of age.⁵ Differential treatment can't begin much earlier than that.

As children begin to read, the storybook characters become the images and the models that little boys and little girls aspire to become. What kind of role does the female play in the world of children's literature? The fact is that there aren't even very many females in that world. One survey ⁶ found that five times as many males as females appear in the titles of children's books; the fantasy world of Doctor Seuss is almost entirely male; and even animals and machines are represented as male. When females do appear, they are noteworthy primarily for what they do *not* do. They do not drive cars, and they seldom even ride bicycles. In one story in which a girl does ride a bicycle, it's a two-seater. Guess where the girl is seated! Boys in these stories climb trees and fish and roll in the leaves and skate. Girls watch, fall down, and get dizzy. Girls are never doctors, and although they may be nurses or librarians or teachers, they are never principals. There seemed to be only one children's book about mothers who work, and it concludes that what mothers love "best of all" is "being your very own Mommy and coming home to you." And although this is no doubt true of many daddies as well, no book about working fathers has ever found it necessary to apologize for working in quite the same way.

As children grow older, more explicit sex-role training is introduced. Boys are encouraged to take more of an interest in mathematics and science. Boys, not girls, are usually given chemistry sets and microscopes for Christmas. Moreover, all children quickly learn that mommy is proud to be a moron when it comes to math and science, whereas daddy is a little ashamed if he doesn't know all about such things. When a young boy returns from school all excited about biology, he is almost certain to be encouraged to think of becoming a physician. A girl with similar enthusiasm is usually told that she might want to consider nurse's training later on, so she can have "an interesting job to fall back upon in case—God forbid—she ever needs to support herself." A very different kind of encouragement. And any girl who doggedly persists in her enthusiasm for science is likely to find her parents as horrified by the prospect of a permanent love affair with physics as they would be either by the prospect of an interracial marriage or, horror of horrors, no marriage at all. Indeed, our graduate women report that their families seem convinced that the menopause must come at age 23.

These socialization practices take their toll. When they apply for college, boys and girls are about equal on verbal aptitude tests, but boys score significantly higher on mathematical aptitude tests—about 60 points higher on the College Board Exams.⁷

⁵ E. B. Thoman, P. H. Leiderman, and J. P. Olson, "Neonate-Mother Interaction during Breast Feeding," *Developmental Psychology* 6 (1972), 110–118.

⁶ E. Fisher, "The Second Sex, Junior Division," *The New York Times Book Review,* May 1970.

⁷ For example, R. Brown, *Social Psychology* (New York: Free Press, 1965).

Moreover, for those who are convinced that this is due to female hormones, it is relevant to know that girls improve their mathematical performance if the problems are simply reworded so that they deal with cooking and gardening, even though the abstract reasoning required for solution remains exactly the same.[8] That's not hormones! Clearly, what has been undermined is not a woman's mathematical ability, but rather her confidence in that ability.

But these effects in mathematics and science are only part of the story. The most conspicuous outcome of all is that the majority of America's women become full-time homemakers. And of those who do work, nearly 80 percent end up in dead-end jobs as clerical workers, service workers, factory workers, or sales clerks. Again, it is this "homogenization" of America's women which is the major consequence of America's sex-role ideology.

The important point is not that the role of homemaker is necessarily inferior, but rather that our society is managing to consign a large segment of its population to the role of homemaker—either with or without a dead-end job—solely on the basis of sex just as inexorably as it has in the past consigned the individual with a black skin to the role of janitor or domestic. The important point is that in spite of their unique identities, the majority of American women end up in virtually the *same* role.

The socialization of the American male has closed off certain options for him, too. Men are discouraged from developing certain desirable traits such as tenderness and sensitivity, just as surely as women are discouraged from being assertive and, alas, "too bright." Young boys are encouraged to be incompetent at cooking and certainly child care, just as surely as young girls are urged to be incompetent at math and science. The elimination of sex-role stereotyping implies that each individual would be encouraged to "do his own thing." Men and women would no longer be stereotyped by society's definitions of masculine and feminine. If sensitivity, emotionality, and warmth are desirable *human* characteristics, then they are desirable for men as well as for women. If independence, assertiveness, and serious intellectual commitment are desirable *human* characteristics, then they are desirable for women as well as for men. Thus, we are not implying that men have all the goodies and that women can obtain self-fulfillment by acting like men. That is hardly the utopia implied by today's feminist movement. Rather, we envision a society which raises its children so flexibly and with sufficient respect for the integrity of individual uniqueness that some men might emerge with the motivation, the ability, and the opportunity to stay home and raise children without bearing the stigma of being peculiar. Indeed, if homemaking is as glamorous as women's magazines and television commercials would have us believe, then men, too, should have that option. And even if homemaking isn't all that glamorous, it would

[8] G. A. Milton, "Sex Differences in Problem Solving as a Function of Role Appropriateness of the Problem Content," *Psychological Reports* 5 (1959), 705–708.

probably still be more fulfilling for some men than the jobs in which they now find themselves forced because of their role as breadwinner. Thus, it is true that a man's options are also limited by our society's sex-role ideology, but as the "predictability test" reveals, it is still the woman in our society whose identity is rendered irrelevant by America's socialization practices.

Further Psychological Barriers

But what of the woman who arrives at age 21 still motivated to be challenged and fulfilled by a growing career? Is she free to choose a career if she cares to do so? Or is there something standing even in her way?

There is. Even the woman who has managed to finesse society's attempt to rob her of her career motivations is likely to find herself blocked by society's trump card: the feeling that one cannot have a career and be a successful woman simultaneously. A competent and motivated woman is thus caught in a double-bind which few men have ever faced. She must worry not only about failure, but also about success.

This conflict was strikingly revealed in a study which required college women to complete the following story: "After first-term finals, Anne finds herself at the top of her medical-school class." [9] The stories were then examined for concern about the negative consequences of success. The women in this study all had high intellectual ability and histories of academic success. They were the very women who could have successful careers. And yet, over two-thirds of their stories revealed a clear-cut inability to cope with the concept of a feminine, yet career-oriented, woman.

The most common "fear-of-success" stories showed fears of social rejection as a result of success. The women in this group showed anxiety about becoming unpopular, unmarriageable, and lonely:

Anne starts proclaiming her surprise and joy. Her fellow classmates are so disgusted with her behavior that they jump on her in a body and beat her. She is maimed for life.

Anne is an acne-faced bookworm. . . . She studies twelve hours a day, and lives at home to save money. "Well, it certainly paid off. All the Friday and Saturday nights without dates, fun—I'll be the best woman doctor alive." And yet a twinge of sadness comes through—she wonders what she really has. . . .

Anne doesn't want to be number one in her class. . . . She feels she shouldn't rank so high because of social reasons. She drops to ninth and then marries the boy who graduates number one.

In the second "fear-of-success" category were stories in which the women seemed concerned about definitions of womanhood. These stories expressed guilt and despair over success and doubts about their femininity and normality:

[9] M. S. Horner, "Fail: Bright Women," *Psychology Today,* November 1969.

Unfortunately Anne no longer feels so certain that she really wants to be a doctor. She is worried about herself and wonders if perhaps she is not normal. . . . Anne decides not to continue with her medical work but to take courses that have a deeper personal meaning for her.

Anne feels guilty. . . . She will finally have a nervous breakdown and quit medical school and marry a successful young doctor.

A third group of stories could not even face up to the conflict between having a career and being a woman. These stories simply denied the possibility that any woman could be so successful:

Anne is a code name for a nonexistent person created by a group of med students. They take turns writing for Anne. . . .

Anne is really happy she's on top, though Tom is higher than she—though that's as it should be. Anne doesn't mind Tom winning.

Anne is talking to her counselor. Counselor says she will make a fine nurse.

By way of contrast, here is a typical story written not about Anne, but about John:

John has worked very hard and his long hours of study have paid off. . . . He is thinking about his girl, Cheri, whom he will marry at the end of med school. He realizes he can give her all the things she desires after he becomes established. He will go on in med school and be successful in the long run.

Nevertheless, there were a few women in the study who welcomed the prospect of success:

Anne is quite a lady—not only is she top academically, but she is liked and admired by her fellow students—quite a trick in a man-dominated field. She is brilliant—but she is also a woman. She will continue to be at or near the top. And . . . always a lady.

Hopefully the day is approaching when as many "Anne" stories as "John" stories will have happy endings. But notice that even this story finds it necessary to affirm repeatedly that femininity is not necessarily destroyed by accomplishment. One would never encounter a comparable story written about John who, although brilliant and at the top of his class, is "still a man, still a man, still a man."

It seems unlikely that anyone in our society would view these "fear-of-success" stories as portraits of mental health. But even our concept of mental health has been distorted by America's sex-role stereotypes. Here we must indict our own profession of psychology. A recent survey of seventy-nine clinically-trained psychologists, psychiatrists, and social workers, both male and female, revealed a double standard of mental health.[10] That is, even professional clinicians have two different concepts of mental health, one for men and one for women; and these concepts parallel the sex-role stereotypes prevalent in our society. Thus, according to these clinicians, a woman is to be regarded as healthier and more mature if she is: more submissive, less independent, less adventurous, more easily influenced, less aggressive, less competitive, more excitable in minor crises, more susceptible to hurt feelings, more emotional, more conceited about her appearance, less objective, and more antagonistic toward math and science! But this was the very same description which these clinicians used to characterize an unhealthy, immature man or an unhealthy, immature adult (sex unspecified)! The equation is clear: Mature woman equals immature adult.

Given this concept of a mature woman, is it any wonder that few women ever aspire toward challenging and fulfilling careers? In order to have a career, a woman will probably need to become relatively more dominant, independent, adventurous, aggressive, competitive, and objective, and relatively less excitable, emotional and conceited than our ideal of femininity requires. Is she were a man (or an adult, sex unspecified), these would all be considered positive traits. But because she is a woman, these same traits will bring her disapproval. She must then either be strong enough to have her "femininity" questioned; or she must behave in the prescribed feminine manner and accept second-class status, as an adult and as a professional.

And, of course, should a woman faced with this conflict seek professional help, hoping to summon the strength she will need to pursue her career goals, the advice she is likely to receive will be of virtually no use. For, as this study reveals, even professional counselors have been contaminated by the sex-role ideology.

It is frequently argued that a 21-year-old woman is perfectly free to choose a career if she cares to do so. No one is standing in her way. But this argument conveniently overlooks the fact that our society has spent 20 years carefully marking the woman's ballot for her, and so it has nothing to lose in that 21st year by pretending to let her cast it for the alternative of her choice. Society has controlled not her alternatives (although discrimination does do that), but more importantly, it has controlled her motivation to choose any but one of those alternatives. The so-called freedom-to-choose is illusory, and it cannot be invoked to justify a society which controls the woman's motivation to choose.

Biological Considerations

Up to this point, we have argued that the differing life patterns of men and women in our society can be chiefly accounted for by cultural conditioning. The most common counterargument to this view, of course, is the biological one. The biological argument

---

[10] I. K. Broverman et al., "Sex-Role Stereotypes and Clinical Judgments of Mental Health," *Journal of Consulting and Clinical Psychology* 34 (1970), 1–7.

suggests that there may really be inborn differences between men and women in, say, independence or mathematical ability. Or that there may be biological factors beyond the fact that women can become pregnant and nurse children which uniquely dictate that they, but not men, should stay home all day and shun serious outside commitment. What this argument suggests is that maybe female hormones really are responsible somehow. One difficulty with this argument, of course, is that female hormones would have to be different in the Soviet Union, where one-third of the engineers and 75 percent of the physicians are women.[11] In America, by way of contrast, women constitute less than 1 percent of the engineers and only 7 percent of the physicians. Female physiology *is* different, and it may account for some of the psychological differences between the sexes, but America's sex-role ideology still seems primarily responsible for the fact that so few women emerge from childhood with the motivation to seek out any role beyond the one that our society dictates.

But even if there really were biological differences between the sexes along these lines, the biological argument would still be irrelevant. The reason can best be illustrated with an analogy.

Suppose that every black American boy were to be socialized to become a jazz musician on the assumption that he was a "natural" talent in that direction; or suppose that parents and counselors should subtly discourage him from other pursuits because it is considered "inappropriate" for black men to become physicians or physicists. Most Americans would disapprove. But suppose that it *could* be demonstrated that black Americans, *on the average,* did possess an inborn better sense of rhythm than white Americans. Would *that* justify ignoring the unique characteristics of a *particular* black youngster from the very beginning and specifically socializing him to become a musician? We don't think so. Similarly, as long as a woman's socialization does not nurture her uniqueness, but treats her only as a member of a group on the basis of some assumed *average* characteristic, she will not be prepared to realize her own potential in the way that the values of individuality and self-fulfillment imply that she should.

The Presumed Incompatibility of Family and Career

If we were to ask the average American woman why she is not pursuing a full-time career, she would probably not say that discrimination had discouraged her; nor would she be likely to recognize the pervasive effects of her own sex-role conditioning. What she probably would say is that a career, no matter how desirable, is simply incompatible with the role of wife and mother.

As recently as the turn of the century, and in less technological societies today, this incompatibility between career and family was, in fact, decisive. Women died in their forties and they were pregnant or nursing during most of their adult lives. Moreover, the work that a less technological society requires places a premium on mobility and

[11] N. D. Dodge, *Women in the Soviet Economy* (Baltimore: Johns Hopkins Press, 1966).

physical strength, neither of which a pregnant woman has a great deal of. Thus, the historical division of labor between the sexes—the man away at work and the woman at home with the children—was a biological necessity. Today it is not.

Today, the work that our technological society requires is primarily mental in nature; women have virtually complete control over their reproductive lives; and most important of all, the average American woman now lives to age 74 and has her last child before age 30. This means that by the time a woman is 35 or so, her children have more important things to do with their daytime hours than to spend them entertaining some adult woman who has nothing fulfilling to do during the entire second half of her life span.

But social forms have a way of outliving the necessities which gave rise to them. And today's female adolescent continues to plan for a nineteenth-century life style in a twentieth-century world. A Gallup poll has found that young women give no thought whatever to life after forty.[12] They plan to graduate from high school, perhaps go to college, and then get married. Period!

The Woman as Wife

At some level, of course, this kind of planning is "realistic." Because most women do grow up to be wives and mothers, and because, for many women, this means that they will be leaving the labor force during the child-rearing years, a career is not really feasible. After all, a career involves long-term commitment and perhaps some sacrifice on the part of the family. Furthermore, as every "successful" woman knows, a wife's appropriate role is to encourage her husband in *his* career. The "good" wife puts her husband through school, endures the family's early financial difficulties without a whimper, and, if her husband's career should suddenly dictate a move to another city, she sees to it that the transition is accomplished as painlessly as possible. The good wife is selfless. And to be seriously concerned about one's own career is selfish—if one is female, that is. With these kinds of constraints imposed upon the work life of the married woman, perhaps it would be "unrealistic" for her to seriously aspire toward a career rather than a job.

There is some evidence of discontent among these "selfless" women, however. A 1962 Gallup poll revealed that only 10 percent of American women would want their daughters to live their lives the way they did.[13] These mothers wanted their daughters to get more education and to marry later. And a 1970 study of women married to top Chicago-area business and professional men revealed that if these women could live their lives over again, they would pursue careers.[14]

[12] G. Gallup and E. Hill, "The American Woman," *The Saturday Evening Post,* 22 December 1962, pp. 15–32.

[13] Ibid.

[14] M. Ringo, "The Well-placed Wife" (Chicago: John Paisios & Associates, 332 South Michigan Ave., Unpublished manuscript).

Accordingly, the traditional conception of the husband-wife relationship is now being challenged, not so much because of this widespread discontent among older, married women, but because it violates two of the most basic values of today's college generation. These values concern personal growth, on the one hand, and interpersonal relationships on the other. The first of these emphasizes individuality and self-fulfillment; the second stresses openness, honesty, and equality in all human relationships.

Because they see the traditional male-female relationship as incompatible with these basic values, today's young people are experimenting with alternatives to the traditional marriage pattern. Although a few are testing out ideas like communal living, most seem to be searching for satisfactory modifications of the husband-wife relationship, either in or out of the context of marriage. An increasing number of young people claim to be seeking fully equalitarian relationships and they cite examples like the following:

"Both my wife and I earned college degrees in our respective disciplines. I turned down a superior job offer in Oregon and accepted a slightly less desirable position in New York where my wife would have more opportunities for part-time work in her specialty. Although I would have preferred to live in a suburb, we purchased a home near my wife's job so that she could have an office at home where she would be when the children returned from school. Because my wife earns a good salary, she can easily afford to pay a housekeeper to do her major household chores. My wife and I share all other tasks around the house equally. For example, she cooks the meals, but I do the laundry for her and help her with many of her other household tasks."

Without questioning the basic happiness of such a marriage or its appropriateness for many couples, we can legitimately ask if such a marriage is, in fact, an instance of interpersonal equality. Have all the hidden assumptions about the woman's "natural" role really been eliminated? Have our visionary students really exorcised the traditional ideology as they claim? There is a very simple test. If the marriage is truly equalitarian, then its description should retain the same flavor and tone even if the roles of the husband and wife were to be reversed:

"Both my husband and I earned college degrees in our respective disciplines. I turned down a superior job offer in Oregon and accepted a slightly less desirable position in New York where my husband would have more opportunities for part-time work in his specialty. Although I would have preferred to live in a suburb, we purchased a home near my husband's job so that he could have an office at home where he would be when the children returned from school. Because my husband earns a good salary, he can easily afford to pay a housekeeper to do his major household chores. My husband and I share all other tasks around the house equally. For example, he cooks the meals, but I do the laundry for him and help him with many of his other household tasks."

Somehow it sounds different, and yet only the pronouns have been changed to protect the powerful! Certainly no one would ever mistake the marriage *just* described as equalitarian or even very desirable, and thus it becomes apparent that the ideology about the woman's "natural" place unconsciously permeates the entire fabric of such "pseudo-equalitarian" marriages. It is true the wife gains some measure of equality when she can have a career rather than have a job and when her career can influence the final place of residence. But why is it the unquestioned assumption that the husband's career solely determines the initial set of alternatives that are to be considered? Why is it the wife who automatically seeks the part-time position? Why is it *her* housekeeper rather than *their* housekeeper? Why *her* household tasks? And so forth throughout the entire relationship.

The important point is not that such marriages are bad or that their basic assumptions of inequality produce unhappy, frustrated women. Quite the contrary. It is the very happiness of the wives in such marriages that reveals society's smashing success in socializing its women. It is a measure of the distance our society must yet traverse toward the goal of full equality that such marriages are widely characterized as utopian and fully equalitarian. It is a mark of how well the woman has been kept in her place that the husband in such a marriage is almost always idolized by women, including his wife. Why? Because he "permits her" to squeeze a career into the interstices of their marriage as long as his own career is not unduly inconvenienced. Thus is the white man blessed for exercising his power benignly while his "natural" right to that power forever remains unquestioned. Such is the subtlety of America's ideology about women.

In fact, however, even these 'benign" inequities are now being challenged. More and more young couples really are entering marriages of full equality, marriages in which both partners pursue careers or outside commitments which carry equal weight when all important decisions are to be made, marriages in which both husband and wife accept some compromise in the growth of their respective careers for their mutual partnership. Certainly such marriages have more tactical difficulties than more traditional ones: It is simply more difficult to coordinate two independent lives rather than one-and-a-half. The point is that it is not possible to predict ahead of time *on the basis of sex,* who will be doing the compromising at any given point of decision.

It should be clear that the man or woman who places career above all else ought not to enter an equalitarian marriage. The man would do better to marry a traditional wife, a wife who will make whatever sacrifices his career necessitates. The woman who places career above all else would do better—in our present society—to remain single. For an equalitarian marriage is not designed for extra efficiency, but for double fulfillment.

The Woman as Mother

In all marriages, whether traditional, pseudo-equalitarian or fully equalitarian, the real question surrounding a mother's career will probably continue to be the well-being of the children. All parents want to be certain that they are doing the very best for their children and that they are not depriving them in any important way, either materially or psychologically. What this has meant recently in most families that could afford it was that mother would devote herself to the children on a full-time basis. Women have been convinced—by their mothers and by the so-called experts—that there is something wrong with them if they even want to do otherwise.

For example, according to Dr. Spock, any women who finds full-time motherhood unfulfilling is showing "a residue of difficult relationships in her own childhood." [15] If a vacation doesn't solve the problem, then she is probably having emotional problems which can be relieved "through regular counseling in a family social agency, or if severe, through psychiatric treatment . . . Any mother of a pre-school child who is considering a job should discuss the issues with a social worker before making her decision." The message is clear: If you don't feel that your two-year-old is a stimulating, full-time, companion, then you are probably neurotic.

In fact, research does not support the view that children suffer in any way when mother works. Although it came as a surprise to most researchers in the area, maternal employment in and of itself does not seem to have any negative effects on the children; and part-time work actually seems to benefit the children. Children of working mothers are no more likely than children of non-working mothers to be delinquent or nervous or withdrawn or antisocial; they are no more likely to show neurotic symptoms; they are no more likely to perform poorly in school; and they are no more likely to feel deprived of their mothers' love. Daughters of working mothers are more likely to want to work themselves, and, when asked to name the one woman in the world that they most admire, daughters of working mothers are more likely to name their own mothers! [16] This is one finding that we wish every working woman in America could hear, because the other thing that is true of almost every working mother is that she *thinks* she is hurting her children and she feels guilty. In fact, research has shown that the worst mothers are those who would like to work, but who stay home out of a sense of duty. [17] The major conclusion from all the research is really this: What matters is the quality of a mother's relationship with her children, not the time of day it happens to be administered. This conclusion should come as no surprise; successful fathers have been demonstrating it for years. Some fathers are great, some fathers stink, and they're all at work at least eight hours a day.

Similarly, it is true that the quality of substitute care that children receive while their parents are at work also matters. Young children do need security, and research has shown that it is not good to have a constant turnover of parent-substitutes, a rapid succession of changing baby-sitters or housekeepers. [18] Clearly, this is why the establishment of child-care centers is vitally important at the moment. This is why virtually

[15] B. Spock, "Should Mothers Work?" *Ladies' Home Journal,* February 1963.

[16] F. I. Nye and L. W. Hoffman, *The Employed Mother in America* (Chicago: Rand McNally, 1963).

[17] M. R. Yarrow et al., "Child-rearing in Families of Working and Non-Working Mothers," *Sociometry* 25 (1962), 122–140.

[18] E. E. Maccoby, "Effects upon Children on Their Mothers' Outside Employment," in *Work in the Lives of Married Women* (New York: Columbia University Press, 1958).

every woman's group in the country, no matter how conservative or how radical, is in agreement on this one issue: that child-care centers ought to be available to those who need them.

Once again, it is relevant to emphasize that child-care centers, like the other reforms advocated, are not merely for the benefit of middle-class women who wish to pursue professional careers. Of the 31 million women in the labor force, nearly 40 percent of them are working mothers. In 1960, mothers constituted more than one-third of the total woman labor force. In March 1971, more than 1 out of 3 working mothers (4.3 million of them) had children under 6 years of age, and about half of these had children under 3 years of age. And most of these women in the labor force—like most men— work because they cannot afford to do otherwise. Moreover, they cannot currently deduct the full costs of child care as a business expense as the executive can often deduct an expensive car. At the moment, the majority of these working women must simply "make do" with whatever child-care arrangements they can manage. Only 6 percent of their children under 6 years of age currently receive group care in child-care centers. *This* is why child-care centers are a central issue of the new feminist movement. This is why they are not just an additional luxury for the middle-class family with a woman who wants to pursue a professional career.

But even the woman who is educationally and economically in a position to pursue a career must feel free to utilize these alternative arrangements for child care. For once again, America's sex-role ideology intrudes. Many people still assume that if a woman wants a full-time career, then children must be unimportant to her. But of course, no one makes this assumption about her husband. No one assumes that a father's interest in his career necessarily precludes a deep and abiding affection for his children or a vital interest in their development. Once again, America applies a double standard of judgment. Suppose that a father of small children suddenly lost his wife. No matter how much he loved his children, no one would expect him to sacrifice his career in order to stay home with them on a full-time basis—even if he had an independent source of income. No one would charge him with selfishness or lack of parental feeling if he sought professional care for his children during the day.

It is here that full equality between husband and wife assumes its ultimate importance. The fully equalitarian marriage abolishes this double standard and extends the same freedom to the mother. The equalitarian marriage provides the framework for both husband and wife to pursue careers which are challenging and fulfilling and, at the same time, to participate equally in the pleasures and responsibilities of child-rearing. Indeed, it is the equalitarian marriage which has the potential for giving children the love and concern of two parents rather than one. And it is the equalitarian marriage which has the most potential for giving parents the challenge and fulfillment of two worlds—family and career—rather than one.

In addition to providing this potential for equalized child care, a truly equalitarian marriage embraces a more general division of labor which satisfies what we like to call "the roommate test." That is, the labor is divided just as it is when two men or two women room together in college or set up a bachelor apartment together. Errands and domestic chores are assigned by preference, agreement, flipping a coin, alternated, given to hired help, or—perhaps most often the case—left undone.

It is significant that today's young people, so many of whom live precisely this way prior to marriage, find this kind of arrangement within marriage so foreign to their thinking. Consider an analogy. Suppose that a white male college student decided to room or set up a bachelor apartment with a black male friend. Surely the typical white student would not blithely assume that his black roommate was to handle all the domestic chores. Nor would his conscience allow him to do so even in the unlikely event that his roommate would say: "No, that's okay. I like doing housework. I'd be happy to do it." We suspect that the typical white student would still not be comfortable if he took advantage of this offer because he and America have finally realized that he would be taking advantage of the fact that such a roommate had been socialized by our society to be "happy" with such obvious inequity. But change this hypothetical black roommate to a female marriage partner, and somehow the student's conscience goes to sleep. At most it is quickly tranquilized by the comforting thought that "she is happiest when she is ironing for her loved one." Such is the power of an unconscious ideology.

Of course, it may well be that she *is* happiest when she is ironing for her loved one. Such, indeed, is the power of an unconscious ideology.

THE OPPRESSION OF CHILDREN

Shulamith Firestone

. . .

We have seen how the increasing privatization of family life brought ever more oppression to its dependents, women and children. The interrelated myths of femininity and childhood were the instruments of this oppression. In the Victorian Era they reached such epic proportions that finally women rebelled—their rebellion peripherally affecting childhood. But the rebellion was destroyed before it could eliminate these myths. They went underground to reappear in a more insidious version, complicated by mass consumerism. For in fact nothing had changed. . . .

The pseudo-emancipation of children exactly parallels the pseudo-emancipation of women: Though we have abolished all the superficial signs of oppression—the distinct and cumbrous clothing, the schoolmaster's rod—there is no question that the myth of childhood is flourishing in epic proportions, twentieth-century style: whole industries are built on the manufacture of special toys, games, baby food, breakfast food, children's books and comic books, candy with child appeal, etc.; market analysts study child psychology in order to develop products that will appeal to children of various ages; there is a publishing, movie and TV industry built just for them, with its own special literature, programs and commercials, and even censorship boards to decide just which cultural products are fit for their consumption; there is an endless proliferation of books and magazines instructing the layman in the fine art of child care (Dr. Spock, *Parents' Magazine*); there are specialists in child psychology, child education methods, pediatrics, and all the special branches of learning that have developed recently to study this peculiar animal. Compulsory education flourishes and is now widespread enough to form an inescapable net of socialization (brainwashing) from which even the very rich can no longer entirely escape. Gone are the days of Huckleberry Finn: Today the malingerer or dropout has a full-time job just in warding off the swarm of specialists studying him, the proliferating government programs, the social workers on his tail.

Let's look more closely at the modern form this ideology of childhood takes: Visually it is as beefy, blonde, and smiling as a Kodak advertisement. As is the case with the exploitation of women as a ready-made, consumer class, there are many industries eager to profit from children's physical vulnerability (e.g., St. Joseph's Aspirin for children); but even more than their health, the key word to the understanding of modern childhood is *happiness.* You are only a child once, and this is it. Children must be living embodiments of happiness (sulky or upset or disturbed children are immediately disliked; they make of the myth a lie); it is every parent's duty to give his child a childhood to remember (swing sets, inflated swimming pools, toys and games, camping trips, birthday parties, etc.). This is the Golden Age that the child will remember when he grows up to become a robot like his father. So every father tries to give his son whatever it was he missed most himself in what should have been a most glorious stage of his own life. The cult of childhood as the Golden Age is so strong that all other ages of life derive their value from how closely they resemble it, in a national cult of youth; "grownups" make asses of themselves with their jealous apologetics ("Of course I'm twice your age, dear, but . . ."). There is the general belief that progress has been made because at least in our time children have been freed from the ugly toils of child labor and many other traditional exploitations of past generations. In fact there is even the envious moan that children are getting too much attention. They are spoiled. ("When I was your age . . ." parallels "It's a woman's world . . .")

A major bulwark for this myth of happiness is the continued rigid segregation of children from the rest of society; the exaggeration of their distinctive features has made of them, as it was designed to, almost another race. Our parks provide the perfect metaphor for our larger age-segregated society: a special playground for the Tender Untouchables, mothers and young children (one seldom finds anyone else here, as if by taboo), an athletic field or swimming pool for the youth, a shady knoll for young couples and students, and a bench section for the elderly. This age segregation continues throughout the life of every modern individual; people have very little contact with children once they have outgrown their own childhood. And even within their own childhood, as we have seen, there are rigid age segregations, so that an older child will be embarrassed to be seen with a younger one. ("Tag-along! Why don't you go play with someone your own age!") Throughout school life, and that is a rather long time in our century, a child remains with others only a year or two in age from himself. The schools themselves reflect these increasingly rigid gradations: junior junior high, senior junior high, etc., marked by a complex system of promotions and "graduations"; lately even graduations from nursery school and/or kindergarten are common.

So by the time a child grows old enough to reproduce himself he has no contact whatever with those outside his own narrow adult age group, and certainly not with children. Because of the cult surrounding it he can barely remember even his own childhood, often blocking it entirely. Even as a child he may have attempted to mold himself to the myth, believing that all other children were happier than he; later, as a teenager, he may have indulged in a desperate joyousness, flinging himself into "fun"—when really adolescence is a horror to live through—in the spirit of "you're only young once." (But true youth is unaware of age—"youth is wasted on the young" —and is marked by real spontaneity, the absence of precisely this self-consciousness. The storing up of happiness in this manner to think of when you no longer have it is an idea only old age could have produced.) Such an absence of contact with the reality of childhood makes every young adult ripe for the same sentimentalization of children that he himself probably despised as a child. And so it goes, in a vicious circle: Young adults dream of having their own children in a desperate attempt to fill up the void produced by the artificial cutoff from the young, but it is not until they are mired in pregnancies and Pampers, babysitters and school problems, favoritism and quarreling that they again, for a short period, are forced to see that children are just human like the rest of us.

So let's talk about what childhood is *really* like, and not of what it is like in adult heads. It is clear that the myth of childhood happiness flourishes so wildly not because it satisfies the needs of children but because it satisfies the needs of adults. In a culture of alienated people, the belief that everyone has at least one good period in life free of care and drudgery dies hard. And obviously you can't expect it in your old age. So it must be you've already had it. This accounts for the fog of sentimentality surrounding any discussion of childhood or children. Every one is living out some private dream in their behalf.

Thus segregation is still operating full blast to reinforce the oppression of children as a class. What constitutes this oppression in the twentieth century?

Economic and Physical Dependence. The natural physical inequality of children to adults—their greater weakness, their smaller size—is reinforced, rather than compensated for, by our present culture: children are still "minors" under the law, without civil rights, the property of an arbitrary set of parents. (Even when they have "good" parents, there are just as many "bad" people in the world as "good"—and the "bad" people are considerably more likely to bear children.) The number of child beatings and deaths every year testifies to the fact that merely unhappy children are lucky. A lot worse could happen. It is only recently that doctors saw fit to report these casualties, so much were children at the mercy of their parents. Those children without parents, however, are even worse off (just as single women, women without the patronage of a husband, are still worse off than married women). There is no place for them but the orphanage, a dumping ground for the unwanted.

But the oppression of children is most of all rooted in economic dependence. Anyone who has ever observed a child wheedling a nickel from its mother knows that economic dependence is the basis of the child's shame. (Relatives who bring money are often the best liked. But make sure you give it *directly* to the kid!) Though he may not be starving to death (neither would he be if children had their own employment; black children who shine shoes, beg, and cultivate various rackets, and working-class white boys who sell papers, are envied in their neighborhood) he is dependent for his survival on *patronage,* and that's a bad state to be in. Such extreme dependence is not worth the bread.

It is in this area that we find one of the pivots of the modern myth: we are told that childhood represents great progress—immediately calling to mind Dickensian images of poor, gaunt children struggling in a coal pit. . . . However, middle-class and upper-class children were not laboring at the dawn of the Industrial Era, but were safely ensconced in some dull schoolhouse studying Homer and Latin grammar. The children of the lower class, it is true, were not considered any more privileged than their fathers, sharing the inhuman tortures to which all members of their class had to submit; so that at the same time as there were idle Emma Bovarys and Little Lord Fauntleroys, there were also women destroying their lives and lungs in early textile mills and children roaming, begging. This difference between the lives of children of the different economic classes persisted right up until the days of the women's vote and into our own time. Children who were the reproductive chattel of the middle class were going through soul-squeezing worse than our own; so were women. But they, to offset this, had economic *patronage.* Children of the lower class were exploited, not particularly as children, but generally, on a class basis: the myth of childhood was too fancy to waste on them. Here again we see illustrated just how arbitrary a myth childhood was, ordered expressly for the needs of the middle-class family structure.

Yes, you say, but surely it would have been better for the children of the working class could they too have lived sheltered by this myth. At least they would have been spared their lives. So that they could sweat out their spiritual lives in some schoolroom or office? The question is rhetorical, like wondering whether the suffering of the blacks in America is authentic because they would be considered rich in some other country. Suffering is suffering. No, we have to think in broader terms here. Like, why were their parents being exploited in the first place: what is *anybody* doing down in that coal mine? What we ought to be protesting, rather than that children are being exploited just *like* adults, is that *adults* can be so exploited. We need to start talking not about sparing children for a few years from the horrors of adult life, but about eliminating those horrors. In a society free of exploitation, children could be like adults (with no exploitation implied) and adults could be like children (with no exploitation implied). The privileged slavery (patronage) that women and children undergo is not freedom. For self-regulation is the basis of all freedom, and dependence at the origins of all inequality.

Sexual Repression. Freud depicts the early contentment of the child: the satisfaction of the infant at the breast of the mother, which it then tries to regain for the rest of its life; how, because of adult protection, the child is freer from the "reality principle" and is allowed to play (activity done for the pleasure of it, and not to achieve any other end); how, sexually, the child is polymorphously perverse and only later is so directed and repressed as to make him fit only for adult genital sex pleasure.

Freud also showed the origins of the adult neurosis to be built into the very processes of childhood. Though the prototypical child may have the *capacity* for pure pleasure, that does not mean that he can fully indulge it. It would be more correct to say that though by nature inclined to pleasure, to the degree that he becomes socialized (repressed) he loses this inclination. *And that begins right away.*

The "reality principle" is not reserved for adults. It is introduced into the child's life almost immediately on his own small scale. For as long as such a reality principle exists, the notion of sparing the child its unpleasantness is a sham. At best he can go through a retarded repressive process; but more often the repression takes place as soon as he can handle it, at all levels. It is not as though there is ever a blessed period when "reality" lays off. For in truth the repression begins as soon as he is born—the well-known formula-by-clock feedings only an extreme example. Before the age of eighteen months, says Robert Stoller, the basic sex differentiation has set in, and as we have seen, this process in itself demands inhibition of the sex drive toward the mother. So from the beginning his polymorphously perverse sexuality is denied free play. (Even now, with a campaign to recognize masturbation as normal, many infants are kept from playing with themselves while still in their cribs.) The child is weaned and toilet trained, the sooner the better—both traumatic in child terms. Repressions increase. The mother love that ideally is meant to be such perfect fulfillment ("unconditional") is used in the manner of father love: to better direct the child into socially approved conduct. And finally an active identification with the father is demanded. (In fatherless homes the identification may occur somewhat later, when the child begins school.) From here until puberty the child must lead a sexless—or secretive—life, not even admitting any sexual needs. Such forced asexuality produces a frustration that is at least partially responsible for the extreme rambunctiousness and aggressiveness—or alternately the anemic docility—that often make children so trying to be around.

Family Repression. We don't need to elaborate on the subtle psychological pressures of family life. Think of your own family. And if that isn't enough, if you are actually that one-in-a-million who is truly convinced that you had a "happy family," read some of the work of R. D. Laing, particularly the *Politics of the Family,* on the Game of Happy Families. ("The more smoothly they function the more difficult they are to study.") Laing exposes the internal dynamic of the family, explaining its invisibility to the ordinary family member:

One thing is often clear to an outsider: there are concerted family *resistances* to discovering what is going on, and there are complicated stratagems to keep everyone in the dark, and in the dark that they are in the dark. The truth has to be expended to sustain a family image . . . Since this fantasy exists only in so far as it is "in" everyone who shares "in" it, anyone who gives it up shatters the "family" in everyone else.

And here are a few children speaking for themselves. Again we quote Reik:

I was told of a boy, who, until he was almost four years old, thought that his name was "Shutup."

A boy witnessed a furious quarrel between his parents and heard his mother threaten his father with divorce. When he returned home from school the next day, he asked his mother, "Are you divorced yet?" He remembered later being very disappointed because she had not gotten divorced.

A boy of nine years was asked by his visiting father at camp if he felt homesick, and the boy replied, "No." The father then asked if the other boys felt homesick. "Only a few," said the child, "those who have dogs at home."

What is amusing about these anecdotes, if indeed they are amusing, is the candor of children unable to understand or accept the masochistic hell of it all.

Educational Repression. It is at school that the repression is cemented. Any illusions of freedom remaining are quickly wiped out now. All sexual activity or physical demonstrativeness is barred. Here is the first heavily supervised play. Children's natural enjoyment of play is now coopted to better socialize (repress) them. ("Larry did the best fingerpainting. What a good boy! Your mother will be proud of you!") In some liberal schools all the way up, it is true, good teachers try to find subjects and activities that will truly interest children. (It's easier to keep the class in order that way.) But as we have seen, the repressive structure of the segregated classroom itself guarantees that any natural interest in learning will finally serve the essentially disciplinary interests of the school. Young teachers entering the system idealistic about their job suddenly are up against it: many give up in despair. If they had forgotten what a jail school was for them, it all comes back now. And they are soon forced to see that though there are liberal jails and not-so-liberal jails, by definition they are jails. The child is forced to go to them: the test is that he would never go of his own accord. ("School's out, School's out, Teachers let the fools out, No more pencils, No more books, No more teacher's dirty looks.") And though enlightened educators have devised whole systems of inherently interesting disciplined activities to lure and bribe the child into an acceptance of school, these can never fully succeed, for a school that existed solely to serve the curiosity of children on their own terms and by their own direction would be a contradiction in terms—as we have seen, the modern school in its structural definition exists to implement repression.

The child spends most of his waking hours in this coercive structure or doing homework for it. The little time that is left is often taken up with family chores and duties. He is forced to sit through endless family arguments, or, in some "liberal" families, "family councils." There are relatives at whom he must smile, and often church services that he must attend (all those grudging hours spent by children at prayer!). In the little time left, at least in our modern middle class, he is "supervised," blocking the development of initiative and creativity: his choice of *play materials* is determined for him (toys and games), his *play area* is defined (gyms, parks, playgrounds, campsites); often he is limited in his *choice of playmates* to children of the same economic class as himself, and in the suburbs, to his schoolmates, or children of his parent's friends; he is organized into more groups than he knows what to do with (Boy Scouts, Cub Scouts, Girl Scouts, Brownies, camps, after-school clubs and sports); his *culture* is chosen for him—on TV he is often allowed to watch only pap children's programs (father knows best) and is barred from all adult (good) movies; his books and literature are often taken from corny children's lists. *(Great American Men and Women. The Annals of Babe Ruth. Lassie. Nancy Drew.)*

The only children who have the slightest chance of escape from this supervised nightmare—but less and less so—are children of the ghettos and the working class where the medieval conception of open community—living on the street—still lingers. That is, historically, as we have seen, many of these processes of childhood came late to the lower class, and have never really stuck. Lower-class children tend to come from large immediate families composed of people of many different ages. But even when they don't, often there are half-brothers and sisters, cousins, nieces, nephews, or aunts, in a constantly changing milieu of relatives. Individual children are barely noticed, let alone supervised: children are often allowed to roam far from home or play out on the streets until all hours. And on the street, if by chance their family size is limited, there are hundreds of kids, many of whom have formed their own social groupings (gangs).* They do not often receive toys, which means they create their own. (I have seen ghetto kids devise ingenious slides out of cardboard and put them up against old tenements with missing steps; I have seen others make go-carts and pulleys out of old

* Gangs are the only modern children's groups that are self-directed: The term *gang* has an ominous sound for good political reasons.

tire wheels and string and boxes. No middle-class child does that. He doesn't need to. But as a result he soon loses that ingenuity.) They explore far afield of their own few blocks, and much more often than their middle-class contemporaries make the acquaintance of adults on an equal level. In class they are wild and unruly, as indeed they ought to be—for the classroom is a situation that would make any even partially free person suspicious. There is a lingering disrespect for school in the lower class, for, after all, it is a middle-class phenomenon in origin.

Sexually, too, ghetto kids are freer. One fellow told me that he can't remember an age when he didn't have sexual intercourse with other kids as a natural thing; everyone was doing it. Those who teach in ghetto schools have remarked on the impossibility of restraining child sexuality: It's a groovy thing, the kids love it, and it far surpasses a lesson about the Great American Democracy or the contribution of the Hebrews who developed One God (why develop one at all?) or coffee and rubber as the chief exports of Brazil. So they do it on the stairs. And stay away from school the next day. If, in modern America, free childhood exists in any degree, it exists in the lower class, where the myth is least developed.

Why then do they "turn out" worse than middle-class kids? Perhaps this is obvious. But I shall answer from my experience living and teaching in the ghettos: Ghetto kids are not lower in intelligence until they reach adulthood, and even this is debatable; lower-class children are some of the brightest, brassiest, and most original children around. They are that way because *they are left alone.* (If they do not do well on tests, perhaps we ought to reexamine the tests and not the children.) Later, in confronting a "reality principle" very different from the middle-class one, they are drained and smashed; they will never "outgrow" their economic subjection. Thus it is day-by-day oppression that produces these listless and unimaginative adults, the ubiquitous restrictions on their personal freedom to expand—not their wild childhood.

But children of the ghettos are only relatively free. They are still dependent, and they are oppressed as an economic class. There is good reason that all children want to grow up. Then at least they can leave home, and (finally) have a chance to do what they want to do. (There is some irony in the fact that children imagine that parents can do what they want, and parents imagine that children do. "When I grow up . . . ." parallels "Oh to be a child again. . . .") They dream of love and sex, for they live in the driest period of their lives. Often when confronted with their parents' misery, they make firm vows that when *they* grow up, *that* won't happen to them; They build glorious dreams of perfect marriages, or of no marriage at all (smarter children, who realize the fault lies in the institution, not in their parents), of money to spend as they please, of plenty of love and acclaim; They want to appear older than they are and are insulted if told that they appear younger than they are. They try fiercely to disguise the ignorance of affairs that is the peculiar physical affliction of all children. Here is an example from Reik's *Sex in Man and Woman* of the little cruelties to which they are constantly subjected:

I had some fun with a boy four years old, whom I told that a certain tree in his parents' garden bore pieces of chewing gum. I had bought some chewing gum and had hung the sticks by strings on the lower bough of the tree. The boy climbed up and picked them. He did not doubt that they grew on the tree, nor did he consider that they were wrapped in paper. He willingly accepted my explanation that the sticks of gum, blossoming at different times, had various flavors. In the following year when I reminded him of the chewing-gum tree, he was very ashamed of his previous credulity and said, "Don't mention that."

Some children, in an attempt to fight this constant ridicule of their gullibility—when they see that their painful ignorance is considered "cute"—try to cash in on it, in much the same way that women do. Hoping to elicit that hug and kiss, they purposely take things out of context, but it seldom works the second time, perplexing them: What they don't understand is that the ignorance itself is considered "funny," not its specific manifestations. For most children don't understand the arbitrary adult order of things, inadequately explained even when there *is* a sound explanation. But, in almost every case given the amount of information the child begins with, his conclusions are perfectly logical. Similarly if an adult were to arrive on a strange planet to find the inhabitants building fires on their roofs, he might assume an explanation; but his conclusions, based on his dissimilar past, might cause the others some amusement. Every person in his first trip to a foreign country, where he knows neither the people nor the language, experiences childhood.

Children, then, are not freer than adults. They are burdened by a wish fantasy in direct proportion to the restraints of their narrow lives; with an unpleasant sense of their own physical inadequacy and ridiculousness; with constant shame about their dependence, economic and otherwise ("Mother, may I?"); and humiliation concerning their natural ignorance of practical affairs. Children are repressed at every waking minute. *Childhood is hell.*

The result is the insecure, and therefore aggressive/defensive, often obnoxious little person we call a child. Economic, sexual, and general psychological oppressions reveal themselves in coyness, dishonesty, spite, these unpleasant characteristics in turn reinforcing the isolation of children from the rest of society. Thus their rearing, particularly in its most difficult personality phases, is gladly relinquished to women—who tend, for the same reason, to exhibit these personality characteristics themselves. Except for the ego rewards involved in having children of one's own, few men show any interest in children. And certainly not enough to include them in any books on revolution.

So it is up to feminist (ex-child and still oppressed child-women) revolutionaries to do so. We must include the oppression of children in any program for feminist revolution or we will be subject to the same failing of which we have so often accused men: of not having gone deep enough in our analysis, of having missed an important substratum of oppression merely because it didn't directly concern *us*. I say this knowing full well that many women are sick and tired of being lumped together with children: that they are no more our charge and responsibility than anyone else's will be an assumption crucial to our revolutionary demands. It is only that we have developed, in our long period of related sufferings, a certain compassion and understanding for them that there is no reason to lose now; we know where they're at, what they're experiencing, because we, too, are still undergoing the same kind of oppressions. The mother who wants to kill her child for what she has had to sacrifice for it (a common desire) learns to love that same child only when she understands that it is as helpless, as oppressed as she is, and by the same oppressor: then her hatred is directed outward, and "motherlove" is born. But we will go further: our final step must be the elimination of the very conditions of femininity and childhood themselves that are now conducive to this alliance of the oppressed, clearing the way for a fully "human" condition. There are no children yet able to write their own books, tell their own story. We will have to, one last time, do it for them.

ANIMAL LIBERATION *

Peter Singer

I

We are familiar with Black Liberation, Gay Liberation, and a variety of other movements. With Women's Liberation some thought we had come to the end of the road. Discrimination on the basis of sex, it has been said, is the last form of discrimination that is universally accepted and practiced without pretense, even in those liberal circles which have long prided themselves on their freedom from racial discrimination. But one should always be wary of talking of "the last remaining form of discrimination." If we have learned anything from the liberation movements, we should have learned how difficult it is to be aware of the ways in which we discriminate until they are forcefully pointed out to us. A liberation movement demands an expansion of our moral horizons, so that practices that were previously regarded as natural and inevitable are now seen as intolerable.

Animals, Men and Morals is a manifesto for an Animal Liberation movement. The contributors to the book may not all see the issue this way. They are a varied group. Philosophers, ranging from professors to graduate students, make up the largest contingent. There are five of them, including the three editors, and there is also an extract

* This article originally appeared as a book review of *Animals, Men and Morals*, edited by Stanley and Roslind Godlovitch and John Harris.—Eds.

from the unjustly neglected German philosopher with an English name, Leonard Nelson, who died in 1927. There are essays by two novelist/critics, Brigid Brophy and Maureen Duffy, and another by Muriel the Lady Dowding, widow of Dowding of Battle of Britain fame and the founder of "Beauty without Cruelty," a movement that campaigns against the use of animals for furs and cosmetics. The other pieces are by a psychologist, a botanist, a sociologist, and Ruth Harrison, who is probably best described as a professional campaigner for animal welfare.

Whether or not these people, as individuals, would all agree that they are launching a liberation movement for animals, the book as a whole amounts to no less. It is a demand for a complete change in our attitudes to nonhumans. It is a demand that we cease to regard the exploitation of other species as natural and inevitable, and that, instead, we see it as a continuing moral outrage. Patrick Corbett, Professor of Philosophy at Sussex University, captures the spirit of the book in his closing words:

. . . we require now to extend the great principles of liberty, equality and fraternity over the lives of animals. Let animal slavery join human slavery in the graveyard of the past.

The reader is likely to be skeptical. "Animal Liberation" sounds more like a parody of liberation movements than a serious objective. The reader may think: We support the claims of blacks and women for equality because blacks and women really are equal to whites and males—equal in intelligence and in abilities, capacity for leadership, rationality, and so on. Humans and nonhumans obviously are not equal in these respects. Since justice demands only that we treat equals equally, unequal treatment of humans and nonhumans cannot be an injustice.

This is a tempting reply, but a dangerous one. It commits the non-racist and non-sexist to a dogmatic belief that blacks and women really are just as intelligent, able, etc., as whites and males—and no more. Quite possibly this happens to be the case. Certainly attempts to prove that racial or sexual differences in these respects have a genetic origin have not been conclusive. But do we really want to stake our demand for equality on the assumption that there are no genetic differences of this kind between the different races or sexes? Surely the appropriate response to those who claim to have found evidence for such genetic differences is not to stick to the belief that there are no differences, whatever the evidence to the contrary; rather one should be clear that the claim to equality does not depend on IQ. Moral equality is distinct from factual equality. Otherwise it would be nonsense to talk of the equality of human beings, since humans, as individuals, obviously differ in intelligence and almost any ability one cares to name. If possessing greater intelligence does not entitle one human to exploit another, why should it entitle humans to exploit nonhumans?

Jeremy Bentham expressed the essential basis of equality in his famous formula: "Each to count for one and none for more than one." In other words, the interests of every being that has interests are to be taken into account and treated equally with the like interests of any other being. Other moral philosophers, before and after Bentham, have made the same point in different ways. Our concern for others must not depend on whether they possess certain characteristics, though just what that concern involves may, of course, vary according to such characteristics.

Bentham, incidentally, was well aware that the logic of the demand for racial equality did not stop at the equality of humans. He wrote:

The day *may* come when the rest of the animal creation may acquire those rights which never could have been withholden from them but by the hand of tyranny. The French have already discovered that the blackness of the skin is no reason why a human being should be abandoned without redress to the caprice of a tormentor. It may one day come to be recognized that the number of the legs, the villosity of the skin, or the termination of the *os sacrum,* are reasons equally insufficient for abandoning a sensitive being to the same fate. What else is it that should trace the insuperable line? Is it the faculty of reason, or perhaps the faculty of discourse? But a full-grown horse or dog is beyond comparison a more rational, as well as a more conversable animal, than an infant of a day, or a week, or even a month old. But suppose they were otherwise, what would it avail? The question is not, Can they *reason?* nor Can they *talk?* but, Can they *suffer?* [1]

Surely Bentham was right. If a being suffers, there can be no moral justification for refusing to take that suffering into consideration, and, indeed, to count it equally with the like suffering (if rough comparisons can be made) of any other being.

So the only question is: do animals other than man suffer? Most people agree unhesitatingly that animals like cats and dogs can and do suffer, and this seems also to be assumed by those laws that prohibit wanton cruelty to such animals. Personally, I have no doubt at all about this and find it hard to take seriously the doubts that a few people apparently do have. The editors and contributors of *Animals, Men and Morals* seem to feel the same way, for although the question is raised more than once, doubts are quickly dismissed each time. Nevertheless, because this is such a fundamental point, it is worth asking what grounds we have for attributing suffering to other animals.

It is best to begin by asking what grounds any individual human has for supposing that other humans feel pain. Since pain is a state of consciousness, a "mental event," it can never be directly observed. No observations, whether behavioral signs such as writhing or screaming or physiological or neurological recordings, are observations of pain itself. Pain is something one feels, and one can only infer that others are feeling it from various external indications. The fact that only philosophers are ever skeptical about whether other humans feel pain shows that we regard such inference as justifiable in the case of humans.

Is there any reason why the same inference should be unjustifiable for other animals? Nearly all the external signs which lead us to infer pain in other humans can be seen in other species, especially "higher" animals such as mammals and birds. Behavioral

[1] *The Principles of Morals and Legislation,* Ch. XVII, Sec. 1, footnote to paragraph 4. (Italics in original.)

signs—writhing, yelping, or other forms of calling, attempts to avoid the source of pain, and many others—are present. We know, too, that these animals are biologically similar in the relevant respects, having nervous systems like ours which can be observed to function as ours do.

So the grounds for inferring that these animals can feel pain are nearly as good as the grounds for inferring other humans do. Only nearly, for there is one behavioral sign that humans have but nonhumans, with the exception of one or two specially raised chimpanzees, do not have. This, of course, is a developed language. As the quotation from Bentham indicates, this has long been regarded as an important distinction between man and other animals. Other animals may communicate with each other, but not in the way we do. Following Chomsky, many people now mark this distinction by saying that only humans communicate in a form that is governed by rules of syntax. (For the purposes of this argument, linguists allow those chimpanzees who have learned a syntactic sign language to rank as honorary humans.) Nevertheless, as Bentham pointed out, this distinction is not relevant to the question of how animals ought to be treated, unless it can be linked to the issue of whether animals suffer.

This link may be attempted in two ways. First, there is a hazy line of philosophical thought, stemming perhaps from some doctrines associated with Wittgenstein, which maintains that we cannot meaningfully attribute states of consciousness to beings without language. I have not seen this argument made explicit in print, though I have come across it in conversation. This position seems to me very implausible, and I doubt that it would be held at all if it were not thought to be a consequence of a broader view of the significance of language. It may be that the use of a public, rule-governed language is a precondition of conceptual thought. It may even be, although personally I doubt it, that we cannot meaningfully speak of a creature having an intention unless that creature can use a language. But states like pain, surely, are more primitive than either of these, and seem to have nothing to do with language.

Indeed, as Jane Goodall points out in her study of chimpanzees, when it comes to the expression of feelings and emotions, humans tend to fall back on non-linguistic modes of communication which are often found among apes, such as a cheering pat on the back, an exuberant embrace, a clasp of hands, and so on.[2] Michael Peters makes a similar point in his contribution to *Animals, Men and Morals* when he notes that the basic signals we use to convey pain, fear, sexual arousal, and so on are not specific to our species. So there seems to be no reason at all to believe that a creature without language cannot suffer.

The second, and more easily appreciated way of linking language and the existence of pain is to say that the best evidence that we can have that another creature is in pain is when he tells us that he is. This is a distinct line of argument, for it is not being denied that a non-language-user conceivably could suffer, but only that we could know

---

[2] Jane van Lawick-Goodall, *In the Shadow of Man* (Houghton Mifflin, 1971), p. 225.

that he is suffering. Still, this line of argument seems to me to fail, and for reasons similar to those just given. "I am in pain" is not the best possible evidence that the speaker is in pain (he might be lying) and it is certainly not the only possible evidence. Behavioral signs and knowledge of the animals's biological similarity to ourselves together provide adequate evidence that animals do suffer. Ater all, we would not accept linguistic evidence if it contradicted the rest of the evidence. If a man was severely burned, and behaved as if he were in pain, writhing, groaning, being very careful not to let his burned skin touch anything, and so on, but later said he had not been in pain at all, we would be more likely to conclude that he was lying or suffering from amnesia than that he had not been in pain.

Even if there were stronger grounds for refusing to attribute pain to those who do not have a language, the consequences of this refusal might lead us to examine these grounds unusually critically. Human infants, as well as some adults, are unable to use language. Are we to deny that a year-old infant can suffer? If not, how can lanaguage be crucial? Of course, most parents can understand the responses of even very young infants better than they understand the responses of other animals, and sometimes infant responses can be understood in the light of later development.

This, however, is just a fact about the relative knowledge we have of our own species and other species, and most of this knowledge is simply derived from closer contact. Those who have studied the behavior of other animals soon learn to understand their responses at least as well as we understand those of an infant. (I am not just referring to Jane Goodall's and other well-known studies of apes. Consider, for example, the degree of understanding achieved by Tinbergen from watching herring gulls.) [3] Just as we can understand infant human behavior in the light of adult human behavior, so we can understand the behavior of other species in the light of our own behavior (and sometimes we can understand our own behavior better in the light of the behavior of other species).

The grounds we have for believing that other mammals and birds suffer are, then, closely analogous to the grounds we have for believing that other humans suffer. It remains to consider how far down the evolutionary scale this analogy holds. Obviously it becomes poorer when we get further away from man. To be more precise would require a detailed examination of all that we know about other forms of life. With fish, reptiles, and other vertebrates the analogy still seems strong, with molluscs like oysters it is much weaker. Insects are more difficult, and it may be that in our present state of knowledge we must be agnostic about whether they are capable of suffering.

If there is no moral justification for ignoring suffering when it occurs, and it does occur in other species, what are we to say of our attitudes toward these other species? Richard Ryder, one of the contributors to *Animals, Men and Morals,* uses the term "speciesism" to describe the belief that we are entitled to treat members of other species

[3] N. Tinbergen, *The Herring Gull's World* (Basic Books, 1961).

in a way in which it would be wrong to treat members of our own species. The term is not euphonious, but it neatly makes the analogy with racism. The non-racist would do well to bear the analogy in mind when he is inclined to defend human behavior toward nonhumans. "Shouldn't we worry about improving the lot of our own species before we concern ourselves with other species?" he may ask. If we substitute "race" for "species" we shall see that the question is better not asked. "Is a vegetarian diet nutritionally adequate?" resembles the slave-owner's claim that he and the whole economy of the South would be ruined without slave labor. There is even a parallel with skeptical doubts about whether animals suffer, for some defenders of slavery professed to doubt whether blacks really suffer in the way that whites do.

I do not want to give the impression, however, that the case for Animal Liberation is based on the analogy with racism and no more. On the contrary, *Animals, Men and Morals* describes the various ways in which humans exploit nonhumans, and several contributors consider the defenses that have been offered, including the defense of meat-eating mentioned in the last paragraph. Sometimes the rebuttals are scornfully dismissive, rather than carefully designed to convince the detached critic. This may be a fault, but it is a fault that is inevitable, given the kind of book this is. The issue is not one on which one can remain detached. As the editors state in their Introduction:

Once the full force of moral assessment has been made explicit there can be no rational excuse left for killing animals, be they killed for food, science, or sheer personal indulgence. We have not assembled this book to provide the reader with yet another manual on how to make brutalities less brutal. Compromise, in the traditional sense of the term, is simple unthinking weakness when one considers the actual reasons for our crude relationships with the other animals.

The point is that on this issue there are few critics who are genuinely detached. People who eat pieces of slaughtered nonhumans every day find it hard to believe that they are doing wrong; and they also find it hard to imagine what else they could eat. So for those who do not place nonhumans beyond the pale of morality, there comes a stage when further argument seems pointless, a stage at which one can only accuse one's opponent of hypocrisy and reach for the sort of sociological account of our practices and the way we defend them that is attempted by David Wood in his contribution to this book. On the other hand, to those unconvinced by the arguments, and unable to accept that they are rationalizing their dietary preferences and their fear of being thought peculiar, such sociological explanations can only seem insultingly arrogant.

II

The logic of speciesism is most apparent in the practice of experimenting on nonhumans in order to benefit humans. This is because the issue is rarely obscured by allegations that nonhumans are so different from humans that we cannot know anything about whether they suffer. The defender of vivisection cannot use this argument because he needs to stress the similarities between man and other animals in order to justify the usefulness to the former of experiments on the latter. The researcher who makes rats choose between starvation and electric shocks to see if they develop ulcers (they do) does so because he knows that the rat has a nervous system very similar to man's, and presumably feels an electric shock in a similar way.

Richard Ryder's restrained account of experiments on animals made me angrier with my fellow men than anything else in this book. Ryder, a clinical psychologist by profession, himself experimented on animals before he came to hold the view he puts forward in his essay. Experimenting on animals is now a large industry, both academic and commercial. In 1969, more than 5 million experiments were performed in Britain, the vast majority without anesthetic (though how many of these involved pain is not known). There are no accurate US figures, since there is no federal law on the subject, and in many cases no state law either. Estimates vary from 20 million to 200 million. Ryder suggests that 80 million may be the best guess. We tend to think that this is all for vital medical research, but of course it is not. Huge numbers of animals are used in university departments from Forestry to Psychology, and even more are used for commercial purposes, to test whether cosmetics can cause skin damage, or shampoos eye damage, or to test food additives or laxatives or sleeping pills or anything else.

A standard test for foodstuffs is the "LD50." The object of this test is to find the dosage level at which 50 percent of the test animals will die. This means that nearly all of them will become very sick before finally succumbing or surviving. When the substance is a harmless one, it may be necessary to force huge doses down the animals, until in some cases sheer volume or concentration causes death.

Ryder gives a selection of experiments, taken from recent scientific journals. I will quote two, not for the sake of indulging in gory details, but in order to give an idea of what normal researchers think they may legitimately do to other species. The point is not that the individual researchers are cruel men, but that they are behaving in a way that is allowed by our speciesist attitudes. As Ryder points out, even if only 1 percent of the experiments involve severe pain, that is 50,000 experiments in Britain each year, or nearly 150 every day (and about fifteen times as many in the United States, if Ryder's guess is right). Here then are two experiments:

O. S. Ray and R. J. Barrett of Pittsburgh gave electric shocks to the feet of 1,042 mice. They then caused convulsions by giving more intense shocks through cup-shaped electrodes applied to the animals' eyes or through pressure spring clips attached to their ears. Unfortunately some of the mice who "successfully completed Day One training were found sick or dead prior to testing on Day Two." [*Journal of Comparative and Physiological Psychology*, 1969, Vol. 67, pp. 110–116]

At the National Institute for Medical Research, Mill Hill, London, W. Feldberg and S. L. Sherwood injected chemicals into the brains of cats—"with a number of widely different substances, recurrent patterns of reaction were obtained. Retching, vomiting, defaecation, increased salivation and greatly accelerated respiration leading to panting were common features.". . .

The injection into the brain of a large dose of Tubocuraine caused the cat to jump "from the table to the floor and then straight into its cage, where it started calling more and more noisily whilst moving about restlessly and jerkily . . . finally the cat fell with legs and neck flexed, jerking in rapid clonic movements, the condition being that of a major [epileptic] convulsion . . . within a few seconds the cat got up, ran for a few yards at high speed and fell in another fit. The whole process was repeated several times within the next ten minutes, during which the cat lost faeces and foamed at the mouth."

This animal finally died thirty-five minutes after the brain injection. [*Journal of Physiology,* 1954, Vol. 123, pp. 148–167]

There is nothing secret about these experiments. One has only to open any recent volume of a learned journal, such as the *Journal of Comparative and Physiological Psychology,* to find full descriptions of experiments of this sort, together with the results obtained—results that are frequently trivial and obvious. The experiments are often supported by public funds.

It is a significant indication of the level of acceptability of these practices that, although these experiments are taking place at this moment on university campuses throughout the country, there has, so far as I know, not been the slightest protest from the student movement. Students have been rightly concerned that their universities should not discriminate on grounds of race or sex, and that they should not serve the purposes of the military or big business. Speciesism continues undisturbed, and many students participate in it. There may be a few qualms at first, but since everyone regards it as normal, and it may even be a required part of a course, the student soon becomes hardened and, dismissing his earlier feelings as "mere sentiment," comes to regard animals as statistics rather than sentient beings with interests that warrant consideration.

Argument about vivisection has often missed the point because it has been put in absolutist terms: would the abolitionist be prepared to let thousands die if they could be saved by experimenting on a single animal? The way to reply to this purely hypothetical question is to pose another: Would the experimenter be prepared to experiment on a human orphan under six months old, if it were the only way to save many lives? (I say "orphan" to avoid the complication of parental feelings, although in doing so I am being overfair to the experimenter, since the nonhuman subjects of experiments are not orphans.) A negative answer to this question indicates that the experimenter's readiness to use nonhumans is simple discrimination, for adult apes, cats, mice, and other mammals are more conscious of what is happening to them, more self-directing, and, so far as we can tell, just as sensitive to pain as a human infant. There is no characteristic that human infants possess that adult mammals do not have to the same or a higher degree.

(It might be possible to hold that what makes it wrong to experiment on a human infant is that the infant will in time develop into more than the nonhuman, but one would then, to be consistent, have to oppose abortion, and perhaps contraception, too, for the fetus and the egg and sperm have the same potential as the infant. Moreover, one would still have no reason for experimenting on a nonhuman rather than a human with brain damage severe enough to make it impossible for him to rise above infant level.)

The experimenter, then, shows a bias for his own species whenever he carries out an experiment on a nonhuman for a purpose that he would not think justified him in using a human being at an equal or lower level of sentience, awareness, ability to be self-directing, etc. No one familiar with the kind of results yielded by these experiments can have the slightest doubt that if this bias were eliminated the number of experiments performed would be zero or very close to it.

III

If it is vivisection that shows the logic of speciesism most clearly, it is the use of other species for food that is at the heart of our attitudes toward them. Most of *Animals, Men and Morals* is an attack on meat-eating—an attack which is based solely on concern for nonhumans, without reference to arguments derived from considerations of ecology, macrobiotics, health, or religion.

The idea that nonhumans are utilities, means to our ends, pervades our thought. Even conservationists who are concerned about the slaughter of wild fowl but not about the vastly greater slaughter of chickens for our tables are thinking in this way—they are worried about what we would lose if there were less wildlife. Stanley Godlovitch, pursuing the Marxist idea that our thinking is formed by the activities we undertake in satisfying our needs, suggests that man's first classification of his environment was into Edibles and Inedibles. Most animals came into the first category, and there they have remained.

Man may always have killed other species for food, but he has never exploited them so ruthlessly as he does today. Farming has succumbed to business methods, the objective being to get the highest possible ratio of output (meat, eggs, milk) to input (fodder, labor costs, etc.). Ruth Harrison's essay "On Factory Farming" gives an account of some aspects of modern methods, and of the unsuccessful British campaign for effective controls, a campaign which was sparked off by her *Animal Machines* (Stuart: London, 1964).

Her article is in no way a substitute for her earlier book. This is a pity since, as she says, "Farm produce is still associated with mental pictures of animals browsing in the fields, . . . of hens having a last forage before going to roost. . . ." Yet neither in her article nor elsewhere in *Animals, Men and Morals* is this false image replaced by a clear idea of the nature and extent of factory farming. We learn of this only indirectly, when we hear of the code of reform proposed by an advisory committee set up by the British government.

Among the proposals, which the government refused to implement on the grounds that they were too idealistic, were: *"Any animal should at least have room to turn around freely."*

Factory farm animals need liberation in the most literal sense. Veal calves are kept in stalls five feet by two feet. They are usually slaughtered when about four months old, and have been too big to turn in their stalls for at least a month. Intensive beef herds, kept in stalls only proportionately larger for much longer periods, account for a growing percentage of beef production. Sows are often similarly confined when pregnant, which, because of artificial methods of increasing fertility, can be most of the time. Animals confined in this way do not waste food by exercising, nor do they develop unpalatable muscle.

"A dry bedded area should be provided for all stock." Intensively kept animals usually have to stand and sleep on slatted floors without straw, because this makes cleaning easier.

"Palatable roughage must be readily available to all calves after one week of age." In order to produce the pale veal housewives are said to prefer, calves are fed on an all-liquid diet until slaughter, even though they are long past the age at which they would normally eat grass. They develop a craving for roughage, evidenced by attempts to gnaw wood from their stalls. (For the same reason, their diet is deficient in iron.)

"Battery cages for poultry should be large enough for a bird to be able to stretch one wing at a time." Under current British practice, a cage for four or five laying hens has a floor area of twenty inches by eighteen inches, scarcely larger than a double page of the *New York Review of Books*. In this space, on a sloping wire floor (sloping so the eggs roll down, wire so the dung drops through) the birds live for a year or eighteen months while artificial lighting and temperature conditions combine with drugs in their food to squeeze the maximum number of eggs out of them. Table birds are also sometimes kept in cages. More often they are reared in sheds, no less crowded. Under these conditions all the birds' natural activities are frustrated, and they develop "vices" such as pecking each other to death. To prevent this, beaks are often cut off, and the sheds kept dark.

How many of those who support factory farming by buying its produce know anything about the way it is produced? How many have heard something about it, but are reluctant to check up for fear that it will make them uncomfortable? To non-speciesists, the typical consumer's mixture of ignorance, reluctance to find out the truth, and vague belief that nothing really bad could be allowed seems analogous to the attitudes of "decent Germans" to the death camps.

There are, of course, some defenders of factory farming. Their arguments are considered, though again rather sketchily, by John Harris. Among the most common: "Since they have never known anything else, they don't suffer." This argument will not be put by anyone who knows anything about animal behavior, since he will know that not all behavior has to be learned. Chickens attempt to stretch wings, walk around, scratch, and even dustbathe or build a nest, even though they have never lived under conditions that allowed these activities. Calves can suffer from maternal deprivation no matter at what age they were taken from their mothers. "We need these intensive methods to provide protein for a growing population." As ecologists and famine relief organizations know, we can produce far more protein per acre if we grow the right vegetable crop, soy beans for instance, than if we use the land to grow crops to be converted into protein by animals who use nearly 90 percent of the protein themselves, even when unable to exercise.

There will be many readers of this book who will agree that factory farming involves an unjustifiable degree of exploitation of sentient creatures, and yet will want to say that there is nothing wrong with rearing animals for food, provided it is done "humanely." These people are saying, in effect, that although we should not cause animals to suffer, there is nothing wrong with killing them.

There are two possible replies to this view. One is to attempt to show that this combination of attitudes is absurd. Roslind Godlovitch takes this course in her essay, which is an examination of some common attitudes to animals. She argues that from the combination of "animal suffering is to be avoided" and "there is nothing wrong with killing animals" it follows that all animal life ought to be exterminated (since all sentient creatures will suffer to some degree at some point in their lives). Euthanasia is a contentious issue only because we place some value on living. If we did not, the least amount of suffering would justify it. Accordingly, if we deny that we have a duty to exterminate all animal life, we must concede that we are placing some value on animal life.

This argument seems to me valid, although one could still reply that the value of animal life is to be derived from the pleasures that life can have for them, so that, provided their lives have a balance of pleasure over pain, we are justified in rearing them. But this would imply that we ought to produce animals and let them live as pleasantly as possible, without suffering.

At this point, one can make the second of the two possible replies to the view that rearing and killing animals for food is all right so long as it is done humanely. This second reply is that so long as we think that a nonhuman may be killed simply so that a human can satisfy his taste for meat, we are still thinking of nonhumans as means rather than as ends in themselves. The factory farm is nothing more than the application of technology to this concept. Even traditional methods involve castration, the separation of mothers and their young, the breaking up of herds, branding or ear-punching, and of course transportation to the abattoirs and the final moments of terror when the animals smells blood and senses danger. If we were to try rearing animals so that they lived and died without suffering, we should find that to do so on anything like the scale of today's meat industry would be a sheer impossibility. Meat would become the prerogative of the rich.

I have been able to discuss only some of the contributions to this book, saying nothing about, for instance, the essays on killing for furs and for sport. Nor have I considered all the detailed questions that need to be asked once we start thinking about other species in the radically different way presented by this book. What, for instance, are we to do about genuine conflicts of interest like rats biting slum children? I am not sure of the answer, but the essential point is just that we *do* see this as a conflict of interests, that we recognize that rats have interests too. Then we may begin to think about other ways of resolving the conflict—perhaps by leaving out rat baits that sterilize the rats instead of killing them.

I have not discussed such problems because they are side issues compared with the exploitation of other species for food and for experimental purposes. On these central matters, I hope that I have said enough to show that this book, despite its flaws, is a challenge to every human to recognize his attitudes to nonhumans as a form of prejudice no less objectionable than racism or sexism. It is a challenge that demands not just a change of attitudes, but a change in our way of life, for it requires us to become vegetarians.

Can a purely moral demand of this kind succeed? The odds are certainly against it. The book holds out no inducements. It does not tell us that we will become healthier, or enjoy life more, if we cease exploiting animals. Animal Liberation will require greater altruism on the part of mankind than any other liberation movement, since animals are incapable of demanding it for themselves, or of protesting against their exploitation by votes, demonstrations, or bombs. Is man capable of such genuine altruism? Who knows? If this book does have a significant effect, however, it will be a vindication of all those who have believed that man has within himself the potential for more than cruelty and selfishness.

Suggested Readings

Benston, Margaret. "The Political Economy of Women's Liberation," *Monthly Review* 24 (September 1969).

Bookchin, Murray. *Post-Scarcity Anarchism.* Berkeley: Ramparts Press, 1971.

Gratus, Jack. *The Great White Lie.* New York: Monthly Review Press, 1973.

Knowles, Louis L., and Kenneth Prewitt (eds.). *Institutional Racism in America.* Englewood Cliffs, N.J.: Prentice-Hall, 1969.

Marcuse, Herbert. *Essay on Liberation.* Boston: Beacon Press, 1969.

Merriam, Eve (ed.). *Growing Up Female in America: Ten Lives.* New York: Doubleday, 1971.

Mitchell, Juliet. *Woman's Estate.* New York: Pantheon, 1972.

Wolfe, Alan. *The Seamy Side of Democracy: Repression in America.* New York: David McKay, 1973.

section two

killing and murder

A. Abortion

ABORTION: PARAMETERS FOR DECISION [1]

R. J. Gerber

"Babies," remarked Mrs. Jill Knight, a Conservative, Protestant member of Parliament during a debate in the House of Commons in 1966, "are not like bad teeth to be jerked out just because they cause suffering. An unborn baby is a baby nevertheless."

"There ought to be no special laws regulating abortion," wrote psychiatrist Thomas Szasz in the same year. "Such an operation should be available in the same way as, say, an operation for the beautification of a nose." [2]

Such dialectics mark the two issues central in the abortion debate now on appeal before the Supreme Court and before the entire nation. One view sees the unborn child

---

[1] Occasion for this article is offered by the recent appearance of the following three major works on the subject: John T. Noonan, Jr., ed., *The Morality of Abortion: Legal and Historical Perspectives* (Cambridge, Mass.: Harvard University Press, 1970), with an introduction by the editor, pp. xviii + 276, $8.95; Daniel Callahan, *Abortion: Law, Choice, and Morality* (New York: Macmillian Co., 1970), pp. xv + 524, $14.95; Germain G. Grisez, *Abortion: The Myths, the Realities, and the Arguments* (New York: Corpus Books, 1970), pp. 559, $6.95 (paper).

[2] "The Ethics of Abortion," *Humanist,* July 22, 1966.

possessing inviolable rights, including the right to life, from the moment life begins in the womb. The other view sees the unborn child as less than human, often as merely "a part of the mother's body," whose rights necessarily yield to the convenience of its parents and society at large.

These contemporary attitudes on taking fetal life are organic developments of two fundamentally different legal mentalities, the Hellenistic-medieval, epitomized by Thomas Aquinas, and the modern, epitomized by Roscoe Pound, Ashley Montagu, and others. In the abortion debate, it is not merely two individuals facing each other; it is a confrontation between the world views of two fairly distinct cultures, one traditional and dated, the other new and untested.

The debate now centers on a practical legal question: should existing laws against abortion be relaxed to make abortions easier to obtain? Dr. Szasz states the issue clearly: "If abortion is murder . . . , it is an immoral act which the law must prohibit." On the other hand, if abortion is not murder, if it is nothing more serious than any other medical procedure, there is no reason why it should concern the law at all. In that case, "the proper remedy must be sought not in medically and psychiatrically 'liberal' abortion laws, but in the repeal of all such laws." Obviously, the law should not tolerate murder; but, by the same token, neither should the law show more alarm about the removal of a blob of nonhuman tissue from the womb than it shows about the removal of a sore tooth or the beautification of a nose.

Central to the abortion debate is the question: how define human value? The various answers to that question tend, in general, to pit individualist approaches against social criteria in ways reminiscent of not only Hans Driesch but also Herman Melville's and Thomas Mann's novels. For example, is humanity determined by structure or by function? By genetic code or by social interaction? By an a priori deduction or by an inference from social activity? In a larger context, is human value a metaphysical conclusion of an abstract system such as natural law, or is it attested only in the pragmatic, social interests emphasized by sociological jurisprudence?

Before we approach such large questions, much less answer them, some qualifications must be made about the convictions underlying the following pages. The first is that the abortion question is not primarily a religious issue. The debate is not furthered by quotations from the Bible or by edicts from Rome. It is a secular, moral matter best resolved by secular, moral arguments. The second conviction is that the abortion movement in the United States will almost certainly succeed within five years in realizing at least a modified form of abortion on demand. Such a result is not wholly bad: benefits will ensue from such liberalization, such as the emancipation of women, the elimination of illegal abortion rings, a possible reduction in population rate, and a decrease in unwanted children. While admitting such positive and realistic benefits however, one can also be convinced that such liberalization will involve detriments beyond the loss of fetal life. Third, it is likely that abortion on demand will see its demise at some future date when the population rate has diminished, when contraceptives have become more commonplace, and when human consciousness belatedly extends ecological and environmental protection to the human womb.

. . .

Parameters for Decision

. . . In the first place, the abortion controversy involves two prime participants, the unborn child and the pregnant mother. Any argument that enters the lists on either side should acknowledge the arguments on the other side. Second, with the exception of the dubious privacy argument, it is apparent that the arguments on the side of the mother are primarily social in nature: population, woman's sexual freedom, quality of life, reduction of ADC payments. Third, it is apparent that the arguments favoring the fetus are primarily individual-oriented and involve an incongrous interweaving of metaphysics and genetics. The metaphysical notion of human potentiality and the genetic DNA structure together suggest that the status of humanity fits the very early fetus but that his social value as a person has yet to be achieved.

In this light, any decision touching on abortion must take into account two values: first, the value of an isolated individual whose humanity is attested only by structure, not by function; second, the value of socially interacting human beings—ourselves— whose humanity is attested by social functions supportive of society at large. What this implies is that our criterion of humanity must embrace both structure and function, both genetics and sociology. To define human value exclusively by structure or by function is to court trouble. To deny the genetic structure as an index of humanity would be to limit humanity to social and technological functioning, a view against which Gabriel Marcel, Alfred North Whitehead, Charles Reich, and a host of modern authorities warn; for, as Nietzsche observes, an individual does remain human once his function ceases. On the other hand, to deny some potentiality for social functioning as an index of human value would involve a priori abstractions investing test-tube babies and genetic monsters with the values of an Artistotle, a Churchill, a Kennedy.

The proabortionist is tempted to define human value in terms of adult achievements and to contrast these achievements with the *tabula rasa* of the unborn child. Underlying this attempt is the conviction that human value is, in Ashley Montagu's words, "an achievement rather than an endowment,"[3] in the sense that no comparison exists between an adult who acts in the world and an unborn fetus who has months to travel before achieving his first social act at birth. At bottom, this kind of thinking puts the premium on activity; it judges value pragmatically by social consequences. In this view, human potentiality is prized only when it acts significantly. But the question then arises of how to explain the careful nurture, rearing, and education accorded a child in our

---

[3] Letter to the editor, *New York Times,* March 9, 1967, p. 38, col. 6.

society for the first ten or fifteen years of his life. Rarely, if ever, is such a child valued for his great achievements or his great contributions to society, or for his prowess in the lists of love or rationality; yet our society has always treated him as a human being of great value because of the untapped promise he holds for such functioning in the future. The careful education tendered the young in our society suggests that we do, in fact, prize human potential for what it may actually achieve in the distant future. The parallel between the child of three years and the fetus of three months should be obvious: their differing potentials are only matters of degree and of time.

If that parallel be considered a first touchstone in approaching the abortion dilemma, then a second principle would be this: nothing should be done arbitrarily to cut off human life as long as less drastic solutions exist. Is there a less drastic solution to the abortion dilemma on the side either of the fetus or of the mother? The fetus once conceived has no alternative but to continue to grow, just as he had no choice in his parents' engaging in sex or his becoming conceived or growing up blond or blue-eyed. The fetus is the *de trop* of the Sartrean enigma; he is without recourse and without remedy.[4] The same cannot be said for the mother, who faces at least three alternatives to the abortion decision: initial will power, grossly out of fashion today; contraceptives, which deserve to be more grossly fashionable; and finally, the transfer of the unwanted, living infant to a Birthright Center after birth. While this view does not totally resolve the continuing confrontation of abortion, it does suggest that it is the fetus, not the mother, who is the ineluctable victim and that it is the mother, not the fetus, who controls the origins of life and should take the precautions necessary to avoid unthinking creation and destruction of it.

Finally, an ideal approach to abortion should be characterized by true liberality. One would suspect that a true liberal of the sort who would attack the senseless killing of peasants in Vietnam, of babes in arms at My Lai, of students at Kent State, would favor laws broadening life and oppose those limiting life to narrow, arbitrary classifications. A truly liberal law is one which seeks to enhance and preserve the most varied expressions of life; a restrictive law is one which seeks to categorize who is and who is not human. While this principle does no more to lighten the individual burden of abortion, it does suggest that the self-styled liberals who would "liberalize" the abortion laws to the point of "destruction of life on demand" seek to impose on society an arbitrary definition of humanity inconsistent with values we already prize. Surprisingly, the humanity of the fetus is often too speculative an affair for many who pronounce with papal conviction on the immorality of war, the rights of conscientious objectors, the inhumanity of violence, and the cruelty and novelty of capital punishment by gas and electrocution, not to mention those who devote themselves to protecting oil-coated sea gulls and innocent seal pups. Yet to decide humanity on the basis of external signs leads

---

[4] See J. P. Sartre, *Nausea*, trans. Lloyd Alexander (New York: New Directions Publishing Corp., 1949), esp. pp. 170–82, wherein *de trop* signifies the absurdly superfluous.

to results whose awkward logic only history can dispel. Montesquieu once observed that there could be no humanity in the majestically passive people of black skin in Africa: "It is so natural," he said, "to think that it is color which constitutes humanity that the people of Asia always doggedly deny to the Blacks any rapport with us humans."

While "sanctity of life" is a term of impenetrable meaning, it is fleshed out somewhat by a famous passage by Albert Schweitzer, who spent his life enhancing the lives of those who did not function well on Wall Street standards: "Let a man once begin to think about the mystery of his life and the links which connect him with the life that fills the world and he cannot but bring to bear upon his own life and all the other life that comes within his reach the principle of reverence for life and manifest by his principle the ethical affirmation of life. Existence will thereby become harder for him in every respect than it would be if he lived for himself, but at the same time it will be richer, more beautiful, and happier." [5]

The central issue—whether there should be abortion laws—is still open, and it is worth recalling, again, that both good and evil will flow from either alternative. Yet it is worth noting that the moral aspirations of the law are minimal. Law seeks to establish and maintain only that minimum of actualized morality necessary for the healthy functioning of the social order. It enforces only what is minimally acceptable and in this sense socially necessary. Mindful of its nature, the law is required to be tolerant of many evils morality condemns. The question thus remains: is there any social necessity that the law adopt and protect minimal standards of what constitutes humanity?

For example, it is often suggested that legalization of abortion will merely put the law in a position of neutrality with respect to fetal life. Given the obvious effects of liberalization, a position of "neutrality" with respect to fetal life is hardly more tenable than to maintain that removal of civil rights laws would be "neutral" toward the lives of blacks. Removal of a law is tantamount to approving what the removal sanctions. Justice Brandeis's warning in a famous dissent is apposite: "Our Government is the potent, the omni-present teacher. For good or for ill, it teaches the whole people by its example. Crime is contagious." [6]

Whatever the answer to the legal question, it seems that the teaching function (as opposed to the coercive function) of the law should emphasize that our society does not exclude from its ranks the children and cripples and infirm whose endowment is human potential rather than human achievement. Herein lies a great danger in the abortion movement, a danger which does not touch the fetus as much as it does those already born. Well beyond the loss of fetal life there looms in nearly all abortion arguments an implication invidious to certain classes of extrauterine human beings.

[5] *Out of My Life and Thought* (New York: Macmillan Co., 1963), p. 179.
[6] Olmstead v. United States, 277 U.S. 438, 485 (Brandeis, J. dissenting).

The basic argument for relaxing the abortion laws essentially relies on Ashley Montagu's notion that humanity is an "achievement" which results from social interaction.[7] In this view, human rights are social in the sense that they derive from social interplay, not from a priori conditions either logically or chronologically precedent to such interplay. Where the philosophical wellsprings of this theory lie involves an exploratory task worthy of an inner-space program of the most ambitious sort, but the guess may be defended that the contemporary popularity of the "I-thou" interpersonal relationship has come home to roost with a vengeance—a vengeance touching those who, for varied reasons, cannot come up to the demands of instant intersubjectivity. Fertilized by some fifty years of the work of thinkers like Gabriel Marcel, Martin Buber, Emmanuel Levinas, Victor Frankl, Carl Rogers, and Harvey Cox,[8] the mentality of the average Westerner of even modest intelligence is preoccupied if not obsessed with concern over his interpersonal rating chart. The ringing injunction to "make love not war" has spurred a secret war on those who cannot love: if they cannot love, one surmises, how can they be human? The cry for communal sharing of mountains, forests, and living quarters suggests the inhumanity of those who cannot share—those, for example, whose greatest curse is always to receive rather than to give: receive the care of a nurse, take food from a needle, accept welfare checks, take nourishment through an umbilical cord. The examples are as endless as they are intriguing and pathetic, but the fact seems clear: so obsessed is the average mind with the communal quest for interpersonal fulfillment that it has come to suspect any speculative thesis about human value that cannot be verified inductively in one's own intersubjective experience.

The concentration on shared experience, abstracted from the given structures making it possible, has forged new ethical patterns rooted largely in a shift from quantity to quality, from a structural to a functional humanism, from a natural law to a sociological jurisprudence, wherein people are not created equal but become equal through what Roscoe Pound calls the socialization of their interests.[9] Isolated nature no longer is a finished vessel whose given nature one must respect in order to utilize. Nature is clay to be broken and remolded responsibly and creatively to one's Faustian desires. Such is the cyclopean view of the otherwise laudable "I-thou" mentality: a resolute focusing on interpersonal dealings, a refusal to look to a priori considerations to downstage intersubjectivity, and a consequent sense of responsibility for humanizing to the utmost the pattern of interpersonal relations. Life is no longer merely *vita;* it must be *la dolce vita.*

Accordingly, while the modern mind reacts strongly to the experience of persons going to death in death row or undergoing harsh treatment in prisoner of war camps

---

[7] Montagu, n. 3 above.

[8] For a representative discussion of the I-thou theory, embodying the insights of all these authors, see E. Levinas, *Totality and Infinity* (Pittsburgh: Duquesne University Press, 1969).

[9] See esp. Pound, "A Theory of Social Interests," *Proceedings of the American Sociological Society* 15 (May 1921): 24.

or suffering the shame of public poverty, this same mind sees little carry-over from those values to a fetus for whom there is no overt sign of interpersonal activity. After all, its existence is still shrouded in the dark waters of the womb, and its creative self-project will not begin for a long time even after birth. The implication is obvious: we are putting a premium on social utility. Speaking in favor of the euthanasia bill in England last year, Lord Dawson of Penn invoked the *dolce vita* argument: "This is a courageous age, but it has a different sense of values from the ages which have gone before. It looks upon life more from the point of view of quality than of quantity. It places less value in life *when its usefulness has come to an end.*"[10]

Whether it be a heritage of existentialism, phenomenology, or humanist psychology, the interpersonal mentality lies at the heart of the "quality-of-life" arguments for abortion. Whether couched in terms of fetal dependency, deformity, inchoacy, nonviability, or uselessness, the basic argument implies that valuable human life is independent, viable, well-oiled, and capable of what Maslow and Rogers call those "self-actualizing" acts which lead to "peak experiences." It is a Nietzschean view, indeed, a view of man as a sociological superman. In his famous letter to the *New York Times,* Ashley Montagu contended: "The embryo, the fetus, and newborn of the human species, in point of fact, do not really become functionally human until humanized in the human socialization process. . . . Humanity is an achievement, not an endowment. The potentialities constitute the endowment, their fulfillment requires a humanizing environment."[11]

What that socialization argument does indeed suggest is precisely the difficulty with a haunting by-product of the abortion reform movement: humanity has been subtly redefined in terms of degrees of achieved social involvement. Man is not vested with human rights at creation or at birth or even as a "newborn" but only much later when he contributes to the "quality" of life. As Montagu put it: "I consider it a crime against humanity to bring a child into the world whose fulfillment as a healthy human being is any way menaced or who itself menaces . . . the quality of the society into which it is born."[12]

Dr. Garret Hardin, in similar vein and with similar convictions, states: "If the total circumstances are such that the child born at a particular time and under particular circumstances will not receive a fair shake in life, then she (the mother) should know— she should feel in her bones—that she has no right to continue the pregnancy. . . . It may seem a rather coldhearted thing to say, but we should make abortions available to keep down our taxes. . . ."[13] The unfortunate corollary of those statements is that

---

[10] Quoted in R. Ayd, "Voluntary Euthanasia: The Right to Be Killed," *Medical-Moral Newsletter* (January and February 1970), p. 17.

[11] Montagu, n. 3 above.

[12] Ibid.

[13] Address delivered at the Second Annual California Conference on Abortion, May 11, 1969, quoted in the *New York Times,* May 12, 1969, p. 66, col. 5.

the quality of life and the rate of taxes are influenced less by the unborn and much more by many classes of persons already born. The day may come when coercive measures are taken to insure that some individuals do not threaten the "quality" of the rest of our lives. One need only recall one of the blacker marks on American jurisprudence, *Buck* v. *Bell*,[14] wherein the Supreme Court in the person of Oliver Wendell Holmes sanctioned the compulsory sterilization of mental defectives. Bearing in mind current "scientific" claims that blacks are genetically inferior,[15] one might anticipate an argument for compulsory abortion of the disadvantaged and compulsory elimination of nonquality individuals along the lines of the infamous argument in *Buck:* "We have seen more than once that the public welfare may call upon the best citizens for their lives. It would be strange if it could not call upon those who already sap the strength of the State for these lesser sacrifices, often not felt to be such by those concerned, *in order to prevent our being swamped with incompetence.* "[16]

The argument that social importance or societal "value" or "interaction" constitutes protected degrees of humanity offers no threat to the Nixons, Johnsons, Calleys, and J. Edgar Hoovers of this world of power. They all can point to their social involvements to assert their claim to a humanity supposedly engendered by those involvements. Such involvement, however, is no help to the unborn fetus who has yet to meet his mother, to the husband in a womblike iron-lung, to the senile grandmother who will never again recognize a person. Neither is that argument much help to the Helen Kellers, Ludwig Beethovens, Friedrich Nietzsches, and Lord Byrons whose physical disabilities retard their social interactions and consequently diminish their social importance, while raising everyone else's taxes.

The New York abortion debate provides a case in point. The proposed bill would have permitted abortion "when there is medical evidence of a substantial risk that the foetus, if born, would be so grossly malformed, or would have such serious physical or mental abnormalities, as to be permanently incapable of caring for himself." [17] In 1969, Martin Ginsberg, a New York State assemblyman who is crippled by polio incurred as an infant and who uses metal crutches and hand and leg braces to move, made the following observation to the Assembly: "What this bill says is that those who are malformed or abnormal have no reason to be part of our society. If we are prepared to say that a life should not come into this world malformed or abnormal, then tomorrow we should be prepared to say that a life already in this world which becomes malformed or abnormal should not be permitted to live." [18]

The real effect of the abortion laws as they seem certain to appear in five years is

[14] 274 U.S. 200 (1927).

[15] See J. Edson, "Jensenism," *New York Times Magazine,* August 21, 1969, p. 10, col. 1.

[16] Buck v. Bell, 274 U.S. 200, 207 (1927).

[17] Quoted in Grisez, p. 342.

[18] Ibid.

not so much the loss of the unborn. We may survive that with calluses on top of our psychic scars. The real danger lies in the possible diminution of value and humanity accorded to the socially deprived among the born: the infant of six months, the spastic teenager, the adult in an iron lung, the woman in a wheelchair, the lunatic in an asylum, the convicted criminal, the recluse, the hermit. On the scales of social intercourse the humanity of each of these individuals either never appears or registers only at inferior levels. If a little legal logic goes a long way, it seems likely that the practical as well as the logical distinctions will shortly disappear among abortion, infanticide, and the various sociological conveniences called "mercy killing"—to the detriment of the extra- as well as of the intrauterine life. Once again, the English experience may become American precedent: those who pushed for a liberalized abortion law in Britain three years ago are now pushing for a euthanasia bill defeated in the House of Lords by only sixty-one votes to forty last year. The entire experience might suggest that there is no such stage as "just a little bit pregnant," or "a little less human," or a "little more equal," or a "little less constitutional." The quantitative differentiations of the yard-stick, the scales, the Gallup Polls, and the welfare and tax rolls are close cousins to a functional and technological assessment of humanity, the entirety of which may constitute a sociological disposal system, a *dolce vita* smoother and more antiseptic than ever devised by any tyrant or Führer.

ABORTION AND INFANTICIDE [1]

Michael Tooley

This essay deals with the question of the morality of abortion and infanticide. The fundamental ethical objection traditionally advanced against these practices rests on the contention that human fetuses and infants have a right to life. It is this claim which will be the focus of attention here. The basic issue to be discussed, then, is what properties a thing must possess in order to have a serious right to life. My approach will be set out and defend a basic moral principle specifying a condition an organism must satisfy if it is to have a serious right to life. It will be seen that this condition is not satisfied by human fetuses and infants, and thus that they do not have a right to life. So unless there are other substantial objections to abortion and infanticide, one is forced to conclude that these practices are morally acceptable ones. In contrast, it

[1] I am grateful to a number of people, particularly the Editors of *Philosophy & Public Affairs*, Rodelia Hapke, and Walter Kaufmann, for their helpful comments. It should not, of course, be inferred that they share the views expressed in this paper.

may turn out that our treatment of adult members of other species—cats, dogs, polar bears—is morally indefensible. For it is quite possible that such animals do possess properties that endow them with a right to life.

I. Abortion and Infanticide

One reason the question of the morality of infanticide is worth examining is that it seems very difficult to formulate a completely satisfactory liberal position on abortion without coming to grips with the infanticide issue. The problem the liberal encounters is essentially that of specifying a cutoff point which is not arbitrary: at what stage in the development of a human being does it cease to be morally permissible to destroy it? It is important to be clear about the difficulty here. The conservative's objection is not that since there is a continuous line of development from a zygote to a newborn baby, one must conclude that if it is seriously wrong to destroy a newborn baby it is also seriously wrong to destroy a zygote or any intermediate stage in the development of a human being. His point is rather that if one says it is wrong to destroy a newborn baby but not a zygote or some intermediate stage in the development of a human being, one should be prepared to point to a *morally relevant* difference between a newborn baby and the earlier stage in the development of a human being.

Precisely the same difficulty can, of course, be raised for a person who holds that infanticide is morally permissible. The conservative will ask what morally relevant differences there are between an adult human being and a newborn baby. What makes it morally permissible to destroy a baby, but wrong to kill an adult? So the challenge remains. But I will argue that in this case there is an extremely plausible answer.

Reflecting on the morality of infanticide forces one to face up to this challenge. In the case of abortion a number of events—quickening or viability, for instance—might be taken as cutoff points, and it is easy to overlook the fact that none of these events involves any morally significant change in the developing human. In contrast, if one is going to defend infanticide, one has to get very clear about what makes something a person, what gives something a right to life.

One of the interesting ways in which the abortion issue differs from most other moral issues is that the plausible positions on abortion appear to be extreme positions. For if a human fetus is a person, one is inclined to say that, in general, one would be justified in killing it only to save the life of the mother.[2] Such is the extreme conservative position.[3] On the other hand, if the fetus is not a person, how can it be seriously wrong

---

[2] Judith Jarvis Thomson, in her article, "A Defense of Abortion," *Philosophy & Public Affairs* 1, no. 1 (Fall 1971): 47–66, has argued with great force and ingenuity that this conclusion is mistaken.

[3] While this is the position conservatives tend to hold, it is not clear that it is the position they ought to hold. For if the fetus is a person it is far from clear that it is permissible to destroy it to save the mother. Two moral principles lend support to the view that it is the fetus which should live. First, other things being equal, should not one give something to a person who has had less rather than to a person who has had more? The mother had had a chance to live, while the fetus has not. The choice is thus between giving the mother

to destroy it? Why would one need to point to special circumstances to justify such action. The upshot is that there is no room for a moderate position on the issue of abortion such as one finds, for example, in the Model Penal Code recommendations.[4]

Aside from the light it may shed on the abortion question, the issue of infanticide is both interesting and important in its own right. The theoretical interest has been mentioned: it forces one to face up to the question of what makes something a person. The practical importance need not be labored. Most people would prefer to raise children who do not suffer from gross deformities or from severe physical, emotional, or intellectual handicaps. If it could be shown that there is no moral objection to infanticide the happiness of society could be significantly and justifiably increased.

Infanticide is also of interest because of the strong emotions it arouses. The typical reaction to infanticide is like the reaction to incest or cannibalism, or the reaction of previous generations to masturbation or oral sex. The response, rather than appealing to carefully formulated moral principles, is primarily visceral. When philosophers themselves respond in this way, offering no arguments, and dismissing infanticide out of hand, it is reasonable to suspect that one is dealing with a taboo rather than with a rational prohibition.[5] I shall attempt to show that this is in fact the case.

II. Terminology: "Person" Versus "Human Being"

How is the term "person" to be interpreted? I shall treat the concept of a person as a purely moral concept, free of all descriptive content. Specifically, in my usage the sentence "X is a person" will be synonymous with the sentence "X has a (serious) moral right to life."

This usage diverges slightly from what is perhaps the more common way of interpreting the term "person" when it is employed as a purely moral term, where to say that X is a person is to say that X has rights. If everything that had rights had a right to life, these interpretations would be extensionally equivalent. But I am inclined to think that it does not follow from acceptable moral principles that whatever has any rights

---

more of an opportunity to live while giving the fetus none at all and giving the fetus an opportunity to enjoy life while not giving the mother a further opportunity to do so. Surely fairness requires the latter. Secondly, since the fetus has a greater life expectancy than the mother, one is in effect distributing more goods by choosing the life of the fetus over the life of the mother.

The position I am here recommending to the conservative should not be confused with the official Catholic position. The Catholic Church holds that it is seriously wrong to kill a fetus directly even if failure to do so will result in the death of *both* the mother and the fetus. This perverse value judgment is not part of the conservative's position.

[4] Section 230.3 of the American Law Institute's *Model Penal Code* (Philadelphia, 1962). There is some interesting, though at time confused, discussion of the proposed code in *Model Penal Code—Tentative Draft No. 9* (Philadelphia, 1959), pp. 146–162.

[5] A clear example of such an unwillingness to entertain seriously the possibility that moral judgments widely accepted in one's own society may nevertheless be incorrect is provided by Roger Wertheimer's superficial dismissal of infanticide on pages 69–70 of his article "Understanding the Abortion Argument," *Philosophy & Public Affairs*, 1, no. 1 (Fall 1971): 67–95.

at all has a right to life. My reason is this. Given the choice between being killed and being tortured for an hour, most adult humans would surely choose the latter. So it seems plausible to say it is worse to kill an adult human being than it is to torture him for an hour. In contrast, it seems to me that while it is not seriously wrong to kill a newborn kitten, it is seriously wrong to torture one for an hour. This *suggests* that newborn kittens may have a right not to be tortured without having a serious right to life. For it seems to be true that an individual has a right to something whenever it is the case that, if he wants that thing, it would be wrong for others to deprive him of it. Then if it is wrong to inflict a certain sensation upon a kitten if it doesn't want to experience that sensation, it will follow that the kitten has a right not to have sensation inflicted upon it.[6] I shall return to this example later. My point here is merely that it provides some reason for holding that it does not follow from acceptable moral principles that if something has any rights at all, it has a serious right to life.

There has been a tendency in recent discussions of abortion to use expressions such as "person" and "human being" interchangeably. B. A. Brody, for example, refers to the difficulty of determining "whether destroying the foetus constitutes the taking of a human life," and suggests it is very plausible that "the taking of a human life is an action that has bad consequences for him whose life is being taken." [7] When Brody refers to something as a human life he apparently construes this as entailing that the thing is a person. For if every living organism belonging to the species homo sapiens counted as a human life, there would be no difficulty in determining whether a fetus inside a human mother was a human life.

The same tendency is found in Judith Jarvis Thomson's article, which opens with the statement: "Most opposition to abortion relies on the premise that the fetus is a human being, a person, from the moment of conception." [8] The same is true of Roger Wertheimer, who explicitly says: "First off I should note that the expressions 'a human life,' 'a human being,' 'a person' are virtually interchangeable in this context." [9]

The tendency to use expressions like "person" and "human being" interchangeably is an unfortunate one. For one thing, it tends to lend covert support to antiabortionist positions. Given such usage, one who holds a liberal view of abortion is put in the position of maintaining that fetuses, at least up to a certain point, are not human beings. Even philosophers are led astray by this usage. Thus Wertheimer says that "except

---

[6] Compare the discussion of the concept of a right offered by Richard B. Brandt in his *Ethical Theory* (Englewood Cliffs, N.J., 1959), pp. 434–441. As Brandt points out, some philosophers have maintained that only things that can *claim* rights can have rights. I agree with Brandt's view that "inability to claim does not destroy the right" (p. 440).

[7] B. A. Brody, "Abortion and the Law," *Journal of Philosophy,* LXVIII, no. 12 (17 June 1971): 357–369. See pp. 357–358.

[8] Thomsom, "A Defense of Abortion," p. 47.

[9] Wertheimer, "Understanding the Abortion Argument," p. 69.

for monstrosities, every member of our species is indubitably a person, a human being, at the very latest at birth." [10] Is it really *indubitable* that newborn babies are persons? Surely this is a wild contention. Wertheimer is falling prey to the confusion naturally engendered by the practice of using "person" and "human being" interchangeably. Another example of this is provided by Thomson: "I am inclined to think also that we shall probably have to agree that the fetus has already become a human person well before birth. Indeed, it comes as a surprise when one first learns how early in its life it begins to acquire human characteristics. By the tenth week, for example, it already has a face, arms and legs, fingers and toes; it has internal organs, and brain activity is detectable." [11] But what do such physiological characteristics have to do with the question of whether the organism is a person? Thomson, partly, I think, because of the unfortunate use of terminology, does not even raise this question. As a result she virtually takes it for granted that there are some cases in which abortion is "positively indecent." [12]

There is a second reason why using "person" and "human being" interchangeably is unhappy philosophically. If one says that the dispute between pro- and anti-abortionists centers on whether the fetus is a human, it is natural to conclude that it is essentially a disagreement about certain facts, a disagreement about what properties a fetus possesses. Thus Wertheimer says that "if one insists on using the raggy fact-value distinction, then one ought to say that the dispute is over a matter of fact in the sense in which it is a fact that the Negro slaves were human beings." [13] I shall argue that the two cases are not parallel, and that in the case of abortion what is primarily at stake is what moral principles one should accept. If one says that the central issue between conservatives and liberals in the abortion question is whether the fetus is a person, it is clear that the dispute may be either about what properties a thing must have in order to be a person, in order to have a right to life—a moral question—or about whether a fetus at a given stage of development as a matter of fact possesses the properties in question. The temptation to suppose that the disagreement must be a factual one is removed.

It should now be clear why the common practice of using expressions such as "person" and "human being" interchangeably in discussions of abortion is unfortunate. It would perhaps be best to avoid the term "human" altogether, employing instead some expression that is more naturally interpreted as referring to a certain type of biological organism characterized in physiological terms, such as "member of the species Homo sapiens." My own approach will be to use the term "human" only in contexts where it is not philosophically dangerous.

---

[10] *Ibid.*

[11] Thomson, "A Defense of Abortion," pp. 47–48.

[12] *Ibid.,* p. 65.

[13] Wertheimer, "Understanding the Abortion Argument," p. 78.

III. The Basic Issue: When Is a Member of the Species Homo Sapiens a Person?

Settling the issue of the morality of abortion and infanticide will involve answering the following questions: What properties must something have to be a person, i.e., to have a serious right to life? At what point in the development of a member of the species Homo sapiens does the organism possess the properties that make it a person? The first question raises a moral issue. To answer it is to decide what basic [14] moral principles involving the ascription of a right to life one ought to accept. The second question raises a purely factual issue, since the properties in question are properties of a purely descriptive sort.

Some writers seem quite pessimistic about the possibility of resolving the question of the morality of abortion. Indeed, some have gone so far as to suggest that the question of whether the fetus is a person is in principle unanswerable: "we seem to be stuck with the indeterminateness of the fetus' humanity." [15] An understanding of some of the sources of this pessimism will, I think, help us to tackle the problem. Let us begin by considering the similarity a number of people have noted between the issue of abortion and the issue of Negro slavery. The question here is why it should be more difficult to decide whether abortion and infanticide are acceptable than it was to decide whether slavery was acceptable. The answer seems to be that in the case of slavery there are moral principles of a quite uncontroversial sort that settle the issue. Thus most people would agree to some such principle as the following: No organism that has experiences, that is capable of thought and of using language, and that has harmed no one, should be made a slave. In the case of abortion, on the other hand, conditions that are generally agreed to be sufficient grounds for ascribing a right to life to something do not suffice to settle the issue. It is easy to specify other, purportedly sufficient conditions that will settle the issue, but no one has been successful in putting forward considerations that will convince others to accept those additional moral principles.

I do not share the general pessimism about the possibility of resolving the issue of abortion and infanticide because I believe it is possible to point to a very plausible moral principle dealing with the question of *necessary* conditions for something's having a right to life, where the conditions in question will provide an answer to the question of the permissibility of abortion and infanticide.

There is a second cause of pessimism that should be noted before proceeding. It is tied up with the fact that the development of an organism is one of gradual and continuous change. Given this continuity, how is one to draw a line at one point and declare it permissible to destroy a member of Homo sapiens up to, but not beyond, that point? Won't there be an arbitrariness about any point that is chosen? I will return

---

[14] A moral principle accepted by a person is *basic for him* if and only if his acceptance of it is not dependent upon any of his (nonmoral) factual beliefs. That is, no change in his factual beliefs would cause him to abandon the principle in question.

[15] Wertheimer, "Understanding the Abortion Argument," p. 88.

to this worry shortly. It does not present a serious difficulty once the basic moral principles relevant to the ascription of a right to life to an individual are established.

Let us turn now to the first and most fundamental question: What properties must something have in order to be a person, i.e., to have a serious right to life? The claim I wish to defend is this: An organism possesses a serious right to life only if it possesses the concept of a self as a continuing subject of experiences and other mental states, and believes that it is itself such a continuing entity.

My basic argument in support of this claim, which I will call the self-consciousness requirement, will be clearest, I think, if I first offer a simplified version of the argument, and then consider a modification that seems desirable. The simplified version of my argument is this. To ascribe a right to an individual is to assert something about the prima facie obligations of other individuals to act, or to refrain from acting, in certain ways. However, the obligations in question are conditional ones, being dependent upon the existence of certain desires of the individual to whom the right is ascribed. Thus if an individual asks one to destroy something to which he has a right, one does not violate his right to that thing if one proceeds to destroy it. This suggests the following analysis: "A has a right to X" is roughly synonymous with "If A desires X, then others are under a prima facie obligation to refrain from actions that would deprive him of it." [16]

Although this analysis is initially plausible, there are reasons for thinking it not entirely correct. I will consider these later. Even here, however, some expansion is necessary, since there are features of the concept of a right that are important in the present context, and that ought to be dealt with more explicitly. In particular, it seems to be a conceptual truth that things that lack consciousness, such as ordinary machines, cannot have rights. Does this conceptual truth follow from the above analysis of the concept of a right? The answer depends on how the term "desire" is interpreted. If one adopts a completely behavioristic interpretation of "desire," so that a machine that searches for an electrical outlet in order to get its batteries recharged is described as having a desire to be recharged, then it will not follow from this analysis that objects that lack consciousness cannot have rights. On the other hand, if "desire" is interpreted in such a way that desires are states necessarily standing in some sort of relationship to states of consciousness, it will follow from the analysis that a machine that is not capable of being conscious, and consequently of having desires, cannot have any rights. I think those who defend analyses of the concept of a right along the lines of this one do have in mind an interpretation of the term "desire" that involves reference to something more than behavioral dispositions. However, rather than relying on this, it seems preferable to make such an interpretation explicit. The following analysis is a natural way of doing that: "A has a right to X" is roughly synonymous with "A is the sort of thing that is a subject of experiences and other mental states, A is capable

---

[16] Again, compare the analysis defended by Brandt in *Ethical Theory*, pp. 434–441.

of desiring X, and if A does desire X, then others are under a prima facie obligation to refrain from actions that would deprive him of it."

The next step in the argument is basically a matter of applying this analysis to the concept of a right to life. Unfortunately the expression "right to life" is not entirely a happy one, since it suggests that the right in question concerns the continued existence of a biological organism. That this is incorrect can be brought out by considering possible ways of violating an individual's right to life. Suppose, for example, that by some technology of the future the brain of an adult human were to be completely reprogrammed, so that the organism wound up with memories (or rather, apparent memories), beliefs, attitudes, and personality traits completely different from those associated with it before it was subjected to reprogramming. In such a case one would surely say that an individual had been destroyed, that an adult human's right to life had been violated, even though no biological organism had been killed. This example shows that the expression "right to life" is misleading, since what one is really concerned about is not just the continued existence of a biological organism, but the right of a subject of experiences and other mental states to continue to exist.

Given this more precise description of the right with which we are here concerned, we are now in a position to apply the analysis of the concept of a right stated above. When we do so we find that the statement "A has a right to continue to exist as a subject of experiences and other mental states" is roughly synonymous with the statement "A is a subject of experiences and other mental states, A is capable of desiring to continue to exist as a subject of experiences and other mental states, and if A does desire to continue to exist as such an entity, then others are under a prima facie obligation not to prevent him from doing so."

The final stage in the argument is simply a matter of asking what must be the case if something is to be capable of having a desire to continue existing as a subject of experiences and other mental states. The basic point here is that the desires a thing can have are limited by the concepts it possesses. For the fundamental way of describing a given desire is as a desire that a certain proposition be true.[17] Then, since one cannot desire that a certain proposition be true unless one understands it, and since one cannot understand it without possessing the concepts involved in it, it follows that the desires one can have are limited by the concepts one possesses. Applying this to the present case results in the conclusion that an entity cannot be the sort of thing that can desire that a subject of experiences and other mental states exist unless it possesses the concept of such a subject. Moreover, an entity cannot desire that it itself *continue* existing as

---

[17] In everyday life one often speaks of desiring things, such as an apple or a newspaper. Such talk is elliptical, the context together with one's ordinary beliefs serving to make it clear that one wants to eat the apple and read the newspaper. To say that what one desires is that a certain proposition be true should not be construed as involving any particular ontological commitment. The point is merely that it is sentences such as "John wants it to be the case that he is eating an apple in the next few minutes" that provide a completely explicit description of a person's desires. If one fails to use such sentences one can be badly misled about what concepts are presupposed by a particular desire.

a subject of experiences and other mental states unless it believes that it is now such a subject. This completes the justification of the claim that it is a necessary condition of something's having a serious right to life that it possess the concept of a self as a continuing subject of experiences, and that it believe that it is itself such an entity.

Let us now consider a modification in the above argument that seems desirable. This modification concerns the crucial conceptual claim advanced about the relationship between ascription of rights and ascription of the corresponding desires. Certain situations suggest that there may be exceptions to the claim that if a person doesn't desire something, one cannot violate his right to it. There are three types of situations that call this claim into question: (i) situations in which an individual's desires reflect a state of emotional disturbance; (ii) situations in which a previously conscious individual is temporarily unconscious; (iii) situations in which an individual's desires have been distorted by conditioning or by indoctrination.

As an example of the first, consider a case in which an adult human falls into a state of depression which his psychiatrist recognizes as temporary. While in the state he tells people he wishes he were dead. His psychiatrist, accepting the view that there can be no violation of an individual's right to life unless the individual has a desire to live, decides to let his patient have his way and kills him. Or consider a related case in which one person gives another a drug that produces a state of temporary depression; the recipient expresses a wish that he were dead. The person who administered the drug then kills him. Doesn't one want to say in both these cases that the agent did something seriously wrong in killing the other person? And isn't the reason the action was seriously wrong in each case the fact that it violated the individual's right to life? If so, the right to life cannot be linked with a desire to live in the way claimed above.

The second set of situations are ones in which an individual is unconscious for some reason—that is, he is sleeping, or drugged, or in a temporary coma. Does an individual in such a state have any desires? People do sometimes say that an unconscious individual wants something, but it might be argued that if such talk is not to be simply false it must be interpreted as actually referring to the desires the individual *would* have if he were now conscious. Consequently, if the analysis of the concept of a right proposed above were correct, it would follow that one does not violate an individual's right if one takes his car, or kills him, while he is asleep.

Finally, consider situations in which an individual's desires have been distorted, either by inculcation of irrational beliefs or by direct conditioning. Thus an individual may permit someone to kill him because he has been convinced that if he allows himself to be sacrificed to the gods he will be gloriously rewarded in a life to come. Or an individual may be enslaved after first having been conditioned to desire a life of slavery. Doesn't one want to say that in the former case an individual's right to life has been violated, and in the latter his right to freedom?

Situations such as these strongly suggest that even if an individual doesn't want something, it is still possible to violate his right to it. Some modification of the earlier account of the concept of a right thus seems in order. The analysis given covers, I believe, the paradigmatic cases of violation of an individual's rights, but there are other, secondary cases where one also wants to say that someone's right has been violated which are not included.

Precisely how the revised analysis should be formulated is unclear. Here it will be sufficient merely to say that, in view of the above, an individual's right to X can be violated not only when he desires X, but also when he *would* now desire X were it not for one of the following: (i) he is in an emotionally unbalanced state; (ii) he is temporarily unconscious; (iii) he has been conditioned to desire the absence of X.

The critical point now is that, even given this extension of the conditions under which an individual's right to something can be violated, it is still true that one's right to something can be violated only when one has the conceptual capability of desiring the thing in question. For example, an individual who would now desire not to be a slave if he weren't emotionally unbalanced, or if he weren't temporarily unconscious, or if he hadn't previously been conditioned to want to be a slave, must possess the concepts involved in the desire not to be a slave. Since it is really only the conceptual capability presupposed by the desire to continue existing as a subject of experiences and other mental states, and not the desire itself, that enters into the above argument, the modification required in the account of the conditions under which an individual's rights can be violated does not undercut my defense of the self-consciousness requirement.[18]

To sum up, my argument has been that having a right to life presupposes that one is capable of desiring to continue existing as a subject of experiences and other mental states. This in turn presupposes both that one has the concept of such a continuing entity and that one believes that one is oneself such an entity. So an entity that lacks such a consciousness of itself as a continuing subject of mental states does not have a right to life.

It would be natural to ask at this point whether satisfaction of this requirement is not only necessary but also sufficient to ensure that a thing has a right to life. I am inclined to an affirmative answer. However, the issue is not urgent in the present context, since as long as the requirement is in fact a necessary one we have the basis of an adequate defense of abortion and infanticide. If an organism must satisfy some other condition before it has a serious right to life, the result will merely be that the

[18] There are, however, situations other than those discussed here which might seem to count against the claim that a person cannot have a right unless he is conceptually capable of having the corresponding desire. Can't a young child, for example, have a right to an estate, even though he may not be conceptually capable of wanting the estate? It is clear that such situations have to be carefully considered if one is to arrive at a satisfactory account of the concept of a right. My inclination is to say that the correct description is not that the child now has a right to the estate, but that he will come to have such a right when he is mature, and that in the meantime no one else has a right to the estate. My reason for saying that the child does not now have a right to the estate is that he cannot now do things with the estate, such as selling it or giving it away, that he will be able to do later on.

interval during which infanticide is morally permissible may be somewhat longer. Although the point at which an organism first achieves self-consciousness and hence the capacity of desiring to continue existing as a subject of experiences and other mental states may be a theoretically incorrect cutoff point, it is at least a morally safe one: any error it involves is on the side of caution.

. . .

VI. Summary and Conclusions

Let us return now to my basic claim, the self-consciousness requirement: An organism possesses a serious right to life only if it possesses the concept of a self as a continuing subject of experiences and other mental states, and believes that it is itself such a continuing entity. My defense of this claim has been twofold. I have offered a direct argument in support of it, and I have tried to show that traditional conservative and liberal views on abortion and infanticide, which involve a rejection of it, are unsound. I now want to mention one final reason why my claim should be accepted. Consider the example mentioned in section II—that of killing, as opposed to torturing, newborn kittens. I suggested there that while in the case of adult humans most people would consider it worse to kill an individual than to torture him for an hour, we do not usually view the killing of a newborn kitten as morally outrageous, although we would regard someone who tortured a newborn kitten for an hour as heinously evil. I pointed out that a possible conclusion that might be drawn from this is that newborn kittens have a right not to be tortured, but do not have a serious right to life. If this is the correct conclusion, how is one to explain it? One merit of the self-consciousness requirement is that it provides an explanation of this situation. The reason a newborn kitten does not have a right to life is explained by the fact that it does not possess the concept of a self. But how is one to explain the kitten's having a right not to be tortured? The answer is that a desire not to suffer pain can be ascribed to something without assuming that it has any concept of a continuing self. For while something that lacks the concept of a self cannot desire that a self not suffer, it can desire that a given sensation not exist. The state desired—the abence of a particular sensation, or of sensations of a certain sort—can be described in a purely phenomenalistic language, and hence without the concept of a continuing self. So long as the newborn kitten possesses the relevant phenomenal concepts, it can truly be said to desire that a certain sensation not exist. So we can ascribe to it a right not to be tortured even though, since it lacks the concept of a continuing self, we cannot ascribe to it a right to life.

This completes my discussion of the basic moral principles involved in the issue of abortion and infanticide. But I want to comment upon an important factual question, namely, at what point an organism comes to possess the concept of a self as a continuing subject of experiences and other mental states, together with the belief that it is itself such a continuing entity. This is obviously a matter for detailed psychological investigation, but everyday observation makes it perfectly clear, I believe, that a newborn baby does not possess the concept of a continuing self, any more than a newborn kitten possesses such a concept. If so, infanticide during a time interval shortly after birth must be morally acceptable.

But where is the line to be drawn? What is the cutoff point? If one maintained, as some philosophers have, that an individual possesses concepts only if he can express these concepts in language, it would be a matter of everyday observation whether or not a given organism possessed the concept of a continuing self. Infanticide would then be permissible up to the time an organism learned how to use certain expressions. However, I think the claim that acquisition of concepts is dependent on acquistion of language is mistaken. For example, one wants to ascribe mental states of a conceptual sort—such as beliefs and desires—to organisms that are incapable of learning a language. This issue of prelinguistic understanding is clearly outside the scope of this discussion. My point is simply that *if* an organism can acquire concepts without thereby acquiring a way of expressing those concepts linguistically, the question of whether a given organism possesses the concept of a self as a continuing subject of experiences and other mental states, together with the belief that it is itself such a continuing entity, may be a question that requires fairly subtle experimental techniques to answer.

If this view of the matter is roughly correct, there are two worries one is left with at the level of practical moral decisions, one of which may turn out to be deeply disturbing. The lesser worry is where the line is to be drawn in the case of infanticide. It is not troubling because there is no serious need to know the exact point at which a human infant acquires a right to life. For in the vast majority of cases in which infanticide is desirable, its desirability will be apparent within a short time after birth. Since it is virtually certain that an infant at such a stage of its development does not possess the concept of a continuing self, and thus does not possess a serious right to life, there is excellent reason to believe that infanticide is morally permissible in most cases where it is otherwise desirable. The practical moral problem can thus be satisfactorily handled by choosing some period of time, such as a week after birth, as the interval during which infanticide will be permitted. This interval could then be modified once psychologists have established the point at which a human organism comes to believe that it is a continuing subject of experiences and other mental states.

The troubling worry is whether adult animals belonging to species other than Homo sapiens may not also possess a serious right to life. For once one says that an organism can possess the concept of a continuing self, together with the belief that it is itself such an entity, without having any way of expressing that concept and that belief linguistically, one has to face up to the question of whether animals may not possess properties that bestow a serious right to life upon them. The suggestion itself is a familiar one, and one that most of us are accustomed to dismiss very casually. The line of thought advanced here suggests that this attitude may turn out to be tragically mistaken. Once one reflects upon the question of the *basic* moral principles involved in the ascription of a right to life to organisms, one may find himself driven to conclude that our everyday treatment of animals is morally indefensible, and that we are in fact murdering innocent persons.

B. Political Violence and Terrorism

THE FORCE OF NONVIOLENCE

Howard Zinn

Four instances of violence come to my mind. One I read about in the newspapers; another I witnessed; in a third I was on the receiving end; in the fourth, the most brutal of them all, I was a perpetrator.

The first took place an hour's drive from my home in Atlanta, Georgia, when a mob in Athens, screaming epithets and hurling rocks, attacked the dormitory occupied by the first Negro girl to enter the University of Georgia.

The second I saw years ago as I walked through a slum area of the lower East Side of New York: a little old Jew with a beard, pulling his pushcart, was arguing with a Negro who was demanding payment for his work. The bearded man said he didn't have the money and the Negro said he needed it and the argument grew, and the Negro picked up a stick of wood and hit the old man on the side of the head. The old man continued pushing the cart down the street, blood running down his face, and the Negro walked away.

In the third instance, I took my wife and two-year-old daughter to a concert given in an outdoor area near the town of Peekskill, New York. The concert artist was Paul Robeson. As he sang under the open sky to an audience of thousands, a shouting, angry crowd gathered around the field. When the concert was over and we drove off the grounds, the cars moving in a long slow line, we saw the sides of the road filled with cursing, jeering men and women. Then the rocks began to fly. My wife was pregnant at the time. She ducked and pushed our daughter down near the floor of our car. All four side windows and the rear window were smashed by rocks. Sitting in the back was a young woman, a stranger, to whom we had given a lift. A flying rock fractured her skull. There were dozens of casualties that day.

The fourth incident occurred in World War II when I was a bombardier with the Eighth Air Force in Europe. The war was almost over. German territory was shrinking, and the Air Force was running out of targets. In France, long since reoccupied by our troops, there was still a tiny pocket of Nazi soldiers in a protected encampment near the city of Bordeaux. Someone in the higher echelons decided, though the end of the war was obviously weeks away, that this area should be bombed. Hundreds of Flying Fortresses went. In each bomb bay there were twenty-four one-hundred-pound fire-bombs, containing a new type of jellied gasoline. We set the whole area aflame and obliterated the encampment. Nearby was the ancient town of Royan; that, too, was almost totally destroyed. The Norden bomb sight was not that accurate.

These four instances of violence possess something in common. None of them could have been committed by any animal other than man. The reason for this does not lie alone in man's superior ability to manipulate his environment. It lies in his ability to conceptualize his hatreds. A beast commits violence against specific things for immediate and visible purposes. It needs to eat. It needs a mate. It needs to defend its life. Man has these biological needs plus many more which are culturally created. Man will do violence not only against a specific something which gets in the way of one of his needs; he will do violence against a symbol which stands for, or which he believes stands for, that which prevents him from satisfying his needs. (Guilt by association is high-level thinking.)

With symbolic violence, the object of attack is deprived of its particularity. Only in this way can man overcome what I believe is his natural spontaneous feelings of oneness with other human beings. He must, by the substitution of symbol for reality, destroy in his consciousness the humanness of that being. To the angry crowds outside the dormitory in Athens, Georgia, their target was not Charlayne Hunter, an extremely attractive and intelligent young woman, sitting, brave and afraid, in her room. She was a "dirty nigger"—a symbol abstracted from life. To the Negro who committed violence on the streets of New York, this was not a pathetic old Jewish immigrant, forced in the last years of his life to peddle vegetables from a pushcart, but a dehumanized symbol of the historic white exploiter who used the Negro's labor and refused to pay him a just wage. To the screaming rock-throwers of Peekskill who fractured the skull of a young woman returning from a concert, the people in the car they attacked were not a family on an outing; in this car were people who had gone to hear a black-skinned communistic singer and who therefore were all congealed into a symbol representing a nigger-loving communism. And as I set my intervalometer, and toggled off by bombs over the city of Royan, I was not setting fire to people's homes, crushing and burning individual men, women and newborn babies. We were at war, we always dropped bombs on the enemy, and down there was the enemy.

The human ability to abstract, to create symbols standing for reality, has enabled man to compound his material possessions, to split the atom and orbit the earth. It also enables him to compound his hatreds, and expands his capacity for violence. But while there is no incentive to distort in the scientific process which changes reality to symbol for purposes of manipulation, and back to reality for purposes of realization, there *is* incentive, in social relations, for distorting the symbols of communication. With man's use of symbols, the potentiality for hatred and therefore for violence is enormously, logarithmically, magnified. And with word-symbols the possibility for distortion is infinite. In fact, distortion is inherent here, for while particles of light are sufficiently similar so that we can express the speed of all of them in a useful mathematical equation, human beings are so complex and particular, and their relationships so varied, that no generalized word can do justice to reality.

War is symbolic violence, with all people who happen to reside within the geographical boundaries of a nation-state constituting "the enemy." Race persecution is symbolic violence directed against all individuals, regardless of their specific characteristics, who can be identified with an abstracted physical type. In the execution chamber, the state puts to death anyone, regardless of individual circumstance, who fits the legal symbol: murderer. The law forcibly deprives of freedom everyone who falls within the symbolic definition of a criminal; sentences are sometimes meted out to individuals, but mostly to dehumanized lawbreakers whose acts match an abstract list of punishments.

There is symbolism also in the use of violence to effectuate desirable social change, whether through revolution, labor struggle, "just" wars or desegregation. This creates the probability that there will be only a partial correspondence between the specific obstacle to progress and the generalized, symbolized object of violence (the head of Marie Antoinette, the $50-a-week scab, the civilian population of Dresden, the poor white in Mississippi). It may hurt the revoluntionary reformer to think so, but the fact of symbolization in human violence creates a common problem for *all* users of violence, regardless of their ends. And it may displease the pacifist to say so, but these different ends do matter in deciding how much violence we should countenance in the rearrangement of the social structure.

Symbolism, with its inevitable distortions, complicates an already tough problem: developing an approach to nonviolence that is both realistic and moral. We need a rational approach that avoids both the blurred thinking shown by some advocates of nonviolence and the easy paths to brutality constructed by the "realists." I infinitely prefer the absolute pacifist to the sharp, cool *realpolitik* character who is found so often these days in academia, journalism and the government, but the same absolutism sometimes infects the nonviolence people, who emerged only recently out of the American desegregation battles and whose theories are less developed than their actions. The nonviolence people in America have been saved the consequences of a muddy theory by the favorable circumstances attending Southern desegregation, and because their technique has not been tested on more difficult problems.

The absolutism of some nonviolence spokesmen weakens their position, I believe, because people know, deep inside, even if they can't articulate the reasons, that there are times when violence is justifiable. For nonviolence seen as absolute pacifism is only one of a pair of linked values which humanitarian people share—peace and social justice. The desirability of the one must constantly be weighed against the need for the other. Also, the problem is subject to internal contradiction: sometimes the failure to use a measure of violence may make inevitable a far greater violence. Would it have been wrong to assassinate Hitler at that moment in the war when this might have brought a halt to general hostilities and the extermination of the Jews?

It is not true, as some say, that bad means always corrupt the ends. If the amount of evil embodied in the means is tiny and the amount of good created by the end is huge, then the end is not corrupted—either objectively in the result or subjectively in the conscience of the doer. This matter of conscience is often pointed to by the absolutist pacifist. Certainly, if a man sees a neighbor stealing his son's bicycle and knocks him unconscious with a baseball bat, the wielder of the bat may recover from his anger and say: What a terrible thing I have done to save a bicycle! But if he should see his neighbor—whom he knows to have a violent temper—pointing a shotgun at his wife and children, and does the same thing—will his conscience bother him then? Is the end corrupted by the means?

The Freedom Riders behaved nonviolently. But their action did bring violence against themselves, and against others. Nonviolence theorists will insist that the responsibility for the violence rests with those who committed it. But this dodges the question; the fact is that there was more violence in the world *after* the Freedom Riders began their rides than *before*. And for this there is only one justification: that the amount of violence was insignificant compared to the amount of justice won.

In a world of great injustice, we need social change. Social change requires action. Action may result, either by design or by accident, in violence. The fact must be faced. And violence is an evil, along with injustice. The only way, then, to decide upon a course of action is to weigh the damage of violence against the damage of social injustice. The nonviolent absolutist, in all logic, may have to forgo social change, putting himself in the contradictory position of maintaining a *status quo* that tolerates violence like capital punishment and police brutality against Negroes. On the other hand, people who are prepared to pursue any course of action leading to social change may find themselves in the contradictory position of using such violent and uncontrollable means that there is no society left to enjoy the benefits of the changes they seek. Our values are multiple; they sometimes clash; and we need to weigh, weigh, weigh.

Yet, I must admit that there is a powerful and humane motive impelling the absolutist position: that once you give nervous, hostile and ill-informed people a theoretical justification for using violence in certain cases, it is like a tiny hole in the dike: the rationales rust through in a torrent, and violence becomes the normal, acceptable solution for a problem.

This happened in the area of free speech. When Justice Holmes, perceptively noting that free speech is not an absolute right, came up with his famous example—should a man be allowed to shout "Fire!" in a crowded theatre?—the gates were down, and the witch-hunters rushed through. The "clear and present danger" doctrine became a "fairly clear and one-of-these-days danger" doctrine. We began to persecute Communists even though their ineffectualness indicated that they were stammerers shouting fire in a foreign language to a deaf audience. Now that the absolute and unequivocal dictum of the First Amendment has been pushed aside, anything goes. This is why Justice Black insists on an absolute defense of free speech. And this may be why pacifists insist on an unequivocal rejection of violence.

I think, however, that it is in the nature of speech that the exceptions to an absolute defense of its freedom would be very few, whereas in the complex sphere of social action, there may be many situations requiring some measure of force or of pressure that produces counterforce. Moreover, in the area of free speech, most situations allow polar solutions; you either permit the speech or deny it. In the tactics of social change, however, there are countless intermediate positions between total passivity and total violence. Still, it is terribly important to understand that our starting point should be pacifism, that the burden of proof should be placed on the arguer for violence. Just as a man should be considered innocent until proved guilty, a policy should be automatically nonviolent until the weight of reason, undistorted by symbolism, argues otherwise. And even here we need a court of appeals, because a cardinal fact about violence is that, once initiated, it tends to get out of hand. Its limits are not predictable.

The actual process of weighing violence versus injustice differs in each specific case. Symbols distort the weighing, but the amount of distortion depends on how far the symbol is from the reality. Sometimes people can refer fairly easily to the specific human situation, as was the case in the 1930s, when the epithets of "socialism" directed at the New Deal could not fool people in the presence of hunger. Such is the situation in the desegregation campaigns today, where visible and appealing Negroes push through the old stereotypes to confront white America. Desegregation is a self-propelling process, because as it proceeds it brings more and more whites into contact with human beings instead of racist symbols.

The most notable contribution of the desegregation movement to other worthy causes is as a showcase for nonviolence under conditions where the technique is shown in the best light. It indicates the possibility, heretofore not clearly enunciated by either pacifists or revolutionists, of using minimum force to achieve maximim justice. Here is nonviolence at its best—a golden mean between passivity and violence. Such techniques have been used countless times in the history of reform—in labor struggles, farmers' movements, etc.—but never yet accompanied by a theory which enables transfer to other social problems.

The weighing is easy, too, in another aspect of American life, but has here been ignored. This is in the area of legal violence against criminals and suspected criminals: capital punishment, police brutality, the murder of burglary suspects. Here, symbolism is still unassaulted by reason and humanity. Last month, in Atlanta, an eighteen-year-old boy was shot and killed while running away from the scene of a vending-machine robbery that had netted him $3.84. The policeman who shot him was not firing at a human being, but at a symbol: a thief, an enemy of society. The policeman was defending another symbol: private property. As symbols, abstracted from flesh and blood, the solution is simple: private property must be protected. As reality, it looks different: the life of a eighteen-year-old boy against the loss of $3.84.

In capital punishment, too, we are not weighing how much justice will be accomplished by the act of judicial murder. If we did, the answer would be obvious: execution of a human being—no matter how foul his deed—cannot bring more happiness, more justice, into the world. But the figure in the electric chair is not a human being, and the act is not weighed in terms of human values. He is a part of a mathematical equation in our law books which says simply that a person who has violated a certain kind of law must be murdered. Our law is symbolic, not human, so abstracted from life that it is capable of the most horrible injustice.

With regard to revolution as a means of changing the social order, the weighing of violence against injustice is more difficult, and the complexity of the problem varies from case to case. Though the American Revolution took seven years and tens of thousands of lives, we are so infatuated with the results that we don't dare question its desirability. Is it possible that methods short of all-out war might have eased Britain off the backs of the colonist? Probably not, except over a long period of time and with constant nonviolent harassment. My point here is not to pass judgment on what is a most complicated revolutionary situation, but to argue that the use of violence as a corrective is so ingrained in the human psychology that we don't even question it. The French, Russian and, more recently, the Cuban revolutions, involving shorter bursts of violence against more uncompromising and backward regimes, are easier to justify; and the fact that each brought on its own brand of Bonapartism does not vitiate the fact of long-term social transformation in a positive direction. Yet these revolutions may have shed more blood than was necessary to achieve their results. You are grateful even for an inept surgeon who removes a festering appendix, but will look next time for someone who will accomplish surgery with less damage.

. . .

It is in large-scale, international wars that the pacifist can hardly go wrong, for here the violence is so massive, so symbolic, so unfocused on specific targets, that even a tremendous turn for the better in the conditions of millions of people does not make easy a judgment for war. World War I, which caused 20 million deaths, is a classic example of mass murder for dubious gain; it was probably the most stupid war in history.

World War II assaults our emotions as we begin to weigh the result in terms of social justice against the degree of violence employed. The reality of Nazism was as close to the symbol of total evil as any phenomenon in human history. In no other war have the issues seemed as clear-cut. Because of this we were able to pass lightly over massive immorality on the part of the Allies—the killing of hundreds of thousands in indiscriminate bombing raids on cities, climaxed by the horrible deeds at Hiroshima and Nagasaki. Altogether, 40 million persons' lives were wiped out. Could we have defeated

Hitler at a lesser cost? With so many lives at stake, could we not have exploited every alternative, sane or wild? Could we not have used nonviolence in a thousand different ways? Perhaps we might have let Hitler take territory after territory, allowed his empire to become bloated and sick, meanwhile organizing an underground against him everywhere. I am not at all sure of this, but what I want to do is to challenge the automatic acceptance of the traditional response to evil. Not only conservatives, but liberals and social revolutionaries as well, are paralyzed by habit.

There are clearly many cases where the weighing of nonviolence against social justice is difficult. Ironically, however, in the situation today, involving rocket-propelled missiles and hundred-megaton warheads, the decision should be obvious and easy—and the peoples of the world have not made it. A fundamental reason is that it is always harder to check up on the reality behind the verbal symbol in international affairs than it is in domestic issues. And the passions of the cold war have created symbolic distortions on an unprecedented scale. This is seen in both elements of the slogan that sums up much of American thinking: that we must "fight" to save the "free world."

It should be apparent to anyone who coldly surveys the effects of multi-megaton weapons—the fire ball, the explosion, the fallout, the mass cremation—that the word "fight" is a monstrous euphemism, and that no possible combination of evils in the world today can balance on the scales the mammouth irretrievable evil of a nuclear way. But we do not have an electronic mechanism to conjure up the right pictures as soon as the word "fight" is heard. Thus, whenever some political issue arises which is subject to inflammation, whether it is Berlin or Formosa or Cuba, we begin to talk of "fighting" or "making our stand here." Americans hearing the word "fight" think, perhaps, of the last war, never of annihilation, never of agony beyond the imagination. We need somehow to push aside these verbal symbols and let people confront with open eyes what Giraudoux in *Tiger at the Gates* has Hecuba describe as the face of war: the backside of a baboon, hairy and red with a fungus growth. The Russians and the Chinese, their memories of death more pervading, may have less trouble than we do with symbolic obstacles. Yet, Marxist terms like "struggle," which they use constantly, are loose enough to becloud a variety of dangerous actions. In every country of the world, it needs to be stated flatly now and through all present crises and possible crises: there is no piece of territory in the world, no city, no nation, no social system, whose preservation is worth a thermonuclear war.

. . .

We find ourselves at a point in history full of paradoxes: H-bombs have, by their test explosions alone, obliterated the traditional revolutionary idea of a "just war" and suggest caution to advocates of social upheaval. Yet, social injustice is everywhere in the world, crying for correction. At this very moment the technique of nonviolence is brought to our attention by the sit-ins of the American South, by the sailors of the *Golden Rule,* by the demonstrators in Trafalgar Square. It is no one method, but an arsenal of methods, all of which start beyond passivity and stop short of war. It recognizes honestly that once passivity is renounced, some degree of force may enter the situation, but it is determined to keep this to a minimum, and starts always from the assumption of zero violence. Nonviolent activists win over the onlookers of the world, and make things more difficult for the perpetrators of violence and injustice. They know the value of words as the tools of symbolic distortion which prevent people from perceiving reality; but they are especially concerned with human contact—interracial and international—as a way of directly smashing through the walls of symbol. While violence is blunt and undiscriminating, nonviolence is sharp, particularized, focused, flexible.

Out of the Southern battles have come the first stalwarts of nonviolent action who may be the forerunners of a new world force. These are the young men and women of the Student Non-Violent Coordinating Committee, white and Negro, of all backgrounds. They have been beaten and jailed and beaten and jailed; they have developed the proper disrespect for authority, and also the self-discipline of martyrs without the professional martyr's predilection for defeat. They fit neither of the old American types of bull-headed radical or suffering pacifist. They come from no particular community and, one of these days, may come from no particular nation. Because they are both mobile and quick to sink roots, they are neither outsiders nor natives wherever they work. They are more than a peace corps and less than an army; they are the guerrilla fighters of social reform.

The Negro in the South has given the cue, but the nation has not taken it. That beautiful balance embodied by the sit-ins and Freedom Rides is cautiously condoned, but not emulated, by the government. And yet, it is especially in the United States that the technique of nonviolence is demanded, at a time when domestic injustice and stupidity in foreign policy require assault. Ironically, our government is missing the golden mean of nonviolence on both counts, for it is passive in domestic affairs which it *can* control, and violent abroad in situations it *can't* control.

The truth is that our entire political system is geared towards a strange inversion. The antiquated structure of Congress—its committee system operating by seniority, the gerrymandered state legislatures—is only the manifestation of a basic political malaise that operates to make our legislative bodies representative of the most backward elements of the population. Our cumbersome lawmaking machinery, its controls supervised by Southern reactionaries, is not geared to the swift pace and zooming expectations of the twentieth century. This is shown in instance after instance where the President cannot get the mildest pieces of social-welfare legislation through Congress, or secure a petty amount of cash to support the United Nations. In foreign policy, on the other hand, he has a free hand. The result is that he is quicker to assault Cuba than to assault Congress.

George Kennan and others have argued convincingly that the most effective thing we can do in foreign affairs is to create a magnificent social system at home. The plain fact is, that despite our superfluity of autos and television sets, we cannot really come before the world and say: here is your ideal social system, where the wealth of the nation is distributed in such a way as to eliminate poverty and insecurity, where the aged are taken care of and the sick are cured regardless of their finances, where all who want education can get it, where artists, poets, musicians and writers can achieve as much economic security as the man who designs a new yo-yo.

It was the feeble ineptitude of the strongest government on earth that brought on the sit-in movement. That 700 Negroes in Albany, Georgia, had to demonstrate in the streets to put into effect an Interstate Commerce Commission ruling that had not been enforced by the government is embarrassingly representative of the years since 1954.

What the Southern Negro has done for desegregation can also work for freedom of speech and assembly, for medical care, against capital punishment. Nonviolent techniques—the kind already used and many kinds still germinating in our imaginations—seem the only sensible answer to a world sitting in a mine field and yet needing to move. They can be effective in the swamp of representative government and within the stone walls of Communist bureaucracy. They employ humor, kindness, pressure, flexibility, attack and retreat—guerrilla warfare in time of peace. Today, when force is absolute, we may have to live, and advance, by our wits.

Man, separated from his fellow man by symbolic distortion, has been violent for most of his history. But he has also shown the ability to break through symbols, to make direct contact with other human beings and to renounce violence. He is not determined inexorably in either direction, the social psychologists and cultural anthropologists tell us. Perhaps here is our chief hope. Man is open to suggestion. And nonviolence uses neither compulsion nor silence. Calmly, powerfully, it suggests.

VIOLENCE AND REVOLUTION

Michael Lerner

Can the American Revolution occur without violence? This is a crucial question, which worries most socialists. And for good reason. We detest violence. In fact, part of the reason for the revolution is to decrease the amount of violence in the world. More particularly, many of us who are currently deeply involved in revolutionary activity suspect that violence will claim our own lives and the lives of those we love. Any way that violence can be avoided and our mission still accomplished will be sought out and explored.

But when the question of violence is addressed to the Left, it is only to distort reality. The real question must be asked of the rulers of this country: will *they* allow their system of unequal power and wealth to be overthrown without violence? This is an empirical question, and part of the answer is already in: the rulers constantly use violence to maintain their social order, and that social order reeks with violence. Let us explore this question a bit more carefully.

The fact that American capitalism has promoted the use of one word—"violence" —to apply to such different phenomena as the torture of North Vietnamese prisoners by American soldiers and the throwing of a rock through the window of a branch of the Bank of America shows how contorted language can become. Only in a capitalist society could we have a language that can see no difference between human pain and the alleged right to property. The revolution rejects this identification: violence must be understood as the causing of unnecessary pain to human beings.[1] Because we view human suffering as a primary concern, we see pain inflicted on human beings and destruction of material objects that cannot suffer pain as entirely different. Of course, there can be a connection between the destruction of property and the creation of human pain, and it must have been this connection that originally provided the cover under which violence became redefined to include property. For instance, if you use herbicides against the crops of Vietnamese peasants and bomb their homes you have deprived them of their means of survival, and hence you are the cause of the physical pain they will soon suffer. It might then be reasonably argued that the meaning of "violence" should extend to include destruction of that property the absence of which will immediately lead to the creation of unnecessary human pain. It is with this kind of violence that I am concerned, and it is this kind of violence that the revolution aims to reduce or eliminate, by destroying the most violent social system ever known to man.

Capitalism is not just violent when it feels itself threatened, as in the war in Vietnam. It is violent in its *normal* operations. And this institutionalized violence is usually overlooked by people who ask revolutionaries why they introduce violence into politics. The fact is that violence of a greater magnitude than could ever be perpetrated by the revolutionary already exists as an integral part of American capitalism.

Consider the domestic violence perpetrated by the capitalist system. In the United States, close to 12 million people suffer from malnutrition and are on the verge of starvation. But the government pays people not to grow food so that there will not be a surplus that would adversely affect prices on the market. That is violence—and the people who participate in that decision have caused violence. The capitalist economic system creates classes of people whose members do not have enough money to provide themselves with adequate food, housing, and health care. In San Francisco

---

[1] We want to distinguish, however between two types of "necessity." Some pain will be necessary to achieve people's goals for themselves, and they will voluntarily undergo the pain for that purpose. For example, if they allow doctors to cause pain to them in order to cure them of some malady, we would not say that the doctors had committed violent acts. On the other hand, pain may be inflicted without the consent of the people involved, for the sake of achieving some social good that they may or may not accept. In this case, one might want to argue that pain was still "necessary" because there was no other way to achieve the desired and desirable goal. But it would add greater clarity if we agreed to call this "violence," and then simply added that there are going to be some cases in which we will want to say that violence is justified, rather than sophistically arguing that it is not violence at all.

recently it was reported that the infant mortality rate among blacks was three times that among whites. That is violence—and all who help to sustain American racism, from the government to the bosses to the unions, help to maintain that violence. When abortion is illegal and women are forced to seek help from unskilled practitioners, all of them suffer pain, many of them are permanently injured, and some of them die. That is violence. When auto manufacturers resist improvements that could make cars safer because it might decrease their profits, they cause violence. And when they use their considerable influence and money to oppose the funding of mass transportation that would cut pollution and make travel safer—again because it would cut into their profits—they are violent. When food manufacturers use chemicals whose long-term effects on human health have not yet been tested and which later turn out to be deleterious, they are violent. When state coverage of health programs is reduced and people are thrown out of hospitals or kept from seeking medical help because they do not have enough money, the people who supported these cuts are acting violently. When newspapers refuse to print statements by black radicals about the actual conditions of ghetto life, suggesting instead that there is something strange and deplorable about black people who follow revolutionary leadership, they help create a white backlash that often manifests itself in violence. Nor am I engaging here in debaters' tricks—these are all legitimate instances of the violence embedded in the normal functioning of American capitalism. And the fact that it is never talked about is a testimony to the complete success of the rulers in so mystifying their system that many people do not even perceive themselves as the victims of violence. The newspapers, the media, the schools, all make consideration of this sort of question impossible. Every newsman asks the Left, "But what about violence?" But no newsman has ever asked the President, "Do you believe it is right to use violence in pursuit of your foreign policy aims—as you have done in Vietnam—or in pursuit of your domestic aims—as you are doing in raising unemployment in order to deal with inflation, thereby ensuring that more people will be unable to afford adequate health care, housing, food, etc.?"

Although the internal violence of the system is tremendous, it does not compare with the violence that capitalism creates around the world. . . . [We have already] discussed the ways this violence works: through preventing countries to industrialize, or forcing them to industrialize only in accord with the needs of American capitalism and extracting from them a great deal of wealth, particularly in the form of raw materials. But we have not adequately stressed the meaning of this whole system for the average peasant in India, Bolivia, or Ghana. The wealth extracted by General Electric, Standard Oil, the Bank of America, United Fruit, or any other imperialist venture is wealth that could have been used to feed, clothe, house, and give medical care to the hundreds of millions of people who live in those countries. Nor can this violence be measured simply by the additional money the colonial people would have if the imperialists did not take it from them. Equally important is the social system the imperialists have to sustain in the exploited country in order to ensure a government that permits them to continue their exploitative relations at the same high level of profit. These social systems would be overturned very quickly if they were not sustained by American economic and military aid—and these social systems bring incredible suffering to the people who must live under them. Then, you may ask, why don't these people rebel? They do, all the time. American weapons and, as in Vietnam or the Dominican Republic, American troops put these rebellions down. Every day, tens of millions of people are hungry who need not be, get no medical care when it could have been available, have inadequate housing and clothing—all directly as a result of the American economic system. Nor should we abstract this system—for its operations are manned by human beings who every day make concrete choices which help to sustain it. The pleasant gentleman on the Long Island Railroad reading his *Wall Street Journal* or the quiet technician working in Palo Alto or on Route 128 in Massachusetts, the Wall Street banker or the assistant secretary of state or agriculture or defense, the professor of political science who runs the institute on Latin America or the liberal senator—all participate daily in making decisions that sustain the daily violence upon which this system rests. If it was right to try Eichmann and other officials of the Nazi regime for crimes against humanity, even though they did not personally kill anyone, then surely the violent men who surround us, with their gentle manners and sweet smiles and well-manicured lawns and all the rest of the petty concealments that hide a life of "honorable" crime, should be tried for their crimes by the peoples of the world. It is on practical, not moral, grounds that we think such trials should not take place.

Until now we have discussed only institutionalized violence—the violence that occurs when the system is working smoothly and no one is questioning it. But the system has an army and police forces to deal with the situation when people no longer accept their exploitation. The police use violence all the time against people who, having been deprived by the system of any way to achieve what they need, resort to stealing or other illegal means to get money. Violence is constantly used in defense of property, because the people who control the government and make the laws believe that property is more important than human life, or, more to the point, that *their* property and the property of the people they represent is more important than human life. Violence is constantly used to enforce the authority of the rulers—hence they will forcefully imprison people for marijuana use because these people have challenged the authority of the rulers by flaunting one of their irrational rules.

Politically, violence is the key to the system's ability to maintain itself. Violence is used against strikers to keep them in line, against political demonstrators to frighten them, and against revolutionaries to suppress them. This violence takes two forms: beatings and murder and jailings. Jailing people is a form of violence: it works because people know that if they resist arrest, guns and clubs will be used against them. Behind the majesty of the courts stands the violence of the police and the jails, and very few people would pay much attention to a legal system so obviously biased in favor of maintaining the established order if that legal system did not have guns and clubs to enforce its decisions. The jails are filled with people who, in a just political system, would be free—people who were faced with the choice of slowly being destroyed by the system or taking a risk and doing something that exposed them to the destruction imposed by the jails. The killings at Kent State, Jackson State, People's Park, and in countless ghetto uprisings, the systematic assassination of leaders of the Black Panther party, the jailing and beating of political protestors—all must be added to the calculus of the ways in which this society is violent.

The police force operates under certain restraints: it cannot bomb a campus, for fear it might also hit the professors and students from ruling-class families. But no such restrictions exist on the counterinsurgency operations engaged in worldwide by the military in order to suppress people who want to run their own country for their own benefit. So the military and the CIA can proudly display the remains of a Che Guevara or some other rebel leader—after all, that's what CIA and military business is all about. Consider the Vietnam war—it is already responsible for the death of over a million civilians, the wounding of millions more, and the forcible removal from their land of many millions more. Professor Samuel Huntington of Harvard University recommends the best way to win the war: force the Vietnamese into the large cities and bomb the countryside until the bomb craters are running with the blood of Southeast Asians. In 1972, President Nixon began full-scale bombings of the cities of North Vietnam, coupled with minings of harbors and bombings of dikes. Every power plant, every bridge, every factory was to be leveled. Special antipersonnel bombs were introduced with pellets that had been designed so that when they entered a human body they could not be traced by X ray. In 1972, mass murder and destruction was the public policy of the United States. And then, even the liberals would turn around and focus more attention on some outraged youth who had smashed a window in exasperated protest, rather than deal with the massive horror created by American capitalism. When the war ends people will say, "Oh, that was all in the past." But a system that causes that kind of suffering is not in the past until fundamental changes are made that make such behavior unnecessary in the future. The only effective change would be the elimination of the economic structure that requires the exploitation of the peoples of the world. Until the overthrow of capitalism the American capitalist system will use its military power to keep people from struggling for their independence. It will prefer, of course, to have armies from dependent countries fight the American battle for America, since this will cause fewer internal political tensions. But it will not cause a decrease in violence, only a change in the victims of that violence. The whole strategy of Vietnamization and the attempt to create a multinational army in Latin America are part of this clever device to get Third Worlders to fight Third Worlders, in support of local elites that could not on their own resist popular forces within their countries.

The question of violence is being answered for us every day by the ruling class. Will they allow us to revolutionize the world nonviolently? Absolutely not. On the contrary, they will fight to the last drop of *our* blood and the blood of every mercenary they can buy or coerce.

Revolutionary violence must be understood in this context. The aim of revolutionary violence is completely defensive: to defend people from the violence inherent in the capitalist system and the violence unleashed against those who attempt to change it. It is crucial to understand that when a revolutionary picks up a gun he is responding to the violence that already exists in the system. The aim of revolutionary violence is always to eliminate the total amount of violence that exists in the world by creating a social system that no longer depends on exploitation, underdevelopment, sexism, racism, and powerlessness.

But isn't there a paradox in this position? Is not the revolutionary introducing more violence into the world? The United States would be perfectly happy with a Pax Americana: if everyone quietly accepted American control over most of the world, there would be less violence. When the Viet Cong picked up their guns they were raising the level of violence. This argument holds true for the short run, but the revolutionary is, by definition, someone who stands back and looks at the long run, and realizes that he must be willing to sacrifice his life in the short run for the sake of a better world in the long run. Every year imperialism imposes, let us say, 13 units of violence on my country (or an American revolutionary might say that he sees his country imposing, say, 143 units of violence across the world) in the course of its normal functioning. Now, for the course of the next four years we will try to make a revolution, say, and we know that the imperialists can double the level of violence by adding overt violence to their covert violence. But when, after four years the revolution succeeds, the level of violence will decrease to two units of violence (what remains being the legacy of underdevelopment which will be eliminated after twenty more years of internal economic progress). So, in the long run revolutionary action will significantly decrease the total amount of violence. Obviously, if this were just a fantasy, it would not justify violence. But one need look only at China, where the total level of violence has dropped astoundingly over the past twenty years, and then at India, where wide-scale starvation is still accepted as a fact of life in a social system that cannot break its ties with imperialism.

Sometimes it is argued that the use of violence as a means will inevitably create a violent society, because once people get used to violence as part of their life, they start to re-create it. But there is no reason to believe this is true. Once the institutions that create violence have been undermined, the continuation of violence is highly unlikely. "Sure," one might argue, "but once people become involved in violence, they will never set up institutions that will undercut it. Look at the Soviet Union: it started out with all sorts of good intentions, but because of its violent start the men who formed its institutions merely prepared the way for violence in a different form." This argument, however, is both abstract and ahistorical. The Bolsheviks took power in a virtually bloodless coup, and their first act was to end the war and bring the troops home, thus significantly decreasing the level of violence. Violence became a significant factor again only after the civil war started, and in that case it was fostered by the invasion of troops from the United States, Britain, and France. During the civil war institutions emerged which did in fact create the possibility of later violence, but it was the concrete circumstances of the world, particularly the emergence of hostile forces committed to defeating the revolution, which were primarily responsible for pushing the Soviet Union in the bad direction it finally went. To generalize from that situation to all situations misses the point. Consider Cuba. Cuba's revolution was brought about by a violent struggle, but the general level of violence in Cuba has markedly decreased since the revolution and there is much less needless suffering in Cuba today than there was before the revolution. Perhaps this will change as the economic pressures become greater and the maneuvers of the U.S. capitalists to destroy Cuba become more ruthless. In dealing with this issue, the specific circumstances, not some abstract theory, are crucial, and in the case of the American revolution, at least one factor will be very different. The United States is the center of the imperialist system; its machinations have been responsible for increasing the level of violence in the revolutions that have occurred in other countries. When that center itself becomes the target, no outside forces will come in and raise the general level of violence. On the contrary, revolution in America would set up a series of events that would lead to revolution all around the world. The collapse of the American economy attendant on wide-scale struggle here would create international havoc and thus the conditions for significant struggle in all of the advanced industrial societies, where revolutionary forces would find it easy to seize the moment. At the same time, the lack of U.S. military support would cause many dictatorships and colonial regimes to topple. The international revolutionary ferment would undoubtedly spread to Eastern Europe, and the Soviet Union, far from being able to come to the aid of the ruling class in America, would ultimately be involved in internal revolutionary struggle as well. So a violent revolution in the United States might well lead to the elimination of violent social structures all over the world.

. . .

But we are far from the day when a majority of the people will want a revolution. There is every good reason to think that a revolution will not occur in this country before fifteen or twenty years, and it may be as far as thirty years away. There is no way to predict these things in the abstract—much depends on the rate of success of other struggles around the world. Even more depends on how successful the revolutionary movement is in this country in providing intelligent and courageous leadership. In the immediate period ahead the primary job is to change people's consciousness, *not* to engage in armed struggle.

I contend that very few acts are right in themselves, and that it is always crucial to ask how a particular militant act advances revolutionary consciousness and for whom. The criteria for assessing any form of militant action must be whether it will be understandable to the relevant communities and whether it will make those who do not understand react in a way that seriously impedes the revolutionary development of those who do.

Underlying these criteria is the assumption that one always aims to increase the number of "relevant communities" wherever revolutionary consciousness is being advanced. Nor is it enough to argue that relevant communities could be made to understand a militant action; the action can be justified only when reasonable steps are taken to ensure that it will be understood. It will often be impossible to know in advance exactly how a particular action will be distorted by the media. This should never be used as an excuse for avoiding struggle, but reasonable assessments should be made, and one should always be sensitive to the understandability criterion. "Understandability" also provides a guide for terrorist activity. For instance, most Weatherman trashing activity (particularly trashing car windows parked along the street—something Weatherman did during its "Days of Rage") clearly should be avoided. On the other hand, one might well criticize those involved in People's Park for not taking more definitive action against the oppressors when the whole community saw itself as resisting an occupying army. "Understandability" does not mean comprehensibility to the press or the bourgeoisie. We must avoid the ruling-class notion of one undifferentiated community, with similar sets of needs and interests. But we must make our actions understandable to potential allies in the struggle to overthrow capitalism. The criteria proposed will require subtle and intelligent application, not mechanical formulas. We will have to study the period carefully, its potentialities and its problems, before deciding what kind of tactics will be appropriate. One can defend revolutionary violence in the abstract without feeling that it is appropriate at any particular moment in the struggle.

It is my assessment of the present period, that the revolutionary movement should rely primarily on a strategy of non-violence probably at least for the next ten years. Such a strategy will undercut the capitalists' ability to confuse people by pointing to a few broken windows or a few bomb explosions. Although it is quite true that the facts should speak for themselves—compare the destruction of some windows with the destruction caused in Vietnam by a single hour of bombing—it is nevertheless true that people are confused on this topic. Since violence in the period ahead cannot possibly be used effectively enough to stop the imperialists, it would be better to avoid it altogether. Or, when it is used, it should be made clear that it is used in self-defense, as, for example, in defense of the ghetto from invading police. Nonviolent action can help to pull the wool away from many people's eyes.

A focus on nonviolence in the movement would do much to overcome the rather sick tendency to glorify armed struggle and the gun that characterizes some factions. It is quite true that eventually we must resort to armed struggle and self-defensive violence, because it will be the only way to act in solidarity with our brothers and sisters around the world and to create a new American society. But this violence will be accompanied by great sadness. The revolutionary hates violence and hates to see innocent people killed. It is precisely out of this hatred of violence that the revolutionary is willing to take great personal risk so that violence can be permanently eliminated or vastly reduced. The revolutionary must always be infused with love and respect for human life, and, all other things being equal, should always opt for the path that causes the least amount of hurt to other human beings. It is this very love for human life that forces a revolutionary to resort to self-defensive (i.e. revolutionary) violence. A tactical use of nonviolence might help put these issues in perspective again.

But nonviolence does not mean passivity. Too often in the past few years the pacifists have been passivists as well. They have had a few militant spokesmen, like Dave Dellinger, but they rarely acted as a militant force. This has tended to discredit the whole notion of nonviolence. Nonviolence should be adopted by the movement for revolutionary change as a tactic. But that does not mean the revolutionary movement should take its political leadership from professional pacifists. Nonviolence must be used militarily, to clog up the operations of the war machine, to challenge the functioning of government, war factories, welfare bureaucracies, universities, polluters, etc. The focus must be on action, but with the clear announcement that it is intended as nonviolent action. Such action must also be distinguished from the moral witnessing in which principled pacifists have been involved. It is not my intention to suggest *individual* acts of heroism or submission to arrest as a proof of strong feelings. Politically, these tactics are often stupid: the risk of jail sentences is seldom worth the publicity the action may create. Rather, mass actions should be planned which involve mobile tactics and which aim both to disrupt nonviolently and also to avoid arrest if possible. It is not my intent to lay down a formula applicable to every situation, even for the immediate future, but to advance arguments for publicly stating our nonviolent position when we involve ourselves in demonstrations over the next few years.

It would be both dishonest and unwise to pretend that we are nonviolent in principle. On the contrary, at every possible moment the arguments about violence should be taken on and defeated. We must carefully explain to people the nature of this society and its violence, and why the rulers will probably make violence inevitable for us just as they have made it a necessity for peoples of the Third World. People must be prepared for the fact that the ruling class has it in its power to make the revolution in this country bloody and violent. And they must learn that we do not welcome violence and that the only way to avoid violence is for enough people to move decisively to the side of the revolution. The rulers must come to understand that if there is to be a sea of blood, it will be made of their blood as well. The one thing that can make the American revolution *less violent* is the clear and public determination of a majority of people to defend that revolution with violence.

. . .

Suggested Readings

Brandt, R. B. "The Morality of Abortion," *The Monist* 56 (October 1972).

Fanon, Frantz. *The Wretched of the Earth.* New York: Grove Press, 1968.

Held, Virginia, Kai Nielsen, and Charles Parsons (eds.). *Philosophy and Political Action.* New York: Oxford University Press, 1972. See Part 1, "Reform, Revolution, and Violence."

Merleau-Ponty, Maurice. *Humanism and Terror.* Translated by John O'Neill. Boston: Beacon Press, 1969.

Murphy, Jeffrie G. *Civil Disobedience and Violence.* Belmont, Calif.: Wadsworth, 1971.

Nagel, Thomas. "War and Massacre," *Philosophy and Public Affairs* 1 (Winter 1972).

Purtill, Richard. "On the Just War," *Social Theory and Practice* 2 (Spring 1971).

Shaffer, Jerome A. (ed.). *Violence: Award-Winning Essays in the Council for Philosophical Studies Competition.* New York: David McKay, 1971.

Thomson, Judith Jarvis. "A Defense of Abortion," *Philosophy and Public Affairs* 1 (Fall 1971).

Wasserstrom, Richard (ed.). *War and Morality.* Belmont, Calif.: Wadsworth, 1970.

Wells, Donald. "Is 'Just Violence' Like 'Just War'?" *Social Theory and Practice* 1 (Spring 1970).

section three

work and play
and the protestant ethic

WORK IN AMERICA

Report of Special Task Force to Secretary of Health, Education and Welfare

Homo Faber

It is both humbling and true that scientists are unable, in the final analysis, to distinguish all the characteristics of humans from those of other animals. But many social scientists will agree that among those activities most peculiar to humans, work probably defines man with the greatest certainty. To the archaeologist digging under the equatorial sun for remains of the earliest man, the nearby presence of primitive tools is his surest sign that the skull fragment he finds is that of a human ancestor, and not that of an ape.

Why is man a worker? First of all, of course, man works to sustain physical life—to provide food, clothing, and shelter. But clearly work is central to our lives for other reasons as well. According to Freud, work provides us with a sense of reality; to Elton Mayo, work is a bind to community; to Marx, its function is primarily economic. Theologians are interested in work's moral dimensions; sociologists see it as a determinant of status, and some contemporary critics say that it is simply the best way of filling up a lot of time. To the ancient Greeks, who had slaves to do it, work was a curse. The Hebrews saw work as punishment. The early Christians found work for profit offensive, but by the time of St. Thomas Aquinas, work was being praised as a natural

273

right and a duty—a source of grace along with learning and contemplation. During the Reformation, work became the only way of serving God. Luther pronounced that conscientious performance of one's labor was man's highest duty. Later interpretations of Calvinistic doctrine gave religious sanction to worldly wealth and achievement. This belief, when wedded to Social Darwinism and laissez-faire liberalism, became the foundation for what we call the Protestant ethic. Marx, however, took the concept of work and put it in an even more central position in life: freed from capitalist exploitation, work would become a joy as workers improved the material environment around them.

Clearly, work responds to something profound and basic in human nature. Therefore, much depends on how we define work, what we conceive work to be, what we want work to be, and whether we successfully uncover its meaning and purpose. Our conceptions (and misconceptions) of ourselves, the wisdom with which public policy is formulated on a range of issues, and the rationality with which private and public resources are allocated are influenced greatly by the degree to which we penetrate the complex nature of work.

Because work, as this report illustrates, plays a pervasive and powerful role in the psychological, social, and economic aspects of our lives, it has been called a basic or central institution. As such, it influences, and is influenced by, other basic institutions—family, community (particularly as a political entity), and schools—as well as peripheral institutions. Work, then, provides one institutional perspective—but a broad one—from which to view these interrelationships that affect ourselves and our society.

Toward a Definition of Work

We measure that which we can measure, and this often means that a rich and complex phenomenon is reduced to one dimension, which then becomes prominent and eclipses the other dimensions. This is particularly true of "work," which is often defined as "paid employment." The definition conforms with one readily measurable aspect of work but utterly ignores its profound personal and social aspects and often leads to a distorted view of society.

Using housework as an example, we can see the absurdity of defining work as "paid employment." A housewife, according to this definition, does not work. But if a husband must replace her services—with a housekeeper, cook, baby sitter—these replacements become workers, and the husband has added to the Gross National Product the many thousands of dollars the replacements are paid. It is, therefore, an inconsistency of our definition of work that leads us to say that a woman who cares for her own children is not working, but if she takes a job looking after the children of others, she is working.

Viewing work in terms of pay alone has also produced a synonymity of "pay" and "worth," so that higher-paid individuals are thought by many to have greater personal worth than those receiving less pay. At the bottom of this scale, a person without pay becomes "worthless." The confusion of pay with worth is a result of historical events and traditions apparently rooted in the distinction between "noble" and "ignoble" tasks. History might have been otherwise and garbage men, for example, in recognition of their contribution to health, might have been accorded monetary rewards similar to those received by physicians. Certainly, it takes little reflection to conclude that, except in crude economic terms, no one is worth nothing, nor is anyone worth a hundred times more than another merely because he is paid a hundred times as much.

We can come closer to a multi-dimensional definition of work if we define it as "an activity that produces something of value for other people." This definition broadens the scope of what we call work and places it within a social context. It also implies that there is a purpose to work. We know that the housewife is *really* working, whether she is paid or not; she is being productive for other people. Substituting the children a woman cares for does not change the nature of her work, only the "others" for whom she is productive. And voluntary tasks are certainly work, although they are not remunerated. Some people at various stages of their lives may be productive only for themselves, a possible definition of leisure.

The Functions of Work

The economic purposes of work are obvious and require little comment. Work is the means by which we provide the goods and services needed and desired by ourselves and our society. Through the economic rewards of work, we obtain immediate gratification of transient wants, physical assets for enduring satisfactions, and liquid assets for deferrable gratifications. For most of the history of mankind, and for a large part of humanity today, the economic meaning of work is paramount.

Work also serves a number of other social purposes. The workplace has always been a place to meet people, converse, and form friendships. In traditional societies, where children are wont to follow in their parents' footsteps, the assumption of responsibility by the children for one task and then another prepares them for their economic and social roles as adults. Finally, the type of work performed has always conferred a social status on the worker and the worker's family. In industrial America, the father's occupation has been the major determinant of status, which in turn has determined the family's class standing, where they lived, where the children went to school, and with whom the family associated—in short, the life style and life chances of all the family members. (The emerging new role of women in our society may cause class standing to be co-determined by the husband's *and* wife's occupations.)

The economic and societal importance of work has dominated thought about its meaning, and justifiably so: a function of work for any *society* is to produce and distribute goods and services, to transform "raw nature" into that which serves our needs and desires. Far less attention has been paid to the *personal* meaning of work, yet it is clear from recent research that work plays a crucial and perhaps unparalleled psychological role in the formation of self-esteem, identity, and a sense of order.

Work contributes to self-esteem in two ways. The first is that, through the inescapable awareness of one's efficacy and competence in dealing with the objects of work, a person acquires a sense of mastery over both himself and his environment. The second derives from the view, stated earlier, that an individual is working when he is engaging in activities that produce something valued by other people. That is, the job tells the worker day in and day out that he has something to offer. Not to have a job is not to have something that is valued by one's fellow human beings. Alternatively, to be working is to have evidence that one is needed by others. One of these components of self-esteem (mastery) is, therefore, internally derived through the presence or absence of challenge in work. The other component (how others value one's contributions) is externally derived. The person with high self-esteem may be defined as one who has a high estimate of his value and finds that the social estimate agrees.

The workplace generally, then, is one of the major foci of personal evaluation. It is where one finds out whether he is "making the grade"; it is where one's esteem is constantly on the line, and where very effort will be made to avoid reduction in self-evaluation and its attending sense of failure. If an individual cannot live up to the expectations he has of himself, and if his personal goals are not reasonably obtainable, then his self-esteem, and with it his relations with others, are likely to be impaired.

Doing well or poorly, being a success or failure at work, is all too easily transformed into a measure of being a valuable or worthless human being, as Erich Fromm writes:

Since modern man experiences himself both as the seller and as the commodity to be sold on the market, his self-esteem depends on conditions beyond his control. If he is successful, he is valuable; if he is not, he is worthless.[1]

When it is said that work should be "meaningful," what is meant is that it should contribute to self-esteem, to the sense of fulfillment through the mastering of one's self and one's environment, and to the sense that one is valued by society. The fundamental question the individual worker asks is "What am I doing that *really* matters?"

When work becomes merely automatic behavior, instead of being *homo faber,* the worker is *animal laborens.* Among workers who describe themselves as "just laborers," self-esteem is so deflated that the distinction between the human as worker and animal as laborer is blurred. The relationship between work and self-esteem is well summarized by Elliot Jacques:

. . . . working for a living is one of the basic activities in a man's life. By forcing him to come to grips with his environment, with his livelihood at stake, it confronts him with the actuality of his personal capacity—to exercise judgment, to achieve concrete and specific results. It gives him a continuous account of his correspondence between outside reality and the inner perception

[1] Erich Fromm, *The Revolution of Hope,* 1971.

of that reality, as well as an account of the accuracy of his appraisal of himself. . . . In short, a man's work does not satisfy his material needs alone. In a very deep sense, it gives him a measure of his sanity.[2]

Work is a powerful force in shaping a person's sense of identity. We find that most, if not all, working people tend to describe themselves in terms of the work groups or organizations to which they belong. The question, "Who are you?" often solicits an organizationally related response, such as "I work for IBM," or "I'm a Stanford professor." Occupational role is usually a part of this response for all classes: "I'm a steelworker," or "I'm a lawyer." In short: "People tend to 'become what they do.' "[3]

Several highly significant effects result from work-related identification: welfare recipients become "nobodies"; the retired suffer a crucial loss of identity; and people in low-status jobs either cannot find anything in their work from which to derive an identity or they reject the identity forced on them. Even those who voluntarily leave an organization for self-employment experience difficulties with identity—compounded by the confusion of others—as the following quote from an article entitled "Striking Out on Your Own," illustrates:

No less dramatic . . . are those questions of identity which present themselves to the self-employed. These identity crises and situations usually come packaged in little episodes which occur when others find that they have encountered a bona fide weirdo without a boss. . . . You are stopped by a traffic policeman to be given a ticket and he asks the name of your employer and you say that you work for yourself. Next he asks, "Come on, where do you work? Are you employed or not?" You say, "Self-employed." . . . He, among others you meet, knows that self-employment is a tired euphemism for being out of work. . . . You become extremely nervous about meeting new people because of the ever-present question, "Who are you with?" When your answer fails to attach you to a recognized organization . . . both parties to the conversation often become embarrassed by your obscurity.[4]

Basic to all work appears to be the human desire to impose order, or structure, on the world. The opposite of work is not leisure or free time; it is being victimized by some kind of disorder which, at its extreme, is chaos. It means being unable to plan or to predict. And it is precisely in the relation between the desire for order and its achievement that work provides the sense of mastery so important to self-esteem. The closer one's piece of the world conforms with one's structural plans, the greater the satisfaction of work. And it follows that one of the greatest sources of dissatisfaction in work results from the inability to make one's own sense of order prevail—the assembly-line is the best (or worst) example of an imposed, and, for most workers, unacceptable structure.

These observations have been verified a number of times in investigations of mass

[2] Elliot Jacques, *Equitable Payment,* 1961.

[3] Harry Kahn and J. R. P. French, in *Social Issues,* July 1962.

[4] Paul Dickson, "Striking Out on Your Own," 1971.

and protracted unemployment. Loss of work during the Depression was found to produce chronic disorganization in the lives of parents and children, as documented in several studies of the 1930's. Cynicism, loss of self-confidence, resentment, and hostility toward the Federal Government, helplessness, and isolation are all experienced during such difficult periods. According to Charles Winick,

> Inasmuch as work has such a profound role in establishing a person's life space, emotional tone, family situation, object relations, and where and how he will live, either the absence of work or participation in marginal work often makes it likely that he will develop a pervasive *atonie*.[5]

Atonie is a condition of deracination—a feeling of rootlessness, lifelessness, and dissociation—a word which in the original Greek meant a string that does not vibrate, that has lost its vitality.

Besides lending vitality to existence, work helps establish the regularity of life, its basic rhythms and cyclical patterns of day, week, month, and year. Without work, time patterns become confused. One recalls the drifting in T. S. Eliot's "The Wasteland":

> What shall I do. . . . What shall we do tomorrow?
> What shall we ever do?

When duration of unemployment has been prolonged, unemployed workers progress from optimism through pessimism to fatalism. Attitudes toward the future and toward the community and home deteriorate. Children of long-term unemployed and marginally employed workers uniformly show poorer school grades. And, despite the popular notion that unemployed people fill their "free" time with intensified sexual activities, the fact is that undermined egos of former breadwinners lead to diminished libidos. "There are so many unconscious and group needs that work meets," Winick writes, "that unemployment may lead not only to generalized anxiety, but to free-floating hostility, somatic symptoms and the unconscious selection of some serious illnesses." [6]

Many of the studies revealing the disorganizing effects of unemployment during the Depression have found echoes in recent "ghetto ethnographies." Such studies as Liebow's *Tally's Corner* show these effects to be as much a function of unemployment and marginal employment *per se* as of economic catastrophe. This is so because to be denied work is to be denied far more than the things that paid work buys; it is to be denied the ability to define and respect one's self.

It is illusory to believe that if people were given sufficient funds most of them would stop working and become useless idlers. A recent economic analysis shows that as people increase their earnings and acquire wealth they do not tend to decrease the time and energy that they invest in work. In another study, when a cross section of Ameri-

---

[5] Charles Winick, "Atonie: The Psychology of the Unemployed and Marginal Worker," 1964.
[6] *Ibid.*

cans were asked if they would continue working even if they inherited enough to live comfortably without working, 80% said they would keep on working (even though only 9% said they would do so because they enjoyed the work they were doing). Some people may not want to take specific jobs—primarily because of the effects on their self-esteem—but working, "engaging in activities that produce things valued by other people," is a necessity of life for most people.

Some of the most compelling evidence about the centrality of the functions of work in life comes from the recent efforts of women to fill what some interpret as a void in their lives with the sense of identity derived from work. As some social critics have noted, the desire for all that work brings to the individual is at the foundation of the women's liberation movement.

There is also considerable evidence that work has the same meaning among the poor and among welfare recipients that it has for middle-class and employed individuals:

A recent study for the Labor Department on the work orientations of welfare recipients found that "the poor of both races and sexes identify their self-esteem with work to the same extent as nonpoor persons do." The study found that although people on welfare are as committed to the work ethic as middle-class people, their attitudes differ in that they are not confident that they can succeed on a job. After experiencing failure, they are more likely to accept the dependence on welfare.

A recent study in South Carolina of 513 underprivileged workers found that the poor did not differ markedly from the middle class in the kind of satisfactions that they derived from work.

The Office of Economic Opportunity has sponsored a three-year study to assess the validity of the assumption that the working poor would stop working if they were guaranteed an annual income. *Preliminary* findings have shown little slackening in work effort among those urban families receiving a guaranteed income. In fact, hourly earnings appear to be higher for those in the experiment than for those in a control group. Although it is too early to assess the results of the experiment, there are signs that withdrawal from work effort is not as extensive as some had feared.

In this regard, it must be realized that although *work* is central to the lives of most people, there is a small minority for whom a *job* is purely a means to a livelihood. To them a job is an activity that they would gladly forgo if a more acceptable option for putting bread on their table were available. What little evidence there is on this point indicates that for most such individuals the kinds of jobs that they see open to them do little to provide the sense of self-esteem, identity, or mastery that are the requisites for satisfying work. These individuals turn to other activities (music, hobbies, sports, crime) and other institutions (family, church, community) to find the psychological rewards that they do not find in their jobs. In effect, these activities, for these people, become their real work. This unusual phenomenon helps to explain the small amount of job withdrawal that occurs among welfare recipients. For example, welfare mothers may choose the personally fulfilling work of raising their children to the alternative of a low-level, unchallenging job—the only kind available to them.

The Change in Attitudes Toward Work

Although social scientists have long disputed the precise contribution of the Protestant ethic to the genesis of capitalism, they generally agree that thrift, hard work, and a capacity for deferring gratification historically were traits widely distributed among Americans. Moreover, as part of the legitimacy of the economic system, individual members of our society were to be credited or blamed for their own circumstances, according to the degree of their prosperity.

But the ethic, or what has passed for it, appears to be under attack. Some futurists tell us that automation will make work unnecessary for most people, and that we may as well ignore work and look to other matters, such as "creative leisure." More immediately, our attention is drawn to these alleged signs of work's obsolescence:

The growth in the number of communes
Numerous adolescents panhandling in such meccas as Georgetown, North Beach, and the Sunset Strip
Various enterprises shifting to 4-day workweeks
Welfare caseloads increasing
Retirement occurring at ever earlier ages.

All of these are relatively benign signs; more malignant signs are found in reduced productivity and in the doubling of man-days per year lost from work through strikes. In some industries there apparently is a rise in absenteeism, sabotage, and turnover rates.

Ironically, many of these symptoms have increased despite the general improvements in physical conditions and monetary rewards for work. In comparison with the dreary lot of most workers during the industrial revolution and, indeed, until quite recently, the workplace today is an Elysian field. Sweatshop conditions have all but disappeared. The extreme dangers of work appear to have declined in most industries. Women and children are seldom engaged in back-breaking drudgery. Arbitrary wage cuts and dismissals are relatively rare, and enlightened laws, personnel policies, and labor unions protect the worker in a variety of ways.

Quantitatively, the lives of workers away from work similarly have improved. Real income, standard of living, health status, and life expectancy have all risen markedly. Among most classes of workers, homes and cars are owned in abundance, and bank accounts continually grow. For those without work, there is social security, unemployment compensation, workman's compensation, and an income floor will very likely be established under welfare compensation. On the average, then, no workers have ever been as materially well-off as American workers are today. What, then, is wrong?

Social scientists are suggesting that the root of the problem is to be found in the changing needs, aspirations, and values of workers. For example, Abraham Maslow has suggested that the needs of human beings are hierarchical and, as each level is filled, the subsequent level becomes salient. This order of needs is:

1. Physiological requirements (food, habitat, etc.)
2. Safety and security
3. Companionship and affection
4. Self-esteem and the esteem of others
5. Self-actualization (being able to realize one's potential to the full).

It may be argued that the very success of industry and organized labor in meeting the basic needs of workers has unintentionally spurred demands for esteemable and fulfilling jobs.

Frederick Herzberg suggests an alternative way of looking at the needs of workers —in terms of intrinsic and extrinsic factors. Under this rubric, job satisfaction and dissatisfaction are not opposites but two separate dimensions. Extrinsic factors, such as inadequate pay, incompetent supervision, or dirty working conditions may lead to dissatisfaction, which may be reduced in turn by such "hygienic" measures as higher pay and "human relations" training for foremen. But such actions will not make workers satisfied. Satisfaction depends on the provision of intrinsic factors, such as achievement, accomplishment, responsibility, and challenging work. Satisfaction, then, is a function of the content of work; dissatisfaction, of the environment of work. Increases in productivity have been found to correlate in certain industries and occupations with increases in satisfaction, but not with decreases in dissatisfaction. Hence, hygienic improvements may make work tolerable, but will not necessarily raise motivation or productivity. The latter depends on making jobs more interesting and important.

A recent survey, which lends some support for this emphasis on job content, was undertaken by the Survey Research Center, University of Michigan, with support from the Department of Labor. This unique and monumental study . . . is based on a representative sample of 1,533 American workers at all occupational levels. When these workers were asked how important they regarded some 25 aspects of work, they ranked in order of importance:

1. Interesting work
2. Enough help and equipment to get the job done
3. Enough information to get the job done
4. Enough authority to get the job done
5. Good pay

6. Opportunity to develop special abilities
7. Job security
8. Seeing the results of one's work.

What the workers want most, as more than 100 studies in the past 20 years show, is to become masters of their immediate environments and to feel that their work and they themselves are important—the twin ingredients of self-esteem. Workers recognize that some of the dirty jobs can be transformed only into the merely tolerable, but the most oppressive features of work are felt to be avoidable: constant supervision and coercion, lack of variety, monotony, meaningless tasks, and isolation. An increasing number of workers want more autonomy in tackling their tasks, greater opportunity for increasing their skills, rewards that are directly connected to the intrinsic aspects of work, and greater participation in the design of work and the formulation of their tasks.

Who Is Dissatisfied?

When we cite the growing problem in the country of job dissatisfaction using the criteria laid out above, are we talking about 5% or 50% of the workers in the country? It is clear that classically alienating jobs (such as on the assembly-line) that allow the worker no control over the conditions of work and that seriously affect his mental and physical functioning off the job probably comprise less than 2% of the jobs in America. But a growing number of white-collar jobs have much in common with the jobs of autoworkers and steelworkers. Indeed, discontent with the intrinsic factors of work has spread even to those with managerial status. It is, however, almost as difficult to measure these feelings of discontent about work as it is to measure such other basic feelings as pride, love, or hate. Most of the leading experts on work in America have expressed disappointment over the unsophisticated techniques commonly used to measure work dissatisfaction.

The Gallup poll, for example, asks only "Is your work satisfying?" It is not surprising that they get from 80% to 90% positive responses (but even this crude measure shows a steady decrease in satisfaction over the last decade). When a similar question was asked of auto and assembly-line workers, 60% reported that their jobs were "interesting." Does this mean that such high percentages of blue-collar workers *are really satisfied* with their jobs? Most researchers say no. Since a substantial portion of blue-collar workers (1) report being satisfied with their jobs *but also indicate they wish to change them* and (2) report they would continue working even if they didn't have to *but only to fill time,* then this can only mean that these workers accept the necessity of work but expect little satisfaction from their specific jobs.

Those workers who report that they are "satisfied" are really saying that they are not "dissatisfied" in Herzbergian terms—i.e., their pay and security are satisfactory, but this does not necessarily mean that their work is intrinsically rewarding. This distinction is illustrated by an interview sociologist George Strauss held with a blue-collar worker on a routine job. This worker told Strauss, in a rather offhand way, "I got a pretty good job." "What makes it such a good job?" Strauss responded. The worker answered:

> Don't get me wrong. I didn't say it is a *good* job. It's an O.K. job—about as good a job as a guy like me might expect. The foreman leaves me alone and it pays well. But I would never call it a good job. It doesn't amount to much, but it's not bad.[7]

Robert Kahn suggests that the direct question of satisfaction strikes too closely to one's self-esteem to be answered simply:

> For most workers it is a choice between no work connection (usually with severe attendant economic penalties and a conspicuous lack of meaningful alternative activities) and a work connection which is burdened with negative qualities (routine, compulsory scheduling, dependency, etc.). In these circumstances, the individual has no difficulty with the choice; he chooses work, pronounces himself moderately satisfied, and tells us more only if the questions become more searching. Then we learn that he can order jobs clearly in terms of their status or desirability, wants his son to be employed differently from himself, and, if given a choice, would seek a different occupation.[8]

More sophisticated measures of job satisfaction designed to probe the specific components of a job offer great contradictions to simple "Are you satisfied?" surveys. When it asked about specific working conditions, the Michigan survey found that great numbers of "satisfied" workers had major dissatisfactions with such factors as the quality of supervision and the chance to grow on a job. A 1970–71 survey of white, male, blue-collar workers found that less than one-half claimed that they were satisfied with their jobs most of the time. The proportion of positive responses varied according to the amount of variety, autonomy, and meaningful responsibility their jobs provided.

Over the last two decades, one of the most reliable single indicators of job dissatisfaction has been the response to the question: "What type of work would you try to get into if you could start all over again?" Most significantly, of a cross section of white-collar workers (including professionals), only 43% would voluntarily choose the same work that they were doing, and only 24% of a cross section of blue-collar workers would choose the same kind of work if given another chance (see Table 1). This question, some researchers feel, is a particularly sensitive indicator because it causes respondents to take into account the intrinsic factors of the job and the very personal question of self-esteem. Those in jobs found to be least satisfying on other measures seldom would choose their present occupation again.

Another fairly accurate measure of job satisfaction is to ask the worker the question:

[7] George Strauss, "Is There a Blue Collar Revolt Against Work?," 1972.

[8] Robert Kahn, "The Meaning of Work: Interpretation and Proposals for Measurement," 1972.

Table 1. Percentages in Occupational Groups Who Would Choose Similar Work Again

Professional and Lower White-Collar Occupations	%	Working-Class Occupations	%
Urban university professors	93	Skilled printers	52
Mathematicians	91	Paper workers	42
Physicists	89	Skilled autoworkers	41
Biologists	89	Skilled steelworkers	41
Chemists	86	Textile workers	31
Firm lawyers	85	*Blue-collar workers, cross section*	*24*
Lawyers	83	Unskilled steelworkers	21
Journalists (Washington correspondents)	82	Unskilled autoworkers	16
Church university professors	77		
Solo lawyers	75		
White-collar workers, cross section	*43*		

"What would you do with the extra two hours if you had a 26-hour day?" Two out of three college professors and one out of four lawyers say they would use the extra time in a work-related activity. Strikingly, only one out of twenty nonprofessional workers would make use of the extra time in work activity.

We are able, then, to differentiate between those jobs that are satisfying and those that are dissatisfying to the people who hold them. The prestige of an occupation is often an accurate predictor of the level of satisfaction found in a job (while the ranking of occupations by prestige does not correspond exactly with either salary or the amount of education needed to perform well on the job). Moreover, prestige ranking of jobs is nearly identical with the ranking of jobs according to who would choose the same work again. Evidently, people know what work is satisfying and what work is not, even if they are unable to articulate the characteristics of each.

We also find that the jobs people find most satisfying contain most or all of the factors cited previously that workers find important in their jobs. The dissatisfying jobs contain only some or none of these factors. (Those jobs with highly dissatisfying aspects are found to correlate with social problems such as physical and mental illness. . . .)

Demographic factors also play a part in the difference between satisfaction and dissatisfaction in the workplace. Young workers and blacks were found to be the most dissatisfied segments of the population in the University of Michigan Survey of Working Conditions. But even dissatisfaction among these groups was often found to correlate with specific kinds of jobs and job situations. For example, highly trained women in low-level jobs were often extremely dissatisfied, but women and men with the same training in the same jobs were equally satisfied.

Sources of Dissatisfaction

Based on what we know about the attitudes of workers toward their jobs, we can identify the following two factors as being major sources of job dissatisfaction: the anachronism of Taylorism and diminishing opportunities to be one's own boss.

THE ANACHRONISM OF TAYLORISM

Frederick Winslow Taylor, father of time and motion studies and author of *Principles of Scientific Management,* propagated a view of efficiency which, until recently, was markedly successful—so long as "success" was measured in terms of unit costs and output. Under his tutelage, work tasks were greatly simplified, fragmented, compartmentalized, and placed under continuous supervision. The worker's rewards depended on doing as he was told and increasing his output. Taylor's advice resulted in major, sometimes spectacular, increases in productivity.

Several events have occurred to make Taylorism anachronistic. Primarily, the workforce has changed considerably since his principles were instituted in the first quarter of this century. From a workforce with an average educational attainment of less than junior high school, containing a large contingent of immigrants of rural and peasant origin and resigned to cyclical unemployment, the workforce is now largely native-born, with more than a high school education on the average, and affluence-minded. And, traditional values that depended on authoritarian assertion alone for their survival have been challenged.

Simplified tasks for those who are not simple-minded, close supervision by those whose legitimacy rests only on a hierarchical structure, and jobs that have nothing but money to offer in an affluent age are simply rejected. For many of the new workers, the monotony of work and scale of organization and their inability to control the pace and style of work are cause for a resentment which they, unlike older workers, do not repress.

Attempts to reduce the harmful effects of Taylorism over the last two generations have not got at the nub of the problem. For example, the "human relations" school attempts to offset Taylor's primacy of the machine with "tender, loving care" for workers. This school (which has many adherents in personnel offices today) ignores the technological and production factors involved in a business. This approach concentrates on the enterprise as a social system—the workers are to be treated better, but their jobs remain the same. Neither the satisfaction of workers nor their productivity is likely to improve greatly from the human relations approach. Alternatives to Taylorism, therefore, must arise from the assumption that it is insufficient to adjust either people to technology or technology to people. It is necessary to consider both the social needs of the workers and the task to be performed. This viewpoint challenges much of what passes as efficiency in our industrial society.

Many industrial engineers feel that gains in productivity will come about mainly through the introduction of new technology. They feel that tapping the latent productivity of workers is a relatively unimportant part of the whole question of productivity. This is the attitude that was behind the construction of the General Motors auto plant in Lordstown, Ohio, the newest and most "efficient" auto plant in America. Early in 1972, workers there went out on strike over the pace of the line and the robot-like tasks that they were asked to perform. This event highlights the role of the human element in productivity: What does the employer gain by having a "perfectly efficient" assembly-line if his workers are out on strike because of the oppressive and dehumanized experience of working on the "perfect" line? As the costs of absenteeism, wildcat strikes, turnover, and industrial sabotage become an increasingly significant part of the cost of doing business, it is becoming clear that the current concept of industrial efficiency conveniently but mistakenly ignores the social half of the equation.

It should be noted that Taylorism and a misplaced conception of efficiency is not restricted to assembly-lines or, for that matter, to the manufacturing sector of the economy. The service sector is not exempt. For example, in the medical care industry, the phenomenal growth in employment over the past decade or so has occurred largely in lower-level occupations. This growth has been accompanied by an attempt to increase the efficiency of the upper-level occupations through the delegation of tasks down the ladder of skills. This undoubtedly results in a greater efficiency in the utilization of manpower, but it rigidifies tasks, reduces the range of skills utilized by most of the occupations, increases routinization, and opens the door to job dissatisfaction for a new generation of highly educated workers.

As we have seen, satisfying jobs are most often those that incorporate factors found in high-status jobs—autonomy, working on a "whole" problem, participation in decision making. But as Ivar Berg and others have noted, as a result of countless public and private policies and decisions that determine our occupational structure, growth in occupational opportunities has occurred largely in middle and lower levels. The automation revolution that was to increase the demand for skilled workers (while decreasing the need for humans to do the worst jobs of society) has not occurred. What we *have* been able to do is to create such jobs as teacher aides, medical technicians, and computer keypunch operators—not jobs with "professional" characteristics. Undoubtedly, these jobs have opened opportunities for many who would otherwise have had no chance to advance beyond much lower-skilled positions. But it is illusory to believe that technology is opening new high-level jobs that are replacing low-level jobs. Most new jobs offer little in the way of "career" mobility—lab technicians do not advance along a path and become doctors.

This problem of a fairly static occupational structure presents society with a formidable barrier to providing greater job satisfaction to those below the pinnacle of the job pyramid. Without a technological revolution there is little hope of flattening out this structure in order to give more workers higher-status jobs. It then becomes crucial to infuse middle- and lower-level jobs with professional characteristics, particularly if we plan to continue offering higher and higher degrees of education to young people on the assumption that their increased expectations can be met by the world of work.

DIMINISHING OPPORTUNITIES TO BE ONE'S OWN BOSS

Our economic, political, and cultural system has fostered the notion of independence and autonomy, a part of which is the belief that a hardworking person, even if he has little capital, can always make a go of it in business for himself. Or, to put it another way, if things get too bad in a dependent work situation, it has been felt that the individual could always strike out on his own.

This element of the American Dream is rapidly becoming myth, and disappearing with it is the possibility of realizing the character traits of independence and autonomy by going into business for oneself. The trend of the past 70 years or more, and particularly in recent years, has been a decrease in small independent enterprises and self-employment, and an increase in the domination of large corporations and government in the workforce. In the middle of the 19th century, less than half of all employed people were wage and salary workers. By 1950 it was 80%, and by 1970, 90%. Self-employed persons dropped from 18% in 1950 to 9% in 1970. Individual proprietorships in service trades declined from 81% to 78% in only five years—from 1958 to 1963. From 1960 to 1970, government workers increased from 12% of the civilian labor force to more than 15%. Out of 3,534,000 industrial units employing 70% of the civilian labor force, 2% of the units accounted for 50.6% of the employees, and more than 27% of the employed were accounted for in 0.3% of the units.

Among a class of occupations notable for their autonomy—managers, officials, and proprietors (excluding farms)—self-employment fell from 50% in 1950 to 37% in 1960. On the farms, wage and salary workers increased as a percentage of all farm workers from 61% in 1950 to 80% in 1960. Even among authors, self-employment dropped from 62% to 38% in this period, while self-employed photographers declined from 41% to 34%. Although the percentage of self-employed lawyers has remained almost constant, in 1967 nearly half reported working in firms having 8 to 50 or more lawyers, suggesting some limitation on their autonomy and independence.

As these data attest, the trend is toward large corporations and bureaucracies which typically organize work in such a way as to minimize the independence of the workers and maximize contol and predictability for the organization. Characterologically, the hierarchical organization requires workers to follow orders, which calls for submissive traits, while the selection of managers calls for authoritarian and controlling traits. With the shift from manufacturing to services—employment has gone from about 50–50 in 1950 to 62–38 in favor of services in 1970—the tyranny of the machine is perhaps being replaced by the tyranny of the bureaucracy.

Yet, the more democratic and self-affirmative an individual is, the less he will stand for boring, dehumanized, and authoritarian work. Under such conditions, the workers either protest or give in, at some cost to their psychological well-being. Anger that does not erupt may be frozen into schizoid depressed characters who escape into general alienation, drugs, and fantasies. More typically, dissatisfying working environments result in the condition known as alienation.

Alienation exists when workers are unable to control their immediate work processes, to develop a sense of purpose and function which connects their jobs to the over-all organization of production, to belong to integrated industrial communities, and when they fail to become involved in the activity of work as a mode of personal self-expression.[9]

Social scientists identify four ingredients of alienation: (1) powerlessness (regarding ownership of the enterprise, general management policies, employment conditions and the immediate work process), (2) meaninglessness (with respect to the character of the product worked on as well as the scope of the product or the production process), (3) isolation (the social aspect of work), and (4) self-estrangement ("depersonalized detachment," including boredom, which can lead to "absence of personal growth"). As thus broken down, alienation is inherent in pyramidal, bureaucratic management patterns and in advanced, Taylorized technology, which divides and subdivides work into minute, monotonous elements. The result of alienation is often the withdrawal of the worker from community or political activity or the displacement of his frustrations through participation in radical social or political movements.

It seems fair to conclude that the combination of the changing social character of American workers, declining opportunities to establish independence through self-employment, and an anachronistic organization of work can create an explosive and pathogenic mix.

. . .

ALIENATED LABOR

Karl Marx

. . .

We shall begin from a *contemporary* economic fact. The worker becomes poorer the more wealth he produces and the more his production increases in power and extent. The worker becomes an ever cheaper commodity the more goods he creates. The *devaluation* of the human world increases in direct relation with the *increase in value* of the world of things. Labour does not only create goods; it also produces itself and the worker as a *commodity,* and indeed in the same proportion as it produces goods.

This fact simply implies that the object produced by labour, its product, now stands opposed to it as an *alien being,* as a *power independent* of the producer. The product

---

[9] Robert Blauner, *Alienation and Freedom,* 1964.

of labour is labour which has been embodied in an object and turned into a physical thing; this product is an *objectification* of labour. The performance of work is at the same time its objectification. The performance of work appears in the sphere of political economy as a *vitiation* of the worker, objectification as a *loss* and as *servitude to the object,* and appropriation as *alienation.*

So much does the performance of work appear as vitiation that the worker is vitiated to the point of starvation. So much does objectification appear as loss of the object that the worker is deprived of the most essential things not only of life but also of work. Labour itself becomes an object which he can acquire only by the greatest effort and with unpredictable interruptions. So much does the appropriation of the object appear as alienation that the more objects the worker produces the fewer he can possess and the more he falls under the domination of his product, of capital.

All these consequences follow from the fact that the worker is related to the *product of his labour* as to an *alien* object. For it is clear on this presupposition that the more the worker expends himself in work the more powerful becomes the world of objects which he creates in face of himself, the poorer he becomes in his inner life, and the less he belongs to himself. It is just the same as in religion. The more of himself man attributes to God the less he has left in himself. The worker puts his life into the object, and his life then belongs no longer to himself but to the object. The greater his activity, therefore, the less he possesses. What is embodied in the product of his labour is no longer his own. The greater this product is, therefore, the more he is diminished. The *alienation* of the worker in his product means not only that his labour becomes an object, assumes an *external* existence, but that it exists independently, *outside himself,* and alien to him, and that it stands opposed to him as an autonomous power. The life which he has given to the object sets itself against him as an alien and hostile force.

Let us now examine more closely the phenomenon of *objectification;* the worker's production and the *alienation* and *loss* of the object it produces, which is involved in it. The worker can create nothing without *nature,* without the *sensuous external world.* The latter is the material in which his labour is realized, in which it is active, out of which and through which it produces things.

But just as nature affords the *means of existence* of labour, in the sense that labour cannot *live* without objects upon which it can be exercised, so also it provides the *means of existence* in a narrower sense; namely the means of physical existence for the *worker* himself. Thus, the more the worker *appropriates* the external world of sensuous nature by his labour the more he deprives himself of *means of existence,* in two respects: first, that the sensuous external world becomes progressively less an object belonging to his labour or a means of existence of his labour, and secondly, that it becomes progressively less a means of existence in the direct sense, a means for the physical subsistence of the worker.

In both respects, therefore, the worker becomes a slave of the object; first, in that he receives an *object of work,* i.e. receives *work,* and secondly, in that he receives *means of subsistence.* Thus the object enables him to exist, first as a *worker* and secondly, as a *physical subject.* The culmination of this enslavement is that he can only maintain himself as a *physical subject* so far as he is a *worker,* and that it is only as a *physical subject* that he is a worker.

(The alienation of the worker in his object is expressed as follows in the laws of political economy: the more the worker produces the less he has to consume; the more value he creates the more worthless he becomes; the more refined his product the more crude and misshapen the worker; the more civilized the product the more barbarous the worker; the more powerful the work the more feeble the worker; the more the work manifests intelligence the more the worker declines in intelligence and becomes a slave of nature.)

Political economy conceals the alienation in the nature of labour in so far as it does not examine the direct relationship between the worker (work) and production. Labour certainly produces marvels for the rich but it produces privation for the worker. It produces palaces, but hovels for the worker. It produces beauty, but deformity for the worker. It replaces labour by machinery, but it casts some of the workers back into a barbarous kind of work and turns the others into machines. It produces intelligence, but also stupidity and cretinism for the workers.

The direct relationship of labour to its products is the relationship of the worker to the objects of his production. The relationship of property owners to the objects of production and to production itself is merely a *consequence* of this first relationship and confirms it. . . .

Thus, when we ask what is the important relationship of labour, we are concerned with the relationship of the *worker* to production.

So far we have considered the alienation of the worker only from one aspect; namely, *his relationship with the products of his labour.* However, alienation appears not merely in the result but also in the *process* of *production,* within *productive activity* itself. How could the worker stand in an alien relationship to the product of his activity if he did not alienate himself in the act of production itself? The product is indeed only the *résumé* of activity, of production. Consequently, if the product of labour is alienation, production itself must be active alienation—the alienation of activity and the activity of alienation. The alienation of the object of labour merely summarizes the alienation in the work activity itself.

What constitutes the alienation of labour? First, that the work is *external* to the worker, that it is not part of his nature; and that, consequently, he does not fulfil himself in his work but denies himself, has a feeling of misery rather than well-being, does not develop freely his mental and physical energies but is physically exhausted and mentally debased. The worker, therefore, feels himself at home only during his leisure time, whereas at work he feels homeless. His work is not voluntary but imposed, *forced labour.* It is not the satisfaction of a need, but only a *means* for satisfying other needs.

Its alien character is clearly shown by the fact that as soon as there is no physical or other compulsion it is avoided like the plague. External labour, labour in which man alienates himself, is a labour of self-sacrifice, of mortification. Finally, the external character of work for the worker is shown by the fact that it is not his own work but work for someone else, that in work he does not belong to himself but to another person.

Just as in religion the spontaneous activity of human fantasy, of the human brain and heart, reacts independently as an alien activity of gods or devils upon the individual, so the activity of the worker is not his own spontaneous activity. It is another's activity and a loss of his own spontaneity.

We arrive at the result that man (the worker) feels himself to be freely active only in his animal functions—eating, drinking and procreating, or at most also in his dwelling and in personal adornment—while in his human functions he is reduced to an animal. The animal becomes human and the human becomes animal.

Eating, drinking and procreating are of course also genuine human functions. But abstractly considered, apart from the environment of human activities, and turned into final and sole ends, they are animal functions.

We have now considered the act of alienation of practical human activity, labour, from two aspects: (1) the relationship of the worker to the *product of labour* as an alien object which dominates him. This relationship is at the same time the relationship to the sensuous external world, to natural objects, as an alien and hostile world; (2) the relationship of labour to the *act of production* within *labour*. This is the relationship of the worker to his own activity as something alien and not belonging to him, activity as suffering (passivity), strength as powerlessness, creation as emasculation, the *personal* physical and mental energy of the worker, his personal life (for what is life but activity?), as an activity which is directed against himself, independent of him and not belonging to him. This is *self-alienation* as against the above-mentioned alienation of the *thing*.

We have now to infer a third characteristic of *alienated labour* from the two we have considered.

Man is a species-being not only in the sense that he makes the community (his own as well as those of other things) his object both practically and theoretically, but also (and this is simply another expression for the same thing) in the sense that he treats himself as the present, living species, as a *universal* and consequently free beings.

Species-life, for man as for animals, has its physical basis in the fact that man (like animals) lives from inorganic nature, and since man is more universal than an animal so the range of inorganic nature from which he lives is more universal. Plants, animals, minerals, air, light, etc. constitute, from the theoretical aspect, a part of human consciousness as objects of natural science and art; they are man's spiritual inorganic nature, his intellectual means of life, which he must first prepare for enjoyment and perpetuation. So also, from the practical aspect, they form a part of human life and activity. In practice man lives only from these natural products, whether in the form of food, heating, clothing, housing, etc. The universality of man appears in practice in the universality which makes the whole of nature into his inorganic body: (1) as a direct means of life; and equally (2) as the material object and instrument of his life activity. Nature is the inorganic body of man; that is to say nature, excluding the human body itself. To say that man *lives* from nature means that nature is his *body* with which he must remain in a continuous interchange in order not to die. The statement that the physical and mental life of man, and nature, are interdependent means simply that nature is interdependent with itself, for man is a part of nature.

Since alienated labour: (1) alienates nature from man; and (2) alienates man from himself, from his own active function, his life activity; so it alienates him from the species. It makes *species-life* into a means of individual life. In the first place it alienates species-life and individual life, and secondly, it turns the latter, as an abstraction, into the purpose of the former, also in its abstract and alienated form.

For labour, *life activity, productive life,* now appear to man only as *means* for the satisfaction of a need, the need to maintain his physical existence. Productive life is, however, species-life. It is life creating life. In the type of life activity resides the whole character of a species, its species-character; and free, conscious activity is the species-character of human beings. Life itself appears only as a *means of life.*

The animal is one with its life activity. It does not distinguish the activity from itself. It is *its activity.* But man makes his life activity itself an object of his will and consciousness. He has a conscious life activity. It is not a determination with which he is completely identified. Conscious life activity distinguishes man from the life activity of animals. Only for this reason is he a species-being. Or rather, he is only a self-conscious being, i.e. his own life is an object for him, because he is a species-being. Only for this reason is this activity free activity. Alienated labour reverses the relationship, in that man because he is a self-conscious being makes his life activity, his *being,* only a means for his *existence.*

The practical construction of an *objective world,* the *manipulation* of inorganic nature, is the confirmation of man as a conscious species-being, i.e. a being who treats the species as his own being or himself as a species-being. Of course, animals also produce. They construct nests, dwellings, as in the case of bees, beavers, ants, etc. But they only produce what is strictly necessary for themselves or their young. They produce only in a single direction, while man produces universally. They produce only under the compulsion of direct physical needs, while man produces when he is free from physical need and only truly produces in freedom from such need. Animals produce only themselves, while man reproduces the whole of nature. The products of animal production belong directly to their physical bodies, while man is free in face of his product. Animals construct only in accordance with the standards and needs of the species to which they belong, while man knows how to produce in accordance with the standards of every species and knows how to apply the appropriate standard to the object. Thus man constructs also in accordance with the laws of beauty.

It is just in his work upon the objective world that man really proves himself as a *species-being*. This production is his active species-life. By means of it nature appears as *his* work and his reality. The object of labour is, therefore, the *objectification of man's species-life;* for he no longer reproduces himself merely intellectually, as in consciousness, but actively and in a real sense, and he sees his own reflection in a world which he has constructed. While, therefore, alienated labour takes away the object of production from man, it also takes away his *species-life,* his real objectivity as a species-being, and changes his advantage over animals into a disadvantage in so far as his inorganic body, nature, is taken from him.

Just as alienated labour transforms free and self-directed activity into a means, so it transforms the species-life of man into a means of physical existence.

Consciousness, which man has from his species, is transformed through alienation so that species-life becomes only a means for him. (3) Thus alienated labour turns the *species-life of man,* and also nature as his mental species-property, into an *alien* being and into a *means* for his *individual existence.* It alienates from man his own body, external nature, his mental life and his *human* life. (4) A direct consequence of the alienation of man from the product of his labour, from his life activity and from his species-life, is that *man* is *alienated* from other *men.* When man confronts himself he also confronts *other* men. What is true of man's relationship to his work, to the product of his work and to himself, is also true of his relationship to other men, to their labour and to the objects of their labour.

In general, the statement that man is alienated from his species-life means that each man is alienated from others, and that each of the others is likewise alienated from human life.

Human alienation, and above all the relation of man to himself, is first realized and expressed in the relationship between each man and other men. Thus in the relationship of alienated labour every man regards other men according to the standards and relationships in which he finds himself placed as a worker.

. . .

"WORK" AND "PLAY"

Richard Burke

"All work and no play makes Jack a dull boy." Most jingles rhyme better than this one, but no proverb is truer. The complement is also true. I venture to add, without argument, a new item to our store of conventional wisdom: "All play and no work makes Jack a big jerk." We don't so often realize, however, that simply alternating between work and play is not very satisfying either, if the work is drudgery and the play is merely recuperation to enable us to go back to work again. This has been the lot of most people throughout history, and it is not an enviable one. The lucky few are not the leisure class, if that means "all play and no work," but those whose activities combine elements of both. We all know someone whose job is so satisfying, so rewarding to him that he would rather "work" than do anything else, regardless of product or profit. And some people are so serious about their leisure activity, whether it be golf, bridge, or the piano, that it absorbs more of their energy and discipline than their work does. I wish to maintain in this essay that the most satisfying kind of work shares in the freedom and plasticity of play; that the most satisfying kind of play (in the long run) is purposeful and disciplined, like work; and that the good life for both individuals and societies must include plenty of both kinds of activities. As John Dewey put it, "Both [play and work] are equally free and intrinsically motivated, apart from false economic conditions which tend to make play into idle excitement for the well to do, and work into uncongenial labor for the poor." [1]

I. Definitions

The above thesis sounds plausible, I suppose; but any attempt to justify it runs into the notorious difficulty of defining both "play" and "work." The *Random House Dictionary* lists fifty-three different meanings of "play" and thirty-nine of "work," not counting idiomatic uses like "He made a play for my girl" or "Let's give him the works." [2] We speak of playing a game, a role, or a musical instrument; of the solitary play of infants and animals; of the play of light on the waves. Can there be anything common to all these? "Work" can be physical labor, but it can also be the functioning of a machine, any paid occupation, an artistic product, or (in physics) any transfer of energy through force. Wittgenstein has suggested, using the word "game" as his example, that the most we should expect in such cases is a "family resemblance" among the various uses, rather than a single definition applying equally to all; [3] and even this may be too much to ask for here.

To make matters worse for my thesis, the same dictionary gives only one antonym for "play" ("work"), and only two for "work" ("play" and "rest"). While this offers some hope for reducing the meanings of each term to one or two basic ones, it also suggests that an activity combining both work and play is somehow a contradiction in terms. And "the man in the street" would probably bear this out. Work is difficult and unpleasant, he might say, while play is easy and fun. But we have already seen that neither of these is necessarily true: that they reflect what Dewey called "false economic conditions." Some people enjoy their work, some have easy jobs, and some even prefer work as a way of spending their leisure time: in a recent study asking

---

[1] John Dewey, *Democracy and Education* (New York: Macmillan Co., 1916), pp. 205–6.

[2] *Random House Dictionary of the American Language* (New York: Random House, 1967), s.v. "play" and "work."

[3] Ludwig Wittgenstein, *Philosophical Investigations* (Oxford: Basil Blackwell, 1953), pp. 31–32.

automobile workers how they would spend additional leisure time if they were to get it, 96.8 percent mentioned "work around the house," as compared with 48.8 percent for attending spectator sports, 42.4 percent for hunting and fishing, 24.8 percent for engaging in athletics, 53.6 percent for travel.[4] On the other side, play can be very demanding: think of intercollegiate football. And it can be distinctly unpleasant when one is playing poorly or when one's companions are irritating.

Another dichotomy, equally unsatisfactory, results from defining both in economic terms: work is whatever you get paid for, and play is everything else. This idea is seldom expressed that crudely; but it lurks beneath the assumption that a professional athlete, musician, or actor is working rather than playing, although his activity may be distinguishable from that of an amateur solely by the fact that he gets paid for it. The fact that a man "plays" baseball, "plays" in an orchestra, or acts in "plays" suggests that his activity is in *some* sense play, even if he is a *good* enough player to earn a living at it. And of course a great deal of work is not paid in our society, as any housewife would be quick to point out. Whether work or play is remunerated seems to be purely a matter of convention, varying from one society to another (how would it apply in premonetary cultures?) and having little to do with the nature of the activities themselves.

What might be called the "common-sense dichotomy" between work and play, then, need not detain us very long. The two terms are not necessarily mutually exclusive, despite the fact that they are often antonyms. Nor are they exhaustive of the range of human activities: eating, sleeping, praying, fighting are normally neither work nor play, and this list could easily be extended. They are simply two of the activities of man, each with a characteristic structure which I am trying to discover.

A number of recent theories give more cause for despair, by using both terms in such extended or paradoxical ways that they threaten to rob them of all meaning. Everyone seems to be talking about "playing games" these days. The mathematical "game theory" of von Neumann and Morganstern is used by some social scientists as a model of rational behavior, useful in devising strategies for business, international diplomacy, and war: [5] a range of activities about as far from "play" as one can imagine. Eric Berne, on the other hand, in his best-selling *Games People Play,* defines a "game" as an interpersonal transaction in which the participants are governed by ulterior motives of which they are unaware and which are invariably self-destructive.[6] Such behavior is utterly serious and utterly irrational; indeed, Berne's purpose is to get us to *stop*

---

[4] William A. Faunce, "Automation and Leisure" (1954), reprinted in E. Smigel, ed., *Work and Leisure* (New Haven, Conn.: College and University Press, 1963), p. 92. These figures must be interpreted with caution. The workers interviewed were evidently allowed to mark as many activities as they chose from a list. Also, some presumably felt they needed more time to fulfill their *responsibilities* at home rather than *preferred* "work" as a way of spending leisure time.

[5] John von Neumann and Oscar Morganstern, *Theory of Games and Economic Behavior* (Princeton, N.J.: Princeton University Press, 1944).

[6] Eric Berne, *Games People Play* (New York: Grove Press, 1964), pp. 48–50.

playing games with each other. In philosophy, Wittgenstein's introduction of the term "language game" [7] is having an enormous influence. Even morality, which Kant considered the ultimate in seriousness and therefore diametrically opposed to play,[8] is now being treated as a kind of game with rules, strategies, spectators, etc.[9]

David Riesman has shown that Freud, reflecting a widespread bourgeois attitude, associated the world of work with the "reality principle" and regarded play as wish fulfillment through fantasy—tolerable and even useful in childhood but hardly appropriate for mature adults.[10] Piaget, after defining intelligence as an equilibrium between accommodation (to reality) and assimilation (to the self), defines play as "the primacy of assimilation over accommodation." [11] There is an important idea here, as we shall see, but it is vastly oversimplified and far too broad, since it would presumably include autistic behavior of all kinds, even that of psychotics. Many studies of animal and human development have emphasized the function of play in the development of physical and mental faculties and in the socialization process. In some species, play even seems to be *necessary* for normal development.[12] Isn't there a paradox here? Finally, Johan Huizinga's classic *Homo Ludens* goes even further, concluding that all of man's most serious activities—religion, art, philosophy, government, war—must be regarded as forms of play.[13]

In such a confusing situation, it would really help if we could attach some clear and consistent definitions to these terms. But what kind of definition is appropriate here? We have seen that lexical definitions, of the kind found in a dictionary, do not take us far: there are too many different uses of these terms, and some of them are already highly metaphorical. I have dismissed several common-sense notions, on the ground that they were not necessary or not sufficient (or both) to account for common usage. But is this not assuming just what I questioned above, that each term must have one and only one basic meaning? Why couldn't we simply agree to stipulate a pair of definitions and accept the consequence that some of their ordinary uses will fall outside? Logic textbooks often assert that this is the process of definition employed in the sciences and suggest that it should also be followed in all rigorous thinking. I will not venture into the controversial issue of the nature of definitions in science; [14] surely what we want here is to move back and forth, dialectically, between lexical and stipulative

[7] Wittgenstein, p. 23.

[8] Immanuel Kant, *Critique of Judgment*, trans. J. H. Bernard (New York: Hafner Publishing Co., 1951), pp. 176–77.

[9] For example, John Rawls, "Two Concepts of Rules," *Philosophical Review*, vol. 64 (1955).

[10] David Riesman, "The Themes of Work and Play in the Structure of Freud's Thought" (1950), reprinted in *Individualism Reconsidered* (Glencoe, Ill.: Free Press, 1954), pp. 326–31.

[11] Jean Piaget, *Play, Dreams, and Imitation in Childhood*, trans. C. Gattegno and F. M. Hodgson (New York: W. W. Norton & Co., 1962), p. 87.

[12] See Susanna Millar, *The Psychology of Play* (New York: Penguin Books, 1968), chaps. 3–7.

[13] Johan Huizinga, *Homo Ludens*, English trans. (London: Paladin, 1970).

[14] See Peter Achinstein, *Concepts of Science* (Baltimore: Johns Hopkins Press, 1968), chaps. 1–2.

definitions—to *clarify* the meanings of play and work by finding formulations which include as many of their actual uses as possible, especially the most common ones, under as few as possible clear, consistent concepts—preferably those which suggest *why* each term has the range of uses it does. For this purpose, we must agree on a few *paradigm* uses of each term which any acceptable definition must include.

II. "Play"

I submit that the following activities are all clearly examples of "play" and that a definition which excludes any of them is therefore inadequate.

1. A one-year-old child rolling a toy across the floor or wearing his cereal on his head instead of eating it—or a kitten, puppy, or young chimpanzee doing the same things
2. A five-year-old boy engrossed in building a tower by himself or a girl making a dress for her doll
3. A pair of ten-year-old boys wrestling but laughing and taking care not to hurt one another—or two wolves doing the same thing
4. Two or more people of any age playing a game or sport, whether of skill or of chance, whether for money, for a prize, for the satisfaction of winning, or simply "for the fun of it"
5. A lone person playing a game or sport, etc.
6. Impersonation of someone or something else ("playing a role") without the intent to deceive
7. Variation for the sake of novelty, such as "doodling" while taking notes or decoration of a utilitarian object
8. Making a game out of a monotonous activity to avoid boredom, such as counting the red cars passed while driving home from the country
9. Putting on a performance for the amusement of an audience, whether for money, etc. (see no. 4)

This list is not intended to be exhaustive or exclusive: numbers 7 and 8 may be the same phenomenon, or numbers 6 and 9. It is simply a list of *examples* of play, chosen to be as uncontroversial as possible. There are interesting borderline cases, such as hiking or swimming, an evening of casual conversation, practicing a musical instrument, sexual "foreplay," the song of birds.[15] For our purpose, however, the above list is long enough. Several observations follow directly from it:

a) Play cannot be a distinct type of observable behavior, since several of the paradigms (nos. 2, 6, 9) can involve almost any sort of behavior. A Martian would often fail to recognize play when he saw it, without some knowledge of the motives of the participants. This rules out a behaviorist approach.

---

[15] Even more interesting is the case of reading for pleasure, which is *not* normally considered play, although it is hard to see why not. The absence of bodily activity, perhaps; but what about chess? Or someone pretending to be a statue?

b) Adults play as well as children, and not only when they are being childish (nos. 4–9); so we cannot define play as essentially a preparation for more mature activity.

c) Not all play is competitive, or social, or governed by rules (nos. 1, 2, 5, 7, 8); our definition must include free exploration of one's environment and experimentation with one's own faculties.[16]

Let me try to formulate a definition that will include all the paradigms on the list. A few common features emerge: freedom from compulsion, completeness of the activity itself apart from its result, and a certain artificial or "pretend" quality which is unobservable and hard to pin down but which is nevertheless present, I think, in the organized games and performances of adults, and even in the random exuberance of the child. I would define "play," therefore, as *activity which is free, complete in itself, and artificial or unrealistic.* I might add that play is often governed by rules, either explicit (as in a game) or implicit (there are rules of impersonation, for example); and that it often involves a test or contest. These two are not necessary criteria, nor are they sufficient. Morality is governed by rules, and war is a contest; but I would distinguish both from play.[17] The three criteria I have given—freedom, intrinsic completeness, and artificiality—*are* necessary, and together I think they are sufficient, to set play apart from man's other activities. Each of them requires further discussion.

By "free," I mean free from both inner and external compulsion. If an activity is dictated by instinct, like the mating behavior of insects and fish, it is not play. (The song of birds probably falls in this category.) If one is hungry or frightened enough, play becomes impossible. An interesting illustration of this is the transition from sexual "foreplay" (which I *would* consider play) to the orgasm itself: normally a smile gives way to a serious expression, and bodily movements become less exploratory, more stereotyped. Likewise, if one is forced to engage in an activity by someone else, either directly or through fear of consequences, it ceases to be play. A spy whose life depends on his successfully impersonating someone is not playing; nor is a girl raped at gunpoint, whatever she may be required to do. Friedrich Schiller's *Letters on the Aesthetic Education of Man* is still well worth reading on the relationship between play and freedom. "Man," he says, "plays only when he is in the full sense of the word a man, and he is only wholly man when he is playing." The "play impulse" combines sensibility, which as part of nature is governed by physical necessity, with reason, which in itself is ruled by logical and moral necessities. In play, man gives shape to the former by means of the latter, and the result of this is Beauty. Only in this way does he achieve true freedom.[18]

My second criterion, that play is complete in itself and pursued for its own sake,

---

[16] By this formula, the fine arts are forms of play, whether professional or amateur (but see p. [306]).

[17] In saying this, I am disagreeing with Huizinga. I will discuss the matter further in connection with my third criterion.

[18] Friedrich Schiller, *On the Aesthetic Education of Man,* trans. R. Snell (New Haven, Conn.: Yale University Press, 1954), pp. 74–80.

may seem to be contradicted by professional athletes and performers (paradigms 4 and 9), by gambling for money (paradigm 4), by the biological and socializing functions of the play of the young (paradigms 1–3), and by the very wording of paradigms 7 and 8. I will take up each of these challenges in order.

A professional baseball player or actor must in some sense be playing, as I said earlier. (He is also working: my thesis, remember, is that the most satisfying activities combine elements of both work and play, and these are prime examples.) He is playing because the activity is *in itself* "artificial or symbolic" (see below) and because he enjoyed it so much that he got good enough at it to be paid. The pay is extrinsic to the activity, which was engaged in for its own sake long before the idea of becoming a professional suggested itself and would most likely be engaged in whether paid or not. The determining perspective should not be that of the economist, who treats all activities from one point of view (exchange value), but that of the participant, who distinguishes them according to their experiential structures. A professional athlete's or performer's work *may* become burdensome to him, of course, and probably does to all of them at times; but it remains an activity which is by its nature intrinsically complete and satisfying, apart from external rewards like money or fame.[19]

Roger Caillois, in his otherwise admirable little book *Les jeux et les hommes,* simply assumes that "professionals . . . are not players but workers." He also stresses the importance of games of chance in many cultures, and the necessity for any definition of play to take into account the fact that the player is far from disinterested in the results of his activity.[20] Here, unlike the stakes in baseball, the stakes are the *raison d'être* of the game. We cannot define play, then, as activity having no consequences at all, but we *can* call it activity pursued for its own sake, and in that sense complete in itself. Many people enjoy gambling when they break even, and even when they lose. When the stakes become so high that one cannot afford to lose, or if someone perfects a "system" that assures him of winning, he passes beyond "play" to more realistic activities.

The same sort of answer can be given to the argument that, since the play of young children (and animals) serves to develop their abilities, it is not pursued for its own sake. This time it is the perspective of the biologist, anthropologist, or developmental psychologist which is falsely given priority over that of the participant. A parallel fallacy is common in the treatment of religion by social scientists: the fact that religion forms a social bond or gives an individual a feeling of security is taken to imply that this is what religion "really" is, despite the protests of believers that this misses the essence of the phenomenon. There is a basic issue in epistemology here, which I cannot go into further without hopelessly distorting the balance of this essay. I will simply say that some sort of phenomenology seems more appropriate to the study of play (and

---

[19] Paul Weiss, *Sport: A Philosophic Inquiry* (Carbondale: Southern Illinois University Press, 1969), chap. 12.

[20] Roger Caillois, *Man, Play, and Games,* trans. M. Barash (Glencoe, Ill.: Free Press, 1961), pp. 5–6.

work) than any form of reductionism, and that phenomenologically play is complete in itself, although it may serve other purposes as well.

Paradigms 7 and 8 mention what seem to be extrinsic purposes in their very wording: "for the sake of novelty," "to avoid boredom." Here the ulterior motive seems to be a part of the phenomenological structure of the act itself. They are far from trivial cases for my general thesis, too: the opportunity to introduce novelty into one's work or to make a game out of it is just what distinguishes many satisfying occupations from dispiriting ones (see below). On closer examination, however, the difficulty turns out to be purely verbal. In both cases, by "playing" with an activity which is in itself a mere means to something else, we transform it into something interesting in its own right. From an objection, this point becomes another argument in favor of my definition.

Now I must defend my assertion that play is artificial, or less than fully realistic. Here I have ranged against me the current uses of the term "game" in mathematical game theory, in psychological role theory, and in Wittgensteinian linguistic analysis. Needless to say, I am not questioning the value of any of these as intellectual tools; I am simply trying to clarify the concepts of "play" and "game" involved. Games are ordinarily thought of as one kind of play: one may play without playing a game, but one may not participate in a game without playing.[21] What von Neumann and Morganstern, Berne, and Wittgenstein have done is noticed *analogies* between games and serious, realistic activities and extend the term "game" to cover the entire field of the analogies. This is misleading, because either they must extend "play" also, creating intolerable paradoxes—insanity or war as forms of play—or they must violate usage by speaking of games which are participated in but not "played." If the analogies are really strong enough—and this is still a controversial question in each case—I think it would have been better to coin a cumbersome term like "gamelike activity."

Huizinga's thesis is different, because he specifically insists on the *play* element in cultural activities like religion, art, and war. By this he means not only the "gamelike" element but also the qualities of freedom and intrinsic satisfaction that I have been discussing as essential to play. He demonstrates that the words for play, game, contest, and ritual interpenetrate in many languages. Drawing on Nietzsche's *Birth of Tragedy* and Granet's studies of ancient China, he detects "agonistic" forms (struggle, contest) in music, drama, sculpture, prosody, myths, rituals, aristocratic manners, legal procedures, usages of war, and the dialectical method in philosophy, which he traces to the riddle contests of ancient India and Europe. I regard all this as extremely valuable. But it is one thing to discover an *element* of play in all these things, as he puts it in more cautious moments, and another to say that they are *nothing but* play. When he says that civilization "does not come *from* play like a babe detaching itself from the womb: it arises *in* and *as* play and never leaves it," [22] I must demur.

[21] *Random House Dictionary of the American Language,* s.v. "game."

[22] Huizinga, p. 198.

Huizinga himself, in his latest chapter, bemoans the fact that "civilization today [i.e., since the nineteenth century] is no longer played, and even where it still seems to play it is false play." [23] But even in chapter 1, in the course of formulating his definition of play, he says that one of its defining characteristics is that "play is not 'ordinary' or 'real' life. It is rather a stepping out of 'real' life into a temporary sphere of activity with a disposition all of its own." This exactly the point I am trying to make. He continues:

Every child knows perfectly well that he is "only pretending," or that it was "only for fun." . . . This "only pretending" quality of play betrays a consciousness of the inferiority of play compared with "seriousness," a feeling that seems to be something as primary as play itself. Nevertheless . . . the consciousness of play being "only a pretend" does not by any means prevent it from proceeding with the utmost seriousness, with an absorption, a devotion that passes into rapture and, temporarily at least, completely abolishes that troublesome "only" feeling. . . . The inferiority of play is continually being offset by the corresponding superiority of its seriousness. Play turns to seriousness and seriousness to play. Play may rise to heights of beauty and sublimity that leave seriousness far beneath.[24]

Huizinga first admits too much—I doubt that every playing child knows "perfectly well" that he is only pretending—then gets hopelessly confused by using "serious" in two different senses in the same paragraph, so that play is both serious and not serious, both "inferior" and "superior" to seriousness. The passage is useful, however, because this distinction between two senses of "serious" is just what I need to justify my claim that play is "artificial" activity.

The distinction is between the nature of an activity in itself and the attitude of the participants on a given occasion. In itself, play is "not serious" in the sense that it contrasts with hard, everyday reality; with more earthy activities like eating, working, fighting, sex. It can be, however, and often is pursued with an attitude or rapt concentration and dogged persistence that surpasses these "more serious" activities. The difference is not in the degree of absorption involved, or in the value placed on the activity by the participant, but in its relationship to the life of man. Play is not just an attitude of mind: it is a type of *activity* in the world, normally associated with a certain attitude but not reducible to it. Play involves a representation or rehearsal of life, especially its agonistic aspects, according to tacit rules of simplification and projection.[25] A child's play world is composed of elements drawn from his experience but rearranged so as to be more manageable and meaningful. The same is true of many sports and games, whether of skill or chance: each generates a finite microcosm, where the things that can happen are strictly delimited. Not only do they take place in delimited areas—stadium, court, casino, board, etc.—and within fixed time limits, but

[23] Ibid., p. 233.

[24] Ibid., pp. 26–27.

[25] See Richard Grathoff, *The Structure of Social Inconsistencies* (The Hague: M. Nijhoff, 1970), chaps. 6–7, for a fuller discussion of the "symbolic" nature of play.

according to rules which artificially equalize the conditions of competition between players and specify which few of their countless characteristics and actions will count as relevant to each game. The result is an artificially simplified world, in which each act has one and only one meaning. Each game is a system of symbolic acts, the meanings of which are drawn from real life but then refined and purified of connotations and ambiguities so that they can be combined in new and interesting ways. The best example is probably chess, drawn from military tactics in ancient India. Performances and impersonations likewise take place in microcosms, governed by the symbols and conventions of the theater. This description applies equally well, however, to the exploratory play of small children, except that the simplification is not for the sake of novelty and amusement but results from the child's inability to deal with more complex situations. Freud and Piaget are relevant here, but they adopt a patronizing attitude toward those who love this simpler world of symbols and conventions. As Huizinga has shown, the kinship between this world and the equally symbolic worlds of the arts, of myth and ritual, and of philosophical speculation is a close one.

Here lies the true significance of play in the life of man: in its more complex forms, it develops his creative, imaginative ability, enabling him to live not only in the "real" world but also in countless symbolic worlds of his own making. No doubt this makes him a more efficient solver of practical problems; but it also enables him to endow his life with form and meaning. What art, religion, and philosophy are for the few, play is for the many: a free, intrinsically satisfying activity governed by rules of man's own making and giving rise to a finite, meaningful world that man can call his own. Perhaps this is what Plato meant in a fascinating passage in *The Laws:* "What, then, is the right way of living? Life must be lived as play [παιδία], playing certain games, making sacrifices, singing and dancing, and then a man will be able to propitiate the gods, and defend himself against his enemies, and win in the contest." [26]

One more problem about my definition remains to be faced. I [have] assumed that animals as well as humans play. My discussion throughout, however, has referred to mental states; and what do we know of the mental states of animals? Although I argued that play is not just an attitude but a type of activity, without the attitude the activity would be fundamentally different. It seems I must either modify the definition or refuse to apply it to animals. But anyone who has watched a kitten with a ball of yarn *knows* it is playing, just as surely as he knows it about a boy with a toy truck. Or does he? The kitten certainly *seems* to be playing, by which I think we mean that it seems to have the same attitude as, or at least an attitude similar to, that of humans at play. But isn't it after all conceivable that its consciousness is quite different from anything we imagine and that there is nothing remotely resembling the human play attitude in it? Descartes must have seen young animals gamboling about; yet it was his considered

---

[26] Plato *The Laws* 7, 803. Huizinga (pp. 37–38) quotes this passage in support of his own thesis apparently failing to notice the contrast with seriousness implied in the last lines.

opinion that they are mere automatons, devoid of thought and even feelings. Experiments may some day be devised which prove that a kitten cannot distinguish between a ball of yarn and a mouse and that what we call "playing with a mouse" is inherited, functional, and impossible to extinguish; would we still want to call it play? All we can say, I think, is that certain animals engage in playlike activity, but we cannot be sure that they are really playing. One or two of our paradigms (nos. 1, 3) must yield in the end, then, to the definition reached with their help. Thus does philosophical dialectic differ from a formal system!

III. "Work"

We have already established certain things about work: it is not necessarily difficult or unpleasant, and it is not necessarily paid. Some of our other conclusions about play, such as that it is better defined phenomenologically than behaviorally, with the corollary that animals only *seem* to play, *may* also apply to work. It is tempting to define work as simply the opposite of play: activity which is compulsory, a means to an extrinsic end, and realistic. But we cannot assume that the two terms are parallel just because the dictionary defines them as antonyms. My main thesis, that some highly satisfying activities partake in both work and play, obviously depends on their being compatible.

Perhaps "work" refers to an entirely different aspect of activity, different from play but not incompatible with it. In order to see whether this is true, let me begin again and assemble another list of paradigms, this time of work:

1. Physical toil, such as digging, hauling or lifting heavy objects, etc.
2. Physical toil performed by an ant or a mule [27]
3. Physical toil performed by a machine
4. Any repetitive task, physical or mental, such as turning a screw on an assembly line or adding up columns of figures in an office
5. Assembling, arranging, or shaping materials into a product (and the product of such assembling or shaping) [28]
6. Problem solving, practical or theoretical, such as untying a knot or designing a scientific experiment
7. Supervising the work of others
8. The proper functioning of any part of any machine
9. Providing a service for others, as does a butler or a babysitter
10. Any occupation for which one gets paid, either in money or in kind [29]

[27] I include this, although we *may* have to retract it later, because it is unquestionably a paradigmatic use of the word.

[28] This too is performed by some animals (e.g., nest building), and by machines.

[29] Not all work is paid, but all paid activity is work—in one important sense, anyway. I objected to *defining* work in terms of pay, but this is surely *one* of the paradigmatic uses of the word.

This list tells us that work can be either physical or mental, either repetitive drudgery (nos. 1, 4) or creative activity (nos. 5, 6). It can apparently be performed by persons, animals, or machines (nos. 2–5, 8, even 6). Note that it need not be active in any overt way (nos. 6, 7, and some forms of nos. 9 and 10), so that a Martian would also fail to recognize these types of work when he saw them. The most striking thing about this list, however, is the way the various activities fall into clusters: paradigms 1–4 are of exhausting or repetitive activity; 5–7 all involve arranging parts (materials, ideas, or people) so that they form a whole; and 8–10 refer to the functioning of a part in a whole. In paradigms 9 and 10, the "whole" is a social nexus in which one person takes the part (or part of the part) of another, or in which people participate in a common task and share in a common product (wealth). Is there a common idea underlying all three clusters?

The last two clusters are obviously related; let us see whether the first is related to the others. There are really only two paradigms of work here: physical toil and repetitive labor. But why does one engage in either of these unappetizing activities? Clearly because they *add up* to a result which is desired and because this is the only available means to that end. The act, then, should be defined in terms of the desired result ("digging a grave," "keeping the books"), and the digging or adding is simply the series of parts making up the whole act. The only difference between this and paradigms 5 or 6 is that here all the parts are the same, whereas in building a house or solving a scientific problem a variety of different acts are required. The same principle applies to repetitive acts performed by a lone individual: a boxer punching a bag or a musician practicing scales is working, not because the activity is boring and unpleasant—he may even enjoy it—but because it is part of the larger task of perfecting his skill.

A single formula, then, seems to cover all types of work: *activity which is part of a larger whole or serves to unite parts into a whole.*[30] This applies to intellectual as well as physical work and to supervisory as well as menial functions. At the minimum, being paid for any activity proves that one is at least part of an economic whole to which others are willing to acknowledge one's contribution, even if the activity itself seems quite unproductive, like that of a business or government sinecure. An activity can be *for the sake of the whole,* then, regardless of whether this is the motive of the participant on any given occasion.

If this is indeed a necessary characteristic of work, is it also sufficient? Can one function as part of a whole, or arrange parts to make a whole, without working? Of course, we are all parts of a thousand "wholes": the population of our community, of our nation, of the world; various ecological systems; the set of people with brown (or blue) eyes; etc. Likewise, we create verbal syntheses every time we speak; our bodies

---

[30] To define work in terms of "means to an end" in general, as some writers have, is too broad: it includes all purposive activity whatsoever, such as reaching for a cigarette.

are continually synthesizing chemical compounds; and in dozens of other ways we "unite parts into a whole" every day without "working" at it. Our definition is still too broad. There must also be a factor of *effort* involved; of consciousness of an end and an attempt to achieve it. The activity need not be guided at every moment by a clear idea of its purpose, but the idea must be there at *some* time, and the whole activity becomes disciplined or structured by that end. Work, then, is activity which is part of a whole *and which is governed by a discipline imposed on the parts by that whole.*

Like play, then, work must be defined partly in terms of an attitude of mind. It follows that we should say of animals that they (sometimes) engage in "worklike" activities, but we cannot tell whether they are really working because they may not be conscious of the whole. To be consistent, this must apply not only to a beaver "building a dam," and to a bird "building a nest," but also to a draft horse pulling a plow. That seems strange, because we want to say that the farmer arranged to have the horse do the work instead of him, and the work got done, so the horse must have done it. A more accurate formulation, I submit, is that the farmer *separated* the work into its two components, neither of which alone is work: the consciousness of the whole and the activity making up the whole. The farmer *uses* the horse in his own work, but the horse's activity by itself is not strictly work.

The same analysis applies to machines (paradigms 3, 4, 8, and even 6). They have been designed by men to help them in their work—to perform one part of the task with less effort, more speed, regularity, etc.—but by themselves the machines do not really work, any more than a computer programmed to make the optimal responses in checkers or chess is really playing. What is missing in both cases is the consciousness of what one is doing and the implied freedom not to do it.

Work has turned out *not* to be the simple opposite of play. Like play, work is the activity of a free agent. The discipline imposed on work by the whole of which it is a part, or which it is producing, is a freely accepted discipline; indeed, the concept of "discipline" applies only to a will that is free not to accept it. Play, too, may involve acceptance of the discipline of a whole—as a member of a team, or with an effort to perfect one's game—and to this extent it shares in the nature of work. The term "teamwork" is perfectly accurate and points to a whole range of activities which partake in both work and play.

Nor is work necessarily an activity incomplete and unsatisfying in itself, a mere means to an end. At the outset we noted that there is a kind of satisfaction from many kinds of work: Veblen called it "the instinct of workmanship." We can now see that this satisfaction must be derived from having helped to bring a new "whole" into existence. Whether this whole is a "work of art" or not, the feeling is an aesthetic one.

Finally, there is a kind of work which is not "realistic": in which the imagination soars to create ideal realms of truth, goodness, and beauty which give order and purpose to our mundane lives. In religion, art, science, and philosophy man creates symbols and values which transcend actual existence and are thus "artifice"; but there is no activity which better "serves to unite parts into a whole."

IV. Conclusion

What, then, is the true relationship between work and play? We must conclude, I think, that each is a characteristic human activity associated with a characteristic attitude but that these are such as to be perfectly compatible with each other in the same activity at the same time. An athlete or a musician striving to perfect his technique, or to function smoothly in a team or an orchestra—regardless of whether he is a professional—can be said to be "working at playing." An architect experimenting with aesthetic effects, or a factory worker making a game out of his monotonous task, might equally well be said to be "playing at working" (except that in English, at least, this suggests that he is only pretending to work).

Caillois has shown that play can be ranged on a continuum from *paidia,* or childlike exuberance, to *ludus,* or strictly organized and regulated games; and that the impulse to create artificial constraints and challenges, turning *paidia* into *ludus,* coincides with the development of civilization.[31] The effect of this channeling of the play impulse is to introduce an element of work into play, thus lending tension and fiber to what would otherwise become tedious for mature adults. Conversely, critics of industrial society from Fourier and Marx to Daniel Bell and Hannah Arendt have stressed the dehumanizing nature of modern labor and the need to provide workers with more scope for imagination and creativity.[32]

There are some activities which are either "working at play" or "playing at work," and it is hard to tell which. The fine arts have all the characteristics of play, but people work so hard at them and *typically* take them so seriously—in our culture, anyway—that they seem to pass beyond the bounds of my definition. It is difficult to think of Michelangelo or Dostoevsky as "playing" when they created their somber masterpieces; but how about Paul Klee? Or John Cage? Twentieth-century art in general seems to be recapturing the spirit of play, together with discipline, that has characterized the arts among many peoples. Similarly, while the free play of imagination is essential to creativity in mathematics, philosophy, and the sciences, the element of discipline is so important that it seems impertinent to call them forms of play.

There are occupations which allow for autonomy, intrinsic satisfaction, and creativity, thus participating in the nature of play. My own occupation, that of a college professor, is one of these; and there are many others (but not enough) in business and the professions, in the arts and journalism, in certain crafts. There are also games which

[31] Caillois, chap. 2.

[32] Daniel Bell, "Work and Its Discontents," in *The End of Ideology* (Glencoe, Ill.: Free Press, 1960); Hannah Arendt, *The Human Condition* (Chicago: University of Chicago Press, 1958).

call for every ounce of intelligence, resourcefulness, and perseverance a man can muster. These continue to fascinate whole populations of mature adults; they are not just "recreation" but valuable activities in their own right.

I have tried to show that there are elements of both work and play in certain very satisfying activities and that it is the combination of these elements that accounts for their powerful and lasting fascination. In order to do this, I have had to define both terms and to show that there is no contradiction in applying both of them to the same activity at the same time. What matters is not to decide whether a free, satisfying, creative activity in which parts are disciplined by participation in a whole should be called basically "work" or "play" but to see to it that more people get to spend more of their time this way! My formula for utopia is simple: it is a community in which everyone plays at work and works at play. Anything less would fail to satisfy me for long.

Suggested Readings

Arendt, Hannah. *The Human Condition*. New York: Doubleday, 1959.

Buckingham, Walter. *Automation*. New York: New American Library, 1961.

Goodman, Paul. *Growing Up Absurd*. New York: Random House, 1960.

Marcuse, Herbert. *Eros and Civilization*. New York: Random House, 1962.

Russell, Bertrand. "In Praise of Idleness," in Erich Fromm (ed.), *Socialist Humanism*. New York: Doubleday, 1966.

Sparshott, F. E. "Work—The Concept: Past, Present, and Future," *Journal of Aesthetic Education* 7 (October 1973).

Weber, Max. *From Max Weber: Essays in Sociology*. Translated by Hans H. Gerth and C. Wright Mills. New York: Oxford University Press, 1946.

section four

sexual morality

RATIONALITY IN SEXUAL MORALITY

Albert Ellis

I

What constitutes a rational approach to sexual morality? "Rational," according to the dictionary, means based on or derived from reasoning. More specifically, an argument is rational when it takes into account the facts of reality, is based on empirical evidence, is not merely rooted in fantasy and wishful-thinking, and is logically consistent with its own basic premises. Applied to human affairs, rational does not mean rationalistic: for rational*ism* is the doctrine of accepting reason as the *only* or *absolute* authority in determining one's opinions or course of action, and it is the belief that reason *rather than* the senses is the true source of knowledge. Rationalism, because of its dogmatism and absolutism, can actually be—as it is, for example, in the philosophy of Ayn Rand—an irrational, religious creed. Rationality, on the other hand, includes reasonableness, practicality, moderation, open-mindedness, provision for change, no allegiance to supernaturalism, and lack of condemnation of individuals who have opposing views.

The main thesis of this article is that if sexual morality is to be rational, it would better be a consistent subheading under the main heading of general morality. Sexual behavior is only an *aspect* of human behavior; and although it is an important aspect, it is not unique, special, and all-important. Indeed, it usually cannot be divorced from socializing, relating, communicating, and various other forms of human contact and collaboration. Consequently, a sex act is immoral, unethical, or irrational not merely because it is *sexual*, but because it is also in some respect nonsexually wrong, mistaken, or inefficient. Even rape, which by practically any code is almost always immoral, is not wrong because it involves intercourse, but because it consists of forceful, freedom-depriving, injurious intercourse; and it is its breach of human consent rather than its sexuality which constitutes its wrongness.

What are the main principles of humanistic ethics, from which principles of sexual ethics can be logically derived? No one seems to know for sure, since invariant and absolutistic ethical ideals do not seem to be achievable; nor are they particularly *human*. Utopias, as recent sociological thinkers have been pointing out, are unrealistic and unattainable, because one of the main characteristics of men and their societies is that they change over the years. Nonetheless, I shall attempt to establish some general ethical postulates which I believe are rational—meaning reasonable—and humanistic today, and which are even likely to have some relevance for the near, and perhaps even more distant, future.

In stating these rational moral postulates I shall try to abide by a principle which seems to me to be based upon empirical evidence and logical reasoning: namely, the principle of duality or plurality. Man tends to think in monolithic, one-sided ways; to look for absolute rules, for certainty. But practically every idea or answer seems to have at least a two-sided, and often a many-faceted, aspect. Thus, human behavior is adequately explained by both heredity and environment; personality includes cognition and emotion; sexual happiness stems from stable and varietist relationships; people would better be concerned with here and now experience and future pains and pleasures. To understand what makes individuals tick without examining and taking into account the variegated influences upon them is to arrive at a narrow and unrealistic view of what they are and could be.

It is my thesis that a dualistic or many-sided point of view can be applied to the ticklish and still highly unresolved problem of human morality. It is also my thesis that although moral codes generally emphasize an individual's harming others, they usually ignore the equally important question of his defeating his own best interests; and they often forget that he may be just as unethical in the latter as in the former case. In the following attempt at stating moral principles, I shall, therefore, include propositions that concern themselves with self-defeatism as well as social sabotage, and I shall consider a pluralistic approach to "right" and "wrong." Using this framework, I hypothesize that an ethical code that includes the following rational ideas would hardly be perfect, but it would be more practical than various other codes that have been dogmatically iterated over the centuries.

II

(1) An individual would better strive primarily for his own welfare (usually, for continued existence and for maximum satisfaction and minimum pain); but since he almost invariably lives in a social group and his satisfactions and annoyances are importantly

bound up with group living, he had better also refrain from unduly interfering with the welfare of others.

(2) A person would better try to live in the here and now and to enthusiastically enjoy many immediate or short-range pursuits; but he had also better keep an eye on tomorrow and give up some immediate gains for longer-range, future satisfactions.

(3) A moral code would better be constructed on the basis of as much empirical evidence about human beings and their functioning as it is possible for the morals-makers to obtain; but they had better realize that morality is also based on a value system or set of assumptions: such as the assumptions that pleasure is "good" and pain is "bad."

(4) There probably cannot ever be any absolutely correct or proper rules of morality, since people and conditions change over the years and what is "right" today may be "wrong" tomorrow. Sane ethics are relativistic and situational. However, the nature of human beings and their environment is, and is likely to continue to be for some time to come, so ordered that a few moral rules will probably remain fairly stable for most groups under most circumstances. For example, "do not kill, lest you be killed," "love begets love," and "work hard to change the obnoxious conditions that you can change but gracefully lump those that are inevitable," are likely to retain some degree of truth for a long time to come.

(5) It is generally better for one to follow the customs and laws of his social group, the flaunting of which will bring real and noxious penalties. But to some degree one would better determine in his own mind the customs he thinks are insane and the laws he considers unjust and try to change or avoid them, even at the risk of some penalty.

(6) No person, group, or thing is holy, sacred, all-important, or godly; nor is any person, group, or thing totally villainous, demoniacal, worthless, or hellish. But many things are more valuable for certain purposes than others. Thus, freedom and justice are not necessitous; and slavery and injustice are not completely horrible. But for most of the people most of the time freedom and justice are important, desirable conditions.

(7) Moral codes would better be democratically applied to all individuals and groups within a given community; but discriminative morality, which is differentially enforced on elite and nonelite groups, may have advantages as well as disadvantages and need not be entirely bad.

(8) In a well-ordered and reasonably fair society, the citizens would better resort to verbal protest, the ballot box, and peaceful demonstrations in order to try to effect desired changes in social processes; but in an unfair or ill-ordered society, resort to force, violence, or mob rule may sometimes help effectuate progressive change.

(9) Man would better base his morality on humanistic precepts: on the nature of man and his desires (rather than the assumed nature of supernatural gods and their supposed desires), and on the fulfilling of these desires in the present, near-future, and more distant future. But man also has the power to significantly change some of his "nature," "desires," and "humanity." It is "natural" and "human," for example, for

man to be hostile, destructive, and warlike; and a rational ethical code may therefore include, as one of its purposes, the goal of trying to teach him to be less "natural" and "human" in these respects, and more "natural" and "human" in other more collaborative respects.

(10) Humanistic ethics include the primacy of human over subhuman goals, desires, and satisfactions. Cattle, for example, can ethically be raised and slaughtered for human food. But man would also better be duly humane and uncruel to animals because in being needlessly brutal to them, he also tends to become callous to human suffering and slaughter.

(11) Rational ethics include provision for slight and serious modification of virtually all moral codes, especially as environmental conditions change and perhaps the biological nature of man changes too. But the alteration of ethical postulates would better be carefully approached, with considerable concomitant fact-finding and discussion, since more harm than good may easily be wrought in the process.

(12) Immorality would better not be defined in terms of an individual's harming or acting unfairly toward another, but in terms of his *needlessly* or *gratuitously* injuring this other. For in the normal course of social living and consequent competition for jobs, sporting victories, sweethearts, or status, it is impossible for a person not to harm another—unless, of course, he is always a loser. However, in determining whether A necessarily and therefore justifiably harmed B (as, for example, when he ran off with the most desirable girl at a party when B very much wanted this girl for himself) or whether A needlessly and unjustifiably harmed B (as when he ran off with B's girlfriend, even though he already had one of his own), it is frequently difficult to decide exactly what is and is not necessary to A's happiness. A could contend that he "needed" the girl B wanted in both these instances; and if he were actually madly in love with B's girl even when he already had a perfectly "satisfactory" girl of his own, many objective observers would uphold his "need." Although it is easy to say that one individual is immoral when he "needlessly" and "gratuitously" and "unfairly" injures or deprives another, it is difficult to give exact and invariant meanings to these modifying terms; so that "true" immorality is often most difficult to determine or measure.

(13) A major concern of humanistic ethics would better be the facilitation of interpersonal relationships. As Lester Kirkendall and Curtis Avery have noted, "Whenever thought and choice regarding behavior and conduct are possible, those acts are morally good which create trust, and confidence, and a capacity among people to work together cooperatively." But man does not live by interpersonal relationships alone. His intracommunications are an integral part of his intercommunications; and he can enjoyably relate to and become absorbed in nonhuman organisms and things. Ethics includes his whole range of activity and not only his relationships with others. *I-Thou* relationships, as Martin Buber has pointed out, are highly desirable and uniquely human; but they arise out of and are experienced in the context of *I-It* relations. As Buber states: "In all the seriousness of truth, hear this: without *It* man cannot live . . . The commu-

nal life of man can no more than man himself dispense with the world of *It,* over which the presence of the *Thou* moves like the spirit upon the face of the waters."

(14) Man is to some degree individually responsible for his actions. Theoretically, he has a measure of so-called free will and can, at least if he works very hard at thinking and acting, choose to perform or not to perform certain intrapersonal and interpersonal acts. But he is also powerfully influenced by his inherited biological tendencies and his social environment; consequently, although he is partly responsible for, or causes, his own behavior, he is never entirely accountable for it.

(15) When an individual commits a wrong, mistaken, inefficient, self-defeating, or antisocial act, he may justifiably be termed a wrongdoer or—more accurately—a person who has performed this or that incorrect deed. As a fallible human, it is an unscientific overgeneralization to say that he is an evil or bad person. This statement implies that he was born to be more immoral than the vast majority of other people, will inevitably continue to be wrong, deserves to be severely punished or damned as a total human being for being mistaken, and if there were some kind of life after death, should be eternally consigned to the tortures of hell for having committed misdeeds. These statements cannot be empirically validated; and there is some factual evidence that some of them are often false.

III

Assuming that the foregoing general rules of ethics have some degree of validity, what are their correlates in terms of more specific rules of sexual morality? As far as I can see, they are along the following lines:

(1) An individual would better strive primarily for his own sex-love satisfaction; but since he lives in a social community and is going to be importantly affected by the sexual pleasures and annoyances of others, he had better also refrain from unduly interfering with the sex-love welfare of these others. This means, negatively speaking, that he had better not be dishonest with his potential or actual sex partners; that he had better not take advantage of minors or incompetents merely for his own satisfaction; that he is immoral if he coerces unwilling individuals to have relations with him; and that it is generally wise for him to follow the sex laws of his community if these are actually enforced with harsh penalties. On the more positive side, it would be better if he fully and freely expressed his feelings to his sex-love partners; genuinely was interested in their satisfactions as well as his own; sincerely tried to help them with their general and sexual problems, including their puritanism, sex phobias, compulsiveness, and inability to relate; and tried in some ways to help create the kind of a world in which other people were sexually alive, unblocked, and ethical.

This does *not* mean that the moral individual would necessarily go along with and bolster the prolongation of others' sex-love guilt, shame, and self-deprecation as many puritans urge him to do. He might not, for example, "respect" a female's virginity, or her tendency to feel terribly hurt if he first loved and then left her, or her horror of his using "dirty" words. He might either decide to stay away from her and look for less disturbed partners; or he might decide, keeping in mind her own good as well as his possible satisfactions with her, to help depropagandize her, induce her to surrender her sex-love hangups, and enable her to widen her potentialities for living. In these "seduction" attempts, he would take the same attitude as he would take in trying to influence or "seduce" another individual to change his or her conservative political, economic, or religious views and to become more liberal.

(2) A person would better try to have sex-love relations in the here and now and to enthusiastically enjoy many immediate or short-range sexual pursuits; but he had also better keep an eye on tomorrow and give up some immediate sex-love gains for longer-range, future satisfactions. This means that the individual is often wiser if he gives up present erotic pleasures for future ones. Thus, he may refrain from having intercourse with a minimum of foreplay in order to enjoy longer-lasting and deeper gratifications by employing more foreplay; forego some amount of sex today because prolonged participation (and lack of sleep) may sexually knock him out for several days to come; resist going to bed with an easily available girl because he might enjoy himself much more thoroughly with one not so easily bedded; and forbear having mere sex relations for sex that is combined with companionship, love, or other values.

The individual is often a saner, long-range hedonist if he gives up present sex-love pleasures for future nonsexual gains. Thus, he may leave his girlfriend relatively early in the evening because he has an important test to take or conference to attend the next morning; choose to live with X rather than Y because, although she is not as good a sex partner as Y, she is much easier to get along with domestically; or decide that love relationships with women take up too much time in his very busy life and therefore refrain entirely from having affairs or honestly enter only casual sex relationships with females.

(3) A code of sexual morality would better be constructed on the basis of as much empirical evidence about human beings and their functioning as it is possible to obtain. Historical, anthropological, and psychological studies tend to indicate that human beings are quite varietist or nonmonogamic in their sex desires. They are easily attracted to each other sexually on very short notice, but their vital interest significantly wanes after prolonged sexual contact and shared domesticity, at least in many instances. Although they may like intense sexual attraction, passionate romantic love between two people rarely outlasts a few years of living together. People who lust after each other sexually may detest each other in many nonsexual ways. Those who have notable nonsexual compatibility may lust for one another minimally. Moreover, large numbers of people can sexually desire and even be intensely amatively attached to two or more members of the other sex simultaneously. If these are common sex-love realities, then certain ethical codes—as lifetime devotion and sexual fidelity to a single member of the other sex—are, although advantageous in some respects, almost impossible for the

average individual to achieve; and they would better be significantly altered or made preferential rather than mandatory.

When all is said and done, sexual morality still has to be related to some underlying value system that is not completely determined by empirical findings. Some typical values that a humanist assumes in his sex codes are that human life and its survival are good, that pleasure is better than pain, self-acceptance better than self-deprecation, tolerance better than bigotry, societal change better than inflexibility and stasis; and that human beings are more important than lower animals, than external objects, and than assumed gods. Given these assumptions, and the known and probable facts about people and their social relations, a fairly consistent and "rational" code of sex ethics can be constructed. But if other assumptions are made—such as the premise that people will be rewarded in some kind of afterlife if they meekly bear pain and deprecate themselves during their earthly existence—a quite different sexual code might logically follow.

(4) There probably cannot ever be any absolutely correct or proper rules of sex morality, since people and conditions change over the years. When man lived in an agrarian-pastoral society, where contraception was virtually unknown, young people married in their early teens, there were no good medical methods for combatting venereal diseases, and it may well have been wise to interdict premarital intercourse and adultery. Today it may be equally idiotic to ban these forms of sex.

At the same time, considering what the nature of human beings is and is likely to continue to be for a considerable time to come, it is unlikely that rape, sexual murder, or an adult's taking advantage of a young child will be considered a perfectly justifiable and ethical act. Nor is it likely that, from the standpoint of ethical self-interest, extreme sexual dissipation or the individual's neurotically and rigidly sticking to a single limited form of sex activity will be considered a desirable or good mode of sexual comportment. Although the act of sex can practically never be deemed bad or immoral, the manner in which the individual performs this act may well be self-defeating or antisocial, and hence immoral.

(5) Normally, it is better for an individual to follow the sex customs and laws of his social group whose flaunting will bring real and noxious penalties. Thus, if he is highly likely to be socially ostracized, fired from his job, or jailed for engaging in nonmarital sex relations or homosexuality he had better give serious consideration to refraining from such activities—no matter how silly or unjust he may consider the laws of his community to be. He would be wise, of course, to work very hard, through speaking, writing, and political activity, to change the laws of his society; but while they still exist and are being enforced, he may well have to obey them.

If, on the other hand, the individual is vigorously opposed to the sex rules and laws of his land and objectively perceives he can fairly easily get away without fully heeding them, he may often be wise in discreetly or secretly flaunting them. Thus, although adultery and noncoital sex relations leading to orgasm (legally termed "unnatural sex practices" or "sodomy") have been banned in many of our states for the past century, there are virtually no indictments or convictions under such laws; and though technically illegal, it is generally quite safe to unobtrusively ignore them. Again, although it has long been considered "wrong" or "illicit" for young people in our culture to have premarital intercourse, most males and many females actually achieve reputation and status by having them. Disobeying the sex rules of one's community is often sane and moral, especially when one is convinced that these rules themselves are essentially insane and immoral.

(6) No sex act is holy, sacred, all-important, or god-impelled, except by arbitrary definition. Sexual intercourse is hardly holy, since abstinence, masturbation, and noncoital sex relations are legitimate practices that have distinct value to many people. Marriage is not a sacrament, unless a couple think it is; and when it is viewed in this manner it has enormous limitations, problems, and anxieties attached to it. Even love between the sexes is never all-important, as many individuals live happy existences with minimal or no experience of it. Whenever, in fact, a sex, love, or marital act is deemed to be sanctified, it tends to become more important than the human individuals partaking in it; and from a humanistic standpoint, immorality, or the needless sabotaging of human satisfaction, then tends to occur.

On the other hand, many sex acts are more valuable for certain purposes than are other activities. Thus, sex with companionship or love may, at least in the long run, be more enjoyable than sex without affection (and an hour in bed with a new partner may be more exciting than an hour with one's usual partner). A rational individual will try to maximize, without unduly attempting to deify, his sexual enjoyments; and he will similarly try to help his partner achieve the more important, rather than the all-important, satisfactions. Similarly, the rational individual will try to minimize sexual constraints and annoyances, without ridiculously amplifying them or damning those who are instrumental in sexually frustrating him.

(7) Sex codes would better be applied undiscriminatingly to all competent adults in a given community, and applied under a single standard that pertains to both males and females. Women, for example, would not, under a rational code, be criticized and penalized more severely than men for unconventional sex behavior or for illegitimacy. Nor would teenagers and younger children be arbitrarily and unduly held in check sexually, except for special reasons (such as their diminished ability to take proper contraceptive precautions). Sexual discrimination, however, may never be completely eradicable and may even have some advantages. Thus, in almost any conceivable society in the present and near future females are more likely to select as sex partners males who are handsome, strong, sexually competent, bright, and self-accepting. A total sexual democracy, where there is equal justice for all, therefore is probably not going to exist.

(8) In a well-ordered and reasonably fair society, the citizens would better resort to verbal protest, the ballot box, and peaceful demonstrations in order to try to effect

desired sexual changes. Thus, feminist movements have helped win a good many rights for women during the last fifty years that they had previously not had; and some powerful organizations are presently still working for greater equality of the sexes and are doing so in peaceful ways, using due processes of law. But it is conceivable that if sexual tyranny reigned—if males, for example, began physically subjugating and violating women or if people taken in fornication or adultery were literally killed (as the Old Testament recommended in the case of females caught in adulterous acts) —then violent revolt against the oppressors might possibly at times be in ethical order.

(9) Man would better base his sex morality on humanistic precepts rather than the assumed nature of supernatural gods and their supposed sexual rules, and on the fulfilling of human desires in the present and future. The fact that the lower animals have certain sexual proclivities and the supposition that Jehovah and Jesus had certain hard and fast sex rules have nothing to do with humanistic sex ethics. Our sexual morality would better be based on human biology and social learning. If men and women frequently enjoy oral-genital relations, they can hardly be deemed to be immoral on the grounds that such relations are "bestial" or "ungodly."

But man also has the power to significantly change some of his sexual "nature." He can train himself to be sexually constant in spite of his natural varietism. He can employ modern technology (such as electric vibrators, electronic music, and strobe lights) to affect his sexuality. He can use drugs, hormones, and other substances to make himself more or less sexual. There seems to be no good reason why he should not experiment in various ways to modify his sexual desires and potentialities, as long as he can increase his satisfactions in this manner without unduly surrendering or minimizing other advantages and benefits.

(10) Humanistic ethics include the primacy of human over subhuman sex goals, desires, and satisfactions. If lower animals are employed, for example, for purposes of bestiality, for the obtaining or sex hormones or stimulants, or for other purposes, this is normally an ethical pursuit of man. But humans would better be duly humane and uncruel to animals in any sexual use they make of them, because otherwise intrahuman values tend to suffer.

(11) Rational ethics include provision for slight and serious modification of virtually all sex codes, especially as environmental conditions change and perhaps the biological nature of man changes too. If we discover, for example, an entirely harmless, perfect method of birth control, codes which now make it unethical or illegal for fourteen-year-olds to have sex relations with each other or for adults to have intercourse with young teenagers might well be liberalized; while if new forms of venereal disease break out and are rampant, more stringent rules regarding nonmarital relations might be in order. But the alteration of sex customs and laws would better be carefully and intelligently approached.

(12) Sexual immorality would better be defined not in terms of an individual's acting

unfairly toward or harming another but in terms of his *needlessly* or *gratuitously* doing so. A boy may harm a girl if he accidentally gets her pregnant; but he may not be unethical unless he has adequate contraceptive means available and he gratuitously and foolishly decides not to employ them. However, since it is easy to interpret the terms "needlessly," "gratuitously," and "unfairly" sloppily, and since a sex-love partner can be exploited with little trouble, people would often do best to lean over backwards not to injure or to take advantage of each other sexually, even when at first blush it appears that they are legitimately and needfully doing so.

(13) It is preferable for partners, in their sex-love affairs, to concentrate on their interpersonal relations and to have *I-Thou* relationships in some instances; but insistence on maintaining deep interpersonal *I-Thou* relationships in all or most instances is unrealistic, impinges on the freedom of choice of the partner, and is likely to cause immense amounts of anxiety and rigid constraint. Sex or sex-love relations of an "exploitative" or *I-It* nature are perfectly ethical as long as they are entered honestly, with the full consent of the "exploited" mate.

(14) Man is to some degree individually responsible for his sex actions and therefore would better accept the penalties of performing them. But he is also powerfully influenced by his inherited biological drives and the social environment in which he is reared; consequently, although he is partly responsible for, or causes, his own sex-love mistakes and misdeeds, he is never entirely accountable for them. With considerable hard work and thinking, he can control many, but never all, of his sex ideas, desires, and acts.

(15) When an individual commits a wrong, mistaken, inefficient, self-defeating, or antisocial sex deed, he may justifiably be termed a wrongdoer or a person who has acted irresponsibly. But because he is a fallible human, it is an unscientific overgeneralization to say that he is an evil or bad person, a rotter or a louse. He is only a a mistake-maker who will tend to make more sexual errors in the future if he is savagely condemned and cruelly punished. It would be far better if he were fully accepted as an imperfect creature, were not totally devaluated or damned, and were encouraged to become more problem-centered rather than self-centered, so that he could work at being a little less error-prone in the future.

IV

Sexual morality, then, when seen in terms of rationality, essentially consists of the individual's following certain sane, sensible, and nondefeating values. He normally wants to live a good life, including a good sex-love life; he also wants to live it, almost always, within the context of some social group. Cunningly, he follows rational rules that will prevent him from foolishly harming himself, and will stop him from senselessly and needlessly harming others, and thereby in the short or long run damaging himself. Sexual morality is merely a subheading under general, humanistic morality.

The fact seems to be, though we often deny it, that human beings are both biologically and sociologically prone to think, emote, and act in self-defeating and immoral ways—in their general and in their more specific sexual behavior. They believe, usually with great vigor and bigotry, several major irrational ideas. For example, they very frequently insanely hold that they positively *must* be loved and approved by others; that they are no damned good as human beings when they perform imperfectly; that other people absolutely should and must act fairly and nicely toward them (and if they do not are complete blackguards who should be utterly damned for all time); and that they should live in a world of supreme certainty instead of the real world of probability and chance.

As a result of these highly irrational ideas, people in our own and other cultures tend to think crookedly about themselves, about others, and about the world. They spend considerable time and energy condemning themselves and others—instead of observing that although a person's deeds or performances may indeed be wrong or inefficient, he as an ongoing process, and as a living human, cannot be legitimately given a report card and thereby deified or damned. And they keep railing at the universe for not being easier to live in than it is—instead of actively working to diagnose its ills and evils and to change them. Consequently, they make themselves inordinately anxious, guilty, depressed, hostile, self-pitying, defensive, and avoidant.

Sexually, people tend to be, if possible, even more irrational than they are nonsexually. They not only condemn themselves and each other for various wrongdoings, but they frequently inaccurately define what is wrong. Thus, if we were to apply the standards of sexual morality listed above to our everyday behavior, we would probably discover that most of the sex acts that have been historically deemed to be sinful in our society—such as masturbation, premarital intercourse, noncoital sex relations leading to orgasm, and occasional homosexuality—are not really unethical, since they do not needlessly harm their participants nor anyone else. But many of the conventional and highly legal sex activities in our culture—such as a husband's insisting that his wife [satisfy] him without his taking any real pains to satisfy her or a wife's refusing to divorce a husband for whom she has little desire or liking—are actually quite immoral.

A genuinely humanistic view of ethics would indicate that people are only wrong or immoral when they *gratuitously* harm themselves and/or injure others; and that this is true for sexual and nonsexual actions. A humanistic outlook would perhaps even more importantly hold that even when he is indubitably wrong, no person is to be damned or condemned for anything he thinks, says, or does. His deeds may very well be foolish or immoral, but he is never a louse for performing them. If he works very hard against his biologically based and socially inculcated tendencies to be an arrant, overgeneralizing, bigoted, religious-minded blamer of himself and other humans, he can enable himself to lead a much more satisfying sex, love, marital, and general existence.

MONOGAMY: A CRITIQUE

John McMurtry

"Remove away that black'ning church
Remove away that marriage hearse
Remove away that man of blood
You'll quite remove the ancient curse."
                                            WILLIAM BLAKE

I

Almost all of us have entered or will one day enter a specifically standardized form of monogamous marriage. This cultural requirement is so very basic to our existence that we accept it for most part as a kind of intractable given: dictated by the laws of God, Nature, Government and Good Sense all at once. Though it is perhaps unusual for a social practice to be so promiscuously underwritten, we generally find comfort rather than curiosity in this fact and seldom wonder how something could be divinely inspired, biologically determined, coerced and reasoned out all at the same time. We simply take for granted.

Those in society who are officially charged with the thinking function with regard to such matters are no less responsible for this uncritical acceptance than the man on the street. The psychoanalyst traditionally regards our form of marriage as a necessary restraint on the anarchic id and no more to be queried than civilization itself. The lawyer is as undisposed to questioning the practice as he is to criticizing the principle of private property (this is appropriate, as I shall later point out). The churchman formally perceives the relationship between man and wife to be as inviolable and insusceptible to question as the relationship between the institution he works for and the Christ. The sociologist standardly accepts the formalized bonding of heterosexual pairs as the indispensable basis of social order and perhaps a societal universal. The politician is as incapable of challenging it as he is the virtue of his own continued holding of office. And the philosopher (at least the English-speaking philosopher), as with most issues of socially controversial or sexual dimensions, ignores the question almost altogether.

Even those irreverent adulterers and unmarried couples who would seem to be challenging the institution in the most basic possible way, in practice, tend merely to mimic its basic structure in unofficial form. The coverings of sanctity, taboo and cultural habit continue to hold them with the grip of public clothes.

II

"Monogamy" means, literally, "one marriage." But it would be wrong to suppose that this phrase tells us much about our particular species of official wedlock. The greatest obstacle to the adequate understanding of our monogamy institution has been the failure to identify clearly and systematically the full complex of principles it involves. There are four such principles, each carrying enormous restrictive force and together constituting a massive social control mechanism that has never, so far as I know, been fully schematized.

To come straight to the point, the four principles in question are as follows:

1. *The partners are required to enter a formal contractual relation: (a)* whose establishment demands a specific official participant, certain conditions of the contractors (legal age, no blood ties, etc.) and a standard set of procedures; *(b)* whose governing terms are uniform for all and exactly prescribed by law; and *(c)* whose dissolution may only be legally effected by the decision of state representatives.

The ways in which this elaborate principle of contractual requirement are importantly restrictive are obvious. One may not enter into a marriage union without entering into a contract presided over by a state-investured official.[1] One may not set any of the terms of the contractual relationship by which one is bound for life. And one cannot dissolve the contract without legal action and costs, court proceedings and in many places actual legislation. (The one and only contract in all English-speaking law that is not dissoluble by the consent of the contracting parties.) The extent of control here—over the most intimate and putatively "loving" relationships in all social intercourse—is so great as to be difficult to catalogue without exciting in oneself a sense of disbelief.

Lest it be thought there is always the real option of entering a common law relationship free of such encumbrances, it should be noted that: *(a)* these relationships themselves are subject to state regulation, though of a less imposing sort; and (much more important) *(b)* there are very formidable selective pressures against common law partnerships such as employment and job discrimination, exclusion from housing and lodging facilities, special legal disablements,[2] loss of social and moral status (consider such phrases as "living in sin," "make her an honest woman," etc.), family shame and embarrassment, and so on.

2. *The number of partners involved in the marriage must be two and only two* (as opposed to three, four, five or any of the almost countless other possibilities of intimate union).

This second principle of our specific form of monogamy (the concept of "one mar-

---

[1] Any person who presides over a marriage and is not authorized by law to do so is guilty of a criminal offense and is subject to several years imprisonment (e.g., Canadian Criminal Code, Sec. 258).

[2] For example, offspring are illegitimate, neither wife nor children are legal heirs, and husband has no right of access or custody should separation occur.

riage," it should be pointed out, is consistent with any number of participating partners) is perhaps the most important and restrictive of the four principles we are considering. Not only does it confine us to just *one* possibility out of an enormous range, but it confines us to that single possibility which involves the *least* number of people, two. It is difficult to conceive of a more thoroughgoing mechanism for limiting extended social union and intimacy. The fact that this monolithic restriction seems so "natural" to us (if it were truly "natural" of course, there would be no need for its rigorous cultural prescription by everything from severe criminal law [3] to ubiquitous housing regulations) simply indicates the extent to which its hold is implanted in our social structure. It is the institutional basis of what I will call the "binary frame of sexual consciousness," a frame through which all our heterosexual relationships are typically viewed ("two's company, three's a crowd") and in light of which all larger circles of intimacy seem almost inconceivable.[4]

3. *No person may participate in more than one marriage at a time or during a lifetime* (unless the previous marriage has been officially dissolved by, normally, one partner's death or successful divorce).

Violation of this principle is, of course, a criminal offense (bigamy) which is punishable by a considerable term in prison. Of various general regulations of our marriage institution it has experienced the most significant modification: not indeed in principle, but in the extent of flexibility of its "escape hatch" of divorce. The ease with which this escape hatch is opened has increased considerably in the past few years (the grounds for divorce being more permissive than previously) and it is in this regard most of all that the principles of our marriage institution have undergone formal alteration. That is, in plumbing rather than substance.

4. *No married person may engage in any sexual relationship with any person whatever other than the marriage partner.*

Although a consummated sexual act with another person alone constitutes an act of adultery, lesser forms of sexual and erotic relationships [5] may also constitute grounds

---

[3] "Any kind of conjugal union with more than one person at the same time, whether or not it is by law recognized as a binding form of marriage—is guilty of an indictable offence and is liable to imprisonment for five years" (Canadian Criminal Code, Sec. 257, [1][a][ii]). Part 2 of the same section adds: "Where an accused is charged with an offence under this section, no averment or proof of the method by which the alleged relationship was entered into, agreed to or consented to is necessary in the indictment or upon the trial of the accused, nor is it necessary upon the trial to prove that the persons who are alleged to have entered into the relationship had or intended to have sexual intercourse."

(Here and elsewhere, I draw examples from Canadian criminal law. There is no reason to suspect the Canadian code is eccentric in these instances.)

[4] Even the sexual revolutionary Wilhelm Reich seems constrained within the limits of this "binary frame." Thus he says (my emphasis): "Nobody has the right to prohibit his or her partner from entering a temporary or lasting sexual relationship with someone else. He has only the right *either to withdraw or to win the partner back.*" (Wilhelm Reich, *The Sexual Revolution,* trans. by T. P. Wolfe [New York: Farrar, Straus & Giroux, 1970], p. 28.) The possibility of sexual partners extending their union to include the other loved party as opposed to one partner having either to "win" against this third party or to "withdraw" altogether does not seem even to occur to Reich.

[5] I will be using "sexual" and "erotic" interchangeably throughout the paper.

for divorce (i.e., cruelty) and are generally proscribed as well by informal social convention and taboo. In other words, the fourth and final principle of our marriage institution involves not only a prohibition of sexual intercourse per se outside one's wedlock (this term deserves pause) but a prohibition of all one's erotic relations whatever outside this bond. The penalties for violation here are as various as they are severe, ranging from permanent loss of spouse, children, chattel, and income to job dismissal and social ostracism. In this way, possibly the most compelling natural force towards expanded intimate relations with others [6] is strictly confined within the narrowest possible circle for (barring delinquency) the whole of adult life. The sheer weight and totality of this restriction is surely one of the great wonders of all historical institutional control.

III

With all established institutions, apologetics for perpetuation are never wanting. Thus it is with our form of monogamous marriage.

Perhaps the most celebrated justification over the years has proceeded from a belief in a Supreme Deity who secretly utters sexual and other commands to privileged human representatives. Almost as well known a line of defence has issued from a conviction, similarly confident, that the need for some social regulation of sexuality demonstrates the need for our specific type of two-person wedlock. Although these have been important justifications in the sense of being very widely supported, they are not—having other grounds than reasons—susceptible to treatment here.

If we put aside such arguments, we are left I think with two major claims. The first is that our form of monogamous marriage promotes a profound affection between the partners which is not only of great worth in itself but invaluable as a sanctuary from the pressures of outside society. Since, however, there are no secure grounds whatever for supposing that such "profound affection" is not at least as easily achievable by any number of *other* marriage forms (i.e., forms which differ in one or more of the four principles), this justification conspicuously fails to perform the task required of it.

The second major claim for the defence is that monogamy provides a specially loving context for child upbringing. However here again there are no grounds at all for concluding that it does so as, or any more, effectively than other possible forms of marriage (the only alternative type of upbringing to which it has apparently been shown to be superior is nonfamily institutional upbringing, which of course is not relevant to the present discussion). Furthermore, the fact that at least half the span of a normal monogamous marriage *involves no child-upbringing at all* is disastrously overlooked

[6] It is worth noting here that: *(a)* man has by nature the most "open" sexual instinct—year-round operativeness and variety of stimuli—of all the species (except perhaps the dolphin); and *(b)* it is a principle of human needs in general that maximum satisfaction involves regular variation in the form of the need-object.

here, as is the reinforcing fact that there is no reference to or mention of the quality of child-upbringing in any of the prescriptions connected with it.

In brief, the second major justification of our particular type of wedlock scents somewhat too strongly of red herring to pursue further.

There is, it seems, little to recommend the view that monogamy specially promotes "profound affection" between the partners or a "loving context" for child-upbringing. Such claims are simply without force. On the other hand, there are several aspects to the logic and operation of the four principles of this institution which suggest that it actually *inhibits* the achievement of these desiderata. Far from uniquely abetting the latter, it militates against them. In these ways:

(1) Centralized official control of marriage (which the Church gradually achieved through the mechanism of Canon Law after the Fall of the Roman Empire [7] in one of the greatest seizures of social power in history) necessarily alienates the partners from full responsibility for and freedom in their relationship. "Profound closeness" between the partners—or least an area of it—is thereby expropriated rather than promoted, and "sanctuary" from the pressures of outside society prohibited rather than fostered.

(2) Limitation of the marriage bond to two people necessarily restricts, in perhaps the most unilateral possible way consistent with offspring survival, the number of adult sources of affection, interest, material support and instruction for the young. The "loving context for child-upbringing" is thereby dessicated rather than nourished: providing the structural conditions for such notorious and far-reaching problems as *(a)* sibling rivalry for scarce adult attention,[8] and *(b)* parental oppression through exclusive monopoly of the child's means of life.[9]

(3) Formal exclusion of all others from erotic contact with the marriage partner systematically promotes conjugal insecurity, jealousy and alienation by:

(a) Officially underwriting a literally totalitarian expectation of sexual confinement on the part of one's husband or wife: which expectation is, *ceteris paribus,* inevitably more subject to anxiety and disappointment than one less extreme in its demand and/or cultural-juridical backing; [10]

---

[7] "Roman Law had no power of intervening in the formation of marriages and there was no legal form of marriage. . . . Marriage was a matter of simple private agreement and divorce was a private transaction" (Havelock Ellis, *Studies in the Psychology of Sex* [New York: Random House, 1963], Vol. II, Part 3, p. 429).

[8] The dramatic reduction of sibling rivalry through an increased number of adults in the house is a phenomenon which is well known in contemporary domestic communes.

[9] One of the few other historical social relationships I can think of in which persons hold thoroughly exclusive monopoly over other persons' means of life is slavery. Thus, as with another's slave, it is a criminal offence "to receive" or "harbour" another's child without "right of possession" (Canadian Criminal Code, Sec. 250).

[10] Certain cultures, for example, permit extramarital sexuality by married persons with friends, guests, or in-laws with no reported consequences of jealousy. From such evidence, one is led to speculate that the intensity and extent of jealousy at a partner's extramarital sexual involvement is in direct proportion to the severity of the accepted cultural regulations against such involvements. In short such regulations do not prevent jealousy so much as effectively engender it.

(b) Requiring so complete a sexual isolation of the marriage partners that should one violate the fidelity code the other is left alone and susceptible to a sense of fundamental deprivation and resentment;

(c) Stipulating such a strict restraint of sexual energies that there are habitual violations of the regulation: which violations *qua* violations are frequently if not always attended by (i) wilful deception and reciprocal suspicion about the occurrence or quality of the extramarital relationship, (ii) anxiety and fear on both sides of permanent estrangement from partner and family, and/or (iii) overt and covert antagonism over the prohibited act in both offender (who feels "trapped") and offended (who feels "betrayed").

The disadvantages of the four principles of monogamous marriage do not, however, end with inhibiting the very effects they are said to promote. There are further shortcomings:

(1) The restriction of marriage union to two partners necessarily prevents the strengths of larger groupings. Such advantages as the following are thereby usually ruled out.

(a) The security, range and power of larger socioeconomic units;

(b) The epistemological and emotional substance, variety and scope of more pluralist interactions;

(c) The possibility of extra-domestic freedom founded on more adult providers and upbringers as well as more broadly based circles of intimacy.

(2) The sexual containment and isolation which the four principles together require variously stimulates such social malaises as:

(a) Destructive aggression (which notoriously results from sexual frustration);

(b) Apathy, frustration and dependence within the marriage bond;

(c) Lack of spontaneity, bad faith and distance in relationships without the marriage bond;

(d) Sexual phantasizing, perversion, fetishism, prostitution and pornography in the adult population as a whole.[11]

Taking such things into consideration, it seems difficult to lend credence to the view that the four principles of our form of monogamous marriage constitute a structure beneficial either to the marriage partners themselves or to their offspring (or indeed to anyone else). One is moved to seek for some other ground of the institution, some ground that lurks beneath the reach of our conventional apprehensions.

IV

The ground of our marriage institution, the essential principle that underwrites all four restrictions, is this: *the maintenance by one man or woman of the effective right to exclude indefinitely all others from erotic access to the conjugal partner.*

---

[11] It should not be forgotten that at the same time marriage excludes marital partners from sexual contact with others, it necessarily excludes those others from sexual contact with marital partners. Walls face two ways.

The first restriction creates, elaborates on, and provides for the enforcement of this right to exclude. And the second, third and fourth restrictions together ensure that the said right to exclude is—respectively—not cooperative, not simultaneously or sequentially distributed, and not permissive of even casual exception.

In other words, the four restrictions of our form of monogamous marriage together constitute a state-regulated, indefinite and exclusive ownership by two individuals of one another's sexual powers. Marriage is simply a form of private property.[12]

That our form of monogamous marriage is when the confusing layers of sanctity, apologetic and taboo are cleared away another species of private property should not surprise us.[13] The history of the institution is so full of suggestive indicators—dowries, inheritance, property alliances, daughter sales (of which women's wedding rings are a carry-over) bride exchanges, legitimacy and illegitimacy—that it is difficult not to see some intimate connections between marital and ownership ties. We are better able still to apprehend the ownership essence of our marriage institution, when in addition we consider:

(a) That until recently almost the only way to secure official dissolution of consummated marriage was to be able to demonstrate violation of one or both partner's sexual ownership (i.e., adultery);

(b) That the imperative of premarital chastity is tantamount to a demand for retrospective sexual ownership by the eventual marriage partner;

(c) That successful sexual involvement with a married person is prosecutable as an expropriation of ownership—"alienation of affections"—which is restituted by cash payment;

(d) That the incest taboo is an iron mechanism which protects the conjugal ownership of sexual properties: both the husband's and wife's from the access of affectionate offspring and the offsprings' (who themselves are future marriage partners) from access of siblings and parents;[14]

(e) That the language of the marriage ceremony is the language of exclusive possession ("take," "to have and to hold," "forsaking all others and keeping you only unto

---

[12] Those aspects of marriage law which seem to fall outside the pale of sexual property holding—for example, provisions for divorce if the husband fails to provide or is convicted of a felony or is an alcoholic—may themselves be seen as simply prescriptive characterizations of the sort of sexual property which the marriage partner must retain in order to retain satisfactory conjugal status: a kind of permanent warranty of the "good working order" of the sexual possession.

What constitutes the "good working order" of the conjugal possession is, of course, different in the case of the husband and in the case of the wife: an *asymmetry* within the marriage institution which, I gather, women's liberation movements are anxious to eradicate.

[13] I think it is instructive to think of even the nonlegal aspects of marriage, for example, its sentiments as essentially private property structured. Thus the preoccupation of those experiencing conjugal sentiments with expressing how much "my very own," "my precious," the other is: with expressing, that is, how valuable and inviolable the ownership is and will ramain.

[14] I think the secret to the long-mysterious incest taboo may well be the fact that in all its forms it protects sexual property: not only conjugal (as indicated above) but paternal and tribal as well. This crucial line of thought, however, requires extended separate treatment.

him/her," etc.), not to mention the proprietary locutions associated with the marital relationship (e.g., "he's mine," "she belongs to him," "keep to your own husband," "wife stealer," "possessive husband," etc.).

V

Of course, it would be remarkable if marriage in our society was not a relationship akin to private property. In our socioeconomic system we relate to virtually everything of value by individual ownership: by, that is, the effective right to exclude others from the thing concerned.[15] That we do so as well with perhaps the most highly valued thing of all—the sexual partners' sexuality—is only to be expected. Indeed it would probably be an intolerable strain on our entire social structure if we did otherwise.

This line of thought deserves pursuit. The real secret of our form of monogamous marriage is not that it functionally provides for the needs of adults who love one another or the children they give birth to, but that it serves the maintenance of our present social system. It is an institution which is indispensable to the persistence of the capitalist order,[16] in the following ways:

(1) A basic principle of current social relations is that some people legally acquire the use of other people's personal powers from which they may exclude other members of society. This system operates in the workplace (owners and hirers of all types contractually acquire for their exclusive use workers' regular labour powers) and in the family (husbands and wives contractually acquire for their exclusive use their partner's sexual properties). A conflict between the structures of these primary relations—as would obtain were there a suspension of the restrictions governing our form of monogamous marriage—might well undermine the systemic coherence of present social intercourse.

(2) The fundamental relation between individuals and things which satisfy their needs is, in our present society, that each individual has or does not have the effective right to exclude other people from the thing in question.[17] A rudimentary need is that for sexual relationship(s). Therefore the object of this need must be related to the one who needs it as owner or not owner (i.e., via marriage or not-marriage, or approximations thereto) if people's present relationship to what they need is to retain—again—systemic coherence.

(3) A necessary condition for the continued existence of the present social formation is that its members feel powerful motivation to gain favorable positions in it. But

---

[15] Sometimes—as with political patronage, criminal possession, *de facto* privileges and so forth—a *power* to exclude others exists with no corresponding "right" (just as sometimes a right to exclude exists with no corresponding power). Properly speaking, thus, I should here use the phrase "power to exclude," which covers "effective right to exclude" as well as all nonjuridical enablements of this sort.

[16] It is no doubt indispensable as well—in some form or other—to any private property order. Probably (if we take the history of Western society as our data base) the more thoroughgoing and developed the private property formation is, the more total the sexual ownership prescribed by the marriage institution.

[17] Things in unlimited supply—like, presently, oxygen—are not of course related to people in this way.

such social ambition is heavily dependent on the preservation of exclusive monogamy in that:

(a) The latter confines the discharge of primordial sexual energies to a single unalterable partner and thus typically compels the said energies to seek alternative outlet, such as business or professional success; [18]

(b) The exclusive marriage necessarily reduces the sexual relationships available to any one person to absolute (nonzero) minimum, a unilateral promotion of sexual shortage which in practice renders hierarchical achievement essential as an economic and "display" means for securing scarce partners.[19]

(4) Because the exclusive marriage necessarily and dramatically reduces the possibilities of sexual-love relationships, it thereby promotes the existing economic system by:

(a) Rendering extreme economic self-interest—the motivational basis of the capitalistic process—less vulnerable to altruistic subversion;

(b) Disciplining society's members into the habitual repression of natural impulse required for long-term performance of repetitive and arduous work tasks;

(c) Developing a complex of suppressed sexual desires to which sales techniques may effectively apply in creating those new consumer wants which provide indispensable outlets for ever-increasing capital funds.

(5) The present form of marriage is of fundamental importance to:

(a) The continued relative powerlessness of the individual family: which, with larger numbers would constitute a correspondingly increased command of social power;

(b) The continued high demand for homes, commodities and services: which, with the considerable economies of scale that extended unions would permit, would otherwise falter;

(c) The continued strict necessity for adult males to sell their labour power and adult women to remain at home (or vice versa): which strict necessity would diminish as the economic base of the family unit extended;

(d) The continued immense pool of unsatisfied sexual desires and energies in the population at large: without which powerful interests and institutions would lose much of their conventional appeal and force; [20]

---

[18] This is, of course, a Freudian or quasi-Freudian claim. "Observation of daily life shows us," says Freud, "that most persons direct a very tangible part of their sexual motive powers to their professional or business activities" (Sigmund Freud, *Dictionary of Psychoanalysis,* ed. by Nandor Fodor and Frank Gaynor [New York: Fawcett Publications, Premier Paperback, 1966], p. 139).

[19] It might be argued that exclusive marriage also protects those physically less attractive persons who—in an "open" situation—might be unable to secure any sexual partnership at all. The force of this claim depends, I think, on improperly continuing to posit the very principle of exclusiveness which the "open" situation rules out (e.g., in the latter situation, x might be less attractive to y than z is and yet x not be rejected, any more than at present an intimate friend is rejected who is less talented than another intimate friend).

[20] The sexual undercurrents of corporate advertisements, religious systems, racial propaganda and so on is too familiar to dwell on here.

(e) The continued profitable involvement of lawyers, priests and state officials in the jurisdictions of marriage and divorce and the myriad official practices and proceedings connected thereto.[21]

VI

If our marriage institution is a linchpin of our present social structure, then a break-down in this institution would seem to indicate a breakdown in our social structure. On the face of it, the marriage institution is breaking down—enormously increased divorce rates, nonmarital sexual relationships, wife-swapping, the Playboy philosophy, and communes. Therefore one might be led by the appearance of things to anticipate a profound alteration in the social system.

But it would be a mistake to underestimate the tenacity of an established order or to overestimate the extent of change in our marriage institution. Increased divorce rates merely indicate the widening of a traditional escape hatch. Nonmarital relationships imitate and culminate in the marital mold. Wife-swapping presupposes ownership, as the phrase suggests. The Playboy philosophy is merely the view that if one has the money one has the right to be titillated, the commercial call to more fully exploit a dynamic sector of capital investment. And communes—the most hopeful phenomenon —almost nowhere offer a *praxis* challenge to private property in sexuality. It may be changing. But history, as the old man puts it, weighs like a nightmare on the brains of the living.

COMMUNES AS EXPERIMENTS IN HUMAN AND SEXUAL RELATIONSHIPS

Carl Rogers

One cannot write . . . on modern marriage without discussing communes, which often provide alternatives to conventional marriage. Yet I approach this [topic] with an uneasiness based on several facts and feelings.
1. The two-to-three thousand communes and intentional communities in this coun-try—the number is only a combination of estimates—keep growing, changing, clos-ing, and starting, with a rapidity which immediately outdates anything which can be written.
2. The variety of communes is so enormous that any general statement one might make is simultaneously true, for some, and false, for others.

---

[21] It is also possible that exclusive marriage protects the adult-youth power structure in the manner outlined on p. 323.

3. A number of excellent books have recently been written about communes, and it seems presumptuous to write only brief[ly] about these diversified groups.
4. Most important is the fact that I have not lived in a commune and hence lack the basic inner experience . . . To offset this, I have been helped by two people, Natalie R. Fuchs and Robert J. Willis, who served as eyes and ears for me.

The Human Relationships as Focus

Naturally I will make no attempt to cover all aspects of these communal groups. There is the economic problem—how to survive. There is the ideological flavor—mystical, behavioristic, wilderness pioneering, an emphasis on women's lib, the search for a higher consciousness, for nonviolent revolution. There are various degrees of organizational philosophy, from wildly hippie to philosophical anarchism to quite strictly ordered. There are a variety of problems in relating to the neighboring community, whether the group lives in an isolated forest or in the heart of a large city. None of these will I touch on . . .

My interest will be . . . to explore the ways of coping with marital, sexual, and other interpersonal relationships in the communal groups. I shall do this in a way which I believe is not identifying of any particular person or commune. Most of it I can do on the basis of taped interviews or from observations by persons whom I know or trust or from letters and reports writted by participants.

Some General Remarks About Communes

Before I begin this undertaking, I should like to clear away certain misapprehensions which may exist in the mind of the reader.

In the first place, communes are not gathering places for "hippies," as that term is understood by the public. They *are* an attempt to live with a set of values different from that which exists in the ordinary community, and frequently this is apparent in their unique and different clothing. But the people quoted in this [article] come from groups made up of people like these: a former industrial engineer, a social worker, a corporation executive, a research scientist, a clinical psychologist, a former computer programmer, a divinity student, a former CIA agent, a person skilled in data processing, a carpenter, an artist, assorted graduates of Radcliffe, Swarthmore, Harvard, and other colleges. Here is a fraction of our intelligentsia, trying to create a revolutionary new world in the midst of the "Establishment" world. They are to be viewed in this light.

A second comment is that most present-day communes—not all—lean toward some degree of an anarchistic philosophy. Since to most people this is synonymous with chaos, lawlessness, and terrorism, a word might be said as to its real philosophical meaning. It rests on a base of self-determination. It involves the rejection of all forms of coercive control and authority, whether governmental or religious. Bertrand Russell caught its spirit when he said of another, "He was inclined to anarchism; he hated system and organization and uniformity." Many commune members would subscribe to this.

In many ways they are, in their philosophy, not unlike the early Christians as described in Acts 2:44–46: "And all that believed were together, and had all things in common; and sold their possessions and goods and parted them to all men, as every man had need . . . and did eat their meat with gladness and singleness of heart." Not all communes give up property to this extent, but many of them go a long way in communal sharing, as one other indication of the fact that they have turned their backs very definitely on the materialistic, competitive culture in which they were raised.

Perhaps the best brief definition comes from the *Merriam-Webster New International Dictionary* (an older edition): "In its more practical forms anarchism . . . [has] for its ideal the formation of small autonomous communes, the members of which respect one another's independence while they unite to resist aggression. At its best it stands for a society made orderly by good manners rather than by law, in which each person produces according to his powers and receives according to his needs." I believe many commune members today would subscribe to this as a goal, while admitting they often fall far short.

In this respect they are very different from the Utopian communes of the last century in this country, in which there was usually a unifying religious ideology, a strong and charismatic leader, and a group of followers whose lives were regulated. In an interesting study of these older communes (Kantor, 1970) it was found that certain items separated sharply the more permanent from the less permanent. (Obviously permanence is not the only criterion by which they might have been judged.)

The outstanding difference between the more and less permanent was that the first practiced either free love or celibacy, while the less permanent did not. In other words, in the lasting communes sexual behavior was clearly decided either by the members or for them. Ranking after these as characteristic of the more permanent were no compensation for communal labor, communal work efforts on a daily routine, daily group meetings, and celebration of special community occasions. It may be of interest to bear these in mind as we examine today's communes.

Nine Brief Examples

I should like now to plunge you into some of the variety which exists. Let me try to give some feeling for the great diversity of groups which are classed as communes by describing a number of them in one brief paragraph each. I have purposely omitted the names of the groups, so that instead of immediately categorizing them, you will be more inclined to imagine what it would be like to live in such a group. All of them are real communes which exist or have existed until very recently.

1. There is a rural commune of eleven adults and six children which functions pretty much as a family. The work gets done, purposes get implemented without any particular organization, just as in the average family. It is not self-supporting and some of the members work for short periods in the city to help balance the budget. Food stamps are also used. No one is in authority. The children are cared for unevenly, but have the advantages of an extended family. The adults are mostly paired, but sexual relationships outside a pair are not prohibited. Interpersonal difficulties are worked out (usually) by very frank interchanges in the group or between the parties involved.

2. One commune "family" is composed of about a dozen professional men and women (and one child) living in a house in the city. They are remodeling the house to give every person more privacy. They all—with the exception of the man who is remodeling the house—hold jobs in the city. They share the communal work. The couples are paired, but there is experimenting outside the pairs, with the knowledge of the group. Encounter group procedures are often used in the handling of interpersonal tensions. Nearly all have had some experience in such groups. The neighbors, at first suspicious, have become much more accepting.

3. A semirural commune was open to anyone who wished to come or stay. Individuals could do whatever they wished in the way of work, or nothing. Drugs were heavily used. The living and sanitary conditions became impossible, and it was eventually closed as a public health menace. The community was enraged by it.

4. There is a coed house near a college, its dozen or more inhabitants mostly students, which has lasted eight years. It has been agreed that all members find their sexual companions outside the house. All work is shared, cooking, etc., regardless of sex. The relationships are similar to brother-sister ties. The aim is to learn to live with one another as human beings. Because these are students, there is considerable turnover, but a great loyalty develops. Meetings are held to deal with tensions which arise. They make much of occasional celebrations or house "rituals," which seem to promote closeness.

5. An urban group is one of those trying the experiment of group marriage, with three men and three women involved. The house is efficiently run. Some work in the city. All come from educated, mostly WASP backgrounds. The group sexuality brought problems, and they finally developed a chart, which shows which man and woman sleep together each night. (The sleeping does not always involve sex.) There is one night per week "free." For some reason the interpersonal interactions, though intended to have an encounter flavor, are often biting and cynical and are aimed at the other person's weak spots. It is far from being a harmonious "marriage."

6. A large group of related communes, with a history going back more than four hundred years, are all farming communities ranging from fifty to a hundred and thirty

members in each. Monogamy is the definite rule. Pacifism has been deep-seated as a policy over the centuries. Religion is a unifying force. Higher education is scorned. There are two leaders in each commune, the preacher and the work boss. Both are elected. I am sure they would be shocked to be included in this list, but they are definitely communal, eating all meals together and sharing all goods in common. They have separate homes or apartments. They have a deep-seated belief in their permanence, strengthened by the fact that they have endured, though expelled from one country after another (including for a time the U.S.) because of the refusal to serve in the armed forces.

7. Another is a clean, orderly, highly organized commune, numbering thirty men and women (only two children), in which everyone must earn a certain number of work credits per day. In order to get *all* the work done, more credit is given for the jobs which people tend to avoid. Some members are also employed outside for two-month periods but they tend to dislike this. Their aim is to build a viable alternative to capitalism (an aim which they take very seriously) and to alter their personal behavior in ways they desire. At first, three planners made all the significant decisions, but gradually the group is moving toward operating by consensus. It started with a small number of individuals (ten) with conventional marital standards. Now nearly every member has a roommate of the opposite sex. An important concern of the group is sexual freedom. Good order is the hallmark of this commune.

8. A sizable number of communes, mostly urban, scattered throughout the country, are bound together by three strong threads: a highly charismatic leader; frequent ideologically based group sessions whose purpose is to attack each person's defenses; and the fact that they have all been drug addicts. The organization is definitely hierarchical and rules are strict. Members are promoted to more responsible posts when they have, in the view of the group and the officials, earned them.

9. A rural commune, limited to twenty-five, is bound together by a combination of Eastern mystical beliefs. Unlike most communes, they focus on the individual rather than the group. There is a great deal of silent meditation and contemplation, though each week there is an ecstatic ritual dance. Work is shared, each member signing up for six "chores." Individuals are a bit remote from each other and any problems are worked out individually. Some members are married, some not. They draw on a number of gurus, but depend on no one guru. Each summer they import a number of these leaders, to absorb their teachings in two-week sessions.[1]

. . .

[1] For those who must know the sources of these descriptions, here they are: (1) High Ridge Farm, described by Houriet [Getting Back Together] in Book II; (2) an East Coast commune, visited and information supplied by Natalie Fuchs; (3) Morningstar, now defunct, described in Gustaitis [Turning On] Chapter 8; (4) in the Northwest, visited and information supplied by Robert J. Willis; (5) Harrad West, from Houriet, Book VI; (6) the Hutterites, described by Allard [The Hutterites—Plain People of the West]; (7) Twin Oaks, modeled after Skinner's *Walden II*, from Houriet, Book VII; (8) Synanon, perhaps best described by Yablonsky [The Tunnel Back: Synanon]; (9) Lama, from Houriet, Book VIII.

Relationships Involving Sexual Partners

Because many communes are departing most sharply from societal norms in the area of sexual relationships, it is not surprising that some of the most troubling problems arise in regard to partnerships, triads, and other arrangements, whether temporary or more lasting.

It would be possible to give many examples of different individuals with different sexual and partnership problems. Yet so much is contained in an interview with Lois, a member of a city communal group, that I believe it may be more profitable to see many facets of these issues through her eyes, as she has *experienced* them in her own relationships. It is interesting that in spite of all her experiences, she thinks of herself as quite "straight." For the next several pages I will let Lois speak for herself, with no interruption except subheadings to indicate the topics to which she addresses herself.

Lois is about thirty years old, professionally trained, from a middle-class background. She has been married and divorced and has one young son. She has been in encounter groups and has led them. She was part of a summer community group which was something of a preparation for her life in the commune. After her divorce she was threatened by deep commitments, and though she felt very close to Boris, a man who was much involved with her, she did not want to commit herself. But she and Boris entered the commune together, where they have lived for a year with approximately fifteen people. The interviewer raised the question as to whether jealousy was ever a problem, and Lois's initial denial led to a deep exploration of the many aspects of man-woman and other relationships in the commune.

JEALOUSY OF PARTNER'S "AFFAIRS"

LOIS: Male-female jealousy? I don't think that is much of an issue here. I am trying to think . . . I certainly feel jealous when Boris makes love with somebody else. I am really perverse in this sense, in that I would rather know about it and I would rather know *all* about it, including the details, and somehow that makes me feel better, if only in the end I am reassured that he loves me more and he would rather make love to me. But if I know about it, I am more reassured; it's funny though, he's just the opposite. But such things are pretty open here.

INTERVIEWER: Is that part of the group norm that it's open if there's any change in male-female relationships within the house?

LOIS: Well, just let me say, we are definitely middle class. We're not like hippie freaks at all. We're much closer to the monogamous and cheating couples in the suburbs. For example, about a month or two ago Boris and I decided we had been monogamous for a long period of time, but it was becoming sort of destructive and we were taking advantage of each other and feeling obligated to each other, and it wasn't feeling good, and we decided we were going to end, at least for a while, the monogamy of our relationship. And we talked about it in our house meeting. Particularly since he really felt like going out and balling some chicks. Picking them up and balling them, and that was his thing, but that's just not my thing at all. I'd rather make love to somebody that I am close to, so that likelihood was much more for me in the house, you know. So we talked about it in the house meeting, and the main question that came up was, "Well, you know, are you going to be mad?" If Enrico said, "Well, I'm going to make love with Lois, and you know, you better have those feelings about me." Well, it wasn't like the minute that the door was opened everybody just rushed around, you know, and reshuffled themselves.

THE HURT INVOLVED IN SHIFTING PARTNERS

We're pretty straight. There is a norm that you can sleep with anyone you want to here in the house. In fact, I can't think of anybody who at least intellectually speaking doesn't agree with that, but what makes me laugh so is that people think there won't be any problems about it. That you can take on a norm like that intellectually and say, "Oh fine, this is just what we happen to do." There is a problem every time. Someone feels hurt or someone feels threatened or someone feels less important. But I have never once felt it has produced a bummer, you know, or it has set people far, far apart.

INTERVIEWER: Somehow you have managed to work most of that out . . . ?

LOIS: Yeah. It also isn't all that frequent. Most people here, when they're in a relationship, they're in that relationship, or they are being single and they are making it with everybody or anybody, you know. It's not like after dinner—you know, I think people sometimes fantasize that after dinner everyone looks around the table and says, "Well, I guess I'll sleep with so-and-so tonight," and just trundle up to bed. It isn't like that.

THE POSSIBILITY OF AN ORGY

We've always talked about having an orgy, you know, just a big group thing, but we've never done it yet. I'm sure we probably will. We've had things that verge on it, but we've never had just a big group with everybody screwing everybody else but we probably will, because there's enough in everybody's head and I think it would be fun, you know. Especially being a girl. I think that would really be nifty—all night long, you know (*chuckling heartily*).

LOVE BETWEEN FEMALES—AND JEALOUSY

Well, I'll tell you one thing that's different, and this has to do with the only time I have really felt jealous, since living here in the house, and that's intimacy. That's a thing. You know, you become closer and closer to people and it's more and more natural to make love with them to express it physically and I've felt that with women here in the house and particularly one woman—I'm very close to her—and a couple of times have made love with her and another guy—once because I was a little drunk and another time because I really wanted to do that with Boris—I mean he didn't have any idea this was coming. We just sort of decided to go to bed together and we went and got into Boris's bed. That's been probably the newest and most exciting sexual experience I've had here, in really feeling very much like wanting to express myself physically to another woman. It's just amazing, you know, just the experience of rubbing another body like your own. It's not a heavy thing, but it freaks me a little bit.

That one night I discovered an awful lot about it. I could tell Jan really wanted to sleep with me. I literally locked myself in the bathroom. I just couldn't decide, you know, whether or not that felt *safe* to me. And I took on this very passive role, which I don't like to think of myself as doing. It was really interesting—it turned out to be just like a male-female relationship, you know. Then at other times I've been more aggressive and she's been more passive. It's really sort of an interesting experience and then you get into jealousy. Like one time I thought maybe she had made love with another girl and I really felt bad. And then it turned out she hadn't, but it was a funny feeling to have.

JEALOUSY OF CLOSENESS

The other thing is Boris. He has some interesting feelings about that, like *really* being turned on by it and enjoying it. It's sort of like being a masturbatory fantasy thing with him, feeling not jealous of the sexuality between Jan and me but the *closeness,* and his feelings are resentful of that. Jealousy has been a hard thing in that way too because he's felt a lot of times jealousies of my relationships with someone else. He's sort of possessive, and he's gotten jealous of the closeness of other people too, when I like to spend time with them, instead of just spending all my time with him. But we've worked that through pretty well. I *think* pretty well.

WAYS OF DEALING WITH SUCH PROBLEMS

INTERVIEWER: You've worked that through mostly by yourselves, or in the group . . . ?

LOIS: Well, I like it better to work it through ourselves. I don't really have any belief at all that anybody in this house understands my relationship with Boris. I really don't, you know. I have this feeling people don't know him very well, and that he is the kind of person that is there on a one-to-one level because he is so sort of involved with me. He has sort of focused all his attention and energy on me and he hasn't gotten to know other people that closely. Therefore people haven't gotten to know him that well either.

I think people misjudge our relationship a lot. We fight a lot and we hit each other and we scream and then we make up, you know. That feels really good to me, but there isn't anything else like that going on around here. That sort of gets it out for me, and then I feel good and loving. But I think it really sort of frightens other people. They don't understand that and don't know what's happening in our relationship. I think we're better off working on it by ourselves or by getting another couple, or a few other people who are close to us, to come and work it out with us.

I don't have a sense that the group is in fact very helpful to us as a couple. I have more of a sense that it is destructive to us as a couple and that there are even some people here who feel that it might even be better if everybody wasn't a couple. They do as much to put in misinformation between us as helpfulness. I really think that's true, sad as it may sound. Especially it has been true I think when for a while other people felt possessive of me. At least two or three other people would have as soon had us split up, 'cause they resented Boris coming up to me and saying, "Lois, come on, I want to be with you now," and me getting up and going, and they'd make trouble. Like Robin would tell me something Boris said to Tommy, my son. Then I'd get mad and then of course I'm mad at Boris, and sometimes she has been absolutely right, and that's exactly what happened, but it was a funny thing to do.

THE LIBERATED WOMAN

INTERVIEWER: There are . . . what . . . three couples in the house?

LOIS: There's one married couple, Robin and Ben. They have changed an awful lot since moving into the house. They were monogamous completely for seven years, since they have been married, and when I first met them three years ago, Ben wanted to get it together with some other girls and Robin was *terribly* threatened by that and terribly upset. When I first met her, she was afraid Ben would get turned on by me and she just didn't like me in the least and just thought I was awful—and I wasn't in fact at all interested in Ben. But that's a sample of how completely freaked out she was by it.

Then last summer he did have an affair and she was *really* upset and I spent time with her that day. It's funny. I wasn't threatened by that situation. I mean someone had to do it for me, when Boris turned around and made love with someone else. I spent the day with her, sort of saying, what did she really want? Like she had an empty space and she could paint a beautiful picture in it, or else she could just get so focused on this, you know, act resentfully and sort of dejectedly, and not have what she wanted in the first place. And as a result of that their marriage has really opened up, maybe even more than any couple in the house. Robin has more affairs and more dates and more going out and doesn't spend too much time here in the house. She does more of that than anyone else in the house, including the single men. And I'm not sure what I think about that, I guess it's not the kind of relationship I'd want—I *know* it's not the kind of relationship I want. But it seems to be making her really happy right now, to be doing that. I guess part of my resentment about it is that she's not around enough because she's always out on some date. But I also worry, like, that maybe Ben is lonely.

I also worry deeply that it's not *really* what Robin wants to be doing. You know, maybe she feels that she *should,* because that's the new social code. I'm not really convinced at all. She talks a lot about wanting to have a baby. They're two very different things. One is running around all the time and the other is tied up to a baby. They're *very* different things.

My Reactions

There are a number of things which strike me about Lois's account. There is, for instance, the complete intellectual commitment to open sexual experimentation, though this is not, in many instances, backed by an equal experiential commitment. Boris and Lois, Ben and Robin can choose to try other than a monogamous life for a time. The single members can try out various relationships on a temporary or more lasting basis. Lois and Jan can experience a homosexual relationship with no feeling of guilt. Lois is even gleeful about the possibility of a sexual orgy in the house. In short, one of the elemental facts about many communes is that they are experimental laboratories where—without guilt, without public knowledge outside of the group, without a commitment to any one mode of behavior—a variety of sexual unions can be tried. What is, for many people, a fantasied variety of sexual experiences is here brought alive in reality.[2]

But all of this experimentation is not without cost. The senses of loss, of hurt, of jealousy, of self-pity, of anger, of desire for retaliation are experienced time and time again by those involved in the experimentation. No matter how "modern" the person's point of view, or his or her intellectual commitment, someone is hurt in one way or another, as Lois makes clear, every time partnerships shift. And jealousy does not necessarily relate simply to sexual behavior, but to such things as a loss of closeness, such as Boris feels about the relationship between Lois and Jan, even though he also finds it exciting.

[2] It is of interest that, as far as I am aware, relationships between man and man are much less common in communes than between woman and woman. I was unable to obtain a satisfactory *inner* account of such a union, though I know that they occasionally exist as part of the experimentation in communes. Somehow male homosexuality seems more threatening to many persons than female homosexual contact.

But the laboratory has its curative elements too, to assuage these hurts. Lois helps Robin in her jealousy and pain, just as someone helped Lois previously in a similar situation. And the impression, from her account and from other experiences, is that very frequently these hurts are also moments of potential growth. It is impressive that Lois believes the experimentation has never once "produced a bummer" or "set people far, far apart." Undoubtedly this is too sweeping a statement, but the fact that a person experiences unpleasant hurts is certainly not synonymous with saying he or she has been permanently damaged.

Another element which needs pointing up is that the group has both its constructive and destructive possibilities. This was mentioned in the brief earlier account of the acrimonious group marriage. Lois makes it more specific by stressing the group's lack of understanding of her stormy but vital relationship with Boris. And, as in any group, there are those who are quite capable of causing trouble through inputs of inappropriate information, whether accurate or inaccurate.

Here, as in so many situations, we have the knowledge which would improve such situations, but we fail to utilize it adequately. A facilitative person, if he is at the right place at the right time, can help to resolve hurts and jealousies and backbiting. But we are far from such a millennium.

One note which strikes me in Lois's account is the vital necessity of knowing, accepting, and trusting one's feelings. Is Robin really blissfully happy in her carefree sexual life? Lois questions this and so do I. Her behavior sounds too much like retaliation, which in turn is a cover for her hurt. Here again she almost certainly needs facilitative help in discovering, beneath whatever defenses she may have, her true feelings. Then she can act as a unified and real person. Whether she will wish for or find such assistance is an open question.

Another element which seems clear from Lois's statement and from much other knowledge, is that most people have a continuing need for a secure relationship. When Lois points out that experimentation "isn't all that frequent," and that most people when they are in a relationship value that relationship, she is expressing something which is, I believe, very widely and profoundly true.

Another Example of Experimental Relationships

Sam is thirty-eight, divorced, and now married to Rita. There are two sets of children. They moved from a suburb into an urban commune because, as Rita says:

I was very isolated. When Sam went off to work, unless I had a particular thing to do or to go to, I just felt very isolated, in a house very separate, you know, from the people across the street or the neighbors. And here people are going in and out—it's just a world by itself.

Later Rita describes the man-woman relationships:

We don't feel that we have to have sexual relationships with every member in the house. The fact that we are nonmonogamous is the fact that we are open to other relationships with other people, but if there were people in the house who felt very strongly that they *were* monogamous and that is something they really believed in—they could probably make it work. . . .

SAM: . . . This woman the other night expressed it in this way. She said, "Well, I don't have the idea of coming into a commune with the expectation of having sex in the house, but if something developed that might be nice. And I wouldn't want to encourage her nor discourage her. . . .

Rita and Doug, another house member, are involved in a sexual relationship, and this has not been easy for Sam. One senses tension in Rita's relationship to him.

INTERVIEWER: How do you handle the jealousies and the feelings? Or have you managed to relieve yourselves of these feelings . . . ?

SAM: No. We are still handling them. At a meeting one night the chairwoman said, "If anybody has had nonmonogamous relationships and has worked them out, will you please tell us." So Doug, who lives in the house, said, "Has anybody worked out their whole life?" So, we're still working it out. And from my point of view in terms of Rita, Doug, and myself, one of the things that makes it easier for me is that Doug tries to be a friend to me as well as to Rita and we do consider each other friends. And his relationship with Rita—it isn't meant to cut me down or push me aside or to make me feel bad, but it is just another thing that has a validity all of its own. I have to keep telling myself that, especially, you know, during the time when they might be having an upswing in their relationship and I'm more or less alone.

INTERVIEWER: That sounds like it could be very hard to handle . . .

SAM: Yeah, and when you've had years and years of conditioning . . . a sort of romantic complex, you learn you don't play around or whatever. But the other side of the coin is that I've never met anybody who didn't spend at least some energy in having fantasies of a relationship with someone other than his or her spouse. So I think what we save is a lot of energy from playing the fantasy game and in our actual relationships working it out, and also it's pretty open, which I think is a *far* healthier thing. Better than sneaking off and pretending we are not having a relationship when we are having one. In some ways I think it made my relationship with Rita probably better than it was . . . I can see my relationship better than it used to be at any point. Better now. Then I think that the fact that she developed this outside relationship has helped. I think it has helped her to feel more worthy as a person, and curiously, it has helped *me* to think of her and to feel about her as being more worthy.

INTERVIEWER: Is what he said true?

RITA: It's not the way I think of it.

Rita doesn't explain this contradiction between them, but goes on to talk about some aspects of sharing, which leads Sam into that topic.

SAM: Yeah. I don't like to go for walks very much. But Rita likes to walk and Doug likes to walk, so some people like to go for walks. That's fine. So, some people who like to walk probably need some walking. So, people who like to sit can sit.

INTERVIEWER: It doesn't put the pressure on to be everything to one person. . . .

RITA: Yeah.

SAM: Yeah. I have a relationship with another woman that doesn't live in the commune and it's not a terribly good relationship and it's a person who I don't think I selected as carefully as I might, but I went into it at a time when I was feeling half lonely after this relationship between Rita and Doug started. But it's fairly good. I guess I'm envious that I didn't start a relationship with someone else living in the same house. Because it's very hard for me to sustain this relationship with this person that is just more than an occasional sexual encounter. If I really spent a lot of time with her, well, I feel that whether Rita is explicit about it or not, she knows the answer. And you see, it's easy to spend time with someone you care about who lives in the same house without making a big deal about it.

At a later point Sam adds, speaking of relations outside the partnership, "You can run a risk when you do this sort of thing. But you run a risk when you get married."

If there is any comment to be made about Rita and Doug, Sam and his outside girlfriend, it is simply that there is always a price to be paid for experimentation in the forming of sexual relationships outside a partnership. But as Sam wisely points out, there is risk in marriage too. And the outside relationship does free each spouse from trying to be everything, to meet *every* need, of the other.

. . .

Why Join?

But why do intelligent, educated, sophisticated individuals, with all the opportunities ahead of them which our society offers, join communes? Let me try to set down a few of the motives which I believe are operative.

One is to escape the increasing alienation and individual isolation in our society. They long to escape from punch-card dehumanization to a place where they can personally *belong*. . . . They desire to be a part of deep, sharing relationsips, which, as we have seen, can occur in marriages as well as in communes.

Certainly another reason is that communes offer an opportunity to be the whole self in a unified way, a very rare opportunity in modern life. All aspects of the person tend to be valued—physical strength, occupational skills, parental aptitudes, intellectual ideas, feelings and emotions, ideals and religious or mystical interests, can all be lived simultaneously. Life is much less fractionalized. This can happen in marriage, as we have observed. It can, to a limited degree, occur in encounter groups. But a commune is another—and perhaps more difficult way—of trying to achieve this new expression of the whole self in a unified life.

Frequently a prominent reason is to find a sanction for all kinds of sexual relationships: in marriage, in partnerships of varying durations, in all kinds of combinations—man-woman, woman-woman, man-man. This experimentation is simply not freely possible in the ordinary community. In the commune it usually finds a supportive climate and can be carried on without guilt—though not, as we have seen, without pain.[3]

Another motive which is perhaps gradually discovered by the person is that the living group is, whether consciously or unconsciously, an experiment in some philosophy of social organization (or nonorganization). Free of the "rat race," it is a chance to build a functioning group in which things get done. So from anarchy to controlled behaviorism, a whole crop of new societies is germinating, each different from the other. The group must wrestle with problems of survival, of authority, of work distribution, of the management of interpersonal differences, of relationship to a very different outside world.

This leads to another realization: that this is not a closed-end experiment, but an opportunity for *learning*. Here is an opportunity for a changing personal development—an opportunity which by no means always occurs, but which stands as a hope.

Finally, there is great drawing power in the dropping of roles. Early in the [article] I mentioned the many backgrounds and work experiences from which these persons are drawn. But in a commune a person is not primarily a Radcliffe graduate or a computer specialist or a psychologist or whatever. A person is a person. A man is a man. A woman is a woman. There is a basic equality which makes movements such as women's lib obsolete, since each woman—and each man—can carve out the personal niche she or he desires in the group. (Interestingly, the women very frequently opt for "feminine" functions.)

All these motives sound appealing. Yet people leave these groups, communes fail or become destructive or fall apart. Why?

One of the most prominent reasons, I believe, is that they have frequently given insufficient thought to the ways in which interpersonal conflicts and hurts and cross purposes may be handled. We have seen . . . that they can also excel in a curative function, but this does not happen necessarily.

Frequently they have simply failed to solve the problem of self-support, but this is a bit outside the realm of this [article].

Jealousy is often an underestimated problem which can undermine a group. Indeed, I wonder whether jealousy is something simply conditioned by the culture or actually has a basic biological foundation, like territoriality?

Related to this is, I believe, a similar underestimation of the need of each person for a reasonably secure, continuing, one-to-one relationship. This need seems to run very deep and may be considered too lightly.

It has been borne in on me—by material I have gathered, by the reading I have done, and by the very intimate accounts [I have received]—that it is far more difficult to sustain a healthy and satisfying relationship in a triad or a group marriage of four or

---

[3] The sexual experimentation in a commune is vastly different from that of a group of "swingers." Evidence shows that swingers try to avoid anything approaching deep involvement or more than casual relationships.

more than it is to sustain it in a two-person marriage (as if that were not difficult enough!). Consequently, communes have fallen apart because of the inability to resolve the problems of highly complex relationships.

Sometimes there is a failure to recognize the great need of each individual for privacy. This can be provided in a commune, but sometimes it is not, with very negative results.

Often, in my judgment, there is no recognition that an anarchistic philosophy, beautiful though it may be, can operate with some degree of success only when the group is composed of people with a high degree of psychological maturity. Hence the attempt to live anarchistically, when the group is made up of individuals badly warped by family and society, can be a resounding flop.

There is sometimes failure to recognize that all ideologies are greatly modified in practice. Thus, Twin Oaks, fashioned on B. F. Skinner's theories, is no longer run by three planners but largely by consensus. The environment is no longer set to condition certain behaviors, but the individual *chooses* which behaviors he desires to change and *chooses* the rewards which are meaningful for him. All this has little resemblance to *Walden II,* Skinner's fictional utopia.

So communes have their full share of problems and failures. But they are process failures from which one can learn. They seem to be performing a most important function in our culture. They are, at little psychological or financial cost to all of us, conducting the laboratory experiments to determine what place marriage, partnerships, interpersonal relations, technology, and social organization may have in the future. Our culture, in all probability, cannot continue as it is. The flaws and fissures, the injustices and hypocrisies are too great. What, then, *will* it become? Communes, with all their mistakes and privations and failures and regroupings, seem to be exploring the way.

. . .

Suggested Readings

Atkinson, Ronald. *Sexual Morality.* New York: Harcourt, Brace, 1965.

Barnhart, J. E., and Mary Ann Barnhart. "Marital Faithfulness and Unfaithfulness," *Journal of Social Philosophy* 4 (April 1973).

Heller, Agnes. "On the Future of Relations Between the Sexes," *International Social Science Journal* 21 (1969).

Rimmer, Robert H. *The Harrad Experiment.* New York: Sherbourne Press, 1966.

section five

medical and psychiatric ethics

PHILOSOPHICAL REFLECTIONS ON EXPERIMENTING WITH HUMAN SUBJECTS

Hans Jonas

When I was first asked to comment "philosophically" on the subject of human experimentation, I had all the hesitation natural to a layman in the face of matters on which experts of the highest competence have had their say and still carry on their dialogue. As I familiarized myself with the material, any initial feeling of moral rectitude that might have facilitated my task quickly dissipated before the awesome complexity of the problem, and a state of great humility took its place. Nevertheless, because the subject is obscure by its nature and involves fundamental, transtechnical issues, any attempt at clarification can be of use, even without novelty. Even if the philosophical reflection should in the end achieve no more than the realization that in the dialectics of this area we must sin and fall into guilt, this insight may not be without its own gains.

The Peculiarity of Human Experimentation

Experimentation was originally sanctioned by natural science. There it is performed on inanimate objects, and this raises no moral problems. But as soon as animate, feeling beings become the subjects of experiment, as they do in the life sciences and especially in medical research, this innocence of the search for knowledge is lost and questions of conscience arise. The depth to which moral and religious sensibilities can become aroused is shown by the vivisection issue. Human experimentation must sharpen the issue as it involves ultimate questions of personal dignity and sacrosanctity. One difference between the human experiments and the physical is this: The physical experiment employs small-scale, artificially devised substitutes for that about which knowledge is to be obtained, and the experimenter extrapolates from these models and simulated conditions to nature at large. Something deputizes for the "real thing"—balls rolling down an inclined plane for sun and planets, electric discharges from a condenser for real lightning, and so on. For the most part, no such substitution is possible in the biological sphere. We must operate on the original itself, the real thing in the fullest sense, and perhaps affect it irreversibly. No simulacrum can take its place. Especially in the human sphere, experimentation loses entirely the advantage of the clear division between vicarious model and true object. Up to a point, animals may fulfill the proxy role of the classical physical experiment. But in the end man himself must furnish knowledge about himself, and the comfortable separation of noncommittal experiment and definitive action vanishes. An experiment in education affects the lives of its subjects, perhaps a whole generation of schoolchildren. Human experimentation for whatever purpose is always *also* a responsible, nonexperimental, definitive dealing with the subject himself. And not even the noblest purpose abrogates the obligations this involves.

Can both that purpose and this obligation be satisfied? If not, what would be a just compromise? Which side should give way to the other? The question is inherently philosophical as it concerns not merely pragmatic difficulties and their arbitration, but a genuine conflict of values involving principles of a high order. On principle, it is felt, human beings *ought not* to be dealt with in that way (the "guinea pig" protest); on the other hand, such dealings are increasingly urged on us by considerations, in turn appealing to principle, that claim to override those objections. Such a claim must be carefully assessed, especially when it is swept along by a mighty tide. Putting the matter thus, we have already made one important assumption rooted in our "Western" cultural tradition: The prohibitive rule is, to that way of thinking, the primary and axiomatic one; the permissive counter-rule, as qualifying the first, is secondary and stands in need of justification. We must justify the infringement of a primary inviolability, which needs no justification itself; and the justification of its infringement must be by values and needs of a dignity commensurate with those to be sacrificed.

"Individual Versus Society" as the Conceptual Framework

The setting for the conflict most consistently invoked in the literature is the polarity of individual versus society—the possible tension between the individual good and the common good, between private and public welfare. Thus, W. Wolfensberger speaks of "the tension between the long-range interests of society, science, and progress, on one hand, and the rights of the individual on the other." [1] Walsh McDermott says: "In essence, this is a problem of the rights of the individual versus the rights of society." [2] Somewhere I found the "social contract" invoked in support of claims that science may make on individuals in the matter of experimentation. I have grave doubts about the adequacy of this frame of reference, but I will go along with it part of the way. It does apply to some extent, and it has the advantage of being familiar. We concede, as a matter of course, to the common good some pragmatically determined measure of precedence over the individual good. In terms of rights, we let some of the basic rights of the individual be overruled by the acknowledged rights of society—as a matter of right and moral justness and not of mere force or dire necessity (much as such necessity may be adduced in defense of that right). But in making that concession, we require a careful clarification of what the needs, interests, and rights of society are, for society—as distinct from any plurality of individuals—is an abstract and as such is subject to our definition, while the individual is the primary concrete, prior to all definition, and his basic good is more or less known. Thus, the unknown in our problem is the so-called common or public good and its potentially superior claims, to which the individual good must or might sometimes be sacrificed, in circumstances that in turn must also be counted among the unknowns of our question. Note that in putting the matter in this way—that is, in asking about the right of society to individual sacrifice—the consent of the sacrificial subject is no necessary part of the *basic* question.

"Consent," however, is the other most consistently emphasized and examined concept in discussions of this issue. This attention betrays a feeling that the "social" angle is not fully satisfactory. If society has a right, its exercise is not contingent on volunteering. On the other hand, if volunteering is fully genuine, no public right to the volunteered act need be construed. There is a difference between the moral or emotional appeal of a cause that elicits volunteering and a right that demands compliance—for example, with particular reference to the social sphere, between the *moral claim* of a common good and society's *right* to that good and to the means of its realization. A moral claim cannot be met without consent; a right can do without it. Where consent is present anyway, the distinction may become immaterial. But the awareness of the many ambiguities besetting the "consent" actually available and used in medical research prompts recourse to the idea of a public right conceived independently of (and valid prior to) consent; and, vice versa, the awareness of the problematic nature of such a right makes even its advocates still insist on the idea of consent with all its ambiguities: An uneasy situation exists for both sides.

[1] W. Wolfensberger, "Ethical Issues in Research with Human Subjects," *World Science,* Vol. 155 (January 6, 1967), p. 48.

[2] *Proceedings of the Conference on the Ethical Aspects of Experimentation on Human Subjects,* November 3–4, 1967 (Boston, Massachusetts; hereafter called *Proceedings*), p. 29.

Nor does it help much to replace the language of "rights" by that of "interests" and then argue the sheer cumulative weight of the interests of the many over against those of the few or the single individual. "Interests" range all the way from the most marginal and optional to the most vital and imperative, and only those sanctioned by particular importance and merit will be admitted to count in such a calculus—which simply brings us back to the question of right or moral claim. Moreover, the appeal to numbers is dangerous. Is the number of those afflicted with a particular disease great enough to warrant violating the interests of the nonafflicted? Since the number of the latter is usually so much greater, the argument can actually turn around to the contention that the cumulative weight of interest is on *their* side. Finally, it may well be the case that the individual's interest in his own inviolability is itself a public interest such that its publicly condoned violation, irrespective of numbers, violates the interest of all. In that case, its protection in *each* instance would be a paramount interest, and the comparison of numbers will not avail.

These are some of the difficulties hidden in the conceptual framework indicated by the terms "society-individual," "interest," and "rights." But we also spoke of a moral call, and this points to another dimension—not indeed divorced from the societal sphere, but transcending it. And there is something even beyond that: true sacrifice from highest devotion, for which there are no laws or rules except that it must be absolutely free. "No one has the right to choose martyrs for science" was a statement repeatedly quoted in the November, 1967, *Dædalus* conference. But no scientist can be prevented from making himself a martyr for his science. At all times, dedicated explorers, thinkers, and artists have immolated themselves on the altar of their vocation, and creative genius most often pays the price of happiness, health, and life for its own consummation. But no one, not even society, has the shred of a right to expect and ask these things. They come to the rest of us as a *gratia gratis data*.

The Sacrificial Theme

Yet we must face the somber truth that the *ultima ratio* of communal life is and has always been the compulsory, vicarious sacrifice of individual lives. The primordial sacrificial situation is that of outright human sacrifices in early communities. These were not acts of blood-lust or gleeful savagery; they were the solemn execution of a supreme, sacral necessity. One of the fellowship of men had to die so that all could live, the earth be fertile, the cycle of nature renewed. The victim often was not a captured enemy, but a select member of the group: "The king must die." If there was cruelty here, it was not that of men, but that of the gods, or rather of the stern order of things, which was believed to exact that price for the bounty of life. To assure it for the community, and to assure it ever again, the awesome *quid pro quo* had to be paid ever again.

Far be it from me, and far should it be from us, to belittle from the height of our enlightened knowledge the majesty of the underlying conception. The particular *causal* views that prompted our ancestors have long since been relegated to the realm of superstition. But in moments of national danger we still send the flower of our young manhood to offer their lives for the continued life of the community, and if it is a just war, we see them go forth as consecrated and strangely ennobled by a sacrificial role. Nor do we make their going forth depend on their own will and consent, much as we may desire and foster these: We conscript them according to law. We conscript the best and feel morally disturbed if the draft, either by design or in effect, works so that mainly the disadvantaged, socially less useful, more expendable, make up those whose lives are to buy ours. No rational persuasion of the pragmatic necessity here at work can do away with the feeling, mixed of gratitude and guilt, that the sphere of the sacred is touched with the vicarious offering of life for life. Quite apart from these dramatic occasions, there is, it appears, a persistent and constitutive aspect of human immolation to the very being and prospering of human society—an immolation in terms of life and happiness, imposed or voluntary, of few for many. What Goethe has said of the rise of Christianity may well apply to the nature of civilization in general: *"Opfer fallen hier, / Weder Lamm noch Stier, / Aber Menschenopfer unerhoert."* [3] We can never rest comfortably in the belief that the soil from which our satisfactions sprout is not watered with the blood of martyrs. But a troubled conscience compels us, the undeserving beneficiaries, to ask: Who is to be martyred? in the service of what cause? and by whose choice?

Not for a moment do I wish to suggest that medical experimentation on human subjects, sick or healthy, is to be likened to primeval human sacrifices. Yet something sacrificial is involved in the selective abrogation of personal inviolability and the ritualized exposure to gratuitous risk of health and life, justified by a persumed greater, social good. My examples from the sphere of stark sacrifice were intended to sharpen the issues implied in that context and to set them off clearly from the kinds of obligations and constraints imposed on the citizen in the normal course of things or generally demanded of the individual in exchange for the advantages of civil society.

. . .

The Fundamental Privilege of the Sick

In the course of treatment, the physician is obligated to the patient and to no one else. He is not the agent of society, nor of the interests of medical science, the patient's family, the patient's co-sufferers, or future sufferers from the same disease. The patient alone counts when he is under the physician's care. By the simple law of bilateral contract (analogous, for example, to the relation of lawyer to client and its "conflict of interest" rule), he is bound not to let any other interest interfere with that of the

---

[3] *Die Braut von Korinth:* "Victims do fall here, / Neither lamb nor steer, / Nay, but human offerings untold."

patient in being cured. But manifestly more sublime norms than contractual ones are involved. We may speak of a sacred trust; strictly by its terms, the doctor is, as it were, alone with his patient and God.

There is one normal exception to this—that is, to the doctor's not being the agent of society vis-à-vis the patient, but the trustee of his interests alone—the quarantining of the contagious sick. This is plainly not for the patient's interest, but for that of others threatened by him. (In vaccination, we have a combination of both: protection of the individual and others.) But preventing the patient from causing harm to others is not the same as exploiting him for the advantage of others. And there is, of course, the abnormal exception of collective catastrophe, the analogue to a state of war. The physician who desperately battles a raging epidemic is under a unique dispensation that suspends in a nonspecifiable way some of the strictures of normal practice, including possibly those against experimental liberties with his patients. No rules can be devised for the waiving of rules in extremities. And as with the famous shipwreck examples of ethical theory, the less said about it the better. But what is allowable there and may later be passed over in forgiving silence cannot serve as a precedent. We are concerned with nonextreme, nonemergency conditions where the voice of principle can be heard and claims can be adjudicated free from duress. We have conceded that there are such claims, and that if there is to be medical advance at all, not even the superlative privilege of the suffering and the sick can be kept wholly intact from the intrusion of its needs. About this least palatable, most disquieting part of our subject, I have to offer only groping, inconclusive remarks.

The Principle of "Identification" Applied to Patients

On the whole, the same principles would seem to hold here as are found to hold with "normal subjects": motivation, identification, understanding on the part of the subject. But it is clear that these conditions are peculiarly difficult to satisfy with regard to a patient. His physical state, psychic preoccupation, dependent relation to the doctor, the submissive attitude induced by treatment—everything connected with his condition and situation makes the sick person inherently less of a sovereign person than the healthy one. Spontaneity of self-offering has almost to be ruled out; consent is marred by lower resistance or captive circumstance, and so on. In fact, all the factors that make the patient, as a category, particularly accessible and welcome for experimentation at the same time compromise the quality of the responding affirmation that must morally redeem the making use of them. This, in addition to the primacy of the physician's duty, puts a heightened onus on the physician-researcher to limit his undue power to the most important and defensible research objectives and, of course, to keep persuasion at a minimum.

Still, with all the disabilities noted, there is scope among patients for observing the rule of the "descending order of permissibility" that we have laid down for normal subjects, in vexing inversion of the utility order of quantitative abundance and qualitative "expendability." By the principle of this order, those patients who most identify with and are cognizant of the cause of research—members of the medical profession (who after all are sometimes patients themselves)—come first; the highly motivated and educated, also least dependent, among the lay patients come next; and so on down the line. An added consideration here is seriousness of condition, which again operates in inverse proportion. Here the profession must fight the tempting sophistry that the hopeless case is expendable (because in prospect already expended) and therefore especially usable; and generally the attitude that the poorer the chances of the patient the more justifiable his recruitment for experimentation (other than for his own benefit). The opposite is true.

Nondisclosure as a Borderline Case

Then there is the case where ignorance of the subject, sometimes even of the experimenter, is of the essence of the experiment (the "double blind"–control group–placebo syndrome). It is said to be a necessary element of the scientific process. Whatever may be said about its ethics in regard to normal subjects, especially volunteers, it is an outright betrayal of trust in regard to the patient who believes that he is receiving treatment. Only supreme importance of the objective can exonerate it, without making it less of a transgression. The patient is definitely wronged even when not harmed. And ethics apart, the practice of such deception holds the danger of undermining the faith in the *bona fides* of treatment, the beneficial intent of the physician—the very basis of the doctor-patient relationship. In every respect, it follows that concealed experiment on patients—that is, experiment under the guise of treatment—should be the rarest exception, at best, if it cannot be wholly avoided.

This has still the merit of a borderline problem. This is not true of the other case of necessary ignorance of the subject—that of the unconscious patient. Drafting him for nontherapeutic experiments is simply and unqualifiedly impermissible; progress or not, he must never be used, on the inflexible principle that utter helplessness demands utter protection.

When preparing this paper, I filled pages with a casuistics of this harrowing field, but then scratched out most of it, realizing my dilettante status. The shadings are endless, and only the physician-researcher can discern them properly as the cases arise. Into his lap the decision is thrown. The philosophical rule, once it has admitted into itself the idea of a sliding scale, cannot really specify its own application. It can only impress on the practitioner a general maxim or attitude for the exercise of his judgment and conscience in the concrete occasions of his work. In our case, I am afraid, it means making life more difficult for him.

It will also be noted that, somewhat at variance with the emphasis in the literature, I have not dwelt on the element of "risk" and very little on that of "consent." Discussion of the first is beyond the layman's competence; the emphasis on the second has been lessened because of its equivocal character. It is a truism to say that one should strive to minimize the risk and to maximize the consent. The more demanding concept of "identification," which I have used, includes "consent" in its maximal or authentic form, and the assumption of risk is its privilege.

No Experiments on Patients Unrelated to Their Own Disease

Although my ponderings have, on the whole, yielded points of view rather than definite prescriptions, premises rather than conclusions, they have led me to a few unequivocal yeses and noes. The first is the emphatic rule that patients should be experimented upon, if at all, *only* with reference to *their* disease. Never should there be added to the gratuitousness of the experiment as such the gratuitousness of service to an unrelated cause. This follows simply from what we have found to be the *only* excuse for infracting the special exemption of the sick at all—namely, that the scientific war on disease cannot accomplish its goal without drawing the sufferers from disease into the investigative process. If under this excuse they become subjects of experiment, they do so *because,* and only because, of *their* disease.

This is the fundamental and self-sufficient consideration. That the patient cannot possibly benefit from the unrelated experiment therapeutically, while he might from experiment related to his condition, is also true, but lies beyond the problem area of pure experiment. Anyway, I am discussing nontherapeutic experimentation only, where *ex hypothesi* the patient does not benefit. Experiment as part of therapy—that is, directed toward helping the subject himself—is a different matter altogether and raises its own problems, but hardly philosophical ones. As long as a doctor can say, even if only in his own thought: "There is no known cure for your condition (or: You have responded to none); but there is promise in a new treatment still under investigation, not quite tested yet as to effectiveness and safety; you will be taking a chance, but all things considered, I judge it in your best interest to let me try it on you"—as long as he can speak thus, he speaks as the patient's physician and may err, but does not transform the patient into a subject of experimentation. Introduction of an untried therapy into the treatment where the tried ones have failed is not "experimentation on the patient."

Generally, there is something "experimental" (because tentative) about every individual treatment, beginning with the diagnosis itself; and he would be a poor doctor who would not learn from every case for the benefit of future cases, and a poor member of the profession who would not make any new insights gained from his treatments available to the profession at large. Thus, knowledge may be advanced in the treatment of any patient, and the interest of the medical art and all sufferers from the same affliction as well as the patient may be served if something happens to be learned from his case. But this gain to knowledge and future therapy is incidental to the *bona fide* service to the present patient. He has the right to expect that the doctor does nothing to him just in order to learn.

In that case, the doctor's imaginary speech would run, for instance, like this: "There is nothing more I can do for you. But you can do something for me. Speaking no longer as your physician but on behalf of medical science, we could learn a great deal about future cases of this kind if you would permit me to perform certain experiments on you. It is understood that you yourself would not benefit from any knowledge we might gain; but future patients would." This statement would express the purely experimental situation, assumedly here with the subject's concurrence and with all cards on the table. In Alexander Bickel's words: "It is a different situation when the doctor is no longer trying to make [the patient] well, but is trying to find out how to make others well in the future." [4]

But even in the second case of the nontherapeutic experiment where the patient does not benefit, the patient's own disease is enlisted in the cause of fighting that disease, even if only in others. It is yet another thing to say or think: "Since you are here—in the hospital with its facilities—under our care and observation, away from your job (or, perhaps, doomed), we wish to profit from your being available for some other research of great interest we are presently engaged in." From the standpoint of merely medical ethics, which has only to consider risk, consent, and the worth of the objective, there may be no cardinal difference between this case and the last one. I hope that my medical audience will not think I am making too fine a point when I say that from the standpoint of the subject and his dignity there is a cardinal difference that crosses the line between the permissible and the impermissible, and this by the same principle of "identification" I have been invoking all along. Whatever the rights and wrongs of any experimentation on any patient—in the one case, at least that residue of identification is left him that it is his own affliction by which he can contribute to the conquest of that affliction, his own kind of suffering which he helps to alleviate in others; and so in a sense it is his own cause. It is totally indefensible to rob the unfortunate of this intimacy with the purpose and make his misfortune a convenience for the furtherance of alien concerns. The observance of this rule is essential, I think, to attenuate at least the wrong that nontherapeutic experimenting on patients commits in any case.

[4] *Proceedings,* p. 33. To spell out the difference between the two cases: In the first case, the patient himself is meant to be the beneficiary of the experiment, and directly so; the "subject" of the experiment is at the same time its object, its end. It is performed not for gaining knowledge, but for helping him—and helping him in the *act* of performing it, even if by its results it also contributes to a broader testing process currently under way. It is in fact part of the treatment itself and an "experiment" only in the loose sense of being untried and highly tentative. But whatever the degree of uncertainty, the motivating anticipation (the wager, if you like) is for success, and success here means the subject's own good. To a pure experiment, by contrast, undertaken to gain knowledge, the difference of success and failure is not germane, only that of conclusiveness and inconclusiveness. The "negative" result has as much to teach as the "positive." Also, the true experiment is an act distinct from the uses later made of the findings. And, most important, the subject experimented on is distinct from the eventual beneficiaries of those findings: He lets himself be used as a means toward an end external to himself (even if he should at some later time happen to be among the beneficiaries himself). With respect to his own present needs and his own good, the act is gratuitous.

On the Redefinition of Death

My other emphatic verdict concerns the question of the redefinition of death—acknowledging "irreversible coma as a new definition for death." [5] I wish not to be misunderstood. As long as it is merely a question of when it is permitted to cease the artificial prolongation of certain functions (like heartbeat) traditionally regarded as signs of life, I do not see anything ominous in the notion of "brain death." Indeed, a new definition of death is not even necessary to legitimize the same result if one adopts the position of the Roman Catholic Church, which here for once is eminently reasonable—namely that "when deep unconsciousness is judged to be permanent, extraordinary means to maintain life are not obligatory. They can be terminated and the patient allowed to die." [6] Given a clearly defined negative condition of the brain, the physician is allowed to allow the patient to die his own death by *any* definition, which of itself will lead through the gamut of all possible definitions. But a disquietingly contradictory purpose is combined with this purpose in the quest for a new definition of death, in the will to *advance* the moment of declaring him dead: Permission not to turn off the respirator, but, on the contrary, to keep it on and thereby maintain the body in a state of what would have been "life" by the older definition (but is only a "simulacrum" of life by the new)—so as to get at his organs and tissues under the ideal conditions of what would previously have been "vivisection." [7]

Now this, whether done for research or transplant purposes, seems to me to overstep what the definition can warrant. Surely it is one thing when to cease delaying death, but another when to start doing violence to the body; one thing when to desist from protracting the process of dying, but another when to regard that process as complete and thereby the body as a cadaver free for inflicting on it what would be torture and death to any living body. For the first purpose, we need not know the exact borderline with absolute certainty between life and death—we leave it to nature to cross it wherever it is, or to traverse the whole spectrum if there is not just one line. All we need to know is that coma is irreversible. For the second purpose we must know the borderline; and to use any definition short of the maximal for perpetrating on a *possibly* penultimate state what only the ultimate state can permit is to arrogate a knowledge

---

[5] "A Definition of Irreversible Coma," Report of the *Ad Hoc* Committee of Harvard Medical School to Examine the Definition of Brain Death, *Journal of the American Medical Association,* Vol. 205, No. 6 (August 5, 1968), pp. 337–40.

[6] As rendered by Dr. Beecher in *Proceedings,* p. 50.

[7] The Report of the *Ad Hoc* Committee no more than indicates this possibility with the second of the "two reasons why there is need for a definition": "(2) Obsolete criteria for the definition of death can lead to controversy in obtaining organs for transplantation." The first reason is relief from the burden of indefinitely drawn out coma. The report wisely confines its recommendations on application to what falls under this first reason—namely, turning off the respirator—and remains silent on the possible use of the definition under the second reason. But when "the patient is declared dead on the basis of these criteria," the road to the other use has theoretically been opened and will be taken (if I remember rightly, it has even been taken once, in a much debated case in England), unless it is blocked by a special barrier in good time. The above is my feeble attempt to help doing so.

which, I think, we cannot possibly have. *Since we do not know the exact borderline between life and death,* nothing less than the maximum definition of death will do— brain death plus heart death plus any other indication that may be pertinent—before final violence is allowed to be done.

It would follow then, for this layman at least, that the use of the definition should itself be defined, and this in a restrictive sense. When only permanent coma can be gained with the artificial sustaining of functions, by all means turn off the respirator, the stimulator, any sustaining artifice, and let the patient die; but let him die all the way. Do not, instead, arrest the process and start using him as a mine while, with your own help and cunning, he is still kept this side of what may in truth be the final line. Who is to say that a shock, a final trauma, is not administered to a sensitivity diffusely situated elsewhere than in the brain and still vulnerable to suffering? a sensitivity that we ourselves have been keeping alive? No fiat of definition can settle this question.[8] But I wish to emphasize that the question of possible suffering (easily brushed aside by a sufficient show of reassuring expert consensus) is merely a subsidiary and not the real point of my argument; this, to reiterate, turns on the indeterminacy of the boundaries between *life and death,* not between sensitivity and insensitivity, and bids us to lean toward a maximal rather than a minimal determination of death in an area of basic uncertainty.

There is also this to consider: The patient must be absolutely sure that his doctor does not become his executioner, and that no definition authorizes him ever to become one. His right to this certainty is absolute, and so is his right to his own body with all its organs. Absolute respect for these rights violates no one else's rights, for no one has a right to another's body. Speaking in still another, religious vein: The expiring moments should be watched over with piety and be safe from exploitation.

I strongly feel, therefore, that it should be made quite clear that the proposed new definition of death is to authorize *only* the one and *not* the other of the two opposing things: only to break off a sustaining intervention and let things take their course, not to keep up the sustaining intervention for a final intervention of the most destructive kind.

There would now have to be said something about nonmedical experiments on human subjects, notably psychological and genetic, of which I have not lost sight. But having overextended my limits of space by the most generous interpretation, I must leave this for another occasion. Let me only say in conclusion that if some of the practical implications of my reasonings are felt to work out toward a slower rate of progress, this should not cause too great dismay. Let us not forget that progress is an

---

[8] Only a Cartesian view of the "animal machine," which I somehow see lingering here, could set the mind at rest, as in historical fact it did at its time in the matter of vivisection: But its truth is surely not established by definition.

optional goal, not an unconditional commitment, and that its tempo in particular, compulsive as it may become, has nothing sacred about it. Let us also remember that a slower progress in the conquest of disease would not threaten society, grievous as it is to those who have to deplore that their particular disease be not yet conquered, but that society would indeed be threatened by the erosion of those moral values whose loss, possibly caused by too ruthless a pursuit of scientific progress, would make its most dazzling triumphs not worth having. Let us finally remember that it cannot be the aim of progress to abolish the lot of mortality. Of some ill or other, each of us will die. Our mortal condition is upon us with its harshness but also its wisdom—because without it there would not be the eternally renewed promise of the freshness, immediacy, and eagerness of youth; nor, without it, would there be for any of us the incentive to number our days and make them count. With all our striving to wrest from our mortality what we can, we should bear its burden with patience and dignity.

ON THE BIRTH OF A SEVERELY HANDICAPPED INFANT *

Warren T. Reich and Harmon Smith

Case No. 149

Missy, the daughter of Mike and Sue B., was born with spina bifida with meningomyelocele, a defect which occurs approximately once in every 500 live births. Spina bifida refers to an abnormal opening in the spine, and meningomyelocele is a condition in which portions of the spinal cord, as well as meninges and spinal fluid, have slipped out through the abnormal opening and are enclosed in a sac which protrudes from the backbone. Up until ten years ago, almost 80 percent of these babies were certain to die in early infancy. Today, surgical treatment is available to ameliorate the condition, and about 75 percent now survive, although affected children all face a lifetime of illness, operations and varying degrees of disability, including mental retardation.

Soon after Missy's birth, a physician consulted with Mike B., giving full details of the severity of the condition which, in her case, already included spastic paraplegia, incontinence of urine and feces, and club feet. He explained the necessary treatment, costs and prognosis and urged that immediate surgery be performed to prevent further nerve damage. Without surgery, he said, Missy would probably contract meningitis which, if untreated, would either lead to more severe

---

* This is one of a series of case studies raising ethical dilemmas in medicine and the life sciences. The case and the commentaries are excerpts from a discussion which was originally presented at the International Congress of Learned Societies in the Field of Religion, September 1972.

    While this case represents an actual medical situation, the content and other identifying material are fictionalized.

handicaps or even be fatal. He explained further that if Missy survived an operation, she would never be able to walk without the aid of braces and crutches, that she would have to undergo extensive physical therapy all her life, and that she had a 90 percent chance of developing hydrocephalus ("water on the brain").

The parents were well-educated, with a good income and comprehensive medical insurance. Their three-year-old daughter was healthy. Each had known families with abnormal children.

Sue and Mike decided not to have Missy treated.

After her discharge from the hospital, Sue returned daily to feed and hold her child. Both she and Mike spent much of their time caring for Missy in the hospital and became very attached to her. When at the age of two weeks Missy began to develop symptoms of meningitis, Mike and Sue reversed their decision and asked to have her treated.

Surgical repair of the meningomyelocele was successful and Missy was discharged. When she was 4 months old low-grade hydrocephalus developed and a shunt was inserted to drain the cerebrospinal fluid from her brain. At age 6 months she was able to sit up with the aid of a special splint, and her personality was emerging, although it was too soon at that time to test her mental development. Mike and Sue seemed to have adjusted well to Missy and tried to treat her as much like a normal child as possible.

Have the doctors and the parents acted in Missy's best interest?

Warren T. Reich

The advantage of the case-study method is that a fairly typical combination of circumstances, usually involving some rather clear-cut alternatives, can be reflected upon in such a way as to shed light on the issues and judgments involved in similar cases. Each case of spina bifida, however, tends to be atypical, with the result that one set of "solutions" cannot readily be applied to other cases.

One way of discussing the questions surrounding "to treat or not to treat" is to examine whether the "working principle" of the licitness of withholding "extraordinary means" can be applied to a case of this kind. It is my opinion that this is an appropriate methodology for decision-making, and that in spite of the problems associated with the "extraordinary means" model (or perhaps because of them), this method avoids the two extremes of always using heroic measures and resorting to pediatric euthanasia.

A basic question in these cases is whether the responsible party has the obligation to preserve life in all situations and at all costs. One response is that we are always obliged to employ ordinary means to preserve life, even in hopeless cases; but that we are not obliged to use extraordinary means. This "principle" does not provide a checklist of specific medical procedures which are to be considered unusual and hence optional in all cases. The distinction between ordinary and extraordinary means is a device, based on relative factors, for assessing what should be considered obligatory and what should be considered elective in a particular situation where one is faced with the opportunity of prolonging a human life.

I believe that in some instances "extraordinary means" may be omitted in pediatric care, even if this means the newborn will die. This means that, in a case such as Missy's, full and adequate treatment should normally be given the newborn, but that in some instances, when the prognosis is very poor, it may legitimately be decided that surgery and other subsequent exceptional treatment should not be performed, and that only supportive care be given. However, this "principle" can only be applied to the newborn by taking into account the following five problems.

1. The concept of withholding extraordinary means has, up to the present, usually been applied to the elderly dying. If the concept is to be applied to the other end of life, one must take account of the fact that we are not necessarily speaking of a *dying* newborn, and that we are always speaking of one who has not had the opportunity of living a full life. There should be a general presumption that pediatric patients have a higher moral claim on "extraordinary" medical care than do adult or elderly patients.

2. The decision not to treat is a decision made on behalf of the newborn patient who cannot give or withhold consent, and who never has been able to make a prior expression of personal preference. I would take the position that the agent responsible for deciding on the child's behalf has the right to make a similar but not identical decision to the one he might make on his own behalf if he were dying.

3. It is usually assumed in this line of ethical reflection that the decision to withhold "extraordinary care" is a decision to let the infant die. In many cases of meningomyelocele, however, if comprehensive care including the initial surgery is withheld, the infant does not die: he/she may survive, the spinal condition may be worsened, complications may set in, and even more "extraordinary" care may be required than in the newborn's first condition. This possibility must be taken into account in making the decision, but it is not justification for pediatric euthanasia. Ethically speaking, the decision of parents and physician does not assume that they have full and prior dominion over the life of the newborn. Rather, their decision is rightly focused only on the feasibility (or non-feasibility) of a certain kind of care, in light of the expected consequences of the treatment.

4. "The treatment" of spina bifida does not simply involve a one-time corrective surgery immediately after birth. Adequate corrective care means "comprehensive" care: it begins with spinal surgery at birth and usually extends over many years. If, let us say, five to ten major interventions have to take place to prolong the life of the infant, does the question of administering vs. withholding treatment get resurrected each time?

Missy's parents made their initial decision on the basis of "objective" advice and prior experience. By the time they had made their second and final decision, they had learned something of the motivation and power that can come from the affective experience of the parent-child relationship. Although the decision to treat or not to treat a neonate should normally not be repeated, the reversal of the decision by Missy's parents was, in the circumstances, both understandable and praiseworthy.

5. It is assumed that the decision in favor of treating the infant is based on the conviction that there is "reasonable hope of success," whereas a decision against treatment is justified by the expectation that the surgery and subsequent treatment do not hold hope of such success. This raises the question: What is a "successful outcome"? The answer cannot come from medicine alone for it requires a value judgment on the "quality of life" of a newborn, the foreseen consequences of whose treatment can only partly be anticipated with accuracy at the present time.

It appears that Missy's parents did make their decision on the basis of what would appear to be extraordinary in the circumstances. They seemed to accept a basic responsibility to care for their child, and to acknowledge limits to their power over their offspring's life. The ambiguity and clumsiness of their decision, while unfortunate, is evidence of the relativity of the "principle" we have discussed.

Harmon Smith

Before the advent of surgical treatment for Missy's abnormality, her death or life would have been beyond human control and unaccompanied by the anguish of uncertain choice. Now the situation is different. The former circumstance was tragic; but it was tragedy in the classical conventions of theodicy, and largely a problem for speculative philosophy and theology. The present situation is also tragic in that ancient sense, but the tragedy in Missy's case is now compounded by another dimension: the human choice to elect an alternative which will almost certainly prolong her life but at probable costs and benefits which cannot yet be assessed.

We can begin by asking about medical responsibility. What is it, how does it function, what are its limits? On the face of it, the medical options appear to be fairly clear: (1) do not treat Missy's condition and allow her to contract meningitis which will (a) cause her death or (b) surviving that infection, leave her in an even more severely handicapped condition; or (2) treat her condition in the hope that mental retardation and physical handicap can be minimized by prompt action. In both options, the extent of damage cannot be precisely predicted.

For a long time now, it has been held that the doctor's obligation toward his patient is to prolong the patient's life and relieve pain. However, it is sometimes impossible to do both—life can be prolonged only at the expense of some distress, or pain can be relieved only at the eventual cost of life itself. According to the Hippocratic Oath, the highest good is the patient's well-being. In this case, the doctor's obligation is pre-eminently to "Missy herself" in a holistic interpretation of that phrase. The function of his responsibility is to achieve her well-being; the limit is her treatment and care. Other considerations, I would think, are beyond the immediate range of the physician's competence and obligation. To argue this is not to reduce the role of the physician to that of a technician. Rather, I would argue that the physician has his own special contribution to make to the decision for Missy but that his role in decision-making is proportional to the measure in which he will not or cannot be accountable for the consequences.

We can also inquire into parental responsibility, how it functions and what are its limits. In this case, the parents initially decided against treatment for Missy, and then reversed their decision. Interestingly, we are given some clues to account for the first decision, but not for the second. It almost appears that the details necessary to justify or excuse the first decision are irrelevant when the second decision is taken—that parental love for a baby is self-evident reason for electing to do everything possible to keep the child alive! Happily for the parents (and perhaps for Missy as well), their second decision seems to have resulted thus far in acceptable consequences. Still, it was a risk; the outcome might just as well have been different. In that event, we could also ask questions appropriate to parental responsibility; principally whether the parents were in fact carrying through with the consequences of their choice, for it is only in accountability for the consequences of choices that decisional responsibility can be fully evaluated.

The social aspects of the decision have already been hinted at. If the choice is made to prolong Missy's life, her life will impinge upon other lives. Can we say the benefits to Missy of her treatment are proportional to the investment of time, energy, resources, personnel, and all the rest? Is the social cost of providing these kinds of services to this kind of patient appropriate in view of our society's full range of needs for medical care? Will Missy be a contributing member to society; or is that less important than society's obligation to care for a certain number of its members who are non-contributory?

The difficulty with questions of this sort is that the rhetoric of our society suggests we have answered them when in fact there is both popular and professional diffidence toward discussing them. So we speak of the "inestimable worth of a single human life" but know full well that this is symbolic language and seldom functional in the pragmatic choices in our medical centers. Maybe that has been not only tolerable in our society, but necessary in the way that myths tend to safeguard sanity. I suspect, however, that we are answering these questions in operational ways that are not usually accompanied by articulate and coherent moral reasoning.

The dominant attitude in Western culture and Western medicine has been a denial of tragedy; we have looked instead to the expansion of knowledge and technology to give us progressive control of the world, and we have supposed that there is no mystery which defies an adequate human resolution. Insofar as this is true, we have undermined and repressed the human capacity for experiencing and affirming the tragic vision, or meaninglessness, or essential conflictedness. Missy's case is tragic in this sense because we see both sides, and having seen both sides, we can never again see the resolution of her situation in only one way. It is at the interface of the struggle for mastery and the awareness of tragedy that ethical theory and moral practice most clearly express the meaning of grace. Grace, in this context, is the capacity to act decisively without the self-justifying choices we would like to have had. I know this is a strange way of speaking in a technocracy, but unless we can discriminate between choosing decisively and choosing definitively, we have already abdicated the moral struggle and an important dimension of what it means to be men and women, and not gods.

PSYCHOSURGERY

Vernon L. Mark

. . .

My own position regarding the appropriateness of neurosurgery can be illustrated in terms of three alternatives. The first two of these I unequivocally reject:

The first of these positions holds that medical means should be undertaken to improve *any* behavior, wherever possible, be the behavior normal or abnormal. Although neurosurgery is not in a position now to improve normal behavior, some people advocate the use of drugs—amphetamines, for instance—for that purpose. The advantage of this position is that it avoids the obvious difficulties in defining normality. The grave disadvantage is that it makes the medical men authorities on improvement and the good life, which they are not, at least under our present social arrangement. Moral values are social concerns, not medical ones in any presently recognized sense.

A second position holds that any *abnormal* behavior should be treated by whatever medical means are available. Often argued by psychotherapists, this position says that, regardless of any *organic* abnormality, what is undesirable in abnormal behavior is the behavior, not its organic base. The criteria for alteration should refer to the behavior, irrespective of whether the organic base is normal or abnormal. Should an unusual brain abnormality produce a 50 point I.Q. *rise,* no one would suggest ablating it: its behavioral product is desirable. (With regard to neurosurgical control of violent behavior, I am *against* the principle that it could be used to treat abnormal behavior when there is no organic abnormality of the brain.)

A third position, then, is that medical procedures like neurosurgery should be used only when behavior is abnormal, and bad, as the result of an abnormality in the brain. As I shall repeat below, violent behavior *not* associated with brain disease should be dealt with politically and socially, not medically.

With this brief positioning of what I take to be support for a very circumscribed domain for neurosurgical procedures, I now want to deal with some common criticisms of neurosurgery. Most of the criticisms either construe neurosurgery to be capable of more than it is, or assume that it would be used in areas I believe to be inappropriate. Like any technological power, neurosurgery can be misused, and setting the limits of its use is more than a medical problem.

Political versus Personal Violence

Implicit in many of the criticisms of the surgical treatment of violent epileptics is the fear that this treatment will be used against political protestors. This fear is based on a semantic confusion about the word "violence." Many activities in our society are called violent. The "establishment" tends to view as violent any protest movement against the war, unfair living conditions, or the prison system. Protestors view the reaction of police and the National Guard as violent. Minority groups have indicated that social or job discrimination is a form of violence.

The kind of violent behavior for which I might approve neurosurgery, however, has a much narrower definition: *personal violent behavior; unwarranted and usually unprovoked acts that directly attempt to, or actually do injure or destroy another person or thing.* And, as I have said, I would not approve neurosurgery even in such cases unless the personal violence could be traced to organic brain disease and could not be treated by non-surgical methods.

Some political psychiatrists have argued that social injustice provokes individual acts of violence which seem "senseless" but which, in reality, are political protests against the social system. As Goebbels showed, political violence of mass proportions can be culled up without counting on people with diseased brains. However, the person whose violence is related to brain disease and is used by a Hitler or Goebbels is a danger to himself and his loved ones, and cannot be counted on to rage only in politically strategic situations. Thus, the morality of preventing such an individual from seeking proper medical diagnosis and care is certainly in question.

Biological Factors in Personal Violence

Many sociologists believe that brain dysfunction does not have a role in such behavioral abnormalities as intractable depression, thought disorders, paranoia, or aggressive assaultive behavior of the sort I am concerned with. In the last case, however, there is *solid* medical evidence to link aggressive behavior to focal brain disease. This behavioral symptom is often present in such clinical disorders as temporal lobe epilepsy, temporal lobe tumors, infections of the brain (such as rabies and post-encephalitic syndromes), and serious brain injuries which affect the under-surfaces of the frontal lobes and the anterior tips of the temporal lobes (usually a transient phenomenon in the last disorder).

The most frequent occurrence of brain dysfunction in violent behavior is in brain poisoning, the most serious and ubiquitous of which is caused by alcohol. Alcohol is a specific brain poison and individuals acutely poisoned with alcohol may have as much dysfunction during the poisoning as would be caused by a brain tumor, infection or injury. The only difference between the former and the latter is that alcohol poisoning is temporary.

The violence in automobile accidents caused by drunk drivers takes a far greater toll than the violence in political protest or repression. A drunk driver suffers from a temporary brain abnormality. Although I certainly do not advocate neurosurgery for the treatment of alcoholism, nor for all kinds of organic brain disease, it is clear that violence is sometimes a function of brain abnormalities, and should be viewed as such.

. . .

Dangers in a Medical Model of Violence

All sorts of dire predictions have been made about the outcome of brain research directed toward the understanding and treatment of emotional disorders, and especially those related to violent behavior. Shades of 1984! "The neurosurgeons want to put electrodes in everyone's brain to keep them from protesting!" "They're going to develop a new drug that will completely destroy the will!" "Man's dignity will be shattered and his innate human quality will be destroyed!" These would indeed be serious statements if they were true. But it is important to see just what the issues are.

It is one thing to advocate neurosurgical procedures for certain kinds of violent behavior caused by organic brain disease or dysfunction. It is quite another to advocate them as general methods of behavior control. My own belief is that no form of conditioning, drug therapy, or surgery is necessary or desirable to control normal-brained members of our society, no matter what their political views are or how they express them.

Of course it is true that behavior control techniques developed to be used in a circumscribed sphere might be adapted to widespread and immoral ends by unscrupulous people. No greater lesson is needed than that provided by Nazi Germany.

But interestingly enough, the controls Goebbels used were environmental ones, not direct alterations of the brain. No drugs were needed to seduce the German population. The S.S. storm troopers did not have little electrodes implanted in their limbic systems.

Although Joseph Goebbels might have reduplicated Skinner's experiments in the best conditioning traditions, he did so before, rather than after, the fact. As a clinician living among the German people for two years after the war, I could find nothing in them that would distinguish them from other human beings.

Can one imagine the most advanced brain electrode technology of the future, or even a new and much more sophisticated group of psychic drugs, that could produce a more perfect form of behavior control than that initiated by environmental "natural" factors in the Third Reich?

One of the important factors to emerge from our own research on the relative influence of deep electrical brain stimulation versus environmental "natural" stimuli is the importance, in terms of effectiveness, of the latter. Of course, effective electrical brain stimulation in target areas can produce pronounced behavioral effects. However, even in susceptible individuals with brain disease, the effect of nonconvulsing doses of electrical stimulation can be remarkably altered and suppressed by giving the subject a demanding and attention-absorbing task during electrical brain stimulation.

My thesis that behavior control through the direct manipulation of the brain is not as dangerous for mass abuse as environmental forms of control should not be taken to imply that it has no dangers whatsoever for mass abuse. But the social limitations on who performs neurosurgery or administers drugs, on whom, and for what reasons, ought to be set through public discussion and social decision. My own claim is that the dangers of mass abuse are not sufficient to warrant preventing the very development of the techniques that might have very great therapeutic value for patients with organic brain disease.

Moral Problems in Neurosurgery

If neurosurgery is not much of a danger as a political tool, there still are serious problems with its medical use. I would like to address two of these.

First is the problem of neurological diagnosis. The emphasis I have been placing on the neurological side of the problem of violence ought not be taken out of the context of environmental factors also. Due to the very fundamental problem of specialization in medicine, it is very difficult to maintain a biological-social model of violence in actual practice. The neurologists are in one place and the psychiatrists and social workers are in another.

Yet if the model is worthwhile, treatment of a patient should involve not only his brain but his family, living conditions, job and role in society. It is very important, therefore, to imbed a neurological diagnosis of problems of violence into a larger integrated approach to human behavior. The social forms for this holistic therapy are yet to be worked out, although my own group has tried to include psychiatric and social psychiatric diagnosis along with the neurological.

From my reading of the present situation, however, I believe the greater danger is that the neurological side will be left out. Recently, for example, an airplane hijacker killed one pilot and shot another before he himself was subdued with a blow to the head. Examination of this man afterward revealed he had been a neurological cripple for eleven years, ever since receiving a gunshot wound of the brain. Yet repeated tests, including hours of brainwave examinations, psychological testing, psychiatric and neurological assessment, failed to reveal the tremendous damage that had occurred in this man's emotional center or limbic brain.

The difficulties of diagnosis had their classic but tragic expression in the case of George Gershwin. This talented composer was seen and treated psychiatrically for a long time while a tumor in the limbic system of his brain grew to an unmanageable and untreatable size. The George Gershwin syndrome of the thirties is still being treated in the seventies. Recently eighteen patients were committed to a mental hospital at one of our best university centers who turned out to have tumors of their limbic brains. In some cases, the true nature of this illness was not recognized until the tumor had caused the patient's death.

Second, after the diagnosis of brain disease has been confirmed, *what are the problems of proper consent to treatment?* Does the patient consent to the treatment? Does he know the dangers of the treatment, and how those dangers compare with letting him pass without treatment? What are the wider factors involved in informed consent when the patient is mentally incompetent? [1]

Usually close members of their families are the sources of consent. But in cases of surgery for violence, I believe the patient and his family should have the assistance of an impartial, noninvolved professional group to determine whether surgery or other forms of treatment should be undertaken. In practical terms, this means that a committee of some sort, composed of physicians, or in some cases, physicians and informed laymen, should be present to monitor the medical, psychiatric, and/or surgical treatment. [2]

In my own practice, I and my group do not accept patients for treatments who do not want therapy, and we do not believe that the public good or public interest should intrude upon the personal medical model in terms of protecting the public against violent individuals.

Free Will and Behavior Control

Radical critics of the biological-social model of violence often construe human violence to be an expression of free will. In line with this they consider the medical correction of brain disease that would, as a secondary result, stop violent episodes, to have an unnatural and degrading effect on human dignity. As a physician I find this view particularly inappropriate, not because I deny free will, but because I prize the quality of human life.

Many of the patients who come to us with focal brain disease associated with violent behavior are so offended by their own actions they have attempted suicide. They feel their human dignity has been lost precisely because of uncontrollable behavior patterns they find unnatural and repugnant.

Because our work, and that of other physicians, has indicated a clinical relationship between limbic brain disease, such as temporal lobe epilepsy, and aggressive assaultive behavior, *I believe the correction of that organic condition gives the patient more rather than less, control over his own behavior.* It enhances, and does not diminish, his dignity. It adds to, and does not detract from, his human qualities.

---

[1] Prison inmates suffering from epilepsy should receive only medical treatment; surgical therapy should not be carried out, because of the difficulty in obtaining truly informed consent.

[2] In conjunction with Dr. David Allen, we are exploring "consumer advocacy" utilizing a group with religious, legal and community representatives in addition to physicians.

Finally, it is appropriate to return to the specter of a tryrannical government controlling a submissive population through neurosurgery and electrical brain stimulation. Even though this is technically unlikely now, it is a possibility to be conjured with. In the face of this possibility I still have great confidence that the neurological research in behavior control now being done will lead to a better understanding of brain mechanisms, and that when this occurs, *it should be possible for brain scientists to devise techniques for making behavior control of one individual by another more difficult or even impossible.*

In other words, one of the expected benefits of increased brain research will be the creation of new techniques enabling each individual better to control or govern his or her behavior, without unwarranted or unwanted interference by other individuals or devices.

There is already enough knowledge of environmental and psychopharmacological drugs to control a vast segment of our population, without invoking brain surgery or electrical brain stimulation. The great hope of emotional brain research is that it will free us from our present tyrannies and future dangers of control. To this end brain scientists need the help of philosophers, ethicists, theologians, social scientists and jurists, working in concert.

PRISON PSYCHIATRY: THE CLOCKWORK CURE

Bernard Weiner

San Francisco

The doctor straps the straitjacketed patient into a chair, injects the drug Prolixin, and tightens the eyelid clamps so that the patient cannot avoid watching the screen. The film begins. Each time an act of sex or violence is observed, the patient becomes progressively more nauseated. After enough of these treatments, he is "cured" of his aggressive impulses.

Aversion therapy, such as that paraphrased above from Stanley Kubrick's supposedly futurist film, *A Clockwork Orange,* is employed frequently in prisons and hospitals around the world. Armed with a battery of new behavioral drugs and techniques, doctors can go even further in "adjusting" antisocial personalities to behavioral norms. The new technology is upon us well in advance of 1984; the ethical problems associated with it are only beginning to demand attention.

A new prison facility in California provides a good example of the technological-moral conflict. It is called the Medical-Psychiatric Diagnostic Unit (MPDU) and is part of the Department of Correction's Medical Facility at Vacaville. It has eighty-four beds, and is designed to handle eventually all 600 to 700 inmates from the various prison

Adjustment Centers (maximum-security wings) around the state. According to the Department of Corrections, the new facility will be used to diagnose and treat inmates with problems and then, it is hoped, return them as better individuals to the prison mainline, perhaps ultimately to the outside world. That sounds benevolent, but inmates and their supporters view the MPDU as a laboratory of behavioral "torture," which in practice will be performed primarily upon militant black and Chicano organizers in the prison population.

There is room for either interpretation, depending upon one's assumptions. If you believe that the primary function of penal administration is to operate a smooth-running system, then anything done to quiet the present hair-trigger prison situation is good. In addition, you may think it obviously humane to help violence-prone inmates adjust to a system that may eventually parole them and accept them on the outside. However, many inmates believe that the prison system—perhaps by design, certainly in practice—denies them the essential prerogatives of consideration as human beings, and they are accordingly alarmed by any medical-psychiatric facility aimed at curing them of "problems" the prison doctors think they detect in failures to adjust to a basically inhumane system.

Which interpretation is nearer the truth? What follows is a history of the MPDU controversy at Vacaville (Cowtown).

On November 19, 1971, the California Department of Corrections (DOC) invited a group of psychologists, psychiatrists, researchers and prison officials to meet at the University of California (Davis) to discuss prison violence and a possible new psychiatric unit at Vacaville. At the meeting, DOC officials were entirely vague as to what kind of treatment they envisioned at the proposed new facility. Pointed questions about electroshock therapy, aversion techniques and the like were evaded; several DOC officials even hastily disappeared when the questioning became too direct. What the invited participants didn't know was that, a week before standing host to the meeting at Davis, the DOC had submitted a detailed proposal for the Vacaville facility. "Looking back on it now," said one of the participants, "it is clear that we professionals were brought in to, as it were, 'legitimize' a decision that had already been made."

One of those present was Dr. Edward Opton, senior research psychologist at the Wright Institute, Berkeley. He pressed prison officials to deal with the ethical questions associated with a new psychiatric facility for prisoners—issues such as the voluntary nature of treatment, the use of aversion therapy drugs, electroshock, and so on—but was told by the DOC's research director, Dr. Lawrence Bennett, that "those who wish to discuss so-called moral and ethical questions should leave."

Shortly after Davis, the press picked up a story that the DOC contemplated brain surgery for certain "violence-prone" inmates. When this news made the headlines, the DOC maintained that it was speaking only of possible electrocauterization (by inserting needles into the brain) for a small number of inmates who might have temporal lobe epilepsy, a rare and difficult-to-diagnose disease which often results in violent behavior. That might have been accepted as a reasonable explanation, if inmate support groups had not obtained a copy of a letter, dated September 8, 1971, from Raymond K. Procunier, head of the DOC, to the California Council on Criminal Justice, which would arrange the financing of the project. Procunier's letter made no reference to temporal lobe epilepsy; it spoke only of surgery for "aggressive, destructive" inmates—to prison guards and wardens that could mean any prisoner who refused to knuckle under to the system.

The proposal offered by the DOC on November 11, a week before the gathering at Davis, refers to "serious management problem inmates" as one of its main reasons for setting up the MPDU at Vacaville:

The control and management of these segregated inmates have become a serious problem, as shown by the recent episodes of violence and disturbance in different prisons where Adjustment Centers have been established. It appears that the present method of handling these cases through the existing Adjustment Centers has been inadequate and the problem remains unsolved. New ways and perceptions are now urgently needed to provide a better approach for handling of these cases.

The statewide uproar over the proposal to cauterize parts of the brains of "management problem" inmates was strong enough to make the DOC back off. The brain surgery plan was shelved, but DOC officials refused to dismiss it completely, the implication being that it might be reactivated at a more appropriate time.

Enough information was getting out—through Dr. Opton and stories in the underground and then the regular media—to stimulate the formation of inmate defense groups. The Bay Area chapter of the Medical Committee for Human Rights became interested, along with ex-prisoner groups, a prison law project, and an ad hoc organization, the Committee on Psychiatric Experimentation on Prisoners. This last group, made up of professionals, convened a meeting in Berkeley in December, to which it invited key DOC officials. In the main, the members wanted to know how the consent of the prisoners was obtained, and the type of psychotherapy to be performed at Vacaville.

They felt they had reason to be suspicious, especially given the DOC's previous use of the drug Anectine. Prolixin makes one nauseated; Anectine (succinylcholine chloride) paralyzes one's voluntary muscles for one-and-a-half to two minutes. According to those who have been injected, the patient is overwhelmed by a feeling of suffocation, of drowning, of sinking into death. While in this fearful state, the inmate is told that when next he has an impulse to smash or attack, he will stop and think and remember the sensation he is experiencing under Anectine.

Anectine was used by the DOC on about thirty prison inmates in the late 1960s. When a psychiatrist asked about consent, the DOC medical director, Dr. John Gorman, wrote that "every one of these patients had signed an informed consent." However, a report made for the DOC by two researchers, Drs. Arthur Mattocks and Charles Jew, states that "the patient was requested to sign a statement of consent. On five patients, consent was not received from the patient himself, but was granted by the institution's Special Treatment Board. Thus, these five patients were included in the treatment program against their will." (These prisoners have since sued the state.) The Anectine is still being stored on the shelf, and the inmates know it. Remembering the statement of the Vacaville superintendent (he is in fact a solicitous warden), Dr. L. J. Pope, they might have some doubts about the motives of their therapists. Said Pope: "If they don't want to take the drug, they don't have to. If they want to stay cuckoo and stay locked up all their lives, that's all right with us."

The DOC tends to see violence and mental disturbance either as organic malfunction or as the result of some outside conspiracy. Like prison administration everywhere, it will rarely acknowledge that the prison system itself produces the violence.

If it is organic or fomented from outside, then the obvious remedies are to devise physical and psychological "therapy," or to come down hard on the prisoners and their supporters. Electroshock therapy was administered at Vacaville nearly 500 times in 1971; Prolixin was injected 1,093 times in 1970. Reports out of the California State Hospital for the Criminally Insane at Atascadero repeatedly mention that genital electoshock was used on sexual offenders as aversion therapy. (Reportedly, the inmates are shown movies of explicit sexual content. If they begin to display evidence of sexual arousal, their gentials are shocked. This program is entitled "Errorless Extinction of Penile Responses.") And there is Procunier's letter, seeking funds to cauterize the brains of "aggressive" inmates. "You don't have to wait until they turn on the gas when you see them building showers with gas nozzles on them," Dr. Opton told me as he summed up the DOC's past record and contemplated what might go on at the new MPDU facility at Vacaville.

After several delays, the MPDU opened its doors (to the prisoners, not the press) in mid-February. All attempts to speak with responsible officials were rebuffed and reporters were shunted off to the Vacaville public relations officer who would say nothing but promised a press release. That statement, accompanied by snapshots of parts of the MPDU facility, says that "medication will be administered only to those inmates who are obviously hallucinating or functioning within a well-established delusional system. Only those drugs which are routinely used for such cases in other institutions within the Department of Corrections and the Department of Mental Health will be employed in the treatment of such symptoms. *No* new or experimental drugs will be evaluated or introduced. . . ."

That statement is more interesting than it looks at first glance. The original MPDU proposal, a copy of which I possess, requests funds in the amount of $9,360 for tranquilizers, stating, "it is estimated that an average of sixty of the eighty-four beds will be filled with an individual requiring medication. The estimated cost per patient per week is $3." In other words, at any given moment, about three-fourths of the inmates are expected to be doped on tranquilizers. As Dr. Philip Shapiro, a psychiatrist who was present at the original Davis meeting, observes, that is hardly a situation lending itself to adequate psychiatric diagnosis.

The DOC press release is also somewhat ambiguous on aversion therapy drugs and techniques. It is possible that it refers solely to tranquilizers, but Prolixin and Anectine have been used at both Vacaville and Atascadero, and thus the DOC statement that "no new or experimental drugs will be . . . introduced" would be technically true.

The press release goes on to state categorically that "there will be *no* surgical procedures employed other than those ordinarily needed in the treatment of natural diseases or injury. No electric shock treatments and no aversive therapy—in short, no physical or psychiatric-psychological experimentation—is planned. . . ." However, critics of the facility are quick to point out that until all the negative publicity broke, the DOC definitely was planning to go ahead with brain cauterization and that the DOC has never stated categorically that it has abandoned the idea. (DOC planning director Walter Barkdull said the brain surgery project is a "second-phase thing," to be reconsidered if an overall study indicates that it would be desirable.)

If no experimental therapy is to be performed by MPDU at Vacaville, what *will* the doctors be doing to the prisoners there, and why all the outlay of money? According to one of the research psychiatrists most heavily involved, Dr. George Bach-y-Rita, the MPDU program will involve little more than intensive diagnosis through electroencephalogram and traditional doctor-patient and group therapy discussions; also perhaps some training in Alpha-wave meditation. The way he describes it, MPDU sounds like an Esalen behind the bars. The Vacaville facility, he says, is merely a convenience; it is near San Francisco and doctors can get there easily, whereas they might not be so eager to make long trips away from their practices to each of the state prisons to work with Adjustment Center inmates.

That seems a frank explanation, but there is some reason to doubt that even Dr. Bach-y-Rita believes it. I have seen a copy of a strong 5-page letter he has sent to his DOC superiors, raising many of the ethical objections voiced by outside critics. He says, in notably blunt language, that he will work at Vacaville only in the traditional forms of psychotherapy and will have nothing to do with any of the more extreme treatments used by the DOC in the past or contemplated for the future. (These would include not only electroshock and Prolixin and Anectine but sex hormone injections, brain cauterization, sound-wave control techniques, and lithium carbonate. Of the latter, "We don't really know exactly what it does," says Dr. Joseph Tupin, who has administered it for years to manic-depressive prisoners at Vacaville. Despite that ignorance, and despite the press release that promises no experimental drugs, the MPDU funding proposal reads: "There has been, for an example, a study in the California

Medical Facility to determine the usefulness of lithium carbonate in treating hyperaggressive, acting-out patients. Further follow-up in this area would make a significant contribution.")

"Look," Dr. Opton told the members of the Committee on Psychiatric Experimentation on Prisoners, "either the Department of Corrections has built this expensive, fancy super-Adjustment Center isolation hole as a research and treatment facility and has no idea what it's going to do (Can we believe that? Are they really that dumb?), or they do know what they're going to do . . . and they're not telling us. . . . This worries me a great deal. It reminds me very much of Soviet psychiatric medicine as applied to political prisoners."

Dr. Bach-y-Rita—a young, Harvard-trained psychiatrist who is a member of the American Psychiatric Association's Task Force on Violence—discussed with me another sore point for scrupulous doctors working within the prison system. That is the nonconfidentiality of their medical records. A psychiatrist at Soledad State Prison last year, Dr. Frank Rundle, refused to turn over to the DOC his confidential medical records of therapy discussions he had held with a prisoner under suspicion for murder within the prison. Acting under an advisory opinion from the State Attorney General that all prison records are the property of the State of California, the authorities seized Dr. Rundle's medical records while he was surrounded by armed guards. How, I asked Dr. Bach-y-Rita, will such tactics help to develop trust between already hypersuspicious prisoners and their psychiatrist counselors? It won't, he said. How, then, will the therapy be conducted and how will the records be kept confidential? "I intend to take very few notes," he said with a bitter grin.

The MPDU at Vacaville raises still another question. According to its public position, the aim of the MPDU is, if possible, to "cure" the inmate and return him to the prison mainline; if he doesn't respond to the therapy, he will be returned to the Adjustment Center whence he came. However, the MPDU funding document contains a third, more ominous possibility, which has not been publicly revealed: "Those inmates who are found to be mentally ill may have to be reclassified for appropriate treatment." Nothing is said as to who will judge the inmate's mental state, on what basis, or what the "appropriate treatment" might be. Indeed, so many questions are raised by the secrecy surrounding the MPDU that the Berkeley City Council recently instructed the city attorney to investigate the possibility of initiating some legal proceedings to halt the program until clear answers can be obtained.

According to the DOC press release, "admission to this program will be voluntary on the part of the inmate, and he will be carefully evaluated for acceptance. . . ." But even in the MPDU's opening weeks of operation, prisoners complained of being under pressure to sign the consent forms for transfer to Vacaville. Several have filed class-action suits to prevent all inmate transfers to the MPDU. One San Quentin prisoner says he was told by a guard, "You'll stay in here until you die if you don't sign that consent form." Another inmate said that he signed the form while drugged on the tranquilizer Thorazine, and that it was never made clear to him what it was he was "volunteering" to do.

Prisoners have traditionally been used as "volunteers" (read: guinea pigs) for a variety of medical experiments—testing vaccines, drugs, therapy techniques, etc.—usually to earn some extra money or to increase their chances for an early parole or a reduction in their indeterminate sentence. However, even a former San Quentin associate warden, Douglas Rigg, doubts the voluntary nature of any of these programs. "There is a real question in my mind," he told me, "whether any prisoner can be considered, in the true sense of the word, a volunteer for any program. The possibilities for direct or subtle coercion are all too obvious."

Yet, the DOC is seeking voluntary consent forms from the most embittered and suspicious inmates held in California's prisons. The "Adjustment Centers" were originally conceived in grand behavioral terms, to be staffed with "a large, highly skilled team of rehabilitation experts," where unadjusted men "would be allowed to take full advantage of the educational, vocational, medical and psychiatric resources of the prison system." The reality is different. The ACs today are, to a large extent, simple segregation lockups where many of the most militant prison organizers are kept apart from the mainline. Far from being rehabilitated, a *Sacramento Bee* report states, prisoners are forced to live in the ACs "under conditions which prison psychiatrists say have driven normal men mad."

On March 10, ten Folsom Prison inmates filed suit in federal court to seek a restraining order which would prevent California prison officials from arbitrarily locking up prisoners in the Adjustment Centers. The suit asserted that many of the inmates so segregated are blacks and Chicanos, placed in the ACs because of their political views. Two of the inmates, L. Wayne Benner and Phillip Eder, charged that they were put in the AC as "agitators" because of letters they had written to California legislators urging them to act on prison reform. ("Attica is coming to this prison," they warned in their letters.) A DOC spokesman, commenting on the suit, said racially militant inmates are not confined to the ACs "as long as they're not trying to propagandize" other inmates. In other words, if you're quiet and submissive to the prison system, you're in no trouble; the minute you begin to sound off, or even to discuss your constitutional rights with other inmates, you can be classified as an "agitator" and popped into the AC segregation cell, thereby risking the denial of favorable parole consideration.

That is what bothers the various inmate support groups. According to Dr. Shapiro, a leader in the Bay Area chapter of the Medical Committee for Human Rights, the MPDU seems to be aimed precisely at black and Chicano militants within the ACs, and at those in general who refuse to accept the dehumanizing prison system. One San Quentin guard, for example, recently told an inmate scheduled for transfer to Vacaville that when he came back back from the MPDU, "you won't be a militant anymore."

No doubt, there are prisoners in the AC holding-tanks who are mentally ill, and who could be helped by intensive diagnosis and therapy at the MPDU in Vacaville. But how are the really insane to be separated from those whom the prison authorities regard as "mentally disturbed" because they refuse to abandon their dignity to the repressive nature of the prison system? Dr. Bach-y-Rita candidly admits that "of course, there will be mistakes, there will be misdiagnoses and misuse of tranquilizers" at the MPDU facility, but feels they will be few and can be corrected. Prisoners suspect that the more politically active inmates will be the ones most frequently "misdiagnosed." Dr. Stephen Sheppard, who heads the MPDU facility, agrees that thère is "the potential for abuse. . . . All I can say is as long as I'm in charge it's not going to happen." His superior at Vacaville, Dr. Pope, laments: "There's no trust in us. What's happened to trust in this country?"

What's happening at Vacaville is only a sample of what's happening all over the world, as technological tools come into the hands of psychiatrists and bureaucrats. Female sex hormones are injected into male sex offenders in Australia; 100,000 brain operations were performed last year, many of them on ordinary neurotics; drugs are dispensed to hyperactive (or hyper-bored) kids in schools to slow them down; prisoners are subjected to the most horrifying aversion therapy. (Says Dr. Arthur Nugent, who administered Anectine to prisoners at Vacaville, "The prison grapevine works fast and even the toughest have come to fear and hate the drug. I don't blame them—I wouldn't have the treatment myself for the world.") More and more, political considerations become paramount in psychiatry—openly within the Soviet Union, more subtly perhaps in the United States.

THE MYTH OF MENTAL ILLNESS

Thomas S. Szasz

On Feb. 28, 1966, the Unites States Court of Appeals for the Second Circuit handed down a decision which displaced the time-honored M'Naghten Rule as a test of criminal insanity, and substituted for it a new rule recommended by the American Law Institute.

The M'Naghten Rule dates from 1843, when one Daniel M'Naghten shot and killed a man named Drummond, the private secretary of Sir Robert Peel, whom M'Naghten had intended to kill. At M'Naghten's trial, evidence was introduced showing that he "was laboring under an insane delusion" of being hounded by enemies, among them Peel. The jury found him "not guilty, on the ground of insanity."

De jure, M'Naghten was acquitted; *de facto,* he was sentenced to life imprisonment in an insane asylum. He died in 1865, having been incarcerated for the last 22 years of his life.

The new ruling (binding on Federal courts in New York, Connecticut and Vermont) provides that: "A person is not responsible for criminal conduct if at the time of such conduct as a result of mental disease or defect he lacks substantial capacity either to appreciate the wrongfulness of his conduct or to conform his conduct to the requirements of law."

Both of these tests—and others, whatever their semantic differences—rest on the premise that the human mind may become "diseased," and that a person who has a "diseased mind" may, because of it, commit criminal acts unintentionally, not know the difference between right and wrong, or be unable to restrain himself from engaging in conduct prohibited by law. The value of all psychiatric tests of criminal responsibility thus hinges on the soundness of this underlying concept of "mental disease."

But what exactly is mental disease? If it is an illness, what kind is it? And if it is not an illness, what is it and why is it called an illness? Because of the frequency with which issues of mental health and illness arise not only in criminal cases but in matters of everyday life, it is important that we ask these questions and intelligently debate various possible answers to them.

I submit that mental illness is a myth. Bodies are physical objects; minds, whatever they may be, are not physical objects. Accordingly, mental diseases (such as depression or schizophrenia) cannot exist in the sense in which bodily diseases (such as broken bones or ulcerated skins) exist.

My disbelief in mental illness does not mean that I reject any facts of human behavior. "A myth," says the British philosopher Gilbert Ryle, "is not a fairy story. It is the presentation of facts belonging in one category in the idiom belonging to another. To explode a myth is accordingly not to deny facts, but to reallocate them." To say that mental illness is a myth is therefore not to *deny* facts (such as sadness or fear) but to *reallocate* them (from the category of mental illness to the category of personal conduct). Insofar as men are human beings, not machines, they always have some choice in how they act—hence, they are always responsible for their conduct. There is method in madness, no less than in sanity.

As long ago as the early nineteen-twenties, George H. Mead formulated the thesis that social situations—and human behavior in them—are analogous to games which must be played by certain "rules." In life, the games are infinite. As social conditions undergo rapid change, old games are constantly scrapped and new ones started. But most people are totally unprepared to shift from one type of game playing to another. They have early in life learned one set of rules—or, at most, a few—and find themselves forced to play new games by the old rules. This fundamental conflict leads to various problems in living—some severe enough to be commonly diagnosed as "mental illness" or "disease." It is these problems in living that the psychiatrist is usually called on to treat.

"But surely," someone might say, "a dope fiend, a rapist, or a Lee Harvey Oswald is not a *normal* person. What difference does it make whether we call him sick or something else?"

It makes, of course, all the difference in the world, for what we call things, and especially people, will shape our attitudes and justify our actions toward them. For example, when socially threatening behavior is called "witchcraft," it is handled by means of theological sanctions; when it is called "crime," it is handled by means of judicial sanctions, and when it is called "mental illness," it is handled by means of psychiatric sanctions.

The practices of modern American psychiatrists originate from two principal sources: hospital psychiatry and psychoanalysis.

Institutions for the care of the insane have existed since antiquity. However, the systematic confinement of madmen in buildings labeled "hospitals" did not begin until the middle of the 17th century. For about 250 years, from 1650 to 1900, the psychiatrist worked almost exclusively in the mental hospital. The alienist, as he was then called, was employed by an institution—a private or, more often, a public insane asylum.

The historical model and social prototype of the modern mental hospital is the French Hôpital Général. According to the distinguished medical historian George Rosen, the purposes of this institutional system were threefold: "In part they were economic: to increase [the] manufacture [of goods], provide productive work for the able-bodied, and to end unemployment; in part social: to punish willful idleness, restore public order, and rid Paris of beggars; and in part, religious and moral: to relieve the needy, the ill and suffering, to deal with immorality and antisocial behavior, and to provide Christian instruction."

A few years after its foundation, the Hôpital Général of Paris alone contained 6,000 persons, or about 1 per cent of the population. Who were these "mentally ill" people? According to regulations issued in 1680, "children of artisans and other poor inhabitants of Paris up to the age of 25 . . . girls who were debauched or in evident danger of being debauched . . . [and] wayward children . . ." were among those listed as proper subjects for confinement. In addition, old people, persons with venereal diseases, epileptics, vagrants, prostitutes—in brief, all of society's *"misérables"*—were incarcerated in the Hôpital Général. Michel Foucault, a French student of psychiatric history, thus concludes: "The Hôpital Général is not a medical establishment. It is rather a sort of semijudicial structure, an administrative entity which, along with already constituted powers, and outside the courts, decides, judges and executes."

The facts I have cited are important in showing us one of the roles of the psychiatrist —indeed, his traditional role: He is a physician working in a mental hospital, employed, as a rule, by the state, and charged with the task of confining and "treating" people who are considered "insane." Although some of his methods have changed, the social role of the institutional psychiatrist has remained what it has always been.

Nor is its importance diminished. At the present time in the United States, approximately 750,000 persons are incarcerated in mental hospitals—90 per cent of them against their will. This is about three times the number of persons imprisoned in jails.

The mental hospital is also important for the psychiatrist: Of 15,200 practicing psychiatrists in the United States, approximately 50 per cent are in institutional practice, most of them in mental hospitals, or in related administrative positions.

I do not imply that the hospital psychiatrist does not try to help his patient, but rather that his interpretation of "helping" is different from the patient's. If one person has the power to confine another, and uses it, it seems inevitable that the confined person will consider the other his jailer. This point of view, often held by mental patients, was expressed by Valentine Alamazov, the protagonist of Valeriy Tarsis's autobiographical novel, "Ward 7." Finding himself incarcerated in a mental hospital, Alamazov had this to say to his psychiatrist:

"I don't regard you as a doctor. You call this a hospital, I call it a prison. . . . So, now, let's get everything straight. I am your prisoner, you are my jailer, and there isn't going to be any nonsense about my health . . . or about examination and treatment."

It was Sigmund Freud who created the second major form of contemporary American psychiatric practice—psychoanalysis.

In the eighteen-eighties, when Freud was a young physician, to be a psychiatrist was to be an alienist or hospital psychiatrist. Traditionally, the psychiatrist was called in by a "mentally healthy" member of the family to treat one of its "mentally sick" members; often this meant removing the sick member from the family and putting him in a mental hospital as a "patient."

Freud departed from this traditional approach. Instead of acting as the agent of the family—ostensibly caring for the patient, but actually protecting the family from him—Freud created a new professional role—the agent of the patient.

He did not accept the situation as it was presented to him, usually by the patient's family. Instead, he listened at length to the patient to ascertain how he perceived his problem; and he tried to help him realize his own aspirations and goals, even if these brought the patient, or Freud himself, into even greater conflict with the family or with society.

Thus, ethically, Freud acted like other physicians, but unlike other psychiatrists: He tried to help his patient, not someone else. By systematically refusing to "treat" patients who did not want to be treated by him, Freud departed from the accepted psychiatric methods of his day. Many psychoanalysts still adhere to this principle in treating patients. Most hospital psychiatrists do not.

It is important to note also that Freud characterized psychoanalytic treatment in humanistic and pedagogic terms and did not regard his work as medical. Psychoanalysis was never intended to make "sick" people "well" again. The analyst's task, in Freud's words, was "to serve the patient . . . as a teacher and educator."

Freud was emphatic that the analyst—and hence also the psychotherapist who only listens and talks and uses no "medical" methods—does not cure disease. Indeed, although the three great pioneers of psychoanalysis—Freud, Adler and Jung—had little good to say about one another's doctrines and methods in later years, they all agreed on one thing: that psychological methods of therapy are *not* medical procedures.

We are now ready to reconsider the question: What is mental illness? In order to do this, it is necessary to understand the principal uses of the concept of mental illness and their social consequences.

First, the term "mental illness" is used to refer to certain types of bodily diseases—that is, to diseases of the brain whose predominant symptoms are abnormalities of behavior (for example, neurosyphilis). According to one school of psychiatric thought, all mental diseases are of this type. Those who hold this view assume that some metabolic, genetic or neurological defect—perhaps a very subtle one—will ultimately be found to explain all disorders of thinking and behavior now called "mental illness."

No one would deny that, like any other part of the body, the brain may be injured or become diseased. Nor are there, to my knowledge, any psychiatrists who would deny that some of the people nowadays diagnosed as mentally ill (and free of demonstrable organic disease) might actually be suffering from the effects of as yet undiscovered neurologic or metabolic disease processes. But for those who regard mental illness as a type of brain disease, the concept of mental illness is unnecessary and misleading. If they mean that people labeled mentally ill suffer from diseases of the brain, it would seem better for the sake of clarity to say that and not something else.

The second major use of the term "mental illness" is to denote a "functional" or "psychological" disorder. Proponents of this view admit that patients called "mentally ill" do not suffer from bodily diseases, but they maintain that such individuals exhibit defects or deformations of their personalities so severe as to justify calling them "ill."

When physicians (or others) label people as "sick" merely because their actions differ from those of their fellows, they speak metaphorically—as poets, not scientists. To be sure, this kind of metaphoric use of the term "sick" is not limited to psychiatry: People also say that our economy is "sick," that a joke is "sick" or that someone they dislike makes them "sick." Yet only in connection with mental illness do we systematically act as if figure of speech were fact. No one believes that "sick economies" require medical help, but nearly everyone believes that "sick minds" do.

The power to name, or to classify, is the basis for the third use of the term "mental illness"—that is, to denote a deviant social role. For our purposes it is necessary only to distinguish between two types of social roles: those that are assumed voluntarily, such as husband or graduate student, and those that are ascribed to a person against his will, such as draftee or convicted criminal.

Roles are social artifacts. Role deviance, therefore, has meaning only in the context of specific social customs and laws. The criminal is deviant because he breaks the law; the homosexual because most people are heterosexuals; the atheist because most people believe—or say they believe—in God. In the same way, the so-called "potential killer" (who, however, has not yet killed anyone) is considered deviant because he appears to be more dangerous than most people; and so is the chronically withdrawn mental-hospital patient, because most people are—and are expected to be—socially more responsive. (I shall say more about the problems that such persons pose for those about them, and for society in general, later on.)

But which kinds of social deviance constitute "mental illness"? The answer is: that conduct which deviates from psychiatrically defined rules of mental health.

However obvious this may be, its implications for our understanding of mental illness seem to be vastly unappreciated. The fact is that every time psychiatrists formulate a new rule of mental health they create a new class of mentally sick individuals. For example, the proposition that prejudice against Jews or Negroes is a manifestation of psychopathology—one of many instances in the contemporary inflation of the concept of mental illness—is nothing but an attempt to expand the category of people who can be legitimately classified as psychologically sick.

Since the consequences of being labeled mentally ill include such penalties as personal degradation, loss of employment, loss of the right to drive a car, to vote, to make valid contracts or to stand trial—and, last but not least, incarceration in a mental hospital, possibly for life—the expansion of the category of people who can be so designated is useful for the increased employment of psychiatric methods of social control.

Labeling someone mentally ill is a special kind of name-calling. In other fields name-calling may constitute libel, but calling someone "mentally sick" does not. The main reason for this is that the psychiatrist who makes a diagnosis of mental illness (especially on an involuntary patient) has more social power than the person he diagnoses.

The role of power in the psychiatric diagnostic process becomes obvious only when the potential patient is a Very Important Person. When someone like Secretary of Defense Forrestal disturbs people by his ideas and actions, it is difficult to get a psychiatrist to label him mentally ill. The reason for this is that by casting the individual in a socially deviant role the psychiatric diagnostician imparts a negative, debased identity to that person. This he cannot do if his intended "patient" is socially more powerful than he is. When a mental-hospital superintendent in Louisiana tried to incarcerate and "treat" Gov. Earl Long, the Governor fired the doctor—and walked out of the hospital.

One of the traditional problems of legal psychiatry, as we saw at the outset, is the determination of criminal insanity. Lawyers and psychiatrists persist in trying to distinguish between "sane" and "insane" criminals, and in finding a "scientific" basis for determining which offenders ought to be "punished" with imprisonment and which "treated" with involuntary mental hospitalization.

I submit that criminal insanity is a metaphorical and strategic concept just as civil insanity is. The effort to distinguish, by psychiatric methods, among different classes of criminals is really an exercise in second-order classification: Having labeled some persons as "criminals," we have the option of labeling them also as "mentally healthy," and dealing with them by means of penal sanctions, or as "mentally ill" (that is, as "criminally insane"), and dealing with them by means of psychiatric sanctions.

I do not believe that insanity should be an "excusing condition" for crime. Lawbreakers, irrespective of their "mental health," ought to be treated as offenders.

Another classic dilemma of psychiatry is the problem of what society should do with its "insane" citizens who, while having committed no crime, lack "insight" into their "illness" and hence do not seek "treatment." Here we should distinguish between two fundamentally different types of psychiatric practice. The person who decides to consult a psychiatrist and pays him for his services is like a graduate student pursuing a course of study: he assumes the role of mental patient (if we wish so to label his role) *voluntarily* and is free to cast it off. By contrast, the person who is coerced into psychiatric treatment by his relatives or by the law, and who does not pay the psychiatrist for this services, is like a prisoner sentenced to a term of servitude; he is placed in the role of mental patient *against his will* and is not free to cast it off.

The psychiatrist thus has a choice between doing something *to* his patient and doing something *for* him. One of the things the psychiatrist can do to this patient is to prescribe certain life games, with the expectation that these will pacify the patient's family and social environment—and perhaps also "help" the patient. Since this kind of treatment is carried out against the wishes of the patient, it requires coercion.

One of the things the psychiatrist can do for his patient is to analyze his life games, with the expectation that this understanding will help the client to lead a life more free and responsible. To do this, however, requires a voluntary, cooperating client. Coercion has no place whatever in this type of psychiatric work. Such a psychiatrist aspires to be on tap, not on top.

The reader who finds this thesis persuasive might wonder about its practical application. If we look upon mental illness as a metaphor and a social role, rather than as a disease, how will this affect what we *do?*

For work with voluntary clients the consequences would be mainly professional and economic: The humanistic view of mental illness would open opportunities for training nonmedical persons (psychologists, social workers and others) in psychotherapy and psychoanalysis, and would eliminate the rationale for preventing such persons from engaging in the independent practice of these skills.

For work with involuntary clients the consequences would be mainly legal and social: The humanistic view of mental illness would remove the justification for involuntary mental hospitalization and treatment; accordingly, it would require the mobilization of fresh personal efforts and social resources to cope with problems now dealt with by means of traditional psychiatric methods.

It would be impossible suddenly to empty out our mental hospitals and to stop all commitments—though, to be sure, I consider these desirable goals. To attain them, however, we must provide suitable alternatives to the present social functions of involuntary mental hospitalization. I must limit myself here to mentioning only a few such alternatives, each directed toward ameliorating a specific type of human problem.

The usual justification for commitment is that the person whose confinement is sought is "dangerous to himself or others." My position is based on a principle enunciated more than 100 years ago by John Stuart Mill: "The only purpose for which power can be rightfully exercised over any member of a civilized community, against his will, is to prevent harm to others. His own good, either physical or moral, is not sufficient warranty."

Suicide, for example, should be recognized as a basic human right. The threat of suicide, or an attempt at suicide, should not be ground for involuntary mental hospitalization. (This does not mean that a physician should not treat a person who, say, is unconscious as a result of an overdose of barbiturates. It does mean that, after the patient has regained consciousness, he should not be confined in a hospital against his will.)

While being "dangerous to oneself" should never be considered a legitimate reason for depriving a person of his liberty, being "dangerous to others"—if it involves breaking the law—is the best reason for doing so. One of the main functions of society is to prevent violence among its members. Thus, if individuals commit violence, or threaten to do so, they should be treated for what they are—lawbreakers.

Judicial sentencing of lawbreakers does not deprive us of the opportunity of also trying to help them. If we truly believe that some lawbreakers are "mentally ill," we could offer them psychiatric help in prison. As always, the clients ought to be free to accept or reject such help.

The social control, by means of psychiatric sanctions, of dangerous behavior is complicated by the fact that people often disagree on what constitutes "dangerousness," and, even if they agree on it, on how such "dangerousness" is to be established. Thus, one group of persons now often committed is composed of individuals who manages their lives more or less adequately, but who break certain laws or social customs, and are therefore considered "dangerous" and treated as involuntary patients.

If we wish to avoid using coercive psychiatric measures against persons of this type, we have two basic options. Instead of constantly proliferating legislation prohibiting various kinds of personal conduct not directly injurious to others (as we now do), we might consider repealing and eschewing such legislation. We would thereby eliminate many types of "crime," and hence the need to define such criminals (as "dope addicts," "homosexuals" and so forth) as mentally sick. Or, if we wish to persist in our efforts to control private behavior by means of criminal sanctions, we might decide that it is more humane to punish persons who transgress these prohibitions by means of penal rather than psychiatric sanctions; the result would be the jailing of many individuals now committed to mental hospitals. (The desirability of confining lawbreakers in mental hospitals rather than in prisons is sometimes advocated on the allegedly humanitarian ground that conditions in mental hospitals are better than in jails. Even if this were true—and as a rule it is not—it would not justify redefining lawbreakers as patients. The proper remedy for inadequate prisons is prison reform.)

In addition to persons whose dangerousness is actual, established by what they have done, there are those whose dangerousness is potential, who are feared for what they might do. We often hear of "potential troublemakers" who, however, have broken no laws, and hence could not be convicted of crime, but whom many would like to "diagnose" as "deranged" and restrain in mental hospitals.

We cannot eat our cake and have it, too: we cannot have a free society and imprison —in jails *or* mental hospitals—people who have broken no law. This does not mean that some people might not be "potentially" dangerous to others (indeed, many, like drunken drivers, are very dangerous); it means only that we cannot restrain such people through our mental-hygiene laws without gravely injuring the entire fabric of our society.

Another large group of persons confined involuntarily in mental hospitals is the aged; in some public mental hospitals as many as one-third of the inmates fall into this group. Yet, even hospital psychiatrists admit that many of these patients do not need mental-hospital care. "Only 50 per cent of the [elderly] patients . . . hospitalized required hospitalization in a mental institution," testified Dr. Dale C. Cameron, superintendent of St. Elizabeth's Hospital in Washington, before a House committee. "For many older patients," he added, "the primary need was found to be for physical rather than psychiatric care."

The fact that public mental hospitals accept geriatric patients—whose "mental illness" is so clearly a strategic concept designed to justify their forcible removal to places of custody—diminishes the pressure on society to provide suitable accommodations for them.

Still another group of involuntarily hospitalized patients is composed of individuals who present so-called psychiatric emergencies. Examples are the young man who becomes uncommunicative, does not leave his room, refuses to eat, perhaps even soils himself; or the young woman who faints and thereafter remains unresponsive and acts as if she were unconscious.

Patients of this type do not object to being hospitalized or to receiving medical care. Moreover, some of them suffer from bodily illness—brain tumor, head injury, uncontrolled diabetes. Others develop medical problems as a result of their behavior—severe dehydration because of failure to eat and drink, for example. Such patients should therefore be hospitalized in medical, not mental, hospitals, and should be treated as medical emergencies. Consent for hospitalization and treatment should be given by relatives, and confinement should last only until the patient has regained his powers.

The application of these principles to the care of chronic mental patients would help us to avoid coercion in their care as well. Regardless of the cause—subtle malfunctions of the brain, the effect of prolonged institutionalization or flight from communal existence into a world of private dreams—people who are almost completely unable to cope with their problems of living will no doubt always be with us. Such "nondangerous" but gravely disabled individuals could be dealt with by offering them care—good and attractive enough so that they would willingly accept it—while leaving them free to make other choices.

In short, the abolition of involuntary mental hospitalization and treatment would mean that psychiatric help, like medical, would (on the whole) have to be restricted to voluntary clients. Furthermore, some persons who are now cast in the role of involuntary mental patients would, if they broke laws, have to be dealt with as offenders, not as patients.

The nominal aim of psychiatry is the study and treatment of mental disorders. The consequences of subscribing to this apparently harmless, conventional definition of "mental-health" work are, in our present age, momentous. Accepting the existence of a class of phenomena called "mental diseases," rather than inquiring into the conditions under which some persons may designate others as "mentally ill," has been the decisive step in embracing what I call the mental-health ethic. In so doing, the study of a large part of human behavior is subtly transferred from ethics to psychiatry, from the free marketplace of ideas to the closed wards of the mental hospital.

The psychiatrist deals with moral and social problems, not with medical diseases. Hence he cannot help being embroiled in the moral conflicts of his patient and of his society. The psychiatrist's role as moral legislator and social engineer is obscured, however, by the rhetoric of mental health and illness which makes his work appear as a species of medical therapy. This evasion of ethical judgments and choices may be reassuring to the laity and comforting to the profession. But can we, as individuals, afford it?

The individual can never escape the moral burden of his existence. He must choose between obedience to authority and responsibility to himself. Moral decisions are often hard and painful to make. The temptation to delegate this burden to others is therefore ever-present. Yet, as all history teaches us, those who would take from man his moral burdens—be they priests or warlords, politicians or psychiatrists—must also take from him his liberty and hence his very humanity.

A humanistic psychiatry must, therefore, repudiate its seemingly therapeutic mandate, the pursuit of which often results, intentionally or unwittingly, in moral tranquility gained at the expense of freedom and responsibility. Instead of trying to diminish man's moral burdens, such a psychiatry must aim at increasing his powers and so making him equal to his task.

And what is this task? No one has stated it better than Albert Camus when he wrote:

"The aim of life can only be to increase the sum of freedom and responsibility to be found in every man and in the world. It cannot, under any circumstances, be to reduce or suppress that freedom, even temporarily."

Suggested Readings

Callahan, Daniel. "Normative Ethics and Public Morality in the Life Sciences," *The Humanist* 32 (September–October 1972).

Halleck, Seymour, M.D., *The Politics of Therapy.* New York: Harper and Row, 1972.

Lasagna, Louis. "Heredity Control: Dream or Nightmare?" *New York Times Magazine,* 5 August 1962.

Margolis, Joseph. *Psychotherapy and Morality.* New York: Random House, 1966.

Skinner, B. F. *Science and Human Behavior.* New York: Macmillan, 1953.

Smith, Harmon L. *Ethics and the New Medicine.* New York: Abingdon Press, 1970.

Szasz, Thomas. *Ideology and Insanity.* New York: Doubleday, 1970.

section six

business ethics and social responsibility

ADVERTISING AS A PHILOSOPHICAL SYSTEM

Jules Henry

Advertising is an expression of an irrational economy that has depended for survival on a fantastically high standard of living incorporated into the American mind as a moral imperative. Yet a moral imperative cannot of itself give direction; there must be some institution or agency to constantly direct and redirect the mind and emotions to it. This function is served for the high-rising living standard by advertising which, day and night, with increasing pressure reminds us of what there is to buy; and if money accumulates for one instant in our bank accounts, advertising reminds us that it must be spent and tells us how to do it. As a quasi-moral institution advertising, like any other basic cultural institution anywhere, must have a philosophy and a method of thinking. The purpose of this [article] is to demonstrate the character of advertising thought, and to show how it relates to other aspects of our culture. In order to make this relationship manifest at the outset I have dubbed this method of thought *pecuniary philosophy*.

The Problem

Since the problem of truth is central to all philosophy, the reader is asked to ask himself, while perusing the following advertising, "Is it literally true that . . ."

. . . everybody's talking about the new *Starfire* [automobile]?

. . . *Alpine* cigarettes "put the men in menthol smoking"?

. . . a woman in *Distinction* foundations is so beautiful that all other women want to kill her?

. . . *Hudson's Bay Scotch* "is scotch for the men among men"?

. . . if one buys clothes at Whitehouse and Hardy his wardrobe will have "the confident look of a totally well-dressed man"?

. . . *Old Spice* accessories are "the finest grooming aids a man can use"?

. . . *7 Crown* whiskey "holds within its icy depths a world of summertime"?

. . . "A man needs *Jockey* support" because *Jockey* briefs "give a man the feeling of security and protection he needs"?

. . . one will "get the smoothest, safest ride of your life on tires of *Butyl*"?

. . . the new *Pal Premium Injector* blade "takes the friction out of shaving" because it "rides on liquid ball bearings"?

. . . *Pango Peach* color by Revlon comes "from east of the sun . . . west of the moon where each tomorrow dawns" . . . is "succulent on your lips" and "sizzling on your finger tips (And on your toes goodness knows)" and so will be one's "adventure in paradise"?

. . . if a woman gives in to her "divine restlessness" and paints up her eyelids with *The Look* her eyes will become "jungle green . . . glittery gold . . . flirty eyes, tiger eyes"?

. . . a "new ingredient" in *Max Factor Toiletries* "separates the men from the boys"?

. . . when the Confederate General Basil Duke arrived in New York at the end of the Civil War *"Old Crow* [whiskey] quite naturally would be served"?

. . . *Bayer* aspirin provides "the fastest, most gentle to the stomach relief you can get from pain"?

Are these statements, bits of advertising copy, true or false? Are they merely "harmless exaggeration or puffing" [1] as the Federal Trade Commission calls it? Are they simply para-poetic hyperboles—exotic fruits of Madison Avenue creativity? Perhaps they are fragments of a new language, expressing a revolutionary pecuniary truth that derives authority from a phantasmic advertising universe. In the following pages I try to get some clarity on this difficult and murky matter by teasing out of the language of advertising some of the components of pecuniary philosophy I perceive there.

Pecuniary Pseudo-Truth. No sane American would think that literally everybody is "talking about the new *Starfire,*" that Alpine cigarettes literally "put the men in menthol smoking" or that a woman wearing a *Distinction* foundation garment becomes

---

[1] An expression used by the Federal Trade Commission in dismissing a complaint against a company for using extreme methods in its advertising.

so beautiful that her sisters literally want to kill her. Since he will not take these burblings literally, he will not call them lies, even though they are all manifestly untrue. Ergo, a new kind of truth has emerged—*pecuniary pseudo-truth*—which may be defined as a false statement made as if it were true, but not intended to be believed. No proof is offered for a pecuniary pseudo-truth, and no one looks for it. Its proof is that it sells merchandise; if it does not, it is false.

Para-Poetic Hyperbole. 7 *Crown* whiskey's fantasies of icy depths, Revlon's rhapsodies on *Pango Peach, The Look*'s word pictures of alluring eyes, and similar poesies are called para-poetic hyperbole because they are something like poetry, with high-flown figures of speech, though they are not poetry. Note, however, that they are also pecuniary pseudo-truths because nobody is expected to believe them.

Pecuniary Logic. When we read the advertisements for *Butyl* and *Old Crow* it begins to look as if *Butyl* and *Old Crow* really *want* us to believe, for they try to prove that what they say is true. *Butyl,* for example, asserts that "major tire marketers . . . are now bringing you tires made of this remarkable material"; and *Old Crow* says that the reason it "would quite naturally be served" to General Duke in New York was because he "esteemed it 'the most famous [whiskey] ever made in Kentucky.' " When one is asked to accept the literal message of a product on the basis of shadowy evidence, I dub it *pecuniary logic*. In other words, pecuniary logic is a proof that is not a proof but is intended to be so for commercial purposes.

There is nothing basically novel in pecuniary logic, for most people use it at times in their everyday life. What business has done is adopt one of the commoner elements of folk thought and use it for selling products to people who think this way all the time. This kind of thinking—which accepts proof that is not proof—is an *essential* intellectual factor in our economy, for if people were careful thinkers it would be difficult to sell anything. From this it follows that in order for our economy to continue in its present form people must learn to be fuzzy-minded and impulsive, for if they were clear-headed and deliberate they would rarely put their hands in their pockets; or if they did, they would leave them there. If we were all logicians the economy could not survive, and herein lies a terrifying paradox, for *in order to exist economically as we are we must try by might and main to remain stupid.*

The problem has now been stated and briefly illustrated: pecuniary thinking can be analyzed into component parts each one of which serves a specific purpose in marketing in our own peculiarly constructed economy. . . .

. . .

Pecuniary Philosophy as a Total System

Every culture produces, in an unbelievably appropriate and rigid way, a philosophy that fits its needs like a glove. Pecuniary philosophy is a total system, embracing, like some great classical school, not only a metaphysics and morality, but also a psychology, a biology, a history, a poetics, and so on. It has also a theory of birth and death—the birth and death of products. Fundamentally what pecuniary philosophy does is place the product in its proper perspective in our culture, for the product and its attached claim are considered central, while the inert consumer, or rather his head (box) is placed where it belongs—in secondary or, perhaps, merely adventitious position. Consumers are necessary to the existence and evolution of products; consumers (like air and water) are the environment in which products (in a way similar to plants and animals) evolve and have their being; and just as deprivation of air and water causes plants and animals to die, so loss of consumers causes the death of products.

Thus advertising rests on a total system of thought and pursues ends that are fundamentally at odds with the traditional academic philosophies of our culture. And because it is at odds with these philosophies and their old-fashioned morality, it is vulnerable to attack from them. On the other hand, however, the contribution pecuniary philosophy makes to our economy is so great that in spite of the fact that it flies in the face of orthodoxy, it needs to be defended. This is accomplished, in great part, through starving the agencies of Government that have been specifically established to supervise it. In 1960, for example, Congress appropriated only $33 million for the Federal Trade Commission, the Federal Communications Commission, and the Food and Drug Administration—about three-tenths of 1 per cent of what was spent for advertising that year.

. . .

The Pecuniary Conception of Man

I have, perhaps, burdened this [article] with too many new expressions; yet it seemed necessary to do this in order to make clear the fact that pecuniary philosophy is a more or less systematic method of thinking, as well as a way to make money. So I have spoken of pecuniary pseudo-truth, a statement nobody is expected to believe but which is set down as if it were to be believed. Pecuniary logic was defined as a statement made to be believed but backed up by shadowy proof, and para-poetic hyperbole was described as being poetry but not quite poetry, its function being to make a product appear rather dreamlike and fey, to transmute it. Pecuniary psychology is the "scientific" base of pecuniary philosophy, and its central concepts are the head or "brain box," penetration, and the claim. Surprisingly enough, pecuniary history emerges as a phase of pecuniary psychology, for the Wars of Pecuniary Claims and the rise and fall of products are indissolubly linked to the concepts of the brain box and of penetration. Being a complete philosophy, pecuniary thought has not only a truth, a logic, a history, and a poetics, but also a biology—the evolution and extinction of products.

This brings us to pecuniary philosophy's conception of man. Man—or, rather, his brain box—is finite, but at the same time, infinite. The brain box is finite with respect to the number of claims it can contain at the same time, but it is infinite in the things it may desire. Claims and perceptions (of products) surge in and out of the brain box like the tides of an ocean moving up and down a passive beach. Put another way, man is inert while the external culture in the form of products and claims molds him to desire. Thus if the culture (i.e., advertising) requires that man stay at home consuming electric organs and barbecue pits, he can readily be gotten to do so if advertising paints mellow pictures of home and family. If, on the other hand, it is desired that he drive around and use up gasoline, man, in the pecuniary conception, will readily be brought to that too, simply through "promoting" the beauties of automobile travel. If he takes his coffee weak, he will drink it strong if advertising admonishes him to do so. If, smoking mentholated cigarettes, he fears for his masculinity, he will lose his fears if he is told that Alpine "put the men in menthol smoking!" [2]

HOW TO SELL HATS

Before Christmas, Bloomingdale's tried a series of five seven-column newspaper advertisements —one a week—built around the idea that the store catered to the "originalist," the person "who loves to shop for or receive the unusual, who appreciates the individual, who looks for the exciting."

The purpose of the advertisement was to get across the idea that Bloomingdale's was loaded with a variety of merchandise that would please the most discriminating taste and be fun to ferret out, in the bargain.

One advertisement had for its art work a cluster of hats on a hat tree. They were not accompanied by any price or description. But from a single such institutional advertisement in a single newspaper, Bloomingdale's, as an immediate reaction, sold $1,000 worth of the hats on the tree—many by mail or telephone.

HOW TO SELL STRAWBERRIES

. . . last winter, Rottelle, Inc., Bucks County, Pa., distributor for Seabrook Farms frozen foods, found itself with a lot of frozen strawberries on hand. . . .

The problem was taken to James H. Williams Jr., national advertising manager of *The Levittown Times* and *The Bristol Daily Courier.* Mr. Williams suggested an advertisement using strawberry-scented ink. In Mr. Williams' words:

"We designed the ad to be appetite appealing, using very little copy and featuring as a focal point a big, juicy red strawberry. When this advertisement arrived in the homes on Jan. 20, the rush was on. . . .

"Rottelle's records show that at the end of the first week, 10,000 packages of Seabrook Farm strawberries were sold." [4]

HOW TO SELL AN ISLAND

[Trans Caribbean Airlines, wanting to increase traffic to Aruba, approached Warwick & Legler, a small advertising agency. Mr. Heller of the agency describes his approach to the problem.]

[2] See, for example the Alpine cigarette advertisements in the *New York Times,* August 2, 1961, and in *Life* magazine, May 26, 1961.

[3] From the *New York Times,* December 30, 1960.

[4] From the *New York Times,* November 6, 1960.

"It is the same sort of approach," Mr. Heller said, "that is used in cosmetics advertising. An effective advertisement for a lipstick does not simply tell a woman that there is a new blushing pink shade available. It tells her that the blushing pink lipstick will make her more beautiful and more appealing to men."

The airline ads for Aruba, Mr. Heller said, attempt to involve the reader in the same way by asking him questions and making specific emotional appeals. . . .

Trans Caribbean is happy with the results of the campaign. The airline's passenger traffic . . . has had a dramatic increase since the campaign. Before the campaign started, flights to Aruba averaged four to five passengers. Four weeks after the campaign was under way . . . . traffic to the island jumped to an average of seventy-five passengers each flight.[5]

People who like to hope that advertising is wasting its money point to the failure of big-car automobile advertising to destroy the American consumer's desire for a smaller car and the consequent encroachment on the market of small foreign cars. But one swallow does not make a summer. It is also important not to forget that the foreign manufacturers were advertising too!

Insatiably desiring, infinitely plastic, totally passive, and always a little bit sleepy; unpredictably labile and disloyal (to products); basically wooly-minded and non-obsessive about traditional truth; relaxed and undemanding with respect to the canons of traditional philosophy, indifferent to its values, and easily moved to buy whatever at the moment seems to help his underlying personal inadequacies—this is pecuniary philosophy's conception of man and woman in our culture. Since it is a very contemptuous one, it appears that Madison Avenue is not so much the "street of dreams," as *McCall's* has called it, but rather the Alley of Contempt, housing thousands who, through the manufacture of advertising, pour their scorn upon the population. The following expresses this with precision: A full page advertisement by a company trying to sell to advertising agencies movies of championship bowling matches, is dominated by a lamp post carrying the sign "54th Street and Madison Avenue." The copy says, in part:

The name of this TV sports series is CHAMPIONSHIP BOWLING. It is an hour show, features the country's top bowlers in head-to-head matches. It is simple to understand, exciting and suspenseful to watch. And once you've got this narcotic TV viewing habit, you're hooked—as witness the fact that every year our ratings climb.

. . . we deliver almost as many people as does Football, week in, week out.[6]

When you are able to talk in a full page ad in the *New York Times* about *delivering* narcotized people, you and the newspaper have almost ceased to think of people as human. On the other hand if advertising, spending almost 12 billion dollars a year, has this conception of the public, there must be some basis for it. After all, this advertisement is from one advertising man talking to the rest, in the comfortable,

[5] From the *New York Times,* August 30, 1961.

[6] *New York Times,* August 7, 1961.

intimate language of a fraternity brother. How could the ad be wrong? Where is the flaw in its assumption that the attitude of "54th Street and Madison Avenue" toward the human race is one of disdain and ridicule? [7]

The only obvious flaw in pecuniary philosophy is its perception of man as expendable, for without man there could be no products—a matter of elementary pecuniary biology.

. . . pecuniary philosophy passes by imperceptible degrees from matters it can handle to materials (drugs, for example) which are beyond its competence because, since it considers human beings expendable, it is unsuited to deal with matters of life and death. Because of this weakness—and all philosophies have some—pecuniary philosophy often leads its followers into errors, such as making improper claims for drugs or trying to put advertisements in the hands of babies. The last is a consequence of pecuniary philosophy's being itself misled through borrowing value words from traditional philosophy. For example, whereas in traditional philosophy "educate" means "to acquaint with ideas and skills," in pecuniary philosophy it has come to mean "to teach to buy a product." In this connection advertising's use of the traditional value words was said to accelerate loss of respect for them and decomposition of their traditional meanings.

In analyzing monetization I said [elsewhere] that "in their wars of survival pecuniary adversaries will use anything for ammunition—space, time, the President, the Holy Bible and all the traditional values"—a discovery that lead to the conclusion that the erosion of traditional values was due in no small part to fear of competition.

The modes of thought and the view of man entertained by pecuniary philosophy . . . derive in great part from fear and contempt. . . . [and] an industry now contributing nearly 12 billion dollars to the gross national product derives much of its dynamism

---

[7] The following correspondence about this ad took place between Mr. V. Redding of the *New York Times* Advertising Acceptability Department and me. (Mr. Redding's letter is reprinted by permission.)

Dear Sir:

I was deeply shocked by the ad on page 11 of Monday, August 7. How can you permit an advertiser to use language like:

"And once you've got this narcotic TV viewing habit, you're hooked. . . ."

Very truly yours,
Jules Henry

Dear Professor Henry:

This will acknowledge your letter of August 9.

We are most regretful that the statement in the Walter Schwimmer advertisement about which you wrote was offensive to you. It did not seem objectionable to us in the degree that would have prompted us to question it.

There are bound to be differences of opinion from time to time as to our judgment. We are not infallible but we can assure you that an earnest effort is made to protect the interests of our readers and we appreciate your taking the time to write.

Sincerely yours,
V. Redding

from contempt and fear. It has also the most radical conception of *Homo sapiens* that has ever been proposed.

. . .

What's to Be Done?

What shall we do? The ideal might seem to be to resocialize all these men, but this is obviously impossible. Ideally we should send them all to a "truth school" where, under the direction of wise and benevolent philosophers of the old tradition, they would have classes in (1) the difference between pecuniary and traditional truth; (2) the nature of values and their social function; (3) the nature of human dignity: problems of human feelings and why they should not be exploited; the importance of shame, female and other; problems in human degradation (self and other). It is unlikely, however, that such retraining would accomplish much. Furthermore, advertising is self-selective, so that youngsters with a traditional ethical sense avoid it; as late as September 20, 1961 Thomas B. Adams, president of the Campbell-Ewald Company, a big Detroit agency, was " 'shocked' at the degree to which promising young men were shunning the advertising profession because they believed it 'dishonorable.' " [8] Those that do not believe it dishonorable can only be young people perfectly socialized to the corrupt system, who will enthusiastically practice the pecuniary ethic of legal innocence. Thus the dishonesties and distortions of advertising are bound to be self-renewing. The most we can expect in the long run, therefore, is some diminution of unlawfulness, some sparking up of the campaigns in order to eliminate dullness and repetition, and more elaborate and whimsical art work—for example, a larger, cuter and more intensely *green* green giant advertising Green Giant vegetables; better looking, more tastefully dressed women occupying more space in advertisements for cosmetics; more realistic and more carefully color-photographed children poring over encyclopedias, et cetera.

Spontaneous moral regeneration is thus impossible for advertising because it does not know what the problem is and is self-selective in recruitment of personnel. Further-more, since business competition will grow more intense (projected expenditures for advertising are about $25 billion by 1970), the chances of self-regulation are illusory. In view of the increasing competition and the expanding operations of advertising, greatly increased budgets of the FDA, FTC, and FCC should be countermoves against advertising's strong inherent tendency to misrepresent. Federal regulatory agencies, however, find it difficult to deal effectively with anything but legal dishonesty. It seems possible, however, to set up, within the FCC a division, the function of which would be perusal of the *non-legal* aspects of the commercial uses of the mass media. If such a unit were to take a project a year or a subject matter a year—toys, women's maga-zines, cosmetics—and publish its findings, it would have a tremendous effect on adver-

[8] *New York Times,* September 20, 1961.

tising through exercising a moral force, bringing the attention of the public to the nature of the corrosive influence. Such publication would be a kind of textbook of clean advertising practice which, over the years, might gradually re-educate the older generation of advertising men while providing fundamental principles to younger personnel. It would have the further effect, through naming agencies and products, of keeping the young job-seeking generation out of companies responsible for copy that is nauseating, insulting, or merely legally innocent.

The fact that advertising expenditures are running currently at 12 billion dollars yearly and will soon double bears repetition, for such enormous expenditures in the mass media exercise great pressure on the morals of the country. It is common knowledge that advertising firms and their clients, in bending the mass media almost exclusively to pecuniary ends, have come to play an important *regulatory* role and have, therefore, usurped the functions of Federal regulatory agencies. The least the Government can do is treat advertising itself as a public utility, and regulate it accordingly.

. . .

COMPETITION AND PLANNING

Friedrich A. Hayek

. . .

The dispute between the modern planners and their opponents is . . . *not* a dispute on whether we ought to choose intelligently between the various possible organizations of society; it is not a dispute on whether we ought to employ foresight and systematic thinking in planning our common affairs. It is a dispute about what is the best way of so doing. The question is whether for this purpose it is better that the holder of coercive power should confine himself in general to creating conditions under which the knowledge and initiative of individuals are given the best scope so that *they* can plan most successfully; or whether a rational utilization of our resources requires *central* direction and organization of all our activities according to some consciously constructed "blueprint." The socialists of all parties have appropriated the term "planning" for planning of the latter type, and it is now generally accepted in this sense. But though this is meant to suggest that this is the only rational way of handling our affairs, it does not, of course, prove this. It remains the point on which the planners and the liberals disagree.

It is important not to confuse opposition against this kind of planning with a dogmatic laissez faire attitude. The liberal argument is in favor of making the best possible use of the forces of competition as a means of co-ordinating human efforts, not an argument for leaving things just as they are. It is based on the conviction that, where effective competition can be created, it is a better way of guiding individual efforts than any other. It does not deny, but even emphasizes, that, in order that competition should work beneficially, a carefully thought-out legal framework is required and that neither the existing nor the past legal rules are free from grave defects. Nor does it deny that, where it is impossible to create the conditions necessary to make competition effective, we must resort to other methods of guiding economic activity. Economic liberalism is opposed, however, to competition's being supplanted by inferior methods of co-ordinating individual efforts. And it regards competition as superior not only because it is in most circumstances the most efficient method known but even more because it is the only method by which our activities can be adjusted to each other without coercive or arbitrary intervention of authority. Indeed, one of the main arguments in favor of competition is that it dispenses with the need for "conscious social control" and that it gives the individuals a chance to decide whether the prospects of a particular occupation are sufficient to compensate for the disadvantages and risks connected with it.

The successful use of competition as the principle of social organization precludes certain types of coercive interference with economic life, but it admits of others which sometimes may very considerably assist its work and even requires certain kinds of government action. But there is good reason why the negative requirements, the points where coercion must not be used, have been particularly stressed. It is necessary in the first instance that the parties in the market should be free to sell and buy at any price at which they can find a partner to the transaction and that anybody should be free to produce, sell, and buy anything that may be produced or sold at all. And it is essential that the entry into the different trades should be open to all on equal terms and that the law should not tolerate any attempts by individuals or groups to restrict this entry by open or concealed force. Any attempt to control prices or quantities of particular commodities deprives competititon of its power of bringing about an effective co-ordination of individual efforts, because price changes then cease to register all the relevant changes in circumstances and no longer provide a reliable guide for the individual's actions.

This is not necessarily true, however, of measures merely restricting the allowed methods of production, so long as these restrictions affect all potential producers equally and are not used as an indirect way of controlling prices and quantities. Though all such controls of the methods or production impose extra costs (i.e., make it necessary to use more resources to produce a given output), they may be well worth while. To prohibit the use of certain poisonous substances or to require special precautions in their use, to limit working hours or to require certain sanitary arrangements, is fully compatible with the preservation of competition. The only question here is whether in the particular instance the advantages gained are greater than the social costs which they impose. Nor is the preservation of competition incompatible with an extensive system of social services—so long as the organization of these services is not designed in such a way as to make competition ineffective over wide fields.

. . .

To create conditions in which competition will be as effective as possible, to supplement it where it cannot be made effective, to provide the services which, in the words of Adam Smith, "though they may be in the highest degree advantageous to a great society, are, however, of such a nature, that the profit could never repay the expense to any individual or small number of individuals"—these tasks provide, indeed, a wide and unquestioned field for state activity. In no system that could be rationally defended would the state just do nothing. An effective competitive system needs an intelligently designed and continuously adjusted legal framework as much as any other. Even the most essential prerequisite of its proper functioning, the prevention of fraud and deception (including exploitation of ignorance), provides a great and by no means yet fully accomplished object of legislative activity.

The task of creating a suitable framework for the beneficial working of competition had, however, not yet been carried very far when states everywhere turned from it to that of supplanting competition by a different and irreconcilable principle. The question was no longer one of making competition work and of supplementing it but of displacing it altogether. It is important to be quite clear about this: the modern movement for planning is a movement against competition as such, a new flag under which all the old enemies of competition have rallied. And although all sorts of interests are now trying to reestablish under this flag privileges which the liberal era swept away, it is socialist propaganda for planning which has restored to respectability among liberal-minded people opposition to competition and which has effectively lulled the healthy suspicion which any attempt to smother competition used to arouse.[1] What in effect unites the socialists of the Left and the Right is this common hostility to competition and their common desire to replace it by a directed economy. Though the terms "capitalism" and "socialism" are still generally used to describe the past and the future

---

[1] Of late, it is true, some academic socialists, under the spur of criticism and animated by the same fear of the extinction of freedom in a centrally planned society, have devised a new kind of "competitive socialism" which they hope will avoid the difficulties and dangers of central planning and combine the abolition of private property with the full retention of individual freedom. Although some discussion of this new kind of socialism has taken place in learned journals, it is hardly likely to recommend itself to practical politicians. If it ever did, it would not be difficult to show (as the author has attempted elsewhere—see *Economica*, 1940) that these plans rest on a delusion and suffer from an inherent contradiction. It is impossible to assume control over all the productive resources without also deciding for whom and by whom they are to be used. Although under this so-called "competitive socialism" the planning by the central authority would take somewhat more roundabout forms, its effects would not be fundamentally different, and the element of competition would be little more than a sham.

forms of society, they conceal rather than elucidate the nature of the transition through which we are passing.

Yet, though all the changes we are observing tend in the direction of a comprehensive central direction of economic activity, the universal struggle against competition promises to produce in the first instance something in many respects even worse, a state of affairs which can satisfy neither planners nor liberals: a sort of syndicalist or "corporative" organization of industry, in which competition is more or less suppressed but planning is left in the hands of the independent monopolies of the separate industries. This is the inevitable first result of a situation in which the people are united in their hostility to competition but agree on little else. By destroying competition in industry after industry, this policy puts the consumer at the mercy of the joint monopolist action of capitalists and workers in the best organized industries. Yet, although this is a state of affairs which in wide fields has already existed for some time, and although much of the muddled (and most of the interested) agitation for planning aims at it, it is not a state which is likely to persist or can be rationally justified. Such independent planning by industrial monopolies would, in fact, produce effects opposite to those at which the argument for planning aims. Once this stage is reached, the only alternative to a return to competition is the control of the monopolies by the state—a control which, if it is to be made effective, must become progressively more complete and more detailed. It is this stage we are rapidly approaching. When, shortly before the war, a weekly magazine pointed out that there were many signs that British leaders, at least, were growing accustomed to thinking in terms of national development by controlled monopolies, this was probably a true estimate of the position as it then existed. Since then this process has been greatly accelerated by the war, and its grave defects and dangers will become increasingly obvious as time goes on.

The idea of complete centralization of the direction of economic activity still appalls most people, not only because of the stupendous difficulty of the task, but even more because of the horror inspired by the idea of everything being directed from a single center. If we are, nevertheless, rapidly moving toward such a state, this is largely because most people still believe that it must be possible to find some middle way between "atomistic" competition and central direction. Nothing, indeed, seems at first more plausible, or is more likely to appeal to reasonable people, than the idea that our goal must be neither the extreme decentralization of free competition nor the complete centralization of a single plan but some judicious mixture of the two methods. Yet mere common sense proves a treacherous guide in this field. Although competition can bear some admixture of regulation, it cannot be combined with planning to any extent we like without ceasing to operate as an effective guide to production. Nor is "planning" a medicine which, taken in small doses, can produce the effects for which one might hope from its thoroughgoing application. Both competition and central direction become poor and inefficient tools if they are incomplete; they are alternative principles used to solve the same problem, and a mixture of the two means that neither will really work and that the result will be worse than if either system had been consistently relied upon. Or, to express it differently, planning and competition can be combined only by planning for competition but not by planning against competition.

. . .

PROFIT VERSUS SOCIAL UTILITY

André Gorz

. . .

Does the man who eats red meat and white bread, moves with the help of a motor, and dresses in synthetic fibers, live better than the man who eats dark bread and white cheese, moves on a bicycle, and dresses in wool and cotton? The question is almost meaningless. It supposes that in a given society, the same individual has a choice between two different life styles. Practically speaking, this is not the case: only one way of life, more or less rigidly determined, is open to him, and this way of life is conditioned by the structure of production and by its techniques. The latter determine the environment by which needs are conditioned, the objects by which these needs can be satisfied, and the manner of consuming or using these objects.[1]

But the basic question is this: what guarantees the adjustment of production to needs, both in general and for a specific product?[2] Liberal economists have long maintained that this adjustment is guaranteed by the mechanism of the market. But this thesis has very few defenders today. Doubtless, if we do not look at the overall picture in optimum human and economic terms, but only at each product taken separately, then we can still maintain that a product totally devoid of use value would not find a buyer. Nevertheless, it is impossible to conclude that the most widely distributed products of mass consumption are really those which at a given stage of technological evolution allow for the best and most rational satisfaction (at the least cost and the least expense of time and trouble) of a given need.

In fact, under capitalism the pursuit of optimum human and economic goals and the pursuit of maximum profit from invested capital coincide only by accident. The

---

[1] "Production furnishes consumption not only with its object. It also gives consumption its definition, its character, its finish. . . . The object is not an object as such, but a specific object, which must be consumed in a specific way, a way which is again determined by production itself. Hunger is hunger, but the kind of hunger that is satisfied with cooked meat eaten with a fork and knife is different from the hunger which bolts down raw meat with hand, tooth, and nail. Therefore production produces not only the object of consumption, but also the manner of consumption, not only objectively but also subjectively. Production thus creates the consumer. Production not only furnishes the object of a need, but it also furnishes the need for an object." Marx, *Grundrisse der Kritik der Politischen Oekonomie* (Berlin: Dietz, 1953), p. 14. [Translated from the German by Martin A. Nicolaus.]

[2] Structure of production; order of priorities between, for example, automobiles, housing, and public services.

pursuit of maximum profit is the first exigency of capital, and the increase of use value is no more than a by-product of this pursuit.

For example, let us take the case of the spread of disposable packaging for milk products. From the viewpoint of use value, the superiority of milk in a cardboard carton or yoghurt in a plastic cup is nil (or negative). From the viewpoint of capitalist enterprise, on the other hand, this substitution is clearly advantageous. The glass bottle or glass jar represented immobilized capital which did not "circulate": empty bottles or jars were recovered and reused indefinitely, which entailed the cost of handling, collection, and sterilization. The disposable containers, on the other hand, allow a substantial economy in handling, and permit the profitable sale not only of the dairy product but also of its container. To increase their profits, the big dairy firms thus forced the consumer to purchase a new product at a higher price although its use value remained the same (or diminished).

In other cases, the alternative between maximum profit and maximum use value is even more striking. The Philips trust, for example, perfected fluorescent lighting in 1938. The life of these fluorescent tubes was then 10,000 hours. Production of these tubes would have covered existing needs cheaply and in a relatively short period of time; amortization, on the other hand, would have taken a long time. The invested capital would be recovered slowly, and the labor time necessary to cover existing need would have declined. The company therefore invested additional capital in order to develop fluorescent tubes which burned for only 1,000 hours, in order thus to accelerate the recovery of capital and to realize—at the price of considerable *superfluous* expenditure—a much higher rate of accumulation and of profit.

The same holds true for synthetic fibers, whose durability, for stockings especially, has decreased, and for motor vehicles, which are *deliberately* built with parts which will wear out rapidly (and cost as much as longer-lasting parts would have).[3]

Speaking generally, and regardless of the objective scientific and technical possibilities, technical development in terms of the criteria of maximum profit is often quite different from development in terms of criteria of maximum social and economic utility. Even when fundamental needs remain largely unsatisfied, monopoly capital objectively organizes scarcity, wastes natural resources and human labor, and orients production (and consumption) toward objects whose sale is most profitable, regardless of the need for such objects.[4]

---

[3] See Vance Packard, *The Waste Makers*, which contains numerous examples of this type.

[4] In 1959 the Canadian government became worried by the fact that the cost of living had risen substantially in the space of a few years, while the price of agricultural and industrial products had remained stable. An investigating committee blamed the spread of supermarkets: after having eliminated independent grocery stores, the supermarkets (often linked to the monopolies of the food industry) established uniformly high prices. Above all, in order to extract the maximum profit per square foot of display area, they pushed the sale of expensive, luxuriously packaged products, to the detriment of products which have the same use value but are less costly.

In general, monopoly capitalism tends toward a model of "affluence" which levels consumption "upward": the products offered tend to become standardized by the incorporation of a maximum of "added value" which does not perceptibly increase their use value. At the limit (a limit attained by an impressive range of products), the usefulness of an object becomes the *pretext* for selling superfluous things that are built into the product and multiply its price; the products are sold above all for their packaging and brand names (that is to say, advertising), while their use value becomes a secondary part of the bargain. The packaging and the brand name, moreover, are expressly designed to deceive the buyer as to the quantity, quality, and the nature of the product: tooth paste is endowed with erotic virtues, detergents with magic qualities, the automobile (in the U.S.) is extolled as a status symbol.

The apparent diversity of the products badly masks their true uniformity: the difference between brands is marginal. All American automobiles are identical with regard to the incorporation of a maximum of "packaging" and false luxury, to the point where an intense advertising campaign is necessary to "educate" the consumer, from school age on, to perceive the differences in detail and not to perceive the substantial similarities. This dictatorship of the monopolies over needs and individual tastes was broken in the United States only from the outside, by the producers of European automobiles. "Upward" leveling, that is, leveling toward the incorporation of a maximum of superfluity, has been carried out in this instance to the detriment of the use value of the product, whose consumers were unable for years to reverse the tendency of an oligopoly to sell goods of a diminishing use value at a constantly increasing price.

The pursuit of maximum profit, to continue with this example of one of the pilot industries of the most developed country, was not even accompanied by scientific and technological fertility. The tendency to prefer the accessory to the essential, the improvement of the profit rate to the improvement of use value, has resulted in *absolute* wastage. None of the four major post-war technical innovations in automobile design: disc brakes, fuel injection, hydro-pneumatic suspension, rotating piston, originated in the American car industry—an industry which with every annual model change brings into conflict the two biggest manufacturing groups in the world. They compete mainly for maximum productivity, not for maximum use value. The notion that competition would be a factor in accelerating technical and scientific progress is thus, in large part, a myth. Competition does not contribute to technical progress unless such progress allows for the growth of profits. Technical progress, in other words, is essentially concentrated on productivity, and only incidentally on the pursuit of a human optimum in the manner of production and in the manner of consumption.

This is why, in all developed capitalist societies, gigantic waste coexists with largely unsatisfied fundamental needs (needs for housing, medical care, education, hygiene, etc.). This is also why the claim that capitalist profit (distributed or consumed) does not represent a great burden for the economy (about five per cent of the French national revenue) is a gross myth.

Certainly the confiscation of the surplus value consumed by the capitalists would not result in a perceptible improvement of the condition of the people or the workers. But nobody claims any longer that in order to transform society the principal attack must be leveled against the profits pocketed by individual capitalists, against the incomes of the great families and the major employers. What must be attacked is not the personal incomes created by capitalist profits; it is rather the orientation which the system and the logic of profit, that is to say of capitalist accumulation, impress on the economy and the society as a whole; it is the capitalist control over the apparatus of production and the resulting inversion of real priorities in the model of consumption.

What must be constantly exposed and denounced is this organized waste of labor and resources on the one hand and this organized scarcity (scarcity of time, air, of collective services and cultural possibilities) on the other hand. On the level of the model of consumption, this combination of waste and scarcity is the major absurdity of the capitalist system. . . .

The effects of capitalist production on the environment and on society are a second source of waste and of distortion. In fact, what was said about the capitalist control over industry holds true *a fortiori* for the orientation of the economy in general. The most profitable production for each entrepreneur is not necessarily the most advantageous one for the consumers; the pursuit of maximum profit and the pursuit of optimum use value do not coincide when each product is considered separately. But if instead of considering the action of each entrepreneur (in fact of each oligopoly) separately, we consider the resulting total of all such actions and their repercussions on society, then we note an even sharper contradiction between this overall result and the social and economic optimum.

This contradiction results essentially from the limits which the criteria of profitability impose on capitalist initiative. According to the logic of this initiative, the most profitable activities are the most important ones, and activities whose product or result cannot be measured according to the criteria of profitability and return are neglected or abandoned to decay. These non-profitable activities, whose desirability cannot even be understood in capitalist terms, consist of all those investments which cannot result in production for the market under the given social and political circumstances, that is to say, which do not result in a commercial exchange comprising the profitable sale of goods and services. In fact this category includes all investments and services which answer to human needs that cannot be expressed in market terms as demands for salable commodities: the need for education, city planning, cultural and recreational facilities, works of art, research, public health, public transportation (and also economic planning, reforestation, elimination of water- and air-pollution, noise control, etc.)—in short, all economic activities which belong to the "public domain" and cannot arise or survive except as public services, regardless of their profitability.

The demand for the satisfaction of these needs, which cannot be expressed in market terms, necessarily takes on political and collective forms; and the satisfaction of these collective needs, precisely because it cannot be procured except by public services belonging to the collectivity, constitutes a permanent challenge to the laws and the spirit of the capitalist system. In other words, there is a whole sphere of fundamental, priority needs which constitute an objective challenge to capitalist logic. Only socialism can recognize the priority nature and assure the priority satisfaction of these needs. This does not mean that we must await the establishment of socialism or fight for socialism only by political campaigning. It means rather that the existence of this sphere of collective needs now offers the socialist forces the chance to demand and to achieve, in the name of these needs, the creation and the development of a sphere of services, a sphere which represents a popular victory and constitutes a permanent antagonism to the capitalist system and permanently restricts its functioning. . . .

The acuteness of this antagonism—and the sharpness of the contradiction between capitalist initiative and collective needs—necessarily grows. It grows principally as a result of the fact that collective needs and the cost of their satisfaction are not in principle included in the cost of capitalist decisions and initiatives. There is a disjunction between the direct cost of the productive investment for the private investor, and the indirect, social cost which this investment creates to cover the resulting collective needs, such as housing, roads, the supply of energy and water; in short, the infrastructure. There is also a disjunction between the computation of direct production costs by the private investor and the social cost which his investment will bring with it: for example, expenses for education, housing, transportation, various services; in short, the entrepreneur's criteria of profitability, which measure the desirability of the investment, and the criteria of human and collective desirability, are not identical. As a consequence, the collective needs engendered by capitalist investment are covered haphazardly or not at all; the satisfaction of these needs is neglected or subordinated to more profitable "priorities" because these needs were not foreseen and included in advance in the total cost of the project.

Thus, when a capitalist group decides to invest in a given project and a given locality, it need not bother to ask itself what degree of priority its project has in the scale of needs, what social costs it will entail, what social needs it will engender, what long term public investments it will make necessary later on, or what alternatives its private decision will render impossible. The decision of the capitalist group will be guided rather by the existing market demand, the available facilities and equipment, and the proximity of the market and the sources of raw materials.

. . .

DETERRING CORPORATE CRIME

Gilbert Geis

Street vs. Suite Crime

An active debate is underway in the United States concerning the use of imprisonment to deal with crime.[1] Enlightened opinion holds that too many persons are already incarcerated, and that we should seek to reduce prison populations. It is an understandable view. Most prisoners today come from the dispossessed segments of our society; they are the blacks and the browns who commit "street crimes" for reasons said to be closely related to the injustices they suffer. But what of white-collar criminals, and the specific subset of corporate violators? If it is assumed that imprisonment is unnecessary for many lower-class offenders, it might be argued that it is also undesirable for corporation executives. In such terms, it may appear retributive and inconsistent to maintain that a law-violating corporation vice president spend time in jail, while advocating that those who work in his factory might well be treated more indulgently when they commit a criminal offense.

I do not, however, find it incompatible to favor both a reduction of the lower-class prison population and an increase in upper-class representation in prisons. Jail terms have a self-evident deterrent impact upon corporate officials, who belong to a social group that is exquisitely sensitive to status deprivation and censure. The white-collar offender and his business colleagues, more than the narcotic addict or the ghetto mugger, are apt to learn well the lesson intended by a prison term. In addition, there is something to be said for *noblesse oblige,* that those who have a larger share of what society offers carry a greater responsibility also.

It must be appreciated, too, that white-collar crimes constitute a more serious threat to the well-being and integrity of our society than more traditional kinds of crimes. As the President's Commission on Law Enforcement and Administration of Justice put the matter: "White-collar crime affects the whole moral climate of our society. Derelictions by corporations and their managers, who usually occupy leadership positions in their communities, establish an example which tends to erode the moral base of the law. . . ."[2]

Corporate crime kills and maims. It has been estimated, for example, that each year two hundred thousand to five hundred thousand workers are needlessly exposed to toxic agents such as radioactive materials and poisonous chemicals because of corporate failure to obey safety laws. And many of the 2.5 million temporary and 250,000

[1] My views on prison reform are set out in *Saturday Review,* December 11, 1971, pp. 47–8, 56.

[2] President's Commission on Law Enforcement and Administration of Justice, *Crime and Its Impact—An Assessment* 104 (Washington, D.C., Government Printing Office, 1967).

permanent worker disabilities from industrial accidents each year are the result of managerial acts that represent culpable failure to adhere to established standards.[3] Ralph Nader has accused the automobile industry of "criminal negligence" in building and selling potentially lethal cars. Nader's charges against the industry before a Congressional committee drew parallels between corporate crime and traditional crime, maintaining that acts which produce similar kinds of personal and social harm were handled in very different ways:

If there are criminal penalties for the poor and deprived when they break the law, then there must be criminal penalities for the automobile industry when its executives knowingly violate standards designed to protect citizens from injuries and systematic fraud.[4]

Interrupted by a senator who insisted that the witness was not giving adequate credit to American industry for its many outstanding achievements, Nader merely drove his point deeper: "Do you give credit to a burglar," he asked, "because he doesn't burglarize 99 percent of the time?"[5]

Death was also the likely result of the following corporate dereliction recounted in the *Wall Street Journal* which, if the facts are as alleged, might well be regarded as negligent manslaughter:

Beech Aircraft Corp., the nation's second-largest maker of private aircraft, has sold thousands of planes with allegedly defective fuel systems that might be responsible for numerous crash deaths—despite warnings years in advance of the crashes that the system wasn't working reliably under certain flight conditions.

Though Beech strongly denies this, it is the inescapable conclusion drawn from inspection of court suits and exhibits in cases against Beech, from internal company memoranda, from information from the Federal Aviation Agency and the National Transportation Board, and from interviews with concerned parties.[6]

After 1970, the fuel systems in the suspect planes were corrected by Beech at the request of federal authorities. Before that, the company had been found liable in at least two air crashes and had settled two other cases before they went to the jury. In one case, tried in California and now under appeal, a $21.7 million judgment was entered against Beech. Of this, $17.5 million was for punitive damages, which generally are awarded in the state only when fraud or wanton and willful disregard for the safety of others

---

[3] *New York Times,* December 27, 1971.

[4] *Los Angeles Times,* May 11, 1971.

[5] *Ibid.* Similarly, Nader has been quoted as saying, "If you want to talk about violence, don't talk of Black Panthers. Talk of General Motors." (*Quoted in* "White-Collar Crime," *Barron's,* March 30, 1970, p. 10.)

[6] G. Christian Hill and Barbara Isenberg, "Documents Indicate 4 Beech Models Had Unsafe Fuel Tanks," *Wall Street Journal,* July 30, 1971, pp. 1, 6.

is believed to exist. At the moment, suits are pending which involve the deaths of about twenty other persons in Beech planes.[7]

Those who cannot afford a private plane are protected against being killed in a crash of a Beech aircraft, but nothing will help the urban resident from being smogged. Again Nader has pointed out the parallel between corporate offenses and other kinds of crime and the disparate manner in which the two are viewed and treated:

The efflux from motor vehicles, plants, and incinerators of sulfur oxides, hydrocarbons, carbon monoxide, oxides of nitrogen, particulates, and many more contaminants amounts to compulsory consumption of violence by most Americans. . . . This damage, perpetuated increasingly in direct violation of local, state, and federal law, shatters people's health and safety but still escapes inclusion in the crime statistics. "Smogging" a city or town has taken on the proportions of a massive crime wave, yet federal and state statistical compilations of crime pay attention to "muggers" and ignore "smoggers.". . .[8]

Corporate crime also imposes an enormous financial burden on society. The heavy electrical equipment price-fixing conspiracy alone involved theft from the American people of more money than was stolen in all of the country's robberies, burglaries, and larcenies during the years in which the price fixing occurred.[9] Yet, perhaps it can be alleged that corporate criminals deal death and deprivation not deliberately but, because their overriding interest is self-interest, through inadvertence, omission, and indifference. The social consciousness of the corporate offender often seems to resemble that of the small-town thief, portrayed by W. C. Fields, who was about to rob a sleeping cowboy. He changed his mind, however, when he discovered that the cowboy was wearing a revolver. "It would be dishonest," he remarked virtuously as he tiptoed away.[10] The moral is clear: since the public cannot be armed adequately to protect itself against corporate crime, those law enforcement agencies acting on its behalf should take measures sufficient to protect it. High on the list of such measures should be an insistence upon criminal definition and criminal prosecution for acts which seriously harm, deprive, or otherwise injure the public.

Obstacles to Public Outrage

The first prerequisite for imposing heavier sanctions on corporate criminals involves the development of a deepening sense of moral outrage on the part of the public. A number of factors have restricted public awareness of the depth and cost of white-collar crime. That the injuries caused by most corporate violations are highly diffused, falling almost imperceptibly upon each of a great number of widely scattered victims is undoubtedly the greatest barrier to arousing public concern over white-collar crime.

[7] *Ibid.* See also, *Warnick v. Beech Aircraft Corp.*, Orange County Superior Ct., File #174046 (Calif. 1971).

[8] Ralph Nader, "Foreword," to J. Esposito, *Vanishing Air* viii (1970).

[9] Nicholas Johnson, quoted in Morton Mintz and Jerry S. Cohen, *America, Inc.* 81 (1971).

[10] Brooks Atkinson, *Broadway* 315–316 (1970).

"It is better, so the image runs," C. Wright Mills once wrote, "to take one dime from each of ten million people at the point of a corporation than $100,000 from each of ten banks at the point of a gun." Then Mills added, with wisdom: "It is also safer." [11] Pollution cripples in a slow, incremental fashion; automobile deaths are difficult to trace to any single malfunctioning of inadequately designed machinery; antitrust offenses deprive many consumers of small amounts, rather than the larger sums apt to be stolen from fewer people by the burglar. It is somehow less infuriating and less fear-producing to be victimized a little every day over a long period of time than to have it happen all at once. That many very small losses can add up to a devastating sum constitutes impressive mathematical evidence, but the situation lacks real kick in an age benumbed by fiscal jumboism.

Take, as an example, the case of the Caltec Citrus Company. The Food and Drug Administration staked out the Company's warehouse, finding sugar, vitamin C, and other substances not permitted in pure orange juice being brought into the plant. Estimates were that the adulteration practices of the Company cost consumers one million dollars in lost value, thereby "earning" the Company an extra one million dollars in profits.[12] For the average customer, the idea of having possibly paid an extra nickel or dime for misrepresented orange juice is not the stuff from which deep outrage springs—at least not in this country at this time.

There are additional problems stemming from the class congruence between the white-collar offender and the persons who pass official judgment on him. The judge who tries and sentences the criminal corporate official was probably brought up in the same social class as the offender, and often shares the same economic views. Indeed, one Washington lawyer recently told a study group examining antitrust violations that "it is best to find the judge's friend or law partner to defend an antitrust client—which we have done." [13] Also, the prosecutor, yearning for the financial support and power base that will secure his political preferment, is not apt to risk antagonizing entrenched business interests in the community. In addition, the corporate offender usually relies upon high-priced, well-trained legal talent for his defense, men skilled in exploiting procedural advantages and in fashioning new loopholes. The fees for such endeavors are often paid by the corporation itself, under the guise that such subsidies are necessary to protect the corporate image, to sustain employee morale, and to provide an adequate defense. Finally, in the extremely unlikely event that he is sentenced to imprisonment, the corporate offender is much more apt to do time in one of the more comfortable penal institutions than in the maximum-security fortresses to which *déclassé* offenders are often sent.

White-collar criminals also benefit from two prevalent, although contradictory, community beliefs. On the one hand, neighbors of the corporate criminal often regard him

[11] C. Wright Mills, *The Power Elite* 95 (1956).

[12] James S. Turner, *The Chemical Feast* 63 (1970).

[13] M. Green, *et al.*, *The Closed Enterprise System* 319 (mimeograph, 1971).

as upright and steadfast; indeed, they will probably see him as solid and substantial a citizen as they themselves are. Witness, for example, the following item in the hometown newspaper of one of the convicted price fixers in the 1961 heavy electrical equipment antitrust case:

A number of telegrams from Shenango Valley residents are being sent to a federal judge in Philadelphia, protesting his sentence of Westinghouse executive John H. Chiles, Jr. to a 30-day prison term. . . .

The Vestry of St. John's Episcopal Church, Sharon, adopted a resolution voicing confidence in Chiles, who is a member of the church. . . .

Residents who have sent telegrams point out Chiles was an outstanding citizen in church, civic and community affairs and believe the sentence is unfair.[14]

At the same time there is a cynicism among others about white-collar crime in general, a cynicism rooted in beliefs that the practices are so pervasive and endemic that reformative efforts are hopeless. "As news of higher immoralities breaks," Mills wrote, "people often say, 'Well, another one got caught today,' thereby implying that the cases disclosed are not odd events involving occasional characters, but symptoms of widespread conditions." [15] Wearied by expected exposé, citizens find that their well of moral indignation has long since run dry. This lack of indignation can clearly benefit the white-collar criminal. For example, the following courtroom speech, delivered by an attorney for Salvatore Bonanno—allegedly a leading figure in the network of organized crime—reflects public leniency toward such offenses: "It does not speak of the sort of activity where the public screams for protection, Your Honor," the lawyer said, his voice rising. "I think that in the vernacular the defendant stands before you convicted of having committed a white-collar crime and, having been convicted of a white-collar crime, Your Honor, I most respectfully . . . suggest to the court that he should be sentenced in conformity whith people who have been convicted of white-collar crimes, and not being sentenced on the basis of his being Salvatore Bonanno." [16]

These are some of the barriers to generating public concern; what are the forces that need to be set in motion to surmount them?

[14] *Sharon* (Pa.) *Herald,* February 8, 1961.

[15] *Supra* note 11, 343–344.

[16] Gay Talese, *Honor Thy Father* 479 (1971). *Note also:*

Last year in Federal court in Manhattan . . . a partner in a stock brokerage firm pleaded guilty to an indictment charging him with $20 million in illegal trading with Swiss banks. He hired himself a prestigious lawyer, who described the offense in court as comparable to breaking a traffic law. Judge Irving Cooper gave the stockbroker a tongue lashing, a $30,000 fine and a suspended sentence.

A few days later the same judge heard the case of an unemployed Negro shipping clerk who pleaded guilty to stealing a television set worth $100 from an interstate shipment in a bus terminal. Judge Cooper sentenced him to one year in jail.

In fact, some judges don't think of white collar criminals as criminals, legal experts say.

Glynn Mapes, "A Growing Disparity in Criminal Sentences Troubles Legal Experts," *Wall Street Journal,* September 9, 1970.

Foremost, perhaps, is the firm assurance that justice can prevail, that apathy can be turned into enthusiasm, dishonesty into decency. History notes that corruption was rampant in English business and government circles until in the late 1800s, when an ethos of public honesty came to prevail, largely through the efforts of dedicated reformers.[17] Similarly, at their origin the British police were a rank and renegade force; today they are respected and respectable. In fact, at least one writer believes that the decency of the English police is largely responsible for the mannerly and orderly behavior shown by the general public.[18] Thus, change can be achieved, and such change can have eddylike effects on other elements of social existence.

Following this alteration in the psychology of the polity, the facts of corporate crime must then be widely exposed and explained. This process requires investigation, analysis, pamphleteering, and continual use of mass media outlets. It is a formidable task, but one made easier by the fact that the ingredients for success are already present: corporate offenses are notorious and their victims—especially the young—are increasingly concerned to cope with such depredations.[19] Also, when confronted with a problem, Americans respond by taking action to resolve the difficulty, an approach quite different from, say, that of the Chinese. As Barbara Tuchman has noted, the Chinese, at least in pre-Communist times, regarded passivity as their most effective tactic on the assumption that the wrong-doer ultimately will wear himself out.[20] The ideological basis of the American ethos was set out by Gunnar Myrdal in his now classic analysis of racial problems in the United States. We had to work our way out of the "dilemma" involved in the discrepancy between our articulated values and our actual behavior, Myrdal believed[21]; that resolution has proceeded, largely through the use of legal forces, though at a painfully slow and sometimes erratic pace.

So too, perhaps, with corporate crime. Part of the public may be unduly sympathetic, and part cynical, toward revelations of such crime, but a latent hostility is also evident. The Joint Commission on Correctional Manpower, for instance, found from a national survey a strong public disposition to sentence accountants who embezzle more harshly than either young burglars or persons caught looting during a riot.[22] Similarly, a 1969 Louis Harris Poll reported that a manufacturer of an unsafe automobile was regarded

---

[17] Ronald Wraith and Edgar Simkins, *Corruption in Developing Countries* 65–170 (1964).

[18] Geoffrey Gorer, "Modification of National Character: The Role of the Police in England," 11 *Journal of Social Issues* 24–32 (1955).

[19] "The corruption of the robber baron days was more direct. Officials made straight deals for big kickbacks and usually admitted they were wrong when caught. Now the deals are comparatively small and oblique, and all proclaim innocence at the end. The effect of this hanky-panky on the restless and critical young generation in America, however, is undoubtedly greater than the spectacular official plunder of the past." James Reston, "Washington: The Supreme Court and the Universities," *New York Times,* May 18, 1969.

[20] Barbara W. Tuchman, *Stillwell and the American Experience in China, 1911–45,* chap. 11 (1970).

[21] G. Myrdal, *An American Dilemma* (1944).

[22] Joint Commission on Correctional Manpower and Training, *The Public Looks at Crime and Corrections,* February 1968, pp. 11–12.

by respondents as worse than a mugger (68 percent to 22 percent), and a businessman who illegally fixed prices was considered worse than a burglar (54 percent to 28 percent).[23]

Corporate offenses, however, do not have biblical proscription—they lack, as an early writer noted, the "brimstone smell." [24] But the havoc such offenses produce, the malevolence with which they are undertaken, and the disdain with which they are continued, are all antithetical to principles we as citizens are expected to observe. It is a long step, assuredly, and sometimes an uncertain one, from lip service to cries of outrage; but at least principled antagonism is latent, needing only to be improved in decibels and fidelity. It should not prove impossible to convince citizens of the extreme danger entailed by such violations of our social compact. "Without trust, a civilized society cannot endure." Marya Mannes has said. "When the people who are too smart to be good fool the people who are too good to be smart, the society begins to crumble." [25]

It should be noted that Americans are perfectly willing to outlaw and to prosecute vigorously various kinds of behavior on social grounds, *i.e.,* in the belief that the behaviors constitute a threat to the social fabric rather than a threat to any prospective individual victims. Thus, possession of narcotics, abortion, homosexuality, and a host of other "victimless" crimes" [26] are proscribed as threats to the moral integrity of our civilization. A reading of historical records indicates without question that class bias and religious intolerance were the predominant forces which gave rise to the laws against such "immoral" behavior.[27] It is now time that the rationale offered for prosecution of victimless crimes—that they threaten the integrity of the society—be applied to where it really belongs: to the realm of corporate offenses. This rationale did not work with victimless crimes because there was no reasonable way to convince nonperpetrators, often members of the perpetrators' general social groups, that what the offenders were doing was wrong. Therefore, eventually and inevitably, the logic of the perpetrators' position moved other groups either to take on their behavior (*e.g.,* the smoking of marijuana) or to take their side (*e.g.,* the performance of abortions). But the rationale *can* work vis-à-vis corporate crime, given its quantifiable harm actually imposed on nonparticipating victims. Also, there is the possibility of isolating the offender from reinforcement and rationalizations for his behavior, of making him appreciate that nobody morally sanctions corporate crime; of having him understand, as the English would put it, that "these kinds of things simply are not done by decent

---

[23] "Changing Morality: The Two Americas," *Time,* June 6, 1969, p. 26.

[24] E. A. Ross, "The Criminaloid," in G. Geis (ed.), *White-Collar Criminal* 36 (1968).

[25] Quoted in Congressional Record, Vol. 111, Part 4 (March 10, 1965), p. 4631.

[26] *See generally,* E. M. Schur, *Crimes Without Victims* (1965).

[27] *See e.g.,* Bonnie and Whitebread "The Forbidden Fruit and the Tree of Knowledge: An Inquiry Into the Legal History of Marihuana Prohibition," 56 *Virginia Law Review* 971 (1970).

people." It is a standard defensive maneuver for criminals to redefine criminogetic behavior into benign terms. "Businessmen develop rationalizations which conceal the fact of crime," Edwin H. Sutherland wrote in 1949 in his classic study, *White Collar Crime.* "Even when they violate the law, they do not conceive of themselves as criminals," he noted, adding that "businessmen fight whenever words that tend to break down this rationalization are used." [28]

By far the best analysis of this process—and the way to combat it—is by Mary Cameron on middle-class shoplifters caught in Chicago's Marshall Field's. Store detectives advised that Field's would continue to be robbed unless some assault on the shoplifters' self-conceptions as honorable citizens was undertaken. The methods used toward this end are described by Cameron:

Again and again store people explain to pilferers that they are under arrest as thieves, that they will, in the normal course of events, be taken in a police van to jail, held in jail until bond is raised, and tried in court before a judge and sentenced. Interrogation procedures at the store are directed specifically and consciously toward breaking down any illusion that the shoplifter may possess that his behavior is merely regarded as "naughty" or "bad." . . . It becomes increasingly clear to the pilferer that he is considered a thief and is in imminent danger of being hauled into court and publicly exhibited as such. This realization is often accompanied by dramatic changes in attitudes and by severe emotional disturbance.[29]

The most frequent question the middle-class female offenders ask is: "Will my husband have to know about this?" Men express great concern that their employers will discover what they have done. And both men and women shoplifters, following this process, cease the criminal acts that they have previously been routinely and complacently committing.[30]

The analogy to the corporate world is self-evident. As a law professor has observed, "Criminal prosecution of a corporation is rather ineffective unless one or more of the individual officers is also proceeded against." [31] A General Electric executive, for example, himself not involved in the price-fixing conspiracy, said that although he had remained silent about perceived antitrust violations, he would not have hesitated to report to his superiors any conspiracy involving thefts of company property.[32] Corporate crimes simply are not regarded in the same manner as traditional crimes, despite the harm they cause, and they will not be so regarded until the criminals who commit them are dealt with in the same manner as traditional offenders.

Harrison Salisbury tells of Leningrad women taking a captured German pilot to a

---

[28] E. H. Sutherland, *White Collar Crime* 222, 225 (1949).

[29] M. O. Cameron, *The Booster and the Snitch: Department Store Shoplifting* 160–162 (1964).

[30] *Ibid.*, p. 163.

[31] G. Williams, *Criminal Law—The General Part* 865 (2nd ed., 1961).

[32] U.S. Senate, Committee on the Judiciary, Subcommittee on Antitrust and Monopoly, *Administered Prices,* 87th Cong., 2nd Sess., 1961, Part 28, pp. 17223–17232, 17287–17288.

devastated part of the besieged city during the Second World War, trying to force him to understand what he had been doing.[33] Persons convicted of drunken driving sometimes are made to visit the morgue so that they might appreciate the kind of death they threaten. Corporate criminals, though, remain insulated from their crimes. F. Scott Fitzgerald made the point well in *The Great Gatsby:* "They were careless people, Tom and Daisy—they smashed up things and creatures and retreated back into their money or their vast carelessness, or whatever it was that kept them together, and let other people clean up the mess they had made." [34]

How can this situation be changed? Taken together, a number of possible strategies involve widespread dissemination of the facts, incessant emphasis on the implications of such facts, and the methods by which the situation can be improved. Specific tactics might include regular publication of a statistical compilation of white-collar crime, similar to the FBI's *Uniform Crime Reports,* which now cover traditional offenses. It is well to recall that in its earliest days the FBI concentrated mostly on white-collar offenses, such as false purchases and sales of securities, bankruptcy fraud, and antitrust violations [35]; it was not until later that it assumed its "gangbuster" pose. Well publicized by the media, these FBI statistical reports form the basis for a periodic temperature-taking of the criminal fever said to grip us. Numerical and case history press releases on corporate crime would publicly highlight such incidents. It is perhaps too much to expect that there will some day be a "Ten Most Wanted" white-collar crime list, but public reporting must be stressed as a prerequisite to public understanding.

Another possibility is the infiltration of criminally suspect corporations by agents of the federal government trained for such delicate undercover work. It would be publicly beneficial to determine why and how such corporations disdain the criminal statutes they are supposed to obey. The cost would be minimal, since the infiltrators would likely be well paid by the corporation, and the financial yield from prosecutions and fines would undoubtedly more than offset any informer fees involved in the operation. To some this tactic may appear too obnoxious, productive of the very kind of social distrust that the corporate crimes themselves create. But so long as infiltration remains a viable FBI tactic to combat political and street crime, its use cannot be dismissed to combat white-collar crime. But perhaps, as an alternative, large companies should have placed in their offices a public servant who functions as an ombudsman, receiving public and employee complaints and investigating possible law violations.

There are, of course, other methods of uncovering and moving against corporate crimes, once the will to do so is effectively mobilized. Mandatory disclosure rules, rewards for information about criminal violations (in the manner that the income tax

[33] H. Salisbury, *The 900 Days: The Siege of Leningrad* 445 (1969).

[34] F. S. Fitzgerald, *The Great Gatsby* 180–81 (1925).

[35] M. Lowenthal, *The Federal Bureau of Investigation* 12 (1950).

laws now operate), along with protections against retaliation for such disclosures, are among potential detection procedures. The goal remains the arousal of public interest to the point where the corporate offenses are clearly seen for what they are—frontal assaults on individuals and the society. Then, journals of news and opinion, such as *Time,* will no longer print stories dealing with the antitrust violations under the heading of "Business," but rather will place the stories where they belong, in the "Crime" section.[36] And judges and prosecutors, those weathervanes of public opinion, will find it to their own advantage and self-interest to respond to public concern by moving vigorously against the corporate criminal.

Alternative Kinds of Sanctions

Sanctions against corporate criminals, other than imprisonment, can be suggested; they are milder in nature and perhaps somewhat more in accord with the spirit of rehabilitation and deterrence than the spirit of retribution. While perhaps less effective instrumentalities for cauterizing offending sources, they at least possess the advantage of being more likely to be implemented at this time.

Corporate resources can be utilized to make corporate atonement for crimes committed. A procedure similar to that reported below for dealing in Germany with tax violators might be useful in inhibiting corporate offenses:

In Germany, . . . they have a procedure whereby a taxpayer upon whom a fraud penalty has been imposed is required to make a public confession, apparently by newspaper advertisement, of the nature of his fraud, that a penalty has been imposed, that he admits the fact, and will not do it again. This procedure is known as *"tätige reue"* [positive repentance].[37]

A former FTC Chairman has said that "the Achilles heel of the advertising profession is that you worship at the altar of the positive image." [38] The same is true of corporations; thus the value of the public confession of guilt and the public promise of reform.

There is, of course, the sanction of the heavy fine. It has been argued that the disgorgement of illegal profits by the corporation—in the nature of treble damages or other multiplicated amounts—bears primarily upon the innocent shareholders rather than upon the guilty officials. This is not very persuasive. The purchase of corporate stock is always both an investment and a gamble; the gamble is that the corporation will prosper by whatever tactics of management its chosen officers pursue. Stockholders, usually consummately ignorant about the details of corporate policy and procedure, presume that their money will be used shrewdly and profitably. They probably

[36] *Time,* February 17, 1961, p. 84.

[37] Harold C. Wilkenfeld, "Comparative Study of Enforcement Policy in Israel, Italy, the Netherlands, the United Kingdom, and Other Countries," unpublished manuscript, Internal Revenue Service, October 7, 1965.

[38] Paul R. Dixon, quoted in *New York Times,* February 10, 1966.

are not too adverse to its illegal deployment, provided that such use is not discovered or, if discovered, is not penalized too heavily. It would seem that rousing fines against offending corporations will at least lead to stockholder retaliations against lax or offending managerial personnel, and will forewarn officials in other corporations that such derelictions are to be avoided if they expect to remain in their posts. The moral to widows dependent upon a steady income will be to avoid companies with criminal records, just as they are well advised to keep their money out of the grasp of other kinds of shady entrepreneurs and enterprises. Then, perhaps, sanctions against white-collar criminality can be built into the very structure of the market place itself.

What of corporate offenders themselves? The convicted violator might be barred from employment in the industry for a stipulated period of time, just as union leaders are barred from holding labor positions under similar circumstances.[39] In the heavy electrical equipment antitrust cases, for instance, one convicted offender was fired from his $125,000-a-year job with General Electric, but was employed immediately upon release from jail by another company at about a $70,000 annual salary. All ex-convicts ought to be helped to achieve gainful employment, but surely nonexecutive positions can be found which would still be gainful. "Business executives in general enjoy the greatest material rewards available in the world today," it has been noted. "The six-figure salaries at the top would be called piratical in any other sphere of activity." [40] A brief retirement by corporate officials from what in other forms of work is disparagingly called the "trough" does not seem to me to be an unreasonable imposition. Why put the fox immediately back in charge of the chicken coop? I recall some years ago the going joke at the Oklahoma State Penitentiary—that Nannie Doss, a woman who had a penchant for poisoning the food of her husbands, was going to be assigned duty as a mess-hall cook and then released to take a job in a short-order cafe. It was a macabre observation, except that similar things happen all the time with corporate criminals.

There have been suggestions that the penalities for corporate crime might be tailored to the nature of the offenses. Thus, the company president who insists that he had no knowledge of the crime could, if found culpable for negligent or criminal malfeasance, be sentenced to spend some time interning in the section of his organization from whence the violation arose. The difficulties inhere, of course, in the possibility of creating a heroic martyr rather than a rehabilitated official, and in problems relating to the logistics of the situation. Yet, veterans on major league baseball teams are dispatched to Class C clubs because of inadequate performance; they then attempt to work their way back to the top. The analogy is not precise, but the idea is worth further exploration.

[39] Joseph E. Finley, *Understanding the 1959 Labor Law* 24 (1960).

[40] Crossland, "Confessions of a Business Dropout," *Wall Street Journal,* December 13, 1967.

The Issue of Deterrence

The evidence gleaned from the heavy electrical equipment case in 1961 represents our best information on the subject of deterrence of corporate crime; no antitrust prosecution of this magnitude has been attempted since, and very few had been undertaken earlier. Government attorneys were then convinced (I interviewed a number of them when I was gathering information on the subject for the President's Commission on Law Enforcement in 1966) that the 1961 antitrust prosecutions had been dramatically effective in breaking up price-fixing schemes by many other corporations. By 1966, however, they felt that the lesson had almost worn off. Senate hearings, conducted after the heavy electrical equipment conspirators had come out of jail, shed further light on the subject of deterrence. One witness before the Senate Antitrust and Monopoly Subcommittee—William Ginn, a former General Electric vice president—granted that the "taint of a jail sentence" had the effect of making people "start looking at moral values a little bit." Senator Philip Hart pushed the matter further, and drew the following remarks from the witness:

HART: This was what I was wondering about, whether, absent the introduction of this element of fear, there would have been any reexamination of the moral implications.
GINN: I wonder, Senator. That is a pretty tough one to answer.
HART: If I understand you correctly, you have already answered it. . . . After the fear, there came the moral reevaluation.[41]

Other witnesses who had done jail time stated with some certainty that they had learned their lesson well. "They would never get me to do it again. . . . I would starve before I would do it again," said another former General Electric executive.[42] Another man, from the same organization, was asked: "Suppose your superior tells you to resume the meetings; will they be resumed?" "No, sir," he answered with feeling. "I would leave the company rather than participate in the meetings again." [43]

These penitents were the same men who had earlier testified that price fixing was "a way of life" in their companies. They had not appreciated, they said, that what they were doing was criminal (though they never used *that* word; they always said "illegal"); and if *they* had not met with competitors, more willing and "flexible" replacements were available. They were men described by one of their attorneys in a bit of uncalculated irony as not deserving of jail sentences because they were not "cutthroat competitors," but rather persons who "devote much of their time and substance to the community." [44] O. Henry's Gentle Grafter, speaking for himself, had put it

[41] U.S. Senate, *Administered Prices, supra* note 32, Part 27, p. 17067.
[42] *Ibid.*, p. 16790.
[43] *Ibid.*, p. 16694.
[44] *New York Times,* February 7, 1961.

more succinctly: "I feel as if I'd like to do something for as well as to humanity." [45]

The corporate executives were model prisoners in the Montgomery County jail. The warden praised them as the best workers he had ever had on a project devoted to reorganizing the jail's record-keeping system. Thus, to the extent that they conduct themselves more honestly within the walls than they have outside, corporate offenders might be able to introduce modern business skills into our old-fashioned penal facilities. Though they were allowed visitors two days a week, the imprisoned executives refused to have their families see them during the time, slightly less than a month, that they were jailed. [46] It was shame, of course, that made them so decide—shame, a sense of guilt, and injured pride. These are not the kinds of emotions a society ought cold-bloodedly and unthinkingly try to instill in people, criminals or not, *unless* it is found necessary to check socially destructive behavior.

What of the financial sanctions? The $437,500 fine against General Electric was equivalent to a parking fine for many citizens. That the corporations still felt the need to alibi and evade before the public, however, was noteworthy for its implication that loss of goodwill, more than loss of money or even an agent or two, might be the sanction feared most. Note, for instance, the following verbal sleight of hand by General Electric about a case that involved flagrant criminal behavior and represented, in the words of the sentencing judge, "a shocking indictment of a vast section of our economy." [47] At its first annual meeting following the sentencing of the price-fixing conspirators, General Electric dismissed suggestions that further actions might be taken to cleanse itself. The idea, advanced by a stockholder, that the Company should retrieve sums paid to the conspirators as "incentive compensation" was said to "ignore the need for careful evaluation of a large number of factors." These factors—the expense of litigation and the morale of the organization—boiled down to a concern that "the best interests of the Company are served." [48] The president of Westinghouse demanded that employees adhere to the antitrust laws *not* because failure to do so was a crime or because it damaged the public. Rather, such behavior was discouraged because "any such action is—and will be considered to be—a deliberate act of disloyalty to Westinghouse." [49]

GE president Ralph Cordiner observed in 1961: "When all is said and done, it is impossible to legislate ethical conduct. A business enterprise must finally rely on individual character to meet the challenge of ethical responsibility." But by then the president had come to understand how the public might achieve what the Company could not: "Probably the strong example of the recent antitrust cases, and their conse-

[45] W. S. Porter, "The Chair of Philanthromathematics," in *The Gentle Grafter* 48 (1908).

[46] *New York Times,* February 25, 1961.

[47] Application of the State of California, 195 F. Supp. 39 (E. D. Pa. 1961).

[48] General Electric Company, *Notice of Annual Meeting of Share Owners,* March 17, 1961, pp. 17–27.

[49] *Sharon* (Pa.) *Herald,* February 12, 1961.

quences, will be the most effective deterrent against future violations," he decided.[50]

So the lesson had been learned—but only partly. It was much like the mother who scolds her children about stealing by saying that their behavior upsets her and might hurt the family's reputation in the neighborhood. After several such episodes, however, and a few prison terms or similarly strong sanctions against her offspring, she might suggest that a more compelling reason for not stealing is that it is a criminal offense, and that when you get caught you are going to suffer for it. When such an attitude comes to prevail in the corporate world, we will have taken a major step toward deterring corporate crime and protecting its innocent victims.

[50] Ralph J. Cordiner, "Comments on the Electrical Antitrust Cases," at 9th Annual Management Conference, Graduate School, University of Chicago, March 1, 1961, p. 9.

Suggested Readings

Harrington, Michael. *The Accidental Century*. Baltimore: Penguin, 1966.

Heilbroner, Robert L. *Between Capitalism and Socialism*. New York: Random House, 1963.

———(ed.). *In the Name of Profit*. New York: Doubleday, 1972.

Hook, Sidney (ed.). *Human Values and Economic Policy*. New York: New York University Press, 1967.

Huberman, Lee, and Paul Sweezy. *Introduction to Socialism*. New York: Monthly Review Press, 1968.

Josephson, Matthew. *The Robber Barons*. New York: Harcourt, Brace, 1934.

section seven

just distribution and the social good

JUSTICE AS FAIRNESS

John Rawls

. . .

The Main Idea of the Theory of Justice

My aim is to present a conception of justice which generalizes and carries to a higher level of abstraction the familiar theory of the social contract as found, say, in Locke, Rousseau, and Kant. In order to do this we are not to think of the original contract as one to enter a particular society or to set up a particular form of government. Rather, the guiding idea is that the principles of justice for the basic structure of society are the object of the original agreement. They are the principles that free and rational persons concerned to further their own interests would accept in an initial position of equality as defining the fundamental terms of their association. These principles are to regulate all further agreements; they specify the kinds of social cooperation that can be entered into and the forms of government that can be established. This way of regarding the principles of justice I shall call justice as fairness.

Thus we are to imagine that those who engage in social cooperation choose together, in one joint act, the principles which are to assign basic rights and duties and to determine the division of social benefits. Men are to decide in advance how they are to regulate their claims against one another and what is to be the foundation charter of their society. Just as each person must decide by rational reflection what constitutes his good, that is, the system of ends which it is rational for him to pursue, so a group of persons must decide once and for all what is to count among them as just and unjust. The choice which rational men would make in this hypothetical situation of equal liberty, assuming for the present that this choice problem has a solution, determines the principles of justice.

In justice as fairness the original position of equality corresponds to the state of nature in the traditional theory of the social contract. This original position is not, of course, thought of as an actual historical state of affairs, much less as a primitive condition of culture. It is understood as a purely hypothetical situation characterized so as to lead to a certain conception of justice. Among the essential features of this situation is that no one knows his place in society, his class position or social status, nor does any one know his fortune in the distribution of natural assets and abilities, his intelligence, strength, and the like. I shall even assume that the parties do not know their conceptions of the good or their special psychological propensities. The principles of justice are chosen behind a veil of ignorance. This ensures that no one is advantaged or disadvantaged in the choice of principles by the outcome of natural chance or the contingency of social circumstances. Since all are similarly situated and no one is able to design principles to favor his particular condition, the principles of justice are the result of a fair agreement or bargain. For given the circumstances of the original position, the symmetry of everyone's relations to each other, this initial situation is fair between individuals as moral persons, that is, as rational beings with their own ends and capable, I shall assume, of a sense of justice. The original position is, one might say, the appropriate initial status quo, and thus the fundamental agreements reached in it are fair. This explains the propriety of the name "justice as fairness": it conveys the idea that the principles of justice are agreed to in an initial situation that is fair. The name does not mean that the concepts of justice and fairness are the same, any more than the phrase "poetry as metaphor" means that the concepts of poetry and metaphor are the same.

Justice as fairness begins, as I have said, with one of the most general of all choices which persons might make together, namely, with the choice of the first principles of a conception of justice which is to regulate all subsequent criticism and reform of institutions. Then, having chosen a conception of justice, we can suppose that they are to choose a constitution and a legislature to enact laws, and so on, all in accordance with the principles of justice initially agreed upon. Our social situation is just if it is such that by this sequence of hypothetical agreements we would have contracted into the general system of rules which defines it. Moreover, assuming that the original position does determine a set of principles (that is, that a particular conception of justice would be chosen), it will then be true that whenever social institutions satisfy these principles those engaged in them can say to one another that they are cooperating on terms to which they would agree if they were free and equal persons whose relations with respect to one another were fair. They could all view their arrangements as meeting the stipulations which they would acknowledge in an initial situation that embodies widely accepted and reasonable constraints on the choice of principles. The general recognition of this fact would provide the basis for a public acceptance of the corresponding principles of justice. No society can, of course, be a scheme of cooperation which men enter voluntarily in a literal sense; each person finds himself placed at birth in some particular position in some particular society, and the nature of this position materially affects his life prospects. Yet a society satisfying the principles of justice as fairness comes as close as a society can to being a voluntary scheme, for it meets the principles which free and equal persons would assent to under circumstances that are fair. In this sense its members are autonomous and the obligations they recognize self-imposed.

One feature of justice as fairness is to think of the parties in the initial situation as rational and mutually disinterested. This does not mean that the parties are egoists, that is, individuals with only certain kinds of interests, say in wealth, prestige, and domination. But they are conceived as not taking an interest in one another's interests. They are to presume that even their spiritual aims may be opposed, in the way that the aims of those of different religions may be opposed. Moreover, the concept of rationality must be interpreted as far as possible in the narrow sense, standard in economic theory, of taking the most effective means to given ends. . . . one must try to avoid introducing into it any controversial ethical elements. The initial situation must be characterized by stipulations that are widely accepted.

In working out the conception of justice as fairness one main task clearly is to determine which principles of justice would be chosen in the original position. . . . It may be observed . . . that once the principles of justice are thought of as arising from an original agreement in a situation of equality, it is an open question whether the principle of utility would be acknowledged. Offhand it hardly seems likely that persons who view themselves as equals, entitled to press their claims upon one another, would agree to a principle which may require lesser life prospects for some simply for the sake of a greater sum of advantages enjoyed by others. Since each desires to protect his interests, his capacity to advance his conception of the good, no one has a reason to acquiesce in an enduring loss for himself in order to bring about a greater net balance of satisfaction. In the absence of strong and lasting benevolent impulses, a rational man would not accept a basic structure merely because it maximized the algebraic sum of advantages irrespective of its permanent effects on his own basic rights and interests. Thus it seems that the principle of utility is incompatible with the conception of social cooperation among equals for mutual advantage. It appears to be inconsistent with the idea of reciprocity implicit in the notion of a well-ordered society. Or, at any rate, so I shall argue.

I shall maintain instead that the persons in the initial situation would choose two rather different principles: the first requires equality in the assignment of basic rights and duties, while the second holds that social and economic inequalities, for example inequalities of wealth and authority, are just only if they result in compensating benefits for everyone, and in particular for the least advantaged members of society. These principles rule out justifying institutions on the grounds that the hardships of some are offset by a greater good in the aggregate. It may be expedient but it is not just that some should have less in order that others may prosper. But there is no injustice in the greater benefits earned by a few provided that the situation of persons not so fortunate is thereby improved. The intuitive idea is that since everyone's well-being depends upon a scheme of cooperation without which no one could have a satisfactory life, the division of advantages should be such as to draw forth the willing cooperation of everyone taking part in it, including those less well situated. Yet this can be expected only if reasonable terms are proposed. The two principles mentioned seem to be a fair agreement on the basis of which those better endowed, or more fortunate in their social position, neither of which we can be said to deserve, could expect the willing cooperation of others when some workable scheme is a necessary condition of the welfare of all.[1] Once we decide to look for a conception of justice that nullifies the accidents of natural endowment and the contingencies of social circumstance as counters in quest for political and economic advantage, we are led to these principles. They express the result of leaving aside those aspects of the social world that seem arbitrary from a moral point of view.

The problem of the choice of principles, however, is extremely difficult. I do not expect the answer I shall suggest to be convincing to everyone. It is, therefore, worth noting from the outset that justice as fairness, like other contract views, consists of two parts: (1) an interpretation of the initial situation and of the problem of choice posed there, and (2) a set of principles which, it is argued, would be agreed to. One may accept the first part of the theory (or some variant thereof), but not the other, and conversely. The concept of the initial contractual situation may seem reasonable although the particular principles proposed are rejected. To be sure, I want to maintain that the most appropriate conception of this situation does lead to principles of justice contrary to utilitarianism and perfectionism, and therefore that the contract doctrine provides an alternative to these views. Still, one may dispute this contention even though one grants that the contractarian method is a useful way of studying ethical theories and of setting forth their underlying assumptions.

Justice as fairness is an example of what I have called a contract theory. Now there may be an objection to the term "contract" and related expressions, but I think it will serve reasonably well. Many words have misleading connotations which at first are likely to confuse. The terms "utility" and "utilitarianism" are surely no exception. They too have unfortunate suggestions which hostile critics have been willing to exploit; yet they are clear enough for those prepared to study utilitarian doctrine. The same should

---

[1] For the formulation of this intuitive idea I am indebted to Allan Gibbard.

be true of the term "contract" applied to moral theories. As I have mentioned, to understand it one has to keep in mind that it implies a certain level of abstraction. In particular, the content of the relevant agreement is not to enter a given society or to adopt a given form of government, but to accept certain moral principles. Moreover, the undertakings referred to are purely hypothetical: a contract view holds that certain principles would be accepted in a well-defined initial situation.

The merit of the contract terminology is that it conveys the idea that principles of justice may be conceived as principles that would be chosen by rational persons, and that in this way conceptions of justice may be explained and justified. The theory of justice is a part, perhaps the most significant part, of the theory of rational choice. Furthermore, principles of justice deal with conflicting claims upon the advantages won by social cooperation; they apply to the relations among several persons or groups. The word "contract" suggests this plurality as well as the condition that the appropriate division of advantages must be in accordance with principles acceptable to all parties. The condition of publicity for principles of justice is also connoted by the contract phraseology. Thus, if these principles are the outcome of an agreement, citizens have a knowledge of the principles that others follow. It is characteristic of contract theories to stress the public nature of political principles. Finally there is the long tradition of the contract doctrine. Expressing the tie with this line of thought helps to define ideas and accords with natural piety. There are then several advantages in the use of the term "contract." With due precautions taken, it should not be misleading.

A final remark. Justice as fairness is not a complete contract theory. For it is clear that the contractarian idea can be extended to the choice of more or less an entire ethical system, that is, to a system including principles for all the virtues and not only for justice. Now for the most part I shall consider only principles of justice and others closely related to them; I make no attempt to discuss the virtues in a systematic way. Obviously if justice as fairness succeeds reasonably well, a next step would be to study the more general view suggested by the name "rightness as fairness." But even this wider theory fails to embrace all moral relationships, since it would seem to include only our relations with other persons and to leave out of account how we are to conduct ourselves toward animals and the rest of nature. I do not contend that the contract notion offers a way to approach these questions which are certainly of the first importance; and I shall have to put them aside. We must recognize the limited scope of justice as fairness and of the general type of view that it exemplifies. How far its conclusions must be revised once these other matters are understood cannot be decided in advance.

The Original Position and Justification

I have said that the original position is the appropriate initial status quo which insures that the fundamental agreements reached in it are fair. This fact yields the name "justice as fairness." It is clear, then, that I want to say that one conception of justice is more reasonable than another, or justifiable with respect to it, if rational persons in the initial situation would choose its principles over those of the other for the role of justice. Conceptions of justice are to be ranked by their acceptability to persons so circumstanced. Understood in this way the question of justification is settled by working out a problem of deliberation: we have to ascertain which principles it would be rational to adopt given the contractual situation. This connects the theory of justice with the theory of rational choice.

If this view of the problem of justification is to succeed, we must, of course, describe in some detail the nature of this choice problem. A problem of rational decision has a definite answer only if we know the beliefs and interests of the parties, their relations with respect to one another, the alternatives between which they are to choose, the procedure whereby they make up their minds, and so on. As the circumstances are presented in different ways, correspondingly different principles are accepted. The concept of the original position, as I shall refer to it, is that of the most philosophically favored interpretation of this initial choice situation for the purposes of a theory of justice.

But how are we to decide what is the most favored interpretation? I assume, for one thing, that there is a broad measure of agreement that principles of justice should be chosen under certain conditions. To justify a particular description of the initial situation one shows that it incorporates these commonly shared presumptions. One argues from widely accepted but weak premises to more specific conclusions. Each of the presumptions should by itself be natural and plausible; some of them may seem innocuous or even trivial. The aim of the contract approach is to establish that taken together they impose significant bounds on acceptable principles of justice. The ideal outcome would be that these conditions determine a unique set of principles; but I shall be satisfied if they suffice to rank the main traditional conceptions of social justice.

One should not be misled, then, by the somewhat unusual conditions which characterize the original position. The idea here is simply to make vivid to ourselves the restrictions that it seems reasonable to impose on arguments for principles of justice, and therefore on these principles themselves. Thus it seems reasonable and generally acceptable that no one should be advantaged or disadvantaged by natural fortune or social circumstances in the choice of principles. It also seems widely agreed that it should be impossible to tailor principles to the circumstances of one's own case. We should insure further that particular inclinations and aspirations, and persons' conceptions of their good do not affect the principles adopted. The aim is to rule out those principles that it would be rational to propose for acceptance, however little the chance of success, only if one knew certain things that are irrelevant from the standpoint of justice. For example, if a man knew that he was wealthy, he might find it rational to advance the principle that various taxes for welfare measures be counted unjust; if he knew that he was poor, he would most likely propose the contrary principle. To represent the desired restrictions one imagines a situation in which everyone is deprived of this sort of information. One excludes the knowledge of those contingencies which sets men at odds and allows them to be guided by their prejudices. In this manner the veil of ignorance is arrived at in a natural way. This concept should cause no difficulty if we keep in mind the constraints on arguments that it is meant to express. At any time we can enter the original position, so to speak, simply by following a certain procedure, namely, by arguing for principles of justice in accordance with these restrictions.

It seems reasonable to suppose that the parties in the original position are equal. That is, all have the same rights in the procedure for choosing principles; each can make proposals, submit reasons for their acceptance, and so on. Obviously the purpose of these conditions is to represent equality between human beings as moral persons, as creatures having a conception of their good and capable of a sense of justice. The basis of equality is taken to be similarity in these two respects. Systems of ends are not ranked in value; and each man is presumed to have the requisite ability to understand and to act upon whatever principles are adopted. Together with the veil of ignorance, these conditions define the principles of justice as those which rational persons concerned to advance their interests would consent to as equals when none are known to be advantaged or disadvantaged by social and natural contingencies.

There is, however, another side to justifying a particular description of the original position. This is to see if the principles which would be chosen match our considered convictions of justice or extend them in an acceptable way. We can note whether applying these principles would lead us to make the same judgments about the basic structure of society which we now make intuitively and in which we have the greatest confidence; or whether, in cases where our present judgments are in doubt and given with hesitation, these principles offer a resolution which we can affirm on reflection. There are questions which we feel sure must be answered in a certain way. For example, we are confident that religious intolerance and racial discrimination are unjust. We think that we have examined these things with care and have reached what we believe is an impartial judgment not likely to be distorted by an excessive attention to our own interests. These convictions are provisional fixed points which we presume any conception of justice must fit. But we have much less assurance as to what is the correct distribution of wealth and authority. Here we may be looking for a way to remove our doubts. We can check an interpretation of the initial situation, then, by the capacity of its principles to accommodate our firmest convictions and to provide guidance where guidance is needed.

In searching for the most favored description of this situation we work from both ends. We begin by describing it so that it represents generally shared and preferably weak conditions. We then see if these conditions are strong enough to yield a significant set of principles. If not, we look for further premises equally reasonable. But if so, and these principles match our considered convictions of justice, then so far well and good. But presumably there will be discrepancies. In this case we have a choice. We can either modify the account of the initial situation or we can revise our existing judgments, for even the judgments we take provisionally as fixed points are liable to revision. By going back and forth, sometimes altering the conditions of the contractual circumstances, at others withdrawing our judgments and conforming them to principle, I assume that eventually we shall find a description of the initial situation that both expresses reasonable conditions and yields principles which match our considered judgments duly pruned and adjusted. This state of affairs I refer to as reflective equilibrium. It is an equilibrium because at last our principles and judgments coincide; and it is reflective since we know to what principles our judgments conform and the premises of their derivation. At the moment everything is in order. But this equilibrium is not necessarily stable. It is liable to be upset by further examination of the conditions which should be imposed on the contractual situation and by particular cases which may lead us to revise our judgments. Yet for the time being we have done what we can to render coherent and to justify our convictions of social justice. We have reached a conception of the original position.

I shall not, of course, actually work through this process. Still, we may think of the interpretation of the original position that I shall present as the result of such a hypothetical course of reflection. It represents the attempt to accommodate within one scheme both reasonable philosophical conditions on principles as well as our considered judgments of justice. In arriving at the favored interpretation of the initial situation there is no point at which an appeal is made to self-evidence in the traditional sense either of general conceptions or particular convictions. I do not claim for the principles of justice proposed that they are necessary truths or derivable from such truths. A conception of justice cannot be deduced from self-evident premises or conditions on principles; instead, its justification is a matter of the mutual support of many considerations, of everything fitting together into one coherent view.

A final comment. We shall want to say that certain principles of justice are justified because they would be agreed to in an initial situation of equality. I have emphasized that this original position is purely hypothetical. It is natural to ask why, if this agreement is never actually entered into, we should take any interest in these principles, moral or otherwise. The answer is that the conditions embodied in the description of the original position are ones that we do in fact accept. Or if we do not, then perhaps we can be persuaded to do so by philosophical reflection. Each aspect of the contractual situation can be given supporting grounds. Thus what we shall do is to collect together into one conception a number of conditions on principles that we are ready upon due consideration to recognize as reasonable. These constraints express what we are prepared to regard as limits on fair terms of social cooperation. One way to look at the idea of the original position, therefore, is to see it as an expository device which sums up the meaning of these conditions and helps us to extract their consequences. On the other hand, this conception is also an intuitive notion that suggests its own elaboration, so that led on by it we are drawn to define more clearly the standpoint from which we can best interpret moral relationships. We need a conception that enables us to envision our objective from afar: the intuitive notion of the original position is to do this for us.

. . .

ECONOMIC JUSTICE

Joel Feinberg

. . .

The term "distributive justice" traditionally applied to burdens and benefits directly distributed by political authorities, such as appointed offices, welfare doles, taxes, and military conscription, but it has now come to apply also to goods and evils of a nonpolitical kind that can be distributed by private citizens to other private citizens. In fact, in most recent literature, the term is reserved for *economic* distributions, particularly the justice of differences in economic income between classes, and of various schemes of taxation which discriminate in different ways between classes. Further, the phrase can refer not only to acts of distributing but also to de facto states of affairs, such as *the fact that* at present "the five percent at the top get 20 percent [of our national wealth] while the 20 percent at the bottom get about five percent." [1] There is, of course, an ambiguity in the meaning of "distribution." The word may refer to the *process* of distributing, or the *product* of some process of distributing, and either or both of these can be appraised as just or unjust. In addition, a "distribution" can be understood to be a "product" which is *not* the result of any deliberate distributing process, but simply a state of affairs whose production has been too complicated to summarize or to ascribe to any definite group of persons as their deliberate doing. The present "distribution" of American wealth is just such a state of affairs.

Are the 5 percent of Americans "at the top" really different from the 20 percent "at the bottom" in any respect that would justicize the difference between their incomes? It is doubtful that there is any characteristic—relevant or irrelevant—common and peculiar to all members of either group. *Some* injustices, therefore, must surely exist. Perhaps there are some traits, however, that are more or less characteristic of the members of the privileged group, that make the current arrangements at least approximately just. What could (or should) those traits be? The answer will state a standard of relevance and a principle of material justice for questions of economic distributions, at least in relatively affluent societies like that of the United States.

At this point there appears to be no appeal possible except to *basic attitudes*, but even at this level we should avoid premature pessimism about the possibility of rational

[1] "T.R.B. from Washington" in *The New Republic,* Vol. CLX, No. 12 (March 22, 1969), p. 4.

agreement. Some answers to our question have been generally discredited, and if we can see why those answers are inadequate, we might discover some important clues to the properties any adequate answer must possess. Even philosophical adversaries with strongly opposed initial attitudes may hope to come to eventual agreement if they share *some* relevant beliefs and standards and a common commitment to consistency. Let us consider why we all agree (that is the author's assumption) in rejecting the view that differences in race, sex, IQ, or social "rank" are the grounds of just differences in wealth or income. Part of the answer seems obvious. People cannot by their own voluntary choices determine what skin color, sex, or IQ they shall have, or which hereditary caste they shall enter. To make such properties the basis of discrimination between individuals in the distribution of social benefits would be "to treat people differently in ways that profoundly affect their lives because of differences for which they have no responsibility." [2] Differences in a given respect are *relevant* for the aims of distributive justice, then, only if they are differences for which their possessors can be held responsible; properties can be the grounds of just discrimination between persons only if those persons had a *fair opportunity* to acquire or avoid them. Having rejected a number of material principles that clearly fail to satisfy the "fair opportunity" requirement, we are still left with as many as five candidates for our acceptance. (It is in theory open to us to accept two or more of these five as valid principles, there being no a priori necessity that the list be reduced to one.) These are: (1) the principle of perfect equality; (2) the principle[s] of need; (3) the principles of merit and achievement; (4) the principle of contribution (or due return); (5) the principle of effort (or labor). I shall discuss each of these briefly.

(i) Equality

The principle of perfect equality obviously has a place in any adequate social ethic. Every human being is equally a human being, and that minimal qualification entitles all human beings equally to certain absolute human rights: positive rights to noneconomic "goods" that by their very natures cannot be in short supply, negative rights not to be treated in cruel or inhuman ways, and negative rights not to be exploited or degraded even in "humane" ways. It is quite another thing, however, to make the minimal qualification of humanity the ground for an absolutely equal distribution of a country's *material wealth* among its citizens. A strict equalitarian could argue that he is merely applying Aristotle's formula of proportionate equality (presumably accepted by all parties to the dispute) with a criterion of relevance borrowed from the human rights theorists. Thus, distributive justice is accomplished between A and B when the following ratio is satisfied:

[2] W. K. Frankena, "Some Beliefs About Justice," *The Lindley Lecture,* Department of Philosophy Pamphlet (Lawrence: University of Kansas, 1966), p. 10.

$$\frac{A\text{'s share of } P}{B\text{'s share of } P} = \frac{A\text{'s possession of } Q}{B\text{'s possession of } Q}$$

Where P stands for economic goods, Q must stand simply for "humanity" or "a human nature," and since every human being possesses *that* Q equally, it follows that all should also share a society's economic wealth (the P in question) equally.

The trouble with this argument is that its major premise is no less disputable than its conclusion. The standard of relevance it borrows from other contexts where it seems very little short of self-evident, seems controversial, at best, when applied to purely economic contexts. It seems evident to most of us that merely being human entitles *everyone*—bad men as well as good, lazy as well as industrious, inept as well as skilled—to a fair trial if charged with a crime, to equal protection of the law, to equal consideration of his interests by makers of national policy, to be spared torture or other cruel and inhuman treatment, and to be permanently ineligible for the status of chattel slave. Adding a right to an equal share of the economic pie, however, is to add a benefit of a wholly different order, one whose presence on the list of goods for which mere humanity is the sole qualifying condition is not likely to win wide assent without further argument.

It is far more plausible to posit a human right to the satisfaction of (better: to an opportunity to satisfy) one's *basic* economic needs, that is, to enough food and medicine to remain healthy, to minimal clothing, housing, and so on. As Hume pointed out,[3] even these rights cannot exist under conditions of extreme scarcity. Where there is not enough to go around, it cannot be true that everyone has a right to an equal share.[4] But wherever there is moderate abundance or better—wherever a society produces more than enough to satisfy the *basic needs of everyone*—there it seems more plausible to say that mere possession of basic human needs qualifies a person for the opportunity to satisfy them. It would be a rare and calloused sense of justice that would not be offended by an affluent society, with a large annual agricultural surplus and a great abundance of manufactured goods, which permitted some of its citizens to die of starvation, exposure, or easily curable disease. It would certainly be *unfair* for a nation to produce more than it needs and not permit some of its citizens enough to satisfy their basic biological requirements. Strict equalitarianism, then, is a perfectly plausible material principle of distributive justice when confined to affluent societies and basic biological needs, but it loses plausibility when applied to division of the "surplus" left over after basic needs are met. To be sure, the greater the degree of affluence, the higher the level at which we might draw the line between "basic needs" and merely "wanted" benefits, and insofar as social institutions create "artificial needs," it is only fair that society provide all with the opportunity to satisfy them.[5] But once the line has been

---

[3] David Hume, *Enquiry Concerning the Principles of Morals* Part III (LaSalle, Ill.: The Open Court Publishing Company, 1947). Originally published in 1777.

[4] Except in the "manifesto sense" of "right" discussed on p. 67.

[5] This point is well made by Katzner, "An Analysis of the Concept of Justice," pp. 173–203.

drawn between what is needed to live a minimally decent life by the realistic standards of a given time and place and what is only added "gravy," it is far from evident that justice still insists upon absolutely equal shares of the total. And it is evident that justice does *not* require strict equality wherever there is reason to think that unequal distribution causally determines greater production and is therefore in the interests of everyone, even those who receive the relatively smaller shares.

Still, there is no way to *refute* the strict equalitarian who requires exactly equal shares for everyone whenever that can be arranged without discouraging total productivity to the point where everyone loses. No one would insist upon equal distributions that would diminish the size of the total pie and thus leave smaller slices for *everyone;* that would be opposed to reason. John Rawls makes this condition part of his "rational principle" of justice: "Inequalities are arbitrary unless it is reasonable to expect that they will work out to everyone's advantage. . . ." [6] We are left then with a version of strict equalitarianism that is by no means evidently true and yet is impossible to refute. That is the theory that purports to apply not only to basic needs but to the total wealth of a society, and allows departures from strict equality when, *but only when,* they will work out to everyone's advantage. Although I am not persuaded by this theory, I think that any adequate material principle will have to attach great importance to keeping differences in wealth within reasonable limits, even after the basic needs have been met. One way of doing this would be to raise the standards for a "basic need" as total wealth goes up, so that differences between the richest and poorest citizens (even when there is no real "poverty") are kept within moderate limits.

(ii) Need

The principle of need is subject to various interpretations, but in most of its forms it is not an independent principle at all, but only a way of mediating the application of the principle of equality. It can, therefore, be grouped with the principle of perfect equality as a member of the equalitarian family and contrasted with the principles of merit, achievement, contribution, and effort, which are all members of the nonequalitarian family. Consider some differences in "needs" as they bear on distributions. Doe is a bachelor with no dependents; Roe has a wife and six children. Roe must satisfy the needs of eight persons out of his paycheck, whereas Doe need satisfy the needs of only one. To give Roe and Doe equal pay would be to treat Doe's interest substantially *more* generously than those of anyone in the Roe family. Similarly, if a small private group is distributing food to its members (say a shipwrecked crew waiting rescue on a desert island), it would not be fair to give precisely the same quantity to a one hundred pounder as to a two hundred pounder, for that might be giving one person all he needs and the other only a fraction of what he needs—a difference in treatment not supported by any relevant difference between them. In short, to distribute

[6] John Rawls, "Justice as Fairness," *The Philosophical Review,* LXVII (1958), 165.

goods in proportion to basic needs is not really to depart from a standard of equality, but rather to bring those with some greater initial burden or deficit up to the same level as their fellows.

The concept of a "need" is extremely elastic. In a general sense, to say that S needs X is to say simply that if he doesn't have X he will be harmed. A "basic need" would then be for an X in whose absence a person would be harmed in some crucial and fundamental way, such as suffering injury, malnutrition, illness, madness, or premature death. Thus we all have a basic need for foodstuffs of a certain quantity and variety, fuel to heat our dwellings, a roof over our heads, clothing to keep us warm, and so on. In a different but related sense of need, to say that S needs X is to say that without X he cannot achieve some specific purpose or perform some specific function. If they are to do their work, carpenters need tools, merchants need capital and customers, authors need paper and publishers. Some helpful goods are not strictly needed in this sense: an author with pencil and paper does not really need a typewriter to write a book, but he may need it to write a book speedily, efficiently, and conveniently. We sometimes come to rely upon "merely helpful but unneeded goods" to such a degree that we develop a strong habitual dependence on them, in which case (as it is often said) we have a "psychological" as opposed to a material need for them. If we don't possess that for which we have a strong psychological need, we may be unable to be happy, in which case a merely psychological need for a functional instrument may become a genuine need in the first sense distinguished above, namely, something whose absence is harmful to us. (Cutting across the distinction between material and psychological needs is that between "natural" and "artificial" needs, the former being those that can be expected to develop in any normal person, the latter being those that are manufactured or contrived, and somehow implanted in, or imposed upon, a person.) The more abundant a society's material goods, the higher the level at which we are required (by the force of psychological needs) to fix the distinction between "necessities" and "luxuries"; what *everyone* in a given society regards as "necessary" tends to become an actual, basic need.

(iii) Merit and Achievement

The remaining three candidates for material principles of distributive justice belong to the nonequalitarian family. These three principles would each distribute goods in accordance, not with need, but with *desert;* since persons obviously differ in their deserts, economic goods would be distributed unequally. The three principles differ from one another in their conceptions of the relevant *bases of desert* for economic distributions. The first is the principle of *merit.* Unlike the other principles in the nonequalitarian family, this one focuses not on what a person has *done* to deserve his allotment, but rather on what kind of person he is—what characteristics he has.

Two different types of characteristic might be considered meritorious in the appropriate sense: skills and virtues. Native skills and inherited aptitudes will not be appropriate desert bases, since they are forms of merit ruled out by the fair opportunity require-ment. No one deserves credit or blame for his genetic inheritance, since no one has the opportunity to select his own genes. Acquired skills may seem more plausible candidates at first, but upon scrutiny they are little better. First, all acquired skills depend to a large degree on native skills. Nobody is born knowing how to read, so reading is an acquired skill, but actual differences in reading skill are to a large degree accounted for by genetic differences that are beyond anyone's control. Some of the differences are no doubt caused by differences in motivation afforded different children, but again the early conditions contributing to a child's motivation are also largely beyond his control. We may still have some differences in acquired skills that are to be accounted for solely or primarily by differences in the degree of practice, drill, and perseverance expended by persons with roughly equal opportunities. In respect to these, we can propitiate the requirement of fair opportunity, but only by nullifying the signifi-cance of acquired skill as such, for now skill is a relevant basis of desert only to the extent that it is a product of one's own effort. Hence, *effort* becomes the true basis of desert (as claimed by our fifth principle, discussed below), and not simply skill as such.

Those who would propose rewarding personal *virtues* with a larger than average share of the economic pie, and punishing defects of character with a smaller than average share, advocate assigning to the economic system a task normally done (if it is done at all) by noneconomic institutions. What they propose, in effect, is that we use retributive criteria of distributive justice. Our criminal law, for a variety of good reasons, does not purport to punish people for what they are, but only for what they do. A man can be as arrogant, rude, selfish, cruel, insensitive, irresponsible, cowardly, lazy, or disloyal as he wishes; unless he *does* something prohibited by the criminal law, he will not be made to suffer legal punishment. At least one of the legal system's reasons for refusing to penalize character flaws as such would also explain why such defects should not be listed as relevant differences in a material principle of distributive justice. The apparatus for detecting such flaws (a "moral police"?) would be enormously cumbersome and impractical, and its methods so uncertain and fallible that none of us could feel safe in entrusting the determination of our material allotments to it. We could, of course, give roughly equal shares to all except those few who have *outstanding* virtues—gentleness, kindness, courage, dilligence, reliability, warmth, charm, consider-ateness, generosity. Perhaps these are traits that deserve to be rewarded, but it is doubtful that larger economic allotments are the appropriate vehicles of rewarding. As Benn and Peters remind us, "there are some sorts of 'worth' for which rewards in terms of income seem inappropriate. Great courage in battle is recognized by medals, not by increased pay." [7] Indeed, there is something repugnant, as Socrates and the Stoics insisted, in paying a man to be virtuous. Moreover, the rewards would offer a

---

[7] Benn and Peters, *Social Principles and the Democratic State,* p. 139.

pecuniary motive for certain forms of excellence that require motives of a different kind, and would thus tend to be self-defeating.

The most plausible nonequalitarian theories are those that locate relevance not in meritorious traits and excellences of any kind, but rather in prior doings: not in what one is, but in what one has done. Actions, too, are sometimes called "meritorious," so there is no impropriety in denominating the remaining families of principles in our survey as "meritarian." One type of action-oriented meritarian might cite *achievement* as a relevant desert basis for pecuniary rewards, so that departures from equality in income are to be justicized only by distinguished achievements in science, art, philosophy, music, athletics, and other basic areas of human activity. The attractions and disadvantages of this theory are similar to those of theories which I rejected above that base rewards on skills and virtues. Not all persons have a fair opportunity to achieve great things, and economic rewards seem inappropriate as vehicles for expressing recognition and admiration of noneconomic achievements.

(iv) Contribution or "Due Return"

When the achievements under consideration are themselves contributions to our general economic well-being, the meritarian principle of distributive justice is much more plausible. Often it is conjoined with an economic theory that purports to determine exactly what percentage of our total economic product a given worker or class has produced. Justice, according to this principle, requires that each worker get back exactly that proportion of the national wealth that he has himself created. This sounds very much like a principle of "commutative justice" directing us to *give back* to every worker what is really his own property, that is, the product of his own labor.

The French socialist writer and precursor of Karl Marx, Pierre Joseph Proudhon (1809–1865), is perhaps the classic example of this kind of theorist. In this book, *What Is Property?* (1840), Proudhon rejects the standard socialist slogan, "From each according to his ability, to each according to his needs," [8] in favor of a principle of distributive justice based on contribution, as interpreted by an economic theory that employed a pre-Marxist "theory of surplus value." The famous socialist slogan was not intended, in any case, to express a principle of distributive justice. It was understood to be a rejection of all considerations of "mere" justice for an ethic of human brotherhood. The early socialists thought it unfair, in a way, to give the great contributors to our wealth a disproportionately small share of the product. But in the new socialist society, love of neighbor, community spirit, and absence of avarice would overwhelm such bourgeois notions and put them in their proper (subordinate) place.

Proudhon, on the other hand, based his whole social philosophy not on brotherhood

---

[8] Traced to Louis Blanc. For a clear brief exposition of Proudhon's view which contrasts it with that of other early socialists and also that of Karl Marx, see Robert Tucker's "Marx and Distributive Justice," in *Nomos VI: Justice,* ed. C. J. Friedrich and J. W. Chapman (New York: Aldine-Atherton Press, 1963), pp. 306–25.

(an ideal he found suitable only for small groups such as families) but on the kind of distributive justice to which even some capitalists gave lip service:

The key concept was "mutuality" or "reciprocity." "Mutuality, reciprocity exists," he wrote, "when all the workers in an industry, instead of working for an entrepreneur who pays them and keeps their products, work for one another and thus collaborate in the making of a common product whose profits they share among themselves." [9]

Proudhon's celebrated dictum that "property is theft" did not imply that all *possession* of goods is illicit, but rather that the system of rules that permitted the owner of a factory to hire workers and draw profits ("surplus value") from *their* labor robs the workers of what is rightly theirs. "This profit, consisting of a portion of the proceeds of labor that rightfully belonged to the laborer himself, was 'theft.' " [10] The injustice of capitalism, according to Proudhon, consists in the fact that those who create the wealth (through their labor) get only a small part of what they create, whereas those who "exploit" their labor, like voracious parasites, gather in a greatly disproportionate share. The "return of contribution" principle of distributive justice, then, cannot work in a capitalist system, but requires a *fédération mutualiste* of autonomous producer-cooperatives in which those who create wealth by their work share it in proportion to their real contributions.

Other theorists, employing different notions of what produces or "creates" economic wealth, have used the "return of contribution" principle to support quite opposite conclusions. The contribution principle has even been used to justicize quite un-equalitarian capitalistic status quos, for it is said that capital as well as labor creates wealth, as do ingenious ideas, inventions, and adventurous risk-taking. The capitalist who provided the money, the inventor who designed a product to be manufactured, the innovator who thought of a new mode of production and marketing, the advertiser who persuaded millions of customers to buy the finished product, the investor who risked his savings on the success of the enterprise—these are the ones, it is said, who did the most to produce the wealth created by a business, not the workers who contributed only their labor, and of course, these are the ones who tend, on the whole, to receive the largest personal incomes.

Without begging any narrow and technical questions of economics, I should express my general skepticism concerning such facile generalizations about the comparative degrees to which various individuals have contributed to our social wealth. Not only are there impossibly difficult problems of measurement involved, there are also concep-tual problems that appear beyond all nonarbitrary solution. I refer to the elements of luck and chance, the social factors not attributable to any assignable individuals, and the contributions of population trends, uncreated natural resources, and the efforts of

[9] Tucker, "Marx and Distributive Justice," p. 310.
[10] Tucker, "Marx and Distributive Justice," p. 311.

people now dead, which are often central to the explanation of any given increment of social wealth.

The difficulties of separating out causal factors in the production of social wealth might influence the partisan of the "return of contribution" principle in either or both of two ways. He might become very cautious in his application of the principle, requiring that deviations from average shares be restricted to very clear and demonstrable instances of unusually great or small contributions. But the moral that L. T. Hobhouse [11] drew from these difficulties is that *any* individual contribution will be very small relative to the immeasurably great contribution made by political, social, fortuitous, natural, and "inherited" factors. In particular, strict application of the "return of contribution" principle would tend to support a larger claim for the *community* to its own "due return," through taxation and other devices.

In a way, the principle of contribution is not a principle of mere *desert* at all, no matter how applied. As mentioned above, it resembles a principle of commutative justice requiring repayment of debts, return of borrowed items, or compensation for wrongly inflicted damages. If I lend you my car on the understanding that you will take good care of it and soon return it, or if you steal it, or damage it, it will be too *weak* to say that I "deserve" to have my own car, intact, back from you. After all, the car is *mine* or my due, and questions of ownership are not settled by examination of deserts; neither are considerations of ownership and obligation commonly outbalanced by considerations of desert. It is not merely "unfitting" or "inappropriate" that I should not have my own or my due; it is downright *theft* to withhold it from me. So the return of contribution is not merely a matter of merit deservng reward. It is a matter of a maker demanding that which he has created and is thus properly his. The ratio—A's share of X is to B's share of X as A's contribution to X is to B's contribution to X—appears, therefore, to be a very strong and plausible principle of distributive justice, whose main deficiencies, when applied to economic distributions, are of a practical (though severe) kind. If Hobhouse is right in claiming that there are social factors in even the most pronounced individual contributions to social wealth, then the principle of due return serves as a moral basis in support of taxation and other public claims to private goods. In any case, if A's contribution, though apparently much greater than B's, is nevertheless only the tiniest percentage of the total contribution to X (whatever that may mean and however it is to be determined), it may seem like the meanest quibbling to distinguish very seriously between A and B at all.

(v) Effort

The principle of due return, as a material principle of distributive justice, does have some vulnerability to the fair opportunity requirement. Given unavoidable variations

[11] L. T. Hobhouse, *The Elements of Social Justice* (London: George Allen and Unwin Ltd., 1922). See especially pp. 161–63.

in genetic endowments and material circumstances, different persons cannot have precisely the same opportunities to make contributions to the public weal. Our final candidate for the status of a material principle of distributive justice, the *principle of effort*, does much better in this respect, for it would distribute economic products not in proportion to successful achievement but according to the degree of effort exerted. According to the principle of effort, justice decrees that hard-working executives and hard-working laborers receive precisely the same remuneration (although there may be reasons having nothing to do with justice for paying more to the executives), and that freeloaders be penalized by allotments of proportionately lesser shares of the joint products of everyone's labor. The most persuasive argument for this principle is that it is the closest approximation to the intuitively valid principle of due return that can pass the fair opportunity requirement. It is doubtful, however, that even the principle of effort fully satisfies the requirement of fair opportunity, since those who inherit or acquire certain kinds of handicap may have little opportunity to *acquire the motivation* even to do their best. In any event, the principle of effort does seem to have intuitive cogency giving it at least some weight as a factor determining the justice of distributions.

In very tentative conclusion, it seems that the principle of equality (in the version that rests on needs rather than that which requires "perfect equality") and the principles of contribution and effort (where nonarbitrarily applicable, and only *after* everyone's basic needs have been satisfied) have the most weight as determinants of economic justice, whereas all forms of the principle of merit are implausible in that role. The reason for the priority of basic needs is that, where there is economic abundance, the claim to life itself and to minimally decent conditions are, like other human rights, claims that all men make with perfect equality. As economic production increases, these claims are given ever greater consideration in the form of rising standards for distinguishing basic needs from other wanted goods. But no matter where that line is drawn, when we go beyond it into the realm of economic surplus or "luxuries," nonequalitarian considerations (especially contribution and effort) come increasingly into play.

. . .

THE ETHICS OF DISTRIBUTION
Milton Friedman

. . .

The ethical principle that would directly justify the distribution of income in a free market society is, "To each according to what he and the instruments he owns produces." The operation of even this principle implicitly depends on state action. Property rights are matters of law and social convention. As we have seen, their definition and enforcement is one of the primary functions of the state. The final distribution of income and wealth under the full operation of this principle may well depend markedly on the rules of property adopted.

What is the relation between this principle and another that seems ethically appealing, namely, equality of treatment? In part, the two principles are not contradictory. Payment in accordance with product may be necessary to achieve true equality of treatment. Given individuals whom we are prepared to regard as alike in ability and initial resources, if some have a greater taste for leisure and others for marketable goods, inequality of return through the market is necessary to achieve equality of total return or equality of treatment. One man may prefer a routine job with much time off for basking in the sun to a more exacting job paying a higher salary; another man may prefer the opposite. If both were paid equally in money, their incomes in a more fundamental sense would be unequal. Similarly, equal treatment requires that an individual be paid more for a dirty, unattractive job than for a pleasant rewarding one. Much observed inequality is of this kind. Differences of money income offset differences in other characteristics of the occupation or trade. In the jargon of economists, they are "equalizing differences" required to make the whole of the "net advantages," pecuniary and non-pecuniary, the same.

Another kind of inequality arising through the operation of the market is also required, in a somewhat more subtle sense, to produce equality of treatment, or to put it differently to satisfy men's tastes. It can be illustrated most simply by a lottery. Consider a group of individuals who initially have equal endowments and who all agree voluntarily to enter a lottery with very unequal prizes. The resultant inequality of income is surely required to permit the individuals in question to make the most of their initial equality. Redistribution of the income after the event is equivalent to denying them the opportunity to enter the lottery. This case is far more important in practice than would appear by taking the notion of a "lottery" literally. Individuals choose occupations, investments, and the like partly in accordance with their taste for uncertainty. The girl who tries to become a movie actress rather than a civil servant is deliberately choosing to enter a lottery, so is the indivdual who invests in penny uranium stocks rather than government bonds. Insurance is a way of expressing a taste for certainty. Even these examples do not indicate fully the extent to which actual inequality may be the result of arrangements designed to satisfy men's tastes. The very arrangements for paying and hiring people are affected by such preferences. If all potential movie actresses had a great dislike of uncertainty, there would tend to develop "co-operatives" of movie actresses, the members of which agreed in advance to share income receipts more or less evenly, thereby in effect providing themselves insurance through the pooling of risks. If such a preference were widespread, large diversified corporations combining risky and non-risky ventures would become the rule. The wild-cat oil prospector, the private proprietorship, the small partnership, would all become rare.

Indeed, this is one way to interpret governmental measures to redistribute income through progressive taxes and the like. It can be argued that for one reason or another, costs of administration perhaps, the market cannot produce the range of lotteries or the kind of lottery desired by the members of the community, and that progressive taxation is, as it were, a government enterprise to do so. I have no doubt that this view contains an element of truth. At the same time, it can hardly justify present taxation, if only because the taxes are imposed *after* it is already largely known who have drawn the prizes and who the blanks in the lottery of life, and the taxes are voted mostly by those who think they have drawn the blanks. One might, along these lines, justify one generation's voting the tax schedules to be applied to an as yet unborn generation. Any such procedure would, I conjecture, yield income tax schedules much less highly graduated than present schedules are, at least on paper.

Though much of the inequality of income produced by payment in accordance with product reflects "equalizing" differences or the satisfaction of men's tastes for uncertainty, a large part reflects initial differences in endowment, both of human capacities and of property. This is the part that raises the really difficult ethical issue.

It is widely argued that it is essential to distinguish between inequality in personal endowments and in property, and between inequalities arising from inherited wealth and from acquired wealth. Inequality resulting from differences in personal capacities, or from differences in wealth accumulated by the individual in question, are considered appropriate, or at least not so clearly inappropriate as differences resulting from inherited wealth.

This distinction is untenable. Is there any greater ethical justification for the high returns to the individual who inherits from his parents a peculiar voice for which there is a great demand than for the high returns to the individual who inherits property? The sons of Russian commissars surely have a higher expectation of income—perhaps also of liquidation—than the sons of peasants. Is this any more or less justifiable than the higher income expectation of the son of an American millionaire? We can look at this same question in another way. A parent who has wealth that he wishes to pass on to his child can do so in different ways. He can use a given sum of money to finance his child's training as, say, a certified public accountant, or to set him up in business, or to set up a trust fund yielding him a property income. In any of these cases, the child will have a higher income than he otherwise would. But in the first case, his income will be regarded as coming from human capacities; in the second, from profits; in the third, from inherited wealth. Is there any basis for distinguishing among these categories of receipts on ethical grounds? Finally, it seems illogical to say that a man is entitled to what he has produced by personal capacities or to the produce of the wealth he has accumulated, but that he is not entitled to pass any wealth on to his children; to say that a man may use his income for riotous living but may not give it to his heirs. Surely, the latter is one way to use what he has produced.

The fact that these arguments against the so-called capitalist ethic are invalid does not of course demonstrate that the capitalist ethic is an acceptable one. I find it difficult to justify either accepting or rejecting it, or to justify any alternative principle. I am led to the view that it cannot in and of itself be regarded as an ethical principle; that it must be regarded as instrumental or a corollary of some other principle such as freedom.

Some hypothetical examples may illustrate the fundamental difficulty. Suppose there are four Robinson Crusoes, independently marooned on four islands in the same neighborhood. One happened to land on a large and fruitful island which enables him to live easily and well. The others happened to land on tiny and rather barren islands from which they can barely scratch a living. One day, they discover the existence of one another. Of course, it would be generous of the Crusoe on the large island if he invited the others to join him and share its wealth. But suppose he does not. Would the other three be justified in joining forces and compelling him to share his wealth with them? Many a reader will be tempted to say yes. But before yielding to this temptation, consider precisely the same situation in different guise. Suppose you and three friends are walking along the street and you happen to spy and retrieve a $20 bill on the pavement. It would be generous of you, of course, if you were to divide it equally with them, or at least blow them to a drink. But suppose you do not. Would the other three be justified in joining forces and compelling you to share the $20 equally with them? I suspect most readers will be tempted to say no. And on further reflection, they may even conclude that the generous course of action is not itself clearly the "right" one. Are we prepared to urge on ourselves or our fellows that any person whose wealth exceeds the average of all persons in the world should immediately dispose of the excess by distributing it equally to all the rest of the world's inhabitants? We may admire and praise such action when undertaken by a few. But a universal "potlatch" would make a civilized world impossible.

In any event, two wrongs do not make a right. The unwillingness of the rich Robinson Crusoe or the lucky finder of the $20 bill to share his wealth does not justify the use of coercion by the others. Can we justify being judges in our own case, deciding on our own when we are entitled to use force to extract what we regard as our due from others? Or what we regard as not their due? Most differences of status or position or wealth can be regarded as the product of chance at a far enough remove. The man who is hard working and thrifty is to be regarded as "deserving"; yet these qualities owe much to the genes he was fortunate (or unfortunate?) enough to inherit.

Despite the lip service that we all pay to "merit" as compared to "chance," we are generally much readier to accept inequalities arising from chance than those clearly attributable to merit. The college professor whose colleague wins a sweepstake will envy him but is unlikely to bear him any malice or to feel unjustly treated. Let the colleague receive a trivial raise that makes his salary higher than the professor's own, and the professor is far more likely to feel aggrieved. After all, the goddess of chance, as of justice, is blind. The salary raise was a deliberate judgment of relative merit.

The operative function of payment in accordance with product in a market society is not primarily distributive, but allocative. The central principle of a market economy is co-operation through voluntary exchange. Individuals co-operate with others because they can in this way satisfy their own wants more effectively. But unless an individual receives the whole of what he adds to the product, he will enter into exchanges on the basis of what he can receive rather than what he can produce. Exchanges will not take place that would have been mutually beneficial if each party received what he contributed to the aggregate product. Payment in accordance with product is therefore necessary in order that resources be used most effectively, at least under a system depending on voluntary co-operation. Given sufficient knowledge, it might be that compulsion could be substituted for the incentive of reward, though I doubt that it could. One can shuffle inanimate objects around; one can compel individuals to be at certain places at certain times; but one can hardly compel individuals to put forward their best efforts. Put another way, the substitution of compulsion for co-operation changes the amount of resources available.

Though the essential function of payment in accordance with product in a market society is to enable resources to be allocated efficiently without compulsion, it is unlikely to be tolerated unless it is also regarded as yielding distributive justice. No society can be stable unless there is a basic core of value judgments that are unthinkingly accepted by the great bulk of its members. Some key institutions must be accepted as "absolutes," not simply as instrumental. I believe that payment in accordance with product has been, and, in large measure, still is, one of these accepted value judgments or institutions.

One can demonstrate this by examining the grounds on which the internal opponents of the capitalist system have attacked the distribution of income resulting from it. It is a distinguishing feature of the core of central values of a society that it is accepted alike by its members, whether they regard themselves as proponents or as opponents of the system of organization of the society. Even the severest internal critics of capitalism have implicitly accepted payment in accordance with product as ethically fair.

The most far-reaching criticism has come from the Marxists. Marx argued that labor was exploited. Why? Because labor produced the whole of the product but got only part of it; the rest is Marx's "surplus value." Even if the statements of fact implicit in this assertion were accepted, the value judgment follows only if one accepts the capitalist ethic. Labor is "exploited" only if labor is entitled to what it produces. If one accepts instead the socialist premise, "to each according to his need, from each according to his ability"—whatever that may mean—it is necessary to compare what labor produces, not with what it gets but with its "ability," and to compare what labor gets, not with what it produces but with its "need."

Of course, the Marxist argument is invalid on other grounds as well. There is, first, the confusion between the total product of all co-operating resources and the amount added to product—in the economist's jargon, marginal product. Even more striking, there is an unstated change in the meaning of "labor" in passing from the premise to the conclusion. Marx recognized the role of capital in producing the product but regarded capital as embodied labor. Hence, written out in full, the premises of the Marxist syllogism would run: "Present and past labor produce the whole of the product. Present labor gets only part of the product." The logical conclusion is presumably "Past labor is exploited," and the inference for action is that past labor should get more of the product, though it is by no means clear how, unless it be in elegant tombstones.

The achievement of allocation of resources without compulsion is the major instrumental role in the market place of distribution in accordance with product. But it is not the only instrumental role of the resulting inequality. We have noted the role that inequality plays in providing independent foci of power to offset the centralization of political power, as well as the role that it plays in promoting civil freedom by providing "patrons" to finance the dissemination of unpopular or simply novel ideas. In addition, in the economic sphere, it provides "patrons" to finance experimentation and the development of new products—to buy the first experimental automobiles and television sets, let alone impressionist paintings. Finally, it enables distribution to occur impersonally without the need for "authority"—a special facet of the general role of the market in effecting co-operation and co-ordination without coercion.

· · ·

TO EACH ACCORDING TO HIS NEEDS

Karl Marx

· · ·

What we have to deal with here is a communist society, not as it has *developed* on its own foundations, but, on the contrary, just as it *emerges* from capitalist society; which is thus in every respect, economically, morally and intellectually, still stamped with the birth marks of the old society from whose womb it emerges. Accordingly, the individual producer receives back from society—after the deductions have been made—exactly what he gives to it. What he has given to it is his individual quantum of labour. For example, the social working day consists of the sum of the individual hours of work; the individual labour time of the individual producer is the part of the social working day contributed by him, his share in it. He receives a certificate from society that he has furnished such and such an amount of labour (after deducting his labour for the common funds), and with this certificate he draws from the social stock of means of consumption as much as costs the same amount of labour. The same amount of labour which he has given to society in one form he receives back in another.

Here obviously the same principle prevails as that which regulates the exchange of commodities, as far as this is exchange of equal values. Content and form are changed, because under the altered circumstances no one can give anything except his labour, and because, on the other hand, nothing can pass to the ownership of individuals except individual means of consumption. But, as far as the distribution of the latter among the individual producers is concerned, the same principle prevails as in the exchange of commodity-equivalents: a given amount of labour in one form is exchanged for an equal amount of labour in another form.

Hence, *equal right* here is still in principle—*bourgeois right,* although principle and practice are no longer at loggerheads, while the exchange of equivalents in commodity exchange only exists *on the average* and not in the individual case.

In spite of this advance, this *equal right* is still constantly stigmatised by a bourgeois limitation. The right of the producers is *proportional* to the labour they supply; the equality consists in the fact that measurement is made with an *equal standard,* labour.

But one man is superior to another physically or mentally and so supplies more labour in the same time, or can labour for a longer time; and labour, to serve as a measure, must be defined by its duration or intensity, otherwise it ceases to be a standard of measurement. This *equal* right is an unequal right for unequal labour. It recognizes no class differences, because everyone is only a worker like everyone else; but it tacitly recognises unequal individual endowment and thus productive capacity as natural privileges. *It is, therefore, a right of inequality, in its content, like every right.* Right by its very nature can consist only in the application of an equal standard; but unequal individuals (and they would not be different individuals if they were not unequal) are measurable only by an equal standard in so far as they are brought under an equal point of view, are taken from one *definite* side only, for instance, in the present case, are regarded *only as workers* and nothing more is seen in them, everything else being ignored. Further, one worker is married, another not; one has more children than another, and so on and so forth. Thus, with an equal performance of labour, and hence an equal share in the social consumption fund, one will in fact receive more than another, one will be richer than another, and so on. To avoid all these defects, right instead of being equal would have to be unequal.

But these defects are inevitable in the first phase of communist society as it is when it has just emerged after prolonged birth pangs from capitalist society. Right can never be higher than the economic structure of society and its cultural development conditioned thereby.

In a higher phase of communist society, after the enslaving subordination of the individual to the division of labour, and therewith also the antithesis between mental and physical labour, has vanished; after labour has become not only a means of life but life's prime want; after the productive forces have also increased with the all-round development of the individual, and all the springs of co-operative wealth flow more abundantly—only then can the narrow horizon of bourgeois right be crossed in its entirety and society inscribe on its banners: From each according to his ability, to each according to his needs!

. . .

ON JUSTICE UNDER SOCIALISM

Edward and Onora Nell

"From each according to his ability, to each according to his need."

The stirring slogan that ends *The Critique of the Gotha Program* is generally taken as a capsule summary of the socialist approach to distributing the burdens and benefits of life. It can be seen as the statement of a noble ideal and yet be found wanting on three separate scores. First, there is no guarantee that, even if all contribute according to their abilities, all needs can be met: the principle gives us no guidance for distributing goods when some needs must go unmet. Second, if all contribute according to their abilities, there may be a material surplus after all needs are met: again, the principle gives us no guidance for distributing such a surplus. Third, the principle incorporates no suggestion as to why each man would contribute according to his ability: no incentive structure is evident.

These apparent shortcomings can be compared with those of other principles a society might follow in distributing burdens and benefits. Let us call

1. "From each according to his ability to each according to his need," the *Socialist Principle of Justice.* Its Capitalist counterpart would be

2. From each according to his choice, given his assets, to each according to his contribution. We shall call this the *Laissez-Faire Principle.*

These two principles will require a good deal of interpretation, but at the outset we can say that in the Socialist Principle of Justice "abilities" and "needs" refer to persons, whereas the "choices" and "contributions" in the Laissez-Faire Principle refer also to the management of impersonal property, the given assets. It goes without saying that some of the "choices," particularly those of the propertyless, are normally made under considerable duress. As "choice" is the ideologically favored term, we shall retain it.

In a society where the Socialist Principle of Justice regulates distribution, the requirement is that everyone use such talents as have been developed in him (though this need not entail any allocation of workers to jobs), and the payment of workers is contingent not upon their contributions but upon their needs. In a laissez-faire society, where individuals may be endowed with more or less capital or with bare labor power, they choose in the light of these assets how and how much to work (they may be drop-outs or moonlighters), and/or how to invest their capital, and they are paid in proportion.

None of the three objections raised against the Socialist Principle of Justice holds for the Laissez-Faire Principle. Whatever the level of contribution individuals choose, their aggregate product can be distributed in proportion to the contribution—whether of capital or of labor—each individual chooses to make. The Laissez-Faire Principle is applicable under situations both of scarcity and of abundance, and it incorporates a theory of incentives: people choose their level of contribution in order to get a given level of material reward.

Principles 1 and 2 can be cross-fertilized, yielding two further principles:

3. From each according to his ability, to each according to his contribution.
4. From each according to his choice, to each according to his need.

Principle 3 could be called an *Incentive Socialist Principle* of distribution. Like the Socialist Principle of Justice, it pictures a society in which all are required to work in proportion to the talents that have been developed in them. Since unearned income is not available and rewards are hinged to contribution rather than need, all work is easily enforced in an economy based on the Incentive Socialist Principle. This principle, however, covers a considerable range of systems. It holds for a Stalinist economy with an authoritarian job allocation. It also holds for a more liberal, market socialist economy in which there is a more or less free labor market, though without an option to drop out or live on unearned income, or the freedom to choose the level and type of qualification one is prepared to acquire. The Incentive Socialist Principle rewards workers according to their contribution: it is a principle of distribution in which an incentive system—reliance on material rewards—is explicit. Marx believed this principle would have to be followed in the early stages of socialism, in a society "still stamped with the birthmarks of the old society."

Under the Incentive Socialist Principle, each worker receives back the value of the amount of work he contributes to society in one form or another. According to Marx, this is a form of bourgeois right that "tacitly recognizes unequal individual endowments, and thus natural privileges in respect of productive capacity." So this principle holds for a still deficient society where the needs of particular workers, which depend on many things other than their productive capacity, may not be met. Although it may be less desirable than the Socialist Principle of Justice, the Incentive Socialist Principle clearly meets certain criteria the Socialist Principle of Justice cannot meet. It provides a principle of allocation that can be applied equally well to the various situations of scarcity, sufficiency, and abundance. Its material incentive structure explains how under market socialism, given a capital structure and a skill structure, workers will choose jobs and work hard at them—and also why under a Stalinist economy workers will work hard at jobs to which they have been allocated.

Under the Incentive Socialist Principle, workers—whether assigned to menial work or to specific jobs—respond to incentives of the same sort as do workers under the Laissez-Faire Principle. The difference is that, while the Laissez-Faire Principle leaves the measurement of the contribution of a worker to be determined by the level of wage he is offered, the Incentive Socialist Principle relies on a bureaucratically determined weighting that takes into account such factors as the difficulty, duration, qualification level, and risk involved in a given job.

There is another difference between societies living under the Laissez-Faire Principle and those following the Incentive Socialist Principle. Under the Laissez-Faire Principle, there is no central coordination of decisions, for assets are managed according to the choices of their owners. This gives rise to the well-known problems of instability and unemployment. Under the Incentive Socialist Principle, assets are managed by the central government; hence one would expect instability to be eliminated and full employment guaranteed. However, we do not regard this difference as a matter of principle on the same level with others we are discussing. Moreover, in practice some recognizable capitalist societies have managed to control fluctuations without undermining the Laissez-Faire Principle as the principle of distribution.

Let us call Principle 4 the *Utopian Principle of Justice.* It postulates a society without any requirement of contribution or material incentives, but with guaranteed minimal consumption. This principle suffers from the same defect as the Socialist Principle of Justice: it does not determine distributions of benefits under conditions either of scarcity or of abundance, and it suggests no incentive structure to explain why enough should be contributed to its economy to make it possible to satisfy needs. Whether labor is contributed according to choice or according to ability, it is conceivable that the aggregate social product should be such that either some needs cannot be met or that, when all needs are met, a surplus remains that cannot be divided on the basis of needs.

On the surface, this Utopian Principle of Justice exudes the aroma of laissez-faire: though needs will not go unmet in utopia, contributions will be made for no more basic reason than individual whim. They are tied neither to the reliable effects of the incentive of material reward for oneself, nor to those of the noble ideal of filling the needs of others, nor to a conception of duty or self-sacrifice. Instead, contributions will come forth, if they do, according to the free and unconstrained choices of individual economic agents, on the basis of their given preferences. Preferences, however, are not "given"; they develop and change, are learned and unlearned, and follow fashions and fads.

Whim, fancy, pleasure, desire, wish are all words suggesting this aspect of consumer choice. By tying the demand for products to needs and the supply of work to choice, the Utopian Principle of Justice ensures stability in the former but does not legislate against fluctuations and unpredictable variability in the latter.

So the Socialist Principle of Justice and the Utopian Principle of Justice suffer from a common defect. There is no reason to suppose these systems will operate at precisely the level at which aggregate output is sufficient to meet all needs without surplus. And since people do not need an income in money terms but rather an actual and quite precisely defined list of food, clothing, housing, etc. (bearing in mind the various alternatives that might be substituted), the *aggregate* measured in value terms could be right, yet the *composition* might still be unable to meet all the people's needs. People might choose or have the ability to do the right amount of work, but on the wrong projects. One could even imagine the economy growing from a situation of scarcity to one of abundance without ever passing through any point at which its aggregate output could be distributed to meet precisely the needs of its population.

So far, we have been considering not the justification or desirability of alternative principles of distribution, but their practicality. It appears that, in this respect, principles hinging reward on contribution rather than on need have a great advantage. They can both provide a general principle of distribution and indicate the pattern of incentives to which workers will respond.

It might be held that these advantages are restricted to the Incentive Socialist Principle in its various versions, since under the Laissez-Faire Principle there is some income—property income—which is not being paid in virtue of any contribution. This problem can be dealt with either, as we indicated above, by interpreting the notion of contribution to cover the contribution of one's assets to the capital market, or by restricting the scope of the Laissez-Faire Principle to cover workers only, or by interpreting the notion of property income so as to regard wages as a return to property, i.e., property in one's labor power. One can say that under capitalism part of the aggregate product is set aside for the owners of capital (and another part, as under market socialism, for government expenditure) and the remainder is distributed according to the Laissez-Faire Principle. Or one may say that property income is paid in virtue of past contributions, whose reward was not consumed at the time it was earned but was stored. Apologists tend to favor interpretations that make the worker a sort of capitalist or the capitalist a sort of slow-consuming worker. Whichever line is taken, it is clear that the Laissez-Faire Principle—however undesirable we may find it—is a principle of distribution that can be of general use in two senses. Appropriately interpreted, it covers the distribution of earned and of unearned income, and it applies in situations both of scarcity and of abundance.

So we seem to have reached the paradoxical conclusion that the principle of distribution requiring that workers' needs be met is of no use in situations of need, since it does not assign priorities among needs, and that the principle demanding that each contribute according to his ability is unable to explain what incentives will lead him to do so. In this view, the Socialist Principle of Justice would have to be regarded as possibly noble but certainly unworkable.

II

But this view should not be accepted. Marx formulated the Socialist Principle of Justice on the basis of a conception of human abilities and needs that will yield some guidance to its interpretation. We shall now try to see whether the difficulties discussed above can be alleviated when we consider this principle in the light of Marxian theory.

Marx clearly thought that the Socialist Principle of Justice was peculiarly relevant to situations of abundance. In the last section we argued that, on the contrary, it was an adequate principle of distribution only when aggregate output exactly covered total needs. The source of this discrepancy lies in differing analyses of human needs.

By fulfillment of needs we understood at least a subsistence income. Needs are not met when a person lacks sufficient food, clothing, shelter, medical care, or socially necessary training/education. But beyond this biological and social minimum we can point to another set of needs, which men do not have qua men but acquire qua producers. Workers need not merely a biological and social minimum, but whatever other goods—be they holidays or contacts with others whose work bears on theirs or guaranteed leisure, which they need to perform their jobs as well as possible. So a principle of distribution according to needs will not be of use only to a subsistence-level economy. Very considerable goods over and above those necessary for biological subsistence can be distributed according to a principle of need.

But despite this extension of the concept of need the Socialist Principle of Justice still seems to face the three problems listed in Section I:

(1) What guarantees are there that even under abundance the *composition* of the output, with all contributing according to their abilities, will suffice to fill all needs? (There may still be scarcities of goods needed to fill either biological or job-related needs.)

(2) What principle can serve to distribute goods that are surplus both to biological and to job-related needs?

(3) What system of incentives explains why each will contribute to the full measure of his abilities, though he is not materially rewarded for increments of effort? Whether or not there is authoritative job allocation, job performance cannot be guaranteed.

Marx's solution to these problems does not seem too explicit. But much is suggested by the passage at the end of the *Critique of the Gotha Program* where he describes the higher phase of communist society as one in which "labor is no longer merely a means of life but has become life's principal need."

To most people it sounds almost comic to claim that labor could become life's principal need: it suggests a society of compulsive workers. Labor in the common view is intrinsically undesirable, but undertaken as a means to some further, typically material, end. For Marx this popular view would have been confirmation of his own view of the degree to which most labor under capitalism is alienating. He thought that under capitalism laborers experienced a threefold alienation: alienation from the *product* of their labor, which is for them merely a means to material reward; alienation from the *process* of labor, which is experienced as forced labor rather than as desirable activity; and alienation from *others,* since activities undertaken with others are undertaken as a means to achieving further ends, which are normally scarce and allocated competitively. Laborers cooperate in production but, under capitalism, compete for job and income, and the competition overrides the cooperation. Hence Marx claims (in the *Economic and Philosophical Manuscripts*) that "life itself appears only as a means to life." Though the horror of that situation is apparent in the very words, many people accept that labor should be only a means to life—whose real ends lie elsewhere; whether in religion, consumption, personal relations, or leisure.

Marx, on the other hand, held that labor could be more than a means; it could also be an end of life, for labor in itself—*the activity*—can, like other activities, be something for whose sake one does other things. We would be loath to think that activity itself should appear only as a means to life—on the contrary, life's worth for most people lies in the activities undertaken. Those we call labor do not differ intrinsically from the rest, only in relation to the system of production. In Marx's view a system was possible in which all activities undertaken would be nonalienating. Nobody would have to compete to engage in an activity he found unpleasant for the sake of a material reward. Instead, workers would cooperate in creative and fulfilling activities that provide occasions for the exercise of talents, for taking responsibilities, and that result in useful or beautiful products. In such a situation one can see why labor would be regarded as life's greatest need, rather than as its scourge. Nonalienated labor is humanly fulfilling activity.

In the course of switching from the conception of alienating labor to that of nonalienating labor, it might seem that we have moved into a realm for which principles of distribution may be irrelevant. What can the Socialist Principle of Justice tell us about the distribution of burdens and benefits in "the higher phase of communist society"?

In such a society each is to contribute according to his abilities. In the light of the discussion of nonalienated labor, it is clear that there is no problem of incentives. Each man works at what he wants to work at. He works because that is his need. (This is not a situation in which "moral incentives" have replaced material ones, for both moral and material incentives are based on alienating labor. The situation Marx envisages is one for which incentives of *all* sorts are irrelevant.)

Though this disposes of the problem of incentives under the Socialist Principle of Justice, it is much less clear whether this principle can work for a reasonable range of situations. Can it cope with both the situation of abundance and that of scarcity?

In the case of abundance, a surplus of goods over and above those needed is provided. But if all activities are need-fulfilling, then no work is done that does not fulfill some need. In a sense there is no surplus to be distributed, for nothing needless is being done. Nevertheless, there may be a surplus of material goods that are the by-product of need-fulfilling activity. In a society where everybody fulfills himself by painting pictures, there may be a vast surplus of pictures. If so, the Socialist Principle of Justice gives no indication of the right method for their distribution; they are not the goal for which the task was undertaken. Since they do not fulfill an objective need, the method for their distribution is not important. In this the higher phase of communist society is, as one might expect, the very antithesis of consumerism; rather than fabricate reasons for desiring and so acquiring what is not needed, it disregards anything that is not needed in decisions of distribution.

There, nevertheless, is a problem of distribution the Socialist Principle of Justice does not attempt to solve. Some of the products of need-fulfilling activity may be things other people either desire or detest. When need-fulfilling activity yields works of art or noisy block parties, its distribution cannot be disregarded. Not all planning problems can be solved by the Socialist Principle of Justice. We shall not discuss the merits of various principles that could serve to handle these cases, but shall only try to delimit the scope of the Socialist Principle of Justice.

This brings us to the problem of scarcity. Can the Socialist Principle of Justice explain why, when all contribute to the extent of their abilities, all needs can be met? Isn't it conceivable that everyone should find fulfillment in painting, but nobody find fulfillment in producing either biological necessities or the canvases, brushes, and paints everbody wants to use? Might not incentive payments be needed, even in this higher phase of communist society, to guarantee the production of subsistence goods and job-related necessities? In short, will not any viable system involve some alienating labor?

Marx at any rate guarantees that communism need not involve much alienating labor. He insists that the Socialist Principle of Justice is applicable only in a context of abundance. For only when man's needs can be met is it relevant to insist that they ought to be met. The Socialist Principle of Justice comes into its own only with the development of the forces of production. But, of course, higher productivity does not by itself guarantee the right composition of output. Subsistence goods and job-related services and products might not be provided as the population fulfills itself in painting, poetry, and sculpture. Man cannot live by works of art alone.

This socialist version of the story of Midas should not alarm us too much. The possibility of starvation amidst abundant art works seemed plausible only because we abstracted it from other features of an abundant socialist society. Such a society is a planned society, and part of its planning concerns the ability structure of the population. Such a society would include people able to perform all tasks necessary to maintain a high level of material well-being.

Nevertheless, there may be certain essential tasks in such a society whose performance is not need-fulfilling for anybody. Their allocation presents another planning problem for which the Socialist Principle of Justice, by hypothesis, is not a solution. But the degree of coercion need not be very great. In a highly productive society the amount of labor expended on nonfulfilling tasks is a diminishing proportion of total labor time. Hence, given equitable allocation of this burden (and it is here that the planning decisions are really made), nobody would be prevented from engaging principally in need-fulfilling activities. In the limiting case of abundance, where automation of the production of material needs is complete, nobody would have to do any task he did not find intrinsically worthwhile. To the extent that this abundance is not reached, the Socialist Principle of Justice cannot be fully implemented.

However, the degree of coercion, experienced by those who are allocated to necessary but nonfulfilling chores, may be reducible if the planning procedure is of a certain sort. To the extent that people participate in planning and that they realize the necessity of the nonfulfilling chores in order for everyone to be able to do also what he finds need-fulfilling, they may find the performance of these chores less burdensome. As they want to achieve the ends, so—once they are informed—they cannot rationally resent the means, provided they perceive the distribution of chores as just.

The point can be taken a step further. Under the Socialist Principle of Justice, households do not put forth productive effort to be rewarded with an aliquot portion of time and means for self-fulfillment. It is precisely this market mentality from which we wish to escape. The miserable toil of society should be

performed gratis for the benefit of society . . . performed not as a definite duty, not for the purpose of obtaining a right to certain products, not according to previously established and legally fixed quotas, but voluntary labor . . . performed because it has become a habit to work for the common good, and because of a conscious realization (that has become a habit) of the necessity of working for the common good. [V. I. Lenin, "From the Destruction of the Old Social System to the Creation of the New," April 11, 1920. From *Collected Works,* English trans., 40 vols. (London: Lawrence & Wishart, 1965), vol. 30, p. 517.]

Creative work should be done for its own sake, not for any reward. Drudgery should be done for the common good, not in order to be rewarded with opportunity and means for creative work. Of course, the better and more efficient the performance of drudgery, the more will be the opportunities for creative work. To realize this, however, is to understand the necessity of working for the common good, not to be animated by private material incentives. For the possibilities of creative work are opened by the simultaneous and parallel development of large numbers of people. To take the arts, poets need a public, authors readers, performers audiences, and all need (though few want) critics. One cannot sensibly wish, under the Socialist Principle of Justice, to be rewarded *privately* with opportunities and means for nonalienated work.

There is a question regarding the distribution of educational opportunities. Before men can contribute according to their abilities, their abilities must be developed. But in whom should society develop which abilities? If we regard education as consumption, then according to the Socialist Principle of Justice, each should receive it according to his need.

It is clear that all men require some early training to make them viable social beings; further, all men require certain general skills necessary for performing work. But we could hardly claim that some men need to be doctors or economists or lawyers, or need to receive any other specialized or expensive training. If, on the other hand, we regard education as production of those skills necessary for maintaining society and providing the possibility of fulfillment, then the Socialist Principle of Justice can determine a lower bound to the production of certain skills: so-and-so many farmers/doctors/mechanics must be produced to satisfy future subsistence and job-related needs. But the Socialist Principle of Justice cannot determine who shall get which of these educational opportunities. One traditional answer might be that each person should specialize at whatever he is relatively best suited to do. Yet this only makes sense in terms of tasks done as onerous means to desirable ends. Specialization on the basis of comparative advantage minimizes the effort in achieving given ends; but if work is itself fulfilling, it is not an "effort" that must be minimized.

In conditions of abundance, it is unlikely that anyone will be denied training they want and can absorb, though they may have to acquire skills they do not particularly want, since some onerous tasks may still have to be done. For even in conditions of abundance, it may be necessary to compel some or all to undertake certain unwanted training in the interests of the whole. But it is not necessary to supplement the Socialist Principle of Justice with an incentive scheme, whether material or moral. The principle already contains the Kantian maxim: develop your talents to the utmost, for only in this way can a person contribute to the limits of his ability. And if a society wills the end of self-fulfillment, it must will sufficient means. If the members of society take part in planning to maintain and expand the opportunities for everyone's nonalienated activity, they must understand the necessity of allocating the onerous tasks, and so the training for them.

III

Perhaps we can make our point clearer by looking briefly at Marx's schematic conception of the stages of modern history—feudalism, capitalism, socialism, communism—where each stage is characterized by a higher productivity of labor than the preceding stage. In feudalism, the principle of distribution would be:

5. From each according to his status, to each according to his status—the *Feudal Principle of Justice.*

There is no connexion between work and reward. There are no market incentives in the "ideal" feudal system. Peasants grow the stuff for their own subsistence and perform traditional labor services for their lord on domain land. He in turn provides protection and government in traditional fashion. Yet, though labor is not performed as a means to a distant or abstract end, as when it is done for money, it still is done for survival, not for its own sake, and those who do it are powerless to control their conditions of work or their own destinies. Man lives on the edge of famine and is subject to the vagaries of the weather and the dominion of tradition. Only a massive increase in productive powers frees him. But to engender this increase men must come to connect work directly with reward. This provides the incentive to labor, both to take those jobs most needed (moving from the farm to the factory) and to work sufficiently hard once on the job.

But more than work is needed; the surplus of output over that needed to maintain the work force (including managers) and replace and repair the means of production (machines, raw materials) must be put to productive use; it must be reinvested, not consumed. In capitalism, station at birth determines whether one works or owns capital; workers are rewarded for their contribution of work, capitalists for theirs of reinvestment. There is a stick as well as a carrot. Those workers who do not work, starve; those capitalists who fail to reinvest, fail to grow and will eventually be crushed by their larger rivals. Socialism rationalizes this by eliminating the two-class dichotomy and by making reinvestment a function of the institutions of the state, so that the capital structure of the society is the collective property of the citizenry, all of whom must work for reward. In this system the connexion between work and reward reaches its fullest development, and labor in one sense is most fully alienated. The transition to communism then breaks this link altogether.

The link between work and rewards serves a historical purpose, namely to encourage the development of the productive forces. But as the productive forces continue to develop, the demand for additional rewards will tend to decline, while the difficulty of stimulating still further growth in productivity may increase. This, at least, seems to be implied by the principles of conventional economics—diminishing marginal utility and diminishing marginal productivity. Even if one rejects most of the conventional wisdom of economics, a good case can be made for the diminishing efficacy of material incentives as prosperity increases. For as labor productivity rises, private consumption needs will be met, and the most urgent needs remaining will be those requiring *collective* consumption—and, indeed, some of these needs will be generated by the process of growth and technical progress. These last needs, if left unmet, may hinder further attempts to raise the productive power of labor. So the system of material incentives could in principle come to a point where the weakened encouragements to extra productivity offered as private reward for contribution might be offset by the accumulated hindrances generated by the failures to meet collective needs and by the wastes involved in competition. At this point, it becomes appropriate to break the link between work and reward. Breaking the link, however, is not enough. Both the Socialist Principle of Justice and the Utopian Principle of Justice break the link between work and reward. But the Utopian Principle of Justice leaves the distinction between them. Work is a means, the products of work are the ends. Given a high productivity of labor, workers would in principle choose their occupations and work-leisure patterns, yet still producing enough to satisfy everyone's needs. This would be a society devoted to minimizing effort, a sort of high-technology Polynesia. Since it neither makes consumption dependent upon work nor regards work as other than a regrettable means to consumption, it fails to explain why sufficient work to supply basic needs should ever be done. The alienation of labor cannot be overcome by eliminating labor rather than alienation.

Breaking the link between work and reward, while leaving the distinction itself in tact, may also lead to the loss of the productive powers of labor. For without reward, and when the object is to work as little as possible, why expend the effort to acquire highly complex skills? What is the motive to education, self-improvement, self-development? A high-technology Polynesia contains an inner contradiction.

By contrast, the Socialist Principle of Justice not only does not make reward depend upon work but denies that there is a distinction between the two. Because man needs fulfilling activity—work that he chooses and wants—men who get it contribute according to their ability.

Yet there still may remain routine and menial, unfulfilling jobs. But who wills the end wills the means. The society must plan to have such jobs done. No doubt, many will be mechanized or automated, but the remaining ones will form a burden that must be allocated.

The Socialist Principle of Justice cannot solve this problem of allocation. But everyone has some interest in getting uncoveted but essential work done. Hence it should not be difficult to find an acceptable supplementary principle of distribution for allocating these chores. For instance, the Principle of Comparative Advantage might be introduced to assign each the drudgery at which he is relatively best. There can be no quarrel with this so long as such alienating work is only a small fraction of a man's total activity, conferring no special status. It is only when alienating work takes up the bulk of one's waking hours, and determines status, that specialization inevitably entails some form of class structure.

The Socialist Principle of Justice cannot solve all allocation problems. But once one understands that it is based on a denial of a distinction between work, need, and reward, it is clear that it can solve an enormous range of such problems. In a highly productive society the only allocation problems the Socialist Principle of Justice cannot solve are the distribution of unmechanized and uncoveted chores and of the material by-products of creative endeavor.

Suggested Readings

Benn, S. I., and R. S. Peters. *The Principles of Political Thought.* New York: Macmillan, 1959.
See chaps. 5 and 6.

Brandt, Richard B. (ed.). *Social Justice.* Englewood Cliffs, N.J.: Prentice-Hall, 1962.

Kaufmann, Walter. "The Origin of Justice," *Review of Metaphysics* 23 (December 1969).

Perelman, C. H. *Justice.* New York: Random House, 1967.

Phelps, Edmund S. (ed.). *Economic Justice.* Baltimore: Penguin, 1973.

Rescher, Nicholas. *Distributive Justice.* Indianapolis: Bobbs-Merrill, 1966.

THANKSGIVING
*Feast
and Festival*

THANKSGIVING
Feast
and Festival

Compiled by

MILDRED CORELL LUCKHARDT

ILLUSTRATED BY RALPH McDONALD

ABINGDON PRESS
Nashville—New York

THE COMPILER AND PUBLISHERS WISH TO THANK INDIVIDUALS AND PUBLISHERS
FOR THEIR PERMISSION TO USE COPYRIGHTED MATERIAL AS FOLLOWS:

Child Guidance for the prayer-song from Kambine, East Africa, by the Rev. Julian S. Rea, copyright © 1945 by The Methodist Publishing House.

Child Life Magazine for "Land of Plenty" and "A Bow to Thanksgiving" by Carolyn Sherwin Bailey, copyright © 1942 and 1946 by *Child Life Magazine* and reprinted with the permission of Mrs. William T. (Carolyn T.) Downey for the estate of Carolyn Sherwin Bailey; and for "Aboard the Sweet Cecile" by Lavinia R. Davis, copyright © 1943 by *Child Life Magazine* and reprinted with the permission of Samuel S. Walker, Jr.

E. P. Dutton & Company, Inc., for "Land of the Pilgrims' Pride" adapted from *The Book of Three Festivals* by Amy Morris Lillie, copyright © 1948 by Amy Morris Lillie. Adapted and reprinted by permission of the author and E. P. Dutton & Company, Inc.

Follett Publishing Company for "Succos," adapted from *All-of-a-Kind Family* by Sydney Taylor, copyright © 1951. Used by permission.

Harcourt, Brace & World, Inc., for "The Departure," abridged from *Pilgrim Kate* by Helen F. Daringer, copyright © 1949 by Harcourt, Brace & World, Inc., and reprinted with their permission.

Harper & Row, Publishers, Inc., for "A Saga of the Prairie," adapted by Margaret Dulles Edwards from *Giants in the Earth* by O. E. Rolvaag, copyright © 1927 by Harper & Brothers, renewed 1955 by Jennie Marie Berdahl Rolvaag; and for the prayers from the Congo, Korea, and

HAPPY THANKSGIVING HARVEST TIME
to
Allison, Amy, Betsy, Bruce, Corell
Douglas, Gordon, Lucy Anne, Marianne
Nan and Richard
and to girls and boys everywhere with
good wishes for peace and contentment

Thank you . . .

In many different lands countless people enjoy happy harvest festivals with thanksgiving. So it is natural that a number of different children and grownups have helped me gather thanksgiving and harvest-home material from many places.

I cannot list all of their names here. As I write this thank you, however, I think pleasantly of each person who has helped me in my writing. School children and their teachers have searched for stories and poems. World travelers and visitors from other countries have told me of harvest feasts or thanksgiving days in Formosa, Borneo, Japan, and other countries, or have sung harvest songs for me.

Here are the names of some persons to whom special thanks is due: Miss Marcia Dalphin, who helped me choose my first library

9

book and advised me with selections for this book; Miss Dorothy Merrick, Director of the Museum of Pilgrim History, Plymouth, Massachusetts; Mr. E. Lawrence Couter, Public Relations Director, and Dr. Arthur G. Pyle, Education Director, of Plimoth Plantation, the replica Pilgrim village at Plymouth, who have supplied material, read and criticized my manuscript, guided my Plantation visit, answered innumerable questions, and who have given me special insights; Miss Maria Cimino, Children's Librarian, and Mrs. Ann Stell, Assistant Children's Librarian, at Central Branch New York Public Library; Dr. Lucy McCafferty, Department of Education, Hunter College, New York; Miss Anne Izard, Children's Specialist, Westchester (New York) Library System; Miss Frances Elrod, Children's Librarian, Mount Vernon Public Library, and Miss Katherine Han from Formosa, who assists Miss Elrod and who told me of the harvest festival in her homeland.

The list grows as persons from far and wide have helped, advised, or encouraged: Miss Lucy Maud Kibler, Department of Speech of Public Schools, Arlington, Virginia, and other librarians and teachers of Arlington who suggested thanksgiving material; Miss Dorothy Fritz, Santa Fe, New Mexico, educator, author, consultant on children's reading, learning, and growth; Mrs. Fannie Bailey, Frenchburg, Kentucky, educator; Mrs. Irma Mazzarella, Orlando, Florida, teacher; Mrs. Carolyn Low, Natick, Massachusetts, teacher; Mrs. Margueritte Bro, Park Forest, Illinois, lecturer and author of many books including *When Children Ask;* Mrs. Ida McMath, teacher in Greenwich, Connecticut, and many others there who have searched with her for thanksgiving material; Miss Betsy Kenney, pupil in Helen Keller Middle School, Easton, Connecticut; Mr. Bruce Kenney, pupil in Joel Barlow High School, Redding, Connecticut, who suggested the book's title; Mrs. Ruth Chelimer, Larchmont,

New York, educator; Mrs. Elizabeth Allstrom, educator, author, and children's book consultant, New York City; Miss Lily Talent-Bateman, Houston, Texas, storyteller known as "Mother Goose."

From Scotland, Miss Kathleen Garscaddon, known to thousands as "Auntie Kathleen" of BBC; Miss Doris Scott, a Librarian of Boys and Girls House, Toronto (Canada) Public Library; Dr. Pierre Brunet, Assistant Dominion Archivist of the Dominion of Canada; Dr. Milton C. Russell, Head of the reference and circulation section, General Library Division of the Commonwealth of Virginia; members of the staff of the Mexican Embassy in Washington; Dr. Richard W. Hale, Jr., Archivist, Commonwealth of Massachusetts.

I must express my appreciation also to the Reverend Francis X. Weiser, S.J., native of Vienna and well-known lecturer, college professor, and author, who was generous in responding to my questions; Mr. Richard McDowell, St. Michael's College in Vermont; Dr. and Mrs. Deane Edwards of Rye, New York, who made available some unusual material; the Reverend Margaret Towner, Kalamazoo, Michigan; Mrs. Mary Barlow and the girls and boys in her class in Midland School, Rye, New York; friendly and knowledgeable librarians in Riverton (New Jersey), Port Chester (New York), Yarmouth (Maine), and Morgantown (North Carolina); Miss Doris Bird, Children's Librarian, Rye Free Reading Room, and other librarians there who suggested material; and my husband, children, and grandchildren, who always cooperate in my writing ventures.

To all who read this book, may the contents which have been gathered from such a variety of people and places add to the joy and the sharing of your harvest feast wherever you are in this wonderful world. Happy Thanksgiving!

MILDRED CORELL LUCKHARDT

Rye, New York, 1966

CONTENTS

PART I

The Pilgrims and Thanksgiving

13

PART II

Thanksgiving and Harvest Time Near and Far

PART I
The Pilgrims and Thanksgiving

The Pilgrims Came

The Pilgrims came across the sea,
And never thought of you and me;
And yet it's very strange the way
We think of them Thanksgiving Day.

We tell their story old and true
Of how they sailed across the blue,
And found a new land to be free
And built their homes quite near the sea.
Every child knows well the tale
Of how they bravely turned the sail,
And journeyed many a day and night
To worship God as they thought right.

The people think that they were sad
And grave; I'm sure that they were glad—
They made Thanksgiving Day—that's fun—
We thank the Pilgrims every one!

—FROM *For Days and Days*
BY ANNETTE WYNNE

The Daring Venture

The farmlands of England were beautiful beneath the golden harvest moon. Within a few days the last sheaves of grain would be brought home, and then would come the merry harvest-home feast. Yet, in many places throughout the land, there would be no feasting. In that early part of the seventeenth century some people did not know from day to day whether the king's soldiers would seize their farms and imprison the owners.

Tonight as some of them slipped quietly through the harvest fields by moonlight they doubted they would ever see another harvest in England. Perhaps not even another springtime. They were hard-working farmers and loved their broad fields and pleasant farmsteads. They loved England, their homeland. But tonight they were going to a secret meeting.

They were in danger of losing their homes and their lives because they refused to attend the national church which the king controlled. They thought the church was not teaching the truth nor helping people to live their best. Instead, the king was using the church to force people to do as he wanted. It appeared that many

21

clergymen were interested only in money and in personal power.

There were other clergymen and many people who were trying to purify and reform the church and to get more complete religious freedom and justice for everyone. These people were jeered at by their enemies who called them "Puritans." These Puritans sent a petition to the king, asking for freedom to worship as they thought right according to the Bible. For answer, the king shouted he would "harry the Puritans out of the land" or do worse. He ordered that certain brave young men be killed for teaching Puritan ideas. Other Puritan leaders were imprisoned in dark damp jails. They had to pay big fines. Then they might be released for a while only to have the king's spies pounce on them again.

William Brewster had been arrested several times. He was Postmaster at Scrooby Manor on the Great North Road, more than one hundred miles north of London, where King James held court and ruled the church. When Brewster had been a student at Cambridge University, he had met many students with Puritan ideas of liberty and especially the right of each person to worship according to his conscience.

Later William Brewster became an aid to the English ambassador to the Netherlands. In Holland, the Dutch had won a bitter struggle against foreign invaders and had gained a truce whereby they were free to worship as they chose. Some English Puritans already had fled to Holland and established a Puritan church there. William Brewster attended that church with the English ambassador.

When he returned to England, Brewster chose to become a Puritan even though it was very dangerous. In time he and his family, and a group of other Puritans, near Scrooby, decided to separate from the national church and hold worship services as a "Separatist" congregation with the Reverend Richard Clyfton as their pastor. He was helped by another young pastor, the Reverend John Robinson, who had been a Cambridge student with William Brewster.

The Scrooby congregation often met at the Brewsters' big home. William Brewster was one of the lay leaders, elected to be an elder. Elder Brewster and his wife were very kind to all those in trouble. They took care of the poor and the sick for miles around.

Tonight there was to be another secret meeting at Scrooby Manor House for the purpose of trying to figure out what was best to do. The meeting would be in the hayloft above the stables of the postriders' horses. The king's spies might not think to look there.

During the chilly autumn and winter evenings the group changed their place of meeting several times. On Sundays the congregation often met in one place for a few weeks; when the king's soldiers or spies were seen, the worshipers found other places to meet in secret. Often they had sad news. Some of their men were jailed because they would not attend the national church. Some had their houses and farms seized by officers of the crown. Nobody knew where terror would strike next.

But everyone knew that the king was especially anxious to arrest William Brewster. Perhaps this time Brewster would be killed. Yet he and his wife never showed their fears and continued to comfort and encourage everyone else. They were especially kind to Will Bradford, a young man who had been orphaned in childhood. Will's uncle had warned Will that if he became a Puritan he might lose the farm his father had left him. But Will Bradford, although only in his teens, replied he would risk everything to have a good conscience in his religion.

Tormented and oppressed continually by the government, the Scrooby congregation determined to risk everything on a daring venture for freedom. Some said, "Let's escape to America and found a settlement there." But others replied, "At present the king hates us so much he would never give us a charter for such a plantation." Others said, "Wherever we go, we will have to go secretly or we'll be arrested, perhaps killed."

Previously some had tried to escape to Holland but were arrested, robbed by the soldiers, and imprisoned for quite a while. Even so Holland seemed to be the only place to which they could flee. Plans were made quietly for chartering a Dutch boat to take them there. The Scrooby congregation now realized that they were like pilgrims, leaving their homes and homeland and beginning a pilgrimage because they would be true to their conscience.

When all the fields blossomed with springtime, the Pilgrims bravely turned their backs on their homes and many friends and relatives. Silently they stepped onto barges moored beneath the willows of a placid stream called Scrooby Water. The men already had loaded on the barges what few possessions could be taken. Down the stream they glided, farther and farther, until the women and children boarded a boat that would take them to the seacoast. The men and older boys tramped fifty miles toward the port where they all would meet and set out on the ship for Holland.

At the port most of the men were rowed to the ship quickly because the boat with the women and children was stuck in the sand at low tide. Before the tide could turn, however, a troop of soldiers ran through the marshes. The ship's captain became frightened, hoisted sail for Holland, and left the frightened and helpless women and children on shore. The soldiers hustled them to the magistrate. They were imprisoned but after a short time they were released, and somehow, after what seemed a long, frightening time, they reached Holland and were met by the men.

The busy, crowded Dutch cities were strange and confusing to the little group of Pilgrims from the quiet English farm country. Few understood the Dutch language. Finding jobs was very hard, for the men were farmers and not trained for city work. They had to learn new trades and, naturally, could not expect high pay. They worked very hard to earn food and shelter for their families.

After a while they moved to the city of Leyden and bought a large old house in Bell Alley near the big cathedral. John Robinson, who was now their pastor, lived in this house, which was known as "the House with the Green Gate." Close by they built little houses crowded together around a small courtyard. They missed their comfortable English homes and rolling fields; but they were glad to be safe and to have religious freedom.

Every Sunday the Leyden Pilgrim families met to worship at "the House with the Green Gate." In time other English people joined them, too. Some French-speaking people who had fled also to Holland for religious freedom became part of the congregation. The Leydeners respected the Pilgrims, for they were kind, honest, hard working, and got along well together and with their neighbors.

To the famous new Leyden University students came from all over Europe. In time William Brewster was able to earn some money teaching English to Danish, German, and other students. This money was needed badly because the Brewster family was large and sometimes William earned barely enough to feed them.

All of the poverty stricken Pilgrims worked hard at whatever jobs they could get, making textiles, hats, buttons, shoes, gloves. Some were barbers, metal workers, printers, working from sunrise to sunset at almost starvation wages. The Brewsters lived in a house on a dark, damp alley called Stink Alley. One of their children died in this unhealthful place. How often the Brewsters and the others longed for sunny, rolling fields and farms where they could raise their own food once more!

Yet, the congregation held together and kept growing, and made friends with many kind Dutch neighbors. Some of the Pilgrims continued to study, too. Will Bradford, although working long hours making a twilled cloth called fustian, learned Dutch and French. He studied Latin and Greek in order to read the Bible in those languages. In Holland, Bible reading was not forbidden.

Every October 3, Leydeners celebrated the victory which had won their freedom in 1574, when Leyden had been saved after a long Spanish siege. At this annual thanksgiving time, there was a big fair in Leyden, to which everyone went. Dressed in holiday clothes, the people watched a pageant of scenes of Leyden courage during the siege. They enjoyed the holiday, riding on the canals, singing, laughing, waving to their friends. They welcomed neighbors and friends and lonely ones into their homes to eat the thanksgiving stew called "hotchpotch." It reminded them of the stew they had eaten when Leyden was saved.

Even amid all the thanksgiving rejoicing for Holland's freedom, some people were worried because the truce would be ended before many years. They feared they might have to fight again for freedom. Already some young men of the Pilgrim congregation were joining the Dutch army along with the Dutch youths they knew. Pilgrim children liked to hear stories of Dutch courage, and many of them were learning much more about Dutch history than the history of their English ancestors.

The older Pilgrims longed for their English homeland. They longed to be surrounded by those who spoke English and to have their children grow up as English. Some kept hoping that soon the king might allow religious freedom and they could go home. Others planned to stay in Holland for the rest of their lives. Many still talked about founding an English colony in America. They visited Leyden's Botanical Gardens and Museum of Natural History and looked at specimens of plants which Dutch navigators had brought back from the East Indies and the West Indies. Then the Pilgrims thought of planting farms across the Atlantic.

Some talked of their dreams for the future. "It doesn't seem that we will be allowed back in England, for the king is getting more intolerant all the time. He has forgotten English justice and English respect for the rights of all citizens. The Dutch have been very good to us and have given us refuge; but we never can hope to build up an inheritance for our children here. We are English farmers and country people at heart. We want lands for ourselves and our children. Why don't we sail for America and make a plantation there?"

They discussed this possibility for some years and watched what was happening in Europe. A religious war was tearing Germany apart. Spain was waiting to invade Holland. Holland would need England's help, and the English king already was beginning to use his power in various ways in Holland.

William Brewster was in new trouble with the king. Since Leyden was a great center of education and publishing and since Brewster was such a learned man, he and a few friends had started a publishing house in the winter of 1616. The press was in an extension of his house where it touched Choir Alley. So they used that address instead of Stink Alley facing the front door.

Quite a few people came to the Choir Alley Press to have books printed. At first that press published several books in Dutch on the Commandments and other religious matters. Then came some books in Latin. They published and sent to England some pamphlets about Puritan ideas of religion, which stirred many people to think of

rights of conscience and the dignity of all men as set forth in the Bible, and of how the present king and a few church leaders were oppressing the people. Then Brewster's publishing house, known as the Pilgrim Press, published in English reports on the way the king had tried to crush the Scotch Presbyterian Church.

These books were considered treason. The king tracked down the publisher and ordered Brewster arrested; Brewster escaped, but his press was raided and closed. Next the king directed his ambassador to Holland to send spies all over that land searching for Brewster. Many Dutch friends and neighbors of the Pilgrims helped Brewster hide and escape. They kept giving the spies false clues. The king was determined to catch this Pilgrim leader and make an example of him and, possibly, frighten the thousands of citizens in England who sympathized with the Puritans.

By royal order both sides of the North Sea and English Channel were searched. But Brewster could not be found. He had escaped into hiding near Scrooby. At the risk of his life he was working quietly in England with other Puritan leaders to get help for the Pilgrims to establish a colony in America, a colony to be sponsored by the London Company.

In time seventy English merchant adventurers raised money for a Pilgrim settlement, or plantation. The settlers were to work together and put their earnings from fishing, farming, and fur-trading into a common fund, which would pay off the company of merchant adventurers in seven years.

When news of the opportunity reached the Pilgrims in Leyden, they talked over very carefully the agreement the merchant adventurers would make. Some of the Pilgrims were afraid to venture into the unknown New World. Some were too frail. Some thought the terms of the agreement harsh. They realized that merchant adventurers could recruit strangers to join the colony of Pilgrims in America.

"We're willing to put what little we have into the common fund," said some, "so we all can be partners in helping buy provisions for the voyage. But we're not sure that everybody should put everything he earns into paying off the common debt. Some people will loaf, and others will work very hard; and the loafers should not be carried along by burdening the hard workers."

The leaders explained that these were the best terms that Robert Cushman and his associates in London could get. Robert Cushman, a deacon of the Leyden church, had been sent to London on the difficult assignment of helping work out some way in which the Pilgrims who wished to could get to America.

During the long weeks while some members of the congregation were discussing the merchant adventurers' proposition and expressing doubts and fears, other Pilgrims already had made up their minds what to do. As William Bradford later wrote, "They lived here but as men in exile and in a poor condition; and as great miseries might possibly befall them in this place (as in America); for the twelve years of truce were now out, and there was nothing but beating of drums and preparing for war, the events whereof are always uncertain." Bradford felt that the enemies of Holland might "prove as cruel as the savages in America, and the famine and pestilence are sore here and there."

After a day of prayer, each member of the congregation voted in a democratic way whether he would join the daring venture or stay in Leyden. About thirty members, including William Bradford, decided to go. Captain Miles Standish, an English soldier who had been sent to help the Dutch about 1600, also joined them. He often worshiped with their congregation but never became a regular member. Decisions were made, and preparations to go were started.

Of course, a patent from the king was necessary. Finally on February 12, 1620, a patent was obtained by the merchant adventurers, covering territory near the Virginia Capes. Then a small ship, the "Speedwell," was chartered to sail from Delft-Haven in Holland, and join the "Mayflower" in England.

The spring of 1620 was very busy with last-minute plans. Some families of the Leyden congregation would be far apart for a while. For instance, William Brewster's wife, Mary, who was now a grandmother, would take their two young sons to America, while the rest of the family would stay in Leyden and go to America later. William Brewster, a hunted man still hiding somewhere in England, would get aboard the "Speedwell" secretly when it reached Southampton.

Since less than one-sixth of the Leyden congregation were going on this first trip to America, Pastor Robinson was to stay in Leyden with the church. The parting of friends and families was very sad. Will Bradford and his wife Dorothy left their five-year-old boy in the care of the Robinsons, and they all cried at parting. It happened that the boy never saw his mother again, for she was drowned a few months later; and he did not see his father for seven years. Almost half of the group who sailed from Leyden were children.

What lay ahead none of them knew. Many of the grown-ups wondered what kind of people the "Strangers" would be who joined the company in England. These Strangers would not be going to America for religious freedom, because most of them agreed with the Church of England. As the little "Speedwell" sailed toward England, everyone was wondering too whether William Brewster would be able to get aboard without being arrested. They were looking forward, also, to seeing old friends who would be going to America on the "Mayflower."

They all wanted to get across the Atlantic Ocean as quickly as possible during the summer season, before wild winds blew down from the north. They planned to build homes in the New World during sunny autumn days so they might be warmly sheltered for the winter.

All such plans came to naught, however, because after the "Mayflower" and "Speedwell" left England, the "Speedwell" proved unseaworthy. It's hard to imagine the worry, disappointment, and terrible loss of time and money caused to them all each time the ships had to sail back to England to get the "Speedwell" repaired. At last, it was decided that the "Speedwell" was unsafe for the voyage. Some of the Strangers and a few of the Leyden people decided to return home.

Finally about 102 passengers crowded onto the "Mayflower," and on September 6, 1620, the Mayflower set sail once more. They would have to brave winter at once, if they ever did arrive in the New World. They were short of food from the start, having had to sell some to pay for "Speedwell" repairs and other unforeseen emergencies. More than one third of the passengers were children, who would have to be protected. There were only about half as many Pilgrims as Strangers. Some people who watched the "Mayflower" sail said God would have to work a miracle if the people aboard ever could start a plantation in the New World.

Since the Pilgrims were a united congregation, they became known by the Old Testament name for such a group, "saints." On the "Mayflower," too, there were several other groups—those known as the Strangers who had been recruited by the merchant adventurers, some orphaned children who were waifs and were allotted to various families, servants, young men who were hired hands to work for one year and had no special interest in the permanent settlement.

It is almost miraculous how, under the most trying conditions, the saints and Strangers in time drew together in brave and friendly co-operation.

At first most seamen on the "Mayflower" jeered at the passengers for getting seasick. The crew, who on the whole were a very rough lot, scorned the Pilgrims for gathering to pray every day and for praying during fierce storms at sea. Later, however, when many passengers and crew were very sick with a mysterious plague, the Pilgrims who could move about nursed the sick seamen just as carefully as they took care of their own families.

For sixty-six days and nights the "Mayflower," commanded by Captain Christopher Jones, plowed through winds and waves, and was blown off course at times. At last the shout arose "Land, ho!" Everyone rushed on deck to catch sight of the green shoreline of Cape Cod in New England. They did not land, however, for their patent called for settlement farther down the coast. So Captain Jones plunged the little ship southward, wallowing madly in powerful currents and shrieking gales.

Some thought they were to start their plantation near the Hudson River; some thought, farther south. Others understood that Thomas Weston, one of the active merchant adventurers, had advised the settlers to go toward Cape Cod where fishing and fur-trading would be good.

However, Captain Jones declared that the ship could not make it southward through the storms and dangerous shallows, and turned back toward Cape Cod. Some sailors started mutiny, demanding that passengers be set ashore at once so the ship could return to England. A few adventurous hotheaded Strangers and hired hands muttered together that when they got ashore nobody could tell them what to do. The patent did not cover this region, so they were free to go off and start a rival colony with rival trading posts. They stirred up others and shouted at the Pilgrim leaders. Mutiny, lawlessness, violence, and murder threatened.

Pilgrim leaders talked with level-headed Strangers. Soon a compact was drawn up to assure everyone fair treatment in a democratic government they would all establish for the common well-being. William Brewster, Will Bradford, Edward Winslow, John Carver and other Pilgrims, together with men like Stephen Hopkins of the Strangers, went about the ship talking to the rebellious groups. They pointed out that unless all stayed together and worked for the common well-being of all in a commonwealth, everything would be lost.

Stephen Hopkins could give hard-hitting advice on the dangers of mutiny. Ten years earlier he had been shipwrecked in Bermuda and condemned to death for leading a mutiny. Somehow, he had escaped. He wanted this new colony to survive and give his children, including the baby Oceanus who had been born on the "Mayflower," new opportunities.

When the Mayflower Compact was ready to sign, everyone crowded into the big cabin, wondering what would happen. Would the discontented refuse to sign, and cause more trouble? William Brewster read the Compact and answered questions. Everyone was uneasy. Then John Carver, one of the kindest, most respected Pilgrims, walked up and signed the paper. Other Pilgrim leaders followed. There was a pause. Up marched Captain Miles Standish, sword clanking, and signed the Compact. Some Strangers followed.

Next came the voting. John Carver, who was wise and able but never got puffed up with power or used it selfishly, was elected unanimously to be the first governer. He was the first governor ever to be elected by the people, themselves, in any English colony.

Previously governors had been appointed by the king and were responsible only to him and the company which had invested money in sending out the colony. Now the Pilgrims dared what very few people ever had dared to do; they started to govern themselves. Through the Mayflower Compact they could choose who would rule for them; and when his term of office was over, they could elect another if they chose.

For some years the Pilgrims had used this democratic method in choosing religious leaders. Now, in following this plan for electing civil officers, they established a custom which would effect democratic ideas as America grew. Elder Brewster was the spiritual leader for the church they would found in the New World. From the beginning, although their civil laws were based on teachings of the Old Testament, their church officers and civil officers and laws were separate. They believed in the right to worship without interference from the government.

Because the "Mayflower" reached America when winter was beginning, the Pilgrims persuaded Captain Jones to stay and let them use the ship for a winter home, especially for the women and children. This took most of the little money left. Meanwhile men were sent in a small boat, a shallop, to scout along the shores for a good place to start the plantation. The weather was so cold that the sea spray froze on their coats; they saw parties of Indians but got away safely each time, although more than once arrows showered all around them.

After several days of exploring, on December 21, the scouts "sounded the harbor and found it fit for shipping, and marched into the land, and found cornfields and little running brooks . . . the best place they could find, and the season and their present necessity made them glad to accept it."

The passengers waiting on the ship were delighted with the

news, and the "Mayflower" sailed for the chosen place. They knew that Captain John Smith had voyaged and surveyed the coast from Cape Cod to Penobscot Bay in 1614. Probably the "Mayflower" had brought a description of that trip and a copy of this map wherein he named the area New England. They could see that the place where they now would land and settle was named Plymouth. This seemed a coincidence, for they had sailed from a port of the same name in old England.

In those days sometimes names were spelled slightly differently by several people, but pronounced alike. Some spelled Plymouth as Plimoth, or Plimouth. Whichever way it was spelled, Plimoth Plantation was begun by people of great courage who, in spite of snow and ice, hunger, hostile Indians, and a plague of sickness, began to build homes in the wilderness.

More than half of the people died during that bitter first winter. By spring only about fifty colonists were alive—twenty-one men, five

women, six sturdy boys, a few older girls, and the rest children. Most of them had lost members of their families; they were hungry, weak, tired, always on guard against Indians. Yet, when the "Mayflower" sailed back to England in the spring, not one of them gave up and went back, too.

Tales of Plymouth courage are told throughout our vast country and elsewhere, especially at thanksgiving time. During the year, hundreds of thousands of visitors go to Plimoth Plantation, the replica village being constructed at Plymouth, Massachusetts, by an organization of present-day Americans. Here, thousands of school children go into various pilgrim houses, climb about the "Mayflower" and watch familiar pilgrim stories come alive. Countless visitors also stand thoughtfully at Plymouth Rock and visit many pilgrim memorials in Plymouth.

Everyone knows the story of Samoset and Squanto, Indians who befriended the first Plymouth colonists, and how Squanto showed them how to plant corn. And noble Massasoit, the Wampanoag chief, made an honorable treaty at Plymouth which was kept on both sides for many years.

Not everyone realizes, though, how the Indians had been studying the Pilgrims. In most cases when people intend to conquer and subdue others, the conquest is begun by a band of armed men. The Indians saw that the Pilgrims had brought their families with them. This meant that they planned a peaceful settlement.

Then, too, it happened that many Indians in the area where the Pilgrims landed had been killed by plague some months before. This left the remaining Indian neighbors weakened, and they welcomed the Pilgrims as allies against some fierce, warlike tribes not far away. Also, word spread of the just and friendly way in which the Pilgrims treated Indians.

Most of the Pilgrims really tried to treat the Indians fairly. Unlike many other colonists, they gave an Indian accused of a crime a fair trial when possible. Records show that an Indian was arrested for a crime that carried the death penalty. During his trial in Plymouth, the judge said the Indian did not know how serious the crime was, and he was released.

One of the favorite stories is of the first thanksgiving harvest feast which the Pilgrims celebrated with Massasoit and ninety of his Indians. After a while, some other tribes tried to cause trouble between his tribe and Plymouth. But when word came to Plymouth that Massasoit was very sick, Edward Winslow and Stephen Hopkins went far into the dark forest to see the suffering chief. Winslow gave Massasoit healing medicines and stayed with him and saved his life.

There were unhappy incidents, too. A shipload of cedar clapboards and beaver pelts worth nearly half the amount the Plymouth colonists owed the London merchant adventurers was captured by a French privateer. Hostile Indians continually caused trouble. The London company sent various shiploads of colonists to Plymouth with no food to sustain them until new crops were ready.

Some newcomers were wild adventurers who stole from the other colonists, robbed their cornfields, and ate their fill before those who had planted the corn got any. One group settled nearby, sold liquor and firearms to the Indians, and when the Indians were drunk, cheated them in trading beaver skins. Plymouth people were called to protect some of those who had done the most harm.

In time Plimoth Plantation spread out into Plymouth Colony, with fishing and trading posts many miles apart. In various parts of New England new colonies were beginning. Some were formed by the Massachusetts Bay Company. This took the name "Massachusetts" from the friendly Indian tribe living near the Great Blue Hill where now Milton, Massachusetts is located. The name in Indian means "Great Hill." To Massachusetts Bay Colony came wealthier Puritans than those who had first fled from England to Holland and then to America. All, however, wanted to break tyranny in government and religion and give representation to the common people.

Because these founders of New England had suffered from oppressive religious intolerance in Europe, they tried to establish colonies where they could worship as they thought right. They made it quite clear that any who wished to join the colonies should worship according to Puritan ideas. They did not pretend to set up a refuge for persecuted people who would not join in Puritan worship.

Other American colonies at that time established forms of worship, and their laws decreed that members of their colony must attend their particular church. For instance, Virginia, which had a governor appointed by the English king, followed English law. This required every man and woman to go to church on Sunday morning and again in the afternoon "for divine service and catechising." If a person were absent, he would lose his provisions for a week. The penalty for a third absence was to "suffer death." For blaspheming God's name in Virginia, the third offense could "receive censure of death."

Today such laws seem cruel. But many of the early colonists were struggling to found communities where people would live decently according to moral law. In comparison with laws in England then and in colonies where the governors were appointed by the king, New England laws were much less harsh. In New England in 1642, twelve or less offenses were punishable by death, whereas English law named at least twenty-five, and the number kept growing.

In Massachusetts, some colonies were darkened by "witch

hunts" and hangings for a few years. A mania for hunting witches had been raging in Europe for many years. One agent appointed by a Pope boasted that he himself had burned more than nine hundred "witches." King James I of England wrote a book about demonology, and sent out many "witch hunters." Historians estimate that during the lifetime of the Plymouth colonist John Alden, 40,000 "witches" were put to death in England.

By comparison the nineteen cruelly killed in Salem village were few. The mania there was overcome very quickly. In Old South Meeting House in Boston, Judge Samuel Sewall made a public confession of his guilt in having taken part in or allowing such "witch hunts." The colonists began to shake off many of the superstitions that darkened Europe at that time.

The Pilgrims of Plymouth were very level-headed about such superstitions. They never killed a witch. In fact, when one woman there accused another of witchcraft, she was fined by the court and whipped. Plymouth seemed also to try to be merciful in most of its punishments. A pillory was never set up there, as it was thought to be too cruel a punishment.

All the colonies were learning new ways and growing. They were jolted into more tolerant thinking when Roger Williams was outlawed in Massachusetts for preaching complete religious toleration and complete separation of church and state. In time, with much struggle, these freedoms have come to the United States of America.

Most historians agree that, in spite of limitations and mistakes, the Pilgrims and Puritans made great contributions to this country. They first brought democratic church government, in which the entire congregation could vote annually. This democratic system was put to use in the New England town meeting, which influenced ideas in planning United States government years later.

Rhode Island championed religious freedom, and Connecticut, civil liberties. Massachusetts led in public education, making it compulsory in 1647. Pilgrims and Puritans introduced and demonstrated the belief that education is the right of each person, not the privilege of a few.

William Bradford, who wrote an account of Plimoth Plantation, said, "We have noted these things so that you may see their worth and not negligently lose what your fathers have obtained with so much hardship."

All records of the early settlement of our country, South and North, show that the founders endured much hardship; and to all colonies many different persons brought ideals of freedom, justice, cooperation, fair opportunity, from which we all have benefited. Because some Virginia statesmen were among the leaders in promoting religious liberty and separation of church and state, these blessings were written into our Constitution as law.

Since the coming of the first colonists, people have migrated to America for many different reasons. Many are guided into port by the huge torch of the Statue of Liberty. In time they celebrate the national Thanksgiving Day. Then it is well for us to be grateful for what the founders and builders in every part of the country "have obtained with so much hardship."

Little did William Bradford think as he wrote thus in his journal that the first president of the United States of America, George Washington of Virginia, would call the whole nation to celebrate its first national harvest feast of thanksgiving, to express gratitude to God and to the early colonists who laid the foundations for the nation.

—MILDRED CORELL LUCKHARDT

Giving Thanks

For the hay and the corn and the wheat that is reaped,
For the labor well done, and the barns that are heaped,
For the sun and the dew and the sweet honeycomb,
For the rose and the song, and the harvest brought home—
    Thanksgiving! Thanksgiving!

For the trade and the skill and the wealth in our land,
For the cunning and strength of the workingman's hand,
For the good that our artists and poets have taught,
For the friendship that hope and affection have brought—
    Thanksgiving! Thanksgiving!

For the homes that with purest affection are blest,
For the season of plenty and well-deserved rest,
For our country extending from sea unto sea;
The land that is known as the "Land of the Free"—
    Thanksgiving! Thanksgiving!

—AUTHOR UNKNOWN

How Young Will Bradford
Made a Great Decision

The blast of the courier's horn sounded gaily across the fields. The postriders were nearing the town of Scrooby on the great North Road from London. Young Will Bradford heard the noise and broke into a run. If he hurried now, he would be just in time to see the riders gallop into the manor courtyard.

William Brewster, the Postmaster of Scrooby, came down the stone steps of the Manor to receive the mail. While Brewster entered the contents of the postbags in his books of registry, the postrider and his bugler were wolfing their dinner.

Having finished the meal, they swung into the saddle and were off. The gay notes of the postman's horn faded sweetly into the distance. The village again settled back into the drowsy dullness of a long afternoon.

Not so William Brewster, who, with his many duties, found little time for idleness. Brewster, as Postmaster at Scrooby, was the great man of the countryside. He was steward of the manor and collected the rents from the tenants of the domain of the Archbishop of York. He was the administrator of law and justice for the district. A man of learning, Brewster had attended Cambridge in his youth where he had studied Greek and Latin.

Later, in the service of Queen Elizabeth, he had accompanied one of her ambassadors on an important mission to the Low Countries. He had seen the great world; yet he had come back to this remote corner of England to be Postmaster at Scrooby where his father had held the same office.

Although Brewster had moved among the great ones of his day, he was neither proud nor vain. He was respected by his neighbors for his wisdom and godliness. When a neighbor was sick or in trouble and needed the help of a friend, he knew that he could find it at the hands of the Postmaster of Scrooby Manor.

No one had felt the warmth of Master Brewster's kindness more than young Will Bradford, who looked to him almost as a father. When the boy had been left an orphan and was long ill, Master Brewster had often traveled the two miles from Scrooby to Austerfield, to visit him and bring presents. As young Will slowly recovered, his friend had helped him in his studies and had given him a copy of the Bible printed in English at Geneva. This Geneva Bible was still a rare and new book in that part of England. Will spent many happy hours absorbed in its wondrous pages. He and the Postmaster often talked together of its beauty and meaning. In hours of loneliness and pain the Book had brought the boy a marvelous comfort and peace.

For some time Will had heard people talking about a preacher at Babsworth who spoke of the Bible with great power. Because Will read and loved the Bible, he decided to hear this man. It was a twenty-mile walk to Babsworth and back, but Mr. Richard Clyfton's preaching was worth all the trouble.

After that first trip Will often walked there to hear Mr. Clyfton read and expound the Scriptures. The boy seldom missed a Sunday, even if his uncles did not approve of reformist preachers.

Later Master Brewster asked Clyfton to preach on Sundays in the great hall at Scrooby Manor. The Postmaster invited friends and neighbors to come and hear Mr. Clyfton preach. It was not long before many people began attending regularly every Sunday. Folks said Mr. Clyfton's discourses woke them up to understand the Scriptures. They came away from these meetings happy and comforted. They began to read and to study their Bible and to try to practice its teaching in their daily lives. Master Brewster explained that in this simple way the first Christian churches began in ancient times.

Within a year the congregation at Scrooby Manor decided to form a church of their own. It was to be entirely separate from the state Church of England and would have no bishops or ceremonies. For this reason they would call themselves Separatists. They would also separate themselves from the Puritans, who wanted to reform the Church of England but not to separate from it.

When young Will Bradford announced to his friends that he would leave the church in which he had been baptized and join the Separatists, people were shocked. His uncles pointed out that he would certainly come to a bad end. Already men had been hung for holding onto such ideas. Friends and relatives argued, pleaded, threatened, warned, but to no purpose. He calmly replied:

"To keep a good conscience and walk in such way as God had prescribed in his Word, is a thing which I must prefer before you all, and above life itself. Wherefore, since it is for a good cause that I am likely to suffer the disasters which you lay before me, you have no cause to be either angry with me, or sorry for me. Yea, I am not only willing to part with everything that is dear to me in this world for this cause but I am thankful that God hath given me heart so to do: and will accept me so to suffer for him."

Plainly the boy was mad.

Spies and informers began to watch the homes and to dog the steps of the members of the Separatist church. The congregation now met secretly at different times and places. One member was arrested and tried by the Archbishop's Court at York. He was imprisoned and then released. Five more members, including Master Brewster, were summoned to appear before the court. William did not need to seek abroad for adventure. Danger waited for him around every corner.

It was becoming clear to the Separatists that there could be no freedom for their religion in England. Already one congregation of Protestants had gone to Holland. Master Brewster said that it was a land where there was perfect freedom of religion, as he had seen in his travels.

The Scrooby Separatists decided to go to Holland, as Master Brewster had advised. However, they knew that no one could leave England or take out goods and money without permission from the government. This meant that they would have to flee secretly like criminals. It was a hard and cruel thing to leave one's home and country in this way and seek a living in a strange land.

—ADAPTED FROM *The Landing of the Pilgrims*
BY JAMES DAUGHERTY

The Departure

Persons in this story who decide to leave their home and country rather than be forced to worship in a manner they think wrong:

Kate Endicott, age sixteen, who fought her conscience a long while before becoming a Puritan

Kate's mother and father and little sister Debbie

Emmy, their young serving maid, who will go with the family

Two who already have fled to Holland for freedom of conscience:

Kate's sister, Meg, who is married to Gerry Neville. Gerry had been imprisoned for his religious beliefs, but he still risks his life to help Puritan families escape.

Some to whom Kate will be especially sad to say goodbye:

Grandfather, who lived in a village not far from Scrooby, the Endicotts' home

Tabby, who had been the Endicotts' servant for many years

Henry, now an old man, who worked for them and had taught Kate to ride

Ginger, a high-spirited horse

Sops-in-wine, their dog, who once had saved Debbie's life

Felicity ("Fairlie") Fitzhugh, from an aristocratic London family, staying for a while at Scrooby Manor because of her mother's health

Hugh, Felicity's brother, who takes a great responsibility for his mother and sister since the father is dead. Kate has become very fond of Hugh.

For the past fortnight, almost since the afternoon of Felicity and Hugh's visit, Kate had been helping Mother and Tabby. The house and its furnishings had been sold. The new owner would take possession on Friday. On the preceding eve the Endicotts would go aboard the bark that was to carry them down the Ryton away from Scrooby and thence down the Idle and Trent. At Hull they would board a Dutch ship for the Netherlands, to join Meg and Gerry and the others of the Scrooby congregation. Master Clyfton and Master Brewster had assisted Father in making arrangements. There were still one or two families of the congregation they must help get away, and then they would join their families in Amsterdam. Meg had written that Mistress Brewster was wondrous kind to her and Gerry, aiding them in many ways.

There was so much work to be done in the house, and Kate was so tired at bedtime that she'd scarcely had time to think what it would be like to leave the farm and Scrooby. The floor rushes all had to be taken out and burned and fresh ones spread on the floors, smelling of the warm July sunshine and scented sweet with sprigs of thyme and rosemary and mint that Mother had Kate gather from the herb garden to strow among the rushes. Emmy and Tabby scraped the pots and scoured them with green rushes, and scrubbed the dairy and brewhouse from ceiling to floor.

Henny helped with the indoor cleaning; 't was too much for

womenfolk to accomplish alone. He took the painted cloths from the walls and shook them well and rehung them, grumbling all the while to himself—though he didn't care who heard him—that 't was a fair waste of time. There'd been no dust settled on them since the Mistress had made him air them and sun them in May. And what was more, t' sun faded their colors.

Kate, kneeling on the long oak table to polish the small leaded panes in the upper part of the bow window, wondered if there would be children in the new family whom Henny would teach to mount and dismount, to pace and canter and trot and gallop. She hoped Henny wouldn't forget her. She would remember him always and how he had winked at her riding Ginger when Father first brought the horse home from the fair. Yea, more than winked; he had aided and abetted her and told her there was nowt to be afeard of. If Master rebuked her, Henny would tell him the horse needed exercise. 'T wasna crime to give a beast exercise! How Sops had yelped with excitement the first time she and Ginger had taken the bars of the meadow gate in one long, smooth leap!

She wished it were possible to take Ginger with them. Father said it would cost too dear. Besides, he thought there was small need for horses in Holland; almost everywhere 't was water. They were taking little with them—two chests filled with linen and clothing, the Great Bible, a few knives and pots and dishes, Mother's spindles and other gear for spinning, a number of packets of seeds and dried herbs, Debbie's hornbook, and a toy or two. Kate was planning to carry, in addition to the loaves and cheese they would require for food on the ship, Meg's lute and Meg's blown glass vase as well as her own Malory book and the tattered book of Master Richard Hakluyt's voyages. Mother thought it was more than Kate could manage, but she had given consent that she might try. Whenever Kate had time to think about it, she willed with all her might and main that she would be able to manage, and mayhap to carry the leather-framed mirror from her wall besides. What she willed, she was bound to succeed in doing, though it might come to pass that she'd have to forego the mirror. She wasn't really including that in her willing, except as a kind of *mayhap*.

Tabby would live with her daughter, Bessie Allnutt. At first she had insisted on going with them to Amsterdam, but Father had dissuaded her. He had done it so gently that Tabby was convinced it was herself who had made the decision that she couldn't bear at her age to pull herself up by the roots and be planted in strange Dutch soil. She wouldn't like it when the Dutch ladies talked and she couldn't make out what they meant any more than if it were gibberish and jabber. She wouldn't like living in a house without a carpet of green English rushes under her two old feet to keep them cool in summer and to warm them in winter.

Moreover she'd heard tell that the roads in the Lowlands were all made of water, fit only for ducks and geese and swimming eels. Nay, 't would never be of her choosing to live in such an outlandish, unaccountable place. 'T wasna fit for a Yorkish person. But if her Mistress had need of her—Tabby dabbed furtively at the tears that escaped to course down the furrows of her old, sunbrowned face— aye, if Mistress needed her, she'd gladly go. With all due respect, Ma'am, she begged leave to point out that 't would be better to take young Emmy, an Emmy should choose to go.

Surprisingly, Emmy did choose. At this very moment Bessie Allnutt was tieing Emmy's clothes into a tight bundle for her to carry, together with a forked twig of blackthorn in the shape of a cross plucked by the light o' the moon on St. John's Eve, a potent charm against evil spirits and witches. Emmy had promised to fetch a St. John's twig for Kate too. Kate had laughed but she hadn't told her not to fetch it.

When Kate had finished polishing the last bull's-eye pane in the bow window, she paused to admire the specklessness of her work. The diamond-shaped panes broke the sunlight into aery patterns that shimmered and dissolved on the surface of the dark oak table as she swung the side casement slowly to and fro. She wondered if the houses in Holland had windows of glass. Meg hadn't said. There were many houses in England that had not glass. Bessie Allnutt's hadn't, nor any of the cots that lay nearest the river where the floods spread at the time of the spring rains.

She wondered what it would be like in Amsterdam. Her mind was double about the Lowlands. Part of her was excited and curious and impatiently pulling at her to go see the tall houses with stair-step eaves crowding beside the cobbled streets, and the roads that were not roads but canals and rivers and deep-digged ditches. The

other part of her—and often it seemed the larger part—wished
to bide at home in Scrooby beside the Great North Road and watch
Mother at her spinning by afternoon sunlight or early candleshine
and firelight and smell Tabby's blackberry tarts baking in the oven
and the joint of beef browning on the spit. And ever as Kate laid
the board for supper she would know that the cows were feeding in
the byre and the horses in stable or pasture. She would know that
when she went on the morn to the paddock, the grass and hedges
would be shining with dew or rain, the mists would be lifting from
the fields, and overhead the rooks would rise from their nests in
the elm tree to caw at her as she ran past. She wondered if there
were rooks in Amsterdam.

Sometimes as she sat with her mending—for all snagged petti-
coats and stockings must be sturdily mended before Mother packed
them in her chest—she puzzled about why it was that God troubled
the consciences of some folk to seek freedom of worship in Holland
and let others bide in comfort at home. She had not wished to
have her conscience troubled. Yet it had been burdened and ill at
ease since the Sabbath morn she had accompanied Meg to the secret
congregation in Scrooby Manor. She had not been able to put from
her mind Master Richard Clyfton's sermon. She had not been able
to forget the pilgrim who was lost in the dark wilderness until the
candle shined upon his head and he heard the Voice say, "Thou
shalt call and I will answer thee."

For a long time she had tried to deny it to herself. She had not
wished to give heed. It was Hugh who had helped her shake off
the blinders she had wilfully held to her eyes. Aye, more than
Father, Hugh had helped her understand. She wondered if Hugh
would think of her sometimes when he was studying at Oxford College. The thread knotted and tangled. She could not see the eye of

the needle to thread it. Dropping the russet kirtle she was stitching, she went to saddle Ginger.

Father told her to take Sops-in-Wine with her. There might not be time on the morrow to take the dog to Gran'fer's. Bid Gran'fer chain him close. It wouldn't do to have him break loose and come seeking them down at the river.

At first Kate did not understand. Put chains to Sops? Then she comprehended. Father proposed to leave Sops behind; not to take him to Amsterdam. How could Father? How—she set her chin and turned her head to keep him from reading her thought, but he read it anyhow. The dog was getting old, Father explained, he would not be happy in a cobbled city. He must have fields to course and deer and conies to trace. In good time Sops would forget to grieve for them; he'd learn to be content with Gran'fer.

Father waited for Kate to speak, but she could not. Had she spoken she would have cried, and she would not that Father should see her cry.

Halfway between Scrooby and Bautry, where the break in the hedge led into the meadow that gave on the boglands, Kate slipped down from the saddle. At her call Sops came loping from the rabbit hole; his black leather muzzle had been nosing under the hedge. 'T was here in this sheep-dotted meadow that she had found Debbie guarded safe. She put her arms around the dog's hairy gray neck and let her sobs have their way. The hound licked her tears with his rough wet tongue and whined and whimpered.

" 'T is not my will that we break faith with thee, Sopsie," she told him when she was again mistress of her voice. And later, before she remounted Ginger, "I promise to keep thee fast in my heart, Sopsie." The three of them made soberly on toward Gran'fer's—Ginger and Kate and old gray Sops-in-Wine.

Almost before she was aware of it, it was the morrow and the blue dusk was beginning to fall, and she and Father and Mother and Debbie and Emmy stood on the deck of the bark looking across at the willows that fringed the bank and shut Scrooby village from view. Master Brewster and Master Clyfton had come down to see that all was well and to wish them God speed ye! There was nobody else save the skipper and his crew and two shepherds taking a score of sheep to market in Hull.

Of a truth, Kate had to remind herself more than once while they waited for the bark to lift anchor, of the veriest truth she ought not be disappointed that no friends had come to bid them farewell. 'T was a secret departure they were making, against the law laid down by the King. 'T would have been a fine kettle of fish if their secret had leaked out; it would have disjointed their plans altogether. They might have been clapped in jail. She was acting like a green girl to let her thoughts run on farewells.

And then, just as she had almost given up hope, she saw the down-hanging boughs of the willow part. She scarce dared breathe lest her hopes prove vain, yet all the while in her heart she was certain. For Hugh was loyal and trusty. Aye, he would ever be true friend to her. He took off his cock's-feather hat and held it high and waved. "Fare thee well and good speed!" he cried.

The anchor was lifted, the bark was beginning to move. He followed along the reedy, close-grown bank, crashing through the alders and willow shrubs. "By God's grace I shall see thee in the Netherlands!" Kate doubted not that the others thought the breathless shout was meant for all the family, but she knew to whom he was giving his promise. Her quilted cap glimmered a darker green than the willow shrubs in the fading light as she snatched it from her hair to wave in token that she had heard.

A bend in the Ryton shut him from sight. After a few minutes Kate turned to face forward, the way they were going. She stood shoulder to shoulder with Mother and Father, leaning against the wind that had begun to blow up from the north. The bark rode free, seeking the ocean where only the far-sailing ships go out.

—ABRIDGED FROM *Pilgrim Kate* BY HELEN F. DARINGER

The Secret in the Brewsters'
Attic in Leyden

For two years the press in the Brewsters' attic in Leyden had been printing books of propaganda sent straight to England. The English government had ordered that the printer of these books be tracked down and arrested. But, so far, nobody had betrayed the secret that William Brewster was the printer and that Thomas Brewer, a member of Leyden University, had helped finance the printing.

One spring day, as Andrew Brewster went toward the attic stairs with his mother, he saw that the worried look she had so often worn lately had returned to her face. She would not feel easy until everything connected with his father's secret printing press was removed entirely.

Andrew remembered what their friend, Israel van Leyden, the Jewish bookseller on Broad Street, had said recently. "If the Dutch refuse free speech to their own, they will not allow refugees to use it. Carleton, the English ambassador at the Hague, will see to that."

Now in the attic, Andrew's mother quickly packed books in a basket and covered them with bundles of herbs. Soon Andrew, carrying the basket, was knocking at the door of Israel van Leyden's bookshop.

No voice called cheerily for him to enter. Israel must be out. Andrew set down the herb-covered basket. Pompey, the dog, nosed his hand, as Andrew reached underneath the ivy for the key hanging on its hidden peg. It was understood that when Israel was out and Andrew brought a basket from the House on the Stinksteeg, he was to unlock the door.

"Who are you? Do you live here?" came a rasping voice.

Andrew swung about quickly. At the bottom of the steps stood a stranger—a sallow, thin man wearing a high-crowned hat. The crown was higher than those worn by Dutchmen, the brim was narrower. When the man spoke harshly again, Andrew saw that the words came from the right corner of his mouth and the expression of the left side of his face did not change. You Old Squint Eye, thought Andrew.

Andrew bowed, saying politely in Dutch, "Goeden Morgen." The man started jabbering in Dutch very fast, and the only word Andrew could understand was book. Andrew blinked and the man began again, in English, slowly and loudly.

"This book? Is it printed in Leyden? The press—it is where?"

He held out a small volume. Andrew was uncertain that if he lifted the plain cover he might see the familiar cut of the Brewster bear on the title page. Of course, neither his father's name nor the place of the press would be there.

Andrew kept a questioning expression on his face, as much as to say, "How would I know where this or any other book is printed?"

Speaking even louder, the stranger demanded, "Is it printed in Leyden?" Andrew's eyes opened wider.

Meanwhile he had forgotten to pick up the basket. Now he saw with horror that Pompey's nose had disarranged the herbs, and disclosed the corner of a book. In size at least, the book was very like the one in the stranger's hand.

"I must put these herbs where they will be cool," Andrew said in Dutch, lifting the basket and quickly covering the book with the herbs. With his foot he opened the door of the bookshop and moved hastily inside. Pompey pushed in, to the stranger's annoyance, since it made him slow his own steps.

Fortunately an open book on Israel's desk caught the man's attention. He bent over to peer at this. Evidently the stranger was very nearsighted. Andrew moved toward the open window at the back of the shop where the canary's cage hung. Outside that window was a stone bench, half hidden with ivy and grape vines. Under their protecting leaves, Andrew hastily pushed the heavy basket.

When he turned back Old Squint Eye was moving about the shop, picking up this book and that and as quickly putting them down. He was most thorough in his search. What shall I do now? wondered Andrew. The time seemed to drag endlessly. After Old Squint Eye had examined all the books in Israel van Leyden's shop would he come peering over to the window? What then?

Just then Israel was coming down the Broad Street with his wife, 'Vrouw Lysbet, like a flower on his arm. The sight of them filled Andrew with relief. Lysbet's hand flew to the "Beggar's Penny" locket she wore. Israel looked up, saw the shop door open, and Andrew coming toward the open door.

"Good morning, young—" Israel began in English. Then Lysbet, who had seen the stranger, pressed her fingers firmly

upon her husband's. The bookseller said "young Williamson," instead of "young Brewster," as he had intended. It was the first time Andrew had been called Williamson, after his father's name, and it pleased him.

Lysbet slipped toward the window, and soon the basket was safe under her shawl. The stranger was demanding of Israel, "This book? It was printed in this town? The ambassador—." He stopped as though he would have caught back the last word. "The ambassador" could mean only Sir Dudley Carleton, ambassador from England at The Hague. Andrew's mother had feared this man would find some way of twisting Dutch laws to England's wishes. She had said, "The day of English secret presses in the Lowlands is over!"

"Come," Lysbet said calmly and moved with Andrew to the door which opened into her own cool, quiet room. Pompey managed to squeeze through the door beside them.

Paying no attention to them, the stranger spat out "This Leyden is a very cesspool for refugees!"

Israel's gentle voice replied, "We refugees, who know what it means to be hunted, speak of Leyden as our City of Refuge. As to your book," he added, handing it back after what had seemed a careful examination, "I have no idea what press it is from."

Andrew whispered to Lysbet who was closing the door "I'm pretty sure it was one which we printed."

She whispered in reply, "Israel cannot see to read a word without his spectacles. Look." She produced them from the depths of her bonnet. "He slipped them in when I went toward the window. He always gives me his spectacles when he wants to be blind."

"Now," she said briskly, "how about some cookies for you and your companion, Andrew? He is such a nice dog."

Pompey was doing tricks for Lysbet and Andrew when, at last, the shop door opened and Israel entered the room, saying, "The ambassador's spy has departed just as wise as when he came. I think he will look a long time for his press. All the same, Andrew, it will be wise to warn your father concerning this man just as soon as he returns to Leyden."

Two men dashed into Israel's shop, crying, "Bad news from The Hague."

They were religious leaders whom Andrew knew well. Israel hurried to meet them, asking "Have they—?"

The door into the shop closed and Andrew heard no more.

The men in the shop were not Puritans, but they too, were struggling for freedom in religion. Andrew was discouraged. He feared for his father's safety. He feared for the safety of all such men. "The torch of liberty burns low," he thought sadly.

—ADAPTED FROM *The Bells of Leyden Sing* BY

CATHERINE CATE COBLENTZ

Andrew Brewster's Own Secret

Andrew Brewster was in the garden with his mother, setting some of the herbs in tiny pots and gathering packets of seeds from others, and bunches of yet other herbs for drying. Mary Brewster was intent on saving all that was possible that autumn, for more than ever she hoped the English folk would leave Leyden. Andrew's sister, Patience, came to them as they were patting the earth in the last pot.

"Professor Polyander has come, with another man whom I do not know. They both look very solemn." Patience was twisting her hands anxiously.

Andrew's heart missed a beat. Had something happened to his father? Had the magistrates detained him when he appeared before them? Or was he ill, perhaps seriously ill, from the night's excitement and the exposure?

The boy's fears increased when he saw Polyander and the stern-looking man with him. Polyander was bobbing up and down, bowing ceremoniously as he refused the chair which Andrew's sister, Fear, offered.

"Ah, madame," began the professor as soon as he saw Mistress Brewster.

At this formality on his part, Andrew saw his mother's hand fly to the knot of her 'kerchief.

Professor Polyander saw this too, for he was instantly at her side. "Pray take this chair yourself, Mistress Brewster," he begged.

The stranger bowed stiffly as the University professor aided her into William Brewster's own seat.

"There is naught to be concerned about," said Polyander. "I am only doing my duty as a member of the University."

"Duties are something very unpleasant," said Mary Brewster, recovering herself. "I am well acquainted with duties." She smiled, taking the sting from her words.

But Andrew stood straight and tall by the stairway. Even before Polyander continued, the boy had sensed what the coming of the two men must mean. Had not Thomas Brewer said that Leyden magistrates were turning the matter concerning himself and the printing press which he had helped finance for Andrew's father over to the University of Leyden to handle? And now Thomas Brewer was under arrest because of the press.

"Madame, you are quite right. Duties are usually unpleasant, but I would take all the unpleasantness possible from this one! I shall therefore come to the point at once. Then we shall talk of more pleasant things. I bear a warrant this day, a warrant from the University of Leyden. It authorizes me to seize certain furnishings and goods located in the attic of your house.

"This, mistress, need cause you no dismay. I assure you there is no need. I have often told you that Leyden is the best place in the world in which to live. And part of Leyden's fame comes from its University.

"Universities as you know have power to protect their members even against kings. And the University of Leyden is not afraid of standing by those rights. I would remind you therefore that Thomas Brewer is a member of Leyden University. I can assure you too that he is in good hands at the moment and in good surroundings. The University has claimed him from the magistrates, and I left him in a comfortable room playing chess with his daughter Trintje. Both were eating dried figs and dates, and both were laughing. Thomas Brewer sends you his personal greetings and assurances that all is well.

"Now." Taking a deep breath Polyander bowed almost to the floor. "With your permission, Mistress, with your permission, I shall read this paper aloud as is the custom, and as my friend here, Doctor Guilielmus Bontius expects. 'Tis merely a formality, you understand. Merely a formality!"

Professor Polyander then read a warrant for him and Doctor Bontius to search Thomas Brewer's library and to seize certain books and his printing press.

"We have," announced Polyander, "already examined Thomas Brewer's library on Bell Alley and have found no such books there. He tells us however that his press is located in your attic, so with your gracious permission, Mistress Brewster, we must search the attic. Will you be so kind as to guide us thither?"

"But you know—" began Mary Brewster, a trifle bewildered, since Polyander had been to the press room in the attic dozens of times.

Andrew broke in. He was very pale, paler than his mother had been but a short time ago. "And what will you do after you have searched the attic, please?"

"We must, following these orders, seize whatever types are

found there, and whatever of printed books, or parts of books we may discover. Then we must nail the attic door shut and seal it. We are ordered then to paste paper over the lock and over the nails and to imprint the seal of the University upon said paper. After that the attic must not be reopened under penalty of the displeasure of the said University."

"Oh," said Andrew. And then quickly, his thoughts racing ahead of his words, "But I have a chest there in the attic, and some private property of my own. May I remove my things?"

"If the chest and the property are yours and not Thomas Brewer's."

"The things I shall take are mine," said Andrew firmly.

"Very well. Remove them. We shall be up presently to carry out our orders. Doctor Bontius, have you by chance seen Mistress Brewster's garden? There are some plants in it which even the University's gardener cannot raise, though I have taken him seeds and cuttings time and time again."

"I will show it to you," cried Patience, eager to be doing something.

Andrew, rapidly ascending the stairs, heard Fear ask her mother whether she might not serve some of the cake which remained. That was like Fear. She did not understand Andrew's plans, but she was giving him time to carry them out.

He heard Polyander's booming voice, but he could not make out what the professor was saying. Doubtless he was boasting about Leyden. Well, as for himself, he would be quite willing that day to listen to Polyander's boasting for as long as the Dutchman chose.

On the way upstairs Andrew stopped long enough to grab a woolen blanket. At the attic door he paused for a moment, his face working. The press before him had been dismantled. It was all ready to be moved to the University later that very day. Had Old Squint Eye not come the night before, it might in fact be on its way.

But now that the dismantled press was about to be sealed in the attic, on orders which the boy knew came from the hated ambassador, Sir Dudley Carleton, Andrew was determined to carry out a plan he himself had made. He had shared that plan with no one but Pompey, his little dog.

Andrew Brewster was going to take that great press screw with him to the New World. Thomas Brewer had declared it was his property. Well, his property then would serve as a beginning for the press which his father had promised the two of them would one day have in that far-off Virginia.

Already he had measured the screw, and he knew it would easily fit in the chest. He lifted it with care, tugged it over to the chest, which he had drawn close to the open door. The blanket lay partially unfolded inside. The head of the screw was flat, and between the tip of the screw and the side of his chest Andrew wedged two small pieces of wood. Now both head and tip fitted into the chest as though the receptacle had been made for it. As he folded the blanket over Jason's handiwork, Andrew doubted that a thickness of paper could be slipped between either end of the screw and the chest itself.

He started to drag his burden through the door, when the sound of laughter made him curious. So he ran to the window overlooking the garden. Polyander and his companion were sitting on the stone bench. Pompey lay at the professor's feet watching for the occasional crumb to come his way.

The Dutchmen were eating cake and talking, while Andrew's

mother and sisters were choosing some potted plants and cuttings for the University gardener to experiment with.

Smiling with relief, Andrew went back to his task. The screw weighed a good deal more in the chest, it seemed, than it had in his arms. And it wasn't at all an easy matter to drag that chest over the threshold. It might have been wiser if he had carried the screw down to his room first and then hauled the chest afterward. But he had not known of course that the two men would linger thus in the garden.

He was glad he had wrapped the screw well, for the chest bumped down the stairs until, judging from the clatter, Andrew felt he might have been removing the whole press. How fortunate that his mother was in the garden! Had she remained in the house, Mary Brewster, even in her present distressed state of mind, couldn't have resisted asking why on earth he need make such a racket. She might even have questioned him as to what he had in the chest.

The last stairs, however, were taken smoothly and swiftly. Andrew dragged the chest into the room which he shared with his brothers and set it at the foot of his cupboard bed. He threw in some things on top, soft things such as his new cape with the braided frogs, his best Sunday hosen, and Pompey's new collar. Then, with a sigh of relief, Andrew locked the chest and went down to the garden.

"It didn't take you long," said Polyander. His eyes rested briefly on Andrew's flushed cheeks.

"And now—" began the professor at last. "We must leave, much as we dislike to break up this pleasant party. So," turning to Andrew, "if you will but guide us to the attic."

Gravely Andrew led the way, and stood by quietly while Polyander and Bontius inventoried with care all that they found there.

Once the professor's right eyebrow went up questioningly. He looked toward Andrew, started to speak, changed his mind just as quickly, and began a vigorous clearing of his throat.

As he passed by Polyander making out the report, Andrew saw in neat and precise letters the words:

One press, minus its screw, and already dismantled.

Ten English books, bound in mottled brown paper.

A small supply of linen paper.

That was all Andrew had time to read. He went to the window and stood looking out until the men had finished. By that time, the books, the types, and the paper had been made into big burlap bundles, which the two men slung over their shoulders. Then, with a final look about the attic, which included even the rafters, they went to the door. Andrew followed last, and he it was who closed the door of the press room.

The bundles were set on the stairs and Polyander was leaning over the rail calling for a hammer, which Fear brought up to him. With two long nails the Dutch professor nailed shut the attic door.

Then, with apologies, he called for a lighted candle. Andrew, who felt the lump in his throat increasing in size by the minute, wondered whether the professor would ever complete his task.

From his pocket Polyander took a piece of paper and a cake of green wax. Between them the two Dutchmen heated the wax over the flame and dripped it thickly over the paper.

Doctor Bontius set the candle down on the stairs and pressed the paper over the lock on the door, working his thumb all along the edge. Meanwhile Polyander held the University seal over the candle flame and, when it was heated, he pressed it on the waxed paper.

And there on the door of the attic was the seal of the University, the sign of authority. Never again would Andrew be able to enter the press room. And the press itself could be used no more in such fashion as might displease King James of England and of Scotland.

The University of Leyden had fulfilled the letter of the law. As to the spirit, Polyander might have told him, that was another matter altogether.

Andrew went downstairs with the others. The last shot in the Battle of Books had been fired from that attic room.

—ADAPTED FROM *The Bells of Leyden Sing* BY

CATHERINE CATE COBLENTZ

Leyden's Day of Thanksgiving

Andrew Brewster looked about the Van Leydens' living room and thought it had never seemed so filled with light and color as on that day.

The brass and crystal of the candelabra shone from much polishing, while the room was warm from the lighted peat fires, and the odors of good things to eat grew more and more enticing.

But better than warmth, better than color and light, better than the smell of food, was the fact that his father was there, sitting in the most comfortable chair and looking well and strong again. When William Brewster spoke, Andrew felt that the sound of his father's voice was the most wonderful sound in all the world.

The Van Leydens were making a thanksgiving in the way they always did. On the third of October, the anniversary of Leyden's first thanksgiving day, they were joined every year by an old friend named Pieter. When he was young, he too had lived in Leyden, but now he lived by the North Sea.

The lively talk and laughter in the room was increasing. Andrew should be perfectly happy, he assured himself over and

over again, as he drew a stool to his father's feet and felt his father's
fingers slipping through his hair. His mother and his sisters were
there, and their faces were aglow with pleasure.

But Andrew was not happy. His conscience was troubling him,
and he had almost made up his mind to do something about it.
Almost, but not quite.

Meanwhile the flow of conversation went on. 'Vrouw van Leyden was explaining to Mistress Brewster that hotchpotch, which was
their chief dish always on the third of October, was a combination
of carrots, potatoes, and onions, cooked with meat and the whole
seasoned with Leyden's best butter.

"If it tastes as good as it smells, it will be delicious," William
Brewster smiled.

"The first time I ate it," said Lysbet, "I thought it tasted
like heaven. You see I had been hungry for so long. And Pieter"—
she turned and smiled at the sturdy Dutchman who sat on the
settle opposite Israel, smoking his long-stemmed pipe—"Pieter
brought a whole kettleful from the Spaniards' fire. They left it when
they fled after the long siege of Leyden. The story of the hotchpotch was told all over the city, and many came to sample it. To
this day, we who remember the siege always serve hotchpotch
on October third, Leyden's day of thanksgiving. On that day all
Leyden enjoys a renewed sense of brotherliness."

"I think such a feast of brotherhood in remembrance to God for
His mercy is an admirable custom, which others might well copy,"
agreed William Brewster. "Personally, I shall always remember
with gratitude the night you opened your home to me."

"Listen—the bells!" broke in Pieter, pausing to blow the smoke
from his pipe upward in a swirl of blue rings.

"Aye, there is the singing note! Always on this day we hear

it." Israel's eyes looked deep into Pieter's, and the two of them sat quietly until the joy bells of the carillon ceased to sound. Lysbet van Leyden too had paused and smiled upon them both.

"You spoke of a singing note the night I came to you for help," began Andrew.

But Israel did not hear. He had begun speaking to William Brewster about a place in Zealand where land had been newly reclaimed from the waters. The Dutch in that locality would be glad to welcome John Robinson's whole congregation, provide them with land and allow them once again to take up the task of farming, as many of them had done in England.

"Such interest and kindness," said William Brewster slowly, "fairly overwhelm me."

"I have yet another suggestion," went on Israel. "There has been, as you know, much talk in this town among some of the Walloons from France, who have settled here, of sailing for New Netherlands on the Hudson River. A fur-trading station is there now. And, since your king is talking of adding more colonies to his Jamestown in Virginia, it behooves Dutchmen likewise to encourage settlement in the New World.

"To be frank, however, the Dutch East India Company can, I think, be made to see how much wiser it would be to send your group to New Netherlands, rather than the Walloons."

Andrew's eyes were popping. Where were they going anyhow? To Zealand? To New Netherlands? He glanced at his mother. Something akin to despair was in Mary Brewster's eyes at this talk of continued settlement among the Dutch. But she tried to hide her dismay.

Israel, however, had seen the expression, and he went on quickly. "These Dutch offers, you understand, might be used as trading points with England. You see, I come from a people who have been known as traders for centuries."

"And known also as the chosen folk of God," put in Brewster quickly. "Having the honor of your friendship, Israel, makes me understand why. You, on your part, realize that in our inmost hearts we English folk have ever longed to dwell on English soil. Our roots there go deep. And we wish our children to remain English both in speech and in ways of thinking.

"More, even than that, we want to forward the work of God's kingdom. We must feel that we are playing our part in the mighty pattern which we have faith is taking shape through the centuries."

There was a knock at the door which connected with the bookshop, and four men entered the room, Master Bradford and Master Robinson, whom the Brewsters had expected. Behind them was Thomas Brewer who had helped pay for the secret printing press on which Andrew's father had printed books of propaganda for religious liberty. The fourth man, Professor Polyander, recently had been sent to the Brewster's attic to seize that press. He had given Andrew time to remove a chest before the attic was sealed up. Today Polyander was beaming, and announced that he was present as Brewer's jailer.

"Tell me all that has happened to you," demanded Brewster, holding Thomas Brewer's hand in both his own. "If it will ease your troubles in the least, I shall give myself up this very day. I have been deeply concerned at the sacrifice you have made."

"Give yourself up and let my efforts and those of the sheriff go for naught?" cried Brewer. "That were indeed poor sense! I am among friends, as you see. While if need be I shall go to England and talk to King James himself. In fact I would rather enjoy it, since I shall always be under the protection of Leyden University.

Therefore I must be returned to this land in as good condition as I go—and this at the king's expense. 'T will hurt poor James mightily.

"I have financed a press. That is all. And that press has printed books. True, no printer in England or Scotland dared print them. But according to the laws of this land, they could be printed here. And of the ways and means whereby those books reached England, I have never known, nor have I inquired. So no man need fear to be put in difficulties by anything I may say."

"Well," Brewster smiled, "since I take my way there soon, I may see you—perchance at the king's court. But do not speak to me in that case, for I must be very careful, even though I do have friends in high places."

Andrew drew a breath quickly. Once again his father would be gone, and there would be weeks, perhaps months of waiting and uncertainty as to his welfare and safety.

His mother spoke. Her voice was low and controlled, but Andrew knew her thoughts were similar to his own just then. "You will take good care of yourself, William!"

"Have no fear. I will take all precautions and I shall be safe there, as safe as I have been before."

"But now your name is associated with the printing of the Scotch book, and the danger, should your identity be discovered, will be the greater. The English ambassador's man, whom Andrew calls Old Squint Eye is still in Leyden, sending forth, no doubt, all the damaging reports he can unearth." Thomas Brewer spoke very seriously.

Israel van Leyden laughed. "I wonder what the ambassador makes of those reports. Old Squint Eye thinks he sees Master Brewster around every corner in Leyden. And, knowing this, there are those who make a game of telling him a tale as often as they think one up. All in all, the ambassador's spy is quite worn from following down the many and varied clues. One day he thinks Brewster is here, and another he is told that he is in England. While perhaps on a third, someone has most certainly seen him at Leyderdorp, and the fourth, according to report, he is at Amsterdam. Probably Sir Dudley Carleton by this time is as puzzled as is his Leyden spy."

"That is why," agreed Polyander, "the ambassador feels he must make the most of the prisoner he has taken—a bird in the hand, you know. He has even persuaded himself that Thomas Brewer can give important information to the king. And for that reason, he is putting heavy pressure on the University authorities to send Brewer to England for the king to question."

Polyander chuckled deeply before adding, "Well, Brewer may go, but he must return. We would not exile any man from such a city as Leyden. I myself shall go with him, if the journey be indeed undertaken, as far as The Hague. And I shall spare no words in making our terms very clear to Carleton. The University can protect its own."

Andrew had been growing more and more anxious as the conversation had continued. If it were true that Thomas Brewer might leave, then he must manage somehow to talk to him privately before he went. He must have reassurance about a certain matter.

Now Israel and Master Brewster began discussing the best way to persuade some group in England to finance them in their next attempt to cross the sea. Polyander was taking out his snuffbox, looking bewildered as he always did when any of his English friends spoke of leaving Leyden. Perhaps, Andrew decided, he had better tell Polyander what he wanted. After all the professor was, according to his own description, Thomas Brewer's jailer.

Andrew went over and took a seat by the Dutchman. "Do you think," he began in a low voice, "that you could manage it so I might speak to Master Brewer, before he goes with you back to the University?"

"But he is here. Why don't you speak to him?" Polyander was clearly puzzled.

"It is a matter of business, of private business between us two," explained Andrew. "I want to talk to him—alone."

"Well," agreed Polyander, wrinkling his brow while his eyes twinkled more than ever, "business should by all means be attended to. That is why the Dutch have prospered. Suppose we go into the shop and I will put Brewer in your charge for a bit." He rose, strolled to the door of Israel's book shop and summoned Thomas Brewer after him. Andrew came too.

Once there, Polyander closed the door of the Van Leyden living room, and bowed formally. "This gentleman has some business to discuss with you, Master Brewer." And the Dutch professor strode to the outer door of the shop, opened it, and stood there looking out, taking great sniffs of the October air, as though he could not have enough of it.

"Do you remember, Master Brewer," began Andrew, "that once we talked about the screw to the printing press?"

"I remember, Andrew."

"And I told you about the part I had in its making and in installing it in the pressroom. Do you remember what you said then, Master Brewer?"

"What did I say, Andrew?"

"You said that since I thought so much of the press screw it was to be my property. And that I was so to consider it."

Thomas Brewer looked troubled. "Yes, Andrew, I remember. I

did say that. But there is naught I can do about the matter now. The door to the pressroom is sealed, and I am a prisoner."

"But the screw is not in the attic, Master Brewer."

"It is not in the attic?"

"No. You said it was my property. So when Professor Polyander came with the warrant, I asked permission first to remove some things of my own, which were in the attic. He said I might, so I put the screw in my chest and took it down to my own room. You see, we shall need the screw, my father and I, if we go to the New World."

"So," said Thomas Brewer, "that was what Polyander meant when he asked me whether the youngest Brewster were not unusually fond of printing. Andrew, you are indeed your father's son. The New World is the very place for the screw. And since it was, as you say, your property, you had a right to do with it as you chose."

Polyander came briskly inside. "Call Israel," he said. "Quickly! You and I, Brewer, must be out of here. The ambassador's man is coming down the street."

There was a quick transfer of people between the Van Leyden living room and the shop. By the time Old Squint Eye arrived, the bookseller and Andrew were alone. Israel was fumbling among his stock, and Andrew was waiting patiently as though to be served, when the ambassador's spy, looking much the worse for his recent illness, came in, demanding, "Have you heard aught lately of that Englishman named Brewster, who ran a press on the Stinksteeg?"

Israel cupped his hand to his ear, though Andrew knew that his hearing was perfect. Old Squint Eye tried him again in English and then in Dutch. Finally he wrote down his question, and Israel, who had, behind the shelter of his great desk, slipped his spectacles into Andrew's pocket, pored helplessly over the paper.

In the room beyond someone muffled a cough, but immediately

the cheerful voice of Lysbet van Leyden broke forth into a little bar of Dutch song. She was joined shortly by the notes of a flute, which Andrew believed the man named Pieter must be playing.

At that moment Andrew's friend Rembrandt came dashing in. At sight of Old Squint Eye he stopped short. But almost instantly a wicked look came into his eyes as he cried out, "Why, I am looking for you! I heard you were seeking a man named Brewster, and I saw someone about his height going down the Stinksteeg."

Old Squint Eye snatched back the piece of paper he had given Israel, and, grumbling to himself, rushed out of the shop and down the street. His broad-brimmed hat looked worse on him, Andrew decided, than the high-crowned one which had fallen in the Leyden canal.

Israel waited until he was certain the man was not returning. Then he smiled at Rembrandt. "You have earned some hotchpotch," he said.

"I've had it once today, but I can eat it again," whispered Rembrandt to Andrew, as Israel locked the shop door. Then the three rejoined the others.

Andrew's spirits were soaring. It was in very truth to him a day of thanksgiving. He could hardly wait for the feasting.

—ADAPTED FROM *The Bells of Leyden Sing,* BY

CATHERINE CATE COBLENTZ

Mayflower Decision

Jamie shivered as he walked along the deck of the "Mayflower." He wondered if the New World would always be so cold. Snow was in the air and wind was rising and small whitecaps were skimming the water.

Only the day before, November 10, 1620, the ship's lookout had shouted, "Land ahoy," bringing everyone to the rail for the first sight of land in the sixty-six days since leaving on this voyage from Plymouth, England.

It had been a day of rejoicing, and now that the ship had dropped anchor, passengers and crew were anxious to go ashore—to place their feet again on firm soil. But no one was yet allowed to leave the ship. Jamie wasn't sure why. He had asked his mother, but she just shook her head. His father would know, but where was he? Jamie hadn't seen him all morning.

Jamie had heard rumors. Some Pilgrims seemed dissatisfied. At sighting land they had clustered in small groups on the deck, muttering and glancing distrustfully at small groups nearby.

Last night Jamie had overheard his parents talking. His father said that some of the "Mayflower" passengers wanted to leave the main group of Pilgrims. Since the ship had landed in New England, rather than Virginia, they felt the Virginia Company should have no power over them.

The Pilgrim leaders were concerned. Every person would be needed once they began to set up their plantation—needed to build homes and to protect each other.

Jamie continued his walk along the deck, glancing into the cabin. Several men were huddled around a table. One seemed to be writing on a large piece of paper. Jamie knew him. He was Mr. Brewster. The others had their backs to Jamie, but he recognized his father's jacket. What were they doing?

Just then Jamie's mother called, "Come help me open the chest. I want some warm clothes from it."

He followed her down to the crowded living quarters and helped her open the heavy oaken chest. Here was stored almost everything they had been able to bring to the New World—dishes, clothing, and family treasures.

After he finished, he sought his friend Jonathan, as it was not quite time for the midday meal. They amused themselves climbing up and down the ladders, pretending they were trees.

Suddenly there was a call for the adult passengers to meet in the captain's cabin. Some girls were left to mind the younger children and babies; but after the adults had assembled, Jonathan and Jamie hurried to the deck to see what was happening.

Did this unexpected meeting mean they might not stay here and settle? Would they go on to find Virginia? Was something else wrong? Perhaps danger of Indian attack?

The boys peeked through the cabin window. The room was filled with people. Mr. Brewster was standing at the front. He

picked up a paper from the table and read ". . . combine ourselves
together . . . for our better ordering and preservation and furtherance of the ends aforesaid . . . constitute and frame such just and
equal laws . . . as shall be thought most meet and convenient for the
general good of the colony. . . ."

"What does this mean?" whispered Jamie. "Some passengers
must be planning to set up their own colony!"

Jonathan replied, "Mr. Brewster wants the people to sign this
paper so everyone will be under one government. But some of the
people won't sign. My father won't sign. And he's right, too."

"He isn't either right. We all need to work together to build a new colony. Do you want to live somewhere else? We wouldn't be able to see each other or play together any more."

"I don't care if we do or not," Jonathan declared. "It's just like my father says—why should we let people in the Virginia Company who don't even live here tell us what to do? Go away. I don't even want to talk to you anymore. You just don't understand at all."

Jamie was silent. Mr. Brewster was saying, "Think about this and return when you are called. We believe this is for the well-being of all those present. We must stay together or all will be lost."

The Pilgrim company quietly left the cabin, and Jamie and Jonathan went their separate ways.

Most people returned to the living quarters in the ship. But Jonathan's father remained above. He paced along the deck in the cold wind. Suddenly Jonathan stepped in front of him.

"What's wrong, Father? You look so very stern." Jonathan's father smiled. Then he explained about the meeting and said he did not want to sign the paper.

"I think you're right, Father," said Jonathan. "I think it will be much better to set up our own colony and make our own rules."

"Do you? But what if it meant leaving your friend Jamie? You might be very lonely. There might be no other children in our colony."

"I don't mind! I don't care if I never see Jamie again! I'll be glad to get away from him."

"Those are very strong words, Jonathan," said his father. "But we'll wait and see how things work out." He moved away to stand beside the rail and look out over the water.

Jonathan walked on. He would miss Jamie . . . they had been good friends a long time. He was sorry they had quarreled. He must talk to Jamie just once more. They could at least leave the ship as friends.

He turned to go below. As he reached the bottom of the ladder, he saw Jamie standing a little away from the group. Jonathan walked over to him. "Jamie, I'm sorry about what I said. And if we leave, I will miss you. Let's stay friends even though we may not be living near each other."

The boys smiled at each other.

Just then there came a call for the passengers to return to the cabin. The boys followed the crowd and posted themselves again by the window. Mr. Brewster said to the group, "I now offer each man an opportunity to sign this document giving the governing power of our new colony to the will of the majority of the people living there. As I call your name, come to the table to affix your signature to the paper."

John Carver stepped forward and signed his name. William Bradford and Edward Winslow followed. Finally it was Jonathan's father's turn. He stepped in front of the table and faced the crowd. Then he began to speak.

"I do not agree with all that this compact sets forth. Therefore, I will not sign it. However, I do agree with Mr. Brewster. We must stay together in this new land to build our homes and plant and gather our food. We must protect each other from dangers which we may encounter. No, I will not sign this paper, but I say to each of you, we must stay together or we will perish."

He turned to Mr. Brewster and held out his hand. Mr. Brewster took it. Another man stepped forward to sign.

Jamie and Jonathan looked at each other, smiling. Each was thinking of the exciting times they could have—together in this new land.

(Note: The Mayflower Compact was signed November 11, 1620, Old Style. Mayflower Compact Day is now observed on November 21, New Style.)

—SUSAN BRINKLEY, ABRIDGED FROM *The Instructor*

The Landing of the Pilgrim Fathers

The Landing of the Pilgrim Fathers
The breaking waves dashed high
   On a stern and rock-bound coast,
And the woods against a stormy sky
   Their giant branches tossed.

And the heavy night hung dark
   The hills and waters o'er
When a band of exiles moored their bark
   On the wild New England shore.

EIGHT LINES FROM *The Landing of
the Pilgrim Fathers in New
England* BY FELICIA DOROTHEA HEMANS

The Mayflower Compact

Cold winds swept down the Atlantic Ocean and rocked a little ship lying at anchor in Cape Cod Bay off the coast of New England. The day was November 11, 1620; the boat, the "Mayflower"; its passengers, homeless emigrants to a strange land. There were no friends to welcome them, no inns where they and their children might find shelter.

Neither was there any government to protect them, nor any laws to guide them. Some members of the group were known as Pilgrims. They had been forced to flee from their home and their native land because they would not attend the church that national law decreed they must attend. People who separated from the national church because of conscience were called Separatists. Even though in every other way they had obeyed the laws and had been good citizens, some had been sent to prison for worshiping otherwise than the law demanded. Some Separatists had been killed by hanging because they spoke bravely for religious liberty.

Persons who were not Pilgrims among the passengers on the little "Mayflower" had come for various reasons. Some were looking for adventure in the New World; some sought new freedom and opportunity for themselves and their families; some were escaping from going to prison for debt, which was the law in their native land. Some felt that now they were free of all law and could go off and do as they pleased.

The people had no governor appointed by the king, nor any church authorities to tell them what to do. The more level-headed men knew they must set up their own government; and they must all cooperate or they never could survive the hardships of the wilderness or attacks by hostile Indians. Also, without law and order, the little new colony might run wild and destroy itself. The Pilgrims had high hopes of establishing a small commonwealth, with a good way of life, obedient to God's laws as shown in the Bible.

So they drew up an agreement, whereby they would make laws necessary for the good of all, and would elect leaders from among themselves, instead of being governed by those appointed by the king. Then into the cabin of the storm-tossed "Mayflower" the 102 passengers crowded that November day while the men signed the historic Mayflower Compact. This is believed to be the first document of its kind in the world whereby persons agreed together on a democratic form of government. And those who signed this compact are known as the Pilgrim Fathers.

They did not realize, nor did their children who crowded in to watch the paper being signed, how great this country would become—based on agreement and free election and opportunity for all people. One young man who signed the Mayflower Compact was William Bradford. He kept a record of the Pilgrims and their colony at Plymouth. Later he was made their governor, and lived long enough to see other colonies planted in the New World.

Of the Plimoth Plantation he wrote, "Out of small beginnings great things have been produced; and, as one small candle may light a thousand, so the light here kindled hath shone to many, yea, in some sort to our whole nation."

Here is a copy of the Mayflower Compact, signed by brave men who valued liberty and just laws.

THE MAYFLOWER COMPACT

In the name of God, Amen. We whose names are underwriten, the loyall subjects of our dread Soveraigne Lord King James by the grace of God, of great Britaine, France, and Ireland king, defender of the faith, etc. Having undertaken, for the glorie of God, and advancement of the Christian faith and honour of our king and countrie a voyage to plant the first colonie in the Northerne parts of Virginia, Doe by these presents solemnly and mutually in the presence of God, and one of another; covenant and combine ourselves togeather into a civill body politic; for our better ordering and preservation and furtherance of the ends aforesaid; and by virtue hereof to enacte, constitute, and frame such just and equall laws, ordinances, Acts, constitutions, and offices, from time to time, as shall be thought most meete and conuenient for the generall good of the Colonie, Unto which we promise all due submission and obedience. In witness whereof we have hereunder subscribed our names at Cap Codd the 11 of November in the year of the reigne of our Soveraigne Lord King James of England, France, and Ireland the eighteenth and of Scotland the fiftie fourth Anno Domini 1620.

Happy Thanksgiving!
(*A story to tell little children*)

Soon Thanksgiving Day will come. People will say "Happy Thanksgiving!" to each other. We will say "Thank you" to God for our food and home and family and friends. We will be thankful for sunshine and rain and everything that makes the world beautiful. And we'll laugh and sing and have a good thanksgiving dinner and a happy time.

Many children will play they are Pilgrim girls and boys who came here long ago and enjoyed their Thanksgiving Day in America. They had sailed across the ocean with their mothers and fathers on a little ship called the "Mayflower." The Pilgrims had left their homes in England because in those days they were not allowed to pray together and worship God in the way they thought was right.

As the "Mayflower" sailed toward America, cold winds whistled through its sails. The Pilgrims kept wondering about this new country where they would live. In that long-ago time there were no cities in America. There were very few people in the big woods or along the seashore.

The Pilgrims knew that Indians lived here. And sometimes the Indians were friendly to people from across the ocean. Often they fought the new people. The Pilgrims were going far from their old homes, but they made up their minds to be brave and work hard. They were determined to make pleasant homes in the new country for their families.

After many weeks at sea someone on the "Mayflower" shouted "Land, ho!" Every one rushed on deck to look. How glad they were to see land after such a long trip on the crowded ship!

Before they went ashore, the Pilgrim leaders talked with every-body. If they wanted to build homes and make little gardens and farms and start a good little town, they must all help each other. So, the men signed a paper promising they would work together for the best good of everyone. And they would obey the laws that were made.

Later some men went to shore in a small boat, to get wood and see what the land was like. They brought back armfuls of sweet-smell-ing pinewood and some sprigs of red holly berries for the children.

Soon the women and children went to shore, bobbing through the water in the small boat. They took great bundles of clothes to be washed. The children ran along the seashore and laughed and shouted and sang. They helped gather wood for fires to heat the wash water. They looked for nut trees. They skipped stones out into the bay. They helped spread the wash to dry on fragrant-smell-ing sassafras bushes and low junipers. They took pine cones and walnuts back to the "Mayflower" with them.

Many days passed, though, before they all left the "Mayflower" to live on land. First the men had to find just the right place to build their homes. They chose a place called Plymouth, on high ground near the shore, with a little brook and springs of water. There they would start the Pilgrim's Plymouth Colony.

Even though winter had begun, the men began to build houses in Plymouth. Their axes sounded "thud, thud" through the woods as they chopped down trees. Soon their hammers pounded as they built some houses.

That winter was very hard for everyone, both those on shore and on the "Mayflower." Many people were very sick. They tried to nurse each other. They were all cold and hungry. Sometimes Indians shot arrows when the Pilgrim men were in the woods. Wolves howled around them. Wild winds blew down part of the houses before they were finished. But the men kept on working, building houses to shelter everyone. And people crowded together in the first houses.

At last springtime was near. Birds began to sing in the woods. Suddenly, one sunny day an Indian came to Plymouth. All alone! The pilgrim children ran to their homes to tell their mothers. Then they peeped from doorways as the Indian walked to the place where the Pilgrim leaders were talking.

The children hurried closer to look and listen. Everyone was surprised when the Indian spoke English as they did. His name was Samoset. He had learned English from fishermen who came to fish at an Island farther up the seacoast. He told them about different Indian tribes; and the Pilgrims gave him roast duck, biscuits, and butter and pudding to eat.

Later, Samoset brought another Indian, named Squanto. The Pilgrims were pleased that Squanto showed them how to plant corn and helped them in many ways. Samoset and Squanto brought the Indian chief Massasoit to meet the Pilgrims. He was a good friend to them. He and they agreed always to be friends and to help each other.

Pilgrim girls and boys worked hard helping plant corn the way Squanto showed them. All summer the Pilgrims worked together fixing their new homes and taking care of their little farms. They wanted to grow enough so they would have extra food to store for next winter.

When leaves on the trees began turning yellow and red, the Pilgrims' little gardens and farms were ready to harvest. They said, "Let's have a harvest feast and thank God for all we have. Let's invite Massasoit and some of his Indians to share the good time."

Everybody in Plymouth got busy for the thanksgiving feast. Some men went into the woods and brought back wild turkeys and geese and other meat. Men and boys went fishing. The children dug clams and picked wild grapes and beach plums. They all helped gather the corn and other vegetables. The women and big girls began cooking the good things to eat.

At last the day of thanksgiving came. Savory smells of roasting meat and of corn and of cakes filled the air. Out of the woods came Chief Massasoit with ninety Indians! They listened quietly while the Pilgrims thanked God for giving them such a good harvest and for taking care of them in this new land.

Then they all gathered around and ate and ate. They laughed and joked together and ate some more. Then the Indians and the Pilgrims ran races and saw how far they could shoot arrows and jumped and wrestled.

Chief Massasoit sent some Indians hunting, and they brought back more meat to roast. So the thanksgiving feast lasted three days. Perhaps during that time some Indians showed the Pilgrim children how to pop corn and gave them corn to pop. Perhaps the Indians sang some of their harvest songs for the Pilgrims, and the Pilgrims sang their songs for the Indians.

That was a Thanksgiving Day the Pilgrims never forgot. In time, all over our great big country people heard the story of the Pilgrims' thanksgiving. And for many years Thanksgiving has been a happy holiday throughout our whole United States of America. Happy Thanksgiving to everybody!

—MILDRED CORELL LUCKHARDT

How the Pilgrims Built
Their Towne in New England

It was mid-December, 1620, when the "Mayflower" weighed anchor and sailed across Cape Cod Bay. When she came within six miles of the mainland, the wind changed and she had to beat out to sea again.

Next day, because the wind was fair, she came into Plymouth Harbor and anchored about a mile and a half offshore. Because of the shallow water, she could get no nearer. The passengers had to ferry from ship to shore through the stormy waters all winter long.

They made their decision to settle in this place by vote in the democratic way. Here by the abundant bay, at long last they would build. This would be their home and haven of rest after many storm-blown wanderings.

Between the sinister forests and the bay they would build a New England with their naked hands and a few tools, with sweat and tears and heartache.

Before starting to build, they planned well. The congregation was separated into nineteen families. Then along a street that led from the hill to the water's edge, the hill slope was divided into plots. The families drew lots for their location. John Carver, who had been their leader aboard the "Mayflower," was confirmed as governor for the coming year.

Twenty men remained ashore in a barricaded camp and began cutting timber for building. The rest lived on the "Mayflower" and went back and forth from the ship to their day's work ashore.

On Christmas Day they worked on the common house, or shelter, which was for storing provisions, ammunition, and clothing. All that day the axes swung. At night the weary builders went back to the ship, leaving twenty men ashore. Between decks on the "Mayflower" they ate a meager dinner with English cheer. Then they sang the old carols, with their hearts back again in merry England, as a storm lashed through the rigging of the "Mayflower" in Plymouth Harbor.

As the winter wore on, hacking coughs and fever and scurvy began to take their toll among the passengers. But whenever the rain and sleet died down, the men who could walk at all went ashore to work on the common house. They began the platform of the fort and the family dwellings along the new street.

When the common house was thatched, provisions and ammunitions were brought ashore and stored in it. In the remaining space the sick beds lay end to end. Here among the stricken lay Bradford and Carver.

One day a spark caught in the dry thatch of the common house, and its roof took fire. At the cries of alarm, the workmen rushed to the burning building and carried out the sick. Before the fire was checked, food and precious stores were damaged, but by the grace of God no lives were lost.

From the top of the mount, Miles Standish gazed grimly across the pine-clad hills in the west to where columns of smoke rose against the gray sky from Indian signal fires.

For this thing called freedom, Standish now well knew, there was a price to pay. Below him in the village, death had taken nearly half of the people. Rose Standish, his wife, was among the first who had died. He had knelt at her side at the last hour. He would rather have taken an arrow through his heart. Fourteen of the eighteen Pilgrim wives had died. They had been buried at night in unmarked graves, so that the savages should not know how few remained. Sometimes there were two or three deaths in a day.

He and a half dozen others still had strength enough to feed the thin soup to the sick, to cheer the wasted forms in the crude beds, to hew wood and carry water so that Plymouth might live.

Bradford from his sick bed had watched the stocky man of war, day and night on his rounds, tending the sick with a woman's tenderness. Years later, rugged old Governor Bradford remembered and wrote this tribute in his blunt prose.

There was but 6 or 7 sound persons, so to their great comendations be it spoken, spared no pains, night or day, but with abundance of toyle and hazard of their owne health, fetched them woode, made them fires, drest them meat, made their beads, washed their lothsome cloaths, cloathed and uncloathed them; in a word did all ye homly and necessarie offices for them which dainty and quesie stomacks can not endure to hear named; and all this willingly and cherfully, without any grudging in ye least, shewing herein their true love unto their friends and brethern. A rare example and worthy to be remembered. Tow of these 7 were Mr. William Brewster, ther Reverend Elder and Miles Standish ther Captein and military commander, unto whom myself and many others, were much holden in our low and sicke condition.

Death had come aboard the "Mayflower." The sickness took one by one the riotous crew who brutally ignored their comrades dying miserably in their bunks. To these men who had cursed and tormented them, the women aboard the ship brought what care and comfort they could with a Christlike compassion.

In the fires and ice of that first winter, their spirits were steel tempered to build a nation of men and women who would never turn back in quest of freedom and justice and of brotherhood.

—ADAPTED FROM *The Landing of the Pilgrims*

BY JAMES DAUGHERTY

The Sailing of the Mayflower

Just in the gray of the dawn, as the mists uprose from the meadows,
There was a stir and a sound in the slumbering village of Plymouth;
Clanging and clicking of arms, and the order imperative, "Forward!"
Given in tone suppressed, a tramp of feet, and then silence.
Figures ten, in the mist, marched slowly out of the village.
Standish the stalwart it was with eight of his valorous army,
Led by their Indian guide, by Hobomok, friend of the white men,
Northward marching to quell the sudden revolt of the savage.

.   .   .   .

Many a mile had they marched, when at length the village of
   Plymouth
Woke from its sleep, and arose, intent on its manifold labors.
Sweet was the air and soft, and slowly the smoke from the chimneys
Rose over the roofs of thatch, and pointed steadily eastward;
Men came from the doors and paused and talked of the weather,
Said that the wind had changed, and was blowing fair for the "May-
   flower";
Talked of the captain's departure, and all the dangers that menaced,

He being gone, the town, and what should be done in his absence.
Merrily sang the birds, and the tender voices of women
Consecrated with hymns the common cares of the household.
Out of the sea rose the sun, and the billows rejoiced at his coming;
Beautiful were his feet on the purple tops of the mountains;
Beautiful on the sails of the "Mayflower" riding at anchor,
Battered and blackened and worn by all the storms of the winter.
Loosely against her masts was hanging and flapping her canvas,
Rent so by many gales, and patched by the hands of the sailors.
Suddenly from her side, as the sun rose over the ocean,
Darted a puff of smoke, and floated seaward; anon rang
Loud over field and forest the cannon's roar, and the echoes
Heard and repeated the sound, the signal-gun for departure!
Ah! But with louder echoes replied the hearts of the people!
Meekly, in voices subdued, the chapter was read from the Bible,
Meekly the prayer was begun, but ended in fervent entreaty.
Then from their houses in haste came forth the Pilgrims of Plymouth,
Men and women and children, all hurrying down to the seashore,
Eager, with tearful eyes, to say farewell to the "Mayflower,"
Homeward bound o'er the sea, and leaving them here in the desert.

—FROM *The Courtship of Miles Standish*
BY HENRY WADSWORTH LONGFELLOW

Paying for the Indian Corn
(*A true story*)

On the eleventh of November, 1620, the "Mayflower" anchored in a harbor at the tip of Cape Cod. As soon as the ship was quiet, the Pilgrims gathered on deck and thanked God that they were safely within sight of land after a voyage of sixty-seven days from England. They were sick of being tossed about by high waves in storms. They were tired of drinking water that had grown stale in the barrels in the ship's hold. They were weary from being crowded together in the cabins and on the deck. They were hungry for something to eat besides hard biscuit and old cheese.

When their thanks were said, some men in the group decided to go ashore on an exploring trip. The women and children gathered at the ship's rail and watched them descend a rope ladder which hung down the side of the "Mayflower."

The men got into a rowboat they had lowered and began to pull toward the shore. Soon they came to shallow water, where they anchored the rowboat and waded up the sandy beach.

The people on the "Mayflower" watched the men disappear

among the dunes and the pines on shore. The children wished they could go ashore, too, and run along the beach. But they knew that this strange land might not be a safe place. They had heard of Indians, from men who had visited earlier. So now they watched for their fathers and their friends to return.

The afternoon passed. Then it began to grow dark, and the mothers looked anxious, till one of the Pilgrim boys cried out, "Here they come!" He pointed toward shore, where the men could be seen wading in the waves. They carried bundles of firewood, holding it high to keep the water from it.

When the exploring party climbed back onto the "Mayflower," the men were so cold that their teeth chattered. The women took the bundles of wood from them and built a fire on a wide box of sand on the deck. Then the men gathered about the fire to warm their hands and dry their clothes.

Everyone asked questions at once. "Did you find food?" "Was there any fresh water?" "What is the new land like?"

William Bradford, one of the younger Pilgrim men, answered. "There is little food growing now, because winter is almost here. But we did see many wild ducks."

"Did you meet any Indians?" the children cried.

"We didn't see an Indian," William Bradford said. "But we plan to go ashore again and explore farther. If we meet Indians, we hope to trade with them. If they will give us food, we will pay them with cloth and knives and other goods which we have brought from England."

Four days later, sixteen of the Pilgrim men went ashore again. Every man carried his musket and sword. No one knew what trouble they might meet in the strange land. They were gone for two days.

When they returned, one of the men said, "We saw several Indians with a dog. They ran into the woods. We followed the path they took, but we could not find them."

"But wait till you see what we *did* find," Governor Carver said. "This is our first discovery in the new world."

The men reached into their pockets now and brought out something which they held in their hands. The other Pilgrims crowded around to look, and saw some kernels of a strange grain. Some of the kernels were yellow, some red, some mixed with blue.

"What is it?" asked several of the Pilgrims.

"Indian corn," said Master Hopkins. He had visited another part of the New World on an earlier voyage, and knew something of the Indians and their ways. "We came upon a heap of sand, newly piled, so we dug and found a basket full of Indian corn. Then we dug deeper and found a big basket that held thirty-six ears of good corn."

"And we found a great iron kettle, which must have been on some exploring ship which stopped here," another of the men said. "We filled the kettle with corn. Two of us carried it back here on a staff."

A boy said, "It must belong to the Indians you saw. They must have buried it."

The Pilgrims looked at one another in silence. It was plain to see that they were troubled about having taken corn which did not belong to them. Master Bradford cleared his throat. "We need this corn very much, for seed," he said. "We must plant the kind of grain which will grow here, or we cannot raise food to live. If we had not found this corn, I do not know where we would get seed."

"We will locate the Indians," the governor said. "We will parley with them, and give them gifts for the corn."

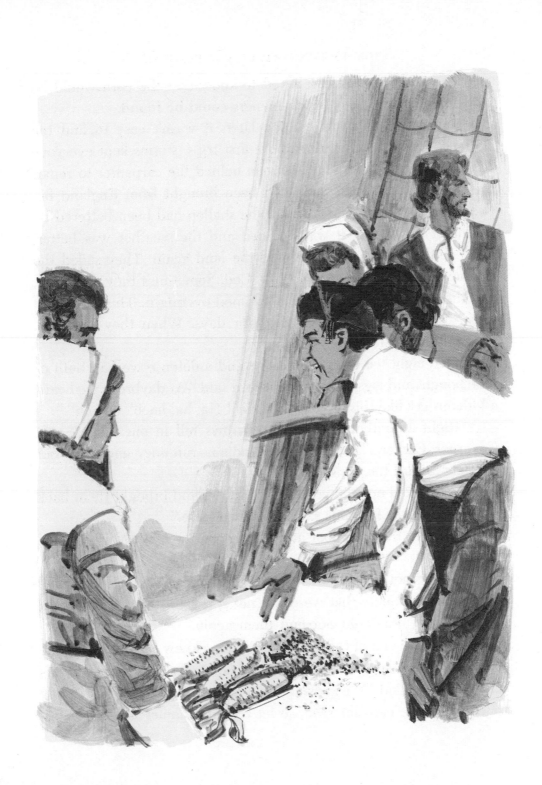

The Pilgrims looked relieved to know that the corn would be paid for as soon as the Indian owners could be found.

But, as the Pilgrims learned later, it wasn't easy to find the Indians. For many days after those first trips, storms kept everyone on board the ship. Some of the men helped the carpenter to repair the shallop, a sailboat which had been brought from England between decks of the "Mayflower." The shallop had been battered by storms at sea. When it was mended and the weather was better, some of the Pilgrim men explored the land again. They sailed the shallop all along the shore of Cape Cod. Sometimes they anchored, and the settlers went ashore and camped overnight. This time they were away from the "Mayflower" for days. When they returned, they told about their new adventure.

"One night we were camped behind a defense we had built of pine boughs and logs," Master Bradford said. "At daybreak we heard a hideous cry like this: 'Woach! Woach! Ha, ha, hach! Woach!'"

"Right after that some Indian arrows fell in our midst," said Governor Carver. "Then we saw Indians running, and shot our muskets toward the trees where they hid."

"We picked up eighteen of their arrows and brought them back with us," Master Hopkins said. "Here they are."

"Did the Indians shoot at you because we took their corn?" a boy asked.

"We do not know," Master Bradford said. "The Indians came upon us so suddenly that we could not speak to them or pay them for the corn. We could not find them again."

Before the end of the year, the Pilgrims knew they must decide upon a place to land and build homes. Some of them wanted to remain on Cape Cod. "We know that the soil here will grow corn," they said. "We have corn for seed, so let us build homes here at once."

But those who had sailed the shallop on the exploring trip said they had found another place which was better. It was called Plymouth. It had a better harbor for ships, and the land near there had taller trees for building, and blacker earth for growing. So the "Mayflower" sailed across Cape Cod Bay and into Plymouth Harbor.

All that winter the men and older boys worked ashore at Plymouth, to cut trees and build homes. Most of the women and children lived on the "Mayflower," anchored in the harbor.

Finally, on a warm day the following spring, the last of the Pilgrims left the "Mayflower" and went ashore to live. They began to plant the seed of the corn they had found on Cape Cod.

Squanto, an Indian who had come to Plymouth, taught the Pilgrims how to plant the corn. Squanto had learned a little English from fishermen whose ships had stopped in the New World. The Pilgrims questioned him about the Indians who owned the corn they had taken. Squanto did not know which tribe had buried the corn.

The Pilgrims met another Indian, great Chief Massasoit. They made a treaty with Chief Massasoit and his men, who agreed to live with the white men as friends. But still the Pilgrims did not find out where the seed corn had come from. Massasoit said that it did not belong to his tribe.

Soon after the red and yellow and blue kernels were planted, green sprouts pushed through the ground. The corn grew and grew. The Pilgrims weeded and hoed, and guarded the fields against deer which might eat the tender stalks.

The corn grew tall. Its leaves rustled in the breeze. Heavy ears hung from the thick stalks. The Pilgrims waited for the grain to ripen, and they were pleased that the crop was good and would feed their people in the year ahead. But one thing troubled them. The seed of the corn was not yet paid for.

Then one day a small Pilgrim boy named John wandered into the woods and was lost. He walked and walked and walked. He grew hungry and thirsty. He wandered up and down for five days, living on berries and whatever else he could find.

At last he came upon some Indians. He tried to tell them he was from Plymouth and that he wanted to go home. But the Indians did not understand him. They put him in a canoe and took the boy to an Indian village, near a sandy beach and dunes. The Indians were

kind to him, and he played with the Indian children. Then one day after John had been at the Indian village for some time, he saw the shallop of his Pilgrim people sailing near the shore. A few minutes later it anchored. Some of the Pilgrim men came into the village. They told the village chief that they were hunting for John, and the boy was returned to them.

As the Pilgrim party prepared to take the lost boy home in the shallop, one of the men noticed a basket beside an Indian house. The basket was woven just like those which had been found with the seed corn! The Pilgrims asked the chief about the basket and told him about finding the corn.

The chief nodded. Yes, the seed corn they had found had belonged to these Indians.

The Pilgrims were pleased. They invited the chief of the village and some of his men to return to their settlement with them.

When the shallop reached Plymouth, the governor greeted the Indians, and the Pilgrim women brought them food.

The Pilgrim men then went to the common house and chose gifts for the Indians. From their sea chests they took colored cloth and knives and beads, and other goods. These they brought and placed before the Indians. "We give these gifts to you in exchange for your corn which we found and took on Cape Cod," the governor said. "Without your corn, we could not have grown food to live. We are grateful for it, and we hope you will be our friends."

And that was how those early American settlers paid their first debt to the Indians.

—WILMA PITCHFORD HAYS

Talking Turkey

Charles Sawyer was a Pilgrim lad
Who, feeling very perky
One misty day, set out to hunt
The wild New England turkey.
He scurried through the brush and bog
And hid himself behind a log;
And there he made a scratchy-squawk
That sounded much like turkey talk. . . .

An Indian, with colored feather,
That very morning wondered whether
He, too, could catch some gobbler game
And through the selfsame woods he came.
On hands and knees, instead of walking,
He crept, and also made a squawking
Till he and Charlie—calling, talking
Back and forth with gibberish word—
Each thought the other was a bird;

And, as they sought each other's place
Of hiding, they came face to face.
Then shots that might have followed after
Were changed to sudden peals of laughter.

The Indian, though just a grunter,
Told Charlie he was quite a hunter;
And Charlie, signing with his hand,
Soon made the red man understand
He much admired his decoying.
So off they went, those two, enjoying

115

Their little joke; and when a jerky
Wattled head peered through the murky
Morning at them, each cried "Turkey!"

The quiet bowshot and the louder
Gunshot with its smell of powder
Brought the bird down in a minute
An arrow and a bullet in it.

Then such a feast the hunters had
Beside the fire! Lad and lad
Forgetting they were enemies
Among the wood anemones.
The fun led to friendly living
And to the Pilgrims' first
THANKSGIVING.

—ROWENA BENNETT

Harvest Home

Before daylight Goodwife Pepperell stood in the doorway of the new house and watched her husband set forth with the men of Cambridge to search the forest for Zeb, and to punish his captors if they should catch them. She had given her husband a good breakfast and filled his pockets with bread for the journey, and when the men came from the village, she gave each a generous piece of pie to eat before starting. There were eight men, all armed.

The Goodwife's lip trembled and then moved in prayer as they disappeared into the dark forest. "God grant they may all return in safety," she murmured. Then, giving herself a shake, she set resolutely about the duties of the day.

Nimrod, their dog, whined and tried to follow his master, but finding himself too weak, lay down again on the hearth and went to sleep. IIe had been beaten cruelly yesterday when the Indians had broken into the house and captured Zeb. Poor Zeb! Not long ago the Pepperells had given him a home and tried to help him forget all the terrors of the slave ship from which he had escaped. Had he been hurt when the Indians carried him off yesterday?

Worrying about Zeb and the safety of those who had gone in search of him, the Goodwife began a patient march back and forth beside the whirling spinning wheel. How thankful she was that the children were safe in their beds in the loft.

Awakened by the whir of the spinning wheel they came scuttling down from the loft. They helped themselves to hasty pudding and milk and took some to Nimrod.

"Nancy," said their mother, "I gave all the pies thou made to the men who have gone to hunt for Zeb. Tomorrow will be Thanksgiving Day, and we shall need more. The mince pies are put away on the shelves, and you can make apple and pumpkin to set beside them. Daniel, go to the field and bring thy sister a fresh pumpkin for the pies. Then hasten to thine own tasks. While thy father is away searching for Zeb, thou must do his work as well as thine own."

"Dost think, Mother, that he will surely bring Zeb back in time for the feast?" asked Nancy anxiously.

"Let us pray, nothing doubting," answered the mother. "If it be God's will, they will return."

All day long they worked, praying as they prepared the feast that they might share it as a united family. Nancy made pies, Dan dressed a fowl, their mother got ready a pot of beans, made brown bread, and steamed an Indian pudding. All day they watched the forest for sign of the returning men. They listened for the sound of guns, but neither sight nor sound rewarded their vigilance. Dusk came on. The Goodwife set a candle in the window, then went back to her spinning. She did not appear anxious, but as she walked beside her wheel, Nancy heard her murmuring, "Because thou hast made the Lord, which is my refuge, even the most High, thy habitation, there shall no evil befall thee, neither shall any plague come nigh thy dwelling."

Supper which Nancy prepared waited—one hour—two—after Dan fed the cattle and brought in the milk. Still no sign of the search party!

Suddenly from his place on the hearth Nimrod gave a sharp bark and, leaping to the window, stood with paws on the sill, peering out into the darkness and whining. Dan was beside him in an instant. He cried joyfully, "I see them, a whole parcel of them, just coming from behind the cow-shed."

Nancy and her mother reached the window at the same moment. As the shadowy figures emerged from behind the cow-shed Mother counted breathlessly, "One—two—three—four—five—."

"There's Father!" shrieked Nancy. "He's carrying something. Dost think it's Zeb?"

"There are ten men when but eight set forth. Praise, God, they have all come back," cried Mother. From the fireplace she snatched a brand of burning pitch pine and holding it high for a beacon, ran to meet them, with Dan, Nancy, and Nimrod at her heels. The torchlight shone on stern and weary faces as the men drew near.

"All's well, wife," came the voice of the Goodman.

"Hast found the lad?" she called.

"Nay—not yet, but we think we have his captors. Hold thy torch nearer and have no fear. The savages cannot hurt thee. Nancy, Daniel, have you seen these faces before?" He thrust forward two Indians with their hands tied behind them.

Nancy shuddered. "I saw them at the window," and Dan added, "This one kicked Nimrod." Nimrod was growling fiercely and snapping at the heels of the taller Indian.

"Call off thy dog," said the Goodman, and Dan shut Nimrod inside the kitchen. The Indians' faces were like stone masks as they stood before their captors with the torchlight shining upon them.

The Pepperells' neighbor, Stephen Day, told Father to go on inside, for there were enough men to guard the Indians. "A night in the stocks may cool their blood and help them remember what they have done with the slave lad."

Father was glad to go into the house. "I am truly spent," he said. He was so weary that his wife and children forebode asking questions until he was a little rested and refreshed. He sank on the settle with Nimrod beside him, and Dan removed his muddy boots and brought water for him to wash, while Nancy and Mother put the long-delayed supper on the table.

After he had eaten a bit, Father said, "We saw no evidence of general uprising among the Indians. I fear they are the same Indians that followed us from Plymouth, to get revenge because I had wounded one when they set upon us in the forest."

"But why was the lad not with them?" asked his wife.

"It may be they have killed him and hidden the body," replied Father. At this dreadful news Nancy covered her face with her hands.

"It may be," went on the Goodman, "they passed him on to someone else to avoid suspicion. We could find no trace. Though they undoubtedly know some English, they refuse to talk, and his fate remains a mystery."

"What further shall you do to find him?" asked the Goodwife, to which her husband replied, "See if we cannot force the Indians to confess."

"Father," asked Dan, "did thou find the gun the Indians took from here?"

"Nay. That causes me to think they have passed it and the boy on to others of their tribe. There is naught to be done now but wait until after Thanksgiving Day."

" 'Twill be a sad holiday," said Mother. "I grieve that evil hath befallen Zeb."

Dan said that he had seen him carrying a burden when he came from behind the cow-shed, and thought it was Zeb, wounded or dead.

"Aye," answered Father, "I almost forgot it. Go and bring it in."

Dan returned soon carrying a huge wild turkey, which Mother said would make a fine addition to tomorrow's feast. "Our preparation has been half hearted."

Next morning they were a solemn little party that left the cabin in Nimrod's care and started across the snowy fields to the Thanksgiving service in the meeting house. The first snow fall, usually a joy to Nancy and Dan, now made them more miscrable. They were glad to see the sun come out as they turned their steps home after the sermon. At least Zeb would not perish of cold if it continued to shine.

They were beginning to climb the home hill when they were surprised to see Nimrod bounding to meet them, barking a welcome.

"How did that dog get out?" exclaimed Mother. "I shut him in the kitchen."

Nancy and Dan raced up the hill and threw open the kitchen door. Comfortably dozing on the settle was their friend Captain Sanders! At his feet lay Zeb! Amazed and delighted, the children burst into the room. Zeb, worn out, slept on, and the sea-captain, as usual, was the first to find his tongue.

He shouted, "Here ye be! I'm hungry enough to eat a bear alive."

Before the children could get in a word, Father, Mother, and Nimrod came in. There was such a babel of noise that Zeb woke and stared about him, dazed. Nimrod jumped upon him and licked his face and Zeb put his arms around the dog.

"What ails ye all?" shouted the captain.

Then Father told the whole story to the captain, and asked, "Where did you find the lad?"

"He was here when I came," said the Captain. "The dog busted out of the house, and as I couldn't get any word out of the lad, I sat by the fire and took forty winks."

The Goodman sat before Zeb and tried to get some account of what had happened in the forest. But Zeb's few words of English were inadequate to tell the terrors of the past twenty-four hours.

"Let the lad be," said the Goodwife. "He's safe, praise God, and we shall have to wait to find out how he escaped and made his way here." She brought out a huge piece of pumpkin pie for Zeb. "He mustn't eat too much at once. Dan, build a fire in the fireplace in the old kitchen. See that Zeb takes a bath. He is crusted with mud. Nancy and I will get dinner."

When all was ready, they took their places at the table. The Goodman asked a blessing and then heaped the trenchers high with what he called the bounty of the Lord. The turkey was a wonder of tenderness, the vegetables done to a turn, the Indian pudding better than its name, and as for the pies, the captain declared they were "fit to be et by the angels and most too good for a sinner like him."

Beside each plate the Goodwife had placed a few kernels of corn, and at the end of the feast the Goodman rose and took them in his hand.

"In the midst of plenty," he said to the children, "let us not forget the struggles of the past and what we owe to the pioneers who first adventured into this wilderness and made a path for those

of us who have followed them. Though they nearly perished of hunger and cold in the beginning, they failed not in faith. When they had but a few kernels of corn to eat, they still gave thanks, choosing like Daniel of old to live on pulse with a good conscience rather than to eat from the king's table. As the Lord prospered Daniel, so hath he prospered us."

Then they all stood with folded hands and bent heads, while he gave thanks for the abundant harvest and prayed that they might be guided to use every blessing to the honor and glory of God. And the captain said, "Amen."

—ABRIDGED FROM *The Puritan Twins* BY LUCY FITCH PERKINS

The First Thanksgiving

Out of the woods the Indians came
into the Pilgrim village,
bringing their gifts of nuts and game,
bearing the fruits of tillage.
Out of the shadows and up the banks
Indians came for the feast of thanks.

"When we were hungered," the Pilgrims said,
lifting their eyes to heaven,
"Father, they showed us the way to bread;
water, and meal, and leaven . . ."
The Indians looked to the heavens, too,
not understanding . . . and yet they knew!

—AILEEN FISHER

The Seed of Liberty Had Taken Root

Governor William Bradford laid his goosequill pen on the desk. At last he had finished it—the story of Plymouth from the beginnings up to now. None knew it better than himself. This was the story of the forty years he had lived since he had joined the Separatists at Scrooby. Those who came after would want to know how it was in the beginning with those who came first.

He had set down the story briefly and plainly, not glossing over any matter, but bluntly stating truth. After Plymouth had prospered, mischievous men had come seeking to sow strife and discord for their own gain. But the Lord's faithful had stood together in unity and had undone their wicked designs. These schemers and rioters had been patiently reproved. Those who had been found guilty after a fair trial had been put out of the colony or sent back to England.

Bradford looked across the bay, sparkling blue in the afternoon sun. His gaze traveled to the horizon; his thoughts went back to his youth, and to Austerfield and Scrooby, where it all began. He had not changed; only that he was surer now and saw truth clearer.

Outside, in the garden, he could see children playing. They had been born in Plymouth, like their fathers and mothers before them. These boys and girls were the grandchildren of the firstcomers. There were still living in this year 1648, by the grace of God, thirty of the old stock who had come in the "Mayflower."

The seed of liberty had taken root in this New England earth. A tree had sprung up that would some day fill the whole world. Truth seekers, like the fowls of the air, would find shelter in its branches. Each year, thousands were coming in crowded ships. New England was dotted with growing towns as far as the Connecticut Valley. Even beyond, young men with axes and plows and Bibles were pushing into the westward forest, saying:

"It is not with us as with other men whom small things can discourage, or small discontentments cause to wish themselves at home again."

—FROM *The Landing of the Pilgrims* BY JAMES DAUGHERTY

PART II
Thanksgiving and Harvest Time
Near and Far

Thanksgiving

The splendor of the harvest
Fills the coffers of the land,
And grateful hearts give thanks
For all the bounty from God's hand.

But let us hold this thought
Before November days depart,
Not just for now—
Thanksgiving is a season of the heart.

—SELECTED LINES FROM *"Thanksgiving"*
BY CATHERINE E. BERRY

Some North American Thanksgivings

"Our harvest being gotten in, our governor sent four men on fowling, that we might after a special manner, rejoice together after we had gathered the fruits of our labors." These words from a very old account of the Pilgrims are part of the story of their first harvest feast in America—at "Plimoth Plantation" in the autumn of 1621.

News of the coming feast spread quickly through the little settlement. Children harvesting big orange pumpkins shouted to those shucking ears of golden corn, "We're going to have a harvest feast!" When they spied fishermen sailing home toward Plymouth, the girls and boys raced laughing down hill to help unload fish and tell the good news of the coming good time. "The women already are planning what we will eat. Chief Massasoit is invited to come and bring some of his Indians, too."

Many grown-ups recalled the jolly harvest-home celebrations of their childhood in England, when the harvest was brought in for the winter with singing, feasting, and thanksgiving. There had been few good times for the Plymouth settlement to enjoy together during the past year. The Pilgrims had suffered from cold, hunger, overwork, fear of Indians, homesickness, sorrow, and a terrible plague which had killed more than half those who had come on the "Mayflower." Now, though, with food stored away for the coming winter, their little houses fairly snug, with the assistance of Chief Massasoit, and a peace pact with the Wampanoag Indians, the Pilgrims were ready to celebrate the harvest feast and play for awhile.

As was the custom of various people throughout the world, some North American Indians had celebrated for many years harvest and thanksgiving. At the Festival of the Green Corn they thanked the Great Spirit for giving them corn and held traditional ceremonies around the council fire. Besides festivals for different crops, some Indians had one festival of thanksgiving for all crops. Massasoit probably understood about such feasts, but the Pilgrims were surprised when he came to their feast bringing a great company of ninety braves. The guests were welcomed, however, even though there were twice as many Indians as Pilgrim men, women, and children. Only five women were alive in Plymouth but they and a few older girls had cooked a real thanksgiving feast. Since early spring everyone had helped with the planting, tending crops, and harvesting. Now, they were proud of the feast they could set forth.

No doubt some of the farmers held up ears of corn with big plump kernels and said to the Indian chief, "Look what a fine crop we harvested because your people taught us how." And perhaps they joked together about how little the Pilgrims had known about corn before they made friends with the Indians. Then Indians and Pilgrims ate the feast together.

Perhaps some of the Plymouth children stuffed themselves so much they felt drowsy. But soon everybody was clapping and cheering while Indians and Pilgrims, men and older boys ran races, jumped, wrestled, shot arrows, and held other contests. Sometimes

an Indian won; sometimes a Pilgrim, but everybody enjoyed the sport. "Let's play stoolball," shouted a young man, and a game was started. Most of those not playing lined up to watch and cheer.

The women, however, were kept busy preparing food, for the Indians stayed three days. Fortunately, their chief sent some out hunting, and they brought back enough venison to feed everyone and have some left over.

This was no solemn time set apart for pious thanksgiving. This was a time of laughter and singing and enjoyment of God's gifts. Every morning, always Pilgrim households gathered to pray and praise God and read the Scriptures.

During these golden autumn days they were especially thankful. Probably they sang some of the special psalms of thanksgiving, and the music floated across the blue waters of Plymouth Harbor as

Indians and newcomers enjoyed a happy harvest festival together.

Although the Pilgrims always tried to keep thankful spirits, they were not able to celebrate harvest thanksgiving feasts regularly every year after that famous one of 1621. During the following year they nearly starved because crops were poor and many new colonists arrived. They brought little clothing and no food. The Pilgrims had to share with these new people what little food they had as well as clothes and bedding. During the spring of 1623, a long drought nearly killed the crops; but in July, rain came at last. Then there was a public thanksgiving for the rainfall.

But a day of special thanksgiving prayers was not the same as a happy autumn harvest thanksgiving festival, when families and friends gathered to share the feast and the fun. Yet in many different places along the Atlantic coast, new arrivals in America from many different lands thanked God together in public for his care and gifts.

From old records one may draw an inspiring picture of different groups kneeling in thanksgiving for a particular blessing. Perhaps Columbus and his men, when they landed on San Salvador that famous day in October, 1492, were the first Europeans who knelt to give thanks in America. We know of that thanksgiving, but it may be that the Vikings, centuries before, had thanked their gods for bringing them safely to Vinland.

While daring explorers from Europe were searching for the passage to Asia, there probably were many times when they held a day of thanksgiving for safety and preservation. *The Ottawa Journal* records that a thanksgiving day was celebrated by Sir Martin Frobisher and his men in Newfoundland in 1578. A search of other old records reveals that from Canada to the islands of the Caribbean explorers, fishermen, and new settlers thanked God for bringing them safely across the perilous sea, for helping them survive and for opening up the New World to them.

Very early in the settlement of the New World, the Virginia colony had special days of prayer and fasting. The day of December 4, 1619, is well known as the day set aside by colonists at Berkeley Hundred to be "perpetually kept holy." After a rough trip at sea, and anxious waiting by those on shore, some new colonists finally had arrived safely. It was natural to hold a special day of thanksgiving. Virginia records show, also, another day of public thanksgiving, March 22, 1623, celebrated after the colony had survived the Indian massacre of the previous year.

Some early Dutch traders along the Hudson River in New Amsterdam of New Netherlands (in what is now New York state) and those along the Delaware River (in the area which now comprises the states of New Jersey, Pennsylvania, and Delaware) may

have celebrated the October Thanksgiving Day of their homeland. This dated from 1574 when Leyden, in Holland, was saved from foreign invaders after many hard battles and long seige. When the Pilgrims lived there before coming to America, they sometimes were invited by Dutch neighbors to share the thanksgiving stew, "hotch-potch."

Dutch and Swedish colonists in New Netherlands also held a special Thanksgiving Day in 1644 after their soldiers returned from battle with Connecticut Indians. And the next year they celebrated a public thanksgiving for an Indian peace treaty.

New Amsterdam was a seaport to which traders came from many lands, including Asia and Africa. Since the Dutch believed in religious toleration, stories are told of how people of many races, languages, and colors joined with the New Amsterdam Dutch to worship. Perhaps they sang to the tune of a Netherlands Folk Song, "We gather together to ask the Lord's blessing," and recalled that this hymn celebrated the victory of Old World Hollanders in their battle for religious and government freedom.

Even though, in time, New Amsterdam came under British rule and was renamed New York, thanksgiving days were held there for years. They began to be associated with harvest feasts more than previously.

Jewish families who came early to live in New Amsterdam brought with them a truly ancient thanksgiving festival, the September Succos, or Feast of Booths. This harvest feast of rejoicing is described in the Bible. As these Jews gathered for this festival in the New World, the voices of men, women, and children mingled in thanksgiving psalms, many of which also were sung by the Pilgrims in Plymouth. "For thou, O Lord, has made me glad . . . at the works of thy hands I sing for joy." Succos is a happy thanksgiving feast, shared to this day by friends and relatives and any strangers who might come.

In the last half of the seventeenth century, part of what earlier had been New Netherlands was granted to William Penn, an English Quaker. These beautiful woodlands were named Pennsylvania. To Pennsylvania, William Penn welcomed many different religious groups who had been persecuted in Europe, for he had insisted that his charter grant religious freedom.

One such group, the Schwenkfelder Society, had suffered religious persecution in Germany for several years after their leader died. Some Schwenkfelders sailed to Pennsylvania, found it a fine place to make their homes, and sent for the others. How happy they all were when nearly two hundred more arrived on September 22, 1734! "This is to be our homeland now," parents assured their children, as they breathed the sweet air of freedom and walked among fields ripening for harvest.

Eager to be good citizens, they went to the state house two days later and promised loyalty to the British crown. Happy to be in America, they spent the rest of the day giving thanks and enjoying this new land. That day, September 24, was named a day of thanksgiving, always to be celebrated by them and their descendants.

About the same time the Schwenkfelders were settling along the Perkiomen Valley in Pennsylvania, Moravians, who had been persecuted in Germany, were beginning settlements not far away along the Lehigh River. After some years there were Moravian settlements in other places also, including North Carolina and Georgia. Moravians were a missionary people who traveled far and wide, helping the poor, the sick, the oppressed. Some went to the Virgin Islands.

Even today people of the Virgin Islands celebrate a special Thanksgiving Day late in October, as well as the United States national Thanksgiving Day. On the October Hurricane Thanksgiving, they give thanks if they have not suffered from hurricanes during the year, and pray for safety from hurricanes for the coming year. After such a Hurricane Thanksgiving service, in Moravian churches the worshipers enjoy a feast of love and good will, with delicious raisin buns and a cool raspberry drink.

To recount all the various special thanksgiving days throughout our country would be interesting, but difficult. For instance, in California, July 1, 1769, a small band of colonists celebrated a special day of thanksgiving. More than three hundred had started from Mexico in various groups by land and sea. Shipwrecks and other disasters killed over half of them. The remaining 126 reached present-day San Diego, half-starved, in danger of hostile natives. They were saved when Father Junipero Serra arrived with soldiers and supplies. On that Thanksgiving Day, Father Serra led their worship;

and they joined in singing "We praise thee, O God . . . All the earth doth worship thee, the Father everlasting."

This is the first recorded time of special thanksgiving on the Pacific coast. But as time went by and people moved from place to place, tales are told of gatherings to give thanks for some special protection or gift from God—among pioneers on the westward trek, or persons born in Alaska or Hawaii, or the vast areas of Canada. In a variety of languages, many used the same thanksgiving psalms sung by Jews, Moravians, Anglicans, Roman Catholics, Pilgrims, and Puritans, and thousands of other persons who came to America. For they had brought with them a reverence for the Creator and thankfulness for his protection.

Many, many years passed, though, before people all over the country celebrated a national Thanksgiving Day. Meanwhile, as more and more people came to the early settlements in New England, they heard of the Pilgrim harvest feast of 1621. Various communities began combining thanksgiving prayers with harvest festivals. On September 18, 1639, the Connecticut government issued a thanksgiving proclamation; and records show that, on the whole, that colony kept a regular autumn Thanksgiving Day for many years. Because of Indian massacre no celebration was held there in 1675.

While our country was growing into a nation, thanksgivings were celebrated in one place or another, often at different times. In 1775, when General Washington commanded American troops in the siege of Boston, he followed the custom there and directed his troops to observe Thursday, November 23, as a "day of public thanksgiving."

Next year the American army suffered terrible defeats, and many more public fasts than thanksgivings were proclaimed. By Autumn, 1777, countless Americans were bitterly discouraged, sad, hungry, ragged. The capital was threatened, and General Burgoyne's powerful army was moving in at the north. Then came new hope! The capital was not captured. Burgoyne's army was defeated! Samuel Adams cried, "This victory calls for a national day of Thanksgiving."

The whole Continental Congress agreed heartily and set Thursday, December 18, 1777, as a day of "Thanksgiving and praise." Postriders carried the proclamation far and wide. Then, for the first time, all thirteen colonies joined in a national day of prayer and feasting. In many places, however, those who would feast were very hungry. The soldiers encamped at Valley Forge had no flour or bread, and little other food. Yet their faith in the cause of freedom and their loyalty to their commander-in-chief kept them from deserting.

After the horrors of that winter, the soldiers at Valley Forge received marvelous news. Early in May a dispatch rider galloped into camp with this message, "France has become our ally!" Supply wagons began lumbering in. French officers appeared, full of enthusiasm. Within a few days General Washington assembled the troops, and the chaplains reported the good news officially. When the cheering quieted, soldiers joined wholeheartedly with chaplains in thankful prayers. The delicious aroma of meat roasting and bread baking floated toward them. Soon the smiling, ragged men walked to a thanksgiving feast they never would forget.

After struggling through more than four years of suffering and warfare, the colonies won independence at last. Then came the difficult task of uniting them all as a nation with a good constitution. Numbers of people had come from many lands, bringing ideals of liberty and justice. At last the ideals were written into the Constitution which begins, "We, the people of the United States, in order to form a more perfect union. . . ." The courage, sacrifices, and great hardships of the early settlers and of all who had struggled for freedom were bearing fruit in this great plan for the nation's government, "which would secure the blessings of liberty to ourselves and our posterity."

The federal Congress asked President Washington to proclaim Thursday, November 26, 1789, as national Thanksgiving Day. In churches and on the streets and around family dinner tables, people read the President's proclamation and talked gratefully of the new Constitution and the growing strength of the new nation. Perhaps some families told stories that had been handed down to them about the first autumn thanksgiving feast in the tiny settlement at Plymouth more than 160 years before.

For some years after President Washington's Proclamation, a time of thanksgiving was celebrated in various parts of the country, not always on the same day. Many people, however, wanted a national Thanksgiving Day that would unite all Americans in enjoying the fruits of the harvest and in thanking God for the nation's blessings. Many states kept a thanksgiving day; others did not.

In 1857, Governor Wise of Virginia issued a thanksgiving proclamation, and the next year governors of eight southern states did the same.

For a long time, though, a number of people in different parts of the country had hoped for an annual nationwide Thanksgiving Day. Mrs. Sarah Josepha Hale, a brave and far-sighted woman of New Hampshire, firmly believed that such a day would help bring everyone in the country together with a feeling of good will. Mrs. Hale had been left a widow with five children. She was eager for them, and for all Americans, to live in a united country.

Sarah Josepha Hale was a clever writer. She became editor of a woman's magazine, *Godey's Lady's Book,* which went into many homes. Through this magazine Mrs. Hale interested some people in the idea of a national Thanksgiving Day to be proclaimed each year by the President. She kept working, writing, and talking about it— and she published delicious thanksgiving recipes. Her hundreds of letters to mayors, governors, senators, and congressmen included one letter to each new President. In an editorial in 1861, during the conflict between the states, Mrs. Hale urged the nation to "lay aside our enmities on this one day and join in a Thanksgiving Day of Peace." Another editorial, in 1863, stated that such a day would help heal "sectional feelings."

Like many others, President Lincoln longed to heal sectional feelings. A few weeks after reading Mrs. Hale's editorial he proclaimed Thursday, November 26, 1863, a "A day of Thanksgiving and Praise to our beneficent Father." Here is part of the proclamation: "The year that is drawing toward its close has been filled with the blessings of fruitful fields and healthful skies." Even though the country was torn by war, the President added, "The ax has enlarged the borders of our settlements . . . the mines . . . have yielded even more abundantly than heretofore." With whatever gifts the nation was blessed, Mr. Lincoln said, "They are the gracious gifts of the most high God, who while dealing with us in anger for our sins, hath nevertheless remembered us in mercy. . . ."

This was the second national thanksgiving proclamation ever made by a chief executive. The United States of America was the first nation in the world to make Thanksgiving a public, legal holiday. In 1941, the Congress of the United States in joint resolution provided that "the fourth Thursday in November in each year after the year 1941 be known as Thanksgiving Day, and it is hereby made a legal public holiday to all intents and purpose." The people of the United States may enjoy with their families and friends, and

with strangers from other lands, the feast and the fun; and they may take part in or watch athletic contests as did the Pilgrims at Plymouth.

Football is a favorite game on Thanksgiving Day throughout the whole country. As in many other states, in Hawaii holiday crowds enjoy football games, and many other games, for songs and dances are part of Hawaii's festival day. When families and friends gather for a thanksgiving luau there, they can recall that the first big thanksgiving feast in Plymouth was cooked and eaten outdoors, too. Of course, in Hawaii birds will be singing, and the countryside will be beautiful with flowers and green trees.

On the other hand when people celebrate the national Thanksgiving Day in Alaska, they are more likely to enjoy eating indoors near a pleasant hearth fire. Yet the same warmth of thankfulness and sharing with others on this special day is felt there as throughout the entire nation. Virginians, Ohioans, Texans, Nebraskans, Mississippians, Californians, people from every state and territory gladly share the feast with friends and family and with the lonely or poor.

Thanksgiving Day has become a time when in all fifty states, territories, and possessions, people of many different races and religious beliefs unite in thanksgiving services. A Pan-American thanksgiving celebration first was held in 1909 at St. Paul's Roman Catholic Church in Washington, D. C. At that time United States President Taft and his Cabinet attended. This was the first time that representatives from all the republics of the Western world met together in religious services. Each year, more and more congregations in every village and town join together in community Thanksgiving Day services.

During World War II, when Americans were in service all

around the world, they brought Thanksgiving Day with them. But nowhere at that time was it celebrated with more deep meaning and enthusiasm than in England. America had shipped tons of turkey across the submarine-infested Atlantic Ocean to England for the great day. And the able-bodied American soldiers there gave it all to American and British wounded in military hospitals. Most of the other Americans ate other meat instead.

Eating, however, was not the most important part of that celebration. Many English people wanted to hear about the American Thanksgiving Day. American officers were invited to some schools to tell about its origin, and American service men and women traveled to see the places from which the Pilgrims had come. The town hall of Chorley in Lancashire flew the American flag for the first time, while servicemen visited the little church where Miles Standish once worshiped. In Lincolnshire, The Lord Mayor of Boston invited one hundred American soldiers to dinner. One American officer laid a wreath on the memorial there to five men who had been born there and later became governors of Massachusetts before the Revolutionary War.

Nearby, an American private placed a wreath in the dark cells where, more than three hundred years before, Pilgrims had been imprisoned after being caught trying to escape to Holland for religious freedom.

At Westminster Abbey, where kings and queens of England have been crowned for centuries, thousands of American service men and women crowded in for a solemn but beautiful thanksgiving service. Some had seen announcements in newspapers, and the word spread fast. Everyone came because he wanted to. Most of them were homesick for Thanksgiving Day in America, as they saw the American flag draped on the high altar and sang together

"America, the Beautiful." Later, some of them wondered together about what the Pilgrims would have thought of such a Thanksgiving Day. Here were Americans, descended from people of many countries of the world, celebrating a great American national festival with friendly, kind-hearted allies whose ancestors may have been living in England when the Pilgrims had to flee for their lives.

In recalling at thanksgiving time the Pilgrim story, Americans near and far realize that "the Plimoth Plantation of 1620 was a 'new planting' where seeds of courage, faith, and devotion to freedom took a firm root. In seeking freedom to work and worship as they pleased, the Pilgrims set a pattern which was duplicated by many other Pilgrims of as many creeds who followed them to new life in America."

Through the centuries countless other such pilgrims have brought to the United States of America many different religious and festival customs. Many of them have held and still hold special thanksgivings; and all of these thanksgivings help enrich the general thanksgiving. All people may share the tradition of the first Pilgrim thanksgiving here, and join together in the great national Thanksgiving Day, not only for the harvests and the bounties of nature, but also for freedom's blessings, opportunities, and responsibilities.

President Washington's first proclamation of thanksgiving was made when our nation was very new. Yet, these words from it have much meaning for us today:

Whereas it is the duty of all nations to acknowledge the providence of Almighty God, to obey his will, to be grateful for his benefits, and humbly to implore his protection and favor . . .

Now therefore I do recommend and assign Thursday, the twenty-sixth of November next, to be devoted by the people of these States to the service of that great and glorious Being . . .

That we may then all unite in rendering unto him our sincere and humble thanks for his kind care and protection of the people of this country . . .

For the civil and religious liberty with which we are blessed, and the means we have of acquiring and diffusing useful knowledge . . . and beseech him to pardon our national and other transgressions . . .

To render our National Government a blessing to all the people, by constantly being a government of wise, just, and constitutional laws, discreetly and faithfully executed and obeyed . . .

To promote the knowledge and practice of true religion and virtue, and the increase of science . . .

And, generally, to grant unto all mankind such a degree of temporal prosperity as he alone knows to be best.

—MILDRED CORELL LUCKHARDT

The Corn Song

Heap high the farmer's wintry hoard!
Heap high the golden corn!
No richer gift has autumn poured
From out her lavish horn!

Through vales of grass and meads of flowers,
  Our ploughs their furrows made,
While on the hills the sun and showers
  Of changeful April played.

We dropped the seed o'er hill and plain,
  Beneath the sun of May,
And frightened from our sprouting grain
  The robber crows away.

All through the long, bright days of June
  Its leaves grew green and fair,
And waved in hot midsummer's sun
  Its soft and golden hair.

And now, with autumn's moonlit eves,
  Its harvest time has come,
We pluck away the frosted leaves
  And bear the treasure home.

But let the good old crop adorn
  The hills our fathers trod;
Still let us, for his golden corn,
  Send up our thanks to God!

—FROM *"The Corn-Song"*
BY JOHN GREENLEAF WHITTIER

Once More the Liberal Year
Laughs Out

Once more the liberal year laughs out
  O'er richer stores than gems or gold;
Once more with harvest song and shout
  Is nature's bloodless triumph told.

O favors every year made new!
  Of gifts with rain and sunshine sent!
The bounty overruns our due,
  The fulness shames our discontent.

Who murmurs at his lot today?
  Who scorns his native fruit and bloom?
Or sighs for dainties far away,
  Beside the bounteous board of home?

And let these altars, wreathed with flowers
  And piled with fruits, awake again
Thanksgivings for the golden hours,
  The early and the latter rain!

—FROM *"For an Autumn Festival"*
BY JOHN GREENLEAF WHITTIER

Land of Plenty

He had lost count of the days since he had escaped from the jail in Philadelphia. Running away from the jailer, old Issachar Davids, had been easy. There were a score or more of orphans like himself there, some of them newcomers waiting for the court orders as to their indentures, others bound-out boys. He, William Aberdeen, had served a hard master for a while; then he had run away. They always locked up runaways. But the jail was poorly guarded, and anyway no one cared much what became of the children, so he had escaped and run away again. Hiding in the forest that lined the Boot Road out from Philadelphia, Will wondered if he had made a mistake.

Peering out between the great trees that shaded the Boot Road, he watched for a clear space in the traffic to allow him to trudge on again. For a rough way the road was well traveled. Women riding on horseback carried butter, eggs, and chickens in baskets, and butterpails hung at the horses' sides. Rude wagons, their clumsy wheels made of sliced logs bound with iron, rumbled along loaded with apples, grain, potatoes, squealing pigs, and cabbages. Other

wagons, returning from the markets of Philadelphia, held purchases:
molasses in fat brown jugs, sugar loaves, tea, spices for gingerbread
and cake, even blue chinaware and lengths of damask and silk.
Everybody was about his own business; no one noticed the ragged
boy, thin and frightened, who stuffed his mouth with another handful of wild berries and shrugged deeper into his worn jacket. Even
the smell of that lush land made a lad hungry, especially when he
had been walking and hiding and sleeping in the chill October woods
for days.

It looked like the Promised Land his Granny had told him it would be that day when the "Soul Seller" had stopped at their cottage in far-away Glasgow to ask for Will.

"You won't really be sold," Granny had told Will. "This man arranges for likely workers to sail to America free of cost. 'Redemptioners,' they are called. When you get there, you will be put to service to pay the captain for your passage. It's just an arrangement, Will. I am sore pained to have you go." She wiped her eyes on her apron.

Will had looked about the bare spaces of the cottage, no peat, no meal. "Then, when I'm through being a 'Redemptioner,' can I send for you? When I'm a rich man, all on my own?"

"So I hope," she had said.

Two months of mast-high storms when he and the rest had been ill in the steerage! His homesickness! The stern master-carpenter of Philadelphia who had bought his services. His stupid handling of precious tools because he had never held any but a hoe or shovel before. No doubt he had deserved the scoldings, the beatings. And there had been his vast longing to see the land. The valley he was wandering through lay like a great horn of plenty curving between the Blue Hills and spilling its riches, corn and wheat, flax and hemp, grapes, plums and peaches, for whoever wanted them. The pastures were white with sheep and tuneful with the tinkling of cow bells. The black earth, Will could see, waited only the turn of the plow to give out its wealth. He would make a living now for Granny, he thought, as he plodded on.

The countryside there in Chester County, about fifteen miles from Philadelphia, fairly smelled and tasted of the farming plenty that was laying the prosperity of our nation. Cress from a little brook beside the road, some sweet chestnuts, a spicy raw turnip, more berries, and dropped apples gave Will his breakfast. Lifting his eyes to the hills colored gold and scarlet as the maples turned, watching a boy his own age guiding a great plow between a field of cornshucks and pumpkins getting ready for the sowing of winter wheat, he gathered hope and new assurance.

He came to a ferry across a creek before he realized it. There was no bridge, only a great flat ferryboat that the ferryman poled and rowed from shore to shore. A wagon with two passengers waited there for the boat which was slowly crossing from the little settlement of Upland that spread like a toy village beyond the water.

One of the men wore a red greatcoat, a brown jacket, a pair of good leather breeches with brass buttons and strings at the knees, a speckled shirt, good shoes, and a tall hat tilted over his tow wig. A bright silk handkerchief stuck out of his pocket, but his dejected looks belied his fine clothes.

"You *will* run away, and wearing your master's best clothes!" Will heard the man's companion saying sternly. "Well, then you shall be returned and an extra term added to your indenture."

Will hid behind a post on the wharf. The first man, he realized, was a runaway "Redemptioner" like himself, except that Will had not taken anything from his master. The other man was his captor— a "Soul Seller," Will guessed. The ferry bumped into the landing and emptied itself of passengers, bags of corn and hops, barrels of apples, and sacks of potatoes. The "Redemptioner's" captor started to bargain for a passage to Upland, but the ferryman shook his head.

"You'll have to wait for the next trip," he explained. "You can ford farther up the shallows."

"May I get aboard?" asked Will. "I haven't any money, but I've strong arms for rowing."

The ferryman considered this as he put on cargo. "Well, come aboard. You can try a few strokes. I haven't had time to read my *American Weekly* yet."

They pushed off, and Will strained at the clumsy oars as the ferryman, a poor but eager reader, spelled aloud the news items. One made Will tremble.

"The year 1760. . . . Wanted: The return of a runaway servant boy named William Aberdeen. He is a lively boy and healthy, of about thirteen years. . . ."

Will pulled out his handkerchief, large, spun and woven by Granny and plainly marked W. A. He mopped his forehead. The sweat came not from the rowing, but from fear. The ferryman looked keenly at him over his spectacles. Then he chuckled.

"And where do ye think ye'll be running to, Will Aberdeen?" he said. "Ye may help me unload when we get to Upland, but next trip there may be a 'Soul Seller' on your tracks if I'm not mistaken. I'll not report ye, but ye'd better run for it!"

As the boat scraped the Upland wharf, Will could see the wagon with its doleful passenger moving toward the shallows on the other side. The little town of Upland with its cobbled streets, tidy stone houses half hidden by trees, late flowering gardens and hedges, gave few hiding places. Will hastily stacked boxes and bales on the wharf for the ferryman, and then ran, ran, through the village.

Presently he left the streets behind and came to a country road. Here the houses were fairly dwarfed by the barns built of red and blue stone, set among great oaks and willows, old apple and pear trees and boxwood. The sound of threshing, the barking of sheep dogs, the tap, tap of apples—pointed Sheepnoses, Newton Pippins of deep yellow shaded to rose, Pound Sweets and snowy-flaked Russets—dropping into barrels drew him on. The smell of boiling cider to be filled with quartered apples to make apple butter; the

sweet breath of the cattle; the scents of quince preserving, of jelly making, of sauer kraut, were tempting. This was the land of plenty, he thought, of which Granny had told him. The earth was bursting with goodness for the stalwart settlers who had braved three thousand miles of sea, from Ireland, Scotland, England, and Germany, to plant it.

"Let a lad find safety here!" he prayed. But the sound of creaking wagon wheels brought his heart to his mouth. It was the "Soul Seller" and his catch, rattling along.

He shivered in the warm October noontime. He felt as if "runaway" were written across his sweating forehead. Just then the biggest barn of all loomed on the horizon in front of him. He dashed through the orchard and inside the wide open door.

It seemed as if the people who had raised the great stones of which this barn was made had loved the building. From the half-circular hole for the swallows up near the gables to the shining horseshoe above and the painting of a wheat field on the door, the barn stood for comfort. Will felt dwarfed as he stood in the center of the vast lower floor where great Percherons and a herd of cattle could be comfortably bedded, where bins were stored with winter vegetables and grain. He looked up, up to the high loft full of sweet-smelling clover. He could hide up there, climb the ladder to safety, he thought, but a slight sound on the sunny side of the door caught his ear. Peering furtively outside he saw the girl.

She wore a close-fitting white cap that could not hide her shining yellow braids, but her long gray dress and white apron told that she was a Pennsylvania Quaker. Will had heard of them, peaceful, industrious farming folk but, he had been told, unfailing strict. He noticed, though, that this girl wore a bright string of coral beads. That was encouraging. The sound he had heard was made by the

corn she was shucking, as it dropped into the bright pan in her lap.
A long smooth husking peg of hickory wood was fastened to her
wrist by an eel skin thong. Her hands flew as she husked and then
pegged off the yellow kernels. But she, too, realized that there was
someone near. She set down the pan on the sturdy resting-bench of
weathered pine where she had been working in the sunshine and
came over to the door.

"Don't send me away!" Will begged. "Wait until the 'Soul Seller' passes!"

She was quick to understand. "Take courage," she said. "Thee will be safe here. This is a farm of Friends, and, anyway, those wicked men who pick up runaways are now outlawed. What would he want of thee?" she went on curiously.

"I ran away," he told her, hanging his head. "I was bound to John Walker of Chester County, but I couldn't abide it. I have been on the road for many days, walking, sleeping in the wilds—."

She laid a kind hand on his ragged sleeve. "Thee must come outside and sit on the resting-bench while I go and speak to my father. It will not take long. Do not fear. I will soon be with you again. I am Magdalena Wade. We are among the first of the Friends to settle in Upland. Thee is in good hands." She ran across to the stone house beside the barn, set within a garden in which great purple autumn crocuses and rosy asters bloomed.

The resting-bench, built on four sturdy oak pegs and placed beside the barn where it was warm almost all day, was surrounded by feathery clucking hens. A sheep dog laid his head on Will's lap, and the fat barn cat jumped up and curled purring beside him. Will felt surprisingly contented, although he knew that he would be returned to jail. A land so rich in food and good farming must, somehow, take him into its peace, he thought, but he could not see how.

He was so lost in that dream that Magdalena had to touch his shoulder. She held a wooden bowl of steaming meat stew. In a basket on her arm were thickly buttered bread, grapes, pears, and seed cookies.

"Eat," she said.

Not until bowl and basket were empty did Magdalena speak. Then, "Come and I will show thee our home," she said.

"If thee were a witch and came around on All-Hallow Eve," she pointed to the horseshoe above the barn door, "and tried to enter our barn to cast spells, thee would have to turn back and count all the footprints made by that shoe before doing us harm. And the picture on the barn door is also to frighten witches. Here is the bake oven. We made the bricks. It will bake two-score loaves and pies at one baking. Here is Mother."

They looked in the dairy where a woman dressed like Magdalena was printing yellow butter pats with wooden molds carved in designs of a tulip, a swan, a bench of wheat and a cow. She smiled at them but turned back to her work.

"Your father?" Will asked fearfully. "Now," he thought, as they came to the door of the house where the sun made the many-paned windows twinkle, "I shall receive sentence."

"Here is Father," Magdalena led the way into the best room, neat and plainly furnished in pine except for books and the carved cherry-wood highboy beside which her father stood. He, too, wore gray, except for a gaily flowered waistcoat and the silver buckles on his shoes. He looked through gold-bowed spectacles at the boy.

"Magdalena, my daughter, tells me thee has done wrong. Thee broke a contract and ran away."

"I did, sir, I did wrong." Will, so full of good food, felt it a comfort to confess. "I was afraid of my master and I was homesick. Now, shall I have to be returned to jail?" he hardly whispered the dreaded word.

There was a short silence. Then Friend Wade lifted his leather money pouch from the highboy, jingling the coins and untying the thong that bound it.

"As I see it, thee is sorry for the fault, and Master Walker we know as a hard master. There is a statute on the books of the

Court that a 'Redemptioner' has the right to change masters under certain circumstances. We Friends need help on the land. Would thee, providing I pay the ship's captain for thy passage, like to work out thy debt here? Magdalena has just put in a strong plea for such an arrangement."

Would he! He felt Magdalena's hand holding his again in happiness. He bowed to his new master; no, his friend. "I will do my best, sir, I want to plant and harvest. I know I can do that."

"And when thy term is over, thee will be a son of our house," Magdalena told him. "We shall give thee a horse on thy coming of age, young and of good mettle; one raised on our farm."

"Stay thy tongue, Magdalena," her father said. "Thy heart is running away with thee. But," he turned to Will. "I am not saying that I might not put such a colt into thy hands for breaking. Thy term with me as a 'Redemptioner' will not be too long. Thy debt will soon be redeemed. Now take this sunny afternoon as a holiday, go nutting or apple-picking. I shall have to think of what excuse I must write to Issachar Davids about one jail breaker named William Aberdeen. Be off with thee, for real work begins at sunrise tomorrow."

"I thank you, sir. I will work hard. I like the land—" he hesitated.

"Well?" his master asked.

"I left Granny back in Glasgow, sir, quite poor and old. I took ship thinking I could make a home for her one day."

"And why not?" Magdalena said. "We have one of the best resting-benches in all Upland. Thy Granny can come to us until thee has thine own farm. Come out and play. All is well with thee."

—CAROLYN SHERWIN BAILEY

A Bow to Thanksgiving
*(A true story of a famous silversmith
and an early Southern Thanksgiving)*

On his way to the waterfront Charles stopped at the Sign of
the Silver Coffee Pot to greet his friend Thomas Sparrow. Thomas
had been an apprentice of Charles's father for some years, working
faithfully at the Sign of Crown and Dial which was a combination
of silversmith shop, inn, and home to the Faris family. But now
Thomas had his own silversmith shop. He was not much older
than Charles, who was fourteen, through school, and sure that the
last thing he wanted to do was to settle down in Annapolis for the
rest of his life, following his famous father's craft.

The day was brisk if warm for late autumn. The thrilling scent
of a sea wind, salty and alluring as the Severn brought it shoreward,
came to Charles. It was the year 1779, and a brig bringing some no-
tables from farther south for their winter in Annapolis had weighed
anchor down at the wharf. Charles was on his way there to see the
unloading, the cargo, and the strangers.

Charles, having grown up in the town, had a mind to go to

sea. There was a large family at home. He would not, he thought, be missed. There were his brothers, William, older, and young Hiram, now ten years old. There were his sisters, Nancy and Abigail. There was even a Faris baby, St. John. All the older boys had had some training as silversmiths, but Charles had taken his work lightly and developed little skill.

The tinkle of Tom Sparrow's hammers, the glint of the sun on his silverware, the small anvil, and his row of shining tools had attracted Charles. He stopped by the open door. Tom called to him.

"Come in, Charles Faris. How is it that you are out strolling

when the rest of us work?" As he spoke, Tom held up a gleaming silver porringer upon which he was welding a delicately designed leaf handle with a thumb hold on which he had engraved the owner's monogram.

Charles leaned against the doorway. "I've done my chores for the day," he told Tom. "Milked the red and white cow, watered and curried the horses, wound the musical clock that stands in the hall. Also I have copied out the week's bills. We expect guests at the inn today, so work started early."

Tom laid his porringer gently on a bench and began stirring

the silver shillings and pence that were melting in his skillet. He consulted a drawing of a silver teapot he had made, pear shaped to hold the heat, slender at the top for beauty, decorated with chased garlands, and having a beaded rat tail for a better grip on the handle. Every new piece of silverware at that time was an adventure to the maker, who studied its use and then combined the shape and the decorations for its purpose. And Thomas Sparrow had benefited by his training. Master Faris, Charles's father, ranked as one of the greatest artists in silver in Maryland.

"Don't you wish you could do as fine work as this?" Thomas asked rather smugly.

Charles kicked the door. "Yes? he scoffed. "After reading up on navigation with the Reverend Jonathan Boucher here at his school, you would have me apprentice myself to my father, one of the hardest taskmasters in Annapolis? You know the oath of the apprentice. Seven years' work with only board and clothing for pay. Moral supervision! The apprentice obeys and keeps the master's secrets."

"But the silversmith ranks with the best of artists," Tom reminded him. "The term of apprenticeship is worth it."

"I should be twenty-one years old when I finished!" Charles sighed. "Let William or Hy learn silversmithing. I'm for adventure. I might take passage for the Canaries this very day as cabin boy."

He turned, but a shadow fell across the threshold of the shop. A foreign scent mingled with the sea breeze. A soft voice drifted over the silence.

"I beg of you not to take ship hastily, young man," the voice urged him. "I assure you that the voyage between the Islands and Maryland is far from pleasant."

Looking at the stranger, a pretty dark-haired girl close to his own age, very stylishly dressed, Charles suddenly felt alien. His stock, he remembered, was not clean. His tongue felt thick. But the girl came to his rescue.

"My name is Judith, and my father is the captain of the brig *Mary Lee,* this morning anchored. I have no mother and have been learning French and the social arts in New Orleans. Our ship is laid up here in the Severn for repairs, and my father and I shall stay at an inn of whose fine hospitality we have heard, the Sign of the Crown and Dial. I precede the captain to see if I like that inn. My luggage is outside in a barrow. But may I rest a moment? I still feel the rolling of the brig." The little lady seated herself on a chair in the shop.

But her indisposition was short. She pierced the shop's glittering store with eager blue eyes. She moved from one piece of silver to another, exclaiming, holding them up to the light.

"A baby's rattle with two little bells in the shape of bluebells. A creamer so delicate in shape that it puts to shame the rich cream it will hold. A comfit dish with a pattern of flowers the bee loves and trailing vines for the handle. A standing salt with hooks for napkins and legs that it may stand firm in the middle of the table for hospitality." Judith stood in admiration before a massive teapot.

"If our table might have that teapot with a creamer, sugar bowl, and tongs to match, we would be the envy of all our friends!"

"I am sorry, miss, but my ware is all ordered and paid for," Thomas Sparrow said. "I weighed the silver shillings and sixpence that went into that teapot, melted them down, designed and wrought the service for a resident of our town."

"Then make the resident of this little country town another tea service," urged Judith, and pouted when Thomas shook his head.

Charles looked admiringly at the pretty girl. He felt a desire to impress her. "My father taught this young man everything he knows," he told her. "He also keeps the inn at the Sign of the Crown and Dial, the one for which you are bound. It will give you excellent accommodations. I," Charles finished with a flourish, "myself, will make you such a silver tea service as Annapolis, or New Orleans either, has never seen. Come with me now." He motioned for Judith to follow him, pretending not to see Thomas Sparrow's amused grin.

Outside Charles gave direction to the sailor who waited with the wheelbarrow that held Judith's hide trunk studded with brass nails and her gay hat box. The air was still sweet with late roses in the gardens and the perfume of the box hedges. The red brick of the houses, the blue water, and the life along the narrow streets, Chancery Lane, Carroll Alley, and the others that radiated like the hubs of a wheel from the ancient grounds of old Saint Anne's Church, entranced Judith. They jostled wealth and fashion; gentlemen whose curling hair fell over their shoulders so that they carried their plumed hats under their arms for vanity, ladies whose pyramids of hair surmounted by feathers and billowing brocades, almost filled the lanes.

"My father is an all-round man," Charles explained, concerned lest Judith ask him what his own training in silversmithing had been. "He is expert in the making of musical clocks. He designs and builds furniture. He grows rare tulips, he keeps the inn well, and he pulls teeth."

Judith gasped, but not a Charles's words. Coming toward them was an odd figure of a man. He stopped, here at a gateway, there at an open door, gossiping with the neighbors, peering into the coaches that brought the winter visitors to Annapolis. A ring of

great jingling clock keys in his hand showed that he was making the rounds of those homes where his timepieces chimed and tinkled, but the news of the morning, as always, delayed him. As a sign that he was a Quaker by faith, he wore no wig, and his braided queue, tied with a black bow, swung along his back like one of his pendulums. His worn brown coat and short clothes were faded, but a row of big silver buttons decorated the coat, and the buckles on his shoes were of finely chased silver. The spectacles, tilted down over his sharp nose, had silver bows.

"Who is that odd little man?" Judith asked.

The man now stopped in front of them, greeting Charles and looking at his companion with interest.

"That," said Charles, looking greatly embarrassed, "is Pa."

Judith curtsied. "Your son here is going to settle my father and myself for a few weeks at your inn, sir. My father is laying up his brig the *Mary Lee*, at the careenage here for repairs. Your son has promised to employ his time until we leave in the making of a silver tea service which I shall take down to New Orleans as a souvenir of my visit."

Charles felt cold sweat beneath his stock. His father's eyes were two swordpoints aimed at him. Finally, wrinkles of amusement began to soften his face. "So!" he agreed. "Well, you will find two lively girls of our own, Nancy and Abigail, to make you welcome. And I doubt not that my eldest son William will take you strolling while our skilled silversmith here is putting in the time necessary for the making of your silverware. Come, it is time I were home. We have a reputation at the Sign of the Crown and Dial for hospitality. The best entertainment and the kindest usage. Gentlefolk meet with polite treatment and hay and oats for their horses. And here we are!"

Charles was silent as Master Faris led them into the garden of

the home, shop, and inn near the church. Four-square, shaded by a
grove of holly trees trimmed in the shape of sugar loaves, the garden
still in bloom with wall flowers, snapdragon, and phlox, the comfort of it charmed sea-faring Judith. Charles's sisters, Nancy and
Abigail, gay in their bright calico frocks and ribbon-trimmed mob
caps, greeted the stranger. Indoors, the neat common room of the
inn with its long dining table, the tall clock made by Master Faris
to play the hours in music, the comfortable rooms with chintz curtains and soft feather ticks on the four poster beds, pleased Judith.

"Make yourself at home," Master Faris told her. "When you
have changed your finery for a plainer dress, the girls will let you
share their preparations for Thanksgiving. They are sugaring the
comfits and stoning the fruit. Each tenth raisin goes into a cook's
mouth."

"Thanksgiving?" Judith looked surprised.

"A fortnight hence," Master Faris told her. "Not the day set
apart by law for church-going such as they decree in New England,
but our Southern day of willing thankfulness for whatever good has
come to us during the past year. Our first Thanksgiving Day was in
1698, when the governor of Maryland decreed a day of thankfulness for the end of the plague that had come upon our people that
year. Since then, we keep Thanksgiving Day when and as we like."

"I must get the gammon of bacon Mother needs," Charles suggested, putting off his moment of doom.

"Ah, no," his father said, "you will need all your spare time for
making that tea service for our guest. Go you into the shop and
begin at once. Mistress Judith will drop in from time to time no
doubt to see your progress." His father's glance was amused. Charles
dragged his feet for shame as he entered the shop of the most skilled
silversmith of the colonies.

A piece of hand-wrought silver at that time was both art and craftsmanship. Master Faris' book of skillfully drawn designs lay on his bench in the shop. The flowers he used in the designs marked the drawings as Charles turned the pages. There were designs for a silver coffee pot, a tankard, some tea cans, a tea kettle, teapot, a widely curving bowl, a soup ladle. Master Faris had favored the tulips he raised in making the designs, but the classic lines of the acanthus leaf and such fancy touches as little animals, a sheep or a dog, for thumb holds, an acorn or pineapple for a cover knob, and pear, melon, and apple shapes for teapots, showed his versatility as an artist.

The shop, whose windows looked out toward the garden and let in the pleasant twitterings of pigeons and martins, had the best supply of tools in all Maryland. Charles touched them: the small anvils, the melting skillets, the specially formed vise, punches, scales, hammers of all kinds, tongs, wood-sinking blocks, and shears. Some of the silver was chased. Other pieces had hammered patterns. Charles sat down on the bench at last. The tools, the gleaming metal, or some unexplained impulse had given him the ambition to be a real silversmith. Whether it was for Judith's sake or for the sake of his father, he could not have explained.

But Charles's knowledge of the craft was superficial. He could not even draw very well. His head drooped into his hands.

But as Charles grew more and more discouraged, a shadow crossed the threshold. His father touched his shoulder.

"Have a hope, Charlie," he said. "There is a piece of work waiting for you that I find tedious in spite of its pretty results." He brought a silver bowl, deep and wide, smooth and unadorned.

"Place it so in this block," he said, "and beat it with this small hammer."

Charles began the tedious work. The silver was tough, and the hammer marks almost too small to be seen at first. But as he beat the surface day after day, Charles saw a transformation. The hammered silver began to reflect the light. As a diamond glitters with its facets, absorbing and sending forth rays, so the bowl became radiant. It brightened the shop. It needed no other decoration than that the hammer gave it. It would shine as brightly by candlelight as in the sunshine of the shop.

Almost every day Judith, wearing one of Nancy's aprons, looked in on the young silversmith. She clasped her hands in front of the bowl, her breath coming in gasps.

"Beautiful, Charles!" she said. "Much nicer than what I had selected. It shall hold the fruits in the center of the thanksgiving table. I can see it filled with apples and pears, grapes and persimmons. Such a dinner as we are planning: wild turkey and sugarcured ham, terrapin, duck and venison, plum pudding, preserves, blancmange, fruit cake, nuts and comfits. And when we leave, it will cheer my father on his long voyages standing on the mess table of the brig."

"Charles has the makings of a fine silversmith in his hands," said Mr. Faris. "We shall see. We shall see."

There was plenty on that long ago thanksgiving board of Maryland. The table in the common room of the Crown and Dial glittered with silver: handwrought spoons and knives, the soup tureens, the tea service, the great standing salt, the gravy boat and ladle, the silver mug. At the head of the table Master Faris glowed with pride in his handwork. At the foot, Mistress Faris wore the silver lace he had made for her. Up and down the sides of the table the Faris boys and girls, Judith, and the guests ate heartily, their good food tasting better for the beauty of the service.

"We have a special cause for thankfulness," announced Master Faris when the blazing plum pudding was brought in, and with it a glowing silver bowl of fruit. "We have a second silversmith in the Faris family. Stand up, Charles, and take a bow. Not all workers can hammer so well."

Judith was the loudest in the hand-clapping for Charles. The silver bowl would go to sea with Judith, but the touch of the silver remained with Charles. It had fired his heart.

And so years later, Charles became one of the famous Faris silversmiths. The Metropolitan Museum in New York shows us Charles's handsome silverware. In a Baltimore museum we may see a delicately curved creamer with three well-balanced legs and a sauce boat with a design of shells that Master William Faris wrought. And Master Faris' yellowing book of designs for silver, the only one that has come down to us, opens its pages to the dried tulip markers that he put in—perhaps the very year that Judith spent Thanksgiving at the Sign of the Crown and Dial.

—CAROLYN SHERWIN BAILEY

The Feast-time of the Year

This is the feast-time of the year,
When plenty pours her wine of cheer,
And even humble boards may spare
To poorer poor a kindly share.
While bursting barns and granaries know
A richer, fuller overflow.
And they who dwell in golden ease
Blest without toil, yet toil to please.

—AUTHOR UNKNOWN

Land of the Pilgrims' Pride

Silvy came home from school humming a tune. It was a tune which had been ringing in her ears since the singing of "America" had closed the school session of this afternoon before Thanksgiving Day. The words were racing through Silvy's mind, partly because they were familiar and she loved them, but mostly because of what Loretta had said.

Her warm red hood, knit by Gran'maw, was tied securely under her chin and made her brown cheeks look more plump than usual. Silvy's dark eyes were thoughtful. Something was troubling her, for she didn't feel the crisp autumn wind nor smell the scent of dry leaves burning.

The troublesome thoughts had started when she was singing with all her heart, "Land where my fathers died, Land of the pilgrims' pride. . . ." Loretta had whispered something to the girl next to her; then they looked at Silvy and laughed. It made Silvy's voice waver, but she went right on, doing her best to "Let Freedom ring," because she was full of the spirit of the play the school was giving, about the first harvest festival of the Pilgrims in Plymouth Colony.

176

Silvy had heard the story before, had studied it in her history lesson. But seeing it dramatized by older boys and girls made Silvy feel herself one with those settlers of the bleak New England shore who gave thanks to God for their first real harvest and celebrated their good fortune with a feast in which the Indians shared. These people were part of her inheritance as an American, Silvy thought happily.

In the cloakroom, when they were getting their coats and hats to go home, Loretta told Silvy, "The Pilgrim Fathers were not your forefathers. They came from England and Holland. Your ancestors were slaves in the South, who came from Africa."

Silvy had known that, but it had seemed that if you were an American, all those first American colonists had given you something of themselves that you could be proud of. And it made no difference what race you belonged to or whether you had a dark skin.

Silvy looked back steadily at Loretta even though her spirit drooped. She did want to claim a link to the Pilgrim Fathers, because she saw something in them that she wanted in herself. She couldn't explain this to Loretta, so Silvy answered, "Yes, I know." Loretta turned away, looking a little uncomfortable.

As Silvy climbed the stairs to the apartment where she lived with Mom, Gran'maw, and her brother Ralph, she still hummed her tune. The humming sounded angry, for she was feeling defiant. She made up her mind she would adopt the Pilgrim Fathers as ancestors no matter what anyone said.

This afternoon she had seen, in a play, daring and courage in men, women, and children which finally won for them a home in the new land after a whole year of struggle and suffering. This little company had crossed a stormy sea with a song of freedom in their hearts. Silvy was hearing that same song, and she wanted the steadfast faith of the Pilgrims in her own heart.

Silvy seldom found anyone but Gran'maw when she came home from school. Mom worked in a department store, and Ralph delivered orders for the grocer on the corner after school. Today Gran'maw was scrubbing the tiny kitchen. Warm odors in the air promised a tasty thanksgiving dinner next day. Silvy sniffed appreciatively. Gran'maw looked tired as she gave one last swab to the floor and pulled herself to her feet with the help of a chair. She did not see Silvy until she wiped the steam from her glasses and put them on again.

"Thought I heard someone coming up the stairs," she said, "but it sounded too heavy-footed for you, Silvy. Sounded like stomping up. Anything wrong?" she asked, noticing the pucker between Silvy's eyes.

Silvy perched herself on the edge of a chair. Her eyes were on Gran'maw, but she hadn't heard Gran'maw's question. Silvy was seeing Gran'maw with a Puritan cap and a white starched kerchief. Instead of her blue gingham apron she wore a full white one like the girls in the play. Gran'maw had been washing the floor of a Plymouth log house. The good cooking odors came from wild turkeys, caught in the woods and roasting in an oven at the back of the huge fireplace.

"What you staring at?" Gran'maw asked, sinking into her shabby rocking chair, her hands cupped over her aching knees.

"Nothing," said Silvy, recalling her thoughts to the present scene with a start. Then she added, "We had a nice play at school, and I was thinking about it."

"You were sort of frowning," said Gran'maw. "What was that play about, Silvy?"

"The first Thanksgiving Day in America," answered Silvy, "when the Pilgrims thanked God their crops had turned out good. They made a big festival and invited the Indian chief with his braves."

Gran'maw rested her head against the back of her chair and said, "I've heard about those Pilgrims and the Indians. I never had much chance to go to school like you're doing so I forgot a lot I used to know, but I reckon people have been thanking God for something since the world began. The Good Book is full of it, and that was written long ago." She began to rock as she crooned softly, "O give thanks unto the Lord, for He is good. For His mercy endureth forever."

Silvy thought that Gran'maw always had her answers straight from the Good Book. But now Silvy wanted to talk about the play, so she raised her voice to keep Gran'maw from drifting into a nap. "The Pilgrims made a very special time of their thanksgiving. Shall I tell you about it?"

Opening her eyes and sitting up straight, Gran'maw said, "What you shouting for? Anyway, your Mom better not find us talking, with a bucket of dirty water in the middle of the floor, when she comes. Put your books and coat and cap where they belong while I put the bucket away. Then tell me anything you want to. I'll be glad to sit awhile."

Silvy put her things away and changed to an older skirt and sweater, then went back to the kitchen. She watched Gran'maw lift two steaming pies from the oven. Together they gloated over the crisp brown crust of one and the satiny top skin, speckled with nutmeg, of the other pie.

"That's mince," said Gran'maw proudly, pointing to the pie with the crust. "I made the mincemeat myself as a surprise for your Mom. The other's sweet potato. That recipe I learned in the South when I was a girl." Gran'maw's eyes had a faraway look.

Silvy was sure no one could make sweet potato pie like Gran'maw. She thought there must be some special cooking magic in this recipe from the South which Gran'maw always spoke about when she baked a pie.

"Gran'maw," asked Silvy, "do you like the South better than the North?"

Gran'maw shut the oven door before she answered. Then she said, "You talk as though North and South were two different countries. It's all the same place—America. I reckon you like it best where your home is, and my home is here with your Mom and you and Ralph. But down there," Gran'maw's eyes were dreamy again, "is where our folks came from, and I remember lots of nice things about Virginia."

"Where our folks came from." That, thought Silvy, was what Loretta had said, only she had not made it sound so nice. Loretta made you feel ashamed; Gran'maw made you feel proud, because you could see that was the way she felt about her folks in the South. Still—there were the Pilgrims whom Silvy wanted for her ancestors. "Gran'maw, may I tell you about the play now?"

"Yes, I'd like to hear it." Gran'maw settled herself in the rocker and stretched her knees with a sigh of relief. Gran'maw was really Mom's grandmother, so she must be pretty old, but Silvy had good times with her.

Silvy didn't sit down, but ran hither and thither showing Gran'-maw how the stage was set, and acting out many of the parts. Gran'maw followed Silvy closely, giving expressions of approval from time to time. They both laughed when Silvy got the old feather duster to show how the Indian Chief and his braves looked.

"What days those must have been!" said Gran'maw. "No big cities, only a few white people and the woods full of Indians. But they all seemed friendly together, eating thanksgiving dinner and playing games. What happened to all the Indians?"

"I don't think they were always friends because after a while the Pilgrims were afraid of them. The pictures in the back of my history book don't look so good, Gran'maw."

"Well anyway," said Gran'maw, "the Pilgrims were good people and brave. They didn't forget who had been taking care of them all the while. I like that part of the play where they all got together to praise and worship God."

"Those are my ancestors, Gran'maw," said Silvy with pride.

"Your what?" asked Gran'maw, in surprise. "Your what?"

"My ancestors," repeated Silvy firmly, "like it says 'Land where my fathers died, Land of the Pilgrims' pride.' I'm an American, aren't I?"

"Sure you are," said Gran'maw, "but when you talk about the Pilgrims being your ancestors you haven't just the right word."

"Gran'maw, I know my folks came from the South, but I'm going to adopt the Pilgrims—like our neighbor Mrs. Jackson adopted George when he was a baby. Why can't I adopt the Pilgrims for ancestors?"

Gran'maw answered slowly. "Ancestors are something you can't pick and choose like that. They're in the past and you can't budge them. They gave you your life, and their blood is in your veins whether you like it or not." Gran'maw stopped rocking and took Silvy's hand. "Your real ancestors were good people. They had a part in making America a great country. You don't need be ashamed of them, honey."

"I didn't mean it like that," Silvy replied. How could she make Gran'maw understand that she wanted that small piece of America which was herself to reach back into the beginnings of her country's history and be joined in spirit with those first brave pioneers who came in search of freedom? "It isn't the blood of the Pilgrims I've been thinking about, but the kind of people they were—what they did and how they felt. I want to be like them."

Gran'maw looked relieved. "There certainly isn't any harm in that. But don't go around saying the Pilgrims are your ancestors because people won't understand, and someone is likely to hurt your feelings."

"I'll keep it to myself, Gran'maw," she promised. "It will be a secret for us two."

They had lots of secrets together because Mom worked all day. Ralph, who was fourteen, didn't pay much attention; and thought Silvy, who was nine, was a "funny kid." Gran'maw was someone you could count on to understand, and she was always home.

Pushing her spectacles on top of her head as she often did when thinking back into the past, Gran'maw said, "I know of an American Negro boy who was born on a plantation in Virginia two years before I was. He worked in a coal mine and went to school at night. But when he was about thirteen, he made his way five hundred miles to a big school at Hampton, Virginia. He worked there as a janitor until he finished his studies and was graduated. Then he was made a teacher and trained lots of boys and girls to be good Americans. At last he became head of a school he started himself at Tuskegee, Alabama."

"That's where Pop came from," cried Silvy, "and you're telling about Booker T. Washington. His name was the same as our first American President."

"Yes, Silvy. And another Negro boy, George Washington Carver, was born five years later in Missouri. His parents were slaves, too. He wanted to study farming and find the best ways to grow good crops, so he worked at Tuskegee and found out that too much cotton growing made soil thin and poor. It needed other crops to make it fertile again. He discovered that planting peanuts and sweet potatoes would do this. Then George Washington Carver set to work making other things out of peanuts and sweet potatoes." Gran'maw shook her finger to emphasize what she said, "He made three hundred different products out of these two."

Silvy's eyes were round with astonishment. "How could he make so many things out of just peanuts and sweet potatoes?"

"You thought they were only what you buy in a bag, or make

into a pie?" asked Gran'maw. "So did lots of people. It took years of studying, and it was all done for the good of other people. When George Washington Carver died a few years ago, he had given all the money he had saved to make it possible for others to carry on his work."

Silvy's eyes were on the sweet potato pie as though expecting any number of items to pop out of it. "What all did he make out of sweet potatoes and peanuts, Gran'maw?"

"I can't rightly remember, Silvy, but there was flour, vinegar, and molasses made from sweet potatoes, and it seems to me he got cheese, milk, coffee, and soap from peanuts. Those are just a few."

"Tell me more about folks you knew in the South," said Silvy, making herself comfortable.

With a smile playing across her face, Gran'maw talked about the cotton fields, the rice fields, the tobacco fields. "The Negroes came from hot countries and could work in the sun better than people from northern lands. If it hadn't been for them, the South would never have been the 'land of cotton.'"

"Our people did help build America, Gran'maw, didn't they?"

"They did!" Gran'maw answered proudly. "They've been part of America ever since the settlers came to Virginia, and that—so they used to tell me down there—was before the Pilgrims landed at Plymouth." Gran'maw looked to see how Silvy would take this, and she noticed the mince pie cooling on the table.

"Silvy, America's kind of like a mince pie. Lots of things go into the making of it. If there were only apples, it would be an apple pie; or just raisins, a raisin pie. But when you mix in all your ingredients, you won't find any pie to come near it for tastiness. There's a lot of work preparing it, but nothing can beat that rich flavor of mince pie."

Gran'maw rocked, enjoying this thought. "Silvy, if only one kind of people had settled in America, it wouldn't be the country it is, but just a copy of the place they came from. People of all races and faiths have brought a bit of their own kind of life into America. Each brought a special flavor, and the mixture is something you can't equal anywhere else in the world."

Silvy was thinking silently of the Pilgrims in the North, the Virginians in the South, and of the people of her own race. All these men, women, and children from faraway shores had learned to love America and call it home. They were different from each other, thought Silvy, yet all alike in living and working together in a new land.

Yes, the Pilgrims were proud of the America they knew, and the southern settlers were proud of their home in the South, and the Negroes were proud of their part in planting and gathering crops which fed and clothed the growing nation. Silvy thought of the Indians, in America before anyone else, and how they shared what they had with the Pilgrims and helped them plant their first corn. She thought of Ah Loo, her Chinese friend at school, and of David, the sad-eyed refugee boy from Europe. Gran'maw was right. America was like a mince pie, all kinds of ingredients blended into one grand, appetizing dish.

Just then Mom came home. "My, what do I smell?" She went to the table and smacked her lips. "Gran'maw, where did you get all the materials you put into your mincemeat? I don't give you much money for extras."

"Ralph was in the secret," Gran'maw laughed. "He worked overtime and took his pay in things we couldn't buy."

Mom looked pleased. Silvy looked through the doorway into the living room at Pop's medal. It had been presented to Ralph in

memory of Pop's bravery when his ship was sunk by a submarine and Pop lost his life saving other men. Ralph had not been a very good boy before this medal was given him by the government, but now he was trying to act like the son of a hero, and it was making Mom's heart much lighter.

Then Silvy told Mom about what she and Gran'maw had been saying about America being like a mince pie. "What you two don't think of!" Ma laughed. "Silvy, since you're part of the pie called America, remember that what goes into the pie can spoil it, as well as add to its flavor, if one little piece is bad or has the wrong kind of taste."

"The Pilgrims were the right kind." Silvy's words tumbled over each other in her haste to make Mom and Gran'maw understand how she felt about this. "And the Virginians, and George Washington Carver, and—and Pop was the right kind, too. I'm going to be like them, Mom. I aim to make the pie better, not spoil it."

Silvy went into the front room and looked out of the window to see if Ralph were in sight. A train rushed past, crowded with people going home. Perhaps, thought Silvy, some were going to homes of relatives or friends to spend the holiday. All over America this would be happening. Tomorrow prayers of thanksgiving would be offered in the churches. Silvy had heard the President's proclamation for a national Thanksgiving Day read in her own church last Sunday. She and Ralph would go to the service tomorrow with Mom and Gran'maw and she would give thanks to God for all the people who had made America a great country.

Silvy's voice had a happy lilt as she sang,

> "Land of the Pilgrims' pride,
> From every mountainside
> Let freedom ring."

—ABRIDGED FROM *The Book of Three
Festivals* BY AMY MORRIS LILLIE

The Harvest Moon

It is the Harvest moon! On gilded vanes
 And roofs of villages, on woodland crests
 And their aerial neighborhoods of nests
 Deserted, on the curtained window-panes
Of rooms where children sleep, on country lanes
 And harvest fields, its mystic splendor rests!
 Gone are the birds that were our summer guests,
 With the last sheaves return the laboring wains.
All things are symbols: the external shows
 Of nature have their image in the mind,
 As flowers and fruits and falling of the leaves;
The song-birds leave us at the summer's close.
 Only the empty nests are left behind,
 And pipings of the quail among the sheaves.

       —HENRY WADSWORTH LONGFELLOW

The Hock Cart or Harvest Home

Come, Sons of summer, by whose toil
We are the lords of wine and oil;
By whose tough labours and rough hands
We rip up first, then reap our lands,
Crowned with the ears of corn, now come,
And to the pipe, sing Harvest Home!

—LINES FROM *"The Hock Cart or Harvest
Home; To the Right Honorable Mildmay,
Earl of Westmorland"* BY ROBERT HERRICK

The Same Language

Ted climbed into the willow tree beside the stream and straddled a limb. From there he could look down the road at the cottages, their gardens brilliant with autumn flowers, and beyond them the square, stone tower of the church. Why on earth was his mother so happy to be spending the winter in this sleepy little English village, and in such a tiny house, too; a pink house with a straw roof? Thatch, they called it, but it was straw for all that. Ted had seen a man putting a new one on, fastening the bundles together and then snipping them off at the eaves, just as if he were giving the roof a haircut.

He drummed with his heels against the trunk of the tree. How quiet it was! The only sound he could hear was a kind of rhythmic squeak—a pleasant squeak, he thought, and rather promising. He flattened himself on the limb in order to see better.

Down the road came a boy about ten years old, trundling a wheelbarrow. He was the right sort of boy in rather dirty blue shorts and a gray sweater, his sandy hair untroubled by brush or comb. Lying in the wheelbarrow was the stuffed figure of a straw man.

"Hi," called Ted, half tumbling from a tree. "What's that?"

"A scarecrow I made for the fair," the boy replied. "There's a three-shilling prize."

"Is there? I hope you win it?"

"I may do," said the boy, with a smile. "As far as I know, there's no one else who has made one."

Ted laughed. "What's your name?"

"Jonathan. You sound like an American."

"Yes, ah'm from Baltimore," drawled Ted, with as much exaggeration as possible. "Spending a whole year in England. We moved in yesterday." He jerked his thumb in the direction of the pink cottage.

"It's a good weekend to move in," said Jonathan. "Sometimes there's not much doing, but tomorrow is the fair, and Sunday's Harvest Thanksgiving."

"Thanksgiving," Ted repeated. "In October?"

"Yes, that's when we have the harvest," Jonathan explained. "Would you like to come? You could. Everybody comes to the Harvest Festival, and you bring a gift, something from your garden, you know."

Ted grunted. "Much we've got," he said. "No one has lived here all summer. The garden's a mess." He stopped suddenly. "Why, I forgot, we do have something, a simply huge squash."

Jonathan burst out laughing. "Not a squash, that's what you drink."

"Well, you wouldn't drink this one," Ted replied. "Even eating it would take a week. I'll show you."

He led the way to the other side of the cottage where there had once been a garden. It was now a mass of nettles, dandelions, and coarse grasses. "Over here in this corner," he said. "There!"

"Oh, that," said Jonathan. "That's a vegetable marrow. It *is* a jolly big one, but I'm afraid it won't do."

"Why not?"

"Vicar says please, no marrows this year."

"Who," asked Ted, coldly, "is Vicar?"

Jonathan opened his eyes wide. "Don't you even know who the vicar is? The parson, the man with the dog collar."

"Oh," said Ted. "But what about the squash? Why won't it do?"

"Oh, the marrow," said Jonathan. "Well, you see, we send all the gifts to the children's home in the city, and everybody's got marrows. The children must be fair sick of them without our taking more. Still, as you're an American, it might make a difference. Shall we ask?"

"No," answered Ted rather crossly. "I'll stay home."

They started back to the road. "It's a shame for you to miss it," said Jonathan. "Perhaps you could take something of ours." He pushed open the gate and went toward his wheelbarrow. "Hey," he cried out. The scarecrow was gone. "Someone's been and taken him," said Jonathan.

Ted looked up and down the road. "We were away only for a few minutes," he said. "Whoever it was must be close by. You run that way, and I'll run this."

They dashed off in opposite directions, glancing into every gate and lane, but when they returned, neither of them had a clue.

"Is there time to make another?" Ted asked sympathetically.

Jonathan shook his head.

"It's funny," said Ted. "A thief might take a wheelbarrow, but why would anyone want the scarecrow?"

"To show in the fair himself, maybe," said Jonathan. "Shall we go to the hall and see if it's there?"

They walked down the street together. The village hall was a one-story building of red brick. Inside there were rows of tables with signs on them: Carrots, Eggs, Preserved Fruit, and so forth. On the stage were the children's classes: Wooden Spoon Dressed as a Doll, Wild Flowers in a Jam Jar, Scarecrow, but no scarecrows were there.

"Many exhibits aren't in yet," said a woman who was bustling about with a placard in her hand that said Largest Vegetable Marrow.

Ted caught hold of Jonathan's arm. "Look at that," he whispered, "I'll give you my marrow. You might win."

Jonathan turned around and read the sign. Then he said rather wistfully, "But it would really be yours."

"Not if I gave it to you. I would never even have heard about all this if you hadn't stopped. Come on, let's get it."

They ran back to the cottage and gave the marrow a good bath. Then they lifted it into the wheelbarrow and off they went to the hall. The bustling lady wrote down Jonathan's name and fastened a number on the marrow.

"Thanks, awfully," said Jonathan. "You'll surely come back for the judging, won't you? I must go home now for my afternoon tea. Cheerio, Ted."

"See you tomorrow," Ted replied, and he, too, returned to his home.

The cottage was still in a turmoil of unpacking, so Ted picked up an apple and went out to the willow tree. As he swung himself over the first branch, he was startled to see a lifeless leg dangling just above his head. Then he chuckled. It's the scarecrow, he thought. Now what do I do? I don't even know Jonathan's last name, let alone where he lives.

He pulled the scarecrow down and looked it over. It seemed none the worse for its experience. When Ted had shaken up its stuffing and brushed off a bit of bark, it looked quite presentable. "I know what," Ted said to himself, and clutching the straw man around the middle, he rushed back to the hall a third time. The bustling lady was also feeling the need of tea, but she was a kindly person, so she took the time to listen to Ted's story and to put the scarecrow on the stage.

You can imagine Jonathan's surprise next day when he saw it there. At first he let out a roar of indignation, believing that the thief had dared to enter the competition, but when Ted ran up and explained what had happened, he laughed. He was happy, too, because no one else had made a scarecrow, so he was bound to get the prize.

"And perhaps you'll win something for the marrow," he said. "They're weighing them now. That's the vicar looking on."

The vicar was easy to recognize by what Jonathan called his dog collar. He looked pleasant enough, but Ted hung back rather shyly when his friend walked up and spoke to him. "Please, sir," Jonathan said, "there's a boy from America, and that marrow is the only thing he has for the Harvest Thanksgiving. Wouldn't you let him bring it?"

The vicar smiled at Ted. "Of course. That's quite a marrow. It seems to be taking second prize. I'm afraid you boys didn't understand that all these exhibits are to be sold for the benefit of the hospital. Otherwise you could certainly bring it to church."

Jonathan's face fell. "Oh, dear. He only put it in the fair to help me." And he told about the scarecrow.

"Well, cheer up," said the vicar. "I know a way out. Take your prize money to the shop and buy some oranges. It's quite the same as giving the marrow, isn't it, and the children will like it much better. Besides, a pile of oranges will look beautiful against the blue of the carpet."

The following afternoon Jonathan arrived to escort his friend to church. He was scrubbed and brushed until he gleamed with cleanliness. The apples he carried were polished, too.

"My mum couldn't come," he said, "because the baby's sick. But I told her we'd be quiet. Don't spill your oranges."

Ted had made a pyramid of them on a paper plate. "I'll be careful," he assured Jonathan. "I've stuck them together with toothpicks."

They went up the lane to the church door and turned the iron ring that served as a doorknob. Then they went in. Ted caught his breath. He had not expected anything like this. "Oh," he said, softly. "Oh, how lovely! It's like Easter."

"A bit like," whispered Jonathan.

Great masses of flowers were on every side. Michaelmas daisies, the wild asters of New England, were banked against the pulpit so that it was almost hidden behind a screen of blue and lavender blossoms. Every window sill was gay with chrysanthemums, and along the aisle stood tall vases of goldenrod and snapdragons.

Jonathan led the way to one of the front pews where other children were sitting. Before long the organ began to play "Come, Ye Thankful People, Come."

"Our hymn," whispered Ted.

"No, ours," said Jonathan firmly. "Whilst they're singing, we march up and lay our gifts before the altar."

Ted joined the procession and carefully placed his plate of oranges on the blue carpet. The vicar was right, they did look pretty. Even when he returned to his seat, he could see them—a bright spot shining among the great heaps of celery, beets, and cauliflower.

Later when they were starting home, they met the vicar in the churchyard. "Did you like the service?" he asked.

"Oh, very much," said Ted. "I don't think I ever saw such a beautiful church, but . . ." He paused as if something were puzzling him, and then he went on. "You people didn't have any Pilgrims, and yet you sing all our hymns. That last was one."

The vicar shook his head. " 'Now Thank We All Our God' happens to have come to us from Germany," he said. "But we do sing your hymns sometimes, and so do you sing ours. The thanksgiving service goes back a very long way," the vicar went on. "The Jews had it in Old Testament times. The Pilgrims had it in your country. Wherever people love God, they must be thankful to him, mustn't they?"

"Why, yes," said Ted slowly. "It's really all the same, isn't it— wherever we are?"

"Wherever we are," said the vicar, "some things are always the same."

—ROBIN PALMER

Thanksgiving in Old Jerusalem

Jonas crept cautiously out between the two tall palm sticks that formed the doorway of their thanksgiving booth. He looked across his roof to their neighbor's flat white rooftop. Thank goodness, Obadiah had gone down the stucco stairs on the other side of the house and was out of sight right now. Jonas couldn't bear to hear Obadiah chatter any more about the fine offering for the harvest festival he was going to present next week at the Temple.

As Jonas reached down for another palm branch to put on top of the sticks, a snowy white dove landed on his shoulder. Then another one came winging down, too, and put its tiny red feet on Jonas' hand. The doves belonged to his older brother, thirteen-year-old Samuel, and he was going to take them to the Temple to present them the day everyone made his harvest offering. Jonas shook the doves off.

It wasn't fair that their family had no harvest this year when Jonas was eleven and should be making his first trip to the Temple. His father had hurt his foot early in the season and could not plant nor reap a harvest, so there was nothing for the family this year.

There was nothing for Jonas to carry up the narrow, cobblestone streets of Jerusalem that led to Solomon's Temple on the high hill above the city.

Jonas heard Obadiah's voice in the street below, "Mother, don't you think this basket would look nicer if we filled that orange gourd you gave me with dates?"

Walking softly to the edge of the roof, Jonas peeked over the parapet between the two big adobe blocks. Obadiah was squatting on the pavement by his own front door. He was arranging things in his thanksgiving basket. As Jonas watched, Obadiah jumped up and ran up the stairs to his roof, two steps at a time. Jonas dodged back into his palm leaf shelter. In a minute he heard a thud close by, then footsteps running on his own roof. Curiosity made him peek out.

"Oh, there you are, Jonas," Obadiah said. "Do you know where I left that big orange gourd I had yesterday? The one with green streaks down the side?"

When Jonas reminded him that Samuel had put it on Obadiah's own Mezuzah by his own front door, Obadiah stretched up to look over the white railing. Obadiah wasn't as big as Jonas, but he was taking an offering to the Temple this year. Obadiah jumped across to his own rooftop and ran down the stairs.

This was Jonas' chance to get away. He didn't care if they did have the nicest thanksgiving booth in the neighborhood, he still wanted to go to the service in the Temple. Jonas remembered his Uncle Malacai was taking care of his sheep outside the city gate and that wasn't far. Uncle Malacai would understand how a boy felt who had attended the Temple school the past season and then couldn't go to the feast with an offering of his own.

As he passed under the big stone arch of the Damascus Gate into the sunshine beyond, Jonas saw his uncle with the sheep.

"Hello, Jonas," Uncle Malacai called. "What is the matter with you? You look as if the world were coming to an end."

Jonas did feel as if everything he cared about had vanished. He blinked hard so that Uncle Malacai wouldn't see the tear that almost spilled down his cheeks. What good had it done to learn the responses they would sing in the pilgrimage up the hill, if he couldn't go to the service like the other boys?

His uncle saw that Jonas felt bad about something, so he started talking about his flocks. "I've got a new baby lamb here, Jonas. Could you help me take care of her?" Uncle Malacai led the way through the flock to the other side of the pasture. "It was born two weeks ago, but its mother died last week. It is hard for me to take care of a baby lamb when I have all the others, too. You may take it home to have for your own, if you will take good care of it."

A lamb of his own! Now the world looked brighter to Jonas. He would have something to rush out to feed right after breakfast, just like Samuel had.

"Oh, yes," Jonas answered gratefully. "I will take good care of it, uncle."

Jonas patted the head of the small white animal. The lamb looked up at him with big, brown eyes and bleated. It seemed as if she knew Jonas would love and care for her. Uncle Malacai said she must have food every few hours while she was little. After awhile the lamb would be ready to eat grass like the older ones, but now she must have milk often.

Walking home with the little lamb following behind on the rope, Jonas swelled up with pride. Obadiah was out in front of the house.

"What have you got there, Jonas?" Obadiah asked.

As Jonas fondled the lamb, the little creature snuggled up against his legs.

"Jonas, can I feed your lamb?" Obadiah asked hopefully.

"Oh, no," Jonas answered. "This is a baby lamb. Its mother is dead, and I must be careful with her. Only one person can feed her while she is tiny. Otherwise she would be frightened."

The next week passed quickly. Samuel and Obadiah were busy getting ready for the trip to the Temple. Jonas was too busy with his lamb to notice.

The day for the festival dawned bright and clear, but it didn't make Jonas feel as happy as such a day should have. His heart was heavy, and his legs dragged because he had no offering to take to the Temple today. God had been good to them even if his father had hurt his leg, but Jonas wasn't expressing his gratitude.

As he sat hunched up by his own front door, Jonas saw Obadiah's mother come out of the house wearing her ceremonial dress with the maroon-colored skirt and bright, embroidered velvet upper part. Over her head was a white veil which hid her face except for her eyes. From the way she looked at him Jonas knew she wished he might go to the Temple, too.

Suddenly, Jonas had an idea and ran in to ask his mother about it. Samuel was taking the doves he raised, why couldn't Jonas give the priests at the Temple his lamb? When it was bigger they could use it to start a flock of sheep and lambs, and then the priests would have meat to give to the poor, hungry people of the town. His mother thought about it a minute and then said he could try it.

Samuel was all ready to go as Jonas dashed into the house to change his clothes. Samuel was wearing a long, flowing garment with stripes of many colors. Jonas thought that might be what Joseph's coat of many colors looked like. But Jonas didn't have time to admire Samuel's new robe. He grabbed the brown and yellow striped one of his own, pulled it over his head quickly, slipped his arms into the orange coat to go over his robe, and he was all ready.

"Jonas, pull down the under robe. It is caught," his mother reminded him.

He yanked at it to get it down.

"Not so hard." His mother was coming across the room to help him. "This cloth is tender because it was once the ceremonial outfit of your father. Please don't tear it."

Obadiah's parents started ahead. Then came the three boys, Obadiah, Samuel, and Jonas. As they went up the narrow streets, the walls of the buildings were so close together and so high that the sun couldn't get into the street at all. It was dark and smelled like many donkeys had been along that way. Up above them sitting on little balconies were women who watched the pilgrims go up the street to the Temple.

As they passed through the Temple gates, Jonas heard music swelling loud and clear:

> Lift up your heads, O gates!
> and be lifted up, O ancient doors!
> that the King of glory may come in.

The singing came from a group of older men over to the left. There were so many people crowding and pushing that Jonas could hardly see them.

Another voice over on the right took up the song: "Who is the King of glory?"

Jonas remembered he should be singing, too, so he joined in the response:

> The Lord, strong and mighty,
> the Lord, mighty in battle!

When Jonas looked to see if Obadiah were singing the responses, he saw that the other boy was having trouble balancing his basket.

Someone had bumped against him and the basket was teetering as if he might drop it. Jonas grabbed one side of the basket to help.

"Stop," Obadiah said, "you'll make me drop this for certain." Obadiah's voice sounded as if he were going to cry. The basket was all in a jumble now.

Just then Jonas heard his lamb bleating in a way she had never done before. When he turned to look, there behind them was a man dressed in a purple robe. Around his neck was a shining, golden chain, and at the end an ornament with jewels in it that flashed in the sunlight. The man turned around in surprise just as Jonas looked up at him.

"Leave my lamb alone," Jonas pushed the man back.

"I'm sorry," the man said. "But what are you doing with a lamb? This is a harvest festival. Where is your grain? Or doves, which are always acceptable?"

Jonas turned his back on the man. He wished he never had thought of the idea of bringing his lamb to the Temple. Perhaps, if he lagged behind Samuel and Obadiah, he could get out of the crowd and go back home. Would the priests think his lamb was not the right kind of offering, too?

But Samuel took hold of Jonas' coat and pulled him along. "What were you thinking of Jonas? That was the head ruler of Jerusalem."

Now Jonas was surer than ever that he never should have brought his lamb to Solomon's Temple. People in the crowd were stepping on its tiny hoofs, so Jonas picked the lamb up and tucked her under his arm. He was sad. He was willing to give God the only thing he had, but it still was not a suitable offering. If he carried the lamb, it would be easier to slip out of the crowd and go back home.

However, Jonas was swept along with the crowd into the main court of the Temple.

Now he couldn't turn back. As Samuel helped him set the lamb down on her feet, he was sick with worry about what the priests would say when they saw him bringing a lamb. The boys helped Obadiah rearrange his basket. Samuel's doves in their wooden cage made a beautiful gift to the Temple.

Ahead of them was an impressive-looking man wearing a red velvet robe. The little lamb hid behind Jonas and snuggled up under his orange coat. It seemed as if the lamb knew she would not be well received.

Samuel nudged Jonas to make him remember his manners. As Samuel bowed low and set his cage of doves on the floor, they cooed as if they were glad to be given as a gift to God. Obadiah's basket looked full, and the bright orange gourd glistened in the sunlight as he set it on the floor. No matter how hard Jonas tried to maneuver the lamb around in front of him so the priest would see her, the lamb still was hidden in Jonas' coat. He was afraid the priest would think he had dared come without an offering at all. He wished he had stayed at home.

Samuel and Obadiah rose. They had made their offerings and were about to leave. Jonas would have to hurry for other pilgrims were waiting their turn. He picked the lamb up, set her in front of the priests, and quickly turned to go.

As he pushed through the crowd Jonas thought he heard his lamb bleating. But he couldn't turn back now. Then he felt a cool nose against his hot hand. Oh, what would he do? He had heard that sometimes soldiers came and arrested anyone making a commotion in the Temple.

"Are you the boy who brought the lamb?" he heard a voice ask.

When he looked up there stood the red-robed priest. Jonas hastened to tell him that the lamb was the only offering he could make this year, that he hadn't meant to disturb the harvest festival. He pointed out that if they kept the lamb until another year, they could have more lambs and maybe meat to give to the poor.

"Have you been taking care of this lamb?" the priest reached down and felt the thickness of her wool.

By now Jonas was ashamed of his offering and afraid because he had talked so boldly to the priest, that all he could do was nod his head.

"The lamb needs better care than we can give it here at the Temple," the priest said. "I will entrust it to your care until harvest-time next year. Then it will be old enough to be an offering to God. You were a good boy to think of giving your only lamb for the benefit of others."

Jonas wanted to tell the priest that he was glad he had some way of expressing his gratitude to God. But the man was turning back. As a last reminder, he said, "Call the lamb 'Segullah' because she is God's own. She is dedicated to God." So saying the priest handed the lead rope to Jonas and was gone in the crowd.

That night as Jonas and Samuel lay on the floor in the palm booth on top of their house, Jonas couldn't sleep. He looked up at the bright stars that shone through the palm leaves. This had been a wonderful day for him after all. His offering had been accepted, and he was commissioned to care for God's own property for a whole year. At last he closed his tired eyes and drifted off to sleep to dream about a red-robed priest and a white baby lamb.

—LOIS TRIMBLE BENEDICT

Some Prayers and Songs of Planting, Harvest, and Thanksgiving from Many Lands

AFRICA

In Kambine, Portuguese East Africa, when the planting season begins, a little group carries seeds and tools to the church and sings this song, asking God's blessing. They leave the seeds and tools at the altar overnight and return at sunrise to sing the last verse. Then they go to their gardens singing.

Seeds, we bring, Lord, to thee,
Wilt thou bless them, O Lord.
Hoes we bring, Lord, to thee,
Wilt thou bless them, O Lord.
Hands we bring, Lord, to thee,
Wilt thou bless them, O Lord.

Ourselves we bring, Lord, to thee,
Wilt thou bless us, O Lord.

—THE REVEREND JULIAN S. REA

Many a Congo woman feels she is working with God in her little garden. She kneels by her hoe and prays this prayer before starting to work:

Father, be with me now as I begin to hoe. You have planned that by working hard people receive their food. Be with me today as I work together with you.

—FROM *The World at One in Prayer*, EDITED BY DANIEL J. FLEMING

KOREA

From a Korean book of prayers is this beautiful expression of thanksgiving at harvest time:

At this time, O Lord, we are especially thankful for the golden ripe grain and for the hundred kinds of red fruits. Where do they come from? The farmers who take them into their barns think they are the result of their own labors. But, O Lord, they are thine. To sustain our lives thou hast given us the needed sunshine and the proper rain; for this we are grateful. Just as the farmers, following the natural law, are diligent in time of sowing that they may reap, so may we follow the laws which thou hast established and sow righteousness day by day.

—FROM *The World at One in Prayer,* EDITED
BY DANIEL J. FLEMING

GREAT BRITAIN

AT PLOWING TIME

Almighty God, of whom first came the wisdom to open and break the clods of the ground, send thy blessing we beseech thee, upon the tillers of the soil, both man and beast, that as they day by day plow the fields, so they may with good success accomplish their labor, to thy praise and to their profit.

—FROM *The World at One in Prayer*, EDITED
BY DANIEL J. FLEMING

HARVEST HOME

Come, ye thankful people, come,
Raise the song of harvest home;
All is safely gathered in,
Ere the winter storms begin!
God, our Maker, doth provide
For our wants to be supplied;
Come to God's own temple, come,
Raise the song of harvest home.

—LINES FROM *"Harvest Home"* BY HENRY ALFORD

GERMANY

Here is the beginning of a song written by Matthias Claudius in Germany about two hundred years ago. As he traveled around among the farms, he realized that God gives the land and all to make it fruitful, but man must do his part to bring forth crops.

> We plow the fields and scatter
> The good seed on the land;
> But it is fed and watered by God's almighty hand;
> He sends the snow in winter,
> The warmth to swell the grain,
> The breezes and the sunshine,
> And soft refreshing rain.
>
> All good gifts around us
> Are sent from heaven above;
> Then thank the Lord, O thank the Lord
> For all his love.

> Now thank we all our God
> With heart and hands and voices,
> Who wondrous things hath done,
> In whom his world rejoices.

More than three hundred years ago a German pastor, Martin Rinkart, taught these words to families during the time when a terrible war laid Germany to waste. Many refugees fled to the walled town where Pastor Rinkart lived and brought with them a deadly plague. Pastor Rinkart went from crowded house to house, nursing the sick and burying the dead. Today, people all over the world sing or speak this song, especially at thanksgiving time.

THE ANCIENT LAND OF PALESTINE

O Lord, my God, thou art very great!
Thou makest springs gush forth in the valleys;
   they flow between the hills,
they give drink to every beast of the field; . . .
Thou dost cause the grass to grow for the cattle,
   and plants for man to cultivate,
that he may bring forth food from the earth, . . .
   and bread to strengthen man's heart. . . .
O Lord, how manifold are thy works! . . .
I will sing praise to the Lord as long as I live; . . .
   for I rejoice in the Lord.

—FROM PSALM 104

Praise is due to thee, O God, . . .
Thou visitest the earth and waterest it,
   thou greatly enrichest it; . . .
Thou crownest the year with thy bounty; . . .
The pastures of the wilderness drip,
   the hills gird themselves with joy,
the meadows clothe themselves with flocks,
   the valleys deck themselves with grain,
   they shout and sing together for joy.

—FROM PSALM 65

Succos

September was almost over. The High Holy Days had come and gone, Rosh Hashana, the Jewish New Year, had been heralded with the blowing of the ram's horn in the synagogue; ten days later Yom Kippur, the Day of Atonement, had been honored with fasting and prayer. There was still another holiday on the calendar which would be celebrated before Jewish folk could once more settle down to a spell of ordinary living.

"My goodness," declared Sarah one day as the children were discussing the coming of Succos, "the Jewish holidays certainly come in bunches."

Succos is a thanksgiving for the harvest, lasting nine days. A part of each of these days is spent in a specially built wooden hut which is known as a Succah. This is to recall the forefathers who had to dwell in wooden huts during their wanderings in the desert after they had left Egypt. The Succah might be built by each family or put up by the local synagogue. In the crowded sections of the lower East Side, there was not much space for any additional building, so many families had to do their celebrating in the Succah built by the congregation. For Mama's family, however, the backyard offered a good chance to celebrate at home.

Preparations for the building had been under way for some time. Even before Yom Kippur, Papa had begun to gather broad planks of wood which he stacked in piles in the backyard. The children had watched the piles grow higher each day. "Soon, soon," they kept telling one another, "Papa will begin building." But it wasn't until the day after Yom Kippur that the "soon" became "to-day."

At lunch Papa said, "I'll close the shop at three today so that I can start work on our Succah."

"Oh, Papa, may we watch you? May we, Papa?" the children clamored excitedly.

"Watch me!" replied Papa. "I should say not!"

Such unhappy looks as appeared on the children's faces! But Papa was only teasing. They soon saw that, for his eyes crinkled merrily in their corners as they always did when he was getting ready to smile. "Watch me, indeed! You'll have to help. I can't do it all by myself."

The children raced home from school that afternoon. Papa was already hard at work in the backyard. Schoolbooks were flung down, afternoon snacks were gobbled up, so eager were they to begin. When the gang of little girls descended upon him, Papa began to issue orders like a master carpenter. Such sawing and hammering and wigglewagging of tongues as went on in Mama's backyard! Mama had to shut the kitchen window to keep out the noise. But the children revelled in it. It was amazing how quickly a tiny wooden house could be put together when everybody helped. By the time Mama called them in for supper, one long and one short wall stood stoutly.

"Well, girls," Papa said, finally, "we'll have to stop now. We'll work some more tomorrow."

At the supper table Sarah said, "You know, Mama, I was telling the library lady about the Succah we're building. She said she never saw a Succah in her whole life! I wish she could see ours."

"Then why don't you invite her?" suggested Mama.

"Can I, Mama? Really? Do you think she'd come?"

"Why not? You can ask her tomorrow."

Everybody thought it was a wonderful idea. "When should she come?" asked Ella. "We don't want her to see the Succah until it's all finished."

"Let me see," said Mama. "Succos eve would be the best time. That's three days from now. The children's room at the library closes early, and she can come right over. Now when you speak to her tomorrow, Sarah, be sure and say that your Mama and Papa would be very pleased if she would come."

They all loved Miss Allen, the library lady. She was so kind and friendly. Once Mama had said, "She's very sweet—and so pretty too! She smiles at you, but somehow the face is wistful." The children thought she must be lonesome because she had no sisters or brothers, and no family to share any troubles with.

The next afternoon when Sarah joined her sisters in the backyard, her face was glowing, and she bubbled over with the news. "She's coming! The library lady's coming to our house on Succos eve! I'm so happy!" and she twirled and turned about the yard.

"Fine, Sarah," said Papa, "but if you want her to see a finished Succah, you'd better get to work."

One more day and the little house was finished. The walls of the Succah had been built of planks laid tightly one against the other, but the roof had only a few planks of wood widely spaced so that broad patches of sky came through. Ever since Papa had built the roof, Gertie had wondered about that. She hadn't said anything because she supposed that it would be finished sooner or later, but here they were already working on the furnishings, and still the roof remained as unfinished as ever. "Papa," she said finally, "what kind of a funny ceiling is that?"

"Exactly the right kind for a Succah," Ella explained. "Papa will spread fresh green branches across the planks of wood, and it will be the loveliest ceiling anyone could possibly want. Sparse enough so that the sun can shine through in the daytime and the stars peep in at night."

Papa nodded approvingly.

"Isn't it nice building the house you're going to live in?" Sarah said earnestly.

"Oh, I wish we could live in it forever!" added Charlotte.

"I hardly think you'd be comfortable in this Succah forever and ever," said Papa. "But I know just how you feel. It *is* nice to be making with your own hands the thing you are going to use. I'll tell you what we'll do. We'll leave the little house up for about a month after the holiday so you can enjoy it."

"Oh, Papa," the children all cried, "how wonderful!"

"We can bring our doll dishes out here and play house, really and truly," Charlotte said.

"We can invite our friends over," added Ella.

"Why, we can use it in a million different ways," continued Sarah.

"And to think it'll be all ours for a whole month," Henny exulted.

"The darling, darling, little house!" Gertie said.

Building over for the day, the family came back into the kitchen once more.

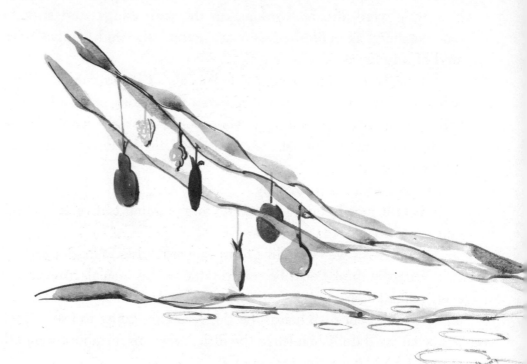

"Well," Mama asked, "how are you getting along?"

"We're almost finished," everybody answered at once.

"Fine," Mama said. "What about the decorations? You know there's only one more day before the holiday begins."

Everybody looked at Ella. Decoration of the Succah was Ella's special job. The others helped, of course, but she was always the designer. Under Ella's direction the children cut different fruits

from cardboard and colored them. They made strings of colored paper chains and crepe-paper flowers.

When they were all made, the children tacked the paper on the walls. Charlie had come over. Charlie was always welcome in their home. He made them all happy. Yet at times Charlie would disappear for many days. Ella and Mama and Papa knew why.

Papa had said, "Charlie quarreled with his parents about a girl he wanted to marry. They wanted him to marry another girl. Charlie's girl learned that his parents opposed their marriage, and she just went away. Charlie has looked for her everywhere he could think of, but couldn't find a trace of her. She was an orphan, and he didn't know any of her people."

But now Charlie was helping decorate their Succah. He strung the bright-colored chains across each other under the roof planks. The paper flowers were arranged in Mama's cut-glass bowl, and when it graced the Succah table, the little house looked festive indeed. The children were enchanted with it.

"Mama!" they called. "You must come out to see it!"

Mama came and admired. "It *is* lovely! I think it's the loveliest Succah we've ever had."

"You girls have done a wonderful job," Charlie praised them.

"I just can't wait till the library lady sees it," said Sarah. "What time is it, Papa?"

"A little after six. She'll be here any minute. You'd better meet her outside. She won't know where the backyard is."

Sarah skipped out joyously. Soon the sound of gay laughter could be heard, and she reappeared, leading the smiling Miss Allen by the hand.

Suddenly Miss Allen stopped. Her laughter stopped too; her face grew pale, and her eyes grew big.

The children looked at her in astonishment, and their gaze followed hers—straight across the yard to Charlie.

"Herbert!" the library lady whispered.

The children knew something was happening, something big. They could feel it. They looked at Mama to see if she understood. But Mama was just as surprised as they were, and so was Papa.

Charlie too seemed to have forgotten where he was. He walked towards the library lady. The yard was still. It was almost as if these two were the only ones alive in it. He took the girl's hands in both of his. "Kathy, Kathy!" he said brokenly. "I had begun to believe you were dead!"

Miss Allen started to laugh, only this time the laugh sounded more as if she were crying. "Oh, I'm very much alive, Herbert."

Sarah spoke up. "His name is Charlie."

For a fleeting moment, Ella felt again the pain of that night when Papa had first told her about Charlie. Was it really only two months ago?

"Herbert is his first name," she told the others. "Charlie is his middle name."

Charlie and Kathy just looked at each other.

"Aren't you going to kiss her?" cried Henny.

"Quiet!" Papa said sternly.

Charlie put his hands around Kathy's face, then bent down and kissed her. It was a wonderful moment.

Kathy looked up at Charlie. There were tears in her eyes as she said, "Oh, my dear, I'm so glad you found me!"

"It was really the children who found you," Charlie said with a radiant face. He turned and looked at the silent group around them. "Thank you, you wonderful family—thank you for Kathy and me."

"I think you can thank yourselves, too," Mama said. "Is it likely that you would have met here tonight if each of you had not been a kind good friend to this family?"

Before Papa left for the synagogue, Mama brought out her shiny brass candlesticks with the holiday candles already in them. Placing them on the Succah table, she lit them and recited a prayer.

With the soft candlelight spread through the wooden hut and the smell of the green branches on the roof planks, the place seemed heavenly to the children who sat there awaiting Papa's return.

"I can't stop thinking about Charlie and the library lady," said Sarah.

"To think that Charlie's lost sweetheart should be our own library lady," Charlotte added dreamily.

"It's just like a storybook come true," added Sarah.

"Why didn't they stay to eat?" Henny asked.

"Kathy wanted to go straight to Charlie's parents and make up with them. I was glad that she felt that way," Mama said. "I know Charlie was glad, too. They promised to come to see us very soon."

Papa had returned. As Mama passed the dishes through the kitchen window, the girls placed them on the Succah table.

"It's fun seeing the dishes come through the window," Ella said. "You can almost imagine that the food is being whisked out of the air and served by magic hands."

She moved one arm in a swinging gesture to illustrate her words. At the end of the swing, she suddenly found a platter of gefüllte fish in her hand.

"This fish was whisked right out of the icebox," Mama said. "Mind you don't drop it, or magic hands will be laid on you."

Everyone laughed as Ella set the fish down with great care. Next out the window came a large soup tureen filled with good hot chicken soup. Inside the tureen floated a Succos delicacy—kreplech (meat-filled dumplings). Then out the window came a covered bowl of vegetables. Next came a platter of chicken.

And last of all, but not out the window, came Mama.

—ADAPTED FROM *All-of-a-Kind Family*
BY SYDNEY TAYLOR

Thanksgiving Farm

Lord of sun and star and cloud,
hear our prayer. It is not loud,
but rises to you from the warm
hearts of children on this farm.

We thank thee for our colored days;
and for the nights Polaris stays
starring the north; for lamplight glow
through shining windows on new snow.

We thank thee for our animals:
the soft-eyed herd; and in their stalls
the quiet horses; and our cat
snitching the chair where Grandpa sat.

We thank thee for our father, mother,
and for each other—sister, brother;
and pray thee keep our hearts, our land,
in the hollow of thy gentle hand.

—FRANCES FROST

Thanksgiving Prayer

Help us, dear Lord, our good to share
With those who have no one to care,
So that they, too, may say
This is a blest Thanksgiving Day!

—EDNA MAE BUSCH

Song of Thanksgiving

Oh, hark to the tune of the droplets of rain
As they go
From the cloud.
For storm on the mountain, for dew on the plain
Sing we low,
Sing we loud.
So green are the meadows and green is the corn
In the rain
Growing tall.
Give thanks for the harvest and praise for the corn,
Singing one,
Singing all.

—BURNHAM EATON

Johnny Appleseed

"Johnny Appleseed, Johnny Appleseed,"
Chief of the fastnesses, dappled and vast,
In a pack on his back,
In a deer-hide sack.

. . . .

Tomorrow's peaches, pears and cherries,
Tomorrow's grapes and red raspberries,
Seeds and tree-souls, precious things,
Feathered with microscopic wings,
All the outdoors the child heart knows.

. . . .

And the evening breeze
Joined his psalm of praise
As he sang the ways
Of the Ancient of Days.
—LINES FROM THE POEM *"Johnny Appleseed,"*
FROM THE BOOK *Johnny Appleseed and
Other Poems,* BY VACHEL LINDSAY

Johnny Appleseed's Coat

"Maybe the boat's not coming, Ma." Seth's face was anxious. Resolutely he turned his back on the empty reaches of the Miami Canal. Perhaps if he could stop looking for the "Silver Bell," she would come.

"Maybe the boat's sunk plumb to the bottom," fretted his twin, Sally. She moped drearily on one of the packing boxes containing the worldly goods of the Rogers family.

"Ma!" Eight-year-old Susan's lips trembled alarmingly.

"Ma!" wailed Shadrach, casting himself upon his mother's knees. "You said we'd ride on the boat! You said—."

"Dry right up, all of you!" scolded Sarah Rogers. "You twins starting such a hullabaloo! Five young 'uns—Seth, Sally, Susan, Shadrach, and Sharon Rogers—and not one of you with a mite of patience. Now hearken to me. Some time or other that packet will come. But when—that's a different matter." Ma suddenly cocked her head, listening. "There now, what did I tell you?" she exclaimed.

From afar came a long-drawn bugling. The forest bordering the canal flung back the echo, clear and lovely. The children shot to

the edge of the landing, tensely watching for the first glimpse of the "Silver Bell." Ma stood up, bright-eyed, holding baby Sharon. And now, as if by magic, the sleepy Ohio settlement of Troy came to life. Eager and noisy, its inhabitants crowded to the landing.

Around the bend, along the opposite towpath, appeared a pair of gray mules. The morning sunlight flashed on their silver-mounted harness. Silver bells swung from their heavy collars. Their driver, but a moment ago plodding through the country quiet, now set his

hat atilt, flourished his whip, and swaggered jauntily. "Giddap!"
he shouted.

In tow of the mules, by means of a long rope attached to their
collars, glided the "Silver Bell." In the water her shadow was reflected in bright broken planes of color. Her underbody was painted
green and red, with accents of black. Dazzling white was her cabin.
Her twenty little windows boasted green shutters. Within hung
crisp curtains of scarlet.

The Rogers children held their breath as the steersman, hand on tiller, guided the boat toward the landing. The captain blew one more blast on his horn. Across the canal the driver bellowed at the mules to halt. The towline grew slack, trailing in the water. As smoothly and silently as a swan, the packet swam to her mooring.

Then what a hubbub of talk as captain and passengers clambered off! "And who might you be, stranger?" inquired the villagers, with kindly curiosity. "What's the news down Cincinnati-way? Nifty outfit you've got there, Captain Brown. 'Bout what speed you making?"

"Three and a half miles an hour," boomed the captain, proudly. "Sometimes as much as four."

"You don't say! Whew!"

The Rogers children could scarcely endure such leisurely talk, such dawdling. But at last they were aboard, bag and baggage, with the other passengers. The boat resumed its way. In no time everyone on the "Silver Bell" knew that the passengers picked up at Troy were Sarah Rogers and her young 'uns from Clare County.

"Bound for Indiana," said Sarah, happily. "We change at Fort Wayne for another packet on the Wabash & Erie Canal. Travel as far as Lafayette, we do, where my man, Steve Rogers, will meet us. He's bought land there and an inn."

Once aboard, the slow, noiseless drifting of the packet seemed to cast a soothing enchantment over the spellbound Seth and Sally, Susan and Shadrach. The grown-up passengers murmured as drowsily as bees; all the nurslings slept; the tramp of the mules came muffled and measured. The children might have thought it a dream journey, had not the captain signaled so lustily at every flouring mill, every tiny settlement, every passing freight and passenger boat.

At noontide he blew the mightiest blast of all. The boat moored.

They all piled merrily off and, at a nearby settler's house, stuffed themselves hugely with savory hot food.

It was mid-afternoon when the "Silver Bell," gliding smoothly among her colored shadows, was hailed from the bank.

"Well, I'll be switched, if it isn't Johnny!" exclaimed a man close to Seth. "Look! And what's come over the old fellow, all fancied up like that?" The speaker turned to his deck companion. "It's dear old Johnny Appleseed. I didn't know he ever traveled by canal boat."

Seth slipped away to find his twin. "It's Johnny Appleseed, Sal," he whispered, and stared with round eyes as the packet sidled up to the shore. Ah, yes, Seth had heard of this odd character, who of his own free will had planted and tended apple orchards all through the new country of the Ohio. When Johnny Appleseed leaped aboard, Seth stood so close he could have touched the pilgrim's coat.

It was the coat that had caused the man on deck to exclaim. For above Johnny's worn moccasins and his tattered deerskin trousers, the coat seemed oddly magnificent. Sky blue it was, very fine and soft, with elegant skirts, standing collar, and silver buttons. Neither did it match the pick ax and spade that Johnny carried. Nor his hat— a cooking pan!

But no one laughed. Not after the word had spread that this was indeed the famous Johnny Appleseed. Now the "Silver Bell" seemed to move with a new pride, as if glorying in the knowledge that she carried one who was already half legend in the annals of the West—Johnny Appleseed, whose history was to outlast his orchards and all of those who journeyed with him this May day on the Miami Canal. The passengers crowded close to see and speak to him.

But as the afternoon shadows lengthened, there came a startling cry, "Man overboard!"

"No, it's a child! See, there he is! He's going under! Look!"

How the passengers pushed and peered! How frantically every mother counted the noses of her flock! The mule driver halted his team. The boat stopped.

Above the wild cries Sarah Rogers heard Sally's scream. "Ma! It's Shadrach! Oh-h-h, Ma!"

Ma reached the stern in time to see Seth plunge to the rescue. Shadrach had disappeared. The channel was only four feet deep, but Shadrach was such a little boy.

"There he is!" yelled the crowd, as the child rose gasping to the surface. Their clamor rang in Seth's ears as with furious strokes he pushed toward his brother. But just as he was ready to grasp Shadrach's collar, he saw the boy lifted out of the water. Some strange giant claw seemed reaching from the sky.

Seth looked up, bewildered. On the deck stood Captain Brown, braced sturdily. He was holding a long pole. At its hook end there dangled, by the seat of his pantaloons, the dripping Shadrach. Amid cheers from the passengers, the youngster was hauled on deck.

Seth was dripping, too, when he climbed aboard. There had been no time, before his frantic plunge, to shed his coat. And when little Shad had been revived, stripped, and wrapped in a blanket, Ma looked ruefully at Seth.

"Soaking wet you are, and that your only decent outfit! Probably won't be dry by morning. What you're going to wear I don't know, nor where I could find it among those boxes. But, there! I believe I do remember where I packed your long red woolens. Sally, lend your pinafore to Seth. He shall wear it over his underpants."

"Ma!" protested Seth, horrified. "A boy as big as me in a girl's pinafore! Everybody will laugh!"

Ma gave Seth a tender pat. "A hero can wear anything he's a mind to, 'thout folks laughing," she whispered.

To be called a hero! Seth was dumbfounded. "Shucks!" he said at last, " 'twas the captain saved Shad, not me."

"But you had the will," insisted Ma. "You made the effort. It's a'most the same. So you needn't mind the pinafore, Son."

Oh, but Seth did mind! And he was feeling not at all like a hero when Johnny Appleseed stepped up. He was pulling off his fine blue coat.

"Please, ma'am," he said, "I'd be proud could your boy wear this while his own clothes dry."

"But, Mister—" Ma cried, though her eyes were warm and deep, "what will you do for the lack of it?"

"A coat's a pesky burden," smiled Johnny. "Specially a fine one like this." He smoothed the sleeves of his shirt, stretching as if he were glad to be free.

Oh, how the sky-blue coat fairly swallowed Seth! And when he had donned his skintight underpants, he was a comical sight, if ever there was one. But every boy aboard gazed at him with envy.

As for him, he was completely dazzled. Even the experience of going through the locks at Junction, where the St. Mary's and St. Joseph's joined to form the Miami, even the knowledge that here the canal became the Wabash & Erie flowing into Indiana—that was certainly exciting, but not so deeply exciting to Seth as the feel of Johnny Appleseed's coat on his shoulders, and the silver buttons under his proud touch. And oh, how everlastingly grateful he was to Johnny for saving him the shame of wearing a girl's pinafore!

At eight-thirty o'clock, there was the drawing of numbers for the sleeping berths. Ma, whose flock had barely escaped disaster that day, looked at Seth anxiously. "You'll have to bide in the men's

cabin, Son. Now do take care of yourself, and mind you, don't sleep in Mister—in Johnny Appleseed's coat."

The berths were tiers of canvas shelves suspended by bars from the cabin walls. Each shelf was equipped with a thin straw pallet, a sheet, and blanket. Seth smothered his giggles as he peered down from his own top berth at the rows of shelves sagging so comically under the weight of the various passengers.

Many slept on the floor. They lay on benches, on and under tables. Their discarded collars and cravets, coats and waistcoats hung on ropes stretched from wall to wall.

But the precious sky-blue coat was not among these garments. Carefully Seth folded it across his body, one sleeve tucked underneath to keep it from slipping. And through all the clumsy settling-down, Seth kept an eye on Johnny. In the dim light he could make out the planter's spare figure. Above him sagged a huge mound of a fellow. There seemed scarcely room for Johnny to draw breath.

Soon there was a steady blast of snores. In Seth's dreams these sounds mingled strangely with the echoes of the packet horn, sweet and mournful and mysterious in the night.

Hours later he wakened. "Pa! Ma! Where am I?" he cried. Then he remembered, and was ashamed of his fear. He felt for the coat. It was safe. Peering through the shadows, he saw that the fat gentleman sleeping above Johnny had sagged yet lower. But Johnny—he was not there!

Tucking the coat under one arm, Seth swung himself down. There were grunts of protests as he picked his way among the sleepers on the floor. At the door he paused. In the half-light of early dawn he could see the shadowy figure of the steersman. On the towpath, mules and driver trod like inky ghosts.

Stealthily Seth tiptoed around the deck. And at the stern end, propped against the cabin's outer wall, lounged Johnny Appleseed. He was not asleep, for he looked up and held out his hand.

"It's you, lad," he whispered. "Couldn't you endure it, either? Put on the coat, and share my blanket. It's chilly. We must be quiet, for the captain, though snug in his cuddy, doesn't allow anyone on deck at night.

"I'll be leaving come morning, lad. I've had my fill of being packed away like a dead pig in a warehouse. Took me a foolish notion to travel by packet once in my life. It'll be the last time." He drew a deep breath.

Seth breathed deeply, too. After the close air of the cabin, how fresh and sweet was the scent of the forest! Little wavelets licked the sides of the packet as gently as kittens' tongues. And while the pale light grew, Seth fell asleep, nestling close to the loving-kindness of Johnny Appleseed.

As the passengers were going ashore for breakfast, Johnny shook hands with Ma. "Now God go with you and yours," he said. "And you may have the coat for keeps, ma'am."

"You would give away such a fine coat as that?" asked Ma.

"I never felt it rightly mine," answered Johnny. "It was but given me in return for some apple seedlings. Besides, it's no coat for the wilderness. Nor for one like Johnny Appleseed, that runs free like a fox."

"I'm much obliged, then, I'm sure, Mister," said Ma, all ashine. "With close contrivin' I can tailor a handsome suit for Shadrach."

"But, Ma!" wailed Seth.

Quietly Johnny drew him aside. "I know, because it was mine, you'd like to keep the coat as it is, Seth, and thank 'ee for the compliment," he said. "But did you see the heartsome looks of your mother, when she saw in her mind's eye her little Shadrach tricked out in blue with silver buttons? Now let her be. *Giving*, lad—why it's one of the blessed things we mortals can do. So now if you'll part with the coat and smile in the doing of it, I'll give you something that's worth far more." Thrusting his hand into the front of his shirt, he drew forth a small buckskin bag. He loosened the string. Into Seth's cupped palms he poured a stream of brown seeds.

"Apple seeds, Seth, to plant in that new place of your pa's on the Wabash. Tend them well, and they'll grow into trees that will last nigh on a hundred years, and the miracle of their fruit will be repeated a hundred times. Think of that, lad!"

Seth lifted glad eyes. "Oh, Johnny, of course I'd rather have the seeds than the coat! 'Cause apple seeds—why, they're *you*, and all I've heard about you my whole life long! An' my pa will be *that* proud!"

"Some day, Seth," continued Johnny, "when there are apples in your pa's orchard, fair beholden I'll be should you give away seeds, too. I shall be gone, but to the folks living then, you must say: 'Remember, when these grow and bear fruit, it will be your turn to give away seeds. Because that was Johnny Appleseed's way, and Johnny Appleseed's faith in the future!'"

"That's not all I'll say," agreed Seth, with shy pride. "I'll say, ' 'Twas Johnny Appleseed told me, when I was a boy and wore his coat, that giving is good.' "

—MABEL LEIGH HUNT

A Saga of the Prairie

Bright, clear sky over a plain so wide that the rim of heaven touched it around the entire horizon.

It was late afternoon, and through the tall grass of this great midwestern American plain, a small caravan was pushing its way. The track that it left behind was like the wake of a boat, except that instead of widening out astern, it closed in again.

"Tish-ah," said the grass. "Tish-ah, tish-ah." It bent under the trampling feet, but it did not complain. Nothing like this had ever happened to it before. "Tish-ah, tish-ah," it cried and rose up in surprise to look at this rough hard thing that had crushed it to the ground so rudely and then moved on.

A stocky, broad-shouldered Norwegian man walked at the head of the caravan. He seemed shorter than he really was, because of the tall grass around him and the broad-rimmed hat of coarse straw which he wore. A few steps behind him followed a boy of about nine years of age. From the looks of these two it was easy to guess that here walked father and son.

Behind them a team of oxen jogged along; drawing a vehicle

245

which looked as if once upon a time it might have been a wagon. Over the wagon box long willow saplings had been bent, six of them in the form of arches. On these arches, and tied down to the wagon body on each side, were spread, first of all, two handwoven blankets, then two sheepskin, which were used for bed coverings at night. The rear of the wagon was stowed full of numberless articles: a large immigrant chest, household utensils, tools, and clothing.

Hitched to this wagon, and trailing behind was another vehicle, home made and curious looking, but solidly constructed. It was loaded full of provisions and household necessities. Both wagons creaked and groaned loudly every time they bounced over a tussock and pulled out of a hollow. "Squeak, squeak," said one. "Squeak, squeak," answered the other, and the sound broke the silence of centuries.

Behind the wagons followed a cow. The caravan moved so slowly that the cow occasionally had time to stop and snatch a few mouthfuls of grass. What little she got this way she sorely needed. She had been jogging along all day. Soon it would be night, and then her part of the work would come—to furnish milk for the little company ahead.

Across the front end of the first wagon lay a rough piece of plank. On the right side of this plank sat a woman with a white kerchief over her head, driving the oxen. Against her side rested the blonde head of a little girl who was stretched out on the plank and was sound asleep. On the left side of the plank, beyond the girl sat a boy about seven years old. With hands folded over one knee he looked straight ahead.

This was the caravan of Per Hansa, who with his family and his possessions was moving from Minnesota to the Dakota territory. There he intended to take up land, and build himself a home; he was going to do something great out there. The boy who followed Per Hansa was named Ola. Beret was his wife, Anna Marie the girl who slept by her side, and Hans the younger boy. The cow who trailed behind, switching and swinging her tail was "Rosie."

Farther and farther the caravan crept, over the boundless prairie toward the skyline. Of road or trail there lay not a trace ahead. As soon as the grass had straightened up again, no one could have told the direction from which the caravan had come or whither it was bound.

For more than three weeks now, well into the fourth, this caravan had been crawling across the plain. At this moment Per Hansa had lost the trail. He did not know where he was, nor how he was to get to the place he had to reach. According to his directions, he should have reached Split Rock Creek before this time. He should have been there two or three days ago, but he hadn't seen anything like the place. If something didn't turn up soon! Well! Per Hansa's eyes wandered over the plain. For a long time the little company had been silent. No one spoke a word, then "Go back, Ola," said Per Hansa to his son without slackening his pace. "Go back and drive for your mother. Talk to her so it won't be so lonesome for her. And be sure to keep as sharp a lookout as you can."

Ola stepped out of the track, Hans jumped down from the wagon, and Ola climbed up and sat down by his mother.

"Have you seen anything?" the mother asked.

"Why no—not yet," answered the boy.

"I wonder if we shall ever see our friends again," she said. "This seems to be taking us to the end of the world—beyond the end of the world."

In front Hans hurried alongside his father and laid his hand in his—he always felt safer thus.

"When I'm a man and have horses, I'm going to make a road over these plains, and put up some posts for people to follow. Don't you think that will be a good idea?"

"Sure thing," answered the father. "You'll manage that all right. I might find time to help you an hour or two, now and then."

At last Per Hansa halted.

"Well, I suppose we can't drive any farther today. We and the animals would both drop pretty soon."

He held up his arms. "Whoa!" The oxen stopped.

Preparations for the night were soon made. Each had his own task and now was well used to it. There was the wood and dry branches strapped under the wagon to be selected. The fire place to fix. Water to be drawn from the keg. The cattle to care for, Rosie to milk. A bed for the whole family to be spread in the wagon. Every member of the family worked fast and yet carefully. There was only enough milk that night for the two youngest children. The others drank water with their porridge. They sat around in silence after the meal was over. Then Anne Marie, the smallest of them, said:

"Thanks to Thee our Lord and Maker."

The glow of the setting sun whose bright colors had spread over the sky grew fainter. In solemn grandeur, the moon swung up above the plain. Never had it seemed so big before. A hush of wonder and reverence fell on their spirits as they watched it rise.

A little while later they all lay under the quilts asleep. All except Per Hansa. Slowly he slipped from the wagon, so as not to wake the others and stood on the prairie in the moonlight. He looked for the North Star, found it, faced about and hurried westward. A ridge lay ahead. He must know what lay beyond it. He walked for an hour, it must have been four miles. Beyond the ridge the land changed. A creek was in sight. Yes, it must be, it was Split Rock Creek. At last Per Hansa knew where he was. He had found the trail. At the edge of the creek he discovered fresh wagon ruts. What a wonderful sight! Now he knew he was near friends: no longer alone and lost on the prairie. At this very spot the other caravans who had started with him must have crossed the creek. The end of the journey was in sight. Nothing mattered now. His weariness was gone. He felt refreshed and strengthened.

The long journey was now soon over. Per Hansa and his family joined their friends, and the little group of immigrants settled down on the western plains. They staked out their lands, and each family set to work. Yes, the long journey was over, but the struggle for existence was just beginning.

It was like going back to the very beginning of things, they thought. How could they manage out here? Untamed nature was round about them: vastness and endlessness on every hand. Water, wood, and food were scarce. Yet dreams of the future were like hidden springs of energy. Per Hansa worked ceaselessly with only five hours of sleep each night. He and his boys began to build a sod house. While they were constructing it, the family lived in the wagon. The walls rose slowly, for besides cutting and piling the sod in straight even rows, the land must be plowed. But before the first snow fell, the sod house was finished, and they were settled in it. There were two rooms. One for the family, one for the animals.

Early in October the first few downy snowflakes fell. The sun had no strength these days. One morning the sun just couldn't get his eye open at all. A chill grayness rested everywhere. By night a cold wind howled around the hut. The snow came down in great swirls. Winter had begun.

The loneliness of the days and nights that followed, the bitter cold, the wild blizzards, the darkness, food and fuel disappearing, the enforced idleness week after week for the little family in their sod hut—these were harder to bear than the long journey, or the hard work of settling. They were glad of the coziness of the animals in the room nearby. The munching of the oxen and the quiet breathing of Rosie made them feel less alone.

On special evenings Per Hansa and the boys sat around the table sifting seed. The wheat they had brought with them lay in small heaps on a white cloth. Every little weed seed, every foreign substance had to be taken out. The seed must be clean.

"The best only for the new soil, be careful, boys! Be careful there! Don't shirk your job!"

It was wonderful to be sitting there handling these precious kernels. These few sacks of grain would not only supply his family with the wheat flour they needed that winter; more than that they would make seed for that year, the next year, and seed again for the year after—thus down all the years to come, always greater and greater abundance of food. What hopes lay in those kernels that had power to create new life over this endless wilderness and transform it into a land of plenty for human beings! Per Hansa's wonder grew as he gazed at the seeds. There they lay so inanimate, yet glowing. Reverently he lifted handful after handful.

Spring came at last. Now if only the ground would dry up. If the sun would only shine warm again tomorrow and tomorrow.

On April 14, Per Hansa began seeding the wheat. Three times that morning he had been out to test the ground; the last time he made his great decision. *Now we will start!*

He filled the seed bag, hung it over his shoulder, and was ready. Per Hansa felt that the greatest moment in his life had come.

He was about to sow wheat on his own ground. He thrust his hand into the bag, and his fingers closed on the grains. Caressingly he took great handfuls, giving them a gentle squeeze.

Now the wheat rained down in yellow semicircles from Per Hansa's hands. The warm rays of the sun struck full across it and seemed to wrap it in golden light. He must work slowly and carefully. The seeding must be even and not too thick. As soon as daylight lasted, Per Hansa kept on sowing. That night he walked home in greatest satisfaction.

Per Hansa's work was not over when his seed was planted. That is not enough to bring any harvest. There were days of work and hours of anxiety. Unexpected cold followed the sowing, when he feared the seed was killed by the frost. In despair he lost all hope of its sprouting. He was afraid to even look at his fields. Then there was the day of overwhelming joy when young Hans came storming in, all out of breath.

"Father, come quick! The wheat is so high!"

Per Hansa rushed to the field. There he stood spellbound, gazing at the sight spread before him. Tears came to his eyes, so that he found it difficult to see clearly. Over the whole field tiny green shoots were quivering in the warm sunshine.

June came and July. Patches of fields were slowly ripening. The kernels were already formed, tiny bodies wrapped in the most delicate green silk. With every day the wheat filled out more and more. At last it was ready to reap. The first harvest in the settlement by Spring Creek was at hand.

—ADAPTED BY MARGARET DULLES EDWARDS FROM
Giants in the Earth BY O. E. ROLVAAG

Singing, the Reapers Homeward Come

Singing, the reapers homeward come, Io! Io!
Merrily singing the harvest home, Io! Io!
Along the field, along the road,
Where autumn is scattering leaves abroad,
Homeward cometh the ripe last load, Io! Io!

Singers arc filling the twilight dim
With cheerful song, Io! Io!
The spirit of song ascends to Him
Who causeth the corn to grow.
He freely sent the gentle rain,
The summer sun glorified hill and plain,
To golden perfection brought the grain, Io! Io!

Silently, nightly, fell the dew,
Gently the rain, Io! Io!
But who can tell how the green corn grew,
Or who beheld it grow?
Oh! God the good, in sun and rain,
He looked on the flourishing fields and grain,
Till they all appeared on hill and plain
Like living gold, Io! Io!

—AUTHOR UNKNOWN

Our Thanks to Thee

For food and shelter and for toil,
For all thy gifts from sun and soil;
For cares that help us to grow strong,
For thought that guides toward right from wrong,
For tears that cleanse, and the need to be
Closer in our touch with thee,
For every care thy love bestows,
For every joy each glad heart knows,
For all good things we feel or see,
Dear loving God, our thanks to thee!

—SOLVEIG PAULSON RUSSELL

Give My Love to Boston

"You're late," said the woman gathering apples from the trees along the stone wall as they went by.

"You're late," said the man fishing from the bridge.

"You're late," said the farmer who pulled up his team to give them more room.

"You're late," said the old man coming down the steps of the corner store.

"You're late," said the boy driving home the cows from pasture. "The last thanksgiving turkeys went by a week ago."

It was usually John who explained. "We got held up. Our father was sick." Molly just listened. The words rang in her ears like a bell, over and over. "You're late, you're late."

Father had said the same thing when they started at dawn.

"You're late getting off. I hope you may get there before snow flies, or you're likely to lose some of the flock. But don't drive them too hard, for they can't stand it. And take care of yourselves."

Mother had run out with a loaf of bread that she had just pulled out of the oven and put into the pack Molly carried. John, who was older, had the heavier blankets and the three dollars and sixty five cents. Grandma stood at the door, waving a dishcloth.

"You'll have a beautiful time," she called. "Give my love to Boston."

She didn't say, "You're late." She was the only one who didn't.

The first day was warm and gentle. There seemed to be no danger in it. John had been to Boston once with Father two or three years ago, but Molly had never been beyond their own valley. When they had climbed the road over the notch, she saw all the world spread out below them in brown and gold woodlands and farms set in emerald-green hay stubble cut in squares. She knew that far to the southeast there lay the great city of Boston and the ocean, but she could scarcely believe that her own eyes could see so much and so far.

"Why, I didn't know the world was like this, John," she said, and he answered in a very grown-up way, "The world is like a lot of things. You'll see."

They went slowly, driving the thirty-four turkeys ahead of them along the grassy edges of the road, so that they might catch crickets and grasshoppers as they went. John took the right-hand side and Molly the left; and with their long switches ended in tufts of leaves, they guided the big birds when they strayed.

The turkeys seemed to enjoy themselves. The sun shone along their bronze feathers and on the blue and purple-red of the cocks' heads and wattles so that they gleamed like metal. Most of the time they flowed slowly along like a river and Molly would say to herself, looking at the little brook tumbling head over heels beside the road, "We're going downhill to Boston." But sometimes the turkeys would be frightened, or try to go into some field, and then the children had to run to head them off.

Old Turk, the leader, tried to help. He had been to Boston three times already and knew the road, his calm figure bringing up the procession, and the sound of the little bell he wore at his neck steadied the flightier birds.

Turk was to come back with them in Samuel Thaxter's wagon after Samuel had unloaded the hams and cheeses he was taking to market.

Sixty miles to go. When a flock started early, they counted on twelve days. But John and Molly were late. It was hard not to urge the turkeys a little. Once or twice, when something scared the flock, John let them run for a while instead of trying to quiet them right away.

"Just that much nearer Boston," he said, as Molly, red-faced and panting, joined him.

"But if they scattered, we'd lose a whole lot of time," she said soberly.

"We have to chance it," replied John.

He was fourteen, going on fifteen, and nearly as tall as Father now, although his arms and legs still looked too long for him.

It was John who was in charge. Molly just helped, for she was only eight. John carried the map their father had drawn to show them the road and good places to stop for the night where the turkeys could roost in the orchard. It was John who decided when to let them take dust baths in the ruts of the road, and when to keep them moving.

It was fun that first day. They must have done well, for they came to the first camping place in good time. The map showed a long stretch of woods beyond, so they didn't try to go further, but asked permission of the farmer to camp in the orchard for the night.

"Sure," said the farmer, and his wife said, "You children can bring your blankets and sleep in the kitchen if you like," but John couldn't leave the flock and Molly wouldn't leave him.

"There's an old haystack at the foot of the orchard," the farmer said then. "You'd better sleep in that." But they ate in the kitchen.

"I know how it is," said the man. "I've taken turkeys to Boston in my time. You young ones are pretty late in getting started, aren't you?"

The hay tickled their faces, but it felt warm and soft as they burrowed deep into it. Several times during the night John roused to look at the flock and to make sure that the dark figures roosting among the branches were quiet and safe, but Molly slept all night long, tired out after the excitement of the day.

The second day was as beautiful as the first, and the turkeys seemed in good humor. The heat had brought out the insects, and the flock drove the grasshoppers before them in a thin green and brown spray. John coaxed them along and kept them going almost until dusk. He passed the camping place marked on the map and found another nearly three miles further down the road.

This time they were barely given permission to let their turkeys sleep in the orchard. "You kids be careful of your fire," the farmer said. "And don't you use any of my fence rails like one crowd did last year."

"And don't pick any apples either," added his wife. Later she put on her shawl and came down to see how they were getting on.

"I don't know but that you could sleep in the old icehouse. It's empty now, and the sawdust's dry. And you could keep an eye on your turkeys from there," she said almost grudgingly. As she turned to go, she took two small eggs from the pocket of her apron.

"Pullet's eggs," she said. "The storekeeper won't take them."

The next day a colder wind blew, and the insects were scarcer. The turkey cocks were more bad tempered. They spread their tails and gobbled and teetered on their horny feet as they passed people and dogs along the way. But Turk kept on steadily, his little bell ringing, and the children drove the flock along steadily, too.

"Might as well get as far as we can while they're fresh," said John.

That evening they went on until they came to the fourth camping place on their father's map; but they had made the distance in three days, not four.

Molly was tired, although the load on her shoulders grew lighter with every day—it was mostly food she carried. Her feet were sore with walking and her back ached, but she didn't complain.

John helped her build the fire in a corner of the stonewall, but it kept flattening in the wind and almost going out.

"Here," he said, "put a blanket over your shoulders. I'm going to the store to get some feed."

"But it will cost money," Molly quavered.

"I got to do the best I can," John explained. "Those turkeys are getting tuckered a little. I got to feed them."

"If only we weren't the last flock."

"Well, we are, and it can't be helped."

Molly sat alone for what seemed to her a long time, with the turkeys roosting about her in the trees. She felt for the first time far away from home and little and lonely. What were the family doing now, she wondered. She didn't seem to care much about Boston. She would have traded Boston and everything in it for a chance to be drying dishes for Mother in the lamplit kitchen at home.

When John came back with the feed in a paper bag, she felt better.

"He let me have it for a quarter," said John, "and I bought us a new loaf of bread for five cents and five cents' worth of rock candy, too.

The rock candy made Molly forget her troubles. And they kept the fire going most of the night and weren't cold either. But the next day it rained, and Turk's bell jingled pretty forlornly behind the flock. The turkeys went well enough, helped on with their morning feed of grain; but the road was muddy, and both children were wet to the skin. At noon they ate cold victuals, standing, and by the time they reached the place marked out for the night, they were all glad to stop. It was a drovers' inn, and John sent Molly to ask how much it would cost to put the turkeys into the barn for the night.

A white-haired woman opened the door. "It won't cost you a cent," she said. "But don't tell anyone, or my husband wouldn't like it. He's gone off to Boston, and I do as I please. Get the turkeys under cover as soon as you can, boy, and come in. Supper's ready."

"But we've got some bread and ham still," protested Molly uncertainly.

"Nonsense," the woman replied. "Haven't I had children of my own? Come in and get warm. You look tuckered out."

That night they ate chicken stew and dumplings, hot potatoes, spinach, and apple pie, and they slept in feather beds.

"You'll have one good night's rest if I know it," declared the woman. "And if it's rainy tomorrow, you shan't stir one foot."

"But we're late, Ma'am," said John. "We've got to go on, rain or shine, before the snow catches us."

Fortunately the next morning cleared to the northwest, bright and cold. There was a white frost on the ground, but the turkeys didn't seem to mind that.

The woman at the inn had fed the flock as well as the children and would take no money. "All I ask is that you'll stop again next year," she told them. "But don't speak of this if my husband should be here."

All day they traveled well. The road was flattening out now. It was no longer downhill, and the farms and villages were closer together. They dreaded the villages, where the dogs ran out of the yards to bark at the turkeys and the flock scattered. That day they lost their first turkey, a young cock which flew over a couple of board fences and disappeared altogether from sight.

"We can't spend half a day chasing him," John decided after nearly an hour's delay. "Father said we'd never get the whole flock there."

The days grew sharper, and the nights were so cold that John insisted Molly must sleep indoors. She agreed, knowing that he could have double the number of blankets if she weren't there. They made good time and lost no more turkeys, but on the ninth day the air seemed too clear to be trusted.

"It's full moon tonight," said Molly. "Father says look for a change after the full moon."

"It it changes, it won't be for rain," muttered John, and all afternoon he kept his eye on the birds more carefully than ever.

"We've only one more day's trip ahead of us, Molly," he said late in the afternoon, "but if it snows tomorrow, maybe we won't be able to get the turkeys through. And if we're delayed for more than a day, we won't have any money left. Do you think you could go on walking by moonlight?"

"I could," said Molly stoutly, "but could the turkeys?"

"We'll have to see."

Before dusk John bought food and gave the turkeys all they

could eat, while he and Molly had a bigger supper than usual by the side of the road. He wrapped her in the blankets and told her to rest until the moon came up. She went to sleep with the turkeys standing uneasily around her. When she woke up, the fire had gone out, and the moon had risen, broad and bright in the sky. John wrapped up the blankets, and they started off.

Old Turk seemed to understand. He drove the turkeys before him down the moonlit road, his bell twinkling like silver in the light. The other turkeys made complaining noises at first, but after a while they quieted down.

The moonlight was so bright that the road showed brown, and the grass had a dark green look in the hayfields. But as the moon rose higher in the sky, a wide ring appeared around it, white and fleecy, and John said, "The moon's wading in snow."

"There're no stars in the ring," said Molly. "It'll snow tomorrow."

But in that bright, windless night it seemed as though they were walking in a dream. The turkeys moved as in a dream, too, not running from side to side after grasshoppers, but walking quietly along in the middle of the road to the sound of Turk's little bell. The moonlight flowed whitely from their polished feathers and caught on the buckles of the straps across John's shoulders and the ends of Molly's shoelaces. The lights went out in the houses. All the world lay sleeping but an owl in the woods and a cat hunting along a ditch.

Still the turkeys went on, and the children followed. When the shadows of the buildings and fences and trees lay almost beneath them and the moon in its dark circle was high overhead, and the mist had spread slowly over the sky, John insisted upon a halt.

"But we can go on," Molly argued. "We'd better go on while we're at it."

"No use running a good thing into the ground," declared John. "We're going to eat now, and so are the turkeys."

"But you don't have to build a fire!"

"Yes, I do. And you're to sit down here and do as you're told."

Once off her feet, Molly thought she'd never get on them again. John wrapped her up and told her to go to sleep, but he wouldn't rest himself. He heated water over the fire and made a hot bran for the turkeys; then he fed them carefully, seeing that the smaller ones got their share. When all had eaten, he stamped out the fire and wakened Molly.

"Let me alone," she kept saying, "there's no school today," but he kept at her until he had roused her at last.

The last half of the night was hard on everyone. Some of the turkeys were limping, and the children had to keep nagging at them.

"That Turk's a wonder," John said, for Turk kept driving the flock ahead as steadily as though he had just started. If John's feet were tired, he never showed it any more than Turk did. But Molly was limping; if she hadn't begun to sing hymns, she might have burst out crying instead. The mist was turning to cloud, and the feel of the air had changed. Any country-bred child would have known that snow was coming. The moon was still shining, but in a startled now-you-see-me and now-you-don't way, and the ring around the moon looked like a band of copper.

About four in the morning they reached Cousin Jonathan Cole's house in Cambridge and knocked, though they hated to waken anyone at that hour. John knew the house by the red barn with the weather vane of a horse jumping a fence, and the bow window on the right side of a white door with a round knocker, just as Father had said.

Cousin Jonathan came downstairs with a candle and let them in.

Then he put on his clothes and helped John get the turkeys under shelter and fed, while Cousin Mattie hurried Molly off to a warm bed.

Neither of the children woke up until noon the next day, and it's a wonder that they woke up then, for the light was dimmed by falling snow, and the earth was silent under a white blanket already two inches thick. Perhaps it was the smell of Cousin Mattie's good dinner which wakened them.

"My, you do look more like yourselves," said Cousin Mattie cheerfully when they appeared washed and dressed at the kitchen door. "You gave me quite a turn when you arrived last night, looking like two ghosts."

"I'd better go see to the turkeys," said John, but Cousin Mattie smiled and shook her head. "Jonathan drove into the market with them this morning in the big cart," she explained. "He's just back and gone to put up the horses. He got a good price for the turkeys on a late market."

"But he didn't take Turk?" asked Molly anxiously.

"No, he understood about Turk. Turk's out at the barn, smelling about, proud of the trip he's made—and well he may be. No one has ever made such good time with a flock to our knowledge, and they brought a better price than they would have last week when the market was full of turkeys. Lots of folks don't think Thanksgiving's Thanksgiving without a turkey on the platter, but there's a lot will leave it till the last minute. Here's your cousin Jonathan. You'd better all eat a good dinner, for you've lots to do and see before Samuel Thaxter stops to pick you up on Monday morning."

—FROM *Up Hill and Down* BY ELIZABETH COATSWORTH

I Praise Thee, Lord

I praise thee, Lord, with humble heart,
For all thy tender good,
For harvest gifts of plenty
From field and vine and wood,
For loving thoughts and laughter,
For tears that cleanse and clear,
For trials that make us stronger
And teach us thou art near.

I praise thee, Lord, for simple things
That bless us every day,
The bird that sings, the butterfly,
The flowers bright and gay.
I thank thee for the kindness
That others show to me,
And for each deep emotion
That turns my thoughts to thee.

—SOLVEIG PAULSON RUSSELL

A Child's Grace

Some hae meat and canna eat
And some wad eat and want it;
But we hae meat and we can eat
And sae the Lord be thankit.

—ROBERT BURNS

The Pudding
That Broke Up the Preaching

Talk about puddings! There never was a more astonishing one than the pudding Ma Tolliver beat up for the all-day preaching that went on down in Possum Hollow Church on Thanksgiving Day. Folks came down to preachings from all over the countryside in those days, from Sandy Creek and Turkey Bottom and Huggins' Crossroads. They brought their dinners with 'em, and between sermons and singing that went on morning and afternoon, they spread their victuals on the ground, picnic fashion, and had a real slapbang good dinner.

Everybody tried to outdo everybody else with their pies and cakes and roast turkey and what not, and Ma Tolliver laid off that Thanksgiving to have a pudding that would top everything else at the preaching. She started on it early Wednesday morning, mixing up her meal and molasses, cutting up peaches and nuts and such fixings to make it extra fancy. After she'd had it on the fire a spell, it came to her that she'd forgot to put the salt in it.

Now every good cook knows a pudding's not right without a pinch of salt, so Ma called out to her oldest girl. "Saphronie!" she says, "I forgot the salt in the pudding, and I'm out here picking a turkey with my fingers all stuck full of feathers. Run in the kitchen for me and put in a good big pinch of salt."

"Lawsy, Ma, I'm a-ironing my dress for the big doings tomorrow. If I stop now my iron'll get all cold." And she went on ironing as hard as she could.

"Hitty, you run in the kitchen and put some salt in the pudding for me," hollered Ma to the next oldest girl.

"I declare to goodness, Ma, I can't do it. I've just been to the witchwoman to get her to take the warts off my hands, and she's smeared axle grease over both my hands and told me not to wash it off till I saw the evening star over my left shoulder. I can't pick up a pinch of salt with axle grease all over my hands."

By this time Ma was mighty nigh wore out with hollering, but she decided to try once more. "You, Lucy! Can't you run in the kitchen and put some salt in the pudding for me?"

"Golly, Ma, I'm a-lying here in bed with cucumber peelings all over my face a-trying to bleach off the freckles before tomorrow. I can't get up now!"

"Sally!" Ma shouted to the youngest girl. "Hump yourself into the kitchen and throw some salt in the pudding for me."

"Goodness sakes, Ma, I'm a-working like fire to get my hair rolled up on old stockings, so's I'll have curls for the doings tomorrow. I ain't got time to salt the pudding!"

Since there weren't any more girls to ask, Ma hollered at her son, "Rufus, please go in the kitchen and throw a spoonful of salt into the pudding." But Rufus was busy, too.

He was a young fellow, just beginning to cotton to girls and do a little courting. "I swan, Ma," he called back, "I'm all full of bear's grease. Been slicking down my hair with it, and now I'm a-greasing my Sunday-go-to-meeting boots. I can't put any salt in the pudding now!"

By that time all the children were used up, and Ma began to holler at her old man. "Lem, can't you stop whatever you're doing and go put a spoonful of salt in the pudding?"

"Shucks, Ma, I'm a-cleaning my gun for tomorrow. S'posing a nice fat rabbit ran across the road whilst we're a-going. If my gun wasn't ready, we'd miss a good rabbit stew for supper. Got my hands full of gun soot. I can't take care of your pudding now."

"Oh, tarnation!" Ma said to herself, clean out of patience. "I'll do it myself!" So she washed the feathers off her hands, and into the kitchen she marched. She got a good big pinch of salt, went over to the hearth where the pudding was boiling away in a pot swung over the fire, and threw it in.

Well, after a while Saphronie got her dress all done up, and she got to feeling a little ashamed that she hadn't done what Ma had asked her to. So she went over to the salt box, got a big pinch, and threw it into the pudding.

Hitty got to feeling bad about refusing Ma, too. "I reckon I could manage to get some salt in that pudding if I tried," she said. So she went into the kitchen, picked up a spoon with her black greasy hands, dipped up a good big dose of salt, and stirred it into the pudding.

Then Lucy, lying back on the bed with her face covered with cucumbers, got to thinking that she hadn't done right, not to help her Ma when she was asked. So she got up, went to the hearth, and put some more salt in the pudding.

No sooner had she got out of the way, than Sally came into the kitchen with her hair done up in knobs all over her head. She got a good-sized pinch of salt and dropped it in the pudding.

Then Rufus got to thinking about it after he'd finished his

boots. So into the kitchen he went and dipped up a heaping big spoonful. Being a man, he didn't know much about such things, and he thought you had to put as much salt in a pudding as in a pot of stew.

Pa's conscience got to hurting him too, and as soon as his gun was all shined up and loaded, he clumped into the kitchen, dipped up a heaping spoonful of salt, and threw it over into the pudding.

At last the pudding was done. Ma took it off the fire. It turned out of the pot as pretty as you please.

"That's as fine a looking pudding as ever I saw!" Ma said. "With a pudding like that, I might even ask the preachers to have some tomorrow."

"Oh yes, do, Ma!" the girls exclaimed.

The next day was sparkling and sunny. Everybody set off, walking to the church. The preaching went fine. As soon as one preacher was winded, another one got up and took his place. By twelve o'clock they were all knocked out, so they called time out for thanksgiving dinner.

Well, sir, Ma was so proud of that pudding that, sure enough, she invited all the preachers over to have some. There were four of 'em, so she cut off four huge hunks and told 'em to dig in.

The first one that took a bite looked at Ma with his eyes popping half out of his head.

"You never tasted anything like it, now did you?" Ma asked proudly.

"No, sister, I never did, and that's a fact," the preacher said.

"Go on, don't be bashful, finish it up!" Ma urged, and the poor fellow, not to hurt her feelings, took another bite and gulped it down.

Those four preachers sure proved their Christian feelings that

day. All four of 'em choked down the pudding without saying a word against it.

After they'd staggered off toward the church, Ma cut some off for herself and passed each of her family a piece. Everybody took a bite and looked up, horrified. Then it came out how each of 'em had gone into the kitchen and salted the pudding.

Ma was mortified. "Too many cooks sure spoilt this pudding!" she said.

They spoilt the preaching too, you can be sure of that. Those preachers didn't save any souls that afternoon. As soon as one of 'em would get himself worked up to a hollering pitch, he'd have to stop and whisper for a glass of water. There was so much water hauled up to the pulpit that day that folks stopped thinking about the preaching and began to wonder what the trouble was. Some took to counting the glasses.

What with preachers plagued with thirst and everybody whispering to each other asking questions, the meeting broke up way ahead of time. The tale about the pudding finally got around, and ever since that time folks around Possum Hollow tell about Ma's pudding that broke up the big Thanksgiving all-day preaching.

—FROM *Tall Tales from the High Hills* BY ELLIS CREDLE

November in the South

The livelong day I listen to the fall
  Of hickory nuts and acorns to the ground,
The croak of rain crows and the blue jay's call,
  The woodman's ax that hews with muffled sound.

And like a spendthrift in a threadbare coat
  That still retains a dash of crimson hue,
An old woodpecker chatters forth a note
  About the better summer days he knew.

Down in the orchard hang the yellow pears,
  Half honeycombed by yellowhammer beaks;
Nearby a dwarfed and twisted apple bears
  Its fruit, brown-red as Amazonian cheeks.

—WALTER MALONE

Thanksgiving Time

When all the leaves are off the boughs,
And nuts and apples gathered in,
And cornstalks waiting for the cows,
And pumpkins safe in barn and bin,
Then Mother says, "My children dear,
The fields are brown, and autumn flies;
Thanksgiving Day is very near,
And we must make thanksgiving pies!"

—AUTHOR UNKNOWN

The Lame Turkey

"What's the matter here?" Michali's father, Yiannis, counted the black turkeys once more. "There should be twenty, but there are only nineteen."

"Let's count them again." Michali did not look his father in the eye. "One-two-three—."

"Aha!" Yiannis saw the strange expression on his son's face. "I think we shall find it is the lame turkey that is missing."

The father waved his arms at the flock of turkeys—not enough to frighten them, just enough to send them fluttering and hopping about. Not one of them walked with a limp.

"So-o-o-o?" Yiannis looked sternly at Michali. "And where is the lame one?"

"Must we sell Napaki?" If Michali had been the crying sort, which of course he was not, there would have been tears splashing all over his face as he asked that question.

Ever since one of the turkeys, as a tiny fluff of feathers, had one leg crushed under the hoof of a donkey, Michali had made a pet of him. He called him Napaki, which is Greek for the Little

274

Lame One. From the very first, the turkey ate out of Michali's hand and rode about on his arm. All the other turkeys seemed rather silly birds. Napaki was different. Michali had petted him and talked to him till the boy was sure the bird understood him.

"Selling Napaki would be almost like selling Marika!" Michali looked at his little sister, standing in the door of their adobe house twirling the spindle of wool from their own sheep. She was spinning yarn for their mother to knit into winter clothes.

The father laughed because he knew Michali did not really mean what he said. "Get Napaki now. Before you start to market, I'll tell you a story they used to tell back in my old village in Asia Minor when I was a boy."

Michali could not hurry today, not even for one of those loved stories remembered from the days before the Greeks of Asia Minor moved into Greece. He dragged himself to the back of the house where Napaki was tethered by his one good leg to a big-leaved fig tree. He tucked Napaki into the crook of his arm and walked slowly back to his father and the turkeys.

"It's a Nasr-ed-Din Hodja story," began Yiannis. Michali stopped frowning. Marika skipped across from her doorway to listen without missing a single twirl of her busy spindle. The children never grew tired of the stories about Nasr-ed-Din Hodja, the man of long-ago Turkey, who was often so wise when he seemed to be foolish, and who did such foolish things while appearing to be very wise.

The story began: Nasr-ed-Din Hodja was carrying a live turkey home from the marketplace, tucked under his arm just as Michali carries Napaki. It was a nice, plump turkey, and the Hodja was proud of it. That is, he was proud till his friend Mehmet joined him. Mehmet was carrying a green-and-red parrot under his arm.

"See my beautiful parrot!" bragged Mehmet. "It can talk." The parrot croaked a few words to prove it.

Suddenly the turkey did not seem so wonderful to Nasr-ed-Din Hodja. He knew his turkeys could say nothing but "Gobble-gobble" in a voice that no fool could mistake for talking. But, as you know, the Hodja never would admit that anyone had the better of him. He was not going to let Mehmet think the parrot was smarter than his own turkey.

Nasr-ed-Din Hodja thought and thought as the two men walked along together through the narrow cobblestoned Turkish street. The Hodja only half-listened as Mehmet bragged about his bird and made the parrot recite all the words he knew. And, as always happened when the Hodja thought his hardest, something popped into his mind that would make everything all right again.

He beamed at Mehmet. "I am glad my turkey does not chatter like your noisy parrot. It must be tiresome to live with a bird that talks on and on with never a thought in her silly green-and-red head. My turkey is much wiser than your babbling parrot."

"Wiser? Prove it!" snapped Mehmet.

"My turkey does not talk. Heaven forbid! But—" and the Hodja stopped to make what he had to say the more impressive. Mehmet stopped too and stared at the Hodja as he went on. "My turkey *thinks* in seven languages!"

So it was with a laugh, after all, that Michali started driving his flock of turkeys to the marketplace in the small town that snuggled beside a hill two miles across the plain.

On the open road, with nobody in sight, he could guide the flock with the hawthorn stick in one hand. It was different when anyone passed or met them: a man on donkeyback, an old woman plodding along with a heavy bag of wheat on her head, a rattling bus loaded till its springs sagged, a truck full of soldiers, boys driving a herd of black goats. Then Michali needed a stick in each hand to guide his gobbling flock safely at the edge of the road.

At these times, Napaki had to hop along as best he could on his one good leg. But Michali would pick him up again as soon as he could manage the flock with only one stick.

He set Napaki down with the flock as they entered the town.

Loaded donkeys, pushcarts, men on horseback, and people milled in all directions. The turkeys huddled close together and looked about stupidly, confused by all the noise and activity. It was a small town, but it seemed like a great city to the boy from a village of thirty mud-brick houses.

He guided the nervous flock straight to the market place. Some merchants had small booths. Others had their goods piled almost in the streets. Others called their wares which they pushed in carts or balanced on trays on their heads.

If he had not known the way to the animal market, he could have found it by the cackling, grunting, and bleating. He looked and was glad to see that no other flocks of turkeys were there ahead of his. Much as he hated to sell Napaki, he knew his family was depending on him to bring home the full price of twenty turkeys.

"Look! A village boy with turkeys!" he heard people say.

Michali had been to market often enough with his father so that he knew just what to do. He knew what price he must get for each turkey and knew that he must begin by asking a higher price. He knew just how far he could let the buyers beat down the price before he clicked his tongue in a firm Greek "no," which meant he could not cut the price another drachma.

One turkey was sold—and another—and another. Of course, Michali saw to it that Napaki was not among the first to go. All over the marketplace there were men and women walking home with turkeys under their arms. The roll of paper drachmas in Michali's pocket felt plump and pleasant. The boy was doing well. Not a single turkey had he sold for less than the sum his father set. Some he had sold for a few drachmas more.

There were only four turkeys left—Napaki and three others. Fat Pedros, who owned the restaurant, came hurrying across the street, bringing the smell of roasting lamb with him. "I'll take all you have left," he puffed.

"Four is a lot for one person to buy, even for a restaurant," said Michali, hugging Napaki close. "Wouldn't three be enough?"

"My soul! What sort of a salesman are you?" asked Pedros, mixing a bit of Turkish with his Greek speech, as many people do in northern Greece.

"Do you come from Asia Minor, like my father?" Michali was saying anything to change the subject. "He is always saying 'My soul!' in Turkish, too, when he is excited."

Pedros laughed. "I do come from Asia Minor. Came here with my family when I was about your size. But that doesn't keep me from buying four turkeys at a time, does it? How much will you take for the four?"

"You wouldn't want this one." Michali held Napaki so that Pedros could see the dangling leg. "You wouldn't want to buy a crippled turkey, would you?"

"What is your game, my boy?" laughed the man. "Are you trying to get a higher price, holding back this way? You must know that a lame turkey roasts as well as any."

Then Michali knew that he was beaten. There was no argument he could give to keep the man from buying his Napaki. Anyway, he must carry home the price of twenty turkeys. He felt like Nasr-ed-Din Hodja, cornered, without an answer.

But Nasr-ed-Din Hodja always found an answer. And so, all of a sudden, did Michali. Because the restaurant owner was from Asia Minor, he would know all the Nasr-ed-Din Hodja stories, just as Michali's father did. At least, he could postpone the sale a minute.

Michali looked up at Pedros with something in his eyes that was halfway between a twinkle and a "please."

"This lame turkey is much too valuable to cook," said Michali. "It is like Nasr-ed-Din Hodja's turkey. You see, this turkey can *think* in seven languages."

And Pedros, who remembered the stories that were told in his village when he was a boy, laughed and laughed. While he laughed, he remembered a little lame duck that he used to have for a pet. By the time he was through laughing, he understood everything.

"I could never roast a bird that thinks in seven languages. Never!" agreed Pedros, still laughing.

Then Michali could laugh with him.

"But what will your father say," asked Pedros, "when you go home with a lame turkey under one arm and too few drachmas in your pocket?"

Michali strugged his shoulders. He had no answer.

But Pedros had an answer. "I can think in only two languages. I'm not smart like your turkey. But I sometimes think well enough in my two languages. I have an idea."

There was something in the man's voice that made Michali listen with hope.

"I need a boy to sweep my restaurant and the street in front of it. I need a boy to run a few errands for me. If a boy worked hard for about five hours, he could earn the price of a lame turkey."

That was why Michali returned to his village at sunset, five hours later than he was expected, with the price of twenty turkeys in his pocket and his lame Napaki dozing comfortably under his arm.

—ALICE GEER KELSEY

Gifts for the Harvest Festival
(*Thanksgiving on the Island of Jamaica*)

"The pigpen is not strong enough, Danny." Esther shook one of the stout upright sticks her brother had used to make the pigpen.

"Stop shaking that stick, Esther." His sister's comments annoyed him, for he had spent hours and hours making sure that he had built a good pen. "I can take care of my pigpen myself. By the time Daddy brings the pig over this evening, the pen will be ready."

Harvest Thanksgiving Festival at the Sharon village church, on the Island of Jamaica, was only a month away. Danny's father had promised him a little black and white pig as a reward for his help on the farm. He was going to give it special care and food because it was to be his gift at the Harvest Festival.

"All right. I was only trying to help you," said Esther, his twin sister. "I have my own troubles. Melita has not brought my chicken."

"I warned you not to give out your hen on the half," said Danny. "I know the plan is to have Melita take care of the hen and give you half the chickens hatched. Surely you can care for your hen better than Melita can."

"I won't have you say such things about my friend," said Esther angrily. "It's not her fault that only two chicks survived this time. She is bringing me a nice healthy one."

"I'm sorry, Esther." Danny left his job of strengthening the sticks and came over to Esther. He put his hand on her shoulder. "What with your Rhode Island chicken, and my black-and-white pig, it's going to be a great Harvest Festival," Danny added, his eyes sparkling with anticipation. "It will be the best on the whole island of Jamaica. Maybe the best in the West Indies."

"It's bad luck to boast." Esther added, "Mamma wouldn't like it."

"Esther, Esther, where are you?" someone was calling. It was Melita.

Esther called out, "I'm coming," and ran up from the backyard around the cottage to find her friend.

Melita, a plump, happy-faced girl, was standing with a little straw basket in her hand. Esther could hear a fluttering in the basket and knew Melita had brought her chicken.

"Oh, Melita, I'm glad you have come and brought my chicken," said Esther, hugging her. "Daddy is giving Danny his pig today, and I was down by the kitchen garden helping him with his pigpen."

"Good for him," said Melita. "Are you going to put this chicken in the big coop?"

"I was going to do that, but Danny says the hens in there will peck at her because she is a strange chicken," said Esther, looking worried.

"Well, haven't you a big wooden box? Maybe Danny or your Daddy would nail some boards across the top and you can keep Teelie—that's what we call her—by herself," Melita suggested.

"Teelie," said Esther. "That's a pretty name. Let me hold her."

Melita took the chicken from the basket and gave it to Esther who patted and stroked it. "In a month she will be big and plump. I am going to feed her a lot of corn," said Esther.

"What are you giving for Harvest Thanksgiving?" asked Esther.

"I am hoping to give an altar cloth," said Melita. "I got the pattern from a magazine and have been crocheting the lace to go around it. It takes a long time to make enough lace to go around such a big cloth."

"Oh, that's wonderful," said Esther. "I wish I could crochet."

"It's quite easy," said Melita. "I will teach you."

"Thank you, Melita. I will get a crochet needle and some cotton. Now come with me to get a box for Teelie." Esther, holding Teelie in one hand, took her friend's hand with the other, and the two went around to the back of the large white cottage.

Esther's mother was very helpful, and soon Esther and Melita had settled Teelie in a big board box and were going down to the well to get some water when Danny came up to them. He greeted Melita casually.

"Look at my chicken, Danny," said Esther. "Isn't she pretty? Her name is Teelie. I would like you to nail three or four boards across the top of her box for me."

Danny bent down and took Teelie in his hands and examined her, moving his hands up and down as if weighing her. "Not bad for a chick," he said. "Almost half a pound."

"Do you think she will weigh two pounds in a month, Danny?" Esther asked anxiously.

"Don't worry about it," Danny said. "Feed her well and give her water."

The girls stood watching Danny. With quick, firm blows of the hammer, he nailed the boards across Teelie's coop. He was nailing the last one in place when Mr. Foster drove up in his old buggy.

Danny held out his hands for the squealing little pig his father took from under the seat. "Stop squealing as if you were going to be put in the pot," said Mr. Foster. "You are in better luck; you're a gift pig, so behave." Then he looked up and greeted the girls, happy to be rid of the pig!

"Thank you, Dad," said Danny. "The pigpen is quite ready. Want to come and see it?"

Father and son walked down the path that led to the pigpen. Esther and Melita got the bucket and rope and went off to get water from the well to put down in the chicken coops. When they had finished this chore, they rushed down to the pigpen to get a good look at Danny's pig. Already Danny was feeding him corn on the cob.

"What are you going to call him?" Esther asked Danny.

Danny scratched his head as he watched his new pet eating greedily. "I think I'll call him Jade," Danny said at last. "I like that name."

"That's a nice name," said Esther. "Don't you think so, Melita?"

"Yes, that's a good name," said Melita. "But you must excuse me now. I have to run off to get on with my altar lace. You both have your gifts settled now."

"I will come with you to the gate, Melita," said Esther, holding her hand. "It will be a job getting Danny away from his treasure."

During the weeks that followed, Danny fed his pig and watched him constantly. He was down at the pen before he went to school, and as soon as he got back from school. He took buckets of water to wash Jade who was soon wallowing in the mud and getting dirty again.

Esther was very happy about Teelie. The chick was growing into a nice, plump hen. Esther could hardly wait until Saturday, when, along with the children and grown-ups of the village, she would be taking her gift to the chapel and Danny, too, would take his pig. Already it was the Tuesday before Thanksgiving. Only four more days!

Esther loved this bringing of all kinds of offerings as a symbol of gratitude to God. Gifts of pigs, chickens, kids, yams, potatoes, corn, all kinds of fruit, pumpkins, melons, corn on the stalks, fancy work—the finest things grown and made—would be crowded at the foot of the altar. How lovely the service would be on Sunday in the decorated chapel. She remembered huge branches of the flowering Poinciana spreading their red radiance along the altar rails. Always Esther felt at this time that all the gifts and flowers were shouting praises to God. Oh, it was good, this time of giving thanks!

"How is Jade, Danny?" asked Esther who was standing by her chicken coop feeding Teelie.

"Not so good," said Danny, looking worried. "He has eaten nothing for the past two days, and that's not like him. He has been eating like a big hog all along. Now he just keeps lying down and grunting."

"Oh, dear, he must be sick. Do pigs get sick?" asked Esther.

"Of course pigs can get sick," said Danny. "Daddy is coming now to give him some medicine."

Just then Mr. Foster came, and Danny rushed him to the pigpen. They both got hold of Jade and examined him. Esther helped Danny hold Jade while Mr. Foster got some medicine down the squealing pig's throat. Mr. Foster tried to cheer Danny up, but the children could see that he too was worried about Jade.

Danny couldn't sleep for worrying. What if Jade got worse? What if Jade died? He had come to love Jade so much. The only thing he could do now was to pray to God to make Jade better.

Thursday night the children slept restlessly. Esther was in a light sleep when a loud barking by the dog next door woke her. She jumped with a start and listened. Then she rushed over to the window and saw in the clear tropical moonlight Jepthah barking fiercely and jumping forward. She ran to wake Father and Danny.

By the time they got to the chicken coop, it was lying on its side. One of the bars Danny had nailed across the top had been torn out. There was a sound of rushing through bushes. Danny ran in its direction, flashing the torch. Mr. Foster followed with his gun.

Esther stood by the coop sobbing, "A mongoose has gone with Teelie—what shall I do? What shall I do? I should have taken her in the house. I know it. I know it." She bent down and picked up a couple of Teelie's feathers.

Mr. Foster and Danny came back from the hopeless chase. "That was a very clever mongoose," said Mr. Foster, turning up the coop and looking at the torn bar by the light of the glowing torch which Danny held.

"He must have been a big, strong one," said Danny. "I thought I had made all the bars very fast." He turned to Esther. "I am very sorry, but never mind, old girl," he said gently. But Esther kept sobbing and was inconsolable.

Esther couldn't go back to sleep, and when she came down to breakfast, her eyes were red and swollen.

When Danny told her that Jade was better, she was glad for his sake, but this made her grief for Teelie even stronger. "Danny, I am glad Jade is better. He is your thanksgiving gift. But what shall I give now that Teelie has been stolen by that wretched mongoose?" Esther began sobbing again.

"Esther dear, don't be so hopeless," said her mother gently.

"I have an idea, a good idea," said Danny. "Come on, Esther. Mom, please excuse us." Danny held Esther's hand and almost dragged her excitedly out of the room.

"Melita is your good friend, isn't she?" he asked Esther.

"Yes she is, you know she is," said Esther, looking at Danny anxiously.

"Well, she can prove it," said Danny with an air of finality. "We are going up there right now, and you are going to ask her to let you have her Rhode Island chicken, the sister of Teelie."

"Oh, but I couldn't take her chicken without paying for it," Esther protested. "Mamma always says never give God a gift that cost you nothing."

"Go and get your pocket money, then," said Danny. "I will get mine too and lend you some if you need it."

The twins almost ran all the way to Melita's cottage. They found her out in the yard giving the hen and chicken water. She was glad to see Esther and noticed she was crying.

"What is the matter, Esther?" she asked anxiously, taking her hand and walking away from Danny who stood looking at the hen and chickens.

"Oh, Melita, a mongoose stole Teelie last night. I have come to ask you to sell me her sister, for I have no gift for the Harvest Festival. Will you do that for me, Melita?" Esther asked anxiously.

"Of course I will," said Melita. "But you must not pay me for Quickie. Take her as a gift from me. I am so sorry about Teelie, poor Teelie."

"You must take some pay, please," Esther pleaded. "You see, I can't give a gift which cost me nothing."

At last Melita gave in and accepted a shilling for Quickie. She ran off to get a basket to put her in. Esther hugged and thanked her.

The twins ran almost all the way home. They were radiantly happy. Despite all the anxieties, they had their gifts for the Harvest Festival. At the Monday Festival sale of all the thanksgiving gifts, their gifts, too, would enrich the Harvest Festival.

—UNA MARSON

A Good Thanksgiving

Said old Gentleman Gay, "On a Thanksgiving Day,
If you want a good time, then give something away."

So he sent a fat turkey to Shoemaker Price,
And the shoemaker said, "What a big bird! How nice!
And, since a good dinner's before me, I ought
To give poor Widow Lee the small chicken I bought."

"This fine chicken, oh see!" said the pleased Widow Lee,
"And the kindness that sent it, how precious to me!
I would like to make someone as happy as I—
I'll give Washwoman Biddy my big pumpkin pie."

"And oh, sure!" Biddy said, " 'Tis the queen of all pies!
Just to look at its yellow face gladdens my eyes!
Now it's my turn," said she, "and a sweet ginger cake
For the motherless Finnigan children I'll bake."

"A sweet cake, all our own! 'Tis too good to be true!"
Said the Finnigan children, Rose, Denny, and Hugh;
"It smells sweet of spice, and we'll carry a slice
To poor little lame Jake, who has nothing that's nice."

"Oh, I thank you, and thank you!" said little lame Jake,
"Oh, what a beautiful, beautiful, beautiful cake!
And oh, such a big slice! I will save all the crumbs,
And will give 'em to each little sparrow that comes!"

And the sparrows twittered, as if they would say,
Like old Gentleman Gay, "On a Thanksgiving Day,
If you want a good time, then give something away!"

—MARIAN DOUGLAS

Around the Hearth on Thanksgiving

When the wind blows thro' the pine trees,
  And comes whistling by the eaves,
When the apples all are gathered,
  When the corn is in the sheaves.

When the geese and ducks fly southward,
  When the whispering pines bend low,
When the flowers, withered, drop to ground,
  And falling is the snow,

Then it's fun to gather round the hearth,
  To sing and laugh and pray,
And say to one another then,
  "This is Thanksgiving Day."
     —BARBARA JEAN BURGETT, age 9,
     KETCHIKAN, ALASKA

Thanksgiving Came on Wednesday

The whole mining camp of Trigger, straggling up the far end of Colorado Gulch, was buzzing with excitement. When school let out, Zulie and Tom Lloyd heard the news before they got as far as the Golden Palace Saloon.

"If only the snow will hold off one more day," everyone said.

Zulie and Tom hurried down the cold, dusty street. At the assay office, where the gulch was wider, Zulie pulled Tom to a stop. She nodded toward a group of miners standing in the doorway, talking.

"I hear there's fifty wagons in the train if there's one," a tall miner was saying. His face was black with whiskers, but his mustache was mostly red.

"Four to eight mules or oxen a-pullin' each wagon. One to two tons to a load. There'll be some tall celebratin' when that freight pulls in."

Zulie looked at Tom. They knew. There wasn't a lemon drop or a peppermint left in Camp. There wasn't a dried apple or a raisin, and if the freight didn't come in time, it would have to be molasses pie for Thanksgiving instead of mince.

"Five days out from Denver and only about twenty more miles to go." It was Martin Speer who said that. Zulie and Tom knew him well. He was a friend of their father. In fact, he had been looking over the mine with Papa the morning of the cave-in, almost two months ago, the morning Papa's legs were hurt and he was taken down to the Center to the hospital.

"Tuesday today," Martin Speer went on. "Didn't I tell you the supplies would get here in time for Thanksgiving?" He clinked some coins in his pocket and tipped back on his toes. "Just in time to celebrate President Grant's thanksgiving proclamation."

"I wouldn't go countin' my chickens," drawled a grizzled old prospector. He sniffed the air. "And I don't like the smell of the weather. Come a heavy snow, they'll never make it up the gulch. Not on a road like that."

Zulie and Tom knew what he meant by a "road like that." It really wasn't a road at all, only a widened pack trail along the creek bed that was usually dry by fall. After all, Trigger Camp wasn't much more than a year old. There hadn't been time to build a real road, when everyone was so busy hunting gold. There had only been time to roll out the biggest boulders from the new trail.

Zulie and Tom knew that except for one icy spot, two miles down where the spring was, the gulch was quite dry. On Saturday, heeding Papa's warning to keep the burros exercised, they had ridden down to the spring. They were surprised to discover that during the week the patch of ice had welled out into a thick lumpy sheet. It was slick and very treacherous. Yet the freight drivers could make their way around safely enough, as long as it didn't snow.

Eager to tell the news to their mother, Zulie and Tom started to move out into the street. But they hadn't gone far before Martin Speer called to them, "Wait right there a minute, you Lloyd kids!"

He left the group of miners and came up smiling. "I know something you're going to have for Thanksgiving," he said.

Tom said, "I know! Mince pie!"

"Something besides that. What's your guess, Zulie?"

"Mama said if there was a nice ham on the freight, we'd have that, with cloves stuck in."

"One more guess," Martin Speer said.

"Is it alive?" asked Tom. "Does it have four feet?" He was always thinking about a dog.

"No, it doesn't have four feet. Fact is, it's lucky to have two." He laughed and leaned down. "It's a secret. You're not to tell your mother, hear? It's to be her thanksgiving surprise . . . if it comes."

Zulie and Tom waited impatiently.

"Saw your Pa last week down at the hospital," he said, trying to make it sound matter-of-fact.

"Is *that* it? Is that it?" Zulie cried. "Is Papa all right? Is he coming on the freight train? Can he walk again?"

"Not so fast, Zulie," Martin Speer chuckled. "Mind you, it's not certain. But the doctor said if there was room on one of the wagons to make a soft bed for your Pa . . . and if the weather stayed nice. . . ." He looked up at the sky. The sun had been moving in and out through clouds all afternoon. Now the clouds seemed to be pushing together, banking over the mountains. "I reckon you could call this nice enough weather, for the end of November." He took out his watch. "The freight ought to be well past Center by now."

"And Papa's on it!" Zulie exclaimed. "I know he's on it. He'll be home for Thanksgiving. Won't he?"

"Good chance, anyway," Martin Speer smiled. "Only don't you breathe a word to your Ma."

Zulie and Tom raced down the road toward a log cabin with a

lean-to kitchen. They burst in at the door. "Freight train's coming," they shouted. But they did not tell their mother what was coming on the train.

"At least fifty wagons. One to two tons to a wagon," Tom said importantly.

"And Martin Speer thinks they've left Center already," Zulie put in.

"At last! Is it really true? Oh, I'm so grateful." Mrs. Lloyd had sensed the excitement in Camp and guessed the news, but she didn't want to spoil the fun. "Now everyone can have a wonderful Thanksgiving. If only . . . if only your father could be here."

That night Zulie woke herself up by trying to call, "Papa! Oh, Papa!" But she couldn't make a sound to warn him. The sides of her neck seemed to press in and choke off her breath. And there was Papa walking over the ice with a cane, limping, trying to get over the slippery humps of boulders. He couldn't make it. He was slipping . . . sliding back down the gulch.

Zulie was hot and trembling. She blinked. What was that strange, fuzzy light outside the window? It almost made her forget her awful dream.

Fully awake now, she sat up in bed and looked out. Snow! Snow, inches deep on the window sill! Zulie gasped. She jumped out of bed and ran over to Tom's cot on the other side of the room. She shook him. "Tom, it's snowing. Snowing," she said.

"Huh?"

"It's snowing . . . and Papa will be stuck in the gulch with the freight."

Snowing! Tom was suddenly awake. And then Mama, hearing voices, called out. "Is anything the matter?" She came in wrapped in her old blue coat, carrying a candle.

"It's snowing . . . and the freight . . . and. . . ." Zulie checked herself. It was hard not to tell the secret.

"Why, so it is." Mama hurried to the window. "And hard, too. But Charley Tremaine will keep the wagons coming. He knows the gulch. He ought to be able to lead the way, even with snow on the ground."

"The ice!" Tom cried suddenly. "It's right in the path of the wagons. He won't know about it because he's been in Center waiting for the freight. And with snow on top, nobody can see it."

"The mules will slip, just the way Papa did in my dreams!" Zulie was horrified. The freight train seemed a million miles away now.

"What can we do about the ice?" Mama's voice was worried. "Is there a way around?"

"Sort of," Tom said. "The gulch is wider there. With a couple more boulders pried out, the teams could get through. But you have to know *where*."

"Dear Lord, we've waited so long for the freight," Mama was saying softly to herself. "What shall we do?"

"Martin Speer. Let's wake him," Tom urged. "He'll know what to do."

That sounded like a good idea. They dressed quickly and hurried out into the snowy night. It was not quite two o'clock. Snow, covering the ground and falling all around, gave a fuzzy brightness to the dark. Though the moon was blotted out, some of its light seemed to come through, riding on snowflakes.

It took considerable knocking and shouting to bring Martin Speer to the door of his little house. But when he saw the snow and heard about the sheet of ice near the spring, he was alert.

"If I know Charley Tremaine," he said, "he'll be making a

forced march up the gulch right this minute. Even with the animals all tuckered out, he won't take a chance on the snow and wait for morning." He nodded at Zulie and Tom. "And of course you're right, he won't know about that icy place. A couple broken mule legs, or a wagon tipped over, could stall the whole train. Someone's got to warn them."

"The freight must get through," Mrs. Lloyd said quietly. "The whole camp's depending on it."

Tom was excited. "I know just where the ice is, and Zulie does too. And we know how to get around it, and what boulders are in the way and. . . ."

"Mrs. Lloyd," Martin Speer said, "will you let the children go down with me? I know it's a mean night, but they can find the place better than I can."

Mama didn't speak for a moment. Then she consented.

It was the kind of night you could never forget. Snow poured out of a heavy sky. Snow piled on the creek bed and on the scrubby bushes along the gulch. Snow mounded over the boulders.

"Charley Tremaine will know this is the last chance to get the freight through," Martin Speer said when they reached the spring and the dangerous patch of ice. "He'll keep coming just as fast as he can. Well, let's build a fire and then start prying away the boulders."

They waited hours, it seemed. Cold, unreal hours with firelight pink on the snow. They waited tensely, eagerly, listening for the sound of wagons. And then . . . at last!

"What's this, a reception committee?" Charley shouted.

No, he didn't know about the ice across the gulch. He'd have tried to go straight ahead.

"Wal, you don't say! The Lloyd kids! Brought a special piece of freight up from Center for you, bundled up in feather beds. Look

now, you lead the way around the ice on your burros, will you? Lead the way, and we'll follow."

Just as the late November dawn was breaking, the first wagons of the freight train pulled into Trigger Camp. In the lead were two plodding burros, a boy riding one and a girl the other. Then came a horse carrying a snow-covered man, with an ax, shovel, and a crowbar strapped to the saddle. Next, Charley Tremaine yelling and shouting at the eight mules hitched to his wagon. Behind came other wagons.

A crowd of people waiting at the livery stable shouted and cheered. The freight! The precious, long-awaited freight!

Zulie and Tom joined their mother at the livery stable. Wagons kept straggling up, drivers calling, "Gee" and "Haw" and "Whoa there." Never had there been such a morning!

Zulie stared nervously at each wagon that pulled up. Which one was hiding Papa under its snowy canvas cover? She strained her eyes, peering through the falling flakes. Then suddenly she saw him. He was limping toward the stable, leaning on a cane. Papa!

She pulled Tom's sleeve. "Look!" she cried. "Oh, look."

"Here comes Thanksgiving!" shouted Tom.

"Well, what do you think of that?" Martin Speer exclaimed, coming out of the livery stable. "Mrs. Lloyd. . . ."

She had been looking the other way. Now she turned and saw. With a surprised cry she ran forward.

Martin Speer put his hand on Zulie and Tom's shoulders to hold them back for a moment. "You're right, Tom," he said. "Here comes Thanksgiving, for you and all of Trigger Camp. But it seems President Grant was plumb wrong about setting the day as Thursday. This year Thanksgiving comes on Wednesday!"

—AILEEN FISHER

Father, We Thank Thee

For flowers that bloom about our feet,
　　Father, we thank thee;
For tender grass so fresh and sweet,
　　Father, we thank thee;
For song of bird and hum of bee,
For all things fair we hear or see,
Father in heaven, we thank thee.

For blue of stream and blue of sky,
　　Father, we thank thee;
For pleasant shade of branches high,
　　Father, we thank thee;
For fragrant air and cooling breeze,
For beauty of the blooming trees,
Father in heaven, we thank thee.

For this new morning with its light,
　　Father, we thank thee;
For rest and shelter of the night,
　　Father, we thank thee;
For health and food, for love and friends,
For everything thy goodness sends,
Father in heaven, we thank thee.

—AUTHOR UNKNOWN

The above poem, sometimes attributed to Ralph Waldo Emerson, may be used for choral speaking or antiphonal speaking, with all joining in "Father, we thank thee." It might be used, also, as a table grace or litany of thanksgiving when the family gathers.

A Sackful of Thanksgiving

Though corn-fodder tepees and golden pumpkins from the neighboring fields decorated the four corners of the fifth-grade room of Lincoln School, Hannah Kruger did not see them.

She didn't even notice the row of plump turkeys that seemed to strut across the chalkboard above the crayon poster of the brave Puritans on their way to church.

All Hannah could see were the two yawning pasteboard boxes perched upon stools beside Miss Anne's desk, and labeled, "Thanksgiving Dinner for the Hillcrest Children's Home."

Such boxes had perched upon such stools beside teachers' desks every Thanksgiving since she had arrived in America, a German refugee, five years ago. Now Hannah loved to hear the story of the first Thanksgiving. Indeed, she sometimes felt like a Pilgrim herself in this strange, new country. And she loved to help fill the boxes. It gave her such a warm feeling, though she did wish that she could put something really nice in the boxes just once.

Why couldn't some newspaper print her picture, she thought, like the picture they took last year of Ruth Turner and her turkey?

What a beautiful picture that was! But who would want to see a picture of her towhead and that everlasting head of cabbage, though it was the largest and firmest one in the cellar, as Mother always reminded her.

Hannah closed her eyes tight and tried to picture the very nicest thing she might bring for the baskets if she had one wish. Her round face puckered, and heavy blond braids bobbed over her shoulders. What would it be? A nice fat goose . . . or a plump turkey . . . or a freezer full of fresh strawberry ice cream . . . or a whole sackful of something . . . or. . . .

Miss Anne opened her notebook. "It's time to list our food gifts for the thanksgiving baskets," she said. Soon the list was growing as fast as an April dandelion in a garden row. Fruit cake, apples, pumpkin pies, chicken, cranberries. Hannah forgot her troubles momentarily. She thought that she could never wait until lunchtime, just listening made her hungry.

But now Miss Anne was in the K's. "Hannah Kruger," she said, with a bright smile in Hannah's direction.

Hannah drew a deep breath, filling her nostrils with the familiar odor of wet leather, damp woolens, and chalk dust. Then her throat closed tight, and she couldn't answer right off. How cheap her gift always sounded. Hearing it would never make anyone hungry.

Then Ruth Turner, who sat across the aisle, said the dreaded words for her in a hissing whisper: "One head of Dutch cabbage . . . homegrown sauerkraut . . . ," she taunted, mimicking Hannah's slow manner of speaking. Some of the children overheard and stifled giggles with their hands.

Hannah wanted to disappear through the keyhole; she felt that small and hurt. Yet she knew that they didn't know how scarce money

was at her home. And no one else had five brothers and sisters as she did. She hoped above all that Miss Anne hadn't heard Ruth's whisper. She would punish her, and then Ruth wouldn't like her at all. She wanted so much to be friends with Ruth and the other girls, but especially Ruth, the leader.

"Food for the Children's Home again?" Mrs. Kruger had asked that morning, laughing good-naturedly. "Already we have a children's home. Is it nicht so?"

Ashamed, Hannah stopped begging to take something extra nice for the boxes.

"And cabbage is gut food," Mrs. Kruger went on, busy with a pile of soapy dishes. "And plenty there is. Lucky you are that your fater is a gartener! And a gut one, too, he is."

Hannah winced. Deep down she wished that her parents would stop using those German words. Some people even mimicked their gutteral accents. Didn't they know English yet after weeks and weeks at night school? Besides, they would all become American citizens soon. If Mother only understood about Ruth Turner, and the new American way of doing things. Were mothers ever young?

Now Ruth's mocking brown eyes were boring inquisitively into Hannah's soft blue ones. "Oh, Miss Anne, I'd like my gift to be a surprise," Hannah burst out. "Maybe—I'll bring them Wednesday —if I can—I—."

Hannah stopped suddenly. Now she had done it. *Bring them.* Why did she say that? And that *maybe* wouldn't help much either. It would probably be cabbage after all. Why, she had let her inner wish slip out as quick as a shooting star!

"Bring *them?*" Ruth whispered at once and tossed her black curls in that proud, sure way she had, but she couldn't hide her sudden new interest in Hannah.

Some of the other girls turned and looked at Hannah admiringly. "A secret! How nice," their smiles seemed to say to her. "Why didn't we think of that?"

Hannah smiled back shyly, glad that they couldn't see the deep inner worry gnawing at her already. Yet she felt so good to be admired and noticed that she couldn't explain she just meant maybe— that she was only wishing out loud.

At intermission the girls crowded around her in the new snow. "Hannah, come play Fox and Geese with us," they begged, but spoiled it for Hannah by adding: "Please tell us your secret."

Oh, she was popular now all right, but how she wished that she had never started the business. Would cole slaw be *them,* she wondered, and knew that it wouldn't. But surely I can solve this some way, she thought in growing desperation.

When dinnertime came, Hannah hadn't thought of a single answer to her problem. This was really serious. Why hadn't she held her tongue and her *maybe's?* And what would Mother say if she knew? Hannah's throat felt so thick that she barely tasted the good beef and noodles.

She slipped off to bed early to think, but Mother followed her. "Hannah, tell Mutter. Your supper you didn't eat. Mit noodles yet." Mrs. Kruger sat down on the bed beside Hannah. "Is it der Dokter I should call?"

"Oh, Mother, I did such a terrible thing at school today," Hannah sobbed. "I just meant that I'd like to—and they took it for granted. And I didn't want to say cabbage again—and—." Then the whole story poured out, and Mother's arms were a wonderful haven. Why, she understood everything, even Ruth Turner, though she never stopped her disapproving cluck.

"A lesson you will learn, Liebekind." Her voice was stern but understanding. And she was puzzled. "Take *them*, Hannah?" she pondered. "Ya . . . I know what . . . and plenty there is in the cellar." She whispered something to Hannah, putting enthusiasm into the word. "Gut ones they are, too."

"But, Mother, you don't understand. I can't take those awful things." Hannah dried her eyes on Mother's blue-checked apron. "They would make more fun of me than ever. I just can't."

Mrs. Kruger looked at Hannah steadily. "And what *is* gut food in this United Staaten?" She rose to her feet to return to the kitchen. "Das is it, or the kohl, Hannah."

"Please, Mother, it's cabbage, not kohl," Hannah explained.

"Ach, Liebekind, hard it is to remember." Mrs. Kruger smiled patiently. "Is it nicht so?"

Wednesday morning came all too quickly. Hannah tried to think of a good excuse to stay home from school, but Mother's clear, understanding eyes squelched that longing. So she reluctantly carried her gift to school, lingering along the way, hoping to be the last one there and no time left for questions.

Miss Anne gave her a quick, inquiring glance and put the gift on her desk. It looked very nice tied with a red ribbon left from last year's Christmas wrappings. The children crowded around to examine the package with their eyes and fingers, but the buzzer sounded and Miss Anne sent them to their desks.

Hannah trembled. How they would laugh when they found out her big secret! Her cheeks went hot. She wanted to run and hide somewhere forever, away from these Americans and their Thanksgiving.

Miss Anne began to check the cartons of food, ignoring the raised hands. Soon the big trucks would stop and pick up all the boxes in the building.

"It's a regular Pilgrims' Thanksgiving," Miss Anne said, "with one exception. We forgot the onions! I just know they had them at the first Thanksgiving feast . . . creamed ones . . . or sliced in vinegar. It's a wonder someone didn't think of onions. The dressing will need them, too."

The children looked at one another apologetically. Why hadn't they brought something that Miss Anne thought so nice.

But Hannah's hand was waving excitedly. "Miss Anne, that's what I brought. Onions. Bermuda onions. A whole sackful of them.

You left them on your desk. But I—." She hesitated and was silent.

The children looked her way admiringly.

"What a thoughtful gift, Hannah," Miss Anne said.

"Mutter—Mother thought of them, Miss Anne," Hannah confessed in some confusion. "I—you know—I—I didn't even want to bring them." Now the whole story, except Ruth's part tumbled out into Miss Anne's sympathetic and understanding ears.

And suddenly Hannah knew that somehow Miss Anne had known all about everything from the beginning—cabbage, onions, Ruth, Mother, and all! Dear, kind Miss Anne. Small wonder they all loved her.

Now Ruth's face was flushed and shamed, and there was a new respect for Hannah in her eyes and real friendliness in her smile.

"I'm so glad that I didn't mention Ruth to Miss Anne," Hannah thought happily. There was a broad smile on her round face. She felt good all over.

"Miss Anne, let's don't keep lists ever again," Ruth suggested with a shyness new to her. "We think of them and forget the day— at least I did." Her eyes wavered in confusion.

Miss Anne made room for the onions atop the biggest box, smiling straight into Hannah's watchful eyes. "No more lists," she said.

Hannah couldn't believe her ears. "No more lists!" she echoed happily. This America. It was getting better all the time.

—NELLIE BLY MIDDLETON

The Heavenly Jam

Craig Moore couldn't remember ever feeling so terrible on Thanksgiving Day. This holiday had always been a happy time. For one thing, the house smelled so good. Mother was extra cheerful as she busied herself with the cooking. Dad was home all day, full of fun and tease. Since Craig had been big enough, it had been his job to help his father stretch the table way out to make room for all the relatives who came to share the thanksgiving feast. In the late afternoon, after the last crumb of bronze pumpkin pie had been eaten, he would join his neighbor-friend, Bob. They would hike into the nearby woods to look over the coming Christmas tree crop. At sunset time they returned home, tingling from the frosty air. The feeling of special good seemed to go through every inch of Craig, making it truly a day for thankfulness.

This year he was over a thousand miles away from Bob. He did have to admit that Mom's cooking smelled as good as ever. But the little beach house that was serving as their new home seemed lonely to Craig. "Even if Bob could be here," he thought, "there sure aren't any woods to hike in."

311

Buttoning his leather jacket, he stepped outside. Looking to the rear of the house, he could see the oil derricks stark and bare on the hills beyond. In front of the cottage, just past a narrow strip of coast, the thundering sea served as frontyard. This Thanksgiving Day the ocean seemed horribly angry. The waves boomed against the shore, crashing loudly, then threw themselves into a foaming spray against a nearby rock.

"There doesn't seem to be as much sand as there was in front of our house. I wonder how far these waves can come up?"

Shivering, he turned and went back into the cottage. "Sure won't have to make the table larger this year!"

The relatives were far away, and there were no friends to ask. As far as Craig could find out, there weren't any people around to be friends. In this section of the beach there were only five houses, and those were scattered. Craig thought there were only two of them that had people living in them during the winter.

He went back into the house, trying hard to shake his lonesome feeling. His Dad looked over his paper at him, the kind face frosted with a sudden frown. "I know it's lonely, Craig-boy, but once you start to school up the coast, there'll be good friends again. And Bob and his sister are coming out for the entire summer."

"Sure, Dad." Craig forced his lips into a smile. He was ashamed of his feelings, but he was terribly homesick.

Craig's mother came in from the kitchen pushing a small serving cart. It was laden with food. Craig went to help her. "I thought it would be nice to have our first Thanksgiving here by the window where we can watch the sea," his mother said.

"Great!" Dad agreed. "This view is the finest part of the house. Need some help carrying?"

"I thought with just us, I'd bring this little tea cart. I have the turkey and everything on it. Now I won't have to be getting up for things during dinner. I'll just enjoy it all. My, those waves seem high and close! Do you think there's any danger?"

Craig began to feel something more than dislike for the ocean roaring out there. He felt a chill deep within him—something he hated to admit—fear. Dad's big voice was full of laughter.

"This house has been here for some twenty years, and the old sea hasn't done much damage yet. The big window is the newest part. This is some view! That sea is on a rampage! We never had anything like this to watch before on Thanksgiving!"

Craig couldn't join his father's enthusiasm. His mother was holding up a large jar of beautiful red jam.

"I've had a caller—Mrs. Dorchester. She lives alone in the very last house up the beach. Look what she brought us! She calls it Heavenly Jam. It's a combination of strawberries and loganberries. If it tastes as good as it looks—it's well named. I'll put some in the crystal dish and then we'll be ready. I've even brought in the pumpkin pie on our cart."

"I sure get hungry in this sea air!" Dad said. "Craig, wouldn't you say the grace? Then we'll be served."

Craig watched Mother getting ready to unscrew the top of the jam. He wondered if he could say the "Thank You" prayer over the big lump in him that was getting colder than an icicle.

Then it happened. The waves rose to a tremendous height against the house. Boom! Bang! Crash! Splinter! Swish!

"The window!" Mother shouted.

Craig heard it and saw the jar of Heavenly Jam go sailing out of his mother's hands, even before he felt the terrible drenching.

It was a strange thing. As Craig saw the waves sweeping the golden-brown turkey up, the lump he had felt disappeared. All he could feel was anger. The sea that he hadn't liked anyway had crashed through the window like some rude, uninvited guest. It had ruined their thanksgiving dinner, to say nothing of trying to drown the whole family and flood the house.

As suddenly as it came, it rolled out and away from the little cottage. Looking out, Craig couldn't see the turkey, but he did glimpse the potato dish, broken in half, riding on the crest of a wave. Without thinking, the boy dashed through the place that had been their picture window. He ran wildly after the waves as though to take back his thanksgiving dinner. Mom had worked over that. Now he wished he had been more thankful.

At the shoreline he saw a jar bobbing in the water. It was the Heavenly Jam. Mom hadn't been able to get the top off. Craig reached out, but the waves tossed the jar away. Soaked, teeth chattering, Craig waded deeper.

"Craig, come back!" his father's voice had "I mean it" tones.

Craig's hand closed firmly on the jar of Heavenly Jam. He started to turn back, but his sodden clothes were heavy in the swirling waves.

"Hi! Need any help here?" It was a voice sort of like Bob's.

Craig thought a wave must have knocked his head, too. No boys lived around. Helping hands propelled him shoreward.

"We came down to help. Our Gran—Mrs. Dorchester—thought you might be in trouble here. She says nothing like this has happened in the twenty years she's been here—probably won't again."

Craig's helpers were two boys who looked exactly alike in slick yellow coats, hats to match, and high black boots. They had big, friendly smiles.

"Here—you're a mess! Take my coat—I've got a jacket underneath. I'm West Dorchester, and this is my twin brother, East—."

"Craig! Let's wrap you in this blanket!" Dad came running with a big car robe.

"Dad, this is East and West," Craig managed between chattering teeth.

The boys all had to laugh at Mr. Moore's surprised face. "He's right, Sir. My name's really Weston—and this is my twin brother, Lawrence. You can sort of see how I got to be West, and the East was a natural."

"They belong to the Heavenly Jam lady," Craig said, handing over his rescued treasure to his father. "I got that away from Old Splash!" Craig glared at the water as it tossed, still noisy, but certainly not so fierce.

"Here comes Gran now and our sister, Sally," East and West shouted together.

Even through his wet clothes, Craig felt warmer looking at their jolly faces.

"Mom didn't tell me you lived here," he told the twins.

"We don't," West answered. "We spend every vacation we can get here."

"We have a lot of fun with what you call 'Old Splash,'" East said. "Tomorrow we'll take you to our cave, and we'll show you our boat."

Mrs. Dorchester and Sally hurried over. Everyone was introduced, and then Craig dashed off to get dry and change.

When Craig returned, the boys were putting sandbags from the storeroom in front of the cottage. Mr. Moore was fastening plyboard over the front window, and there was a fire roaring in the fireplace. Sally was carting off the last of the broken dishes. Dry kitchen chairs were brought in to replace the dampened living-room furniture.

"Boy! Did you save the day!" East said to Craig. "All Gran's Heavenly Jam had been sent up to our place in the city. This last jar she gave to you."

"Something's wrong with the gas at our place," West added, "'so Gran turned off the main valve. No thanksgiving dinner at our house. Absolutely none!"

"Old Splash gobbled ours! Our turkey and the pumpkin pie!" Craig moaned.

"Yes," East agreed, "but your mother says she's going to make some special pancakes on the electric griddle—and with the Heavenly Jam. . . ."

"Boy-o-boy!" West grinned.

They couldn't stretch the table because the wood was still wet. Sally and the boys sat on blankets and cushions on the floor by the fire. The older Moores and Gran managed on the kitchen furniture. Never did Craig feel warmer inside or more thankful as he said grace for this unusual Thanksgiving Day by the sea.

"And thank you, our Dear Lord, for our new friends—and even Old Splash out there. And for Mom's special pancakes and the Heavenly Jam. Amen."

—ESTHER FRESHMAN

A Child's Thought of Harvest

Out in the field which were green last May,
But are rough and stubbled and brown today,
They are stacking the sheaves of the yellow wheat,
And raking the aftermath dry and sweet,
The barley and oats and golden rye
Are safely stored in the granary;
Where the pumpkins border the tall corn rows,
The busy reaper comes and goes;
And only the apples set so thick
On the orchard boughs are left to pick.

What a little time it seems since May—
Not very much longer than yesterday!
Yet all this growing, which now is done
And finished, was scarcely then begun.
The nodding wheat and high, strong screen
Of corn were but little points of green.
The apple blossoms were pink and sweet,
But no one could gather them to eat;
And all this food for hungry men
Was but buds or seeds just planted then.

—SUSAN COOLIDGE

Harvest Time the World Around

Oh, sing for the golden ripened grain;
  Give thanks, and share your cheer;
Rejoice for the fruits of harvesttime,
  The feast-time of the year.

For thousands of years farmers around the world have harvested their crops with joy and songs. And at harvesttime many different people have given thanks for seedtime and harvest, fruit and grain. Countries celebrate in various ways; yet many harvest customs are somewhat alike.

One of the earliest harvest feasts about which we know was celebrated by the Hebrews more than three thousand years ago. It was called the Feast of Booths, or Tabernacles, and still is celebrated in September by Jewish people. It is often called *Succos*. The book of Deuteronomy in the Bible gives plans for this happy season of thanksgiving to God, of family gatherings, feasting, sharing with the poor and lonely. The people were told, "Rejoice in your feast . . . be altogether joyful."

319

Ancient Greeks held a harvest festival to Demeter whom they believed to be the goddess of agriculture. They offered her fruit, honeycombs, and other gifts. Romans called their harvest goddess Ceres and celebrated her festival, Cerelia, in October. They formed gay processions and went through the fields, playing musical instruments and singing. Then they enjoyed the thanksgiving feast, with more singing and dancing and games.

Although many rural customs are changing throughout the world, in some places harvesters still form a procession and go singing through the fields. In parts of Germany farm workers make a large beautiful wreath of wheat and field flowers, called the *Erntekranz*. In a jolly procession they carry it as a gift to the farm owner, and he welcomes them to a harvest feast.

In the Hungarian festival also, when the last sheaf was harvested, the farm workers made a wreath. Laughing and shouting, they fastened it to the door of the landowner's house. And he invited them in to feast and enjoy a merry time singing and dancing.

The Polish harvest festival, *Dozynki,* included a reapers' parade with a wreath for the farm owner and his wife, who welcomed the reapers indoors to feast and to sing traditional songs and dance the old harvest festival dances. The wreath was hung on the wall to remain until next year's harvest.

Harvest home in Czechoslovakia was called *Obzinki,* or sending off summer. There, too, a wreath was made of grain and flowers. Ears of grain in the center symbolized the sun which ripened it. In some localities the woman who bound the last sheaf was called the *Baba.* Sometimes Baba was a doll of grain decorated with flowers and ribbons. Whether woman or doll, Baba was placed in a farm wagon together with gaily trimmed scythes and rakes. Bright ribbons were braided in the horses' manes and tails. All the reapers, dressed

in their best gay-colored clothes, paraded beside the wagon to the
farmer's home. After congratulating him on the good harvest, they
shared in the harvest feast and the fun. There were special square
harvest cakes, filled with plum jam or some other delicious filling.
Sometimes at the end, the Baba was splashed with water so there
would be rainfall for a good harvest next year. Splashing with water
was part of the harvest celebration in many countries.

Everywhere the new grain of harvest has been received with joy. For instance, in old Bulgaria the whole family was happy when the first bread was made from that grain. They took the grain to the mill gladly, brought home the flour proudly, then watched while the mother kneaded it into bread. She pressed a hole in the center of each loaf, praying, "God please bless this bread and each person who eats it. Bad luck blow away like chaff, good luck stay with us."

Each one in the family wanted to taste the new bread. But the first crisp loaves, with butter and cheese in the middle, were put in bowls outside the front door for passersby. Everyone who stopped would say before eating the bread, "God bless this house and give it daily bread. Bless the people who live here; bless their wheat fields with twice as many sheaves."

Meanwhile more loaves with the most tempting fragrance were baking in the courtyard oven and in the indoor fireplace. Soon the family would gather around the table, give thanks, and enjoy the bread from grain they had raised themselves.

Mexico always has been a land of many different crops, and harvest feasts have been held there for centuries. And Mexico is a land of music. When the harvests are brought in; happy songs fill the air in many villages, and people are thankful for God's goodness.

In some South American countries the same harvest dances have been danced for hundreds of years. Whole villages celebrate with music and harvest feasting.

So it is in many places in Africa at planting and harvest time.

One of the happiest occasions for Chinese children is the harvest moon festival. An old tradition says that since the moon influences crops, lovely flowers fall from the harvest moon. Children and grown-ups feast, play games, and enjoy music and a merry time. As far as possible, the foods are prepared in round shapes to honor the moon. Since the tale is told that a rabbit lives on the moon, the children receive presents of toy rabbits. They are given also toy pagodas like the palaces of the moon. Many sweet cakes are bought from bakeries and candy stores. The cakes are round and are decorated with pictures of the moon and its palaces. Some have pictures of the rabbit in the moon. Delightful legends are retold at this happy time.

Thanksgiving Day is celebrated in Japan the first week in November. On this holiday people are grateful for the harvests and for good relationships in business and industry and, of course, for their homes and families.

Diwali, or the Feast of Lights, is celebrated by many Hindus in India on the last night of their autumn festival. They light cotton wicks in clay saucers filled with oil. These soft lights are placed on windowsills, roofs, and along roads and streams. Many people in the northern hill country think that at harvesttime the goddess of prosperity returns to the lowlands. Their lights will guide her, and she may give them a special blessing.

On that night also, numbers of such little lights float on the Ganges River. Silently the women and girls who have set them afloat watch and hope their lighted saucers will reach the other side still glowing. That will mean good fortune.

Great drums boom out the beat for dancers at harvest festivals in Borneo. Dressed in their finest clothing, the merrymakers gather in a large open-air pavilion. They dance and dance until they are weary. The last to keep dancing are cheered loudly and given prizes. Travelers who have watched the Borneo festival say it is much like thanksgiving and harvesttime in countries around the world. Everyone is thankful for the harvest; everyone shares the fun and the feast.

Harvest-home feasts and Thanksgiving Days have been enjoyed in Canada for many years, for most of the people who came to settle Canada brought from their homelands happy harvest customs. Thanksgiving in Canada was first proclaimed a holiday in 1879 and observed November 6. In following years other dates were tried. Preceding the end of World War I it was held on the third Monday of October. After the war it was proclaimed on the Monday of the week in which Armistice Day occurred, and Thanksgiving Day and Armistice Day were merged in 1921. In 1931, the two days became separate holidays again.

Thanksgiving Day in Canada is celebrated on the second Monday in October. In the morning many people attend church. Later, families gather to feast on turkey and other good things. At that time some people whose families were pioneers to the great Canadian wheat lands recall tales of planting, of hard work, of drought, of scanty harvests and bountiful ones. They are proud that their wheat harvest helps feed the world. And so are the families of the Canadian fishermen, farmers, cattlemen, and all who help provide food and comfort to many people.

Many countries have pleasant harvest customs, interesting to think about as harvesttime draws near. The Pilgrims brought to America memories of harvest-home festivals in their homeland, England, and special days of thanksgiving in Holland.

One celebration that probably is much newer than the Pilgrims is held at times in London by the peddlers of fruit and fish. On a Sunday afternoon in harvest season they parade in suits trimmed with countless pearl buttons. The "Pearly King" and "Pearly Queen" are picked because they have the handsomest costumes.

In the British Isles in a few rural areas special harvest-home celebrations have continued for centuries. Now, however, instead of separate celebrations on each farm, many communities hold a harvest-home festival in which they give some of their best farm products or other gifts to be used to benefit the church and the poor.

Old stories of Britain tell that sometimes the last sheaf of grain at harvesttime was hailed as the "kern." It became part of a dressed up image that was hoisted on a pole. Harvesters circled around this "kern baby" as they moved, singing and dancing, to the barn for the harvest-home supper. Often a pretty girl was chosen as the "harvest queen."

Sometimes the last harvest load was taken from the field in a wagon called the hock-cart or horkey. Reapers surrounded it singing to the music of homemade pipes and small drums called tabors. Often some climbed up and rode on top of the horkey-load. One of their old songs that has come down through the years is:

> Harvest home! harvest home!
> We've ploughed, we've sowed,
> We've reaped, we've mowed,
> We've brought home every load.
> Hip, hip, hip, harvest home!

Whatever the music is and wherever the country and whatever way the harvest is gathered—in baskets, or carts, or farm wagons, or by means of motorized reapers and binders and huge trucks— the people of the world rejoice for their harvests. And no matter where we live, throughout the whole year, we enjoy the products of the harvests of many different lands around the world.

—MILDRED CORELL LUCKHARDT

A Thanksgiving to God, for His House

Lord, thou hast given me a cell,
   Wherein to dwell;
A little house, whose humble roof
   Is weather-proof;
Under the spars of which I lie
   Both soft and dry.

Low is my porch, as is my fate;
   Both void of state;
And yet the threshold of my door
   Is worn by th' poor,
Who hither come and freely get
   Good words and meat.

Some brittle sticks of thorn or briar
   Make me a fire,
Close by whose living coal I sit
   And glow like it.

Lord, I confess too, when I dine
   The pulse is thine,
And all those other bits that be
   There placed by thee;

All these, and better, thou doest send
   Me, to this end:
That I should render, for my part,
   A thankful heart.

—ROBERT HERRICK

A Prayer of Thanksgiving

Lord, behold our family here assembled.
We thank thee
For this place in which we dwell;
For the peace accorded us this day,
For the hope with which we expect tomorrow;
For the health, the work, the food
And the bright skies that make our lives delightful,
For our friends in all parts of the earth, and our friendly helpers . . .
Let peace abound in our small company.

—ROBERT LOUIS STEVENSON

A Spaceman's Prayer

Father, thank you . . .

Thank you for letting me fly this flight.

Thank you for the privilege of being able to be in this position; to be in this wondrous place, seeing all these many startling, wonderful things that you have created.

Help, guide, and direct all of us that we may shape our lives . . . trying to help one another and to work with one another rather than fighting and bickering. . . .

Help us to complete this mission successfully.

Be with all our families. Give them guidance and encouragement, and let them know that everything will be okay.

—L. GORDON COOPER

(From the prayer of Major L. Gordon Cooper, during his seventeenth orbit, in the middle of the night over the Indian Ocean.)

Aboard the "Sweet Cecile"

You couldn't have stayed in Bayport Village for ten minutes on the Wednesday before Thanksgiving Day without knowing that something special was going to happen. It wasn't just the red, white, and blue bunting on Town Hall; or the signs in the shop windows; or the excited crowd around the stove in Goodhue's General Store. Newly hung flags gave a festive air even to the splintering old wharfs and the launches in dry dock down at the harbor. Bayport was about to celebrate the most important Thanksgiving in its history. Tomorrow it was to entertain two of the country's naval heroes, recently returned from active duty in the Pacific.

Beanie Bayliss, twelve, and small for his age, hurried up Wharf Street, trying not to see the signs and the bunting. Beanie was the only Boy Scout, probably the only live boy in Bayport, who wouldn't have any part in the festivities.

It had all happened this way. Beanie's father was in the Army. His mother, a trained nurse, had been called away on an emergency case over in Rockland; so for the past two weeks Beanie had been staying at Cousin Mary's. When Old Cap'n Abram Whiting, who lived on a landlocked houseboat south of town, had heard that Beanie's family was going to be away, he had asked Beanie to have Thanksgiving dinner with him. Beanie had accepted. Then the next day word had reached town that the two heroes, who were touring the eastern states for the Government, were coming to Bayport for Thanksgiving.

The whole town had thrown itself into preparations. The Boy Scouts were to form a guard of honor at the railroad station. They were to eat together at the Bayport House, guests of the city, while the two heroes, dined at the mayor's home. Finally, climaxing the whole thing, there was to be an early afternoon reception at Town Hall where Mayor Chase was to present Commander Rice and young Lieutenant Blaine with two beautiful silver cups which the whole town had chipped in to buy.

When Beanie thought about that presentation, a great lump settled in his throat. He was going to miss it all. He couldn't walk all the way down to Bayport inlet where the houseboat "Sweet Cecile" was beached and all the way back and get to Town Hall in time without just swallowing Cap'n Abram's dinner whole and running away, and he wouldn't do that. By the time he could get back, Commander Rice and Lieutenant Blaine would already be on the train heading for Portland where further ceremonies awaited them.

Beanie tipped his Scout hat forward over his forehead and jerked up the collar of his mackinaw. Missing the ceremony was bad enough, but the way people acted about his missing it was worse. Cousin Mary Hedgeman thought he must be sick. Pete Larson, his best friend, thought he was crazy. Even Mr. Penton the scoutmaster didn't understand.

Just a half-hour ago Mr. Penton had asked Beanie if he wouldn't change his mind. "We want the whole troop to turn out," he said.

"I can't come," Beanie had said slowly. "I told Cap'n Whiting I'd eat with him. He's going to have turkey and fixin's."

Mr. Penton's face had looked less sympathetic. "Frankly I don't get it," he had said. "Turkey and fixings don't seem as important to me as Commander Rice and Lieutenant Blaine. Still each person has to make his own decisions."

And didn't *that* make Beanie feel fine!

Even when Thanksgiving Day actually came and Beanie had started out on the four-mile walk past the salt marshes over to the "Sweet Cecile," he twisted uncomfortably at the recollection of Mr. Penton's voice. Everybody thought he just preferred going to Cap'n Abe's. They couldn't seem to understand that he was going because Cap'n Abe was depending on him and a promise was a promise.

It was all such a mess. Not seeing Commander Rice was bad enough, but missing Lieutenant Blaine was almost unbearable. Lieutenant De Witt Blaine was a Maine boy who had actually lived in Bayport for a few years before Bennie was born. Recently he had been in command of a P.T. boat credited with doing almost legendary damage to enemy shipping. The newspapers had acclaimed him as an able commander, hero of three separate encounters in which his small, swift craft had emerged unhurt after sinking his bulkier enemy. But above all they had noted him as a gallant and loyal friend. Beanie's brown eyes had glowed when he had read the account of how De Witt Blaine had gone back, under heavy fire, to rescue a friend of his who had been wounded and washed overboard.

The final irony was that Lieutenant Blaine was an old friend of Cap'n Abram Whiting. For years Beanie had been hearing about the Blaine boys: De Witt and his twin brother Bill. The cabin of the "Sweet Cecile" was plastered with pictures of them. There were the Blaine twins at the age of eight. The Blaines in their first dory. De Witt Blaine fishing from the deck of the "Sweet Cecile." Bill Blaine as a midshipman at Annapolis. The boys looked exactly alike, and both had made records in the Navy. The town had wished it could have both Blaines at the festivities, but Bill was off in his boat somewhere, probably winning new honors.

"Don't surprise me none," Cap'n Abe had said when Beanie had brought him the newspapers with the accounts of the Blaine twins' exploits. "Why, way back in 'twenty-two, I guess it was, they had thanksgiving dinner with me because their folks were called away much the way yours are, and I said to them, 'You boys have got the makin's of first class skippers.' No, sir, you can't fool your Uncle Abram when it comes to boys."

Beanie had grinned as he heard the story. The old tar did love to spin a story. Still Beanie believed him when he talked about the Blaines. Everybody in town knew they were friends. The Invitation Committee had even driven all the way out to the Inlet to ask Cap'n Whiting to go to the banquet. Beanie had hoped the old man would call off his own party after he got the invitation, but he had been adamant.

"Never was much of a hand at that sort of shindig," he had told the Invitation Committee. "And ef De Witt wants to see me, I reckon he knows where to find me. The 'Sweet Cecile' ain't shifted her moorings two feet since he sat on her lower deck lookin' for shedder crabs."

Beanie didn't entirely understand the old man's reasoning, but he rather admired it. Cap'n Abe had always been a recluse. He lived on his pension in the little shore-bound "Sweet Cecile" and bothered no one. Beanie himself had only got to know him because the loss of an oarlock had left him stranded on Bellow's Reef until Cap'n Abe had rowed by and showed him how to scull. That had been three years ago, and since then they had been great friends. Recently the old Captain had become lame and pretty frail, though he refused to admit it. Beanie worried over him and came out frequently on all sorts of trumped up errands.

Beanie was just thinking of all the fun they had had together when he saw a spiral of smoke, white and billowing against the leaden sky ahead of him. He stared over the brownish reeds straight toward the "Sweet Cecile." His heart thumped furiously. The "Sweet Cecile" was on fire! There wasn't a doubt of it. Those great puffy clouds of smoke came straight from her top deck. In another moment the old house boat would be a mass of flames!

Beanie hesitated just long enough to measure the salt marsh with his eye. If he went straight across it, he'd reach the "Sweet Cecile" in a moment, if he didn't sink in. If he kept on by the road, he might not get there until the "Sweet Cecile" was badly burned.

Beanie charged straight through the marsh. He plunged ahead, fighting the whipping reeds, shouting. "Fire! FIRE! Cap'n Abe, get out of the cabin. She's on FIRE!!"

By the time Beanie got alongside the houseboat, the old man had just put his head out of the galley window. "Fire!" Beanie panted. "Get out. Top deck's on FIRE!" At the same moment he reached for an empty pail, plunged it into the icy water of the inlet and hurled it in the direction of the smoke.

The water slapped on the deck and there was a blood-curdling shout of rage! "What is this, a joke?" a voice demanded, and a pair of strong hands gripped Beanie's shoulders and lifted him onto the top deck.

"Fire!" Beanie shouted again, but now the hands moved him

forward, face down, so that his nose was almost over the galvanized iron chimney. Thick steamy smoke came out that chimney spout, billows of it, reeking of clams. Beanie only needed one look to understand about the fire! Somebody was steaming clams, freshly dug and wrapped in wet seaweed, in the wire netting at the top of the cook stove chimney!

Beanie had often cooked clams that way for Cap'n Abe. It had never occurred to him that anyone would be steaming clams if he wasn't there and he had thought the steam was smoke.

Beanie wriggled, but the hands held him firmly. "What'll I do with him, Uncle Abe?" the voice belonging to the hands demanded. "Throw him overboard?"

Cap'n Abram's chuckle was reassuring. "Don't you do any sech thing. I reckon Beanie just thought he was doing a good turn putting out a fire. He didn't calculate on anybody steaming clams for me but himself."

The hands released Beanie, and their owner moved nimbly over the rail that surrounded the upper deck and down the ratlines. "Lend me some duds while these dry will you, Cap'n? And this young pirate needs attention, too," the stranger said, and for the first time Beanie was free to look at him.

One glance showed him an officer's cap, an officer's uniform, and a strangely familiar yet unfamiliar face. The next minute with a feeling that fourteen and a half bricks had just landed on his stomach, Beanie knew who it was. It was Lieutenant De Witt Blaine! Somehow he had managed to get off to visit Cap'n Abe. The hero of the Solomons was very uncomfortable from the water, he, Beanie, Benjamin Aspinwall Bayliss III, had thrown at him!

Beanie's teeth chattered as much from fright as cold as he stuttered his apologies. Cap'n Abe interrupted him, grinning.

"Get next the cookstove, you boys," he ordered. "Never saw a colder lookin' pair of seamen this side of the Arctic."

They did as they were told, and in time Beanie was formally introduced to Lieutenant Blaine. "Meet the best Scout in Greene County," Cap'n Abe said. "Makes a date with an old man for Thanksgiving and don't break it for anybody, reception committee, Scoutmaster, even you, De Witt."

The Lieutenant laughed as he pulled on an old sweater of the Cap'n and hung out his own clothes to dry.

"Stout fella," he said and look questioningly at Beanie's Scout hat. "How'd you get away with it?" he asked. "I thought all the Boy Scouts were meeting the train?"

Beanie hesitated. He had made about as many mistakes as a human being could. He might as well make one more.

"How come *you* got here?" he blurted out. "You're the reason the troop was down there."

Blaine laughed. "I like your friend, Cap'n," he said. "Jumps to conclusions but the kind of chap you can rely on." He turned back to Beanie. "Ever heard of my twin brother, Bill Blaine?" Beanie nodded. Of course he'd heard of Bill Blaine. Who hadn't? Bill was just as famous as De Witt. They'd wanted him at their meeting when they'd heard he might be on shore leave. "He's a lieutenant, too," Beanie said. "On a P.T."

"He was," De Witt said solemnly. "Right now he's serving at the mayor's luncheon. Department of brotherly love. Got off his boat ahead of schedule and offered to pinch hit for me. Good old Bill!"

For a moment Beanie could only flounder like a sally growler in the bottom of a rowboat. And then he understood! "You mean," he got out, "your twin brother's taking your place and nobody knows it?"

"Go to the head of the class," De Witt Blaine said.

For a minute Beanie did not say anything while a bright and uncomfortable red spread up from his freckled neck to his ears. "B-but," he began and didn't know what to say next. A joke was a joke, but somehow Beanie didn't like the sound of it. There was that silver cup that every man, woman and child had helped to buy, and it had De Witt's name on it. Beanie swallowed and tried again. "People are expecting you," he faltered. "It seems sort of—er—."

It was Cap'n Abram who put him out of his misery. "It's all right, sonny," he said. "The lieutenant's turning up in plenty of time for the reception. He's just missing the lunch at the mayor's. He's going to explain the whole thing, how he's been to banquets for two weeks steady and how he just had to have some of his Uncle Abe's steamed clams and home cooked turkey and a few hours of rest. His brother got this leave sudden like so they took the train up together, but De Witt borrowed a jalopy at Bayport Junction and came here, and Bill went on to Bayport. The crowd's going to love it. They get three heroes instead of two, this way."

Beanie let out a deep sigh of relief. "If you're there for the ceremony," he said happily. "Of course it's all right. And in a jalopy you can get there in just a few minutes when the time comes."

The lieutenant looked at Beanie and now he seemed to be mulling over a question of his own. "Cap'n Abe won't go with me," he said. "Though I could take him in the jalopy if he wasn't so pigheaded. I wish I had some sort of bodyguard for company, going to that meeting. The way the big shots have an aide."

"How about you, Beanie?" Cap'n Abe said, but Beanie was too busy looking at his shoes to answer. He was muddied and scraped, and his socks torn from the weeds. What would Mr. Penton say about a guard of honor that looked like that? The same thought seemed to have occurred to Lieutenant Blaine.

"If anybody mentions your clothes we'll tell them you've been fire fighting," he said. "Rice and I didn't look too smart when we got through putting out the flames on the 'Flying Mackerel' back in the Pacific." He grinned and his eyes danced. "After all you thought those clams were a fire, and the way you went at them was worthy of a medal."

Beanie grinned, too. He felt very much at home with the tall officer. "No, sir," he said stubbornly. "I'll tell everybody exactly what happened."

Lieutenant Blaine gave a big shout of laughter. He thrust out his hand. "Stout boy!" he said. "I can see that the good old Pilgrim integrity is still going strong in New England. Well, that's one of the things we're fighting for—the right to be honest, the right to be our true selves and say what we mean and do what we think is right."

Beanie gripped the hand held out to him. It was a big hand, hard and rough, and a long scar, still red and angry looking ran from thumb to wrist. "Yes, sir," said Beanie. "That's so!"

—LAVINIA R. DAVIS

Seeds for Thanksgiving

Peter Nolan's mother was talking on the telephone, and what she said sounded alarming. But finally the receiver clicked, and Mrs. Nolan returned to the supper table where Peter and his father were waiting. "Aunt Min has a virus infection so she won't be able to come for thanksgiving dinner," she said.

Just thinking about Aunt Min being sick made Peter feel sick too, and terribly lonely. Thanksgiving was a time for company, especially relatives, and Aunt Min was his favorite. Now who would have dinner with them?

"She'll be all right soon, but with Thanksgiving only four days away, she thought she shouldn't try to come," said Mrs. Nolan.

"Well," said Mr. Nolan, "if Aunt Min can't be here, we'll go out for thanksgiving dinner. It will save you the bother of getting a big meal."

"Oh, no!" cried Peter. "There's—there's my pumpkin!" His parents turned to look at him.

"I'll make pies of it anyway, Peter," Mrs. Nolan said with a smile. "We can always eat pumpkin pie."

"We can have your pumpkin for supper that evening," said Mr. Nolan.

"Yes," answered Peter, "but it won't be the same. Thanksgiving is for people—for company!"

His mother and father looked at each other. Then his father said, "But we don't know many people here, Peter. We have lived in this town only a short time."

"Long enough to grow my pumpkin," said Peter sadly. "It grew so big, and I was counting on Aunt Min to help eat it on Thanksgiving."

Mrs. Nolan glanced at her watch. "Oh, the P.T.A. meeting! We'll have to hurry! We'll decide about Thanksgiving later. This is Monday. Thanksgiving isn't until Thursday."

Since it was a special program, Peter went with his parents, but he didn't hear much that was going on. He was too busy thinking about Thanksgiving. Then suddenly he heard the P.T.A. president, Mrs. Morton, say, "—and we need people to invite them for Thanksgiving dinner."

There were people needing Thanksgiving dinner? Who? Peter looked at his mother and father—they seemed to be listening intently. "These foreign students should have a chance to get to know us better," Mrs. Morton continued.

"Foreign students! What if we invited one to our house?" thought Peter.

As soon as the program ended, Peter asked his mother, "Couldn't we invite a foreign student to our house for Thanksgiving dinner?"

"Why, I don't know, Peter," said Mrs. Nolan slowly. "What do you think, Andy?" she asked her husband.

"Well, it's all right with me, if you want to fuss with it. I thought going out would save you a lot of work."

"Getting ready is part of the fun," Mrs. Nolan said, smiling. She told Peter, "At least I'll ask."

Peter went with her to talk to Mrs. Morton, who seemed pleased. "Let me send you two boys from India," she said.

"India?" murmured Mrs. Nolan. Peter held his breath. What would students from India be like? Would they like pumpkin pie?

Mrs. Morton was saying, "Many of them are vegetarians, you know."

"But," said Mrs. Nolan, "on Thanksgiving we have turkey for dinner."

"Don't worry." Mrs. Morton laughed. "These boys tell me we have so much food that they find plenty with just the side dishes. They do like rice, though. If you could have rice—and vegetables—."

"Yes, of course—."

"What about pumpkin pie?" Peter interrupted. "I grew the pumpkin myself!"

"That's wonderful!" Mrs. Morton smiled at him. "I shall tell the boys!"

It was all settled, but Peter's mother was still a bit worried. "Peter, this is your dinner," she told him on the way home. "We'll count on you to be the host."

His mother planned the dinner carefully to have many foods beside turkey. "I'll make a rice casserole—I've been wanting to try that—and brussels sprouts and cranberry sauce and sweet potatoes and perhaps some celery. And, of course, pumpkin pie for dessert!"

When Peter saw the two students from India coming up the walk on Thanksgiving Day, he felt a lump in his throat. His tongue seemed tied when he opened the door.

One man was short, with smooth, light brown skin. His hair

was very black, as were his twinkling eyes. The other student was taller, thinner, and darker, with a kind but solemn expression on his face. He wore a yellow turban.

"I'm Peter," said Peter, opening the door wide.

"I'm Chandra," said the man with the turban. He held out his hand to Peter.

The second man shook hands, too, and said, "I am Rama."

Peter tried to introduce the guests to his parents. He stammered over their names, but Mr. Rama smiled and helped him out. Mr. Nolan invited them to make themselves at home.

The students were very quiet and polite. They seemed friendly, but it was hard for Peter to think of anything to say. His father was asking them questions about what they were studying at school. Soon Mrs. Nolan called them to the table.

The big turkey sat in front of Mr. Nolan, waiting to be carved. It smelled delicious, but as Peter looked at the two dinner guests, Thanksgiving was not the way he had always remembered it. "They don't even eat turkey!" he thought.

Mr. Nolan started to carve. "I understand you don't eat meat," he said. "But it is part of our traditional Thanksgiving!"

Mr. Rama smiled. "This is what I wanted to see—to know. I want to learn everything—the custom, the traditions. Turkey? Yes, please, I should like to have some."

The Nolans were pleased. "That's fine!" Mr. Nolan replied, slicing white meat. He spooned dressing onto the plate and handed it to Mr. Rama. Then he asked Mr. Chandra, "Will you have some turkey, too?"

Mr. Chandra bowed his turbaned head. "Thank you, no. You may say I am not as modern as my friend. The rice casserole—yes. The vegetables—fine, thank you."

Peter asked, "Is pumpkin all right? We're having pumpkin pie for dessert.'"

The students' eyes twinkled. "Mrs. Morton told us you grew the pumpkin. That is fine!"

The men enjoyed the food and accepted second helpings. They talked of India. Mr. Chandra was a Sikh. He had gone to the university in Banaras. Mr. Rama had traveled all over his country, and told exciting stories of jungles and tigers and of the cities and people.

"Ours is a big country, too," said Peter proudly.

Mr. Rama nodded, "Before I go back to India, I want to travel all around it."

Mr. Chandra smiled. "Rama is a very modern Indian. You never know with him. For an international student party at school he did our native songs in your jazz time," Mr. Chandra explained.

"Would you for us?" asked Peter, excitedly.

Mr. Nolan exclaimed, "That would be great! You sing and— Emily, where's that guitar of mine? Is it still in that old trunk?"

Peter really was excited. Did his father have a guitar?

Mrs. Nolan was smiling broadly. "I think it's still in that trunk in the basement. I had forgotten about it."

While Mr. Nolan looked in the basement, Peter and the students helped Mrs. Nolan clear the table. It was as though they were all one big family. By the time the table was cleared, Mr. Nolan was back with the guitar. "Come on, everyone! Let's have some music."

Mr. Rama sang, Mrs. Nolan played the piano, and Mr. Nolan the guitar. Peter and Mr. Chandra sat on the floor beating time with their hands. Peter had never had so much fun.

Finally it began to get dark. "Time for some pumpkin pie," announced Mrs. Nolan.

The pie was delicious, everyone agreed. "I should like to take some pumpkin seeds home to India when I go," said Mr. Chandra. "And when they grow, I shall remember today and all of you. And I shall be very thankful."

After Mr. Chandra and Mr. Rama were gone, Peter went to bed. This had been the most wonderful day in his life. Mother came upstairs to say goodnight. But before she turned out the light, she said, "Thank you, Peter. You helped us have a wonderful day. When you planted those pumpkin seeds who would have thought what would happen? We can be truly thankful for today."

—CLARA BALDWIN

Prayer for Thanksgiving

We thank thee for our daily bread,
For faith by which the soul is fed,
For burdens given us to bear,
For hope that lifts the heart's despair.

We thank thee, Lord, for eyes to see
The truth that makes, and keeps, men free;
For faults—and for the strength to mend them,
For dreams—and courage to defend them.

We have so much to thank thee for,
Dear Lord, we beg but one boon more;
Peace in the hearts of all men living,
Peace in the whole world this Thanksgiving.

—JOSEPH AUSLANDER

BIBLIOGRAPHY

SOME BOOKS ABOUT THE PILGRIMS

The original sources of information are *A relation or journal of the beginnings and proceedings of the English plantation settled at Plimoth in New England, written by G. Mourt,* published in London, 1622; *Good Newes from New England, written by Edward Winslow,* published in London, 1624; *Of Plimoth Plantation, 1620-1647,* written by William Bradford. (Bradford worked for twenty years on this history. During the American revolution this handwritten manuscript disappeared, and its whereabouts was not known to Americans until about 1865. In time it was returned to Massachusetts from the Library of the Bishop of London. *Mourt's Relation* is believed to have been written by William Bradford and Edward Winslow during the first year in America. Edward Winslow took *Good Newes from New England* to England in the fall of 1623.)

Versions of these old accounts are available today. Here are three:

Atwood, William Franklin. *The Pilgrim Story from Bradford and Winslow Documents.* Plymouth, Massachusetts: The Memorial Press.

Smith, E. Brooks, and Meredith, Robert. *Pilgrim Courage.* Boston: Little, Brown and Company, 1962.

————. *Mourt's Relation: A Journal of the Pilgrims at Plymouth.* New York: Citadel (Corinth) Press, 1962.

(If you wish to see how the early Pilgrims lived, you may visit Plimoth Foundation at Plymouth, Massachusetts. This authentic replica of their village is having more buildings and exhibits added continually. Every day from mid-April through November families, school groups, and travelers from many lands walk through this village and talk about Pilgrim beginnings in our country. More information may be had by writing Plimoth Plantation, Box 1620, Plymouth, Massachusetts)

SOME BOOKS CONTAINING STORIES ABOUT
THE PILGRIMS, THANKSGIVING, OR HARVEST FESTIVALS

Barksdale, Lena. *The First Thanksgiving*. New York: Alfred A. Knopf, 1942.

Cavanah, Frances, and Pannell, Lucile. *Holiday Round Up*. Philadelphia: Macrae Smith, 1950.

Credle, Ellis. *Tall Tales from the High Hills*. New York: Thomas Nelson and Sons, 1957.

Dalgliesh, Alice. *Thanksgiving Story*. New York: Charles Scribner's Sons, 1954.

Daringer, Helen F. *Debbie of the Green Gate*. New York: Harcourt, World & Brace, 1950.

Daringer, Helen F. *Pilgrim Kate*. New York: Harcourt, World & Brace, 1950.

Daugherty, James. *The Landing of the Pilgrims*. New York: Random House, 1950.

Dobler, Lavinia. *Customs and Holidays Around the World*. New York: Fleet Publishing Company, 1962.

Fleming, Thomas J. *One Small Candle*. New York: W. W. Norton, 1964.

Hall, Elvajean. *Pilgrim Neighbors*. Chicago: Rand McNally, 1964.

————. *Pilgrim Stories*. Chicago: Rand McNally, 1962.

Harper, Wilhelmina, editor. *The Harvest Feast (Thanksgiving)*. New York: E. P. Dutton & Company, 1938.

Hays, Wilma Pitchford. *Pilgrim Thanksgiving*. New York: Coward-McCann, 1955.

Krythe, Maymie R. *All About American Holidays*. New York: Harper & Row, 1962.

Lillie, Amy Morris. *The Book of Three Festivals*. New York: E. P. Dutton & Company, 1948.

Lindsay, Vachel. *Johnny Appleseed and Other Poems*. New York: The Macmillan Company, 1923.

Morison, Samuel Eliot. *Builders of the Bay Colony*. Boston: Houghton Mifflin, 1930.

Rolvaag, O. E. *Giants in the Earth*. New York: Harper & Row, 1927.

Secrist, Elizabeth Hough, and Woolsey, Janette. *It's Time for Thanksgiving*. Philadelphia: Macrae Smith, 1957.

Taylor, Sydney. *All-of-a-Kind Family*. Chicago: Follett Publishing Company, 1951.

Weiser, Francis X., S.J. *The Holyday Book*. New York: Harcourt, Brace, & World, 1956.

Willison, G. F. *Saints and Strangers*. New York: Ballentine Books.

Wyndham, Lee. *Thanksgiving, A Holiday Book*. Scarsdale, N. Y.: Garrard Publishing Company, 1963.

Ziver, F., and Willison, G. F. *Pilgrims and Plymouth Colony*. New York: Harper & Row (American Heritage Junior Library), 1961.

INDEX
of Authors and Titles

349